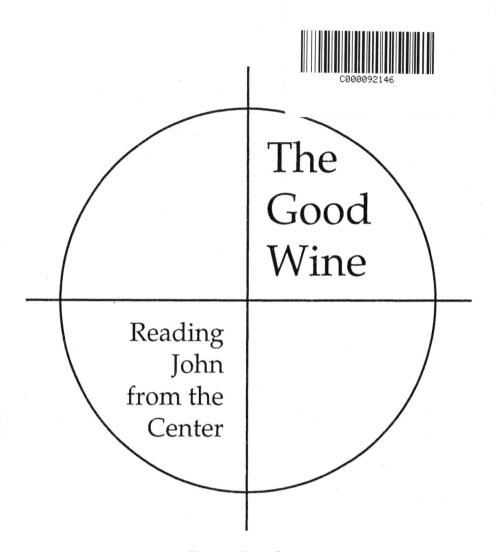

The Good Wine

Reading John from the Center

Bruno Barnhart

WIPF & STOCK · Eugene, Oregon

For my mother and father

Wipf and Stock Publishers
199 W 8th Ave, Suite 3
Eugene, OR 97401

The Good Wine
Reading John from the Center
By Barnhart, Bruno
Copyright©1993 Barnhart, Bruno
ISBN 13: 978-1-60608-340-6
Publication date 12/01/2008
Previously published by Paulist Press, 1993

Contents

PART III. Gospel, Community and World

Acknowledgments

Recognition is due first of all to the members of my community of New Camaldoli, for their warm support and their patience during the protracted time of writing. I am particularly grateful to Fr. Robert Hale, the Prior, for providing the freedom from other responsibilities which was needed to do the work—and for his continual encouragement. Brother Paul Sweringen supplied splendid graphic work. Several friends read the manuscript and supplied valuable criticism, corrections and suggestions: Rev. Cynthia Bourgeault, Carole Marie Kelly, OSF, Jean Marie Pearse, OSB Cam, Richard and Heather Tarnas, Wendy Marie Teichert, and particularly William Yaryan. Without their help the book would have been much less readable. Francis Dorff, O. Praem., suggested the old Celtic design which has become the cover figure.

A number of other people, by their warm response to this interpretive approach in various conferences and classes, have helped to bring the child to birth.

The book owes its initial inspiration and much of its development to the work of John Gerhard, S.J. and Peter F. Ellis, and Professor Ellis' encouragement is much appreciated.

Kevin Lynch of Paulist Press has been continually supportive, and most patient with the repeated delays.

Introduction

When Jesus turned, and saw them following, he said to them, "What are you looking for?" They said to him, "Rabbi . . . where are you staying?" He said to them, "Come and see" (Jn 1:38-39a).

The Jesus who enters our personal world in John's gospel brings, within himself, a promise of plenitude. His gravitational pull stirs unexplored depths within us. This book is intended, first of all, as a reintroduction to John's gospel for those who have experienced this power of the Johannine Jesus and have already given some time to John's text, but don't yet feel that they have begun to enter deeply into John's meaning. It may also be of interest to those who are not yet acquainted with John, but feel drawn to the more contemplative side of Christianity and are seeking a way into the New Testament which corresponds to this attraction.

Our contemporary western culture, with its pragmatic realism and skeptical attitude toward metaphysical truths, has made it more difficult to approach the fourth gospel on its own level. To many it seems a noble relic of some past age of faith—and credulity. Some people of faith have put John aside because it seemed unrelated to the urgencies of human life, to the imperatives of our historical moment.

From somewhere beneath the surface of this history, however, something new—and timeless—is emerging. The west, dominated for centuries by a consciousness evolving toward greater and greater differentiation, is experiencing a rebirth of the *unitive*: unitive vision, unitive thinking, unitive consciousness. This is evident in the ecumenical movement, with its deabsolutizing of the boundaries between Christian communities, in our broad interaction with the eastern religious traditions, in the emergence of a "global village," in our growing planetary ecological sense, and in many other ways, which have been summed up in the concept of the "new paradigm."[1] Within the biblical tradition, John is very probably the deepest point of resonance with this unitive consciousness. The encounter of John's gospel with this growing unitive awareness promises to bring light to both one and the other.

Our interpretation will proceed, then, from a *unitive* perspective. The meaning of this term will become progressively clearer as we go on. From time to time, and particularly in the final chapter, we shall bring alongside the Johannine vision some expressions of the unitive consciousness which is emerging in our contemporary world.

John, the "other disciple," has written an "other gospel."[2] He speaks, from the beginning, in a language of his own, differing from the language of the first three (frequently called the *synoptic* gospels). He proposes his own unique theological vision of the one Christ-mystery.[3] It is this vision which we shall be seeking in his gospel. John's "other" gospel bears the aura of *mystery* which shrouds the "other disciple" in his narrative. At the same time it is in the fourth gospel that the reader encounters Jesus as the light, center and source of a distinctly new way of *knowing*, a new consciousness.

Even more profoundly than the gospel of Luke, John's work presents itself as a carefully and aesthetically crafted *composition*, as a poem, a product of imagination.[4] John's gospel is based upon historical fact, and many of its details, very likely, are historically accurate. A basic assumption of the present work is, however, that John was written with the energy and creative freedom of a theological imagination. If one is to understand the fourth gospel deeply, one must attempt to bring to it something of the same spirit.

We propose in this book, then, an alternative style of interpretation which is attuned to this "other gospel." Our study, while frequently making use of the results of historical-critical scholarship,[5] proceeds in a way which, like that of the pre-modern commentators, relies less on methods of scientific exactitude than on intuition and symbolic imagination, inclining less to analysis than to synthesis. Our work aims to continue, in a contemporary perspective, the sapiential exegesis[6] of the fathers and of the eastern Christian traditions.

The methods of interpretation proposed here are personal choices, and are not proposed as the ultimate way into John. They are, however, a way along which one can penetrate into the Johannine world. Once in that world, the question of method will become less important; one will be experiencing the inner movement of the gospel itself.

What is ultimately important is one's own involvement, one's own journey with the Word. Getting it exactly right—if such a thing is possible—is secondary to the personal engagement and the participatory process. It is in this conviction that these methods are presented. They are offered here because they have been of great help to me personally in getting deeper into the meaning of John.

The commentary will not proceed verse-by-verse,[7] but will focus selectively upon those passages and those elements (persons, scenes, encounters, symbolic actions, places, words) which play major roles in the *convergent* structure and movement of the gospel.

A number of the ideas which appear here originated in the context of classes and retreat conferences on John's gospel. Like many others, I have found in preaching and teaching a very great help in entering into the biblical texts. There is a particular grace of understanding to be had in studying the Word in the context of a community. Yet time after time it will be during one's own silent reflection that the Johannine light will come forth from within.

John's gospel is an initiation into the fullness of the baptismal gift, the Christ-mystery. Our study of the text will tend to become a personal initiation; it is to *us* that the Word speaks as we read it. From the early centuries of our era, Christians have entered into the depths of their faith by taking John's thesis literally, in the sense of conceiving their own journey as the unfolding of a personal relationship with the *Word*.[8]

The book is divided into three parts. Part I will present the methods to be employed in our study of John. In Part II, the body of the book, we shall offer an interpretation of the whole of John's narrative according to these methods. Part III will review the gospel synthetically in the light of John's prologue and of Christian baptism. Finally we shall look at the Johannine unitive revelation in the context of our western history and of our contemporary experience.

It is important that the reader invest the time and attention required to gain a working understanding of the chiastic mandala in Part I, before moving on to the commentary in Part II. Without this framework, the reader who journeys through the gospel by the particular route which we shall follow will frequently lose his bearings, and experience less frequently John's singular union of precision and depth resonance. Once this foundation has been acquired, however, it is the commentary in Part II which invites the reader's intimate participation, and where it is hoped that his or her own imaginative energies will become engaged with the peculiar music of John. The synthetic reflections of Part III should help to bring the gospel as a whole back into a unitive focus. The concluding reflections in the context of history and the present may stimulate the reader's own efforts to bring his or her world into the radius of the Johannine Word.

This book cannot be read by itself. It has been written as a help in reading John, and presupposes a lively interest in that gospel—however limited may have been one's Johannine experience until now. It will be necessary continually to refer to the gospel text. For the numerous biblical quotations, we have used the New Revised Standard Version.[9]

I
UNITIVE MEANING AND CENTRIC METHODS

Chapter One

The Language of Fullness

The Wisdom Gospel

"In the beginning was the Word...." Thus begins John's gospel. Its first eighteen verses, known as the prologue, are very different from the narrative of Jesus' actions and movements, the account of meetings and discourses, healings and dialogues which we expect a gospel to be. We shall approach the fourth gospel from the perspective which is suggested at its beginning, in these first words of the prologue. We shall be concerned with this "Word" (*Logos*) of which John speaks, and which is the key to the meaning of his gospel. To take as principle of interpretation this declaration, "In the beginning was the Word," is to start out upon a path which was well-traveled in the early centuries of the Christian era. Biblical studies during the past few centuries have moved further and further away from this way, however.

Biblical interpretation today continues to be dominated by the scientific approach, which has been developed into a battery of powerful analytical methods: form criticism, redaction criticism, tradition criticism and so on. The purpose of these methods is to arrive at a clear understanding of the literal meaning of the biblical text, in the light of an historical understanding of the time and culture in which it was composed.

This science of the biblical text has succeeded in bringing the Bible into a world of sober rationality, of public verification, of honesty and objectivity: a movement into daylight which cannot be renounced. We now have objective standards which offer some confrontation to our infinite creativity in bending the word to our own inclinations.

At the same time we are more or less conscious that something has been lost, that we have experienced some kind of eclipse. This feeling is particularly acute when we read the fourth gospel today. Centuries ago, the west took a decisive step in the direction of the development of the individual, of human reason and of rational science, which has transformed our civilization and, in our own century, drawn the rest of the world behind us in a rational and technological revolution. The abundant fruits of this progress have themselves made it difficult for us to retain an awareness of that which we have left behind.

This awareness dawns upon many westerners with a shock when they first encounter the depth and power of one of the ancient spiritual traditions of the east: of an authentic embodiment of Hinduism or Buddhism. What have we left behind in our breakthrough into the rationality and individual self-possession of human "adulthood," in our liberating exodus from a world of faith into a world of reason and liberty? Reflection on these ancient traditions is likely to suggest that the answer lies in the word *wisdom.*[1]

The strange solitude which we share in this "postmodern" age is the end-result of our centuries-long "anti-pilgrimage," our movement away from the center. And yet we know that we have been moving forward as well, that history cannot be reversed, that we would not—and cannot—return to an earlier, less rational, less critical, less individuated age. It may be that the cultural task of the west in our time, and particularly of Christianity, is—without rejecting the growth which humanity has achieved on this modern journey—to take one more step forward into a new unitive wisdom.

It is at this point that the importance of John's gospel for our time becomes apparent. Wisdom is John's concern, and it is the perspective from which he presents the life of Jesus. For John, and in a very real sense, Jesus embodies the wisdom of God, and gives it to other human persons in the gift of himself to them.

In his typically sapiential[2] concern for "the beginning," John brings us back to a point of origin which is prior to the division of east and west, and the parting of the ways between contemplative wisdom and creative life.

How this sapiential and unitive orientation distinguishes John from the other three gospels, and determines John's relation to our own historical situation, became apparent to me while preparing to teach a class on John. In the commentary of Raymond Brown, a master of contemporary Johannine exegesis, I read:

> One aspect that immediately sets the Fourth Gospel apart from the other Gospels and gives it peculiar force is its presentation of Jesus as incarnate revelation descended from on high to offer men light and truth....
>
> ...We suggest that in drawing this portrait of Jesus, the evangelist has capitalized on an identification of Jesus with personified divine Wisdom as described in the OT....Just as the NT writers found in Jesus the antitype of elements of the historical books of the OT (e.g., of the Exodus, Moses, David) and the fulfillment of the words of the prophets, so the fourth evangelist saw in Jesus the culmination of a tradition that runs through the Wisdom literature of the OT.[3]

> In the mind of the theologian of the Prologue the creative word of God, the word of the Lord that came to the prophets, has become personal in Jesus who is the embodiment of divine revelation. Jesus is divine Wisdom, pre-existent, but now come among men to teach them and give them life. Not the Torah but Jesus Christ is the creator and source of light and life.[4]

The fourth gospel is a *wisdom gospel* (the unique Johannine sense of this word "wisdom" will gradually unfold in the course of our study). More urgently than the other gospels, therefore, John calls for methods of interpretation which are attentive to a sapiential level of meaning.

Methods

Frank Kermode, preparatory to his profound study of John's prologue, excuses himself and the reader from the vexing questions of authorship, stages of composition, and so on. Anticipating the inevitable charge of "precritical" exegesis, he says,

> ...there is a case for preferring the label "postcritical." In deciding not to be hindered by this immensely powerful tra-

dition of largely disintegrative commentary, one hopes, without forgetting its importance, to regain some of the advantages of the precritical commentators who knew nothing about the Higher Criticism....[5]

Perhaps chief among these advantages is that of a unitive, or sapiential viewpoint. It is time for a recovery of this fundamental approach which will be able to integrate the fruits of modern scientific reason without being intimidated by its cyclopean epistemology.[6] Paradoxically, to enter into the unitive Word is to break out of the "single vision"[7] of a scientistic mentality toward the multiple modalities of consciousness which correspond to the God of Christian tradition, who is one and three.

Our approach to John's gospel will include several component methods, which will be explained at this point only briefly. They may be called the structural, the symbolic and the unitive methods.

Structural analysis, among these three tracks, approximates most nearly to a technique, the well-defined procedure that we usually expect of a *method*. This will demand a greater investment of attention at the outset, and may well raise more questions for the reader, than the other approaches. This is a mode of literary interpretation which has been applied to the Johannine prologue—as well as to other New Testament texts—for many years, and has now been proposed as the key to the entire structure of John's gospel. It proceeds on the supposition that the text has been composed according to a formal pattern of symmetry known as chiasm, and that this design is itself more expressive of the meaning of the text than is the simple chronological order of the narrative. The next three chapters will be devoted to an explanation of this method.

The *symbolic* interpretation of scripture has a very long history: it appears already in the Old Testament, undergoes a great development within the New Testament, and was the dominant mode of exegesis during the first thousand years of Christian history. It operates on the principle that places, things, events and even persons in the biblical narrative have a significance beyond that which belongs to their particularity: that there is another level of meaning beneath the literal sense of the text, and that this deeper meaning is more indicative of the genuine and ultimately intended sense of the passage. John's symbolic system is closely interwoven with his structural pattern, and both of these approaches involve a sensitivity to the relationships or *resonances* between one event and another, one character and another, in the gospel. John's art lies largely in communicating through these resonances a truth which is at once varied in its articulation and one at its core.

The *unitive* approach,[8] while peculiarly appropriate to John, is not so widely exemplified in the history of Christian exegesis. It can be pointed to in some of the eastern Christian fathers (e.g. Origen, Maximus Confessor, and especially Ephrem and other early writers of the Syriac tradition), and emerges in the late medieval western tradition in Meister Eckhart.[9] This approach derives from the sapiential principle that there is *one* ultimate reality, and that the basic intent of the text is to express or communicate this reality.[10] In John's gospel, this unitive[11] reality appears in the *Logos* of the first words of the prologue, and will be manifest finally in the baptismal experience to which the whole of John's text points.

Our fourth methodological principle is difficult to capture in a word. It animates these three lines of method, comprehends them and goes beyond them. It is, indeed, the general approach within which the particular methods operate. I have given a good deal of thought to putting it into words, without much success. This, I believe, is not because it is a vague or confused notion, but because it is rather motion than procedure, spirit than letter. It is an attempt to move with the life itself of the text, which goes beyond any grasp of the materiality of a text or any particular conceptual interpretation. Let us name it for what, at least, it attempts to achieve: *dynamic participation.*

This movement goes beyond the literal text of the gospel in two directions: one might call them upstream and downstream, inward and outward, the apophatic and the creative directions. The Johannine Jesus does not remain in the world in the "literalness" of his earthly human form; he both returns to the Father and returns to the world in another, dynamic form: that of the Holy Spirit.

On the one hand, similarly, we are drawn beyond the literal text of the gospel inward and back, to the underlying "archetypal" structures and ultimately to the unitive silence of God. Our "unitive" method proceeds in this direction. We may sometimes actually arrive at an element, a pattern, a structure, which has not intentionally been introduced into the text by the human author, but which belongs to the inner structure of the mystery of Christ. Here we should also recall that it is not only the words of scripture which are symbolic, but the persons, events, the things themselves.[12] The responsibility of the author does not demand that he consciously construct everything in his text, but rather that he faithfully communicate this inner mystery.

The second direction of "going beyond" the text is outward and forward, corresponding to the movement of the Spirit outward in creation and forward in history. Here we go beyond the "artifact" of the literal textual word or passage into the continuing movement of the Spirit. What is called for is a readiness to follow this movement of the Spirit with mind, heart and imagination, in such a way that the *creative* Word realizes itself also in the present, the moment of reading.

The rabbis and the church fathers read the scriptures in this way instinctively and without hesitation. From the time of our austere baptism of critical reason, however, we are in the position of having to relearn to do it—and now with a more differentiated awareness of what it is that we are doing. Along with the indispensable maturing of critical reason, we have acquired a virus of theological timidity—of spiritual inertia and positivist skepticism which habituates us to *materializing* the word, the text: immobilizing it perfectly within a framework of historical fact and critical analysis. Get it exactly right, whether alive or dead. The simplistic alternative which is easily at hand is not much better: rejection of the precious realism and balance of critical thought, the hard-won adulthood of our culture, in favor of an option for pure vigor, vitality, charismatic power or unction.

Between the accurately labeled skeleton and the blind wave, or rather beyond both of them, there is a way of reading the Word in which it is allowed once again to become the creative Word, flowing forth in a wealth of meaning, but meanings which are always consistent with the inner essence of the Word, and always yielding to its unspoken fullness, its inner authority.

Imagination is another partial name for this forward movement of the Word in human consciousness and speech. There is an imagination which is true, which expresses reality and remains faithful to it, as it faithfully expresses the center of the human person; that center is an organ not only of faith but of generativity, creativity. The psyche's image-making power is an essential quality of the human: this has become a scientifically respectable assertion in our time. What we mean by imagination, however, is not merely the power of generating images, but that creative freedom in this world which is an essential endowment of the human person. This imagination has also a theological component, a theological root: it has to do with the beginning, and is our own vestigial capacity to participate in the role of the creator vis-à-vis the world and our own person.[13]

If the gospel of John differs from the other three gospels in its bold departures from the probable chronological order and exact historical factuality of the events of Jesus' life, it is because John is a work of theological imagination—perhaps the prime expression of Christian imagination. We can enter fully into John's gospel only by *participating* in this act of theological imagination, by realizing its energy and dynamism in our own reading.

⊕

John's gospel, then, is *in movement*—is itself, at its deepest level, the *life* that moves within the arrangement of words as music lives within its pattern of notes. "The words that I have spoken to you are spirit and life" (6:63). It will be helpful to know something of the direction of this movement from the outset. As we often find in the New Testament, this one dynamism, invisible and all-inclusive, can be expressed only through paradoxical statements. Something of this movement which we are to experience can be indicated by the two adjectives, *convergent* and *emergent*.

A certain *convergence* is already evident in the three methods which have just been outlined: the structural, symbolic and unitive methods. This will become much more evident as soon as we begin to consider them more concretely and to apply them. The *structure* of which we speak is a convergent structure, in which the ultimate theological weight lies at the center. The dynamism of this structure is first convergent, or centripetal, and then expansive, or radial. This structure is itself *symbolic*, as is the term "center." And both structure and center are symbolic projections of an ultimate reality which is *unitive*. Structure and symbolism converge upon the unitive reality which is the heart of John's message.[14]

As we journey through John's narrative, we shall become aware again and again of this convergent movement[15] pervading the whole, aware of the powerful presence of an organizing center. We have already been told of this center, from the beginning of the prologue: "In the beginning was the *Word*...." The movement of the gospel becomes a progressive revelation of this center, and concludes by disclosing its presence within ourselves, in the baptismal gift of the Spirit. To the convergence of our three strands of methodology, therefore, corresponds a convergent movement in the gospel itself.

Simultaneous with this convergence is the movement of *emergence*, and this too will be reflected in the process of interpretation. *What we are discovering is itself the principle of interpretation*, and therefore the path of our inquiry, the choices and hypotheses which shape it, will be validated by their fruits rather than by any extrinsic criteria. This affirmation is less banal than it sounds; it is a corollary of the Word's emergence in the midst of this world.

The coming of Christ challenges humanity to a *revolution* in consciousness, and this must be reflected first of all in the way we interpret the gospels themselves. The Word comes into a world which was created through the Word, and within which the Word is already invisibly present. This world, however, has evolved its own structures of thought and of life independently of this forgotten foundation, this disregarded cornerstone. And this *continues to be true* in every age: the confrontation between the Word and these human structures is continually being repeated—even, and particularly, when these structures are the artifacts of a religious culture. The archetypal biblical model of this conflict is the drama which begins when Jesus appears in the midst of the Jewish religious world with its stubborn structures of law and mentality.

At this point there echo, again and again, the words of the Baptist, the man who came first: "He who comes after me ranks ahead of me, for he *was* before me"(1:15); "Among you (in the midst of you) stands one whom you do not know"(1:26). It is the one who comes after, who comes in the middle and stands in the midst, whom we come to know only gradually, that is the first and final Word, and the holiest structures of human thought and custom must give way before him, reorder themselves around him.

He is the *emergent* one in the very process of interpretation. Our methods, like those of the Baptist, can only prepare the way, create a space, point to the signs of his emergence. They must not be so perfect, complete, so complacently effective as to close him out, to exclude the *mystery* in which he comes and in which he continues to dwell. Ultimately they must not translate him into terms *other than himself.*

It is the quality of the vision that emerges, therefore, which will be decisive. And this quality will be intrinsic rather than comparative. Its verification will not, finally, derive from external criteria and structures of meaning, but from within itself. It is the emergent, unitive form itself, the *fruit* of the method, which validates both itself and the method. It is the consistency, the integrity, the beauty and power of the vision, which witness to its truth. Having said this, we must immediately add that this internal "fittingness" is at the same time a fittingness in the implicit context of the universe and of our own being. It is the consonance of all of being around this center which witnesses to its dominion.[16]

⊕

Western science, in its wonderful development during the past two hundred years, has led us nearly to forget the dimension of *depth* in knowing. The spectrum ranges from that certainty which is rigorous but lifeless and superficial, to a knowledge which touches the core of life and yet is inseparable from mystery. On the one hand there is the precise and certain knowledge of a *fact*, and on the other hand there is fullness of *meaning*—here the hard certainty and very limited meaning of the immediate results of positive physical science, and there the deep and inexpressible certainty and the inexhaustible and living meaning of the great spiritual truths.

A "postcritical" exegesis might reflect the uncertainty principle of post-Newtonian physics in crossing the frontier of a rigorous precision of particulars into the region of a final depth and intensity of meaning: the most adequate meaning, the great sly fish who is hidden in the whole sea. It would be a *lectio divina*,[17] ancient and ever new, in which, without offense to the literal meaning of the text, the obsessive insistence upon a *single* clear meaning would yield to that glowing field of energy and creative potentiality from which meanings are ever freshly coming forth. The analogy of an energy field is appropriate, for both around the biblical Word and at the center of its materiality lives the creative Spirit, with its inexhaustible plenitude, its living flux of meaning.

There is a kind of *poetry* which is language in movement, living language, word flaming into spirit, and this could probably come closer to the Johannine Word than our prose paraphrases and commentaries. It is essential to remember as we proceed through the fourth gospel that our analyses and paraphrases, our structural symmetries and symbolic connections, are no more than the dry bones of this Word. What John is communicating conceptually in his Gospel is the new creation which takes place in the Word, in Jesus. The poetic energy of his words, which rises from the page into the consciousness of the reader, tends to realize this same creative act, this birth, within the reader.

As John attempts to convey, insofar as words can do so, the act of new creation in the Word, his gospel corresponds to the new birth which is Christian baptism. To "know" this creative act is to realize it within oneself, within one's life. This is much more than poetry. But insofar as a gospel, a composition of human words, can convey it, it is communicated through the "poetic act," realized in the reader. When poetry itself is alive, it is not mere pattern nor speech, but an act, an event, a birth, a bringing to life and coming to life, an advent of newness. The words of John are the embodiment within this poetic vehicle of another and greater act, another birth.

Our reading of John must ultimately be the offering of an interior space of silence to the birth of this Word within ourselves. We can expect to experience this birth again and again, more and more frequently, as we dwell within the world of John's gospel.

Chapter Two

Cross and Pleroma:
The New Testament Mandala

Very soon in our study of John's gospel, we shall find ourselves moving within a world constituted by *symmetries*. In the next chapter we shall give special attention to one form of symmetry (familiar to us in the shape of a simple hinge)—called *chiasm*—which appears to be a basic structural principle not only of this gospel but of a number of other New Testament writings. The Johannine symmetry goes further than this, however. Our chiastic study leads us to the discovery of a *mandalic* form as the fundamental structural pattern of John's gospel. At this point, we find, John converges both with ancient spiritual traditions of Asia and with the psychological wisdom of our own time. The mandala is the centerpiece of a language of "sacred geometry" which has long flourished outside the Judaeo-Christian tradition. It is an archetypal form which reflects, apparently, the fundamental structure of that reality within which we live.

True sacred geometry is not, as a first glance might suggest, a tedious partitioning of the known. Rather, it is the disclosing of unseen boundaries, and an opening of passages to the unknown, the revelation of a plurality of interrelated worlds. And it is an attempt to represent the whole of reality, including that which is invisible, in relation to its unitive center.[1]

⊕

Among Christian symbols, the *cross* is primary. This sign has often been taken as summing up the heart of the gospel, and as the sign of Christ the Savior himself. But the Latin cross, to which we have become accustomed in western Christianity, has oriented the understanding of this symbol in a particular way. The western cross invites a response of heart and will rather than the contemplative regard of the mind. This is so not only because our modern crucifix brings before us the suffering Christ rather than the glorified Savior; it is related to the form itself of our cross.[2] Significantly, in its passage from east to west the cross has become vertically elongated, so that it is no longer a symmetrical figure.

In moving from the Orient, the image of the cross has evolved from a symmetry which suggested the reconciliation of heaven and earth, and thus the bringing together of all opposites, in the triumph of life over death. Receding from the "Oriental light,"[3] it has become itself less luminous, casting a lengthening shadow, raising the Savior farther from our earth, suggesting the dramatic enactment of a supernatural mystery *before* us rather than the unification of our fractured being—and of the universe itself— *within*, at a point of absolute centrality. We have no longer interpreted the cross as the symbol of the unification of our own being around its ultimate center.

In the period of the New Testament and the fathers, however, the cross was often seen from a sapiential point of view in which it was precisely the figure of the reconciliation of all being, divine and created, in a fullness issuing from the crucified body of Jesus.[4] We may be surprised to discover a convergence between this early Christian tradition and contemporary studies of the ancient figure of the *mandala*.

The Mandala

While the word *mandala* has become familiar in recent years even to western Christians, it still has an exotic sound; this is yet another element from our own tradition which, due to our estrangement from that tradition—and partial immunization against it—must be recovered by importation from abroad.

Our recent contact with the notion of mandala has come from two principal directions: the eastern religious traditions[5] and the Jungian school of psychology.[6] From the former derives the mandala itself, and, from the latter, its contemporary interpretation in terms of human experience.

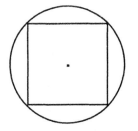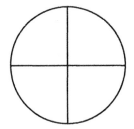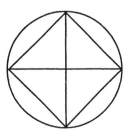

FIGURE 1.1 ELEMENTARY MANDALAS

What is a mandala? In brief, it is a geometrical figure which has a very strongly *centered* character. It combines *circular* form with *quaternity*—combines in some way the circle with the square, and retains within itself the tension of this paradox. It is an image for reflection, for meditation. According to ancient traditions it is an image of the cosmos, the universe, and is also an image of the person, in which all of the levels—bodily, psychological, spiritual—are represented, as well as the journey of the individual toward wholeness.

The Sanskrit word *mandala* means "circle" in the ordinary sense of the word. In the sphere of religious practices and in psychology it denotes circular images, which are drawn, painted, modelled, or danced.... As psychological phenomena they appear spontaneously in dreams, in certain states of conflict, and in cases of schizophrenia. Very frequently they contain a quaternity or a multiple of four, in the form of a cross, a square, an octagon, etc. In alchemy we encounter this motif in the form of *quadratura circuli* (the squaring of the circle).[7]

Mandalas emerge in a situation of psychic disorder, in the role of compensating structures. They present graphically, as it were,

...the "primal order of the total psyche," and their purpose is to transform chaos into cosmos. For these figures not only express order, they also bring it about.[8]

These figures are representations of the archetype of wholeness.

Because of this significance, the "quaternity of the One" is the schema for all images of God, as depicted in the visions of

Ezechiel, Daniel, and Enoch, and as the representation of Horus with his four sons also shows....[9]

The many variants of the mandala all involve a conjunction of square and circular form.

> Their basic motif is the premonition of a centre of personality, a kind of central point within the psyche, to which everything is related, by which everything is arranged, and which is itself a source of energy. The energy of the central point is manifested in the almost irresistible compulsion and urge to *become what one is,* just as every organism is driven to assume the form that is characteristic of its nature, no matter what the circumstances. This centre is not felt or thought of as the ego but, if one may so express it, as the *self.*[10]

The spiritual journey and the journey of psychic integration appear as two faces of the same coin in the mandalic representation.

> The mandala is the center. It is the exponent of all paths. It is the path to the center, to individuation.[11]

This language of the *mandala* is not the language of the *cross.* The mandala will seem to some Christians—profound though it may be—to be the perfect example of a "human" wisdom alien to the fullness that is in Christ.

> See to it that no one takes you captive through philosophy and empty deceit, according to human tradition, according to the elemental spirits of the universe, and not according to Christ. For in him the whole fullness of deity dwells bodily, and you have come to fullness in him... (Col 2:8-10).

The word of the cross, absolute core of reality, challenges with its unthinkable density of truth even a sapiential elaboration of the Christ-mystery itself:

> I did not come proclaiming the mystery of God to you in lofty words or wisdom. For I decided to know nothing among you except Jesus Christ, and him crucified (1 Cor 2:1-2).

... not with eloquent wisdom, so that the cross of Christ might not be emptied of its power (1 Cor 1:17).

Cross and mandala, then—as the latter is explained by its contemporary proponents—may seem at first to represent two contradictory visions. Where the mandala is interpreted in terms of the integration of opposites, the cross seems to represent precisely the conflict of irreconcilable contraries. Harmony and dissonance, peace and the sword, wisdom and paradox, immanence and transcendence: these two geometrical images seem to bring together the religious philosophies of east and west at their point of greatest contrast.

In part this apparent clash results from the incompleteness of our perspective as we view both east and west. We easily fail to see both the presence of the cross in the eastern traditions and the integrating resolution which is represented by the risen Jesus in our full Christian tradition. In part, however, the clash expresses an evolution in cultural history by which the mandala itself undergoes a new birth through the cross, and the cross ripens into its unitive fullness.

It is Paul to whom we owe our theology of the cross. And for Paul the cross is not only conflict but fullness, not only division but resolution. In fact that which distinguishes the "word of the cross" from every teaching that has preceded it is precisely the *divine fullness* which is released into the world through it. Paul places graphically before us the drama of the death and rebirth of wisdom.

Cross and Fullness: The Paschal Mandala

When Paul preaches the word of the cross, we feel the fire at the heart of the gospel. There are probably no words more powerful than these.

> For Jews demand signs and Greeks desire wisdom, but we proclaim Christ crucified, a stumbling block to Jews and foolishness to Gentiles, but to those who are the called, both Jews and Greeks, Christ the power of God and the wisdom of God. For God's foolishness is wiser than human wisdom, and God's weakness is stronger than human strength (1 Cor 1:22-25).

These words, however, proclaim not only the death of wisdom but the birth of the new and ultimate wisdom: a *unitive* wisdom, "to those who are the called, *both Jews and Greeks, Christ...the wisdom of God.*" It is "in Christ" that the new unity is born and grows.

The "power" of the word of the cross is inseparable from the *wisdom*, that is, practically, the *unity* which it contains, and which gives birth to a new world within itself.

> May I never boast of anything except the cross of our Lord Jesus Christ, by which the world has been crucified to me, and I to the world. For neither circumcision nor uncircumcision is anything, but a *new creation* is everything (Gal 6:14-15).

In this new unity between Jews and Gentiles which comes about through the cross, there is signified the birth of a new creation in which the *cosmos* itself finds its final unity in Jesus Christ. Unitive wisdom—and its mandalic representation—are reborn. This figure becomes clearer in the letters to the Ephesians and Colossians.

> So then, remember that at one time you Gentiles by birth ...were at that time without Christ, being aliens from the commonwealth of Israel and strangers to the covenants of promise, having no hope and without God in the world. But now in Christ Jesus you who once were far off have been brought near by the blood of Christ. For he is our peace; in his flesh he has made both groups into one and has broken down the dividing wall, that is, the hostility between us. He has abolished the law with its commandments and ordinances, that he might create in himself one new humanity in place of the two, thus making peace, and might *reconcile both groups to God in one body through the cross,* thus putting to death that hostility through it (Eph 2:11-16).

The center of this figure is Christ on the cross. At this center all of reality is brought together, and this is expressed in terms of two dimensions or axes. First we hear of the joining of Gentiles and Jews at this point; this is the horizontal axis. Then, finally, in the words *"reconcile both groups to God"* we are given the vertical axis. Implicit is the bringing together of all creation as it is joined to God in Christ upon the cross. Because of the pronounced accent upon the reconciliation of Gentiles and Jews here, it is possible to overlook the vertical dimension of union with God.

I pray that, according to the riches of his glory, he may grant that you may be strengthened in your inner being with power through his Spirit, and that Christ may dwell in your hearts through faith, as you are being rooted and grounded in love. I pray that you may have the power to comprehend, with all the saints, what is the breadth and length and height and depth, and to know the love of Christ that surpasses knowledge, so that you may be filled with all the fullness of God (Eph 3:16-19).

The power of this second text from Ephesians develops through a series of geometrical images, gradually constructing the mandalic figure. First the *center* is affirmed—expressed in an avalanche of language: inner man, interior dwelling in the heart, Christ, faith, root, ground, love. Then the four dimensions are extended with rhetorical generality.[12] Finally, with "the love of Christ which surpasses... filled with all the fullness of God," everything is enclosed within the sweep of an exultant circle, inevitable symbol of the fullness.

He himself is before all things, and in him all things hold together. He is the head of the body, the church; he is the beginning, the firstborn from the dead, so that he might come to have first place in everything. For in him all the fullness of God was pleased to dwell, and through him God was pleased to reconcile to himself all things, whether on earth or in heaven, by making peace through the blood of his cross.
And you (i.e. you Gentiles) who were once estranged and hostile in mind, doing evil deeds, he has now reconciled in his fleshly body through death, so as to present you holy and blameless and irreproachable before him... (Col 1:17-22).

Here the spotlight rests upon the center, which is Christ upon the cross. The figure of the cross represents the four dimensions, heaven and earth, Jew and Gentile: God and the world, those first chosen and the totality. It is in the physical body of Christ upon the cross that all of reality is thus brought to unity, for in this body, this center, dwells the fullness of God from which all things have come, in which all things subsist.
A consistent visual image emerges from these texts:[13] a concentric figure consisting of cross and circle superimposed. The center of the

figure is the crucified Christ. The vertical axis of the cross joins heaven and earth, God and his creation, and the horizontal axis brings together Jews and Gentiles: all in the one body of Christ upon the cross. The circle expresses the *plērōma*, or "fullness," emanating from this center.

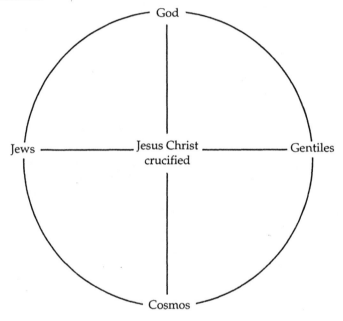

FIGURE 1.2 THE PAULINE MANDALA

While the vertical axis in this figure symbolizes the *ontological* change (that is, the divine-human or divine-cosmic unity finally achieved in Christ), the horizontal axis represents the *historical* progression of this change[14]—in which the new creation comes into being—from the Jewish "center"[15] to the Gentile periphery, or the limits of the world.

As usual in these confrontations between the Christian revelation and other traditions, one may interpret the correspondences in more than one way. Does the Christian expression of the mandala derive from the Oriental traditions through some cultural passage, as yet undiscovered? While possible, this seems unlikely. Does the eastern expression constitute some form of "prophetic anticipation" of that which was to be fulfilled by Christ upon the cross? Certainly, in some sense. Perhaps the most illuminating perspective, however, is to see here a *basic structure of reality*, an archetypal form which is present everywhere, both in the universe and in the human person; and further to see the point of entry of the Word of God into the world, the point of incarnation, occurring precisely at the center of this archetypal form, so that the form of the unfolding of the Christ-mystery in the world corresponds to this pattern. From a Christian perspective, the ultimate archetype of this omnipresent structure is the quaternity of Father, Word, Spirit, and created world.

Fullness, Christian Mandala, and Baptism

The unitive fullness,[16] which the mandala expresses, is born through the cross: that is, through the death and resurrection of Jesus. The person who believes in Jesus enters into both this death and the fullness which it brings into being, through *baptism*. The consciousness of this *baptismal* source of the new experience of unitive fullness seems to be so universal in early Christian tradition that it is most often taken for granted and left unexpressed. Sometimes the author will make explicit the baptismal context of these central texts.

> For in him the whole fullness (*plērōma*) of deity dwells bodily, and you have come to fullness in him, who is the head of every ruler and authority.... When you were buried with him in baptism, you were also raised with him through faith in the power of God, who raised him from the dead ... (Col 2:9-12).

> Was Paul crucified for you? Or were you baptized in the name of Paul? (1 Cor 1:13).

It is through the cross of Jesus and their own baptism that these believers have experienced this fullness.

Cross—Mandala in Christian Tradition

Forms of the archetypal figure appear in Christian writers of the first centuries. Irenaeus of Lyons, one of the earliest and most profound expositors of the Christ-mystery, was a disciple of the great bishop Polycarp, who in turn was known as a disciple of the apostle John. Irenaeus defends the teaching of the church by demonstrating its consistency, its integrity, its symmetry—and, ultimately, one feels, its beauty. When he must express this totality of the mystery, he turns frequently, as if naturally, to one or another image combining *the four and the one.*

Irenaeus argues, for example, that the number of the gospels could not have been other than four. There are four habitable regions in the world, he says, and four principal winds. Therefore there must be four pillars of the church: living pillars which breathe out the spirit of eternal life to humankind.

> From which it is evident that the Word, the Artificer of all, He that sitteth upon the cherubim and contains all things, He who was manifested to men, has given us the Gospel under four aspects, but bound together by one Spirit.

He goes on to recall the vision, in Revelation 4:2-11, of the Lord God enthroned in the midst of four "living creatures, full of eyes in front and behind" with the countenances of a lion, an ox, a man and a flying eagle. Closely reflecting the initial vision of Ezekiel (Ez 1), this quadriform figure of the living creatures in Revelation became consistently applied in the Christian patristic tradition to the four evangelists.

> And therefore the Gospels are in accord with these things, among which Christ Jesus is seated. . . .[17]

> Such, then, was the course followed by the Son of God, so was also the form of the living creatures; and such as was the form of the living creatures, so was also the character of the Gospel. For the living creatures are quadriform, and the Gospel is quadriform, as also is the course followed by the Lord. . . .[18]

Irenaeus elsewhere will write of the *tree*—at once tree of paradise and tree of the cross. This quaternary form, expressing an ultimate fullness, seems to be, for him, the primordial image of the Christian mystery. The Word of God that had been hidden from us—lost through a tree, he says—was revealed to us once again through a tree, "showing the height, the length, the breadth, the depth in itself. . . ." The two hands of Christ, extended upon the cross, represent the gathering of Jews and Gentiles into one; the head of Christ represents the "one God who is above all, and through all, and in us all."[19]

The cross of Jesus reproduces visibly the presence and power of the Word throughout the whole of the universe, which for Irenaeus is quadriform.

So by the obedience, whereby He obeyed unto death, hanging on the tree, He undid the old disobedience wrought in the tree. And because He is Himself *the Word of God Almighty, who in His invisible form pervades us universally in the whole world (sic), and encompasses both its length and breadth and height and depth*—for by God's Word everything is disposed and administered—*the Son of God was also crucified in these, imprinted in the form of a cross on the universe*; for He had necessarily, in becoming visible, to bring to light the universality of His cross, in order to show openly through His visible form that activity of His: that it is He who makes bright the height, that is, what is in heaven, and holds the deep, which is in the bowels of the earth, and stretches forth and extends the length from East to West, navigating also the Northern parts and the breadth of the South, and calling in all the dispersed from all sides to the knowledge of the Father.[20]

Elsewhere Irenaeus will sum up the entire mystery of salvation in a single image of creation: a quaternary figure which is strikingly parallel to the one we have just considered. The Father lifts up to his face a bit of earth with his two hands—the Word and the Spirit—and breathes into it the spirit of life.[21] Irenaeus sees this new human creature as a child, who will be gradually, through the course of history, taught by God to bear the weight of its own vocation to divinity.

⊕

The mandalic pattern of center, cross (or square) and circle, then, is written into the foundations of Christian theological tradition. Here the basic divisions of the biblical vision of reality—between God and creation, between Jew and Gentile—are bridged by the crucified Christ. From the point of consummate rupture, of contradiction and irony—the death of the Son of God—flows the unifying fullness which is new creation. The cosmos is centered in the crucified body of Christ—not statically, but in a continuing emanation of creative power, a continuing process of new creation.

As this comprehensive and cosmic Christian vision fades in the course of history, the dynamic, historical nature of the Christ-event, the new creation, will also be forgotten. Structures—both ecclesiastical and theological, often too inflexibly static and too exclusively exterior —will prevail.

Many other texts could be cited from Christian tradition, but these early ones have a plenitude, a comprehensiveness and balance, which is rarely found after the second century. This mandalic image, however, is a permanent archetypal reality at the heart of the religious psyche of the west. As it surfaces again in our own time, it expresses the same basic dimensions of human reality. Northrop Frye outlines in this way the imaginary framework within which T.S. Eliot's *Four Quartets* are to be understood:

> Draw a horizontal line on a page, then a vertical line of the same length cutting it in two and forming a cross, then a circle of which these two lines are diameters, then a smaller circle within the same centre. The horizontal line is clock time, the Heraclitean flux, the river into which no one steps twice. The vertical line is the presence of God descending into time, and crossing it at the Incarnation, forming the "still point of the turning world"...[22]

The same two axes[23] appear again and again in history, the vertical joining earthly realities with the divine, and the horizontal unfolding the same polarity between part and whole, particular and universal, individual and fullness, along the dimension of time: from "first chosen" to "all creation," from the representative to the totality, from the distinctive to the common. The Word of God must expand from its minute point of entry to fill the whole world. The unitive event of incarnation, which brings God and the creation together seminally in the one person of Christ, must be extended into the whole of the creation, and this historical movement—the inner meaning of human history—is the temporal expression of the inner life of God.

We may speak of these two axes as the Johannine and the Pauline, respectively, even though both John and Paul express the mystery of Christ in the totality of its dimensions. The vertical or ontological line is encapsulated in the words of John's prologue, "and the Word became flesh and dwelt among us," while the horizontal or historical line is expressed again and again in Pauline affirmations like this one to the Ephesians:

> In former generations this mystery was not made known to humankind, as it has now been revealed to his holy apostles

and prophets by the Spirit: that is, the Gentiles have become *fellow heirs, members of the same body, and sharers in the promise* (i.e. the promise hitherto limited to the Jews) in Christ Jesus through the gospel" (Eph 3:5-6).

The interior structure of John's gospel will also be constituted by these two axes. The outward historical movement, which is explicated by Paul and which corresponds to his personal vocation, remains implicit in John, whose narrative focuses continually upon the revelation of the divine fullness which dwells in Jesus. Along a "horizontal axis" in the structure of the fourth gospel, however, we shall find expressed a dramatic tension between the Jewish nucleus of Judea, Jerusalem, chief priests, Pharisees, scribes, Sadducees, on the one hand, and the periphery of Galilee, Samaria, Gentiles, on the other. Along the "vertical axis," meanwhile, the inner fullness of Jesus will be manifested and, finally, poured out.

These "objective" and theological implications of the mandalic figure do not exhaust its meaning. In line with what we have learned from extra-Christian sources, we may also expect to find represented in it both the fundamental structure of cosmic and psychic reality and the inner form of a personal journey.[24]

Chapter Three

Chiastic Structure
in John's Gospel

The discovery of a pervasive geometrical structure in John's gospel opens a dramatically new way into the *meaning* of the text through its literary form.

For many years it had been proposed that the *prologue* of John is constructed in a centered pattern known as *chiasm*.[1] Only quite recently[2] has a thoroughgoing analysis of the entire gospel of John been made in terms of chiastic structure.

Chiastic form can be understood by considering first a simpler form called *inclusion*: the circumscribing of a text by placing the same element at its beginning and at its end—A B A. Chiasm carries this symmetry through an entire text by arranging its elements so that the sequence of the first half of the text is reproduced in reverse order in the second half: A–B–C–B'–A'.

Chiasm is a literary form used widely in the ancient Middle East, and occurring in the Old Testament.[3] A widespread presence of chiastic structure has been asserted also in the New Testament writings: in the gospels of Matthew, Mark and Luke as well as in that of John, in the book of Revelation, in the Pauline letters and in the letter to the Hebrews.

Peter F. Ellis, following the doctoral dissertation of John Gerhard, S.J.,[4] has presented the structure of John's gospel, as it exists in our present text, as completely determined by the laws of chiastic parallelism. (See Figure 1.3)

According to Ellis, the five-part chiastic pattern—A–B–C–B'–A'—prevails not only in the gospel of John as a whole (from the beginning of the narrative in 1:19 through chapter 21), but also within each of the sections (called "*sequences*") into which he divides the gospel.

The gospel is divided into five great parts, each of which is governed by an overall theme.

Part I: 1:19 – 4:3.   Witness and Discipleship

Part II: 4:4 – 6:15.   Response to Jesus: Positive and Negative

Part III: 6:16-21.   The New Exodus

Part IV: 6:22 – 12:11.   Response to Jesus: Positive and Negative

Part V: 12:21 – 21:25.   Witness and Discipleship

Parts I and V are related by chiastic parallelism, as are Parts II and IV; Part III is the center of the chiasm. Within each of Parts I, II, IV and V, the five sections ("sequences") are also related chiastically, and within each of these sequences there is also a chiastic structure. Overall structure, intermediate structure and fine structure are all chiastic, smaller chiasms nesting together within the greater ones.

This basic pattern of chiastic symmetry makes use of a diversity of material:

John creates his parallelisms most often by repeating either the same words or the same content (concepts). Occasionally he creates parallelisms by means of antithetic parallelism, i.e., by contrasting a negative with a positive or a positive with a negative situation or concept. On rare occasions he not only parallels words and content (concepts) but even the literary form of a sequence.[5]

One can quickly perceive the persuasiveness of this chiastic proposal by examining the general plan of the gospel (Figure 1.3). Clear affinities are visible, for example, between the sequence-pairs 1 and 21, 2 and 20, 3 and 19, 5 and 17. These parallelisms can be somewhat deceptive, however, in the light of the disproportionate size of some of the sequences in Part V. One may conjecture that it would be possible to find some parallel for almost any theme within a text which includes chapters 13, 14, 15, 16 and 17 of John's gospel, as does sequence 18.

FIGURE 1.3

THE CHIASTIC STRUCTURE OF JOHN'S GOSPEL

(according to Ellis, *The Genius of John*, pp. 14-15)

PART I: 1:19–4:3
WITNESS AND DISCIPLESHIP

Seq. 1 (1:19-51)
At the Jordan

Seq. 2 (2:1-12)
Mary at Cana

Seq. 3 (2:13-25)
Jesus in the temple

Seq. 4 (3:1-21)
Discourse to Nicodemus

Seq. 5 (3:22–4:3)
Witness of the Baptist

PART V: 12:12–21:25
WITNESS AND DISCIPLESHIP

Seq. 21 (20:19–21:25)
At the lake

Seq. 20 (20:1-18)
Mary at the tomb

Seq. 19 (ch. 18–19)
Jesus' passion

Seq. 18 (ch. 13–17)
Supper discourse

Seq. 17 (12:12-50)
Witness of Jerusalem crowd

PART II: 4:4–6:15
RESPONSE: POSITIVE & NEGATIVE

Seq. 6 (4:4-38)
Samaritan woman

Seq. 7 (4:39-45)
Samaritan men

Seq. 8 (4:46-52)
Pagan official's son cured

Seq. 9 (5:1-47)
Cure of paralytic at feast

Seq. 10 (6:1-15)
Bread multiplied

PART IV: 6:22–12:11
RESPONSE: POSITIVE & NEGATIVE

Seq. 16 (10:40–12:11)
Bethany women

Seq. 15 (10:22-39)
Jesus: "My sheep hear . . ."

Seq. 14 (9:1–10:21)
Cure of man born blind

Seq. 13 (7:1–8:58)
Feast of Booths

Seq. 12 (6:22-72)
Bread discourse

PART III: 6:16-21
THE NEW EXODUS

Seq. 11 (6:16-21)
Jesus walks on the sea

Note: Titles of some individual sequences have been altered.

Application of this chiastic structural analysis to John offers to resolve a number of the major problems which have been posed to scholars by the present text of the fourth gospel. Passages which, according to the logic of narrative order, seem clearly out of place in John's text fall into place from a chiastic perspective. Repetitions (e.g. much of the content of ch. 16 and 17 repeats that of ch. 13 and 14) and unlikely chronological placements (e.g. the cleansing of the temple at the beginning of Jesus' ministry) are explained, and the present state of the text is vindicated without major changes.[6]

Ellis finds the center of the entire gospel in the narrative of the sea-crossing (6:16-21) which, theologically, signifies a *new exodus.*

Only when the reader recognizes the episode as the turning point of the Gospel and as the dramatization of a new exodus constituting a new people of God does it dawn upon him or her that responsive Israel (the disciples and Christians in general) is about to replace unresponsive Israel (the synagogue) as the true Israel of God—the Christian Church.[7]

The theological power of this chiastic thesis appears first of all in the emergence of this *center*[8] in the gospel, and then in the *symbolic relationships* which are suggested by the symmetries of this geometrical form. We shall explore both of these aspects of chiasm in John.

The scheme proposed by Ellis, aside from its promise to give order to the whole of text of John, is attractive because this *centering* which is inherent in the chiastic structure resonates not only with a general impression created by the fourth gospel, but also with a centering dynamism which we shall find in the gospel's symbolic structures. This centering is encountered in a long series of symbols which begins with the *Logos* and the light of the prologue and includes the symbols of temple, of Jacob's well (ch. 4), of the garden of paradise, the vine and its branches, and finally of Jesus' body itself.

It is not possible here to give an adequate idea of the structure and mode of application of the chiastic model of Gerhard and Ellis, nor of its fruitfulness. In Ellis' book, one can easily follow the application of the hypothesis to the whole of John's gospel, chapter by chapter.

This rigorous application of chiastic analysis to John, however, inevitably raises some questions in the reader's mind. We may wonder what contribution many of the smaller chiastic forms make either to the theological understanding of the gospel or simply to the reading of it. One may often wonder whether the comprehensive *formal* unity which has been achieved through chiasm is accompanied by a corresponding *theological* unity, a development of unitive meaning.

In the chiastic grid which results from this method there is a tendency toward rigidity. One suspects that the author of the gospel would find his own scheme inhibiting his freedom in molding the narrative material, and limiting the expressiveness of his text. The system seems often inadequate to the imaginative vitality and subtlety of John. Are there other, more subtle forms of chiastic parallelism in John than the parallels of word, phrase and concept that have been brought out here? Might some of these deeper resonances require a step of *symbolic interpretation*, a further movement within John's symbolic language which has not yet, in these instances, been made? Are some of the chiastic parallels, that is, *implicit*, requiring *development*? Is the chiastic parallelism itself meant to lead—or to impel—us to this deeper reading, as does the enigma of a parable in the synoptic gospels?

Often the proposed chiastic form does deepen the meaning of an episode (as in the parallel of the cleansing of the temple with the passion and death of Jesus). Often too, however, the imposed chiastic form seems arbitrary and tangential to one or both of the texts. The parallel elements may not be related to the central meaning of the texts. This more easily occurs where the matching elements are only words and phrases.

By affirming balance, symmetry and concentricity in John's gospel, the chiastic analysis confirms a tacit conviction which has formed within many a reader. After the lean years of disintegrative criticism, the method seems to offer some promise of a new and more integrative understanding of John. The chiastic analysis by itself, however, does not yet fulfill this promise of depth and unity.

Building upon this invaluable discovery by Gerhard and Ellis of a basic chiastic structure in John's gospel, we shall propose two further steps: first, a quaternary or mandalic development of the chiasm, and, second, the interpretation of this Johannine structure according to a unified symbolic scheme: the seven days of the new creation.

With the discovery of John's chiastic structure, a crucial door has been opened into that fullness of meaning which awaits within the fourth gospel's captivating glow. We have noted the limitations of this first application of chiastic interpretation, however. If we would glimpse the length and breadth, the height and depth of the Johannine mystery, a further journey into "sacred geometry" will be needed.

Chapter Four

The Chiastic Mandala of John's Gospel

From Chiasm to Mandala

The pervasive five-part chiasm which was found by Gerhard and Ellis to govern the structure of John's gospel[1] can be imagined geometrically in more than one way. Besides the simple binary parallelism which appears in the "horseshoe" diagram of the whole gospel (Fig. 1.3), a quaternary figure, or cross-form, centered in Part III, is also conceivable.

The attraction of this quaternary or cruciform chiasm deepens when we discover, in the chiastic arrangement proposed by Ellis, some relationships which point beyond binary chiasm. The most striking of these relationships is that between sequences 2, 20, 6 and 16 (Fig. 1.3; Ellis p. 14). In each of these *four* episodes, Jesus interacts with a *woman*. While a parallelism between seq. 2 and seq. 20 is recognized by Ellis, as well as between 6 and 16, the affinity of all four "Jesus and woman" sequences does not find expression in the scheme. These four episodes seem to constitute a "feminine ring" around the center of the chiasm, and as one reflects upon them a further geometrical pattern begins to emerge.

Following these clues—both the fivefold chiastic pattern and the thematic symmetry among these four Jesus-woman sequences—Ellis' chiastic figure (pp. 14-15) has been rearranged into a quaternary, or cross-form, around the same central sequence 11 (see Figure 1.4).

At first, the resulting figure does not seem to bring to light much symmetry or significance which had not already been manifest in the Ellis arrangement. The key to a dramatically new chiastic vision is in an observation which seems at first trivial. Along this horizontal axis

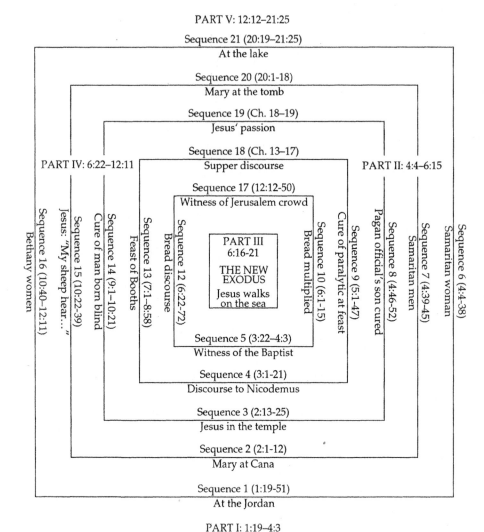

FIGURE 1.4
ELLIS CHIASM IN QUATERNARY FORM

which has been created between seq. 6 and seq. 16, the path from the central seq. 11 to either of the poles, seq. 6 or seq. 16, includes a total of *six* sequences or episodes. When one recalls that it was on the *sixth day of creation*, in Genesis (Gen 1:28), that *man and woman* were created, this sixth position of the episodes of the Samaritan woman and of Mary of Bethany takes on a new significance! In the beginning of John's gospel—a few verses into the prologue—we hear of the *creation* of all things in the divine Word. Once awakened to this theme, we shall encounter it reflected in one way or another throughout the gospel. It begins to appear that there may be more than coincidence in this curious fact of the sixth day.

If one reflects, at this point, upon the *central* episode of the Ellis chiasm—the night sea-crossing of 6:16-21—it is natural to perceive in that scene, besides the exodus symbolism which Ellis has demonstrated, a further meaning. This appearance of Jesus upon the dark waters reflects also *the first moment of creation*, as recounted in Genesis 1:2.

Suddenly the stunning possibility emerges that John's narrative has been composed according to a quaternary figure, centered in the episode of the night sea-crossing, in such a way as to retrace the scheme of the *seven days of creation*!

This hypothesis has great potential for an ordered structuring and a theological centering of the gospel narrative. Much of this promise derives from the profound suggestiveness of the first verses of the Genesis creation narrative. The creation of light, through the Word of God, upon the dark waters where the Spirit hovers, resonates with the theological center of the New Testament, as we shall see.

This structural hypothesis of the seven days of creation was not immediately borne out by most of the other episodes. The experiment was then made of moving the divisions between some of the Gerhard-Ellis sequences, with the aim of arriving at a greater degree of symmetry and correlation: not so much between key words, phrases and concepts, but between the themes and symbols which governed the individual episodes (see Table 1.1).

It was not found necessary to make any changes in the sequences which lie upon the vertical axis, except the provisional removal of chapter 21 from the chiastic scheme.[2] Aside from this exclusion of ch. 21, only seven sequences were modified: 6, 7, 8, 9, 14, 15 and 16. The criterion which guided these adjustments was basically that of bringing *similar episodes*—seen as symbolic wholes united around a particular thematic core—into chiastic symmetry with one another.

In this process the only chiastic relationships which were considered were those *between* sequences or episodes; the smaller chiastic relations *within* the sequences themselves were disregarded.[3] It was hoped that this loosening up of the framework of precise formal parallelism would allow the deeper symbolic-theological symmetries between the episodes to appear.

For the sake of a clear distinction from Ellis' *sequences*, these new divisions of the text have been called *sections*. They have also been numbered differently. Section 1 (6:16-21) is the *center* of the mandala, and successive sections proceed outward from this center, rather than following the narrative order of the gospel. Thus the movement outward from section 1 to section 21 corresponds to the progression through the seven days of the new creation. Within each concentric ring, representing one "day of creation," the numbering sequence is from Part I to II to IV to V. The result of these changes can be seen in Figure 1.5. In Table 1.1 the twenty-one sections are placed alongside the corresponding sequences of Ellis.

This quaternary chiasm naturally takes the form of a *mandala*:[4] a cruciform figure enclosed by a circle. Planetary circles representing the respective days of creation radiate from the common center. Ellis sequences 1 and 21 (the latter without chapter 21) have been brought outside the mandala proper, constituting the "seventh day." Since this results in a deficiency of two sequences along the vertical axis, the second day, consisting of sequences 10 and 12 of chapter 6, the bread narrative, has been allotted spaces along the vertical as well as the horizontal axis. Together, days one and two constitute a double center for the entire figure. By the term "center," however, we shall ordinarily refer only to the first day (Section 1:6:16-21).

Relationships Within the Chiastic Mandala

The mandalic chiasm of Figure 1.5 will provide the structure for the central and largest part of this book, in which we shall examine the whole of John's narrative from this perspective of the seven days of creation. First, let us try to get a general understanding of how the mandalic chiasm "works." We shall take a first look at the principal symmetries and other relationships which emerge from the figure. Some lines of interpretation will be suggested by this preliminary view.

The ultimate center of the pattern is taken to be the *egō eimi* or *I Am* spoken by Jesus in 6:20. This expression evokes the divine *name*;[5] Jesus is the creative Word that was "in the beginning" (prologue, 1:1), who appears now, moving like the Spirit over the waters of the

TABLE 1.1

DIVISION OF TEXT: MANDALIC SECTIONS AND ELLIS SEQUENCES

MANDALIC SECTION (M)		SCENE	CORRESPONDING ELLIS SEQUENCE (E)	
NO.	TEXT		NO.	TEXT
1	6:16-21	SEA	11	E=M
2	6:1-15	BREAD SIGN	10	=
3	6:22-71	BREAD DISCOURSE	12	=
4	3:22–4:3	BAPTIST	5	=
5	5:31-47	WITNESSES	9	5:1-47
6	7:1-53 + 8:12-59	BOOTHS	13	=
7	12:12-50	JERUSALEM	17	=
8	3:1-21	NICODEMUS	4	=
9	5:1-30	PARALYTIC	8	4:46-52
10	9:1-41	BLIND MAN	14	9:1–10:21
11	ch. 13–17	SUPPER	18	=
12	2:13-25	TEMPLE	3	=
13	4:43-54	CHILD	7	4:39-45
14	ch. 10–11	LAZARUS	15	10:22-39
15	ch. 18–19	PASSION	19	=
16	2:1-12	CANA	2	=
17	4:4-42	SAMARIA	6	4:4-38
18	12:1-11	BETHANY	16	10:40–12:11
19	20:1-18	GARDEN	20	=
20	1:19-51	JORDAN	1	=
21	20:19-31	HOUSE	21	20:19–21:25

NOT INCLUDED: Prologue: 1:1-18
Epilogue: 21:1-25

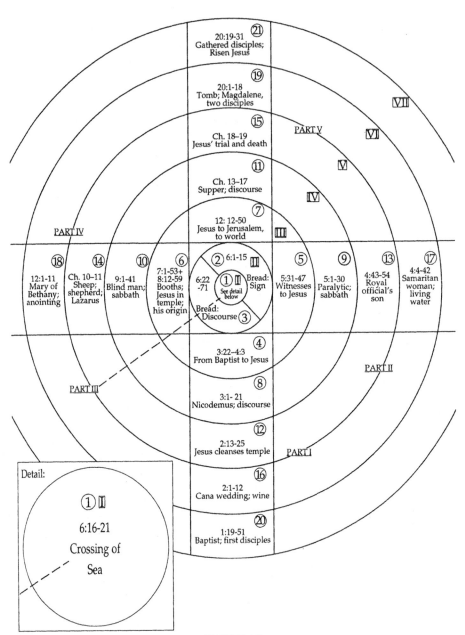

FIGURE 1.5
THE MANDALIC CHIASM OF JOHN'S GOSPEL

primeval chaos of Genesis 1:1. This divine Word, source of all creation (1:3), dwells at creation's center and regenerates it in himself. At this central point of the figure will be fixed the cross, symbol of the death and resurrection of Jesus. Here symbolically occurs the act of faith, the experience of baptism and the passage from darkness to light.

The changes from Ellis' division of sequences occur along the horizontal axis, and have been made in order to allow further symmetries to appear between episodes on the left and right arms of the figure. Thus there is a significant alignment of the *signs* of Jesus in the figure. The four *healing* signs align themselves in two parallel pairs along the horizontal axis in sections 13 and 14, 9 and 10. Two other, *"epiphanic"* signs—the Cana miracle (sec. 16) and the central sea-crossing (sec. 1)—remain aligned with the great sign itself of Jesus' resurrection (sec. 20), along the vertical axis.

The two *sabbaths* have been brought into chiastic parallel, in sections 9 and 10, together with the healings which Jesus performed on these sabbaths: that of the paralytic (ch. 5) and that of the blind man (ch. 9). The two "revivals from death"—that of the royal official's son (sec. 13, ch. 4) and that of Lazarus (sec. 14, ch. 11)—are also brought into chiastic symmetry.

Episodes on the *vertical axis* develop the gospel's central thematic of Jesus' self-revelation against the background of the institutions of the old Israel, and then in the midst of his own disciples. Gradually the trajectory of his life, death and resurrection unfolds, and that which is in him becomes manifest and is transmitted to his chosen followers. Recalling the development of the prologue, this sequence of events expresses the theological core of the gospel. Along this vertical axis are aligned the three *Passovers* of Jesus' ministry, and here unfolds the entire narrative of his final *hour*.

Along the *horizontal* axis, on the other hand, the focus broadens to embrace Jesus' public ministry of teaching and of healing. The scope of the narrative here is more pastoral, more anthropocentric. The nature of Jesus' power is expressed in the overcoming of illness and death. A dramatic conflict builds progressively between this power and the power of the Jewish religious authorities, between faith and unbelief, merciful love and hatred, grace and the hardening of hearts.

There is also a geographical and social movement, from the Samaritan woman and the royal official (probably a Gentile) on the right to the intimate friends of Jesus and the vicinity of Jerusalem on the left, as Jesus' drama approaches its crisis and conclusion. The presence of the four healing signs culminating in the raising of Lazarus establishes an axis of active compassion and power of life, while the mounting and finally murderous opposition of the Jerusalem officials provides the counter-principle. Midway on this line, Jesus, moved by compassion for the hungry crowd that follows him, multiplies for them the bread and the fishes.

It is also possible to characterize each of the *four arms* of the figure. This has been done by Ellis for the five great parts of the gospel, which correspond to the center and the four arms or extremities of our figure. Each part, for Ellis, expresses a particular aspect or segment of the story of Jesus, as is evident in the titles which they are given (see p. 31 above). To Parts I and V, II and IV, respectively, correspond the lower and upper, right and left arms of our mandalic figure. This mandalic figure[6] will bring to light relationships and resonances which are not suggested by the binary chiastic figure—accenting first a center and then quaternary groupings of elements, and introducing a second path of movement through the gospel.

The lower arm of our mandalic figure (Part I) is encompassed by "John the Baptist" sections, while the upper one (Part V) is related, in parallel fashion, to the "disciple whom Jesus loved" (identified with the author of this gospel). This disciple and the Baptist are the central *witnesses* to Jesus.

Along the lower arm we pass a series of symbolic representations of the *old order*, which is to be supplanted by Jesus: the Baptist, the water, the old wine, the temple, Nicodemus the "teacher of Israel," and once again John the Baptist, friend of the bridegroom who has now appeared. The upper arm, correspondingly, is devoted to the birth of the *new order*, which takes place in the *hour* of Jesus, which has now arrived.

Along the right arm (Part II) Jesus interacts with people on the periphery of Israel, signifying the universality of the salvation which he brings. Movement along the left arm, in contrast, is toward the Jewish "center": Judea, Jerusalem, temple, law, and the final hostility of chief priests and Pharisees.

⊕

The *seven days of creation*, as presented in the first two chapters of Genesis, do not immediately leap to the eye in the mandalic figure's seven planetary rings. One by one, these correlations appear, sometimes only with the help of some mediating idea. Correlation is impressive on the first, fifth and sixth days. At the supper which concludes the fourth day, Jesus illuminates those who are to be his "lights" in the world, in conformity with a contemporary interpretation of Genesis 1:14-18. When the risen Jesus returns to his disciples and gives them his "peace" on the first day of the week, we can infer an allusion to the seventh day, the sabbath of God's rest (Gen 2:2-3).

We shall assume, however, that John has conceived the seven days of the new creation *in his own way*, which does not correspond in a literal way with the seven days of Genesis 1–2. He has also *combined the symbolism of the first and second creation accounts* (that is, Gen 1:1–2:4a and Gen 2:4b-25). We shall study John's development of each of the seven days in Part II.

Mandala and Double Reading

The meaning and power of the mandalic figure appear when we contemplate it in the light of John's prologue. The figure expresses geometrically that which is verbally proclaimed in the prologue: the unfolding of a new creation which becomes present and manifest in Christ, replacing the Mosaic law through the coming of that fullness of grace and truth which is the Word. This uncreated light which is the Word dwells anew in the center of the old creation, which it illumines, transforming it through birth in itself.

If the mandalic figure is to deepen our reading of the fourth gospel, we must distinguish the figure's *two movements*. The first is *linear* and historical, following in the usual way the narrative of the life of Jesus, and corresponding to the historical journey of Israel in the Old Testament, particularly in the fundamental exodus experience. Events of the gospel story are presented with continual reference to this biblical, and chiefly exodus, background. The central episode of the figure (sec. 1, the sea-crossing of John 6:16-21) represents the actual Passover event (crossing of the Red Sea) on this plane.

The second movement is not linear but *radial*, proceeding outward from this center of the figure (interpreted now not as the exodus event but as the first moment of creation, as in Genesis 1:1-5), and representing the seven days of the new creation. These seven days are redefined by John in terms of the life, death and immanent creative presence of Jesus, the Word incarnate.

Corresponding to this double movement is the fabric of biblical reference in John's gospel. This is largely woven of two theological components: first, the Mosaic–exodus–Israel historical strand, and, second, the Genesis–new creation strand.[7] To the first relates the linear movement of the historical journey of the gospel narrative toward its conclusion, and to the second relates the breakthrough of the light and power of the creative Word in each episode of the gospel.

The mandala, therefore, points to a reading of the gospel—and ultimately of one's life—*on two levels at once*: both *linearly*, with continual reference to the preceding biblical history, and *centrically*, as a continual emergence and discovery of the creative center, the living Word, present and at each moment displaying a fresh aspect of its activity.

Before committing the time and energy required to master these complexities, the reader will certainly ask: *Is it really there*? Has John's gospel actually been written according to this chiastic-mandalic scheme, or is this just another elaborate structural fantasy being imposed upon the over-compliant Johannine text?[8]

In response, let me first affirm that the chiastic mandala of the seven days is proposed here in all seriousness as a hypothesis for the structure of the fourth gospel.

On the other hand, the reader does not have to become convinced of the scheme's "objective" validity before proceeding to use it. It is offered here, first of all, as an interpretive *tool*, a means of questioning the Johannine texts. I have personally found that this mandalic scheme brings to light more meaning, and more satisfactory meaning, in John's gospel than any other structural proposal which I have explored. Having invested much time and energy in this structural approach, however, I find it difficult to step outside it and critically evaluate it, and impossible to read John from a standpoint outside its influence.

The reader who has not yet become glued to the spider web can regard the chiastic mandala more guardedly, yet without having to reject it. First, the scheme is a hypothesis: it may or may not prove itself to be the skeleton of John's gospel, as one works one's way through the narrative with it. Second—and this is more important—

one may employ the chiastic-mandalic structure functionally, as a convenient scaffolding from which to enter into the symbolic world of John. One is likely to find, at the least, that the combination of a linear-chronological reading with a centric reading brings one closer to the fullness of meaning in John than merely a linear reading. The density of meaning which this geometrical approach discloses in such related Johannine themes as creation and new creation, woman and spiritual interiority, incarnation and unitive symbolism, will open up to the reader new dimensions of the gospel.

Again, one enters into the vibrant fullness of John's gospel by going beyond the issue of certainty and exposing one's spirit and imagination to the wind of the Spirit that moves there. It is frequently by the exploit, the adventure of imagination that one comes closest to John's meaning. We gradually discover in his gospel hidden paths of symbolic imagination of an audacity and reach that astonish us, and that are sealed to the mind which refuses to step off the well-marked path.

One may think of this mandala of the seven days as a boldly constructed ship, an exploratory vessel specially built to carry us into the hitherto unmapped recesses of John. The sole guarantee furnished with it is that it will not fail to bring the reader deep into Johannine country. Or it may be imagined as a listening device, an archetype-antenna, a meaning-detector capable of picking up wavelengths that are excluded by the very design of our more conventional equipment.

From this perspective of depth-geometry—and with the help of our other interpretive methods (Chapter 1 above)—we shall look first at John's prologue and then begin our journey through the Johannine narrative itself.

Chapter Five

Into the Unitive Source:
John's Prologue

John's prologue, a microcosm of the fourth gospel, reproduces in its eighteen verses the structure of the gospel—and therefore the structure of the "Christian mandala" which we have examined. While the prologue provides a vital key to the *meaning* of the gospel narrative, it is the narrative which makes present to us the journey of the Word in flesh and blood, and so gives *life* to the sublime theological procession of the prologue.

The prologue is often referred to by biblical scholars, in whole or in part, as a *hymn*,[1] and it is related to other such concentrated and rhythmic texts in the New Testament.[2] Like these other texts, the hymn of John's prologue is often thought to have pre-existed the gospel. It is also frequently divided into sections of differing origin. Claiming once again the exemption accruing to our literary approach,[3] we shall bypass these bothersome questions and attempt to understand the prologue in its present (and traditional) form.

The word "hymn" implies music, and this is music—though of a strangely timeless quality. The discourse orbits around an unseen center, of which it sings. It circles and casts a spell: its circular motion is incantatory, magical. This is the leisured music of fullness, of an inexpressible plenitude of being which overflows the ring of words, the rings of the chain of words, like a brimming light. The first letter of John, with its circling chant, conveys the same brimming fullness. This letter sheds much light upon John's gospel and particularly upon the gospel's prologue. (Compare, for example, 1 Jn 1:1-5 with Jn 1:1-18.)

And yet the music moves forward; the movement is a spiral. The progression is from fullness to fullness, as we shall see: from a fullness of being through a fullness of revelation to a fullness of life. It moves from an invisible pre-existence to a visible presence and then to an invisible consummation within the believer.

This circular movement is slowed momentarily by the two appearances of John the Baptist. The lean figure in a camel skin is drawn into the dance, whirls for a moment with its movement as he gives his witness, and with a self-deprecating bow detaches himself again. When the music of the prologue has ceased, we shall find ourselves once more with the Baptist. His surprising presence in the prologue is a first clue that this text may itself be related to baptism.

Chiastic Structure in the Prologue

We have mentioned in the third chapter the chiastic form which has been discovered in John's prologue.[4] There has been increasing agreement that the *center* of this chiastic form is in v. 12 or 12+13. Gerhard and Ellis[5] find in the prologue the same five-part chiastic structure which they have found throughout the gospel. We shall use their proposed structure for the prologue. Here we have supplied provisional titles to make evident, from the beginning, some of the symmetry and thematic development.

I. (a) 1:1-8.   The Word before creation; creation; light of Word in the world.

II. (b) 1:9-11.   Light of the Word coming into the world in Jesus, and unrecognized by the world or by "his own," the Jewish people.

III. (c) 1:12-13. All who believe in him are enabled to become children of God.

IV. (b') 1:14.   The Word becomes flesh, dwelling among those who believe in him. These see his glory.

V. (a') 1:15-18. Those who believe in him receive his fullness of grace and truth; they know God by dwelling in God as does he, the Son. This is the new creation.

Some of the chiastic parallels[6] are easily seen. There are two matching sections concerning John the Baptist (vv. 6-8 and v. 15). The prologue begins with the Word which is *with God* (1:1), and concludes with the Son who is *in the bosom of the Father* (1:18). All things were created *through him* (the Word) (1:3) and grace and truth came *through Jesus Christ* (1:17).

Less obvious is the antithetic parallel of the "world" (1:10) which did not know him although he was in it, with the "we" (1:14) who have seen his glory as he dwelt among us.

Quaternary Structure in the Prologue

The five-part chiasm, once again, suggests a cruciform geometry. In Figure 1.6 the prologue has been arranged in an elementary quaternary form, parallel to the figure of the gospel but with no attempt to relate the individual verses to the days of creation.[7]

As this figure is contemplated, its symmetries deepen and relationships are perceived both with the mandalic gospel and with the archetypal "Christian mandala" which is evident in the Pauline letters (above, chapter 2). The mandalic configuration intensifies the importance of the *center*, and this importance is confirmed by the obvious theological weight of v. 12. In Figure 1.7, these *three* figures are shown together in a simplified form for comparison. While relationships between the three are complex, the overall parallelism of the axes or poles of the three figures is evident.

Both Johannine figures represent further theological developments with respect to the simple *Pauline figure* (A). From the Pauline metaphoric image we proceed to a more subtle and implicit image, embedded in the structure and fine symmetries of the Johannine texts. The titles employed for the *gospel mandala* (B) bring out the strong *baptismal* theme which characterizes the vertical axis. Along the left or "Jewish" arm of the horizontal axis, there is a differentiation between those Jews who "receive" Jesus (exemplified by Mary) and those who reject him (exemplified by the chief priests). The central *sea-crossing* correlates well with the Pauline center (in A, Jesus upon the cross) (cf. Jn 8:28: "When you have *lifted up* the Son of man, then you will realize that *I Am...*"), with the baptismal thematic of the vertical axis, and with the passage and separation which occurs along the horizontal axis. (It is clear, however, that the concrete episodes which make up the gospel mandala are open to various interpretations.)

FIGURE 1.6
JOHN'S PROLOGUE
IN
QUATERNARY FORM

who has made him known.

who is (in the Father's bosom),

It is God the only Son,

18. No one has ever seen God.

grace and truth came through Jesus Christ.

PART V

17. The law indeed was given through Moses;

grace upon grace.

16. From his fullness we have all received,

because he was before me.'"

ranks ahead of me

'He who comes after me

PART IV

"This was he of whom I said,

15. John testified to him and cried out,

14. And the Word became flesh and lived among us,

and we have seen his glory,

the glory as of a father's only son,

full of grace and truth.

12. But to all who received him,

who believed in his name,

he gave the power to become children of God,

13. who were born,
not of blood
or of the will of the flesh
or of the will of man,
but of God.

9. The true light, which enlightens everyone, was coming into the world.

10. He was in the world,

and the world came into being through him;

yet the world did not know him.

11. He came to what was his own,

and his own people did not accept him.

but he came to testify to the light.

8. He himself was not the light,

so that all might believe through him.

7. He came as a witness to testify to the light

PART II

PART III

whose name was John.

6. There was a man sent from God,

and the darkness did not overcome it.

5. The light shines in the darkness,

and the life was the light of all people.

What has come into being 4. in him was life,

PART I

and without him not one thing came into being.

3. All things came into being through him,

2. He was in the beginning with God.

and the Word was God.

and the Word was with God,

1. In the beginning was the Word,

FIGURE 1.7
PARALLEL MANDALAS: PAULINE LETTERS, GOSPEL NARRATIVE, PROLOGUE

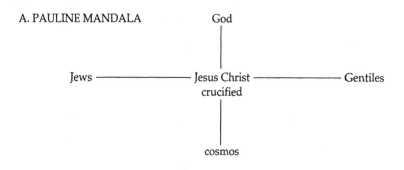

A. PAULINE MANDALA

God

Jews ———————— Jesus Christ ———————— Gentiles
crucified

cosmos

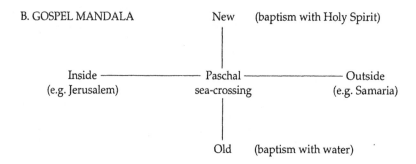

B. GOSPEL MANDALA

New   (baptism with Holy Spirit)

Inside ———————— Paschal ———————— Outside
(e.g. Jerusalem)   sea-crossing   (e.g. Samaria)

Old   (baptism with water)

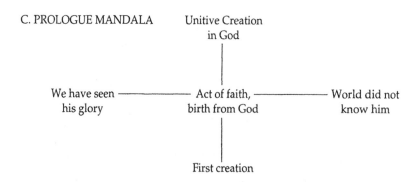

C. PROLOGUE MANDALA

Unitive Creation
in God

We have seen ———————— Act of faith, ———————— World did not
his glory   birth from God   know him

First creation

In the *prologue figure* (C), there is a return to the clarity and simplicity of the Pauline figure, but with the unique theological richness and depth of John's vision. The *center* of this figure correlates very well with the baptismal symbolism of the sea-crossing (B), and thus also with Jesus upon the cross (A). The cosmic scope of the Pauline figure is maintained, but deepened with the thematic of new and immanent *creation*. The contrast between *Jew* and *Gentile* has given way to the contrast between *"we"* who have seen his glory and believed in him, so that he dwells among us as in the new Israel, first fruits of the new creation, and the *"world"* which did not know him when he appeared within it, and so remains merely "world," the untransformed old creation. The divine unitive *fullness* which is implicit in the mandalic structure of these figures becomes explicit in the language itself of the prologue (1:14-16).

We shall return to this prologue figure to develop it further, after our detailed study of the gospel. From the prologue's perspective of final synthesis, we shall then be able to review the narrative as a whole.

Johannine Symbolism in the Prologue

Our second general approach, the reader may recall, is that of *symbolic interpretation*. Just as one is frequently struck, while reading John, by symmetries that suggest an underlying structure, one is aware also of other resonances—a kind of poetic communication between the images and events of the gospel. Many of the characters in John's gospel seem related to one another by some mysterious kinship. The cosmic images of light and of water, and familiar human things like bread and wine, subtly respond to one another as they all take on an aura of meaning beyond their ordinary power of communication.

In our study of John's gospel we shall be continually moving within the language of symbolism. The prologue offers an introduction to this Johannine language as it speaks of ultimate mysteries through a few simple images: word and world, light and darkness, flesh and blood, childbirth, dwelling and the human breast.

In the prologue we are given the "eye" of John's gospel. This brief text supplies, in a subtle and profound way, the viewpoint and the essential concepts with which the gospel is ultimately to be read and understood. These eighteen verses refract, like the facets of a crystal, the unitive light of the *Logos* into the primary colors of the symbolic spectrum or alphabet from which the world of John's gospel will be created.

The *Logos*, or Word, itself appears at the prologue's beginning to begin our initiation into the *new way of knowing* which is the objective of John's gospel and the fruit of the baptismal event. It is in the central solar light of the *Logos* that everything else in this gospel is finally to be understood.

The key to John's *symbolic* language, with its peculiar depth, is in this same creative Word. "All things came into being through him, and without him not one thing came into being" (1:3). The same divine Word which is the source of *creation* is the source and center of John's *symbolism*. From the Word arise all being and all thought, as well as the worlds of language and of symbolism[8] which lie between being and thought.

Unitive Revelation in the Prologue

I have referred to our third approach as a *unitive* method. The meaning of this term[9] will, I hope, gradually fill out for the reader in the course of our study of John. Since the word is intended, practically, to signify the *plērōma*, the fullness of John's meaning, it is necessarily somewhat indeterminate at the outset. But if indeterminate, how can it be used from the start as a method of interpretation? It is available because we know it already with a preverbal knowledge.[10] Within each of us is present the light of this unitive reality, in which we know the oneness of all things, of all being. This light must be led by the hand from its imprisonment within complex structures of inhibition, and this, from one point of view, is the purpose of John's gospel. There is an inevitable circularity in our use of the unitive as an interpretive approach, but this will become less of an obstacle as we proceed. We shall find that the Johannine unitive is intimately related to the mystery of *baptism*.

Logos and Unitive Wisdom

At the beginning of our reading of the prologue, we encounter the Word, the creative *Logos*, which is John's fundamental unitive term. There is a world of Greek thought[11] behind the *Logos* of John's prologue. It seems likely that John himself was influenced by Philo,[12] in whom the Greek and biblical traditions meet. The dominant influence here, however, is the biblical tradition itself. In the Johannine *Logos* the creative Word of God becomes a human person, Jesus, who embodies in himself the totality of divine revelation.

Jesus is divine Wisdom, pre-existent, but now come among men to teach them and give them life. Not the Torah but Jesus Christ is the creator and source of light and life. He is the *Memra*, God's presence among men. And yet, even though all these strands are woven into the Johannine concept of the Word, this concept remains a unique contribution of Christianity. It is beyond all that has gone before, just as Jesus is beyond all who have gone before.[13]

Much of the language of the prologue reflects the Jewish *wisdom* literature.[14] *Sophia*, the feminine Divine Wisdom of the late Old Testament period, bears within herself both the *creative* and the *unitive* power of the Word:

I learned both what is secret and what is manifest, for wisdom, the *fashioner of all things*, taught me (Wis 7:21-22).

For in her there is a spirit that is intelligent, holy, unique, manifold, subtle...*all powerful, overseeing all, and penetrating through all* spirits that are intelligent, pure and altogether subtle....For she is a reflection of eternal light, a spotless mirror of the working of God, and an image of his goodness. Although she is but *one, she can do all things*, and while *remaining in herself*, she *renews all things*... (Wis 7:22-23.26-27).

Centering in the Prologue

A second door to this unitive perspective is through the symbol of *"center,"* which has re-emerged in western spirituality recently.[15] The first words of John's prologue, "In the beginning was the Word," establish a center and its gravitational field. The remainder of the prologue draws out this center into a theological axis along which the deepest meaning of the gospel will unfold.

"In the beginning...": we are led to imagine not only the origin of a history in time, but a continuing source of being, from which the creation continues to radiate as a series of concentric rings upon a liquid surface radiate from their point of origin. The source is light—and source of light—at the center of that human person which is the "rational creation." This light shines in the darkness of incomprehension.

The source itself comes into the world once again, in a physical and visible form (Jesus), and, though unrecognized by that world, becomes anew its *center* through this presence. The light shines in the midst of the darkness with a new intensity as he comes to his own people—a people who had been prepared as the living temple of God in the midst of his creation. They, representing the world, receive him not: the world, centered in itself, will not accept as its center this one who comes from the beginning.

He became a human person, made his earthly dwelling in that being who was created to be the temple of God, the center of that world. We have beheld his glory, as of the only one begotten of the source, as the center. He has opened himself to us, and poured out into us that which is within him: a fullness which manifests itself in grace and truth, in the living fullness and the inner self-validating light of our being.

Through Moses we had been given an external structure to contain and guide our life with God; now the life itself of God has opened, unfolded within us through Jesus Christ. God cannot be seen externally, with human eyes; he—the absolute center who is in God—*has opened the way* into that place for us.[16]

This luminous center, established by the prologue, remains silently present throughout the narrative of the fourth gospel, as each episode, each action and discourse of Jesus, opens new facets, discloses new colors, of the central light. The series of "I am" statements of Jesus, with their changing predicates, constitute an inner sphere around this center. I am the bread of life; I am the light of the world; I am the resurrection and the life; I am the way, the truth and the life: these are the shining faces of the crystal, refracting the central light of the *I Am*. This supreme name of the God of Israel blazes at the center of the whole symbolic structure as the revelation of Jesus' own inner being.

Much of the charm and power of John's narrative derives from the magnetism of this center as it is sensed beneath the surface of one scene after another. "Teacher, where are you staying?" the Baptist's disciples ask Jesus in the first chapter, and the fragrance of this place is already sensed. When Jesus says to Nathanael, "you will see heaven opened, and the angels of God ascending and descending upon the Son of Man," he alludes to Jacob's dream at Bethel of the ladder stretching between heaven and earth. Jesus, we gradually become aware, is this ladder, this cosmic tree joining heaven and earth, God and the universe. He is, as well, the ultimate sacred place, "the house of God, and . . . gate of heaven" (Gen 28:17).

In each of the subsequent episodes, the music of the moving surface of John's narrative, with its tapestry of symbolic images, plays continually over the tonic note of this center. Each major image evokes a resonance of depth, a metaphysical fullness, as Jesus walks through the world as through a garden, awakening within each creature its own fullness by his light. A total presence is continually awakening in these interactions.

In the prologue's juxtaposition of uncreated and created reality, we find that our *symbolic* and *unitive* perspectives *converge*. The embodied symbols which are created things find their source and unitive center in the *Logos*. As John's narrative proceeds, we shall continuously encounter in its images and events a luminosity which opens to symbolic depth, which, in turn, again and again manifests the presence of the same central unitive reality.

Jesus attends a wedding, and at his word there flows a wine which sparkles with the inner light of some unknown feast of final union. He drives the tradesmen from the temple, speaks of the temple of his body, and we feel obscurely that this is to be the heart of the world. He speaks to Nicodemus of a new birth of water and the Spirit, and with the old rabbi we feel the call to a baptism in the Source, a rebirth at the center of our being.

Jesus speaks to a woman beside a well in Samaria, and as we listen to their conversation our eyes are held by the ring of stones that marks this old well: "the water that I will give will become in them a spring of water gushing up to eternal life" (4:14)—something moves deep within our own heart, the waters of the deep spring of God, the center.

Jesus breaks bread in the midst of a hungry crowd, and an invisible creative power works in his hands: the bread flows outward among the seated people. Then when darkness has fallen and his disciples are rowing across the sea against the wind, they see him walking toward them upon the water. "*I Am*; do not be afraid." When they move to take him into the boat, distance somehow vanishes; suddenly they are at the farther shore. "I am the bread of life. Whoever comes to me will never be hungry . . ." he tells the crowd, inviting them too to come into this place, this center.

This continual unitive centering of John's narrative often derives simply from the sovereign power which moves through his gospel in the figure of Jesus and successively disposes each scene around him. It is not something which forces itself upon our attention, nor even constrains us by indisputable evidence to admit it once it has been pointed out. And this will be true of much of what we shall have to say of the fourth gospel.

A further line of unitive centering in John becomes evident in the *structural arrangement* of the gospel narrative. We have already observed that the basic formal pattern of the fourth gospel is a chiastic, that is, symmetrical, or *centered* structure. We shall trace this structure in detail, and explore its implications.

In the prologue this chiastic form channels our understanding into a vision of the movement from the first creation to a new creation, centered in Jesus' conferring, through faith, of the "power to become children of God": to enter into the *unitive generation* of the Son by the Father. The movement of the divine creative Word which the prologue describes is, correspondingly, a progression from being in God to revelation in the world and thence, dramatically, to unitive immanence in those human persons who receive him.

If we call John's prologue the overture or key to his gospel, the musical connotation of these two words is appropriate both to the prologue and to the narrative which it introduces. In this music of light which is the prologue, the gospel drama undergoes a metamorphosis into a strangely abstract and crystalline luminosity, like the glowing stones of that heavenly city where sorrow does not enter and where "there will be no night" (Rev 21:25).

The central expression *"children of God"*[17] expresses the core of the *unitive new creation*: that is, its reality in those who believe in Jesus, those who "receive him." To receive him is to receive him in the unitive mode, since he is the unitive Word, unitive Person: it is to become one with him, and in him to become one with God, and so to become simply *one*. If this verse is the pivot of the prologue, then this *unitive revolution* is the pivot of the gospel as a whole: it is the decisive passage from the first creation to the new creation.

We have noted that "children," however, expresses something besides a vital unity, besides even this entry into the unitive. It connotes also *generation*, and this is an aspect of the new creation which leads us still deeper into the mystery of God. The first creation was a creation "outside" of God. The new creation is a *creation within God, that is, a divine generation*—from creation *through* the Word to creation *in* the Word, the one Son of God.[18]

As we begin to study the gospel narrative itself, we shall encounter again and again the motif of new creation/new birth, and within it these two movements of convergence and emergence (see chapter 1 above, p. 13), of union and of generation.

Chapter Six

The Door in the Waters

The primacy of the *center* in John's gospel, paradoxically, is the primacy also of the *beginning*. And so the *unitive* meaning of John is concretely expressed in *baptism*. The prologue's mysterious opening words have drawn our attention to a beginning before the creation, in God. It is John the Baptist who presides over the beginning of the gospel narrative, and situates it at the Jordan, in a context of baptism. Behind the first scenes of this narrative lies the baptism of Jesus, which emerges as a symbolic door bringing us directly to the center and beginning of the gospel's chiastic organism.

In the movement from prologue to the narrative (which begins at 1:19), we are aware of an abrupt change of rhythm, of style and of scale and focus. Here the *metaphysical poetry* of the prologue becomes *narrative poetry*, a concrete language of subtle suggestion, of symbolic implication.

The moving stream of John's narrative opens from time to time to reveal deeper and larger forms, events and meanings upon other planes. Thus here at the beginning the Baptist's words—to his questioners from Jerusalem and to the others who are present—open to reveal the persisting image of an earlier event, the baptism of Jesus in this same Jordan River.

Jesus' baptism by John does not appear in the fourth gospel (though given a key position in the other gospels[1]); it is the Baptist himself who recalls the event in John's first chapter.

> I myself did not know him; but I came baptizing with water for this reason, that he might be revealed to Israel.... I saw the Spirit descending from heaven like a dove, and it remained on him. I myself did not know him, but the one who sent me to baptize with water said to me, "He on whom

you see the Spirit descend and remain is the one who baptizes with the Holy Spirit." And I myself have seen and have
testified that this is the Son of God (1:31-34).

By these words we are taken back to the moment when Jesus
came to the Baptist at the Jordan, descended into the waters and came
up out of them once again. As he ascended from the water, the voice
of the Father was heard, "You are my Son, the Beloved; with you I am
well pleased" (Mk 1:11; Lk 3:22; cf. Mt 3:17).

All three synoptic gospels recount that at this moment the heavens were opened and the Spirit descended upon Jesus. The presence
of the Spirit upon the waters takes us back once again— this time to a
scene which is recounted in those earliest verses of Genesis to which
the prologue had just recalled us.

In the beginning when God created the heavens and the earth,
the earth was a formless void and darkness covered the face
of the deep, while the spirit of God swept over the face of the
waters. Then God said, "Let there be light"; and there was
light. And God saw that the light was good; and God separated the light from the darkness (Gen 1:1-4).

At the beginning of John's narrative we find ourselves drawn
immediately into this center, this beginning, which is the first day of
creation. As Jesus emerges from the waters, the heavens are opened
once again, the Spirit descends and the light is born. It is at this place
that we shall begin our journey through the progressive stages of the
new creation which constitute the inner structure of John's gospel. In
order to do this we shall here leave behind the narrative order of
John's gospel and move directly to the episode which is the gospel's
chiastic center: the sea-crossing of 6:16-21. It is the *waters* which, like
the four streams of paradise (Gen 2:10-14), bring us from the Jordan to
the center of John's gospel. And it is the symbolism of the waters[2]
which will open to us the gospel's deepest meanings.

We have moved from the theological flight of the prologue to the
concreteness of Jesus' descent into the waters at his baptism. In Part
III, as we attempt a synthetic view of John's gospel, we shall find ourselves tracing a parallel path from the fullness of interior unitive
experience, which is the mandalic gospel's culmination, to the sacramental event of Christian baptism.

In John's narrative order, a first cycle will complete itself in seven
days, recapitulating at the outset the seven days of the new creation.

This first week concludes at the Cana wedding, where Jesus changes water into wine for the guests. The movement from the water of John's baptism, where the uncreated light is first manifested in a human body, to the wine of Cana, with its symbolism of participated fullness, anticipates in abbreviated form both the progression from the first creation to the new creation and from the first day to the seventh day.

Against the background of the Baptist's "I am not," as we begin this journey of the seven days of the new creation, we shall soon hear the solemn words of Jesus, "*I Am.*" These words mark the source and starting point of John's exposition of the new creation.

II

THE UNFOLDING OF THE
NEW CREATION

Chapter One

The First Day:
Light in Darkness

In the beginning when God created the heavens and the earth, the earth was a formless void and darkness covered the face of the deep, while the spirit of God swept over the face of the waters. Then God said, "Let there be light"; and there was light. And God saw that the light was good; and God separated the light from the darkness. God called the light Day, the darkness he called Night. And there was evening and morning, the first day (Gen 1:1-5).

In the day that the Lord God made the earth and the heavens, when no plant of the field was yet in the earth and no herb of the field had yet sprung up—for the Lord God had not caused it to rain upon the earth, and there was no one to till the ground; but a stream would rise from the earth, and water the whole face of the ground—... (Gen 2:4b-6).

⊕

But to all who received him, who believed in his name, he gave power to become children of God ... (Jn 1:12).

Section 1: 6:16-21
The Sea-Crossing

We begin with the briefest of all our episodes, a narration that at first sight seems no more than an interlude between miracle and discourse, graced by the wondrous apparition of Jesus walking upon the sea. The scene reveals its depths of meaning only by its resonance with the whole of the scriptures, the multitudinous waters of the Word.

Both in Mark (6:45-52) and in John, this sea-crossing takes place when Jesus' popular acclaim has risen to a peak. His preaching and the crescendo of his signs, culminating in the multiplication of the bread and fish for the five thousand, have gathered the people of Galilee around him. When he had miraculously fed the multitude, in fact, "...they were about to come and take him by force to make him king..." (6:15). Jesus withdrew to the hills by himself, and his disciples, when evening came, embarked for Capernaum without him.

Jesus will not be forced by his people into the role of an earthly king, ruling by force. The issue of power—of the two contrasting kinds of power, human and divine—which arises here at the very beginning, will generate the dramatic conflict of the gospel. Jesus disappears from view, and then reappears upon the night sea, revealing to his close disciples a glimpse of his true authority. His kingship has to do not with political power but with being; not with external governance, as we shall see, but with creation and the communication of life.

In the synoptic gospels, Jesus calms the turbulent sea, rescuing the hard-pressed disciples from their danger. The accent of the story is upon this demonstration of his power over nature. In John's account, we hear nothing of such a rescue. Attention is focused upon the words of Jesus, "*I Am*" (Gr. *egō eimi*)—and therefore upon the self-manifestation which these words imply—and upon the abrupt arrival of the boat at its destination on the farther shore.

For a long time, without understanding why, I had found a particular fascination in these gospel stories of Jesus and his disciples upon the sea. While the context and details vary, in each of these stories one feels the surging forth of a majesty, a gravitational force, from Jesus, which silently reorders the cosmos around him. Suddenly, in the midst of a churning universe, this man appears, a diminutive light in the immense darkness, and everything comes into harmony around him, all the tumult subsides into a wondering hush where he stands. We find ourselves in the presence of one who seems to have stepped out of John's prologue into the midst of the world's dark disorder, and swallowed it up in his peace. A sovereign center, gently emanating this mysterious power to which all being must respond, is revealed here in Jesus.

If the chiastic proposal of Ellis, upon which we are proceeding, is correct, this sea-crossing episode is *the structural center* of John's gospel. We must expect it, then, to contain an extraordinary *fullness of meaning*. Otherwise the whole structural pattern would seem to relate to the essential content of the gospel in a merely extrinsic way. The logic of our method leads us to expect that depth and fullness of meaning which we sense everywhere in John to be present with maximum density in this central episode.

And yet the importance of the sea-crossing in the narrative of Jesus' life and work seems negligible. We do not see that it has any consequences as the story continues, nor is it accompanied by a discourse of Jesus—as are some of his other signs—opening up a further level of significance. The miracle seems but a rather meaningless display of power, having little resonance with the other signs. It is evident that any greater fullness of meaning here will have to be sought on other than the literal level of the narrative.

⊕

Ellis has brought out powerfully the *symbolic* significance of the sea-crossing as a *new exodus*.[1] The exodus event was the birth of Israel as a people, the primordial act of God on their behalf which became the foundation stone of Israelite faith for all time. This exodus background brings much depth and range of meaning to the Johannine sea-crossing.

The Passover sea-crossing is one of the principal Old Testament types, or symbolic foreshadowings, of the death and resurrection of Christ.[2] Here at the crossing of the sea we begin to see the crucial phases of the history of Israel being taken up into the movement of the gospel and into the person of Jesus. It is in Jesus, and precisely in his "passing over," that the liberation of humanity from sin and death is accomplished.

⊕

The words of Jesus to the frightened disciples, in Greek *egō eimi*, are usually translated "It is I." Their literal meaning, however, is "*I Am*"—

an expression which has an enormous resonance in the Jewish tradition. It is a version of the *name* of God revealed to Moses at the burning bush at Sinai (Ex 3:14), immediately before the liberation of Israel in the exodus from Egypt.

In the Greek Septuagint version of Second Isaiah, *egō eimi* becomes the self-designation of the God who accompanies Israel through history, the "creator of Israel," who is also creator of the universe.

> Listen to me, O Jacob, and Israel, whom I called:
> *I am he (egō eimi)*; I am *(egō eimi)* the first, and I am *(egō eimi)*
>   the last.
> My hand laid the foundation of the earth,
> and my right hand spread out the heavens;
> when I summon them, they stand at attention (Is 48:12-13).

Isaiah is writing for the Israelites in their Babylonian exile. God, he says, will bring them back from Babylon to their own land: this will be a new exodus. The words of the Baptist at the beginning of the gospel, "I am the voice of one crying in the wilderness, 'Make straight the way of the Lord,'" had referred back to Deutero-Isaiah's prophecy of this new exodus through the desert.

What is of crucial importance for our Johannine study is this: the new exodus will be a *new creation*.[3] The "I Am" of Jesus upon the sea evokes at the center of John's gospel this Isaian vision of a transforming passage, a new exodus in which there commences a new creation.

Here is the key to the Copernican revolution which brings the whole of John's gospel into a new and unifying perspective. The crucial step is the interpretation of the sea-crossing of John 6 as a recalling of the *initial creation event*. At this point the words of Genesis, "Let there be light," seem to touch the whole of John's gospel, bringing it to life with a new clarity and power. It is the vision which opens up from this point that we shall develop in the remainder of the book.

> For it is the God who said, "Let light shine out of darkness,"
> who has shone in our hearts to give the light of the knowl-
> edge of the glory of God in the face of Jesus Christ (2 Cor 4:6).

These words of Paul seem to originate from the center of the Johannine vision; in them we feel the power and immediacy of a personal experience of that same reality which is solemnly chanted in

John's prologue. Here Paul affirms the same central knot of the mystery, as he identifies his own transforming illumination by the glorified Christ with the primal moment of the first account of the creation of the world in Genesis—God's creation of light. Inseparable from this initial experience is a continuing act of divine creation within the believer (2 Cor 3:18; 4:16-18; 5:17; cf. Rom 8:18-23), a continuing rebirth in which one experiences the beginning of the re-creation of the world in Christ.

In John, this primal moment is understood as the revelation of the *light* which is Christ. The *"I Am"* is spoken, in the manifestation upon the sea of Galilee, by the creative Word that *was* in the beginning, according to the prologue, and that now appears in Jesus, striding over these dark waters which recall the primeval chaos of Genesis 1:1. The presence of this divine light, and this first moment of creation, become the structural center of the fourth gospel. From this point the work of creation, present symbolically in the successive events of John's narrative, flowers in the expanding concentric circles of the seven days.

The first day, as we find it in the gospel of John, develops from the account in Genesis 1:1-5 in this way: corresponding to the *creation of light* in the first creation is the *manifestation of the uncreated light in the self-identification of Jesus as the I Am*, in the new creation. The material darkness remains, but the light shines for those who believe in him, who "receive him" (compare 6:21[4] and 1:12).

In this "beginning" which includes the first day, all of the following days are virtually contained. Conversely, this primary event will be found within each of the following days and even within each of the twenty subsequent chiastic episodes or sections of the gospel: for at each of these points is manifested the light which is in Jesus.

Here at the center there is represented, first, the hidden being of God and of the *Logos before* the creation, and then the first day itself, the appearance of the uncreated light[5] in Jesus. In the prologue, *light* is identical with *Logos*. Here in the sea-crossing scene the divine light of the *Logos* is not explicit: it is apparent in the self-revelation of Jesus, his *"I Am"* in the midst of the darkness.

> In the beginning was the Word,
> and the Word was with God,
> and the Word was God....
> ... The light shines in the darkness,
> and the darkness did not overcome it....

The true light, which enlightens everyone,
was coming into the world.
He was in the world,
and the world came into being through him;
yet the world did not know him.
He came to what was his own,
and his own people did not *accept* him.
But to all who *received* him,
who believed in his *name*,
he gave power to become children of God....

The disciples who "wanted *to take him* into the boat" when he had identified himself with the words, "*egō eimi*," represent all those who *receive* him, who *believe in his name*, and who consequently receive the power to become children of God. The instantaneous arrival of the boat at the "land to which they were going" signifies the entrance into the promised land, or the garden, of the new creation, the land of divine sonship which is in Jesus himself.

So if anyone is in Christ, there is a new creation: everything old
has passed away; see, everything has become new (2 Cor 5:17).

⊕

John's prologue, we shall find, relates to the structure of his gospel in more than one way. The prologue, that revelation of "beginning," seems to insert itself at this center-point of the mandalic chiasm as an axle fits into the hub of a wheel.[6]

The sea-crossing episode unfolds itself upon successive levels as its imagery and words are reflected upon in the light of these two cardinal theological moments of the Old Testament: first exodus, and then creation. This same axis continues through the central points of the New Testament revelation: the incarnation, baptism, death and resurrection of Jesus, rebirth of the believer through faith and baptism, and the new divine indwelling in the core of the person. From this center, this paradoxical light in darkness, develops the whole of the new creation. Faith, itself a unitive light in darkness, grasps the whole darkly in its center, the immanent *Logos*.

The series of "*I Am*" statements of Jesus[7] serve to carry this presence and power of the Word through the other days of the new creation, as do also the "signs" of Jesus. The symbols of darkness and light, of water and of wind/breath are also arteries which carry the

THE FIRST DAY / 69

influence of this central event to every part of the gospel. The concentric circles of the days, in their planetary progression outward from the center, express the development of this creative presence and act throughout the human person, the human world and ultimately the cosmos itself.

Identified with this structural center, which coincides with the *second Passover* of Jesus' career according to John, are the events of Jesus' *first* Passover—the cleansing of the temple, signifying the sacrificial preparation of the new place of divine indwelling—and of Jesus' *third* Passover, his crucifixion and resurrection.

⊕

"In the beginning..."—John the Baptist called the people of Israel to return to their *beginning* in the desert, a new exodus in which they might hope to re-experience the birth, the creation of Israel. Now Jesus brings his disciples to a moment which has a similar, but more profound symbolic meaning: the *absolute* beginning, the light of the creative *Logos* shining in the darkness, the primal *"I Am."* From this point John's entire gospel will unfold.

Here in the sea-crossing the gospel begins for the second time. If the implicit background of the first chapter of John was the baptism of Jesus by John in the Jordan, that river associated with the history and birth of Israel, here at the sea we are in the presence of a cosmic event, a symbolic baptism or rebirth of the cosmos. We arrive at this second baptismal "illumination" by a paradoxical progression from exodus to creation, which will recur again and again as we journey through the seven days.

The relationship between the Baptist and Jesus was expressed already in the prologue, in words which correspond exactly to the movement from the scene at the Jordan to the scene upon the Sea of Tiberias.

John bore witness to him, and cried, "This was he of whom I said, 'He who comes after me ranks before me, for *he was* before me'" (1:15).

It is the one who rose from the water as the Spirit descended upon him, who now walks on the sea like the creative Spirit that was upon the primeval waters. It is the one who *"was* before me," who says, *"I Am."* And in these words he is manifest as the Word who is the beginning of creation. We have moved from a beginning to *the* beginning.

All beginnings are born together in this place where, in darkness, the light shines over the waters. Here the world originates from nothingness; here the Word is generated from the invisible fullness of the Father, then shines in the night of the creation. Here, again, begins the new creation within the divine darkness and within the darkness of created being.

This meeting place of sea and land, of air and water, of light and darkness, becomes the boundary of boundaries. Here we are placed at the borderline between consciousness and mystery, between conscious mind and the numinous psyche, between creation and creator.

Here upon the dark waters, at this boundary, is the place of awakening, of compunction and metanoia, the place of silent meditation and of creative inspiration. Here in this darkness is the womb of creative light. It is the place of poverty and expectancy, the place of all potential. Here we are all fishers. And here in our poverty we are in touch with the dark depths of God, from which the light is born into our world.

John's theme is the coming of the Beginning, who enters into the middle, dwelling there as the End. His gospel has a beginning, a middle and an end, each of which is a beginning. Each beginning takes place from water: water of the Jordan (Jn 1), water of the Sea of Tiberias (Jn 6), and again the water of this sea (Jn 21). Water, in John, always bears upon its face the brightness of the beginning; it confers this beginning. From this beginning unfolds the structure of John's gospel: fourfold symmetry around a center, which is the beginning.

We can return to this point of the beginning again and again, as John does in his narrative, and each time find the spring flowing forth. This is the first great secret of John: this place in the bosom of the Father and in the opened body of Christ whence continually the light is born from the darkness, whence creation comes forth again, filled with God, where we are born in God.

Here, in the Johannine unitive beginning, is the source of the peculiar simplicity and depth of the fourth gospel. To it correspond the radical inversions of the synoptic gospels and of Paul: "...unless you change and become like children, you will never enter the kingdom..."; "I thank you, Father...for you have hidden these things from the wise and the intelligent and have revealed them to infants..."; "Blessed are the poor in spirit, for theirs is the kingdom of heaven..."; "for whenever I am weak, then I am strong..."; "for God's foolishness is wiser than human wisdom, and God's weakness is stronger than human strength."

⊕

The central liturgical event of the Christian year is the *Easter vigil*. There are striking parallels between this rite and John's sea-crossing narrative, as we have interpreted it. The liturgy begins with the lighting of a new fire, from which the paschal candle itself, representing the newly risen "light of Christ," is ignited. A long series of biblical texts are then read, beginning with the account of the creation in Genesis 1, and including the passage through the Red Sea in Exodus 14, the prophecy of a new divine immanence in Ezekiel 36 and the baptismal theology of Paul in Romans 6. The symbolism of light born in the midst of darkness is inseparable from the symbolism of water, creation, birth and baptism, as we have found on the Johannine first day of creation.

The long service culminates in the *baptism* of the catechumens, and in the early church this sacrament was known not only as new birth but as *phōtismos*, illumination. Like the gospel of John, this holiest of the year's liturgies, which commemorates the resurrection of the Lord, was constructed in the light of the central Christian reality of the *baptismal event*.

⊕

"In the beginning was the Word." This first Johannine episode is *hē archē*, the beginning, in which is manifested, simply, the divine *Logos* which dwells and acts in Jesus. The cosmic and human resonances of this primary "sign" are innumerable. We shall mention, at this point, expressions of two contemporary lines of development of this fontal mystery which, in John's vision, is the first day of the new creation.

A recurring mythological theme reflected in contemporary psychological experience[8] is the *night sea journey*. In many myths the hero must undertake a struggle which then draws him into a strange journey.

More often than not the typical struggle of the hero with the monster (the unconscious content) takes place beside the water.... In the decisive battle the hero is, like Jonah, invariably swallowed by the monster.... But, once inside the monster, the hero begins to settle accounts with the creature in his own way, while it swims eastwards with him toward the rising sun... he kills the monster, which then drifts to land, where the hero, new-born through the transcendent function (the "night sea journey" as Frobenius calls it) steps forth, sometimes in the company of all those whom the monster has previously devoured....[9]

Jesus, as well as Jonah, undergoes this transforming journey, and each of us must sooner or later travel the same route toward the east, to be reborn.[10] Within John's gospel and within the sacramental event of Christian baptism are hidden also the mysteries of the journey of individuation. Jung very often speaks of the mandalic figure as a symbol of this final integration of the person.[11]

If it is in the "east" that John's language is most readily understood, this is true particularly of such Johannine texts as the sea-crossing, with its profound cosmic symbolism.[12] Hindu and Buddhist traditions express themselves quite naturally in the language of fullness, or of the unitive: whether this language be that of a cosmic symbolism or of the paradoxical apophatism[13] of Buddhism.

Jyoti Sahi, an Indian writer,[14] speaks of Jesus coming into a world in which the primal unity, symbolized by the "water mandala," has been broken. (Water and light, for Sahi as for John, are unitive principles.) In contrast to the first creation described in Genesis 1, which proceeded through successive *separations*, Jesus' new creation consists in bringing together again everything that has been divided. To illustrate this reintegrative work of Jesus, he turns by preference to the Johannine sign of the sea-crossing.

One might even say that whereas the Lord of the Tantric Mandala is breaking through the Mandala, like a child breaking through the womb, the Christian Lord of space is entering into the womb in order to create the womb from within. The typical structure of this mode of thinking is to be found in the narrative centering around the fourth and fifth signs, where the distribution of the loaves and fishes on the mountain is followed by Jesus walking upon the waters, appearing in fact at the centre of the lake in a storm. The total action is unitive. The storm is cosmic....The mountain has been separated from the sea. The new Moses does not divide the water (from Moses to Elijah the prophetic word has divided the water) but rather He walks upon it, calming the storm, reminding one of the first creative unity of the Spirit brooding over the waters....[15]

From his Indian perspective, Sahi sees John's gospel itself as a mandala, representing at once the totality of the universe and of the individual person.

The Evangelist, through his careful selection of signs, builds, like the artist of the Mandala, a cosmos, a pictograph at whose centre is revealed the Lord of History, who, through sacrament, enters the heart of his disciple, and establishes his kingdom there.[16]

Chapter Two

The Second Day:
Bread from Heaven

And God said, "Let there be a dome[1] in the midst of the waters, and let it separate the waters from the waters." So God made the dome and separated the waters that were under the dome from the waters that were above the dome. And it was so. God called the dome Sky.[2] And there was evening and there was morning, the second day (Gen 1:6-8).

And the Lord God planted a garden in Eden, in the east; and there he put the man whom he had formed. Out of the ground the Lord God made to grow every tree that is pleasant to the sight and good for food, the tree of life also in the midst of the garden, and the tree of the knowledge of good and evil (Gen 2:8-9).

The Lord God took the man and put him in the garden of Eden to till it and to keep it. And the Lord God commanded the man, "You may freely eat of every tree of the garden; but of the tree of the knowledge of good and evil you shall not eat, for in the day that you eat of it you shall die" (Gen 2:15-17).

And the Word became flesh... (Jn 1:14a).

SECTION 2: 6:1-15
THE SIGN OF BREAD

Alongside the Sea of Galilee, near the time of Passover, Jesus feeds over five thousand people with five barley loaves and two fishes. The crowd acclaims him as "the prophet" and wants to seize him and make him their king. While the miracle appears in all four gospels, a number of features in this account are peculiar to John.

Only John tells us that "they were about to come and take him by force to make him king," and that this is the reason for Jesus' withdrawal into solitude. The Galileans' desire to make Jesus their king, while it seems an expression of their faith and commitment, is not acceptable to him. It indicates a fundamental misunderstanding of his person and his mission, which Jesus will confront forcefully in the discourse.

The meaning of the *kingship* of Jesus will emerge as a central issue at the time of his trial, on the fifth day. Here on the second day the titles of prophet and king disappear into the title of Son of Man which Jesus himself adopts.

The disciples have been given a hint of the nature of Jesus' true power in his appearance upon the waters; the multiplication of the bread and fishes in his hands was another, more widely visible manifestation of his power. It is a vivid physical image of *creation* (cf. Gen 2:7).

This story, and the discourse and dialogue which follow it, represent a *turning point* in the gospel. Jesus' popularity has been rising, in the course of his preaching and his signs, to a peak. But this acclaim and following is based on a misinterpretation of the nature of his power. They are about to make of him a political leader, and he flees. Then he crosses the sea, as if signifying his distance from their thinking (see Is 55:8-9; John 6 is closely related to this chapter of Isaiah, as we shall see). Some of the people doggedly follow him to the other side, but remain far from him in the quality of their faith and understanding.

SECTION 3: 6:22-71
THE BREAD DISCOURSE

After Jesus' spectacular sign of the loaves and fishes, and his epiphany on the dark sea, Jesus' disciples find themselves once again among people, once again in the busy daylight "world of men." The people press around them, eager to be fed by further works of power, to make this source of plenty their own. The Teacher turns them— and even some of his own followers—away with words of impossible difficulty. Meanwhile the few around him continue to listen almost blindly, sensing themselves filled from within even as he speaks these words that completely elude their understanding. Their world begins to turn inside out as they feed like infants upon this simple knowledge that comes to them from him.

⊕

While John's story of the bread and fishes has not differed fundamentally from the corresponding accounts of the synoptics, the discourse which follows is unlike anything in the other three gospels. We have passed from the common world of the synoptic gospels, with their history of Jesus, to a Johannine world of unitive symbolism, a sapiential world.

Ellis finds numerous chiastic parallels between these two episodes. While we have moved from the single episode of the first day to a pair of episodes, these are so closely related that they border on a simple continuity. To the diptych's first panel depicting the sign of the loaves and fishes corresponds another which explicates the symbolic implications of this action in words.

Jesus' words in the synagogue at Capernaum are spoken in the course of a running dispute, surprising in its acrimony, with the Galileans who had taken the trouble to follow him across the sea. The central issue is Jesus' claim to be the "bread come down from heaven." Related to the question of *food* is that of *work*, which Jesus introduces, and the argument zigzags over this subject too. When Jesus has repeated his assertions in varying forms again and again, the scene changes. We are present at an intense dialogue between Jesus and his own disciples, who have also been shaken by his words to the crowd. While some turn away from him at this point, Peter speaks for those who remain with him, professing his faith in Jesus.

⊕

The two creation stories of Genesis are woven together: while the seven days of the first account provide the basic structure, the symbolic patterns are created by means of the literary resources of the second account.

The second day in Genesis 1 includes the creation of "heaven" (translated also as *firmament* or *dome*). In John 6 Jesus repeatedly speaks of himself as the bread which comes down from *heaven*. The implicit connection of this bread with the tree of life suggests that this tree, identified with Jesus himself, connects heaven with earth (cf. 1:51), thus establishing a paradise in which eternal life is once again accessible to humans.

⊕

On day 2, the *second creation account* of Genesis 2 begins to assert itself strongly, if subtly, in the implicit presence of the *tree of life*. The words which closed the first day, "...and immediately the boat reached the *land* toward which they were going" (6:21b), suggest, in the key of exodus, the promised land. In the creation key, however, they suggest the garden of Genesis 2, at the center of which grows the tree of life. This is the original land, which has been sealed with fire (Gen 3:24) until this Passover sea-crossing has been completed in the death and resurrection of Jesus.

⊕

Section 3 is the first episode of Part IV, the left arm of the mandalic figure (although this is not immediately evident in our diagram, Fig. 1.5). Jesus' discourse in section 3 contains certain parallels with his words to the Samaritan woman in section 17, which is the first episode of Part II, the right arm of the mandalic cross. In Samaria Jesus speaks of the *living water* which he will give, and here he speaks of the *bread of life*. We have already suggested (Part I, ch. 2, p. 25) a correspondence of the figure's two arms with the *Holy Spirit* and with the *Word*.

Jesus' words in the synagogue frequently echo chapter 55 of Isaiah, the conclusion of the Deutero-Isaian "Book of Consolation":

Ho, everyone who *thirsts, come* to the waters;
and you that have no money, *come*, buy and *eat*!
Come, buy wine and milk without money and without price.
Why do you spend your money for that which is not *bread*,
and your *labor* for that which does not satisfy?
Listen carefully to me, and *eat* what is good,
and delight yourselves in rich *food*.

Incline your ear, and *come to me*;
listen, so that you may *live*. . . .

Seek the Lord while he may be found,
call upon him while he is near. . . .

For my thoughts are not your thoughts,
nor are your ways my ways, says the Lord.
For as the *heavens* are higher than the earth,
so are my ways higher than your ways,
and my thoughts than your thoughts.

For as the rain and the snow *come down from heaven,* and do not
return there until they have watered the earth, making it bring
forth and sprout, giving seed to the sower and *bread to the eater,*
so shall my *word* be that goes out from my mouth; it shall not
return to me empty, but it shall accomplish that which I purpose, and succeed in the thing for which I *sent it* (Is 55:1-11).

There follows in Isaiah the description of a new exodus, in the
course of which the wilderness is transformed into a kind of garden,
filled with good trees. (We recall that the opening chapter of the Book
of Consolation (Is 40:3) was quoted by the Baptist in the wilderness
(Jn 1:23) to explain his own mission.) This metamorphosis of the
desert into a garden, we realize, is the work of the *Word.* Here we
have, then, a new *exodus* which immediately becomes a new *creation,*
effected by the Word of God. This Word has come down from heaven
and soaked into the earth like the rain, then to raise up from this earth
bread for the people. There is a very strong resonance here with
John's revelation of the Word of God which is Jesus, become the
bread of life. The wilderness of John the Baptist has become the new
paradise in which this bread is offered. The poet of Deutero-Isaiah
anticipates John in bringing together exodus and creation, the histori-
cal-prophetic and the sapiential traditions.

Jesus appears as a *tree* which is rooted in heaven and, paradoxically, roots itself also on earth: a tree which bears the bread of life, the
tree of life of Genesis 2, which nourishes the new creation. The creation of heaven, or the firmament, by the separation of the upper and
lower elements, is succeeded by a unitive creation in which the higher
becomes the food of the lower.[3] The true bread is precisely the fruit of
the unitive incarnation, the divine Word present and available in a
human person: "heaven" present in earth's matter.

Wisdom, in the book of Sirach, comes down from heaven, from God, and takes root in the holy city Jerusalem as a cedar tree, an olive tree, a vine. The further echoes of this poem of *Sophia* in Jesus' discourse here are unmistakable:

Come to me, you who desire me,
and eat your fill of my fruits. . . .
Those who eat of me will hunger for more,
and those who drink of me will thirst for more (Sir 24:19.21).

"Come to me" is typical language of *Sophia*,[4] and here the words immediately follow *Sophia*'s self-depiction as tree and as vine (vv. 12-17). The same language is used by Jesus in 6:35.44.45.65. He invites the people to come to him as the tree of life and to fill themselves with his fruit, the "bread of life." And this place where the tree appears is the new garden, the new paradise, which is also to be identified with Jesus himself. When he asks the twelve "Will you also go away?" it is as if he is asking them whether they too will leave this tree of the wisdom of life, and this place. "Lord, to whom can we go?" responds Peter, "You have the *words* of eternal life."

The intimacy which we find in the Old Testament between *wisdom* and *creation* (see Prov 8:22-31; Wis 7:22) appears also in John, where the sapiential vision expresses itself preferentially in the imagery of the second creation account of Genesis 2.

The *unitive* wisdom of God which finds expression in John does not recognize some of the divisions which are habitual for us. It is hardly possible to speak of a Johannine *spirituality* which is distinct from Johannine *theology*, and both of these are inseparable from the *symbolic poetry* of this gospel. A life inspired by John's gospel should be drawn together by this same sapiential unity.

$$\oplus$$

The new creation, and the new bread of life, stand in a *twofold contrast* within the biblical tradition. On a first, and more explicit level, this bread is contrasted with the *manna* which Moses obtained for the Israelites. Secondly, it is contrasted implicitly with the *fruit of the tree of the knowledge of good and evil*, which the first parents ate, and consequently died. And then the "fathers" ate and died: their earthly bread was not enough to give them eternal life, as would the tree of life from which they were barred and which is now made accessible once again in Jesus.

Once again we find the double symbolic movement which had appeared on the first day (see p. 68 above). The first movement of symbolic interpretation arrives at the *exodus* level; the second movement proceeds all the way to the *creation* level. While the Mosaic/exodus connections are indispensable for understanding John's text, it is the discovery of the Genesis/creation stratum which opens this gospel to its full depth and luminosity.

What is it that opens when, along the path of sapiential interpretation, we come to this creation symbolism? A door opens into a garden in which we begin to perceive the luminosity of created being itself. From the confining spaces of religion and the narrow corridors of sacred history, we enter this hidden garden which paradoxically opens into unlimited space. The translucent green mansions of our childhood, the living world of innocence surround us once more.

It is here on the second day, under the name of wisdom, that this garden opens for us. The *creative Word*, from which the earth came, is one with the earth and its life, and this creation begins to shine again from within. Words find their body, their ground, the fullness of their sound. The Word has become "nature," and now nature herself speaks wordlessly, with color and sound, as trees do speak with liquid syllables of light. Wisdom, the gift of this day, is the marriage, the rejoining, of spirit and earth, mind and body, light and matter.

⊕

When the Galileans find Jesus at Capernaum and begin to question him, he says to them, "Do not work for the food that perishes, but for the food that endures for eternal life..." (6:27a), and a discussion on the "works of God" follows: both those works which a person must perform to please God and also the miraculous signs which Jesus must perform if he is to satisfy these people. The people, in fact, ask these *two* very different questions about work: what work must *we* do, and then what work can *you* do, what sign will you show us? Both questions will terminate in Jesus himself. The work that God expects of them is to believe in him, and *Jesus himself* is God's ultimate work, the bread from heaven which gives life to the world. Raised up from the earth, he will be God's conclusive sign.

The biblical tradition associates work and works with the observance of the *law*, but also refers to God's saving *miracles* as works. Preeminent among these was the gift of *manna* (see Ex 16)—food from heaven—at the time of exodus and the wandering in the wilderness. God's *first* works, however, were the works of *creation*. Adam had been placed in the garden to cultivate it, and when expelled from the garden his sentence was one of hard labor. This complex tradition underlies the discussion at Capernaum.

The *signs* of Jesus, in John's gospel, are the new works of God which verify Jesus' own identity as the Son. We shall find that a number of them are directly related to the wonders performed by Moses at the time of *exodus*. When Jesus heals on the sabbath, however, he defends this apparent breach of the *law* with the words, "My Father is still working, and I also am working" (5:17), referring to the continuing work of *creation*. The work which is required of humanity now is not the "works" of the law, which belong to the old order which is passing away, but rather the work of faith in Jesus himself. Correspondingly the work of God himself now is the providing of this bread of life which is Jesus, a work which recreates the world. The crowd, however, presses Jesus for some "work" that is more tangible: the thing that they must do to please God, and the thing that Jesus must do to convince them.

According to Jesus' great prayer at the supper (17:2-4), eternal life will consist in the *knowledge* of God and of Jesus himself. Jesus' words "authority over all people, to give eternal life..." refer implicitly to the *work* of Jesus: "I glorified you on earth by finishing the work that you gave me to do..." (17:4). The "bread from heaven" with which Jesus identifies himself is a parallel expression for this work of his which is the communication of eternal life through the *knowledge of God in Jesus himself*: a knowledge which is the fruit of the "work of God" (6:29) which is faith in Jesus.

Here, as in the letter to the Hebrews, *work* is to be understood in relation to *rest*. This rest corresponds both to the promised land of exodus times and also to the garden, the paradise, of the Genesis creation account. This promised land and garden, like the bread and the tree of life, are, ultimately, *Jesus himself*. The crossing of the sea by the people parallels the transition from the multiple works of the law to the *single work of faith*: the *sabbath work* of feeding upon the unitive Word. Work and rest become one (cf. Mt 11:28-30) in the work of faith by which one dwells in this place, in Jesus. Work and rest, work and food are drawn together in the unitive field of the incarnate Word.

⊕

What, precisely, is Jesus talking about when he refers to himself as the *bread of life?* The question has sustained controversy from the Capernaum synagogue to the academic journals of today. The numerous theories on the meaning of the expression "bread of life" seem to be reducible, however, to two interpretations: either the bread signifies *wisdom,* or it means the *eucharist.* Raymond Brown wisely concludes that the meaning of Jesus' words about the bread of life is *both* sapiential and eucharistic. The sapiential first part of the discourse leads as naturally to its eucharistic climax as Jesus' teaching will lead to his death, the breaking of his body. This progression is our first encounter—outside the prologue—with the single many-sided *movement* of John's gospel: from revelation to union, from Word to Spirit. This great figure of the gospel pattern reproduces itself in each of its parts.

The incarnate *Word* of God is *bread.* The Word is already food and drink in the Old Testament, but there the threshold of understanding is lower: the images may be taken as metaphor. Here the metaphor, the symbol, has become a physical reality and even a person. It refuses to be spiritualized or allegorized: I am your food. I have come to be consumed and assimilated: first into your hearts and minds through listening and faith; then into your very bodies which I will transform into my own. This will be a further revolution, in which the *"I Am"* of the first day becomes the new personal center and the life of those who come to him.

These insistent words of Jesus about the necessity of eating his flesh and drinking his blood are apparently his most difficult assertion up to this moment. The challenge in this narrative has not immediately been a *eucharistic* assertion of Jesus, however, but something just as deeply mysterious: Jesus' presentation of himself as *embodying the revelation and the life of God.* And this life of God is to be assimilated by humans in some inconceivable way. Against the background of the Old Testament wisdom literature,[5] Jesus presents himself as the Wisdom of God which has come into the world in the form of flesh and blood to give life to humanity. It is *later* in the discourse (6:51-57) that the language of Jesus can only be understood in the light of his death and subsequent *eucharistic* presence in the world. This second, sacramental challenge to his listeners confronts them along the same way of *incarnational faith* as the first, sapiential challenge: *And the Word became flesh.*

"I am the bread of life": the later *eucharistic* form of this assertion ("Those who eat my flesh and drink my blood have eternal life..."— 6:51-56) only further accents the absoluteness of the revolution in consciousness which is already demanded by this first challenge to faith. Jesus is the divine light and life made visible, audible, touchable (see 1 Jn 1:1ff) and finally ingestible. To "see" him, to listen to his words and believe in him, and thus to feed upon him, is to begin to *surrender the boundaries* of one's own consciousness and one's own being.

$$\oplus$$

In this development of the discourse from incarnate wisdom to eucharist, we can see a movement of *creation*. As divine Wisdom, *Sophia*, was instrumental in the original creation of the universe (see Prov 8:27-30; Wis 7:22), so *Jesus*, the divine Wisdom now incarnate, initiates the second and unitive creation. The bread of life which shall be the body of Jesus will be, like this visible body of Jesus, the matter of this world, cosmic stuff, in which God is immanent in a new way. The body of Jesus, and this eucharistic body which will continue to feed his people, is the first fruits, the *first matter* of the *new creation*.

$$\oplus$$

This movement from wisdom to eucharist in the discourse will have a later parallel in the progression from word to sacrament in the Christian eucharistic liturgy. Already in the gospel, however, the life and teaching of Jesus move steadily toward the supper and the cross, where his life is to be consummated in a physical and sacramental form.

The movement from the first day to the second day is strikingly parallel to the progression from baptism to eucharist: we begin to suspect a sacramental initiatory order in John's developing scheme of new creation. These two sacraments of initiation constitute together a fitting center for the geometric expression of new creation.

The second day completes the center-function of the first day with the imagery of the second creation account in Genesis 2: the garden and the tree. Both will provide a continual symbolic reference for the following days. The figure of the tree, like the cross, also suggests the four dimensions of reality, the fullness of the mandala, further intensifying the centric character of John 6 as a whole. John 1:13 will serve a parallel function in the prologue.[6]

⊕

Throughout John's gospel, this unitive knowledge which is one with Jesus will continue to pound, like a sea of boundless light, upon the confines and defenses of the human mind, until it finally breaks itself upon this wall and saturates the thirsty earth; from then on it gleams everywhere, within and without the ramparts.

⊕

Some of Jesus' language in this discourse, as we have seen, tends to identify him not only with the biblical Wisdom of God and the tree of life, but also with the garden of paradise. The "creation" symbol from Genesis 2 with which he ultimately identifies himself, and which gathers the others into itself, is *Adam*.

While the first day brings us back to the *beginning*, and to the baptismal event, the second day turns us in the direction of the eucharist and the *end*. The Son of Man with whom Jesus identifies himself in the discourse of John 6 (6:27.53.62; Son in 6:40) is the eschatological Man of Daniel 7, who gathers the people of God together in himself.

> Thus it is written: "The first man, Adam, became a living being"; the last Adam became a life-giving spirit. But it is not the spiritual that is first, but the physical, and then the spiritual. The first man was from earth, a man of dust; *the second man is from heaven* (1 Cor 15:45-47).

It is this *man from heaven* (6:38.41.42.50.51.58) who offers his flesh as the bread of life here in John 6. His continual promise to those who come to him and eat this bread is that he will *raise them up on the last day* (6:39.40.44.54). The last day belongs to this Son of Man, and Jesus speaks of him here only in connection with life, with eternal life, with heaven. "What if you were to see the Son of Man ascending to where he was before?" (6:62). Those who eat of his flesh shall have eternal life because they "abide in me and I in them" (6:56).

The symbolism of the bread of life discourse, with its reflections of Genesis, comes together in this second Adam who will, on the last day, give life to those who believe in him and who dwell in him through their participation in his body and blood. The two interpretations of the *bread of life* also converge here: divine wisdom participated[7] by faith and reception of the eucharistic bread are two parallel means of abiding in this Son of Man, the new Adam. On the "last day" of this week of creation, the Son of Man, risen from the dead, will breathe the Spirit of life into his new body (Jn 20:22).

On the second day of the new creation (see Gen 1:6-8; for the traditional *heaven*, newer translations frequently have *sky*), the man from heaven *brings heaven to earth*, brings heaven and earth together in one, by appearing as a human person and giving himself as bread to those who come to him.

$$\oplus$$

Upon what do we finally feed?
The body finds its bread,
And soul through all the senses takes its food.
And will the spirit feed itself on God?

Our fundamental hunger has no bounds: we need *everything*; are famished for all being.

You must want like a God that you may be satisfied like God.
... Be sensible of your wants, that you may be sensible of your treasures.[8]

We hunger for God and for all creation, being endowed—both curse and blessing—with an appetite like God's. We farm the dust, husband specks, and hunger for the world and God. Our sentence is heavy: exclusion from the garden at the center means that we must labor over infinitesimals and decimals, while within us throbs the single hunger of the One.

There are trees in the world, to be sure, and we eat from them. Our culture feeds us, but often leaves us empty and dry. In the middle of human culture is the tree of the *word*, and we are fed by words. Thinker and poet labor, each from his perspective, to build the single word-tree once again. As birds seek seeds, and squirrels nuts, so we constantly gather words, feed through our eyes and ears, wearily graze a scant verbal surface, the gaunt black and white pasture of our exile. Words are food as we are informed, educated, occupied and sustained by our interest, by the life of the mind and soul, uneasily at home in the world. Fact and thought are bread, and poetry is wine, native and congenial in our veins.

Blind in this world, we know not whence we come, and unknowing seek constantly the single golden seed that will tell us who we are. And we know not that we must be fed from whence we come, nourished from the source of our own being.

The tree is a silent companion in our exile. This friend, only a little larger than ourselves, is a quiet parable of what we are, or will be when we see (the half-sighted one in Mark 8:24 saw people like trees walking)—when, once more, we feed with innocent eyes on our world. The tree does not speak; sealed and sworn to opacity, it conceals its brilliant fruit, from which we once did feed, until our eye is opened once again. Cipher of our humanity, the tree stands in its circle of quiet.

Jesus comes: seed, then root, growing at once from our earth and from heaven, single tree joining the divided worlds in one. With our hunger in him, with the hunger of God in him, he reaches out into the four quarters to gather everything into one in himself, God within him gathering the fragments into one. The bread broken is the one tree, and the tree in the center is a man, the Son of Man who is God.

Through the double tree the one life was murdered, creation dismembered and estranged from God within it. The human tree which is Jesus sinks its roots deep and sends its branches high, a manifold bridge of life. It swallows up the separation of sin and death, and the law's distinction of good and evil, in the one, unrejecting life.

Each tree is a prince of creation and image of God's wisdom, the living juncture of all things. Witness standing, moving, in the changing wind and sun, it speaks within us where its likeness lives and grows, joining the worlds in one.

Chapter Three

The Third Day:
His Glory Fills the Earth

And God said, "Let the waters under the sky be gathered together into one place, and let the dry land appear." And it was so. God called the dry land Earth, and the waters that were gathered together he called Seas. And God saw that it was good. Then God said, "Let the earth put forth vegetation: plants yielding seed, and fruit trees of every kind on earth that bear fruit with the seed in it." And it was so. The earth brought forth vegetation: plants yielding seed of every kind, and trees of every kind bearing fruit with the seed in it. And God saw that it was good. And there was evening and there was morning, the third day (Gen 1:9-13).

A river flows out of Eden to water the garden, and from there it divides and becomes four branches. The name of the first is Pishon; it is the one that flows around the whole land of Havilah, where there is gold; and the gold of that land is good; bdellium and the onyx stone are there. The name of the second river is Gihon; it is the one that flows around the whole land of Cush. The name of the third river is Tigris, which flows east of Assyria. And the fourth river is the Euphrates (Gen 2:10-14).

... and (he) lived among us (Jn 1:14b).

The *transition* from the second to the third day involves a movement from Galilee to Judea, and the mention of Judas at the end of section 3 (6:71) may be an intentional link. All four episodes of the third day occur in Judea or involve a going into Judea, and the last two (sections 6 and 7) occur almost entirely in Jerusalem. As in the gospel narrative as a whole, Judea and Jerusalem become the context for the rejection of Jesus and the consequent judgment upon the Judeans which develops in the course of these four scenes. While the narratives of the first and the second days have taken place in Galilee, Judea is the setting for the drama of light and darkness which occupies the third day.

⊕

On the third day, for the first time we have *four* episodes: the fullness of the mandalic tree begins to appear in the realization of this quaternary form, which will persist through the sixth day. As these four episodes of the third day develop we shall discover deep and complex relations between them, and the unfolding of a thematic complex centered in the *manifestation* of Jesus. He reveals himself, is witnessed to and believed in. Those who refuse to believe in him bring judgment upon themselves. Finally he is lifted up into glory. The dramatic movement here is propelled only indirectly by actions (miraculous signs, for example) of Jesus, and more immediately by his appearances and the words with which he reveals his being, his true identity. To Jesus' self-manifestation in these narratives respond the people of Judea, and particularly the Pharisees and chief priests.

SECTION 4: 3:22–4:3
THE BAPTIST AND JESUS

John the Baptist, man of the beginning, has been calling the Jews out into the wilderness to renew themselves symbolically in the waters of exodus, primal historic event of Israel's birth. He preaches a baptism of repentance for sins against the Mosaic covenant, and a return to observance of the law. In contrast to Jesus, John is presented as the man of the *first* beginning, as the *first* Adam. While the Baptist's place in the fourth gospel cannot be reduced to one symbolic role, he does serve to represent the *first* creation in contrast to the *new* creation which is brought by Jesus, the new Adam. John administers a symbolic birth in the beginning; Jesus will offer a new birth in the *divine beginning*, in himself the Word, and hence in God. This is the heart of that "recapitulation" celebrated by Paul (Eph 1:10) and by Irenaeus. John prepares the bride as he baptizes in symbolic waters; Jesus will bring the earthly bride, the new Israel, to her unitive fulfillment through a baptism in the Holy Spirit, the divine Feminine.

John is not the bridegroom but the friend of the bridegroom, as Moses was the friend and intermediary of the God who espoused Israel as bride. The new bride is surely the new Israel, but there is something further here. "No one can receive anything except what is given him from heaven. . . . I said, I am not the Christ, but I have been sent before him. He who has the bride is the bridegroom. . . ." It is the bride that comes from heaven which glorifies the bride that comes from earth, the new Israel gathered from humanity. The bride that comes from heaven, the bride of the Son of Man, is the anointing, the *chrisma* that constitutes him the Christ; it is the Holy Spirit, the divine glory itself, and it is the "feminine" Wisdom of God. The presence of John the Baptist here on the third day underlines the relation between this gift of the Spirit and Christian *baptism*. This theme of the *one gift* will be developed more fully on each of the following days. The focus of the third day is on the manifestation of this glory in Jesus, and the largely negative response to this revelation by "his own"—that is, by the people of Judea.[1]

The "fullness" of John's joy is as the fullness of the *moon*, which must give way to the glory of the rising sun from which its own light comes. Yet Jesus, the sun, will himself follow the way of John, as if he had learned it from John as his master. It is he, the one who comes after, however, who is himself this *Tao*, this dark Wisdom of which Paul speaks: ". . . we speak God's wisdom, secret and hidden . . ." (1 Cor 2:7).

SECTION 5: 5:31-47
THE WITNESSES TO JESUS: SEVERAL AND ONE

Jesus' words focus immediately upon the question of *witness* and on that of *belief*. From Jesus' own witness to himself, and that of the Baptist, he proceeds to speak of a further witness which is at once more mysterious and more definitive. This final witness is interior: the source of that inner conviction which every other witness seeks to elicit. Among these exterior witnesses are, first, the works which the

Father has given Jesus to perform, and then the *Torah*, the words which Moses "wrote of me" (5:46f).

John was a burning and shining lamp, and you were willing to rejoice for a while in his light. Then why do you refuse the light which shines in me and is offered to you? Your failure to find me in your scriptures, the law which you have from Moses, and your blindness to this light in the works which I perform, prove that you have no light within you. And you cannot recognize nor receive what you do not have. This light, which is the Word of God, the love of God, the Spirit of God, is not within you, O most religious of men. Splendid fools, you reject it by preferring the light, the glory, which is reflected to you from outside, from one another. Your inability to recognize the glory of God in me exposes the unreality of the light which you cherish, and judges you finally unworthy of this glory which is the only enduring life.

> For to those who have, more will be given, and they will have
> an abundance; but from those who have nothing, even what
> they have will be taken away (Mt 13:12).

SECTION 6: 7:1-53
THE FESTIVAL OF BOOTHS: I

The revelation of the divine glory in Jesus continues in the rich symbolic context of the feast of Booths, or Tabernacles.[2] Jesus' *hour*, the time for his glorification (see 12:23), has not yet come; it is not yet time for him to "go (literally, "go up") to this festival" (7:8). This phrase "go up" takes on a multiple significance. In the final episode of the third day, when Jesus' hour has finally come, he will solemnly enter Jerusalem. There he will be *lifted up* on the cross, and simultaneously (in John's vision) he will be *raised up* into the glory of the Father.

"I performed one work, and all of you are astonished" (7:21). If on the sabbath day, you yourselves do not hesitate to operate upon a part of the human body in order not to break the law in which you glory (see Gal 6:13), why do you condemn me for making a man's whole body well on the sabbath? The raising up of the paralytic on the sabbath, to which Jesus here refers, is a foreshadowing of the *one work* which he is to perform when his hour has come, and which is but ironically prefigured by circumcision. "For neither circumcision nor uncircumcision is anything; but a new creation is everything" (Gal 6:15).

The *one work* of Jesus, to which the whole of John's gospel is devoted, is the new creation of humanity, of "Adam," through the interior fullness of the Holy Spirit, the bride. This will be finally realized through the shedding of his own blood, in the "circumcision" of the cross, when he is lifted up. The risen Jesus will himself become the *new sabbath*, in whom this fullness will be experienced. Those who condemn his sabbath healings have not understood Moses nor circumcision nor the sabbath.

Can this be the Christ, the Anointed One, the bearer of God's gift? No, we know where this man comes from, we know his parents and his place of birth; he cannot be the Christ. As he speaks to them, and as they recall the signs that he has done, the power that is in him touches them, but then they recall what they know, and the doors of their minds are pulled shut. The witness of the Spirit burning from within him, smoldering within their own hearts, is quenched by what they already know. The eye of wonder, which had begun to open to the intimation of new birth, now once again intimidated, subdued by what must be truth, closes once more.

The superintendents of public truth take steps to arrest him, but he eludes them, as his hour has not yet come. What are these strange words, "Where I am you cannot come" (7:34)? Does he intend to go out from the land of Israel to teach the Greek proselytes? Here the wider radius of the manifestation of Jesus begins to be suggested.

On the last day of the festival, prefiguring his own "great day" shortly to come, Jesus finally speaks directly and lucidly, though still in the language of symbol, of the gift which he is to give. "Let anyone who is thirsty come to me, and let the one who believes in me drink. As the scripture has said, 'Out of his belly shall flow rivers of living water'" (7:37-38). And John immediately translates the symbolism of this *living water*: "Now he said this about the Spirit, which believers in him were to receive; for as yet there was no Spirit, because Jesus was not yet glorified" (7:39). The *Spirit* had not yet been given because Jesus had not yet been *glorified*. The divine Spirit which Jesus is to give is the *glory* of God which he is to receive when he is "lifted up."

This final promise of the gift of the Spirit brings together the symbolism of the *temple* itself, of the *water* ritual and *light* ritual of the feast of Booths, and of the "*one work*" which Jesus had performed in healing the paralytic. The new temple is to be the body of Jesus and the body of humanity, in which the glory of God will dwell. It is the Spirit or glory of God which must, by witnessing *within the human person*, confirm all the other, external and therefore "symbolic" witnesses to Jesus. Similarly, it will be this same unitive gift of the Spirit/glory which will finally transform the symbols into reality and personal experience.

From within *whom* are to flow these rivers of living water? While some commentators believe that it is from the heart of the person who believes in Jesus, others incontrovertibly argue that the waters of the Spirit are to come from within the body of Jesus. Precisely in the deliberate ambiguity of this convoluted saying of Jesus (7:37-38), John is intimating the *unitive* nature of the gift of the Spirit. The one spring flows from within the body of Jesus and within the heart of the disciple: this water is itself the divine *oneness*.

Set in dramatic contrast against the intimacy and prodigality of this gift is the mean-spirited legalism of the chief priests and Pharisees, who find excellent rational and scriptural grounds for rejecting Jesus. *Torah* and temple have become a prison for those who cannot comprehend him, and seek to arrest him. This issue of freedom and servitude will soon be developed further.

SECTION 6: 8:12-59[3]
THE FESTIVAL OF BOOTHS: II

Still apparently in the context of the feast of Booths, with its symbolism of light and its recalling of the liberation of the Israelites from Egypt, Jesus drives his controversy with the Judeans to a climax. He persists in speaking to them of his union with the Father, exposing a murderous hostility rising within their own hearts.

The theme of *witness* is resumed immediately as Jesus' authenticity is questioned, and this time Jesus refers to no other witness than his own and that of his Father. The words which Jesus speaks in the treasury of the temple are not grasped, nor is Jesus apprehended; his *hour*, though it is approaching fast, has not yet arrived.

"You are from below, I am from above" (8:23): these words recall what had been said earlier of Jesus and John the Baptist (3:31), but now with grave implication. "I told you that you would die in your sins, for you will die in your sins unless you believe that *I am*" (8:24). Here is recalled the death of the unbelieving Israelites in the desert, those who "could not enter because of unbelief" (Heb 3:19). "*Who are you?*" they demand (8:25). In reply, Jesus refers them once again to "the beginning." In this series of affirmations Jesus declares once again his own identity in language which appropriates to him the divine Name itself. "When you have lifted up the Son of Man, then you will realize that *I am*" (8:28).

The truth which Jesus offers them, he declares, has the power to make them *free*. The exodus from bondage in Egypt is recalled once again. But these children of Abraham deny any need to be set free. As the crescendo of confrontation between Jesus and these Judeans continues to mount, the debate turns on the issue of *parentage*, becoming an exchange of mortal insults. Implicit in Jesus' words about his Father has been the birth in God which he *is*, and which he offers to communicate. With this divine generation Jesus contrasts first their human descent from *Abraham*, and finally the filiation to the *devil* which their behavior betrays. They oppose this supreme "truth," and like the liar and murderer that is the devil, they seek to kill rather than to communicate it. Abraham, the father of his people, is only an *image* of the divine fatherhood. He can give his children neither true freedom nor eternal life.

What is this truth that will make them free if they "continue in my word"? Is it not, ultimately, the divine Word itself, that is, the Son of God, with which one becomes progressively identified as one "continues in" it? And the freedom is the freedom of this assimilation to the *unitive* reality which is Jesus, the Son.

SECTION 7: 12:12-50
THE FINAL PASSOVER APPROACHES: JESUS ENTERS JERUSALEM

As in the three other gospels, the account of Jesus' passion is introduced by his solemn entrance into Jerusalem, in the midst of an enthusiastic crowd. He is welcomed as the King of Israel, and John tells us that the motive for this acclaim is his raising Lazarus from the tomb. It was this spectacular sign which has brought about the decision of the sanhedrin to put Jesus to death.

"Look, the world has gone after him" (12:19), the Pharisees lament, and it is at this time in fact that some "Greeks," probably Jewish converts from outside Palestine, ask to see Jesus. These "Greeks" represent the "world," all the Gentile peoples. Jesus does not respond by manifesting himself to them. Rather, he seizes the occasion of their coming to define his own path in contrast to the widening road which they open before him. In this way he confirms once again the continuity between his own way and that of the Baptist. Jesus indeed stands at the threshold of his glorification. He enters upon his *hour*. But the drama of this glorification will be played out with an absolute irony. And the one who would follow him to glory must follow him in the same way of diminishment, the same descent into the earth.

While the synoptic gospels recount Jesus' struggle in the garden of Gethsemani, the Jesus of John's gospel does not waver despite the shadow that now weighs upon his soul. "Father, glorify your name" (12:28). The voice which sounds from above in reply to these words recalls the voice which had "glorified" Jesus at his baptism in the Jordan and at his transfiguration on the mountain, in the synoptic narratives. Now the Father is to glorify his name conclusively by raising Jesus into his glory. When this authoritative voice has spoken, Jesus announces that the judgment of this world has come, and that its ruler, the devil, is now to be deposed. At the same time, Jesus is to be raised to his destined glory, from which position he will draw all of humanity (or all creation: the Greek is not clear) to himself. This is to take place as he is *"raised up"* on the cross!

After a final appeal to believe in the light before it is taken away from them, we are told that Jesus "departed and hid from them" (12:36). The time of Jesus' public manifestation is over, and John's "book of signs" now concludes. For the rest of John's narrative Jesus will speak to almost no one but his disciples, and at this moment he is about to enter into his hour. John's "book of glory" is about to open.

The quotations from the prophet Isaiah which John introduces at this point are very significant. That their *Isaian* context is relevant is indicated by the words, "Isaiah said this because he *saw his glory* and spoke about him" (12:41). Here John refers to the initiatory vision of Isaiah (Is 6:1-4) in which he saw the Lord "raised high and exalted" upon his throne in the middle of the temple. At the same time there is reference here (12:38; cf. Is 53:1) to the Isaian servant of Yahweh, who is to die in the midst of the unbelief of his people, then to be vindicated and glorified by God. Here are foreshadowed the passion, the death and the glorification of Jesus. The insistence on the theme of glory continues as once again the diverging ways of the human glory and the glory of God are contrasted (12:42-43). It is *faith* which sees this glory of God in Jesus, and consequently receives this glory.

The progressive revelation of the glory of Jesus on the third day thus ends in the obscurity of the way of the *Baptist*: "I must decrease" (3:30). But precisely at the moment in which Jesus decreases to the point of death, he is to *increase*, to acquire that glory which constitutes the power to draw all to himself.

The cry of the seraphim in the vision of Isaiah, which lies behind the conclusion of this episode and which John has connected with the glory of Jesus, sums up the revelation of the third day:

" . . . the *whole earth* is full of *his glory*" (Is 6:3c).

THE THIRD DAY: SYNTHETIC REVIEW

The whole of the third day can be seen as a conflict between, on the one hand, Jesus—who manifests in himself the glory which is the destiny both of humanity (or "Adam"), and of the earth itself—and, on the other hand, that human world which prefers its own glory and its own certainties.

⊕

Exodus symbolism is maintained continually by the multiple allusions to the Mosaic history, and its liturgical commemorations, throughout the third day. Connections between John's third day and the third day of the first *creation* account in Genesis, though not immediately obvious, are also abundant. On the third day of Genesis 1, the dry land is separated from the waters, and called earth. From the earth then springs forth vegetation, "plants yielding seed, and fruit trees of every kind bearing fruit with the seed in it . . ." (1:11).

Jesus comes from above into the world, onto the earth, as seed; he dies into the earth and simultaneously is lifted up from the earth, to draw to himself "*the whole world*," all those peoples who live on the earth. He becomes the rock, the garden, the *new earth*, from which spring the living waters of the Spirit.

The recurrent distinction between Jesus and John the Baptist in our texts recalls the *separation of the earth from the waters* on the third day of Genesis 1. Still present behind these texts of the third day is the image of Jesus emerging from the waters at his baptism, as the *new earth*, the new promised land, the new garden of paradise.

The second creation account of Genesis 2 is recalled at the climactic moment of the third episode: "out of his belly shall flow *rivers* of living water" (7:38): first, as applied to Jesus himself. We recall the *four rivers that flow from paradise*: in Genesis 2, and in Sirach 24. On the one hand, the *body of Jesus* is the new paradise. The Spirit flows from this earth which is the body of Jesus (see 19:34 and 20:22). And on the other hand, the heart or body of the believer becomes the new paradise.

Jesus speaks these words while teaching *in the temple* (7:14). This temple itself is to be replaced by the same body of Jesus (2:19). It is from the new temple that will flow the living waters, according to the prophecy of Ezekiel (Ez 47:1-2).

In each episode of the third day a central motif is the *coming of Jesus*, whether this is his arrival or appearance at a particular place, his self-manifestation, or his coming into the world. There emerges thus a series of moments, phases or aspects in the movement toward the full revelation, or glorification, of Jesus. This progressive manifestation of Jesus corresponds to the third day because it is, taken generally, a coming into the *world*, a coming to this *earth*. Then, when Jesus finally goes away, he departs to another *place* to *become the new earth*, and to draw "all things" (see 12:32) to himself, to share his glory.

⊕

One direction of movement throughout these four episodes is *inward* or centripetal, from Galilee into Judea, and then to Jerusalem and the temple. This movement proceeds toward the religious center of Israel, of the religion and the people of the *exodus*. The other movement is *outward* or centrifugal, toward the whole world; this becomes apparent as we move through the last two episodes.

The *inward* movement is strengthened by the reference to the sixth chapter of Isaiah in the concluding section 7 (in 12:38-41). The allusion is to the vision of Isaiah of the Lord enthroned in the *temple*, which corresponds to the religious center of Israel. The inward movement, into Judea, Jerusalem, the temple, is consistently *ironic* in John. And while 12:46, "I have come as light into the world," announces (as does 12:32) the opening of this manifestation up to the whole world, in the style of the prologue, it is becoming ominously clear that this full revelation of the light will only come about through a final confrontation between Jesus and the disbelief of "his own," the people— and most especially the religious leaders—of Judea and Jerusalem.

⊕

On the *first day* of the new creation we were brought to a unitive beginning; on the *second day* we were fed, in the midst of our journey, with the unitive divine wisdom which becomes the flesh of the risen Son of Man. Here on the *third day*, having arrived at the threshold of the end, we begin to hear of the divine glory which is to fill the body of this Son of Man, in whom shall dwell all those who have believed in him.

These first three days thus complete a figure within the larger figure of the seven days. The theme of divine glory which is emerging as the central thread of the third day will be developed further in the succeeding days. On the fourth day Jesus will reveal how this glory is to be participated in by his disciples. In his passion on the fifth day, Jesus' descent into humiliation will be at the same time his exaltation into glory (see 8:28; 12:32-33; 17:1). On the sixth day the symbolism of glory will be brought to its fullest development in the symbolic key of a nuptial relation between man and woman. On the seventh day, finally, the glory will be breathed into the disciples to complete the creation of the new dwelling of God: the body of the collective Son of Man.

Without some understanding of the meaning of *glory* (in the Hebrew *kavod*, and in the Greek of the New Testament *doxa*) in the biblical tradition,[4] we can sense little of the richness contained in John's use of the word. The glory is the experienced presence of God, God as perceptible—whether in the cloud that filled the tabernacle in the desert, or in the pillar of fire that guided the Israelites through the desert, or as visibly manifest in the temple.

The glory is God as concrete reality, as appearance, as quality, as palpable presence, God as submitting to human experience and at the same time overwhelming it. It is the distinctive quality of the divine, "Godness," and when seen reflected in a human face—as in that of Moses—it marks that person out as a chosen one, an emissary, of God. The continual controversy in the episodes of the third day about the authenticity, the identity, the origin of Jesus, may be understood in terms of his possession or non-possession of the divine glory.

While inalienably belonging to God—"I am the Lord, that is my name; my glory I give to no other" (Is 42:8; cf. 48:11)—the glory belongs also to the destiny of humanity, created in the image and likeness of God. But "all (i.e. both Jew and Gentile) have sinned and fall short of the glory of God" (Rom 3:23). If it can be truly said that "The essential revelation of the New Testament is the connection of glory with the person of Jesus,"[5] this glory must be understood also as the gift of the "Anointed," the Christ, to humanity.

The work of Jesus—from the incarnation to his death and resurrection—is to *bring humanity into the glory of God*, or, conversely, to bring the divine glory into the human body, to make the divine glory immanent in the creation. Both Paul and John are distinguished by their sense of the glory of Jesus: a consciousness which obviously reflects personal experience of this glory in him. The gospels of Paul and of John may be summarized as their personal accounts of God's communication of this glory to humanity through Jesus Christ.

We cannot here trace the thread of the glory through the successive phases of Old Testament literature,[6] but will note briefly its relation to the two moments of this tradition which are of particular concern to us: *exodus* and *creation*.

Moses was the man who was dignified to a unique degree by the divine glory: it shone from his face after his meetings with the Lord. Both the mighty works of God on behalf of the Israelites during the exodus journey and the presence of God in their midst were expressions of his glory. Together with the ark of the covenant and the manna, both memorials of the exodus experience, the glory would dwell in the temple at Jerusalem once the Israelites had established themselves in the promised land.

"Glory" is not part of the vocabulary of the first chapters of Genesis. The creation of man and woman "*in the image*" of God (Gen 1:26-27), however, suggests that their original condition was not completely alien to the divine glory. Was that which was lost by the "fall" not at least a reflection of the divine glory (see Rom 3:23)? When Adam and Eve discover themselves to be naked after their sin, and hide themselves from God in the garden, is it not because they have been stripped of the vesture of grace, or of divine glory, with which they had been adorned?

This intimate relation of the divine glory with the human condition is very important for understanding John's gospel. The glory which is to crown the work and suffering of Jesus is the destiny not merely of Jesus, but *of every human person*. We are born for glory, but born in an alien land, and our very birth is an image of that one final birth into the light, into the "land of likeness,"[7] which is the divine birth of the Son of Man.

John the Baptist has a particular relation to this glory. Like Moses, the man of exodus upon whom the glory dwelt, he calls the people of Jerusalem out of the city, away from the constructions, the towers and simulacra of human glory, into the chaste wilderness where the human person once again discovers his hunger and thirst for the glory of God. This glory somehow sits upon John as it had rested on the face of Moses: "What did you go out into the wilderness to look at?" (Mt 11:7), Jesus demanded of the crowds who had followed the Baptist into the desert.

Who is this man, then, who is neither the Christ, nor the prophet, nor Elijah, nor Moses, and whose harsh words are salted with the taste of God's glory? Who is this bush burning in the wasteland with a fire other than the fire of human hearths? On the level of creation symbolism, John the Baptist is simply *man*: he is Adam, collective humanity, who *lives in the wilderness the truth of the human condition*, lives with clarity the poverty of Adam who has been stripped of the original glory which he wore unknowing in the garden, and who burns with an inner knowledge, a thirst for glory yet unseen.

The dove which John sees descending upon the young rabbi from Nazareth is a visible expression of this glory. In the synoptic gospels, the glorification of Jesus at the moment of his baptism is signified by the voice from heaven declaring, "This is my beloved Son, in whom I am well pleased" (see Jn 1:14 and the transfiguration narratives: Mt 17:1-8; Mk 9:2-8; Lk 9:28-36).

$$\oplus$$

If we extend our reflection on the glory, this is because of its importance in our initiation into the world of John's gospel. Glory is that which sings from the strings of the gospel word; it is the flame that springs up within us when the word touches the heart. It is the realization for which all our labor of study is a preparation. It is that which is most Pauline in Paul, that which is most Johannine in John, and that which is most deeply and inalienably ourself. And it is God, in this very igniting of structures and bursting of limits—the excess, the pure gratuity in which God is most God for us, most transcendent in being more intimate to us than our own hungry and struggling self.

Can we learn with more precision what may be this glory which is not only of such intense concern to John, but also of urgent importance to Jesus in John's gospel? We have a glimpse of it when Jesus turns the water into wine at Cana, and we hear Jesus asking the Father for it at the end of the supper, when he is about to go to his death.

From the side of *God*, it is God himself as God herself: poured out, given, participated and yet God. The Old Testament begins to hint at this in the figure of *Sophia*, later Judaism knows it as the *Shekinah*, and the eastern Christian theologians speak of this in terms of the "divine energies."

From the point of view of *Jesus*, as Word incarnate, God and man, it is the messianic *anointing* which he is to receive and to impart.[8] It is the *bride* which he is to receive from the Father when he has run his course.

And for *us*? The glory is that which glows at the extremes of experience: at the height and the depth of life. Everything in the world moves toward glory as its flowering, its coming to flame, its truth. Glory is beyond the reach of our distinctions, beyond the conundrums of our dualistic world, in the tranquil sufficiency of the divine being. Beyond the distinction of self and other, of creature and God, it is precisely the movement, the pouring, the freedom which is supremely itself in leaping over these boundaries: in this it is the glory of God.

And so it is the uniqueness which vindicates itself like rain precisely in its commonality (see Is 55 and Prov 8:1ff), in its ability to penetrate everything, to make itself everything. Coming from above, it pulls every single thing down to selfhood, into utter truth.

Glory is that which we seek, beyond what we need. It is the natural term of human desire, and the secret knowledge within that desire. Glory is inseparable from the bread of wisdom, the living bread which is Christ, and yet it is a further aspect, another phase, a companion bringing a new delight, the delight of otherness, the infinite fullness just beyond the wall of self, that every beloved other intimates to us.

The poet, the artist seeks glory as does the lover, the soldier, the thinker or the monk, but each along a different valley, a different stream. The poet, particularly, is concerned with the glory with which the human word is pregnant, and so, in his creative effort, may cross the threshold of theology.

We carry glory in the darkness of our hearts, in this world. We know it in the freedom of sunlight on a wing: those flights and arrivals of the music that we hear. To seek to possess it is the fatal error. "Little children, keep yourself from idols" (1 Jn 5:21). If we could keep faithfully this Johannine "last word," perhaps the golden river would burst free and inundate the world, the tree would burn transfigured in the sun.

Within our insatiable egoism burns an unlimited need for glory—that is, for the gold that is woven in the fibres of our being so that we cannot be without it, even though we may know it only by eclipse and absence. There is the eclipse of *shame*, somehow worse than all, when we know glory by its awful opposite. And there is, on the other hand, the eclipse of poverty and *risk*, when the fire of spiritual freedom which is the inner person may become exultantly manifest. Glory—in this world—is known in this peripheral glow of eclipse.

Shame, some psychologists[9] now say, is the toxic ill of ills, the hole in the container that sabotages every healing and destroys every gift. Shame is an inverse experience of glory, an inverse knowledge of our destiny, in the awful nakedness that we feel without our garment of light.

Beauty is the icon of glory, the light of eternity upon the features of time. People in love are caught by a glimmer of this light blown through an opened window of this world, and see the essential glory of one another before the time of its final blossoming. The resurrection is anticipated for a while, in the grace that sits upon a human face, a human body.[10] We know that this perishable bloom opening within us is something more than normal life; we know that its roots plunge in another earth. In the romance tradition of medieval Europe, the grandeur of the revelatory vocation of the west erupted in a cultural expression of this experience of the divine glory in the love of man and woman.[11]

In Paul, history in all its conflict and turbulence is an alchemy of glory, a transformative process in which is spun this shining thread of glory (see Rom 8:18-23; 2 Cor 3:17–4:18). The inner fire with which Paul speaks witnesses that his own life is propelled by the knowledge of this glory: a knowledge inseparable from his knowledge of Jesus and of the mystery of his cross.

But we impart a secret and hidden wisdom of God, which God decreed before the ages for our glorification. None of the rulers of this age understood this: for if they had, they would not have crucified the Lord of glory. But as it is written,

"What no eye has seen, nor ear heard,
nor the heart of man conceived,
what God has prepared for those who love him,"

God has revealed to us through the Spirit (1 Cor 2: 7-10a).

⊕

In the perspective of John's seven days of the new creation, glory is the culmination of a first cycle—it closes the trinitarian ring of the first three days: origin, sustenance and consummation; birth in light, journey of witness and unitive homecoming; mystery, wisdom and glory.

On the second day of the Genesis account God created *heaven*, and on the third day God created the *earth*. On the second day of John's new creation we find Jesus bringing heaven to earth by presenting himself as the "bread from heaven." On the third day, the movement, in contrast, is upward, as John develops the creation of the new earth in terms of the Son of Man—Jesus and then those who have believed in him—ascending into the divine glory. On both days, the first creation by *separation* is followed by a new creation by *union*. The new heaven and the new earth are complementary aspects of this new union of the created world with God.

Both the wisdom of God and the glory of God seek a *dwelling* on the earth. The body of the Son of Man, the new Adam, is formed from the earth to be the dwelling of the divine glory: the meeting place of earth and glory.

Chapter Four

The Fourth Day:
You Are the Light of the World

And God said, "Let there be lights in the dome of the sky to separate the day from the night; and let them be for signs and for seasons and for days and years, and let them be lights in the dome of the sky to give light upon the earth." And it was so. God made the two great lights—the greater light to rule the day and the lesser light to rule the night—and the stars. God set them in the dome of the sky to give light upon the earth, to rule over the day and over the night, and to separate the light from the darkness. And God saw that it was good. And there was evening and there was morning, the fourth day (Gen 1:14-19).

Now the serpent was more crafty than any other wild animal that the Lord God had made. He said to the woman, "Did God say, 'You shall not eat from any tree in the garden'?" The woman said to the serpent, "We may eat of the fruit of the trees in the garden; but God said, 'You shall not eat of the fruit of the tree that is in the middle of the garden, nor shall you touch it, or you shall die.'" But the serpent said to the woman, "You will not die; for God knows that when you eat of it your eyes will be opened and you will be like God, knowing good and evil." So when the woman saw that the tree was good for food, and that it was a delight to the eyes, and that the tree was to be desired to make one wise, she took of its fruit and ate; and she also gave some to her husband, who was with her, and he ate. Then the eyes of both were opened, and they knew that they were naked; and they sewed fig leaves together and made loincloths for themselves.

They heard the sound of the Lord God walking in the garden at the time of the evening breeze, and the man and his wife hid themselves from the presence of the Lord God among the trees of the garden. But the Lord God called to the man, and said to him, "Where are you?" He said, "I heard the sound of you in the garden, and I was afraid, because I was naked; and I hid myself" (Gen 3:1-10).

From his fullness we have all received, grace upon grace (Jn 1:16).

Christ therefore is "the true light which enlightens every man, coming into this world." From his light the Church itself also having been enlightened is made "the light of the world" enlightening those "who are in darkness," as also Christ himself testifies to his disciples saying: "You are the light of the world." From this it is shown that Christ is indeed the light of the apostles, but the apostles are "the light of the world." ...

... For just as "star differs from star in glory," so also each of the saints, according to his own greatness, sheds his light upon us (Origen[1]).

The fourth day is concerned with teaching and with empowerment. Corresponding to the fourth day of Genesis 1, on which the heavenly lights were set in the sky to illuminate the world, the thematic continuum here relates to instruction, to communication of the light, and to the creation of ministers of the light. On this day the Word incarnate presents himself as light and life, and comes into conflict with the incumbent ministers, the custodians of the *Torah*. The essential confrontation here is between the creative Word which is light and life for human persons, and the mediatory Mosaic Word which has been frozen into the letter which kills. It is the account of the temptation and sin of the first man and woman, in Genesis 3, which provides the symbolic and theological basis for John's development of the dramatic conflict between the "knowledge of good and evil" which has become the legalistic religion of the scribes and Pharisees, and the unitive wisdom of the Word.

SECTION 8: 3:1-21
NICODEMUS

Nicodemus, a *man* (*anthrōpos*) from among the Pharisees, comes to Jesus at night. We are reminded of the *man sent from God* of the prologue, the Baptist, who initiated the third day. Nicodemus is a leader, an *archōn*[2] of the Jews, and a "teacher of Israel," and he comes to Jesus with profound respect as to another teacher who bears the marks of a genuine representative of God. "Rabbi, we know that you are a teacher who has come from God...." He is one of the "authorities" among the Jews who believed in Jesus, as we heard at the end of the third day. There is also a thematic continuity between the third and fourth days, as the accent moves from the authenticity of Jesus and his teaching, from the peculiar "light" that is in him, to the question of *teaching* itself, of the transmission of this light.

Jesus shocks us by responding so brusquely to this dignitary's friendly and earnest inquiry. He immediately confronts the good man with a steep and paradoxical saying: "...no one can see the kingdom of God without being born from above." These words resemble Jesus' reply to the wealthy *archōn* in Luke's gospel (Lk 18:18-25). These two very different stories are nevertheless closely parallel, contrasting nicely the perspectives of Luke and John. *Torah*, teaching and tradition here seem to encounter a blind precipice. Nicodemus in his puzzlement and frustration, repeatedly asks, "But how can...?"

When Nicodemus came in the night to visit this impressive young teacher, he could not have expected such an assault on the foundations of his mental world. Your understanding is worth nothing until you are born again, born from above (the Greek word *anōthen* used here can mean both "again" and "from above," and both meanings are intended here). His knowledge of *Torah* disappears into this precipice. "*How can...?*" protests Nicodemus.

If the first difficult lesson is this swallowing up of holy tradition in an impossible birth, the second lesson, equally baffling, is somehow embodied in the person of this young rabbi himself. The birth of which he speaks has to do with *himself*, is in him. He *is* this birth. Nicodemus can hardly suspect this yet; there are many things in these words of Jesus which are completely beyond him at this moment.

Teaching, knowledge, *Torah*, concludes in *birth*, terminates in a *beginning*. And this beginning is the *one* beginning: the birth in the Word. This Word is present before Nicodemus in Jesus. "For God so loved the world that he gave his only *Son*, so that everyone who believes in him may not perish but may have eternal life" (3:16). The younger teacher is this *Son*—Son of Man, Son of God, in whom the one birth is present. He is the Wisdom of God. "How can anyone be born after having grown old? Can one enter a second time into the mother's womb and be born?" (3:4). The word *can* occurs six times in this dialogue, and when Nicodemus uses it, it bears this sense of vexed impotence. No, you must be born again not of woman, but of water and the Spirit. Water is not woman, the Spirit is not woman, and yet... you are to be born in God as a child is born from a woman. Born not merely from God but in God, born to dwell in God. Yet born from God, born into the world anew from God. This image of a woman giving birth will appear once more near the end of the supper narrative, to enclose within its symbolism the whole of the fourth day.

The position of this *archōn*, this teacher, before the younger rabbi is parallel to that of John the Baptist before Jesus: the older man encounters in the younger man not only the full development of his own ministry, but its very substance, its beginning, its source. Together with Nicodemus, we are carried by Jesus' words back to the first day of the new creation, between water and wind, water and Spirit. The essential word which must resound within Nicodemus' heart if he is to understand this teaching is the "*I Am*" of Jesus upon the waters.

When Jesus speaks of the *serpent* which Moses lifted up in the wilderness, we are to recall the time of the Israelites' exodus from Egypt (Num 21:4-9). Once out in the wilderness the people murmured at the lack of food, and hankered after the plenty of Egypt. God sent among them fiery serpents which bit them and killed many of them—and then offered them, through Moses, a remedy from this scourge: "Make a fiery (or poisonous) serpent, and set it on a pole; and everyone who is bitten shall look at it and live" (Num 21:8).

As Moses lifted up the bronze image of the serpent for the healing of those wounded Israelites who would turn and look upon it, so the Son of Man must be lifted up that whoever believes in him might have eternal life. The bite of the serpent was healed by looking with faith at the elevated likeness of the serpent. The cure comes through the simulacrum of the punishment, to the sinner who looks upon it with faith. But *what* is it that will be healed by looking at Jesus raised up on the cross?

Once again the interpretive movement from exodus to *creation* brings a flood of light. The original serpent's bite, in the symbolic language of the Bible, was the word of the serpent to the first man and woman which persuaded them to eat of the forbidden tree. And when they ate, their eyes were opened, and they saw that they were naked, and they were afraid and hid themselves from God among the trees of the garden (Gen 3:1-10). It was an ambiguous knowledge that they received from the tree of the knowledge of good and evil—an illumination which sent them, out of fear and shame, into hiding in the darkness, and a wisdom which proved to be wedded to death. If there is a knowledge that is death, however, there is also a knowledge that is life, and this is what Jesus offers. This is the living knowledge which comes from looking upon this serpent, Jesus, raised up on the tree of the cross. "For our sake he made him to be sin who knew no sin, so that in him we might become the righteousness of God" (2 Cor 5:21).

The contrast between these two kinds of knowledge will generate the dramatic conflict of the fourth day. On one side, Jesus will be manifesting a truth, a teaching, which is life, as he preaches and as he heals upon the sabbath. At the supper, this teaching will be passed on to his own disciples, empowering them as the teachers and leaders of the new Israel. On the other side, the religious leaders and teachers of Judaism will continually oppose to this teaching their own version of the *Torah*, which they have made a word of death.

It was the *tree of life* which conferred eternal life in the garden, while the tree of the knowledge of good and evil bore the fruit of death. Now Jesus becomes both tree of knowledge and tree of life. To look upon him with faith is to begin to participate in unitive knowledge and in eternal life.

The conclusion of this discourse (3:17-21) is also rooted in the narrative of Genesis 3 (vv. 7-11). "For all who do evil *hate the light* and do not come into the light, so that their deeds may not be exposed." It is the wise and learned men of Israel, the ones whose eyes have been opened by their study of the *Torah*, who will show themselves in the course of this fourth day to hate the light which is life. Nicodemus came to Jesus at night, came blinking and timid into the light, and found that what had been light for him before must now be considered darkness.

The symbolic story of the tree of knowledge expresses a mystery which is woven into our being: intimate to us, both obvious and obscure. Nothing is more familiar to human experience than this entanglement of consciousness and blindness, fear and desire—this ambivalence toward the light—which still tastes of the subtle serpent's poison.

To the radical leap from *teaching* to new birth, new *creation*, corresponds the movement from Mosaic *history* to *creation* symbolism, which we have seen emerging in the latter half of this Nicodemus episode. The movement is once again from a *linear* progression to a *radial* unfolding from an all-containing creative center. John's creation symbolism brings us each time into the liberating breadth and depth, the essential power, of the creative Word itself.

SECTION 9: 5:1-30
THE PARALYTIC

At our second station on the fourth day, alongside a pool in Jerusalem, we come upon a living symbol of "the flesh" and its inertia. The paralytic, helpless until Jesus comes, is healed by the one positive movement which he manages to make: at Jesus' word he rises and picks up his bed. When Jesus has healed his bodily paralysis, though, he shows no signs of coming to life interiorly, but goes on as if walking in his sleep. He tells the Jewish authorities that it was Jesus who healed him on the sabbath, supplying them with one more pretext for their mounting persecution of the young rabbi.

⊕

John's story of the healing of the paralytic is related to several episodes in the synoptic tradition. Most obviously parallel is the story of the similarly helpless man who, on the sabbath, was lowered by his friends through the roof of the house before Jesus, who then healed him, telling him to take up his pallet and walk (Mk 2:1-12). One is also reminded of the story of the woman who had been bent over— "whom Satan bound"—for eighteen years, and was similarly healed by Jesus on the sabbath (Lk 13:10-17).

A third synoptic story helps to bring out some of the symbolic meaning and the power beneath the surface of John's narrative. In the third chapter of Mark, Jesus enters the synagogue on the sabbath, and finds there a man with a withered hand.

They watched him to see whether he would cure him on the sabbath, so that they might accuse him. And he said to the man who had the withered hand, "Come forward." Then he said to them, "Is it lawful to do good or to do harm on the sabbath, to save life or to kill?" But they were silent. He looked around at them with anger; he was grieved at their hardness of heart and said to the man, "Stretch out your hand." He stretched it out, and his hand was restored. The Pharisees went out and immediately conspired with the Herodians against him, how to destroy him (Mk 3:1-6).

Both bodily paralysis and the withered hand—notwithstanding the probable historicity of these events—can be understood also as eloquent symbols of the *impotence of the existing religious tradition*, of the *Torah* as it was being taught and exemplified at that time.

The *Word* of Jesus, on the other hand, immediately effects healing, restores the ability to move and to act. As Jesus knowingly performs this communication of life and movement on the sabbath day, we find ourselves present at a brilliant epiphany of the living Word, in contrast with the dead hand, the grim background of legalistic *Torah*.

"Is it lawful to do good or to do harm on the sabbath, to save life or to kill?" You, Pharisees, are a withered, indeed a withering, murdering hand: in you the Word of the living God has become a law of death. In your hands the *Torah*, the law of the sabbath, spoken by God as a time of refreshment, healing and new life for humanity, has itself become an instrument of slavery and death. Behold the power of the Word of life, behold the living sabbath of God which has come among you. And there is no contradicting this power of life which surges into the man with the crippled hand, and into the paralytic.

The story of the paralytic, then, is about an empowering word, about the communication of the word of God, and about the contrast between the transmission of life by the living Word (see 1:3-4) and a doctrinal and moral tradition which has deadened the living Word and transformed it into a paralyzing and ultimately deadly letter (see 2 Cor 3:6-9; Rom 7:4-13).

While this story does not obviously suggest a symbolic level of meaning, there are indications pointing to an *exodus*-interpretation here. The man has been waiting here for thirty-eight years without "a man" (5:7: Gr. *anthrōpon*), recalling the Israelites who wandered in the wilderness, unable to enter the promised land for "thirty-eight years, until the entire generation of warriors had perished from the camp, as the Lord had sworn concerning them" (Deut 2:14).

> And to whom did he swear that they would not enter his rest (see Ps 95:11), if not to those who were disobedient? So we see that they were unable to enter because of unbelief... (Heb 3:18-19).

Our paralytic is the Israelite who languishes in the wilderness unable to enter the promised land, God's *rest*, because of a lack of faith. These waters, moved from time to time by a spirit, recall the waters of the first day of creation, over which hovered the Spirit. This man's hope is in once again immersing himself in the waters of the beginning. He reminds us of the ancient religious traditions of the world which rest upon a primordial revelation, a "cosmic revelation."

Jesus comes along and heals the paralytic with a word: an empowering command. It is in *doing* this word that he is healed, he rises up and walks. He carries the pallet which had borne him. The life of the beginning, the waters of life which flow through paradise, are in this man Jesus, who heals with the energy of his Word. He is himself the Word who descends into the waters to fertilize them so that they may give birth to the new creation. He is Lord of the sabbath (Mk 2:28; Lk 6:5). This Son of Man, who is himself the future of humanity, reverses the direction of human religion as he appears in this world to impel history forward to its conclusion, the final sabbath of God's rest.

⊕

On the third day, Jesus referred to this healing when he said in the temple, "I performed one work, and all of you are astonished.... If a man receives circumcision on the sabbath so that the law of Moses may not be broken, are you angry with me because I healed a man's whole body on the sabbath?" (7:21-23). It is this *one sabbath work* transcending time which is in question here. This is the union of God and humanity, the raising up of humanity in God which is already present in Jesus himself. "My Father is still working, and I also am working" (5:17), and it is one work, the generation of the Son, that is being done. This is itself the sabbath, and when Jesus walks upon the earth, the sabbath flows into the days of the week.

"For this reason the Jews were seeking all the more to kill him, because he was not only breaking the sabbath, but was calling God his own Father, thereby making himself equal to God" (5:18). It is not, precisely, equality, but *unity* that is in question here. What Jesus is affirming is *the new union of humanity with God*, which is realized in him. This is his one great *work*, which is behind the continual reference to work, to actions, in this episode. And *this work is itself the great sabbath*. "The sabbath was made for humanity..." also in this sense: the day which has been traditionally conserved as a space in which the human person is freed to be with God, "as in the beginning," in the garden, finds its fulfillment in the final union in which the human person is born into the fullness of life in God. The institution of the sabbath is a ritual anticipation of this communion of God and humanity, to be realized once Jesus has made humanity "equal with God" in himself. The Son of Man is the Lord of the sabbath (Mk 2:28; Lk 6:5) as he conducts the sabbath to this consummation. Thus it is the fullness of their own life which they feel compelled to kill. "And this is the judgment, that the light has come into the world, and people loved darkness rather than light because their deeds were evil" (3:19).

This episode turns around the *sabbath* theme, which is related to the Mosaic law—but ultimately to the creation story. The divine word embodied in the law had been virtually paralyzed, and this was exemplified by the legalistic interpretation of the sabbath in terms of complete inactivity. Jesus brings the word of the sabbath back to its original meaning in the sense of *re-creation*, return to the font of life. Once again, the movement from exodus to creation is a movement from human religious structures, imperfect, impotent and sometimes perverse and inimical to life, to a faith which relates the person immediately to God's creative power.

This union with God, humanity's destined new birth, also transforms one's relationship with "the flesh," with nature, with the cosmos. "Stand up, take your mat and walk." That which formerly you rested upon, you must take up, now that you have entered into this sabbath rest of God. That which you formerly depended upon, now you shall carry in the strength of your vocation as God's steward and gardener in the world. Further light on the creation level of meaning in this story emerges, therefore, when it is considered from the aspect of *work*. There is recurrent reference to work in the narrative, since this healing has been done on the sabbath. The man who has been healed is reproached for carrying his pallet on the sabbath (5:10), and Jesus is condemned for healing him on the sabbath.

What is the *work* of humanity? In the narrative of Genesis 2-3, Adam is a cultivator of the garden who must, when he is driven from it, till the unrewarding soil for his bread, while the woman is to "labor" in bringing forth children (Gen 3:16-19). In this way both are God's helpers in the work of creation. But what is the destined *fullness* of this vocation of humanity? Have man and woman been created, ultimately, to be *creators*, in the image of their maker? It is here that the fuller implications of the *unitive* gift of Jesus begin to appear. It is here also that the relationship of this episode to the basic thematic of the fourth day emerges more fully. Jesus will conclude the fourth day by *communicating his own powers to human persons, to his disciples.* The fourth day is about the communication of the fullness of the human destiny which is in Jesus. If one side of this gift is the divine *birth*, the other side is the role of *creator*.

Anticipated in the healing of this sabbath, by which Jesus *raises up* a human person, this transmission of the creator function to his brothers and sisters will be more clearly expressed on the sabbath of the week of creation, the seventh day (Jn 20:22) when one man breathes the spirit of life into others, so that they may do the same. The heart of the new creation is the transmission of this gift of divine life, and Jesus, as human person, both has the power to transmit this gift, and *communicates that power* to his disciples. And so the new temple, the body of the Son of Man, is constructed.

Owen Barfield[3] speaks of the historical moment of incarnation as the moment in history when human persons receive, in Christ, their destined *creative* role toward the cosmos. This is a reversal: what humanity depended upon, lived from, shall now depend upon, live from, humanity. The man takes up and carries the bed which had carried him.

When Jesus says, "My Father is still working, and I also am working" (5:17), and "... he [the Father] will show him greater works than these, so that you will be astonished" (5:20), his words hold meaning also for the human vocation. "... the one who believes in me will also do the works that I do and, in fact, will do greater works than these, because I am going to the Father" (14:12).

Beneath the apparently meager connection of the story of the paralytic with Genesis 2-3, therefore, there lie these strong implications: it is the *power of creation* itself, the destined "work" of a humanity made in the image of its creator, which is being symbolically conferred by Jesus on this fourth day of the new creation. The creative Word has become a human person; and this creativity, Jesus' gift, dwells among us.

Our faith in Jesus is a faith in the *creative Word* of God become one of us. One line of development of this faith is in the direction of the "east," the "beginning," the luminous simplicity and contemplative repose of the center. The corresponding "westward" development may be that secular creativity which reproduces on its own level the divine creative act. The potential for both—the interior *sabbath* and the world-transforming *work*—dwells within each person created in the divine image.

SECTION 10: 9:1-41
THE MAN BORN BLIND

"As he walked along, he saw a man blind from birth." This third narrative of the fourth day, like the first and the second, begins as Jesus encounters a *"man" (anthrōpos)*—this time a blind man begging by the wayside. Blind from his birth, this person is every child of Adam. Nicodemus, the "teacher of Israel," came to Jesus at night, hesitantly approaching the light. The light that he already had, his learning, seemed to pull him back toward the darkness. The man born blind is handicapped by no such learning. His unquestionable physical blindness places him in a position of receptivity to the gift of light: both physical and spiritual. And when he receives the light, he responds to it like a seedling bursting through the ground into the sun.

When Jesus spits on the ground, makes clay and anoints the man's eyes, he recalls once more the first creation: God's molding of Adam from the moist earth (Gen 2:7). Every healing seems to involve a return to this beginning; every healing occurs within this one great work which is the new birth, new creation within the Word which is Jesus. These two healings on the fourth day exemplify a principle which is verified in all of the Johannine signs. The light which bursts forth in each life-giving miracle contains within itself the power of the one great work, the new creation of Adam, of humanity. The man born blind, after many years of darkness, experiences through Jesus' word the first day of creation, the original dawn, the light born out of the darkness. The paralytic lay alongside the pool of Bethzatha, and Jesus sends the blind man to the pool of Siloam. Each episode of the fourth day has been carefully related to *baptism*.

⊕

A comedy begins when the man returns, seeing, to those who had known him when he was blind. They seem not to recognize him; they argue about his identity. Finally he himself affirms, "I am" (*hoti egō eimi*). He has received more than sight, this man who now sees. Burning and shining within him now is something of the one who gave him his sight, and who had identified himself with those syllables reserved to God. And yet he knows only that it was the man Jesus who had given him his sight; he knows neither who Jesus is, nor what is that light, now within him, in which he himself *is*.

The man who was blind is brought to the Pharisees for examination. "Now it was a *sabbath* day when Jesus made the mud and opened his eyes" (9:14). There is going to be trouble. Jesus has violated several sabbath prescriptions. The comedy of light and darkness, of blindness and sight, intensifies. The reasonings of the Pharisees buzz like flies around the immovable fact: "...and now I see." The Pharisees then interrogate the man's parents, who squirm and respond evasively to avoid being expelled from the community. "For the Jews had already agreed that anyone who confessed Jesus to be the Messiah would be put out of the synagogue" (9:22). Once again the Pharisees call the man born blind, and bear down upon him. We are sorry, but it is impossible for you to be seeing. This man is a sinner. Our authoritative and unquestionable light decrees that the light is neither in this man nor, consequently, in you. Please sign here.

But their intimidation and insults fail to move this marvelous man born blind. "Why do you want to hear it again? Do you also want to become his disciples?" He is a rock, this man who now sees, who now *is*. "You are his disciple, but we are disciples of *Moses*...." And the man once blind: "*Never since the world began* has it been heard that anyone opened the eyes of a person born blind..." (9:32). The implication of these words goes beyond Moses, his teaching, the *Torah*, to the *creation*. The man is then thrown out of the synagogue, the Jewish religious community, the Mosaic "church," for the light that has been born in him is not welcome there. It is a light that precedes Moses and the synagogue: the light in which light was created on the first day.

⊕

The accounts of Jesus' *finding* of the two whom he has healed, the paralytic and the blind man (5:14 and 9:35), are perfectly matched. He finds the former paralytic now within the temple, while he finds the man born blind when he has been cast out of the synagogue. The first is admonished to sin no more, under the threat of something worse befalling him, and to the second is offered faith in the Son of Man. One man has returned to the past, upon which he lies as on his bed before he was healed; he has not really begun to walk, to move forward. The other man has been cast out of the past, and now is free to believe in this future, the Son of Man. And so the uncreated light, the ultimate sabbath light, is his.

The crafted symmetry here is precise: to the something *"worse"* than paralysis (5:14)—probably meaning a death which is more than physical—correspond the words, "Do you believe in the Son of Man?" (9:35), in which Jesus offers to the man once blind something *better* than the physical sight which he has received: the vision of faith in the Son of Man which is identical with the gift of eternal life (see 6:40).

The paralytic, healed externally, entered the external temple, but remained unawakened internally. He seemed to prefer the Jewish temple and its society to Jesus, for he promptly informed the authorities that it was Jesus who had healed him on the sabbath. The blind man, healed externally and also internally by Jesus' opening of his eyes, is cast out of the external temple and is received by Jesus. When he responds, "I am," it is suggested that he has begun to enter into the unitive being or temple of this light which is the Word. He will continue this movement into the light with his confession of faith in the Son of Man.

$\oplus$

Implicit in the Genesis 3 story of the "opening of the eyes" of Adam and Eve is the contrast of *two kinds of vision*. The *first* vision, of a reality still undivided against itself, is what was *lost* immediately after eating from the forbidden tree, and this would seem already to resemble in some degree the unitive vision which Jesus imparts. At that same moment of their sin, the eyes of man and woman were opened to the *second* vision, the ironic "knowledge of good and evil." This second vision is immediately manifested in their recognition of their nakedness, and the shame and fear which impels them to cover their bodies with fig leaves and hide behind the trees of the garden. In Jesus' finding of the paralytic and the blind man after he has healed them, we may sense a merest echo of God's seeking and finding the first humans in the garden where they had hidden themselves (Gen 3:8-10).

From this second vision, the knowledge of good and evil, derives the knowledge of these Pharisees, who are such ready judges of who is good and who is evil: "We know that this man is a sinner," "You were born entirely in sins…" etc. They resemble closely the naked and blind ones of the letter to the Laodiceans: "For you say, 'I am rich, I have prospered, and I need nothing.' You do not realize that you are wretched, pitiable, poor, blind and naked…" (see Rev 3:15-17). They have thoroughly covered themselves—covered their nakedness even from themselves. It is the *law*, the Word of God, with which they have wrapped themselves, in becoming professional righteous ones. Thus the law becomes the abettor of this false knowledge of good and evil which is theirs.

On the third day, John discussed this same hypocritical posture in terms of *glory*: trusting in human glory rather than the glory of God. At the end of the Nicodemus discourse, we heard of those who hate the light because their deeds are evil, and will not come into the light. That section was concerned with faith (trust, confidence) in the Son of God who had been sent into the world, and concluded with the confidence of the one who does what is true, and so "comes to the light, that it may be clearly seen that his deeds have been wrought in God."

The Pharisees say *"we see"* (9:41); they are confident in their light, which has become darkness. Confident in their knowledge of the law, they reject the light of the Word. The man born blind has nothing to be confident about; he knows he is blind, he is a beggar. But when he receives his sight, he comes into the marvelous confidence (Gr. *parrēsia*[4]) of faith. He becomes an unshakable witness, like the light itself. The confidence of this man who was blind is the *exact contrary of the fear and shame of the first man and woman after their sin*. They hid themselves from the light of God; this man is filled with the light, comes out into the light, and immediately accepts the light which is offered him afterward by Jesus (9:38).

And so the man born blind corresponds to *Adam*; he is everyone, but with a physical blindness which expresses the common interior blindness. When he receives his physical sight, he receives some degree of participation in the original light, the uncreated light, the *I Am* (9:9). Sight, light and being are here inseparable, as in the *baptismal* experience. The man once blind possesses this unitive light before he has a name for it, and it is this light that is the source of his iron confidence. The light itself is shadowed by no hesitation, no doubt, and it is in him. The light is its own witness. The gospel narrative moves subtly back and forth between physical sight and the spiritual sight which is a participation in the Word: the blind man has received both.

⊕

The story of the man born blind fills out the picture of the vocation, the work of humanity, which we had begun to compose from the narrative of the paralytic. Once he has received his sight, this man has *simply to be the light in the world*, to be witness. It is thus that Jesus will define his own mission in the world (18:37). The man who was blind does this well, standing boldly yet simply transparent to the light that is within him, in the face of the Pharisees' intimidation. Brought out of the darkness into the light, he becomes himself a light in the midst of darkness. This man resembles the disciple[5] who simply remains to witness, in contrast with Peter whose mission is a primarily active one.

⊕

In these two healing narratives, the *sabbath* law functions like Solomon's sword of judgment, dividing the Pharisees and their teaching from Jesus and his teaching. It is the sabbath which is to be interpreted in terms of life or of death, union or separation, love or vindictiveness. Does the love of God demand abstraction from the love of human persons, or is it embodied in this love of humanity? Jesus will finally become manifest *as* the sabbath, in whom God and humanity are inseparably joined. On the seventh day of the new creation, God's rest will be established precisely within the human person. There is some anticipation of this seventh day in the substantive illumination of the man born blind. The gesture of Jesus forming mud to spread upon the blind man's eyes (9:14) will find its complement in his gesture of breathing the Spirit into the disciples on the seventh day (20:22). Together these two actions reproduce the action of God in creating the first human being, in the account of Genesis 2.

⊕

Jesus, who comes not for those who are well but for the sick (Mk 2:17), has come into a world of blind people. Those of them who acknowledge their blindness of spirit may receive from him new eyes, and thus a new birth, new being. For those, on the other hand, who insist that their darkness is light—as the Pharisees have so firmly done throughout this narrative—their darkness, and their guilt, become final. What emerges here in the metaphoric language of blindness and sight is very close to that rejection of the light, of the works of the Spirit, which Jesus calls, in the synoptics, the sin against the Holy Spirit (Mt 12:31-32). It is a blindness which is at some deep level of the heart conscious and voluntary, a definitive rejection of the saving light.

At the conclusion of this episode, the once blind man's confession of faith and Jesus' judgment upon the Pharisees thus define two histories: a movement from darkness into transforming light, and a transformation of light into conclusive darkness. These two histories —interwoven and contrasting—constitute, in turn, an ironic drama which is played out on different levels. First there is the tragic and ironic story of the religious authorities, in their relation to the "little ones" (cf. Mt 11:25) or common people of Israel, and then the parallel inversion which takes place between this chosen people, the Jews, and the other peoples of the earth, the Gentiles "born in utter sin."

⊕

Our transition from an exodus-Mosaic plane to the ultimate creation plane appears to be nearly a *reversal* in this story. This conflict is most sharply evident when the Jews oppose Moses to Jesus in their dispute with the blind man (9:28). The "creation" references are numerous and strong. They include the initial question about the possible sin of the man's "parents" (9:2f); Jesus' reference to the works of God (9:3.4); the anointing of the man's eyes with clay and the expression "opening of the eyes" (9:10.21.32). This phrase is a direct allusion to Genesis 3:5.7. Climactic is the defiant assertion of the man once blind, "Never *since the world began* has it been heard that anyone opened the eyes of a person born blind" (9:32).

⊕

In contrast to the paralytic, the man born blind is created anew, born anew, in true being: "*I am*" (9:9). The light that is in him is the same light that was manifested on the first day of creation, when Jesus identified himself with those same words upon the dark sea (6:20). The man's new vision is one with his being, and at the same time this vision and being are not just a restoration of the "natural" sight and being of the first creation, but already a participation in the new creation—because a participation in the *uncreated light and being of the*

Word. John interweaves here, as often, the literal and symbolic senses of words such as "see" and "blind," so that the two are nearly indistinguishable.

⊕

What is communicated by Jesus to those who believe in him, and what they must communicate to others, is the *unitive* light of the Word. Unlike the ministry of the scribes and Pharisees who shut the kingdom of heaven before the people, neither entering themselves nor allowing others to enter (Mt 23:13-14), the mediation of Jesus' disciples is to be a self-annulling mediation, a communication of freedom. The unitive Word transcends and immediately relativizes all hierarchical distinctions between human persons. We shall see this revolution dramatized by Jesus in the next episode when he washes the feet of his disciples, and then we shall hear it explicated in his discourse on communion at the supper.

⊕

Seeing is holy and immortal. Within the confusion between different levels of sight in this story lies the precious truth that all light participates in the unitive light, the uncreated light, which is the Word and Christ. Light is a grace in the world, a window, an angel of the creation, the beginning and the end burning among us.

Painters and poets find their religion in the *seeing* of what is around them, in the truth of visible reality. Something is consummated between the tree, the eye and the mind. Light itself is unitive, is communication. All light is a vestige, a dew of the light of the Word. The leaf, the tree, the face are revelations of God in the light that blesses us in them, that brings us together. The light which creates a visible world around us is a beginning of communion. There is another light hidden within everything, which is the fullness of communion.

Compared with the light she is found to be superior,
for it is succeeded by the night,
but against wisdom evil does not prevail (Wis 7:29-30).

It is she, this divine wisdom, who has come into the world in Jesus, so that we may see who we are, and, in that unitive seeing, be born.

> There is no longer Jew or Greek, there is no longer
> slave or free, there is no longer male or female; for
> you are all one in Christ Jesus (Gal 3:28).

⊕

Why, then, was this man born blind? Because of that first sin in the garden? "Neither this man nor his parents sinned; he was born blind so that God's works might be revealed in him" (9:3; cf. 11:4). It is for the *glory of God* that this child of Adam is blind. His blindness, the darkness itself, is for the sake of the glory which is to be born within him. It is out of darkness that the Son appears. Out of the darkness that is God and out of the quite different darkness that is humanity comes the Son of God and Son of man, in whom the two become one light and one flesh. The essential movement of meaning here, the dynamism of the Word, is not back through some dark chain of causality but *forward* into the light of the new creation.

SECTION 11: CHAPTERS 13–17
THE SUPPER

The Footwashing

Jesus has finished his public ministry of preaching and healing, and he turns to his own disciples, to complete their instruction in the little time that remains. Here begins the second great division of John's narrative, often called "The book of glory."

John's supper narrative is very unlike that of the synoptics. Here, if ever, the Johannine account requires the complement of the other gospels, and probably presupposes it. John makes no reference to the institution of the eucharist, the central action of Jesus which gives the supper its meaning in the other gospels. John develops the supper narrative in a *sapiential* direction, as we might expect. Here this Johannine vision emerges in its fullness as we find ourselves present not at a sacramental eucharist, but at a eucharist of the *Word*.

John's account of the supper begins as Jesus removes his garments, pours water into a basin, and washes the feet of his disciples. This baptismal gesture signifies a passage, an entering, an initiation, a new beginning. Our journey arrives, like a pilgrimage, at its goal, and we must be washed for the solemn meal. We have arrived at another threshold, like the Jordan of John the Baptist. The water flows gleaming over our feet as we pass over into this new country. Here within this room the life and teaching of Jesus will pool to a fullness.

In the narrative order, this banquet of Jesus, and his washing of the disciples' feet, follows very shortly after another supper, at which Mary of Bethany had anointed Jesus' own feet with precious nard, "and the house was filled with the fragrance of the ointment" (12:3). Judas, "he who was to betray him," complained of this waste. Now Jesus kneels to wash and dry the feet of his disciples, in imitation of this gesture of the woman. It is not Judas this time but Peter who protests at the gesture. Shortly after this, however, Judas will go out to execute his work of betrayal. The movement from signs to glory is accompanied by a movement of Jesus from his *masculine* role of witness, preaching and works of power, the functions of the Word, to a *feminine* mode which is related to the unitive, to the Spirit, to glory, to immanent wisdom.

When Jesus ritually washes the feet of his disciples, and when Jesus speaks repeatedly of *glory* at the supper, we may infer that what is to follow soon after will be a eucharist of the *Spirit*. Rather than the bread and wine of the synoptic and Pauline eucharistic accounts, John invites us to discover that which is beneath the appearances of bread and wine: Word and Spirit. As Jesus crosses the threshold from sign to glory, and washes the feet of his disciples so that they may follow him in this passage, we are brought to the threshold between Word and Spirit. The Word Made Flesh is about to be broken in death, and the Spirit poured into this waiting earth which is humanity.

We have arrived at the *hour* of Jesus. John carefully reminds us that it is "before the festival of the Passover," when Jesus is about to pass from this world to the Father. This is the primary *exodus* parallel here at the supper.

"Having loved his own who were in the world, he loved them to the end." He loved them to the limit of possibility, to the end of his life—yes, but John intends something more profound here. He loved them to the point of bestowing upon them his own *fullness*—the discourses which these words introduce will point to the fullness which is meant here. Jesus' love consummates itself in the communication of *his own being* to those he loves. This is the significance of his last supper with them.

The one clearly ritual action of John's supper narrative is Jesus' stripping himself of his clothing, pouring out water and washing the feet of his disciples. This contrasts strongly with the central ritual action of the institution of the eucharist in the synoptic gospels. We can expect to find in it the same symbolic fullness, however. This plenitude can be explored only by isolating one thread after another.

The action is what it obviously is: a washing. This must signify a cleansing from sin. It is also an example of humility and service, as Jesus himself explains (13:12-16). If the master, Lord and teacher washes the feet of his disciples and servants, then this will be the pattern for relations among the disciples themselves.

Something further, however, is suggested in Jesus' words to the recalcitrant Peter, "Unless I wash you, you have no share with me" (13:8). The washing has to do with relationship, with union.

The comprehensive meaning of Jesus' gesture and words at the supper has been elegantly rendered by Beatrice Bruteau.[6] She sees the supper narratives (not that of John alone) as consisting of *two actions* of Jesus, which constitute together the *"Holy Thursday revolution."* The first action, symbolized by the washing of his disciples' feet, is the destruction of the *"domination* paradigm," and the second action is Jesus' initiation of the *"communion* paradigm," which is signified by the institution of the eucharist in the synoptic gospels and in Paul.

John's supper discourse as a whole, from the end of chapter 13 through the prayer of chapter 17, is an explication in words and symbols of this new economy of *communion* which Jesus is about to inaugurate. On the other hand, Jesus proclaims the abolition of the old order, the order of *domination*, in his symbolic gesture of washing the disciples' feet here at the beginning of the supper narrative.

The domination paradigm, the old order, is a world structured by relationships of power: of master and slave, rich and poor, and even in the traditional sense of teacher and disciple. This order is based upon a perception of reality as fragmented, of other persons as simply separate from ourselves, and it operates through abstraction, distinction, exclusion, comparison and competition. The communion paradigm, in contrast, is based upon participatory, or unitive consciousness.[7]

Within John's gospel, we hear this communion abundantly revealed in the *words* of Jesus at the supper. It is here that words go as far toward the reality of communion as is possible, as when Jesus says, "I do not call you servants any longer... but I have called you friends, because I have made known to you everything that I have heard from my Father" (15:15); this revelation of which he speaks is that of a love which bestows communion.

The communion paradigm, the *new order*, consists of a participation in the unitive reality—which in the Johannine tradition is God himself—and it is constituted by relationships of love. This is the content of the *new commandment* which Jesus proclaims at the supper (13:34; 15:12).

In washing the feet of his disciples, Jesus declares that the old order of domination is ended.

> You know that the rulers of the Gentiles lord it over them, and their great ones are tyrants over them. It will not be so among you; but whoever wishes to be great among you must be your servant, and whoever wishes to be first among you must be your slave; just as the Son of Man came not to be served but to serve, and to give his life as a ransom for many (Mt 20:25-28).

> But you are not to be called rabbi, for you have one teacher, and you are all students. And call no one your father on earth, for you have one Father—the one in heaven. Nor are you to be called instructors, for you have one instructor, the Messiah (Mt 23:8-10).

It is *Peter* who recoils at Jesus' gesture: "You will never wash my feet" (13:8). Why this resistance on the part of the one whom Jesus had singled out among the disciples as the chief shepherd? Something about this action of base servitude is deeply repellent to *him*, the very one who will come to personify authority among the disciples. It is in Peter that the parodox of worldly power and the power of Christ is to be most dramatically played out within the church.

Peter, apparently both a natural leader and the shepherd-to-be, experiences in the movement of his master to wash his feet a shaking of his whole world-view. He is still a citizen of the old order, and understands Jesus and his own relationship with Jesus in the terms of the old order.

Peter's problem here is similar to that of Nicodemus, the "ruler of the Jews" and "teacher of Israel," in the chiastic counterpart to this episode, when Jesus announces that the one who would enter the kingdom of God must be *reborn*. "How can a man be born when he is old?" Nicodemus' world-view is completely subverted by Jesus' strange words. The traditional path of discipleship has suddenly disappeared into a vertical wall of impossibility. When the sacred authority of the teacher is annulled in this manner, where is the disciple to look? To reduce oneself from teacher to infant about to be born; to allow one's teacher to be replaced by a slave—where can this lead?

Jesus' gesture has, at the outset of the supper narrative, proclaimed a break with every former mode of teaching, of the transmission of doctrine, of ministry. No tradition, no method, no pedagogical structure, previous or existing, is adequate for the transmission of this gospel of the Son of Man, for communicating the creative Word. Here there is to be a radical transformation in the meaning of *power*. Institutional structure and power is to be subordinate to, and exist within, the paradoxical "kingdom of God" which is communion in a life received continually from within. It is in Peter's commission, his faith, his failure in this, Jesus' *hour*, and his repentance, that John most clearly expresses the ambiguity which will always accompany a position of power among the disciples of Jesus.

The supper itself, in its symbolic resonance, expresses the meaning of power in the new dispensation which Jesus brings. The power of Christ, as we have seen throughout this fourth day, and will hear throughout the supper, is a power of *life*, of communicating both human life and ultimately the life of God. This is symbolized by food, feeding, the supper itself. Peter, the shepherd who is to follow Jesus, will finally be told simply to "feed my sheep." As Jesus continues to speak to his disciples at this meal, we shall learn more about what this *feeding* may involve.

The concept of the "Holy Thursday revolution," as developed by Bruteau, very nicely brings together the two sides of John's gospel, which are both complementary and opposite to one another. On the one hand is the drama which takes place around the issue of *power;* on the other is the revelation and bestowal of the *unitive gift.*

⊕

This revolution which is signified in the Johannine supper narrative is another expression of that great boundary line which we have traced through the earlier days—between *exodus,* or Mosaic religion, and *creation.* The "Holy Thursday revolution" defines this boundary in the context of human relationship, human society: between *domination* and *communion.* In another context the language will change to that of *law* and *grace,* or *dualism* and *immanence.* In each case the movement is into the spaciousness of the Word.

Jesus' last supper is related symbolically to the first meal related in Genesis: the eating of the fruit of the tree of the knowledge of good and evil by Adam and Eve in the garden (Gen 3:1-7). Jesus spoke to Nicodemus of those who would *enter* the kingdom of God and *see* the kingdom of God. The paralytic was enabled to walk, but did not enter; the blind man, given his sight by Jesus, entered into the sacred place. As the narrative of Jesus' supper begins, we enter the "large upper room, furnished" of the synoptics (Mk 14, Lk 22), which is to be the place of a definitive celebration of intimacy, comparable to a wedding banquet. The ritual of *entering* consists of Jesus' washing the feet of his disciples. The *seeing* will be their participation in the meal itself, this final pouring out of the Word.

Jesus' washing of the feet of his disciples parallels Joshua's leading the Israelites out of the wilderness across the Jordan River into the promised land. In John's narrative it reflects the baptism of Jesus in the Jordan, which itself corresponded to the exodus from Egypt through the Red Sea. The entry into the promised land is also the re-entry into the garden of paradise. Once again it is the Genesis background which opens the Johannine text to its depths.

$$\oplus$$

Woven into John's narrative of the footwashing are Jesus' references to the *betrayer* (13:2.10b-11.18-19), and Jesus turns to this matter when, after his ritual gesture, he resumes his place. The *footwashing* and the *dispatch of Judas*, the betrayer, are twin events in this narrative.

Judas, as John is careful to point out, had the money box (12:6; 13:29) and was a thief (12:6). He is the disciple who does not really believe in Jesus (6:64); he has not been given to perceive the fullness, the glory, that is in Jesus (12:5); he is blind to the light of this glory. Consequently he is still completely in solidarity with the old order, with the powers of this world, and under the dominion of the "ruler of this world" (13:2.27). Judas will betray Jesus into the hands of the *powers*—the chief priests—of the Jewish religious institution. Judas' name itself associates him, for John, with the Judeans, and therefore with Jesus' "own," who will reject and crucify him. "He came unto his own, and his own received him not" (1:11; and see 13:20—Jesus' words between his two predictions of the betrayal). Judas is the individual personification of those whom Jesus *receives*, but who *do not* "*receive*" *him*: that is, by faith. He is the individual in whom the drama of light and darkness is played out to its full negative possibility through disbelief and through the betrayal of love and communion to power and possessiveness.

John's narrative employs three characters, *three disciples*, to dramatize in themselves the conflict between the two *powers*.

It is *the disciple whom Jesus loved* (traditionally *John*) to whom Jesus will give his mother, who is always the first to *know*. He is the first, therefore, to know this life within himself. We do not see him shaken, attracted or intimidated by the power of the world. He knows, somehow, the things of God, the way of God, in the heart of Jesus.

Peter, or "Simon, son of John," in contrast, loves Jesus, but not as completely as he thinks he does, and therefore wavers and falls when the wolf comes near. At the moment of testing in the high priest's court, he denies Jesus. Simon is intimidated by the power of the world and collapses at the sight of Jesus' weakness in the hands of this power. Equivalent in the synoptic gospels is Peter's protest at Jesus' prediction of his coming passion, and Jesus' stern rebuke, "Get behind me, Satan! You are a stumbling block to me; for you are setting your mind not on divine things but on human things" (Mt 16:22-23; see Mk 8:32-33).

Judas, "son of Simon Iscariot" (13:2.26), does not believe in Jesus and finally betrays him. In John he is venal, a thief, and is scandalized by the magnanimity of Mary's anointing of Jesus. He does not know the true anointing of Jesus with the glory of God. Blind to this infinite worth in Jesus, he sells Jesus to the powers of the world, for the currency of the world. Judas is moved by Satan, the devil (13:2.27; see 6:70).

Peter, vacillating in "human things," wavers between John and Judas. He is finally grasped by Jesus on the shore and pulled into the way of God, upon which he will have to follow him, bearing his cross until the day of his own death upon it.

In John 13:21-30 Jesus and these three disciples interact in a Shakespearean scene. John expresses with precision here the lessening closeness to Jesus as we move from the beloved disciple to Peter to Judas. Peter must ask the disciple who the betrayer is: it is to be Judas. Peter is in an ambivalent, intermediate state, devoted and weak, moved at one moment by his love for Jesus and at another moment by his fear and unwillingness. Both the disciple and Judas, on the other hand, are *decided* in their respective, and opposite, responses to Jesus.

The *bread* which Jesus dips and hands to Judas (13:26) seems a dark sacrament, ironic and demonic counterpart to Jesus' self-communication to the disciples through his institution of the eucharist in the synoptic supper accounts. "After he received the piece of bread, Satan entered into him" (13:27).

When one considers both John's explicit parallel to the eucharist here, and his omission of an account of Jesus' institution of the eucharist in his supper narrative, it is natural to suspect a common motivation behind these two deviations from the common gospel tradition. May John, in addition to his sapiential message, have wished to offer a subtle but emphatic criticism of some misunderstanding or "betrayal" of the eucharist in Christian communities of his time (see 1 Cor 6:13-20; 10:16-22; 11:20-34)?

Judas went out to his dark business, and "it was night." It is no longer time for the Son of Man to "work" (see 9:4); it is time for him to be glorified. Jesus himself has set in motion (13:26-30) the process of his passion and death, which is to be simultaneously his elevation into glory. The *hour* has come (see 12:23). The remainder of the supper account will be devoted to Jesus' unfolding of the meaning of this "glory" which he is very soon to receive and to share with his disciples.

⊕

The supper's dramatic action, in its two moments, is quickly finished. Jesus has washed his disciples' feet and dismissed the betrayer into the night to do his work. Now begins the longest discourse of the gospel, a veritable banquet of wisdom. In the intimacy of this last evening with his own, in the shadow of the terrible events which are quickly to begin, Jesus pours himself out in the language of love. He speaks of new things about to come: of a reciprocal indwelling and the coming of a mysterious *other*.

Jesus' discourse at the supper corresponds to the genre of a *farewell speech*, such as were often attributed to famous men just before their departure.[8] The closest biblical parallel is the book of Deuteronomy, which is presented as a series of speeches of Moses to the Israelites just before his death and before their entrance into the promised land.

This, then, is the *Mosaic-exodus* site of the supper discourse. The parallel is close, for Jesus is about to depart and his disciples are about to enter the "promised land" of their new relationship with God. The discourse is an introduction to this new land, and a disclosure of its relationship to the old world.

The *Genesis-creation* equivalent to this promised land is the garden of paradise. As Adam and Eve were ejected from the garden after their transgression so that they could not eat from the tree of life, now the curse will be rescinded and humanity will be admitted into the garden which is this new unitive relationship with God in Jesus. They shall eat freely of the tree of life which is Jesus himself.

Whoever has seen me has seen the Father (14:9b).

I do not call you servants any longer, because the servant does not know what the master is doing; but I have called you friends, because I have made known to you everything that I have heard from my Father (15:15).

The Father's House

The decisive change that occurs in the movement to this creation level of meaning is in the *new immanence*, the mutual indwelling, which is revealed in Jesus' words here at the supper. This new way of being is revealed in chapter 14, where it explicates the image of the *Father's house* (14:2).

Jesus used this expression for the *temple*, when he had ritually cleansed it at his "first" Passover (2:13-25). The supper narrative has begun with an analogous ritual purification of his disciples. Both of these symbolic acts will be fulfilled only in his sacrificial death (17:19). This house of the Father is the final *place*: it is simply *inside*, the dwelling of humanity in God. The whole wide river of biblical history and symbolism moves toward this point, to plunge out of sight *within*: within the one who believes and within God, in a unity beyond word and image.

As Jesus continues to speak to his disciples at the supper, we find our attention wandering. We cannot remain with his discourse, cannot follow this stream of words which becomes circular and rhythmic, speaking of things too deep for us. We are oppressed by a surfeit of language which becomes detached from the moorings of concrete imagery. Human words pool to a fullness within their limits, reach up the walls and fall back, returning upon themselves. Here in this ritual scene the words themselves become a rhythmic, incantatory movement within this room that contains them. Only later will these words individuate themselves, solidify and become the containers for our experience.

The *Father's house*: with this image, Jesus introduces a new language. "Believe me that I am in the Father and the Father is in me" (14:11); "... you will know that I am in my Father, and you in me, and I in you" (14:20). Here is the breakthrough into interiority which reveals the inner significance of this *meal*. Language can go no further. The actuality of this union will leave behind the spatial relationships

suggested by the image of the temple and even by the intimacy of expressions like "abide" (or dwell) *"in."*
"If you love me..." (14:15.21.23.24.28). We need to feel the *strangeness* of these words in the mouth of the young rabbi. This is the language of feminine Wisdom.

> I love those who love me,
>   and those who seek me diligently find me....
> I walk in the way of righteousness, along the paths of justice,
> endowing with wealth those who love me,
>   and filling their treasuries (Prov 8:17.20-21).

> Wisdom is radiant and unfading,
> and she is easily discerned by those who love her,
> and is found by those who seek her.
> She hastens to make herself known to those who desire her
> (Wis 6:12-13).

> ...and love of her is the keeping of her laws (Wis 6:18).

> If you love me, you will keep my commandments (14:15).

The one final *commandment* of Jesus is "that you love one another..." This woman who is the wisdom of God is the icon of the new order of love which is about to begin, flowing from this new presence of Jesus in his disciples.

The Vine

The vine stands at the center of the chiastic[9] supper narrative like the tree in the middle of the garden of paradise (see below, p. 135).
Jesus' words, "I am the true vine..." (15:1), bring his "I am" statements to a culmination here at the center of the supper account. The unitive fullness contained in the *egō eimi* is here explicitly opened to an inhering participation by his disciples. "I am the vine, you are the branches" (15:5). The vine of John 15 reflects the *trees* of Genesis 2 and 3: especially the tree of life which we had found shadowed in the bread of life discourse of John 6. The vine, here at the supper, is a new transmutation of the image of the tree, in a "feminine" sense.
In the scriptures Israel is a vine, and divine Wisdom is a vine. The wider mythological context of the image of the vine, however, relates

it to the cosmic tree at the center of the world which joins heaven and earth and underworld. Behind the Johannine image of the vine may be a parable of Jesus which, like the tree of life in Genesis, lent itself to this interpretation.[10]

In the light of Jesus' first sign, at the Cana wedding banquet, both the vine and the supper itself take on a *nuptial* significance. Upon the tree of the cross Jesus is to be united with his *bride*, however we construe that bride. The anomalous tree which is the vine grows at the boundary of knowledge and life, sobriety and ecstasy, stability and flight, law and spontaneity. Here is form full and bursting with union, with the surpassing of form. Masculine figure or form has become one with feminine movement and life. At this banquet where wisdom is poured out as love, the tree steps beyond its own limits; river and tree are one. The tree of life is one with the four rivers of life, the bread and the water of life. The vine is Word, truth, form, ripening within itself beyond itself into Spirit, interiority, realization, union.

Jesus is about to go to his death on the tree, where he will pour out his blood on the earth. Responding to this will come the wine of the Spirit, to flow within the new vine. The tree of the Word, the tree of life, is about to reach its fullness, when Jesus is "lifted up," having carried the cross-bar upon his shoulders to the stake fixed at the place of execution. Now, at the supper, he brings out this horizontal—or communal—dimension of the tree with great clarity (see 13:34-35; 15:15-17).

The Word is a tree which was in the world in the beginning, and when humanity sinned at the tree and at the tower they were banished from that unitive tree of the Word. But this light of the Word is their life, and without it they die. The human person is a tree which bears the light, the Word, within itself. Speaking, naming, witnessing, preaching, confessing, from Adam to the Baptist to Jesus to Thomas, this is the human vocation in the world: to give witness to the truth. The man born blind, receiving his light from Jesus, witnessed to the light that now had been born within him.

The fullness of this unitive tree is in Jesus, and now with his own disciples he pours out this fullness: the tree of the Word finds its fullest expression, comes into its roundness, bears its fruit. *"Abide in me"*: root yourselves in this central place, and remain rooted here, and my life will flow through you and bear fruit in the world. "Whoever does not abide in me is thrown away (or *cast forth*)..." (15:6)—again the language of expulsion from the garden. Judas went forth in this way.

"I have said these things to you so that my joy may be in you, and that your joy may be complete" (15:11). The wine of glory—of the

Spirit—which is to fill my body will fill you, as you abide in me as the fullness of my body, as my branches.

"I have called you friends, because I have made known to you everything that I have heard from my Father" (15:15). The fullness of the Word is not in a system of cosmic gnosis nor a comprehensive new law, but in this simple commandment of love. The teaching now contracts to this single point of response, coherence, action, which is *to abide* in Jesus; the form becomes movement, Word becomes Spirit, the gospel becomes *koinōnia*, communion.

With this unitive gift, by which Jesus will be present in them, will come also *the world's hatred* which had been concentrated upon him. To this revelation of the fullness of his teaching in the commandment of love will correspond the full hostility of the power of darkness, the "ruler of this world" (14:30), and consequently hatred on the part of the *world* itself, of those who have rejected Jesus and his Word. Thus will proceed the judgment of the world—the separation between those who love the light and come into it, and those who hate the light and are compelled to seek its extinction. The concluding words of the chiastically related Nicodemus episode (3:19-21) are reflected and further developed here.

The Woman in Childbirth

In the chiastic symmetry of the supper narrative (see Figure 2.1, on p. 135 below), the image of the woman in childbirth, which distinguishes this next section, corresponds to the Father's house of chapter 14. To the Father's house correspond also the synagogues, from which the disciples of Jesus will be expelled. To enter into this house, this vine, will mean exclusion from the old house, the old vine, from temple and Israel.

As Jesus speaks more intently of his imminent departure, a mood of sorrow steals over the supper gathering. This grief which they are beginning to feel as he speaks of his going away will be all the heavier now that the outpouring of this evening has brought their relationship to a new depth and intensity. He must go away, however, if the Spirit is to come, and it is the Spirit which will cause the fullness of his joy to be in them. The final great image of Jesus' supper discourse is a *feminine* one:

When a woman is in labor, she has pain, because her hour is come. But when her child is born, she no longer remembers the anguish because of the joy of having brought a human

being into the world. So you have pain now; but I will see
you again, and your hearts will rejoice, and no one will take
your joy from you (16:21-22).

We are reminded here of the woman in childbirth of Revelation
(12:1-6), pursued by the dragon, and of Paul's vision of the universe
itself groaning like a woman in labor as it awaits the "revealing of the
children of God," the new birth of resurrection (Rom 8:18-23).

How can anyone be born after having grown old? Can one
enter a second time into the mother's womb and be born?
(3:4).

Jesus responded to Nicodemus' protesting question, in the chiastic counterpart of the supper narrative, by insisting that whoever
would enter the kingdom of God must be born again of water and the
Spirit. The hour has now arrived when Jesus will initiate this birth for
the disciples. It will be both his birth and their birth: this will be the
one, *unitive* birth.
"On that day..." (16:26). The day of this unitive birth will be the
seventh day, the unitive sabbath. Both woman and child are expressions of the unitive. The woman is the disciples, and she is also Jesus,
arrived at his hour. The child is, similarly, both disciples and Jesus. It
is the child, however, which is the ultimate unitive symbol.[11] It is now
that the human person will be *"begotten of God."*[12]

I have said these things to you in figures of speech. The hour
is coming when I will no longer speak to you in figures, but
will tell you plainly of the Father (16:25).

Surely if Jesus has ever spoken clearly and explicitly, it has been
here at the supper—though he has spoken of things difficult and still
to be disclosed. Now, however, we have arrived at the final limit of
language, whether of word or image. The woman about to give birth
is the last image in the world of images;[13] now we are to pass over into
the world of *reality*, of the realization of that which has been spoken
and depicted. There is an exhilaration in these words of Jesus; they
stir for a moment the great curtain which separates us, through the
whole of our lives, from ultimate reality, from that which simply and
abundantly *is*—and into which our life and our death is a birth.
These disciples, continually misunderstanding him, questioning
him in their confusion and frustration, will soon experience some-

thing new; then their questions will no longer be necessary. In the fullness of this present moment at the supper's end, they suppose that they are already within this experience of the *One*. Very shortly, however, the power of darkness will scatter them like sheep, and leave Jesus "alone." Alone, however, in the *One*; "the Father is with me."

Jesus' Great Prayer

Jesus' concluding words to his disciples led them to the limit of words and figures; from this point, he would communicate with them in the plain speech of the interior *Word*. His discourse had focused to a unitive point, the needle's eye of unitive birth, in the Father.

Now he turns away from the disciples in this same direction, toward the Father, to whom he speaks a final prayer. This prayer is an *epiclesis* (i.e. a calling down of the Holy Spirit) over the bread of words of the Word, the wine of words of the Spirit, which he has set out among them. The bread will be broken, the wine poured, upon the cross. He lifts his eyes and prays that the fire may descend to fill these words and figures with the reality which they have evoked as in shadow.

Jesus' prayer is a sacrificial invocation, a flame which gathers all of the themes and words of the supper into itself, and bears them upward ritually to the Father, calling for the returning flame of the Spirit. The language now is the golden language of glory, of the unimaginable fullness which is to burst forth from the tree, when it has been raised up. The glory for which he prays is the knowledge of God which is in him, conferring eternal life upon "all whom you have given him."

Jesus' mission on earth has been to reveal the *name* of the Father: to open the divinity to participation by human beings through his presence among them as the *I Am* in flesh and blood. As Jesus, while on earth, has made this *I Am*, the unitive divinity, present and visible to the world, now the disciples whom the Father has given him are to be the continuation of this presence. He prays, therefore, that they may be filled with this same unitive being, "that they may be one, as we are one" (17:11). This is to remain in the *I Am*, in the name of the Father. To pray that the disciples may be protected from the evil one is to ask that they may remain in this unitive being. The Johannine prayer contains some close parallels with the versions of the "Lord's Prayer" in Matthew (6:9-13) and in Luke (11:2-4).

Sanctify them in the truth; your word is truth. As you have sent me into the world, so I have sent them into the world. And for their sakes I sanctify myself, so that they also may be sanctified in truth (17:17-19).

The word "sanctify" modulates in meaning as Jesus applies it to himself and then to the disciples. He will offer himself in sacrifice that they may be born in him and remain in him. The individual body of Jesus will become a holocaust for the consecration of the new temple which is to be his inclusive body, the corporate body of his disciples. This, rather than the temple of Jerusalem, will now be the dwelling of the *glory*.

This conclusion of the supper narrative is Jesus' *prayer of consecration for the new temple*[14] which he, the Son of Man, will become by his resurrection from the dead. The disciples will constitute this new house with many mansions, a "house of prayer for all the nations." The fifth day of creation will open in this key, as Jesus cleanses the temple at Jerusalem and speaks of the new temple which will replace it. Jesus' prayer, in which he asks that his disciples may be consecrated in the *truth*, recalls the prayer for *wisdom*[15] attributed to Solomon as he prepared to build the temple.

Jesus has prayed for his own glorification in the Father's presence, then that these first disciples may be kept in this glory. Finally he prays for those who shall hear his Word through them—that is, for all those who are to believe in him. "That they may all be one" (17:21). The *intensive* fullness of his prayer for the consummation of *union* turns to an *extensive* fullness: that this union in the One may embrace humanity as a whole and so, implicitly, the cosmos itself.

Again and again Jesus returns to the golden core of the matter, the divine *glory*. This is the end, the reason for everything.

Symmetry Within the Supper Episode

The chiastic structure of the supper narrative, established by Gerhard and Ellis,[16] is reflected in the dominant symbols and themes of the five parts. At the center of the entire narrative (see Figure 2.1 below) stands the vine, or tree, like the tree in the middle of the garden. The tree of life, which had been the implicit unifying image of the discourse on the bread of life, is replaced by this vine at the center of the supper episode. From this center radiate the other four parts of the narrative.

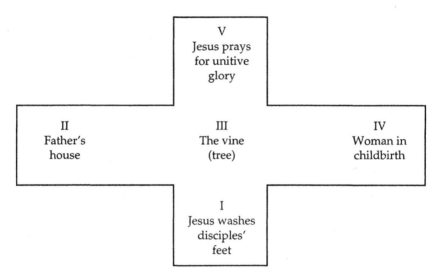

FIGURE 2.1 CHIASTIC STRUCTURE OF THE SUPPER NARRATIVE

The symmetry of parts I and V is antithetic: by contrast. Jesus' humble gesture of servitude, as he bends to wash his disciples' feet, is balanced when, like a priest, he lifts up his eyes to heaven to invoke the Father, in the epiclesis of glory which is his final prayer. This glory may be foreshadowed in the multivalent water of the footwashing.

In Part II we hear of the *Father* and his many-chambered house. In Part IV Jesus speaks with the figure of a *mother*, within whom is a child—a child which is somehow both one and many (cf. Is 66:7-8, 54:1ff). First Jesus acts, then projects three figures, and finally passes beyond figures in his prayer to the Father for glory.

⊕

In the synoptic accounts, Jesus gives his body and blood ritually to the disciples. The Johannine equivalent of this eucharistic action is Jesus' passage from a visible presence and ministry among his disciples to a dwelling within them which is invisible and yet complete: an interior fullness.

There is a certain parallel between these two actions: the eucharistic breaking of bread and the Johannine ritual of the footwashing. Both gestures are able to signify, though differently, the destruction of that visible image of Jesus to which the disciples were accustomed. The footwashing, as a menial service, adds a particular moral and even social dimension to the essential theological sense of both rituals: the departure of the visible Lord and his new dwelling within them. While the breaking of the bread conveys this truth in a eucharistic key, connoting selfless sharing and communion, the footwashing, in a baptismal key, connotes the breaking of an old, "vertical" order of relationship. This "revolutionary" sense of the footwashing gesture is parallel to the revolution which Jesus announced to Nicodemus, who had been teacher and lord in his own circle. The new communion will be the unity of the body of Jesus, broken upon the cross. From this body, pierced upon the cross, will flow the living waters in which all who believe are to be reborn.

Peter is not ready for this shattering of the traditional structure of relationship, and recoils. Within himself, we can imagine, he pulls back from the exposure and the intimacy which are implied in the Master's washing his feet. Unlike the "disciple whom Jesus loved," he is not yet sufficiently assured of the depth of Jesus' acceptance of him to abandon himself to that love. It is the all-accepting, all-forgiving love of Jesus for each of his disciples that is expressed in his washing of their feet. Peter still prefers that the boundary lines between teacher and disciple remain unbroken, rather than offer his feet to these hands, to this water that penetrates the flesh to touch the secret places of his soul. Confident with the solid bread of obedience, he is not yet ready for the wine of union.

It is the woman, Mary, who perfectly anticipates this act of Jesus, with all its overtones, when she breaks the vessel (according to Mark 14:3) and pours the perfume upon Jesus, so that the house is filled with its fragrance.

The bread of Jesus' teaching is broken also when his teaching reduces itself to the single new commandment of love. The bread here also gives way to the wine, becomes the wine. Visible and tangible among them, Jesus has been for them the bread of life, and his words have been the bread of life. Now he is to go away, to be broken and consumed, and they do not yet understand the manner in which he will remain with them. He will remain with them as the wine of interior presence, of shared life.

He is the vine, but the vine will be invisible henceforth except in its branches: in these disciples. The *body* of the vine—the bread of life —will continue to be present in them, in their witness and in their teaching. The *blood* of the vine—the wine which flows within it both as gift and as fruit—will be the Spirit which Jesus now promises, and in which he himself and the Father will dwell in them.

⊕

This long supper narrative, unique to John, is inseparable from the witness of the "*disciple whom Jesus loved.*" It is at the supper that this special intimacy of the disciple with Jesus is most graphically described (13:23). It is by this proximity to Jesus that the same disciple will be identified later (21:20). It is to this same disciple that Jesus entrusts his mother from the cross (19:27). These passages suggest, in the Johannine language, that to this disciple is communicated a unique *fullness.* Tradition has identified this gift with the fullness of wisdom which is contained in the fourth gospel. It is here at the supper that Jesus pours out his teaching, "himself," most fully (cf. 15:15). The fourth gospel itself implies that this "disciple whom Jesus loved," who rested upon his breast at the supper, is the one among the disciples (see 21:24) who grasps this plenitude, and who *bears witness* to it in this gospel.

⊕

Between *Genesis 3* and the Johannine supper, the meaning of the fourth day emerges. The contrast between the eating of the fruit of the forbidden tree by Adam and Eve, and the banquet of wisdom which is Jesus' last supper with his disciples in John, is the contrast between a meal—and a "knowledge"—which *divides* and a meal which *unites.*

The first separation recounted in Genesis 3 was the fracture of trust in God which the serpent inspired in Eve, so that she ventured to transgress his Word and eat the fruit. With the opening of their eyes, man and woman discover a *naked* reality: a world stripped of the grace of *communion.* This is an externalization of the interior break which expressed itself in the sinful act itself. This knowledge of nakedness divides sight from body, self from the light, such that immediately the body must be hidden, clothed. "Who told you that you were *naked*?" The knowledge of nakedness, *naked knowledge,* is the knowledge of the serpent, for whom each being is alone against the background of darkness, rather than existing as a figure in the tapestry of divine wisdom, divine grace, the embrace of the One.

Immediately the whole human reality is fissured: relationships which had been borne within the unitive sea of grace are broken, so that blame, guilt, is transferred instinctively from the self to another: from man to woman, from woman to serpent. In this very brief story the shattering of the "first world" has been profoundly sketched. Lifetimes could be spent following the radical fracture into all its ramifications in human life and human history. Here is the demonic counter-principle of egoism, of division, isolation and suspicion that obliterates all memory of the tree of life, atomizing human life and society. In the "sentences" (Gen 3:14-19) of the serpent, of the woman and of the man, are implicit the enduring oppositions between human persons and between humanity and the earth. The definitive separation of humanity from original unity is signified in the Genesis story by the exclusion from the garden, that place of the central tree of life.

The *reversal* of this dissection is revealed in the words of Jesus at the supper. The two *meals* balance one another quite precisely. To the meal which divides, dissolves the primal unity of creation, corresponds the meal which restores this unity in the Word from which creation arose. This new unity transcends the former unity, however—for the bond, the medium of communion will now be the divine light and life itself, the One. Jesus' words here at the supper speak of this new unity first in one image and then in another: each term and each symbol expressing another of its aspects.

Eve and Adam had eaten from the tree of the *knowledge* of good and evil. The sapiential gospel of John conceives of Jesus as divine Word, as Wisdom, and this Wisdom is the *unitive* divine Mind or Knowledge. The dark knowledge of good and evil is instinctively expressed in the shame of nakedness that impels the man and woman to hide part of themselves as "evil," and to hide themselves from the light in their guilt. This *knowledge* is inherently one with the *division*, the fracturing of reality. On the one hand it brings the division between darkness and light into the human person, so that part of the person must be repressed outside consciousness. On the other hand, it brings the division between one person and another, the privatization of the good and the projection of evil, which generate the injustice and violence in human history and in contemporary society. The primal paranoia which underlies the structure of human pathology, with its psychological and its social dimensions, is represented in this microcosm of the garden and its moral-ontological drama.

The fourth day is concerned with *knowledge and communion*: their inherent relationship, their historical opposition, their reunion in the Word incarnate, which is revealed in the supper discourse of Jesus. There is a knowledge which is division, and there is a knowledge which is communion, and the opposition between these two has constituted the drama of the fourth day.

The virus of the knowledge of good and evil expresses itself in human society largely in the stratification of *shepherds and sheep.*

"Knowledge is power," and man appropriates power to himself and thus divides society into two classes. The upper class is represented in John by the religious authorities; on the fourth day by the scribes and particularly the Pharisees. These men know the *Torah*, and in that knowledge they place themselves—or find themselves—above the contemptible common people who do not know the law, do not possess this divine treasure: the "people of the land." Nicodemus, this teacher of Israel, for all his good will, is such a man, and he must completely die to his wisdom—he must be born again. The Jews who condemn Jesus for healing the paralytic on the sabbath and for telling the man to carry his mat are of this class. The opposition of the upper and lower castes of this split religious society is beautifully presented in the dialectic between the Pharisees and the man born blind, for here it is light, knowledge, that is in question. The simple, invincible light of the beggar makes fools of the Pharisees as they circle around him with their questions, their judgments, the whole of their dualistic wisdom, their knowledge of good and evil.

When Jesus strips himself and pours water upon his disciples' feet, he is initiating them into this simple vision of communion, the "single eye" which was re-created in the man born blind. They have come to know Jesus as the embodiment of wisdom—"You have the words of eternal life," says Peter (6:68)—and now he seems to liquefy before their eyes, bathe their very eyes in a new innocence: "...and you are clean..." (13:10). The words of the discourse which follow will explicate this new vision, new knowledge, but their full illumination will not come until their baptism in the Holy Spirit (20:22; see 16:12-13).

The *progression from wisdom to eucharist*, which we found in the bread of life discourse of John 6, is developed more fully here at the supper, where the Word of God pours himself out first in gesture and then in words and images, expressing this transformation which he himself is about to undergo: from the divine Wisdom seen and heard and touched among them to the communion of divine life experienced *within* them and among them.

This identity, relationship and progression between knowledge and communion (expressing the movement of life between Word and Spirit) is most clearly and concisely expressed in the First Letter of John.

> ...what was from the beginning, what we have heard, what we have seen with our eyes, what we have looked at and touched with our hands, concerning the word of life—this life

was revealed, and we have seen it and testify to it, and
declare to you the eternal life that was with the Father and
was revealed to us—we declare to you what we have seen
and heard so that you also may have fellowship with us; and
truly our fellowship is with the Father and with his Son Jesus
Christ (1 Jn 1:1-3).

The letter proceeds to argue, in one word or image after another,
that the revelation, the *knowledge* of Christ is inseparable from *love*,
communion. "He who says he is in the light and hates his brother is
in the darkness still; he who loves his brother abides in the light" (1:9-
10a). God is light and God is love, and the two are therefore one: if
you are to dwell in God's light, and so be saved, you must remain in
the communion of the brethren.

At the end of the supper, Jesus gathers up into a prayer this progression from knowledge to communion. The Word is about to leave
the world to return to the Father, after having revealed to humans the
knowledge, the "name" of the Father. He prays that they, and all who
shall believe in him through them, may be *one* in the One. This is the
movement from Word, and the words and signs of the Word, to glory:
the Word present within them in this glory which is the Spirit. It is in
the Spirit that humanity enters into a life of communion in the One.

THE FOURTH DAY: SYNTHETIC REVIEW

On the *second day* the unitive wisdom of Jesus began to open into both
a eucharistic fullness and an interior realization: "Those who eat my
flesh and drink my blood abide in me, and I in them" (6:56). The
eucharistic sense of this bread of life remains implicit in the supper
narrative of the *fourth day*, while the interior dimension is fully developed. The movement from bread of life, tree of life, to the vine, is a
parallel development. This development of wisdom will continue on
the *sixth day* in a nuptial key.

In the successive episodes of the fourth day, various dimensions
of this unitive wisdom have been opened up: empowerment, vision,
new birth. At the supper, finally, Jesus' words focus upon the one plenary *gift*, the unitive reality itself. At the outset of the fourth day Jesus
told Nicodemus that one could only *see*, could only *enter* the kingdom
of God when one is *born anew*. The two healing signs pursue these
themes of entering and of seeing, and they are continued implicitly in

the supper narrative. It is at the end of the supper narrative that the image of new birth itself emerges explicitly once more, as the immediate prelude to the death and resurrection of Jesus.

The entering, the seeing, the birth all reflect the imagery of the narrative of Genesis 2–3. Garden, tree, river, and the creation or birth of man and woman give way, during this final supper, to an explicit revelation of Father, Son and Spirit, and of the new creation which will be a birth from figures into reality.

It is here on the central fourth day that the horizontal of the mandalic tree becomes fully visible, the cross-beam is fitted to the tree of the cross. Knowledge moves forward into communion, and knowledge pulls back, resisting this death into communion. The eternal life of the second day and the glory of the third day flow outward along these branches, shared by these guests who represent all of humanity.

The fourth day, as it concludes with the supper, becomes the *ecclesial* day. The ecclesial development here, however, is typically Johannine: expressed in a language not of institutional structure or roles but of interior union—abiding in Jesus' words and so abiding in him. Here the church is adumbrated in the supper itself, in the feast that is Jesus' great discourse, in the one commandment of love and in Jesus' prayer that his glory may be in the disciples so that they may be one.

The revolution consists in this: what belonged only to God, was only in God, is now *in human persons without distinction of class*, and so the old mediations between humanity and the divine, and the old gradations and distinctions of level between persons, are radically invalidated, short-circuited, emptied of their power. The shared life of God, as Jesus has revealed the trinitarian God here at the supper, has now become the shared life of human persons. This radical bridging of the distance between God and humanity—symbolized by the common meal itself—introduces a revolution in the structure of human relationship. The prevailing inequality, the verticality, the ancient hierarchical order of human relations, the "domination paradigm," must give way to the oneness of this shared divine life: must be swallowed up in this ocean of communion.

The long prevalent "vertical representation," the hierarchical representation of God in human society—from parenthood, fatherhood, patriarchy, to empire—must now give way to the primacy of the representation of God through *communion*. At the same time, *representation* is about to be fulfilled as it gives way to *realization*, at this threshold between the revelation of the Word in Jesus and the gift of the Spirit. It is this great change of phase which Jesus is explicating—

and his disciples are hardly beginning to suspect—here at the supper. In the brief dispute between Peter and Jesus at the footwashing (13:6-9) is a lesson which the church must ever begin to learn anew.

The dramatic struggle between power and communion will reach its climax on the fifth day.

Chapter Five

The Fifth Day:
The Living Temple Is the Lamb

And God said, "Let the waters bring forth swarms of living creatures, and let birds fly above the earth across the dome of the sky." So God created the great sea monsters and every living creature that moves, of every kind, with which the waters swarm, and every winged bird of every kind. And God saw that it was good. God blessed them, saying, "Be fruitful and multiply and fill the waters in the seas, and let birds multiply on the earth." And there was evening and there was morning, the fifth day (Gen 1:20-23).

Then the Lord God said, "It is not good that the man should be alone; I will make him a helper as his partner." So out of the ground the Lord God formed every animal of the field and every bird of the air, and brought them to the man to see what he would call them; and whatever the man called every living creature, that was its name. The man gave names to all cattle, and to the birds of the air, and to every animal of the field; but for the man there was not found a helper as his partner (Gen 2:18-20).

What has come into being in him was life, and the life was the light of all people (Jn 1:3c-4).

The transition from the fourth day moves through the *prayer* of Jesus, at the conclusion of the supper discourse, to the cleansing of the temple by Jesus at Passover time in Section 12. The depth of this connection appears when John 17 is understood as Jesus' consecratory prayer at the initiation of the new temple (cf. 1 Kgs 8; 2 Chr 6) which is to be his body (2:21): that is, his disciples. One of the scenes of the fifth day will take place at the portico of Solomon, builder of the first temple, at the feast of the rededication of the temple (10:22ff). At the end of his prayer Jesus indicated the nature of this new temple with his language of divine indwelling: "I made your name known to them (cf. 1 Kgs 8:29), and I will make it known, so that the love with which you have loved me may be *in them*, and *I in them*" (17:26).

We move from the initiation of Jesus' ministers or *shepherds*, at the supper concluding the fourth day, to the climax of his conflict with the *shepherds* of Israel. From the fullness of the light of Jesus shared intimately among his disciples, we proceed to the final struggle with darkness in which the light will be extinguished, to rise again within those who believe in him. The dialectic of knowledge and communion which had pervaded the fourth day becomes on the fifth day a dialectic of power and life.

SECTION 12: 2:13-25
JESUS CLEANSES THE TEMPLE

The fifth day of the new creation, the day of life, begins in the temple of Jerusalem. Worship in the temple was centered in animal sacrifices,[1] to such an extent that in the biblical accounts it sometimes becomes a sacred slaughterhouse.[2] Immediately the relationship between *religion and life* emerges upon the dramatic axis of this day. In the synoptic gospels, Jesus' cleansing of the temple is the immediate prelude to his trial and execution. John, on the other hand, has placed the temple episode near the beginning of his narrative, where it is in chiastic symmetry with the passion account itself. He has introduced the story of the raising of Lazarus, meanwhile, into the place which the temple cleansing occupies in the synoptics—the immediate occasion for the death of Jesus. The cleansing of the temple in John, therefore, symbolically corresponds to the death of Jesus rather than directly bringing it about.

Only John mentions the *sheep and oxen* in the temple precincts, and so recalls the fifth day of Genesis, broadly conceived as embracing the creation of animal life. The two Genesis accounts give different accounts of the creation of the animals. (See the two Genesis texts at the head of this chapter.) John will develop the meaning of the temple from this starting point: the place of animal sacrifice. The body of Jesus, the "Lamb of God," will itself be the definitive *sacrifice*, replacing the incessant animal sacrifices of the temple, and will be also the definitive *temple*, replacing that of Jerusalem.

> But when Christ came as a high priest of the good things that have come, then through the greater and perfect tent (not made with hands, that is, not of this creation), he entered once for all into the Holy Place, not with the blood of goats and calves, but with his own blood, thus obtaining eternal redemption (Heb 9:11-12).

> For it is impossible for the blood of bulls and goats to take away sins. Consequently, when Christ came into the world, he said,

> > "Sacrifices and offerings you have not desired,
> > but a body you have prepared for me...."
> > Then I said, "See, God, I have come to do your will, O
> > God...."

> And it is by God's will that we have been sanctified through the offering of the body of Jesus Christ once for all (Heb 10:4-7.10).

The letter to the Hebrews' solemn tone of sacrifice will be transformed when the old temple is replaced by the body of Jesus.

"I saw no temple in the city, for its temple is the Lord God the Almighty and the Lamb" (Rev 21:22). This new temple is the divine life itself. "I am the resurrection and the life," Jesus will say to Martha (11:25). "And the city has no need of sun or moon to shine on it, for the glory of God is its light, and its lamp is the Lamb" (Rev 21:23).

By this same transformation, the *human body*, the body of the believer, will then become both temple (1 Cor 6:19) and sacrifice: the temple of a continual *living* sacrifice, the worship "in spirit and truth" which Jesus brings. Bodily life will itself become divine worship.

> I appeal to you therefore, brothers and sisters, by the mercies of God, to present your bodies as a living sacrifice, holy and acceptable to God, which is your spiritual worship (Rom 12:1).

> Come to him, a living stone, though rejected by mortals yet
> chosen and precious in God's sight, and like living stones, let
> yourselves be built into a spiritual house, to be a holy priest-
> hood, to offer spiritual sacrifices acceptable to God through
> Jesus Christ (1 Pet 2:4-5).

When Jesus drives the sheep and cattle from the temple, we may
be reminded of Noah and his ark at the time of the flood. When the
waters had subsided, all the living creatures came forth from the confinement of the ark into the new world's green fields. The temple and
the Mosaic worship which it represents may be conceived as a narrow
"ark" of salvation, which is to come to shore in the new creation,
when the Messiah arrives. The pigeons which Jesus commands to be
taken away may recall the dove which was released from the ark
finally to return no more, but to dwell in the new land, a symbol of
the Spirit which is to fill and animate this new creation and its temples, the bodies of men and women. At the end of the fourth day,
Jesus invoked the descent of this Spirit, the glory of God, into these
new temples, to make them one temple.

The animal sacrifices of tent and temple had been established in
the Mosaic legislation of the time of exodus. John has already, at the
outset of this fifth day, directed us back beyond this exodus worship
to the time of *creation*, as recounted in the first chapters of Genesis. In
this vision which is projected back before the ages of bloody sacrifice,
the animals are presented as if created by God as man's companions
in the garden (see Is 11:6-9).

"*Destroy this temple...*" challenges Jesus (2:19), looking forward to
his death—as well as to the actual destruction of the Jerusalem temple, soon to follow. The crucifixion episode which matches this temple narrative will present us with a concentration of creation imagery.
The water flowing from the side of Jesus upon the cross will represent
both the river which flows from the temple (Ez 47:1-12; Rev 22:1) and
the river of paradise (Gen 2:10).

This decisive movement from exodus to creation is, as we have
learned, a passage from *mediated* religion to the *immediacy* of incarnation, of the divine indwelling in the human person. The transition
from temple of stone to the body of the risen Jesus perfectly symbolizes this passing over to an immanent new creation. In this new body
of Jesus as temple, the inclusive *I Am* of the Word will be a physical
reality, the "spiritual body" of First Corinthians (1 Cor 15:44).

The movement of *exodus*, however, continues through the whole
of the fifth day. The temple narrative is not to be interpreted in terms

of a *reform* nor simply as a further *development* of the existing worship of Israel. The movement from old temple to new temple is something more radical: an actual *termination* of the old order. The vehemence of Jesus' action, and his words, in the temple are expressive of the violence of this historical revolution. He comes not merely to purify the institutions of Jewish worship from the corruptions which had gradually transformed them, but actually to *replace* the temple and the whole system of worship that is centered in it, with a new worship "in spirit and in truth" (4:23).

Jesus' action in the temple expresses a radical incompatibility between *worship and commerce*. Since the money-changers supplied the special temple currency in exchange for the diverse kinds of money brought by Jews from abroad coming to worship there, the expulsion of these businessmen may be also interpreted as a symbolic movement from this Jewish religious monopoly to a universal worship.

The contamination of religion by greed will re-emerge when John characterizes Judas, the one who kept the money box, as a thief (12:6). Later on the fifth day, Judas will betray Jesus to the chief priests. It may be that this characterization of Judas is meant to refer also to the priestly elite of Judea.

The Johannine sense of *gratuity*, which we shall find expressed particularly in relation to women in the episodes of Day 6, and the emphasis which John places both on faith and on the love of friends, stands in sharp contrast with the figure of Judas and the money concerns associated with him. The chiastic symmetry of Jesus' expulsion of the temple businessmen and Judas' betrayal of Jesus may be significant.

This apparent hostility between commerce and the spirit is closely related to the opposition, already noted, between *two kinds of power*. Money is power, and is regarded by John—as well as by Jesus[3]—as opposed to the power of the Spirit which is associated with faith, love and *charis* (grace). Money belongs to the great structure of *intermediate* human conventions which will be supplanted by the new creation, with its "laws" of immediacy and communion. Alien to this world of the Word is the quid pro quo relationship characteristic of commerce and of a decadent understanding of the Jewish law.

The issue of *power* will become dominant in the course of the fifth day, as we approach the final battle of the two powers. The dramatic core of the Johannine temple episode is in the symbolic encounter of these two orders, two powers, two temples, two worlds. There is a perfect symmetry and a dense irony here: it will be precisely in being "destroyed" by the "old temple"[4] that the new temple will arise to take its place. What finally emerges through this contrast and conflict of the fifth day is the essentially *life-giving power* and being of the creative Word. This Word, embodied in humanity, becomes the center and form of the worship which rises from the cosmos to its creator.

Against the background of the Genesis creation story, the temple of Jerusalem seems the rigid fortress of a sanguinary religion, hostile and fearful in the midst of a fallen world. This religion of divine revelation had closed upon itself and become a stony prison at the heart of the world. Jesus comes to replace this fortress-prison of religion with the God-filled humanity of his own person. He purifies the temple in humanizing it. Flesh replaces stone; human life becomes the worship of God, and the destiny of humanity is fulfilled as Adam becomes once again the central temple of God from which the light of life emanates to the world.

Section 13: 4:43-54
The Royal Official's Son

The fifth day, the day of life, continues as Jesus brings back two persons from death. The first was on the point of death with fever, while the second will have been four days in the tomb when Jesus comes to get him. First Jesus heals from his mortal illness the son of a "royal official," or *basilikos*—a title which is itself derived from the word for king, *basileus*. The healing is done at a distance as Jesus tells the man, "Go, *your son lives*"(4:50). The man believes Jesus' word, starts toward home and is met by his servants who tell him that his son became well at the seventh hour, the hour when Jesus had spoken those words to him.

This miracle is not found in the other three gospels, but it strongly resembles two of the synoptic healings: the exorcism of the Syrophoenician woman's daughter (Mk 7:24-30) and the healing of the servant of the centurion of Capernaum (Mt 8:5-13; Lk 7:1-10). John's story appears to be a version of the centurion miracle account. Both of these synoptic miracles are performed by Jesus for *non-Israelites*. In Matthew's account, Jesus is astonished by the faith of the centurion and exclaims,

> Truly I tell you, in no one in Israel have I found such
> faith. I tell you, many will come from east and west

and will eat with Abraham and Isaac and Jacob in the kingdom of heaven, while the heirs of the kingdom will be thrown into the outer darkness... (Mt 8:10-12).

John's narrative is to be interpreted against this background of the synoptic tradition: the *basilikos* represents those Gentiles who are to believe in Jesus.

The story also recalls Old Testament miracle accounts involving pagans: Elisha's cure of Naaman the leper (2 Kgs 5), and particularly *Elijah's* resuscitation of the son of the *widow of Zareptha* (1 Kgs 17; see Lk 4:25-26). Elijah lodged in an upstairs room in the widow's house. When her son fell ill and died, and she brought him to Elijah, the prophet carried the dead child to his room and laid him upon his own bed.

Then he stretched himself upon the child three times, and cried out to the Lord, "O Lord my God, let this child's life come into him again." The Lord listened to the voice of Elijah; the life of the child came into him again; and he revived. Elijah took the child, brought him down from the upper chamber into the house, and gave him to his mother; then Elijah said, "See, your son is alive (*your son lives*)" (1 Kgs 17:21-23).

John is careful to point out that the healing of the official's son takes place at *Cana*, "where he had changed the water into wine." His linking of these two miracles of Jesus opens up another line of symbolic meaning in connection with the exodus event itself. These two Cana signs of Jesus correspond to the first and last *plagues* which God wrought on the Egyptians through Moses.

Jesus chides the father, "Unless you see *signs and wonders*, you will not believe" (4:48), and the father replies with a plea from the heart. As the time of the Israelite exodus approached and God was about to afflict Egypt with the series of plagues, he said to Moses, "I will harden Pharaoh's heart, and I will multiply my *signs and wonders* in the land of Egypt" (Ex 7:3).

The first plague worked by Moses upon the Egyptians was the turning of the waters of the Nile into blood, so that they became impossible to drink and the fish in the river perished. At Cana, Jesus turned water into wine. In place of the castigation, his first sign of the new creation was an addition to the joy of a festivity.

The final plague, on Passover night itself, was the slaying of all the firstborn of Egypt.

> At midnight the Lord struck down all the firstborn in the land
> of Egypt, from the firstborn of Pharaoh who sat on his throne
> to the firstborn of the prisoner who was in the dungeon, and
> all the firstborn of the livestock (Ex 12:29).

Here in John, the kingly association of the title *basilikos*, or royal
servant, is the clue that we are to interpret the healing of this boy in
the light of the slaying of *Pharaoh's* firstborn son at the time of exodus.
Here again Jesus reverses the exodus sign, in bringing a child back to
life. The significance of Jesus' words and action in the temple expands
into this world of the Gentiles.

If the Cana wedding signifies the union of God and humanity
wrought in Jesus, and the outpouring of new wine symbolizes the gift
of the life-giving Spirit, the raising of the *basilikos'* son may be seen as
the fruit of this wedding as it flows out to the Gentiles, represented by
Pharaoh and the Egyptians.

Against this background we begin to perceive the outline of a *second exodus* in John's gospel. In the historical exodus, the Israelites
were led out from among the Gentiles (Egyptians) to form a resolutely separate nation, the "people of God." The second exodus will
reverse this movement of isolation, which through the centuries had
hardened and tightened. From the constriction of a national worship,
from the cloister of the Jewish law, the followers of Jesus begin to
move out once again into the fullness of the world, the variety and
richness of the nations. This is the new exodus foretold by Deutero-
Isaiah, which will soon break entirely free of the eggshell of Jewish
religion and culture, and bring to birth the people of God within *every*
nation.

John's brief story does not mention *animals*, but we recall (see Ex
12:29 quoted above) that together with the firstborn of the Egyptians
there were slain at midnight "all the firstborn of the livestock" (Ex
12:29). Pharaoh rose up in the night, summoned Moses and sent the
Israelites away:

> Rise up, go away from my people, both you and the Is-
> raelites! Go, worship the Lord, as you said. Take your flocks
> and your herds, as you said, and be gone (Ex 12:31-32).

In our first episode of the fifth day, Jesus drove from the temple
not only the tradesmen, but their oxen and sheep (2:15). These animals who are driven from the Jewish temple, these flocks and herds
who go out of Egypt with the Israelites, suggest a further aspect of the

new exodus. In the tenth chapter of the Acts of the Apostles, Peter is being prepared for his mission to Cornelius, the centurion (!) who will represent the Gentiles to be baptized and brought into the newborn church. In a vision he sees

> ...something like a large sheet coming down, being lowered to the ground by its four corners. In it were all kinds of four-footed creatures and reptiles and birds of the air. Then he heard a voice saying, "Get up, Peter; kill and eat" (Acts 10:11-13).

Peter refuses to eat "anything that is profane or unclean." And then he is told, "What God has made clean, you must not call profane" (Acts 10:14-15). The dietary restrictions which have been so intrinsic to Jewish life are now terminated. But in addition, these animals somehow represent for Peter the Gentile peoples, themselves "unclean." On this tablecloth, descending to the earth, Peter has been shown the universality of life, which the gospel and the Spirit are to embrace. We may be reminded of the tradition of the four "living creatures" which surround the throne of God (see Ez 1:5ff; Rev 4:6-8).

The various animals indicate, then, the extension of this new exodus to all living creatures, to "the whole creation" (see Mk 16:15) on the fifth day of the new creation. The new exodus is a movement from the confinement of the Jewish law and worship (signified by its dietary restrictions, which distinguished clean from unclean animals) to the fullness of the original creation, the cosmos. In Genesis 2, all the animals were led to Adam to be named; in the second creation, it is Jesus, the second Adam, who will confer their new names upon those who have followed him.

> To everyone who conquers...I will give a white stone, and on the white stone is written a new name that no one knows except the one who received it (Rev 2:17).

Jesus performs this healing at a distance, through his Word, and this too points symbolically to the communication of life to the Gentiles, the widespread peoples of the earth, through the death of the firstborn, the Passover Lamb, at the conclusion of the fifth day. We are told twice that Jesus performed this second Cana sign "after coming from Judea to Galilee." "Galilee of the Gentiles" (Mt 4:15) was considered a hinterland, outside the boundaries of orthodox Judaism. This movement from Judea to Galilee, like the driving of the animals from the temple, resonates with the exodus, though paradoxically. Jesus leads his disciples out from the constriction of Judaism to the fullness of the creation and the immediacy of "worship in spirit and in truth." Luke, in his account of the transfiguration, presents Moses and Elijah speaking with Jesus "of his departure (Gr. *exodos*) which he was about to accomplish at Jerusalem" (Lk 9:31).

In contrast with the series of implicit *enterings* of the fourth day, the fifth day will continue to present us with a series of *exits*: from the Jewish temple, from Judea, from the Jewish people, from the tomb and the bonds of death (Lazarus), and finally from the "old order," the old creation itself, to the cosmic fullness, the freedom and unfettered life of that new creation which will be represented on the sixth and seventh days.

The contrast of *two powers*, which we have seen in the healings of the fourth day and in the temple episode, continues here. The positive *life*-giving power of the creative Word in Jesus emerges by contrast with the destructive power of the old order, exemplified by Moses and the plagues, as well as by Pharaoh himself. The royal official, a man of power like Pharaoh, has been unable to give life to the child who is called his son. Jesus restores life to the dying child immediately and at a distance. The power of the Word incarnate, risen from the dead, will extend to all life.

"Your son lives": these words continue to echo in our minds after we have read John's story. They can be understood in a number of ways; they seem to embrace hope and the future. Turned toward God, they become a confession of resurrection faith. The fifth day of creation springs from this life of the Omega, the Son—of God and of humanity—toward whom history moves.

SECTION 14: CHAPTERS 10–11
THE GATE; LAZARUS

The last and greatest of Jesus' life-restoring signs is the raising of his friend Lazarus from the dead. This immediately precedes Jesus' own death, and in John's account it is this sign which finally brings about the decision of the Pharisees and chief priests to kill him (11:46-53). The Lazarus narrative is also a rehearsal of the death and burial and resurrection of Jesus. It thus stands in the narrative as a gate between the book of signs and the book of glory, gathering up the signs of Jesus in this final act which anticipates the definitive sign of glory,

Jesus' own resurrection. "This illness does not lead to death; rather it is for God's glory, so that the Son of God may be glorified through it" (11:4).

Closely related to the Lazarus story itself is the preceding chapter of John (ch. 10), in which Jesus develops the theme of the *shepherd and sheep*, and then is confronted by the Jews in the temple at the feast of its dedication. In another major departure from Ellis' chiastic scheme, we have joined this section to the Lazarus narrative. Section 14 thus becomes a large five-part chiastic structure, centered in the great sign of the raising of Lazarus.[5]

As Jesus begins to speak in the language of sheep, shepherd and sheepfold, we are explicitly in the world of the fifth day of creation. His words, though metaphoric, refer directly and concretely to contemporary Judaism and to his own struggle with the religious authorities. At the same time, they evoke another, quite tender, picture of the shepherd and his sheep. There is a hint of that close relation of man and animals in the creation account of Genesis 2. The shepherd "calls his own sheep by name," for "they know his voice."

These sheep are human, and yet their world, too, includes thieves and robbers. Jesus' discourse is dominated by the *contrast* between these plunderers and the true shepherd who lays down his life for the sheep. We can distinguish *four categories* of persons in this symbolic complex of sheep and shepherd. On the one side are the ordinary people, or "sheep," and Jesus, their good shepherd. On the other side are the false shepherds—we understand here the chief priests and Pharisees—and somewhere between is the hireling who abandons his sheep in time of danger. Peter and the other disciples, by deserting Jesus and his cause at the time of his arrest, will place themselves for a while in this category.

The line of Old Testament "shepherds" runs down through the middle of biblical history, and includes David, Moses, the patriarchs Abraham, Isaac and Jacob, Abel—and, in the light of Genesis 2:18-20, perhaps Adam himself. The biblical prophets often used this imagery. They described as false or unfaithful shepherds the authorities of the Jewish nation, both civil and religious (see Ez 34; Zech 10–13). The prophets also speak of the true shepherd, the messianic Son of David, who will lead Israel according to God's heart.

⊕

The Lazarus narrative itself is explicitly linked to this series of discourses on the sheep and their shepherds. "Rabbi, the Jews were just now seeking to stone you, and are you going there (into Judea) again?" (11:8). Jesus validates his claim to be the true shepherd by this *work* (10:25); not even death itself can snatch his sheep from his hand (10:28). The concrete symbolic image which best ties the two sections together is the *gate*: gate of the sheepfold and door of the tomb.

$$\oplus$$

The story of Lazarus yields its biblical resonances only gradually, through a series of *chiastic* relationships. First, its chiastic twin, the cure of the *basilikos'* son, complements and illuminates the whole Lazarus episode on the level of *exodus* symbolism. But this emerges clearly only through the internal chiasm of the Lazarus episode itself. Jesus' opening words (10:1ff), about the sheepfold and its door, are clarified by the episode's concluding part, where we are told, "Now the Passover of the Jews was at hand..." (11:55). Both the *basilikos* and the Lazarus episodes are to be understood in the context of the historical *Passover*, and they represent, respectively, the Egyptian or Gentile side and the Jewish side of that event. It was on the night of the slaying of the firstborn of Egypt that the Israelites ate the Passover lamb, and immediately they went forth from Egypt (Ex 12).

Together with the correlation between the two Cana signs and the first and last plagues, these connections suggest a consistent structure of *exodus symbolism* underlying the Johannine text. The *sheepfold*, then, becomes the house of the Israelites, within which they remained shut on the Passover night, and the *gate* of which Jesus speaks becomes the door of that house, upon which the blood of the Passover lamb was sprinkled. Moses is the shepherd who, when morning comes, leads the people out on their exodus journey. Three episodes of our fifth day take place near the Passover time, and the fourth one, the cure of the *basilikos'* son, relates to the Passover symbolically, through the slaying of the firstborn. Passover, the door between one life and another, and the door of death, is essentially connected with the Johannine fifth day of creation.

"I am the good shepherd; the good shepherd lays down his life for the sheep" (10:11). Jesus, the Word incarnate, is the shepherd who becomes lamb, and the paschal lamb who lays down his life for the sheep. The gate of the sheepfold is double: incarnation and death (see Phil 2:6-11). First the shepherd, God's Word, becomes a sheep among the sheep, and then he passes through death as every sheep must, to lead the other sheep through the same gate.

Since, therefore, the children share flesh and blood, he himself likewise shared the same things, so that through death he might destroy the one who has the power of death, that is, the devil, and free those who all their lives were held in slavery by the fear of death (Heb 2:14-15).

"I am the gate for the sheep" (10:7). Having anointed the door with his own blood, Jesus becomes the one door which leads out of this life through death, and then into the next life, the final sheepfold of the Father's house, the new and unitive temple of his body.

$$\oplus$$

"I have other sheep, that do not belong to this fold. I must bring them also, and they will listen to my voice. So there will be one flock, one shepherd" (10:16). The *basilikos* in the twin narrative, representing the "Egyptians," thus represents these *other sheep* who will heed the voice of Jesus and enter into the flock. "The man believed the word that Jesus spoke to him, and started on his way" (4:50). The twin episodes of the *basilikos'* son and of Lazarus are related by a complex symmetry. In both of these healings, it is a question of life and death rather than a particular ailment, as in the two healings on the fourth day. There is an emphasis on distance and on time in both stories. The boy is on the near side of the gate of death, while Lazarus is decisively on the far side: four days dead. In both cases it is the anxious sorrow of the close relatives that stirs Jesus and is the occasion for the healing.

There is an implicit contrast between two categories of *official* here. The *basilikos*, whom we understood to be a pagan, is so ready to believe Jesus that he immediately accepts his word of assurance and goes on his way. The *centurion* of the synoptics is evoked here. This "royal official"—not a religious official—touches our hearts, like the good centurion, with his tender concern for his son. "Sir, come down before my little boy dies" (4:49).

In contrast, the Jewish religious authorities, leaders of the chosen people, refuse to believe in Jesus even after he has raised a man from the dead (11:47.57). We may be reminded of the hardness of heart of the rich man in Luke's Lazarus story. It is, indeed, the signs of Jesus which provoke the chief priests and Pharisees to seek his death (11:47ff). The contrast between these two categories of official further relates the Johannine Lazarus story to the context of *sheep and shepherds*: the good secular, presumably pagan shepherd and the universality of the salvation brought by Jesus is juxtaposed with the heart-less religious shepherds of Israel, who want to put to death both the revivified sheep and the Shepherd who brought him back.

The stories of the *basilikos'* son and of Lazarus thus join the two healings of the fourth day in referring to the *power* thematic. More specifically, they correspond to the *life-power* dialectic of the fifth day.

The plea of the *basilikos*, "Sir, come down before my little boy dies" (4:49), creates a striking resonance with the Lazarus story, in which Jesus precisely does *not* "come down" before Lazarus dies. There is significance in these details of time and distance. In the curing of the *basilikos'* son, which we have interpreted as representing the *Gentile* world, Jesus demonstrates a power over *space*, by healing the boy from a distance. In the raising of the orthodox *Jew*, Lazarus, on the other hand, Jesus triumphs over *time*, for he brings back to life a man who has been dead for four days.

There is probably symbolic meaning here. The creative or life-giving power of the Word extends over the whole *cosmos*, and this is the "spatial" dimension. The power of the Word rules *history*, and this is the temporal dimension. This temporal or historical dimension of God's power is that which predominates in the biblical revelation, and which joins the successive layers of biblical meaning which we encounter in John's narratives. In Jesus, the Word incarnate, the spatial and temporal dimensions meet. Once again, this cross-figure is discovered, woven in the fabric of John's gospel itself. As the Word enters history in Jesus, the cosmos itself is taken up into that "sacred history" which is the central theme—or language—of the biblical revelation.

The stories of *two women*, one a Gentile and one an Israelite, who give hospitality to Elijah and Elisha, and whose sons are then returned to them from the dead by the two prophets, are also reflected in these twin narratives of the fifth day. We have already noted a correspondence between Elijah's raising of the son of the widow of Zarephath (1 Kgs 17) to Jesus' cure of the *basilikos'* son. Both here and in Elisha's raising of the Shunammite's boy (2 Kgs 4), we find a moving image of the incarnation of the Word, of Jesus stretched upon the man-shaped tree, and finally descending into the grave to bring back from death the one whom he loves.

Then he [Elisha] got up on the bed and lay upon the child, putting his mouth upon his mouth, his eyes upon his eyes, and his hands upon his hands; and while he lay bent over him, the flesh of the child became warm (2 Kgs 4:34).

John, by the way in which he relates the death and tomb of Lazarus to the death and tomb of Jesus, invites us to see here a tender image of the unitive mystery which is being consummated when Jesus enters the same dark gate as every child of Adam.

⊕

Our understanding of the dramatic opposition implicit in John's narrative of Lazarus can be enriched by reflecting upon the *parable* of Lazarus and the rich man in Luke (16:19-31). Luke's parable turns around the dramatic contrast between these two characters, and we may wonder if John intends a similar contrast between his Lazarus and the chief priests and Pharisees. The Lucan Lazarus, though a poor man, is a son of Abraham. So is the rich man. But in the end it is Lazarus who rests in Abraham's bosom, while the rich man swelters in hell.

The central point of resemblance between the Lazarus of Luke and that of John appears in the final words of Luke's parable: "If they do not listen to Moses and the prophets, *neither will they be convinced even if someone rises from the dead*" (16:31). Both stories center in this Lazarus, the pitiable man who dies and then rises from the dead.

Reading John's story of Lazarus in the light of the Lucan parable, we find that Lazarus, son of Abraham, contrasts with the *basilikos'* son, understood as a pagan, e.g. the firstborn of Pharaoh in the exodus narrative. The geographical details reinforce this contrast, as in the story of the believing *basilikos* we are told twice that Jesus has just come from Judea into Galilee, and in the story of Lazarus and the disbelieving Jews, Jesus must travel from Galilee into Judea to perform the miracle. Lazarus may signify for John, therefore, faithful Israel. He is called the one whom Jesus loved. In contrast to him, the chief priests and Pharisees would represent the unfaithful leaders of Israel. Quite precisely, these men *are not convinced though someone has risen from the dead* (see Lk 16:31 above).

⊕

The *name* of Lazarus is another clue. It is the Greek version of the biblical name *Eleazar*, which was borne by two representatives of orthodoxy in the Jewish tradition. The first is Eleazar the priest, son of Aaron, who succeeds his father as the *chief priest* of Israel in the time of the sojourn in the desert. Eleazar was the custodian of the worship of Yahweh: the tabernacle and its furnishings, the animal sacrifices. The second Eleazar is also a priest, "one of the foremost teachers of the law," and is martyred when he refuses to eat the flesh of pigs, the meat of pagan sacrifices, in the time of the Hellenistic persecution of the Jews and of the Macchabean rebellion (2 Mac 6). A third Eleazar is mentioned as the great-great grandfather of Jesus, in the genealogy at the beginning of Matthew's gospel (Mt 1:15).

The name Eleazar, or Lazarus, therefore, brings together a number of associations: exodus and the Mosaic law, the priesthood and the animal sacrifices, strict observance of the orthodox liturgical worship, heroic witness to the authority of the law, and finally the lineage of David, from which Jesus is to spring. The town of Bethany, only two miles from Jerusalem, may have been one of the towns where resided the priests and levites who served the temple worship.

In the context of the entire Johannine fifth day, these slender clues assume a broader meaning. Lazarus, as "son of Aaron," and therefore representing the orthodox Jewish priesthood deriving from the exodus-Mosaic legislation, and the Jerusalem temple worship, would symbolize the complex of Jewish priesthood, worship, sacrifice and orthodoxy. Lazarus would stand in contrast to the *basilikos'* son, who in the light of the exodus history is son of Pharaoh, son of the Gentile king, and therefore represents the profane power of empire and army. Lazarus and the *basilikos* may be intended, therefore, to represent those members both of the official class of Judaism and of the pagan civil government who believed in Jesus, and stand in contrast to the unbelieving Jewish and Roman authorities. Eleazar, the Mosaic chief priest, would be recalled in contrast with the chief priests who decide to put both Jesus and Lazarus to death (12:10). At the same time Lazarus may represent a Jewish structure of priesthood and sacrifice and a segregated orthodoxy which will both soon undergo a radical transformation in the death and resurrection of Jesus.

⊕

Within the fifth day's thematic of sheep and shepherds, this division into the *two categories of power*—civil and religious, royal and priestly —will be further developed in the narrative of the passion of Jesus. Jesus will be taken first before the chief priests and then before Pilate, representative of the emperor, the Gentile "king." As we shall see, these figures will provide the dark background to the new kingship and priesthood which are to emerge in Jesus, the Son of Man. Jesus, in turn, will reconstitute the human vocation as a "royal priesthood" (1 Pet 2:9). Adam, humanity, is king and priest in creation, with respect to the other creatures—represented by the animals whom he names—and to God. The Son of Man restores this cosmic mediation of humanity as he restores and brings to its fullness the temple of the human body. Every hierarchical form of mediation and power—whether religious or secular—is now to be subordinated to this restored dignity of the human person—of *every* human person.

⊕

Jesus' *sorrow* as he approaches the tomb of Lazarus (11:33.35) need not be seen as provoked wholly by the death of his friend and the grief of Mary and the other mourners. In just a few days, Jesus will himself enter the nocturnal sheepfold of death to bring out his friend—Adam, humanity. In Jesus' expressions of grief and anguish (see also 12:27), John may be signifying his anticipation of the weight which he is about to take on his shoulders: the totality of human sin and mortal pain, his climactic struggle with the prince of death (see Heb 2:10; 5:7-9).

⊕

The story comes to its dramatic climax when Jesus stands at the door of the tomb and cries, *"Lazarus, come out!"* "The gatekeeper opens the gate for him, and the sheep hear his voice. *He calls his own sheep by name and leads them out*" (10:3).

"Unbind him, and let him go." These words of Jesus are John's signal that Lazarus is identified with *Isaac* (see Gen 22:9 and Lk 16: 22-23); Abraham's *binding* of Isaac is a major motif in Jewish tradition), the son who was spared when another "lamb" (Gen 22:8) was provided for the sacrifice by God himself. As we shall see, John also identifies Jesus himself with Isaac, Abraham's "beloved only son" (Gen 22:2).

"Unbind him, and let him go." The captivity, the confinement and heteronomy of the *old order*—of law and death and fear—is ended. When Jesus brings back Lazarus into the ordinary light of day on this fifth day of the new creation, he symbolically enacts the bringing of humanity, of the "first Adam," through the door of death into the life of this new creation, a participation in the life of God.

It is this sign of life which precipitates the decision of the chief priests and Pharisees to kill Jesus. They fear the loss of their holy place, the temple, and their nation. Indeed, a new temple and a new nation (see 1 Pet 2:9-10) are to be born through Jesus' death. "...and not for the nation only, but to gather into *one* the dispersed children of God" (11:52). The *basilikos*, the Egyptians, all the Gentiles, are gathered into this *one* flock, into this one shepherd who is the new, unitive temple of God.

⊕

While reading Jesus' discourse on the shepherd, the sheepfold and its door, we were aware of strange leaps in thought and clashing assertions. "I am the gate for the sheep." "I am the good shepherd." These conflicting predicates of the basic *I Am* statement impel us beyond the exodus level to a unitive interpretation. As earlier, this unitive level of meaning expresses itself in the imagery of the Genesis creation accounts. "...the sheep hear his voice. He calls his own sheep by name and leads them out" (10:3). "...and whatever the man [Adam] called every living creature, that was its name" (Gen 2:19). Jesus is the new Adam who comes to call each person by name, and as we shall see in the Lazarus story itself, this naming is a gift of new *life* (see 10:27-28).

This ultimate level of interpretation has been developed further in the dispute between Jesus and the Jews at the feast of the *Dedication* of the temple (10:22-39). The Johannine meaning of the temple itself is developed at the same time. To this historical dedication or reconsecration of the temple after its desecration by the Gentiles (see 1 Mac 1:54; 2 Mac 6:1-5; 1 Mac 4:41-61) corresponds the consecration[6] of the new temple of Jesus' body which he will accomplish through his paschal death. Though Jesus is already "consecrated" by his origin from the Father (10:36), he had spoken at the end of the supper of a new self-consecration that "they also may be sanctified [consecrated] in truth" (17:19).

At this point we encounter another startling leap. Jesus has spoken of human persons as *sheep,* and of himself as entering the sheepfold through its low door. Now he begins to speak of humans as *gods!* "If those to whom the word of God came were called 'gods'—and the scripture cannot be annulled..." (10:36). Jesus, the new Adam, is at once shepherd and *Word,* "Name" of God, who is sent to men and women, to call them by name—by their true names in the creative Word, which are godly names, generative of divine being. Those who hear the Word of God are gathered into it and become "gods." Those who receive the Son of God are gathered into him and become children of God (1:12). The violent compulsion which leads Jesus' hearers to take up stones to kill him (10:31) comes from beyond themselves, from one who would only kill and destroy (see 8:40.44); what they rush forward to destroy is the divine-human life which is their own destiny.

"I have other sheep...there will be one flock, one shepherd" (10:16). "The Father and I are one" (10:30). The sheepfold into which Jesus leads those who hear his voice, who hear him speak their new names—whether they have been Jews or Gentiles—is ultimately this One, this *I Am*, which is his own being.

⊕

The contrast—sometimes explicit and always present as a dramatic undercurrent—between Jesus, the true shepherd of Israel, and the false or unfaithful shepherds who are the chief priests, Pharisees, and other rulers of the people, has continued to unfold. We have seen that there is a strong biblical basis for this imagery (see p. 153 above). *Moses*, who had literally pastured sheep before his call to lead the people, was seen as the shepherd of Israel: this is the *exodus level* of symbolic reference. In the light of Genesis 2:18-20, *Adam* himself may be considered the first shepherd in the biblical narrative. The role of shepherd begins to appear as nearly an integral dimension of human life. This makes Jesus' words more shocking still:

All who came before me are thieves and bandits...the thief comes only to kill and destroy; I came that they may have life, and have it abundantly (10:8-10).

Who are these "thieves and bandits" who have preceded Jesus? As we respond to this question at successive levels of depth, the scope of our response will broaden to meet the radicality of Jesus' words. They do not refer only to those leaders of the people who have been patently corrupt. At the time of exodus, Moses and the Israelites extorted from the Egyptian people their precious things: "And so they plundered the Egyptians" (Ex 12:36) "...only to steal and kill and destroy" (10:10): these words can be applied to the violence inflicted upon the Egyptians by Moses and the Israelites in their exodus, and become the background against which the distinctive *life*-giving quality of the new exodus will emerge, on this fifth day.

Jesus' term "thieves and bandits" applies most directly to the Jewish religious leaders of his time. The expression may also be connected with the *temple*, and hence with Jesus' symbolic cleansing of the temple earlier on the fifth day. His words, "You shall not make my Father's house a *house of trade*" (2:16; see Mt 21:13; Mk 11:17), and his expulsion of the moneychangers and other tradesmen, would reflect also upon the more subtle "business" of the chief priests, scribes and Pharisees, who in one way or another profited from their position as shepherds, at the expense of the ordinary folk and to the detriment of true religion.

Perhaps stealing and killing come ultimately to the same thing. In Jesus' prophetic assault upon the leaders of the Jewish people, killing may signify the destroying of people's *faith*, of their spiritual life, their relationship with God. The worst crime of the bad shepherds, the perverse *mediators*, is to transform their own role of mediation into a closed door, an impenetrable wall—or a way leading nowhere.

These hard words of Jesus may be applied also, in a sense, to *every teacher but Jesus*. Every charismatic religious teacher, even in spite of himself, "steals" by drawing the disciple to himself to some degree: that is, both away from God and *away from the disciple's own self* and his own immediate relationship with God. This leads further: only Jesus can confer the life of which he speaks, and this at the center of the person: a living water which is the opposite of all alienation. And so John, who baptizes externally with water, gives way before the one who is to baptize with the Holy Spirit (see 1:33).

"What has come into being in him was life, and the life was the light of all people" (1:4). Only the teacher who is himself light and life can enter into a person as light and regenerate the person from its own center, as life. Jesus is that light of life from the beginning, and enters the door anew as one accepts his death and resurrection through faith.

⊕

As John's gospel approaches its denouement in the death and resurrection of Jesus, the narrative gathers and deepens. We are dimly aware that when Jesus concludes his series of signs by bringing back his friend Lazarus from the dead, we are witnessing a shadowy image not only of Jesus' death but of its fruit. This final sign epitomizes the work of Jesus: by his death he returns Adam—humanity—to life. As in the vision of Paul (Rom 5:12-21; cf. 1 Cor 15:44-49), it is the second Adam who brings the first Adam back from death to a life which is now eternal.

There is a "chiastic" symmetry, an inverse parallel, between the supper of Jesus, followed by the death and burial and resurrection of Jesus, and the death, burial and resurrection of Lazarus followed by the supper at which Mary anoints Jesus. These events bind together the fourth, fifth and sixth days.

The Lazarus story is related to the supper at Bethany and the following events in the narrative order by the delicate fragrance of friendship, of love, which we begin to perceive here. In this climate, we are surprised to see Jesus quite deliberately *waiting* for Lazarus to die before going to him. One motive for this may be, by raising a *dead* Lazarus, to strengthen the faith of his disciples in the power of life that is within him, before the looming darkness of his own death, the terrible night that they will soon undergo (see 11:15). In the synoptic gospels, it is Jesus' own *transfiguration* that enkindles a glimmer of resurrection light to support the disciples through this coming darkness. Lazarus has died only two miles from Jerusalem, where Jesus is to die (11:18). The geographical vector parallels the dramatic vector as Jesus approaches his *hour*. The "sleep" of Lazarus reflects both the sleep of Jesus, upon the cross, and the sleep of Adam, from which he awoke to discover a new, feminine presence in the garden.

$$\oplus$$

As this Lazarus-Adam returns through the door of death, he seems to be all humanity, responding to the voice of Jesus who has himself risen from the tomb. Lazarus, the dying man of Bethany (literally "house of the afflicted"), embodies the totality of human misery and need, the weight of sin and mortality, which Jesus is to take up and transform by his passion. This is suggested in John's narrative as we see the three other healing signs of Jesus, and indeed his whole series of signs, resumed in the raising of this man. Lazarus is brought back to life on the *fifth day*, signifying the new creation of human life, of all life. This is the last and conclusive sign until that great sign which will be Jesus' own resurrection. In the Johannine narrative it is this Lazarus sign which *causes* the death of Jesus. At the same time the raising of this man *expresses* in its fullness the life-giving efficacy of Jesus' death and resurrection. Each of Jesus' signs has manifested the glory of God which is in Jesus, but it is only at the first of them, the Cana miracle (see 2:11), and at this final one (see 11:4) that John speaks explicitly of this glory. Together, these two signs become a diptych representing, in its two panels, the fullness of the work which

Jesus is to accomplish by the final glorious sign of his death and resurrection. Mediating between them is the supper at Bethany, and Mary's gesture.

⊕

Few contemporary commentators[7] would identify Mary of Bethany with Mary Magdalene and with the "sinful woman" who anointed Jesus with perfume in Luke's gospel, although symbolic merging of this kind was common among the fathers and medieval exegetes. While the historicity of this identification may be very doubtful, it is not at all unlike John to merge the three women for a literary-theological motive. We shall see as we continue that John brings the several women who interact with Jesus throughout his narrative together into *one* symbolic figure. In the present instance, identifying Mary of Bethany with the two other women opens in the Lazarus story a deep and rich vein of further meaning, in terms of the symbolism of the narrative of creation and fall in Genesis 2–3. This "sinful woman" (Lk 7:36-50) from whom Jesus cast seven devils (Lk 8:2) is *Eve*. John brings Jesus into the center of the human situation which derives from the sin of the first man and woman: a condition of sin and illness, of diabolic infestation and death. He does this, it appears, by subtly orchestrating elements from the whole of the gospel tradition.

As the paralytic, the blind man, the royal official's son, who represent the totality of human affliction, are gathered into the single figure of Lazarus, or Adam, so the various women, who represent particularly the *interior* aspect of the fallen condition, are gathered together into one representative woman who is Eve. Alongside the physical death of this *man* ("man," however, as comprehending all human persons from one aspect) who has returned through death to the earth from which he was taken, there has taken place, symbolically, in *woman*, the interior death.[8] This is expressed by the connotations attached to the two women in the gospel tradition: the former sinful condition of the woman who anoints Jesus in Luke, and the former indwelling of seven devils in Mary Magdalene. Through faith in Jesus, this woman has already been exorcised, forgiven, cleansed: as is typical in John's gospel, she has received grace before the man, her brother. And now she grieves for him.

The role of woman is reversed. Once temptress to the fruit of death, inviting Adam to eat from the tree of the knowledge of good and evil, she now mediates between her dead brother-spouse and the tree of life who is Jesus (see 11:25). Woman is once again the mediator: first of death, now of life. This role of *new Eve* has traditionally been attributed to that other Mary who is the mother of Jesus.

The woman, however, is split into two sisters, Martha and Mary, who are characterized by John consistently with their presentation in Luke's story (Lk 10:38-42). Luke depicts Martha as the one who busies herself with serving, *feeding* Jesus and his disciples. An assertive person, active in service, she resembles Peter the fisherman. Mary, in contrast, remains at Jesus' feet listening to his words. She is content to *be fed*, like the "disciple whom Jesus loved" who rested in his Master's bosom. Mary recognized the tree of life, the bread of life, the "one thing necessary," and remained at the foot of the tree, eating and drinking of this life.

While Martha does not appear again, it is Mary who will soon anoint Jesus' feet with costly perfume. This gesture, as we shall see, expresses profoundly what is about to take place as John's story flows to its conclusion.

The immediate context of Jesus' raising of Lazarus has been defined by these two sisters. Jesus' death and resurrection will be similarly enclosed by the *women* who have believed in him. At this climactic point in John's gospel, where Lazarus and then Jesus traverse the doors of death and rebirth, woman plays a decisive, though mysterious role.

The first man and woman—their companionship, their sin, their penalty and the glory which they prefigure—will be frequently present beneath the surface of John's narrative as we conclude the fifth day and continue with the sixth and seventh days of the new creation.

SECTION 15: CHAPTERS 18–19
THE PASSION OF JESUS

Structure

The drama of Jesus' passion and death takes place in five distinct acts, each involving a change of place.

A.	18:1-12.	Jesus is arrested in a garden.
B.	18:13-27.	Jesus is tried before the high priests.
C.	18:28–19:16.	Jesus is tried before Pilate, scourged and mocked.
D.	19:17-30.	Jesus is crucified.
E.	19:31-42.	Jesus is buried in a garden.

Ellis[9] has brought out the chiastic symmetry of these five divisions.

A. The Arrest of Jesus: 18:1-12

Like old King David, fleeing from his treacherous son Absalom (2 Sam 15:23), Jesus crosses the brook Kidron with his disciples and enters the garden where he will be betrayed by Judas into the hands of the Jewish officials. Jesus' repeated question to them, "Whom are you looking for?" (18:4.7), recalls with sorrowful irony his question to the first two disciples,"What are you looking for?" (1:38). "Jesus of Nazareth," they reply. "*I Am*," responds Jesus, and the men fall backward to the ground. With these two words he at once affirms his identity as the Jesus of Nazareth they have come to seize (cf. 6:15.20), and as one whose power is of a quite different kind than that which they represent. Then he surrenders himself into their hands. "Unbind him, and let him go" (11:44) had been Jesus' final words concerning Lazarus; now Jesus is bound and led away toward his death. Judas' treachery and Peter's violent resistance are clearly recounted here, recalling the drama of Judas, Peter and the beloved disciple at the supper.

B. Jesus Before the High Priests: 18:13-27

As Jesus is brought to the high priests, he is followed by Simon Peter and another disciple who moves with a certain freedom in this world. Peter is challenged by a serving maid, "You are not also one of this man's disciples, are you?" The words in which he denies his master, "I am not" (*ouk eimi*) (18:17), ironically recall Jesus' own response a little earlier (18:6). Very soon after his violent defense of his master in the garden, Peter, the rock, has abdicated the new *name*, the new identity, which Jesus had communicated to him; he has abjured himself; he *is not*. Peter stands and warms himself at the fire with the servants and the officers who had arrested Jesus. In the light of the position which Peter will assume, it is significant that it is in the court of the Jewish *high priest* that he betrays his master.

We hear no more here of the "other disciple" who brought Peter into the high priest's court. If this is the beloved disciple, as is likely, we are probably to assume that he remained close to the events which follow, until he appears at the cross in 19:35-37. This would maintain the parallel with the roles of the three disciples at their last supper with Jesus. The order of relationship—Jesus–beloved disciple–Peter–Judas—is verified once again here, in the behavior of the three. Judas betrays and disappears; Peter follows, falters, denies, disappears; only the beloved disciple *remains* close to Jesus until the end and witnesses to what he has seen.

There is very little dialogue between Jesus and Annas, who represents the high priestly household; the dramatic attention focuses upon Peter and his denials of his master. When Annas does question Jesus about his teaching and disciples, Jesus refers this public person to the public record, the public memory of his words. Jesus will again refuse to testify or defend himself when he stands before Pilate, but there the words exchanged between the two will be very significant. This brief dialogue between the old high priest and the one high Priest centers upon the *words* of Jesus: and these words are now common property. Jesus has no more to say to these functionaries who represent the blind and deaf "temple" of official Judaism; there remains now only the sacrifice of his body, the destruction of this living temple, to be performed at their insistence.

Jesus as High Priest

John indicates the priestly character of Jesus very subtly, and largely by contrast with the high priests Annas and Caiaphas. His priesthood will differ radically from that of the Jewish religious leaders.

It is in the *letter to the Hebrews*, with which John has strong affinities, that we find an explicit contrast between the traditional priesthood of Israel, in the line of Aaron, and the new priesthood of Jesus. The author insists that the old priesthood could not confer salvation. He speaks of Melchizedek—who appears as an archetypal cosmic priest—and then of Jesus.

> ...another priest arises, resembling Melchizedek, one who has become a priest, not through a legal requirement concerning physical descent, but *through the power of an indestructible life* (Heb 7:15-16).

The sons of Aaron, appointed priests by the Mosaic law, served the altar but for a time and died. Jesus is a priest forever *by virtue of his very being*—which is of an essentially different order because he is Son not merely of man but of God. A church father demands, "When we speak of Christ's priesthood, what else do we mean than the incarnation?[10]"

Here is the meaning of Jesus' priesthood in terms of our fifth day of creation: by the power of his divine and indestructible *life*, Jesus ends the history of animal sacrifices, the ritual destruction of life, and institutes a new union of God and humanity in which humanity *participates the very life of God*, and is therefore immortal.

The high priestly family of Annas and Caiaphas, on the other hand, represents the old Aaronic line, a "priesthood of death" (see Heb 7:23 and 2 Cor 3:6-9), whose final act of office will be to slay the Lamb of God, the priest-victim, and thus liberate this divine life into the world.

Much of John's gospel—in recounting both the signs and the words of Jesus—is occupied in communicating the sense of this gift of divine *life*. The new life will flow first into those persons who believe in Jesus through faith and baptism. In the Johannine vision of new creation, however, this new life is somehow to be participated by the entire cosmos. Paul is more explicit on this:

> ...the creation itself will be set free from its bondage to decay and will obtain the freedom of the glory of the children of God. We know that the whole creation has been groaning in labor pains until now; and not only the creation, but we ourselves, who have the first fruits of the Spirit, groan inwardly while we wait for adoption, the redemption of our bodies (Rom 8:21-23).

The *"priesthood of Adam,"* only faintly adumbrated in Genesis 2, begins to emerge more clearly: it is through the human person that the material creation itself is to be renewed.

Hebrews 7 distinguishes Melchizedek—and hence Jesus—from the Jewish priests in a vertical, platonic-sounding way: through his belonging to *eternity* rather than to genealogy and time. The same distinction can be developed in another direction which is more nearly Johannine: from the Mosaic religion, with its law and other institutions, to *creation*—to the universality and profundity of a creational vision. Thus Jesus, "by the power of an indestructible life," becomes the Priest of *the whole of creation*, and restores the human vocation which was to have been fulfilled by Adam. This vocation has an ontological basis; it is written in the structure of the human person: spirit and matter, "spirit in the world."[11]

In Jesus' "priestly prayer" at the end of the supper, he had spoken of *sanctifying* himself, doubtless through his sacrifice, so that the disciples might be "sanctified in truth" (17:17-19), that is, sanctified in the

Word of God. Through the sacrifice of the Word incarnate, those who believe in him will be joined to him in the one divine life. This word *sanctify (hagiazein)*, used also for the consecration of a temple, conveys this unitive event in another way. When the high priest Caiaphas had spoken of Jesus' death, John commented:

> He did not say this on his own, but being high priest that year he prophesied that Jesus was about to die for the nation, and not for the nation only, but *to gather into one* the dispersed children of God (11:51-52).

Jesus himself had prolonged his prayer at the supper:

> ...also on behalf of those who will believe in me through their word, *that they may all be one.* As you, Father, are in me and I am in you, *may they also be one* in us, so that the world may believe that you have sent me. The glory that you have given me I have given them, so *that they may be one,* as we are one, I in them and you in me... (17:20-23).

In this unitive intercession is expressed the priesthood of Jesus; the unity for which he prays is that of the divine life itself.

C. Jesus Before Pilate: 18:28–19:16

From the court and residence of the Jewish high *priests* we pass to that of the Roman procurator, deputy of the *"king,"* the Roman emperor. The Jewish chief priests have literally handed Jesus over, "betrayed" him, to the Gentiles, the Roman power. This close interaction of priesthood and kingship continues throughout the passion narrative, and is reflected in its chiastic structure (see p. 165 above). We have arrived at the *center* of this chiasm, and here the persistent theme is *kingship*: that of Jesus in contrast to that of the kings of this world. The three parties in this long dramatic narrative are, first, *"the Jews"*—that is, the Jewish religious leaders—secondly, *Pilate,* shuttling to and fro in the middle, and, finally, *Jesus,* the accused "King of the Jews."

The drama within a drama which is this running dialogue between Jesus and Pilate, Pilate and the Jews, is structured in a *sevenfold chiasm*.[12] The chiastic drama is centered in the mockery of Jesus by the soldiers (19:1-3), and plays between scenes *inside and outside the praetorium*. The Jews lead Jesus to Pilate but will not enter the praetorium lest they be defiled and unable to eat the Passover meal. Pilate must therefore go outside the praetorium to speak to them. He travels back and forth from Jesus inside to the Jews outside the praetorium. This movement weaves the dramatic action, and is powerfully symbolic.[13] In the words of Goettmann, the Jews have become "the theological...prototype of the world which opposes Jesus, the agents of the powers of darkness. These are called *exterior darkness* in contrast to the interior light."[14]

Jesus, held within the praetorium, is twice brought outside by Pilate so that he may show him to the Jews who are waiting there. When outside, Pilate struggles with the Jews, and when he returns within the praetorium again, he questions Jesus. Jesus speaks to him only within the praetorium. Pilate vacillates between the inner light which he perceives in Jesus and the outer darkness to which he is already committed by compromise and cowardice.[15]

Here once again there is subtly suggested that *central place* in which Jesus dwells, in John's vision of reality. Peter waited outside the court of the high priest until the "other disciple, who was known to the high priest," brought him inside. Then Peter stood warming himself with the servants and officers at a fire, still manifestly "outside." We receive the impression that Peter is always "outside" while the disciple whom Jesus loved is "inside." Peter had not known the inner Jesus, the high Priest, and so his inner fire was quenched and he denied his Master.

The mockery of Jesus by Pilate's soldiers, the travestied enthronement, also takes place within the praetorium (19:1-3). The praetorium, as Jesus is enthroned within it, becomes the center not merely of the local political power, but of a cosmic power. We have moved from the Jewish *temple*, at the beginning of the fifth day, to this Roman *praetorium*, as the day draws to its conclusion. Jesus has been handed over by the Jewish religious authorities to the power of the Gentiles, the Romans, and thus symbolically has moved from the center of the Jewish religious world to the *center of the cosmos*. The recurrent pattern of this movement from the religion of the Jews to a cosmic creation, here at the end of the fifth day, appears in the drama of Jesus, Pilate and the Jews.

When Pilate brings Jesus out to the Jewish leaders in kingly robes, saying, "Here is the man" (19:5), we behold at once the dishonored King of the Jews—and Adam, *Man*. The responding shout, "Crucify him," the rejection of the Son of Man by the Jewish crowd, is the rejection of the destined life of humanity, which is in him. Pilate finds no crime in him; he is the innocent Lamb of God who comes to bear the sin of the world.

In this scene there are only indirect suggestions of light and darkness: the crowing of the cock and the observation that "it was early." Jesus is hauled before Pilate at dawn. And yet this remains the hour of darkness (11:9-10; 12:35-36; 13:30). The dawn which is in this man, and which is about to open at the center of the creation, and in the hearts of human persons, remains hidden.

> The light shines in the darkness, and the darkness did not overcome it... the true light, which enlightens everyone, was coming into the world (1:5.9).

> For this I was born, and for this I came into the world, to testify to the truth. Everyone who belongs to the truth listens to my voice (18:37).

"What is truth?" Pilate does not hear this voice, and consigns the bearer of life to death by crucifixion.

⊕

The center of the chiastic passion narrative is the long account of the trial before Pilate, which is itself a chiasm. The center of this center is the scourging and mockery of Jesus by the Roman soldiers (19:1-3).[16] "Hail, King of the Jews!" they cried, as they struck him in the face. If we conclude that this must be also the theological center of the whole passion account, then we must find a proportionate depth of *meaning* in this mockery of the King of the Jews. Jesus is mocked by the Gentile soldiers with the title of *King of the Jews*, expressing both his complete rejection by the leaders of his own people, and the helplessness, contempt and abuse which he suffers at the hands of the Gentile power. The center of the passion narrative, then, is the *ironic inversion of Jesus' kingship*.

What is the meaning of *"king,"* then, that its inversion should have such a supreme theological weight? Corresponding to the Johannine christology of Word/Wisdom, we should expect the title to relate to *knowledge*, and this is confirmed by Jesus' response to the question of Pilate (18:37). In the context of our fifth day of creation, Jesus' kingship would logically relate to re-*creation* and particularly to *life*. These inferences are supported by Jesus' own description of his *power* at the beginning of his great prayer.

Father, the hour has come; glorify your Son so that the Son may glorify you, since you have given him authority (*exousia*) over all people, to give eternal life to all whom you have given him. And this is eternal *life*, that they may *know* you, the only true God, and Jesus Christ whom you have sent (17:1-3).

Two Kingships, Two Priesthoods

In the course of the fourth and fifth days, and particularly in connection with Jesus' signs worked upon the blind man and upon Lazarus, John has already had opportunity to contrast the two orders of *shepherd* in Israel, represented on the one hand by the chief priests, the scribes and Pharisees, and on the other hand by Jesus. His principal attention here in the passion episode, therefore, is given not to the question of priesthood but to that of *kingship*. Both terms, "king" and "high priest," however, are repeated here by John with significant insistence.[17] The two "powers," or two shepherd roles, must be considered together. The entire prayer at the supper may be seen as an expression of the intercessory mediation between the Father and humanity which is Jesus' *priesthood*. Here we find together the unitive glory which is the object of Jesus' prayer and the "priestly" language of sanctifying or consecration.

Sanctify them in the truth; your word is truth. As you have sent me into the world, so I have sent them into the world. And for their sakes I sanctify myself, that they also may be sanctified in truth (17:17-19).

Both king and priest had a long development in the history of Israel,[18] and the same personage sometimes functioned in both offices. The patriarch ruled his clan as an autocrat and offered sacrifices from his herds and flocks to his God. Moses, in Jewish tradition, was supposed to have been both king and priest.[19] David was king and at times acted as a priest by offering sacrifice. Both shepherds—priest as well as king—were flogged by the prophets for their selfish exploitation of their own position, their abuse of the people's faith.

Both titles can be applied to Jesus only in a transformed sense. As the true shepherd, he is, in his person, the final prophetic judgment on the kings and priests of this world. While the letter to the Hebrews presents Jesus as high Priest, in John, and particularly in the passion narrative, he is most insistently called *King*, with all the irony which this involves.

The ultimate meanings of king and of priest here may be sought either from below—from the fullness of the human vocation as anticipated, for example, in Adam—or from above—the role of Jesus, the creative Word as a human person in the world (see the letter to the Hebrews). These two aspects come into a new relationship as the "royal priesthood" of Jesus is shared by his brothers and sisters in the world.

> But you are a chosen race, a royal priesthood, a holy nation, God's own people... (1 Pet 2:9).

Priesthood and kingship may be seen as two complementary relational aspects of the same being, two forms of the mediation between God and the cosmos which is the vocation of the human person: to be "God in the world." "Adam" as *king* directs, informs all life in the name and in the Word of God. As *priest*, the human person relates life to God in the Spirit of God, facilitating and symbolically representing the interchange of life between heaven and earth. Both functions are present simply in a life of faith, for the world is in oneself; one's body and soul are a microcosm.

> ...present your bodies as a living sacrifice, holy and acceptable to God, which is your spiritual worship (Rom 12:1).

Human life itself is kingship and priesthood, when infused with the life of God which is the Holy Spirit. The bloody sacrifices and the violent domination of the old order must give way to this new and unitive form of human life in which the divine is *immanent* in the individual person.

Jesus unites these two functions in himself as Word incarnate: king and priest by nature, uniting God and created world in one person. In him first of all the Father finds the worship in spirit and in truth which he seeks: a truth which radiates in the world and informs it; a Spirit which unites the world, within its own depths, to God, through the very life of God.

In opposition to this unitive royal priesthood, we encounter here in John *another kingship* and *another priesthood*. The dark priesthood is represented by the *chief priestly family* of Annas and Caiaphas, noted at the time for its corruption.[20] The dark kingship here is Rome, represented by *Pilate*. The Jewish royalty has been suppressed at this time, and the chief priests of the Jews have taken its place under the Roman secular authority.

The dark priesthood becomes definitively evil at the point at which it closes itself to the obvious truth—to the signs and the words and the person itself of Jesus—espouses its blindness with finality, and resolves to extinguish the light by killing Jesus. Then it "hands him over" to the Roman secular authority to be killed. "The chief priests answered, 'We have no king but the emperor'" (19:15), thus definitively rejecting their heritage, "betraying" Jesus into Gentile hands much as Judas had betrayed him into their hands. The underlying choice has not been between Caesar and Christ at this point but between Jesus and Satan, "ruler of this world" (14:30). The dark kingship, wedded to this world and its power, vacillates between truth and expediency and then surrenders Jesus to death out of fear of *Caesar*, the final visible power of this world.

When the chief priests of the Jews hand Jesus over to the Roman authority, the movement *from exodus to creation* is once again symbolically completed. The Wisdom of God, entrusted to Israel, is renounced as Jesus is given over to the mockery of Gentile soldiers. The Word of God, hitherto restricted to the small circle of Israel, is now released into the whole of humanity, the whole of the creation. The temple is definitively profaned, and the presence of God which it had contained is now released into the body of humanity as a whole.

D. The Crucifixion: 19:17-30

The twofold colloquy between the Jews and Pilate, and Pilate and Jesus, concluded when Pilate gave in to the pressure of the Jewish leaders and handed Jesus over to be crucified. As Jesus arrives at Golgotha, the place of execution, the narrative changes in character. It becomes the precise account of a symbolic ritual. We shall find that the symbols of the crucifixion are related very closely to the narrative of Genesis 2–3.

> Again and again the events of the Passion re-state in dark and cruel form the symbols which originally portrayed the joy and innocence of paradise....[21]

Now that Jesus has arrived at his *hour* and at the place of the cross, we are at a cosmic and historical crossing point, at the center. Here the symbols flow together as well, to speak of *one thing*: the unitive gift which is the substance of Jesus' great work. This unitive symbolism begins to emerge at 19:23, when the controversy between Pilate and the Jews has finally concluded and we are left at the cross with Jesus, the soldiers, his mother and the other women, and the beloved disciple.

⊕

The title "King of the Jews," on which Pilate so stubbornly insists, cannot but recall King *David*. The allusions to the Psalms of David in John's narrative strengthen this suggestion and bring to light in the crucifixion account a further development of the *animal* symbolism which belongs to the fifth day. In his passion narrative, John speaks of the fulfillment of prophecies which are contained in two of the psalms traditionally ascribed to David. We must expect, however, that the citation of one or more verses of a psalm may be intended to bring to the gospel narrative the context of the citation as well—that is, the *entire psalm* containing the cited text.

John quotes, from Psalm 22:

> They divided my garments among themselves,
> and for my clothing they cast lots (Ps 22:24; Jn 19:18).

Unlike Matthew and Mark, John has not quoted the opening words of the same psalm:

> My God, my God, why have you forsaken me? (Ps 22:1).

The verse cited by John is surrounded by metaphoric references to different forms of animal life, now appearing in the darkened atmosphere of the passion.

> But I am a worm and not human;
> scorned by others, and despised by the people....
> Many bulls encircle me,
> strong bulls of Bashan surround me;
> they open wide their mouths at me,
> like a ravening and roaring lion....
> For dogs are all around me....
> Deliver my soul from the sword,
> my life from the power of the dog!
> Save me from the mouth of the lion....

From the horns of the wild oxen you have rescued me
(Ps 22:6.12-13.16.20-21).

John refers to Psalm 69 when Jesus, about to die, has said, "I am
thirsty," and the soldiers have given him sour wine (19:28-30).

They gave me poison for food,
and for my thirst they gave me vinegar to drink (Ps 69:21).

It was this psalm to which John referred Jesus' cleansing of the
temple, central place of the ritual animal sacrifices. "It is zeal for your
house that has consumed me..." (Ps 69:9).

When, finally, the psalmist emerges into the light, he confidently
sings,

I will praise the name of God with a song;
I will magnify him with thanksgiving.
This will please the Lord more than an ox
or a bull with horns and hoofs... (Ps 69:30-31).

Here reflected in the person of David who was shepherd, psalmist
and king, Jesus moves through the depths of tribulation and the shedding of his own blood on this fifth day, into the creation of a new worship which supplants the old ritual sacrifices of animals. The roles of
king and priest become inseparable once more in these songs of the
sacrificial Lamb.

The mention of the seamless *tunic* (19:23-24), which is not to be torn,
alludes to the robe which was to be worn by *Aaron* the priest when he
ministered in the sanctuary (Ex 28:32). This robe, "seamless, woven in
one piece from the top," together with the garments of Jesus which
are divided into four parts by the four soldiers, discloses a powerful
geometric symbolism[22] combining universality, in the quaternity of
dimensions, with an integral unity, "originating from above." The
mandalic figure of John's gospel is forcefully made present here at the
place of the cross.

On the *exodus* level, then, the seamless tunic is a high-priestly garment. Here, however, it is *stripped* from the high Priest, as he prepares
for the final sacrifice in which he himself will be the victim, passing
through his own flesh (Heb 10:20) into the sanctuary. On the *creation*

level, it represents the unitive garment of grace or glory which had covered Adam and Eve before they sinned. It is this which was torn from them by their sin, so that "they knew that they were naked" (Gen 3:7) and were afraid, and hid themselves (see Jn 3:19-21). Jesus, in being stripped of this seamless garment, as he had stripped himself at the supper to wash his disciples' feet, descends symbolically into the "nakedness" of the children of Adam. Soon he will be clothed once again in the seamless wedding garment of glory (see Phil 2: 6-11).

⊕

While in the western Christianity of medieval and modern times the crucifix or the cross has become *the* symbol and representation of Christ, the symbolic power of the cross has largely been eclipsed, as we have seen (Part I, Chapter 2 above). As the full meaning of the *resurrection* of Jesus was gradually eclipsed by his passion and death in the west, a parallel transformation took place in the meaning which was attached to the *cross*. The western tradition of intense personal devotion to the passion, with its focus upon the suffering and sacrifice represented by the cross, has not often been sufficiently aware of the "power of God and the wisdom of God" (1 Cor 1:24) which Paul knew in the crucified Jesus,[23] and in the symbolism of the cross itself. The asymmetry of the elongated western cross, whether in the Catholic or the Protestant tradition, expresses this eclipse of the *sapiential* meaning which both the New Testament and patristic authors had found in it.[24] This quaternary symbolism of the cross, of extreme importance in our mandalic interpretation of John, is reinforced here in the crucifixion episode by the other quaternary symbols: the four soldiers and the four portions of clothing.

⊕

If we see in the four soldiers of the crucifixion a representation of universality, the "four corners of the earth," this universality is gathered into unity through the three (or four; exegetes differ) women, who are also *one woman*: for only one feminine name is mentioned: "Mary." Jesus addresses his mother once again as "*woman*," recalling the woman of Genesis 2 and 3 who is Eve, "mother of the living." He addresses her in the same way at the Cana wedding.

Only one male disciple is mentioned as remaining at the cross, and he is mentioned here only in conjunction with this *woman* who is the mother of Jesus. "Woman, here is your son.... Here is your mother." These words imply the inclusion of the beloved disciple into the representative and unitive identity of Jesus himself. "Woman," in addition, carries an overtone of paradise, and of Adam and Eve.

The gift of the mother of Jesus to the disciple corresponds to the one gift which Jesus is to give to his disciples through his death; and here the one gift appears in the feminine person of divine Wisdom, whom Mary represents. These words (19:25-27) will disclose the richness they contain when we pass, very soon, from the fifth to the sixth day. There we shall immediately encounter Jesus and his mother once again, at the wedding feast of Cana. The correspondences between Cana and the cross, which have often been noted,[25] will find a fuller meaning in the context of the mandalic structure of John's gospel.

The Greek words which are translated as "the disciple took her into his own home" (19:27b) strengthen the reference to that woman who, in the scriptures, is the wisdom of God.

> Therefore I determined to take her to live with me, knowing that she would give me good counsel. . . . Because of her I shall have glory among the multitudes. . . . When I enter my house, I shall find rest with her; for companionship with her has no bitterness, and life with her has no pain, but gladness and joy (Wis 8:9-10.16).

So reflects young King Solomon, in the book that bears his name. Then he turns and prays to God the Creator to send wisdom to him that he may rule well, and that he may build the temple according to the divine will.

> You have given command to build a temple on your holy mountain, and an altar in the city of your habitation, a copy of the holy tent that you prepared from the beginning. . . . Send her forth from the holy heavens, and from the throne of your glory send her, that she may labor at my side, and that I may learn what is pleasing to you. For she knows and understands all things, and she will guide me wisely in my actions and guard me with her glory . . . (Wis 9:8.10-11).

As the divine glory dwelt in the temple of Solomon,[26] this divine wisdom is to come down from the opened heavens to dwell in the new temple of Jesus' body, the new holy place. It will be the special gift of the disciple to know this place and to remain there.

The words "from that hour" (19:27) emphasize that this gift of immanent wisdom originates from the *hour* of Jesus which is the moment both of his passion and of his glorification (see 7:38-39). They further suggest that the beloved disciple may anticipate the other disciples in awakening to this immanent fullness.

⊕

When Jesus cries "*I am thirsty*" (19:28; see Mk 10:38; Lk 12:50), these words are to be understood symbolically, and in the light of that which is soon to follow. Jesus has emptied himself (see Phil 2:6-8), and now thirsts for that "*glory*" for which he prayed in John 17. This glory is the divine presence which is to fill the new temple of his body. Jesus will come to possess it precisely in receiving the power to communicate it to others. This gift is most itself in being poured out. This is also the "authority (*exousia*) over all people, to give eternal life..." which is so closely associated with his glory (see 17:1-2). The sour wine which the soldiers give to Jesus on the cross is a travesty, an *ironic inversion*, of the unitive wine of *glory* (recall the central scene of Jesus' mockery by the soldiers) which we shall shortly see poured out symbolically for the wedding guests (2:10-11). This vinegar also represents the sour fruit of the vine which is Israel (see Is 5:1-4; Jer 2:21), or all of humanity, and which contrasts with that wine of the Spirit which Jesus, the "true vine," will soon yield.

⊕

"When Jesus had received the wine, he said, 'It is finished.' Then he bowed his head and *gave up his spirit*" (19:30). These words which John has carefully chosen can signify either "breathed his last" or "gave over the Spirit." Both meanings are intended, and they bring together into one symbolic act the yielding of Jesus' life and the gift of the Holy Spirit which he will breathe into his disciples on the day of his resurrection. As a human life is yielded up, here at the conclusion of the fifth day, the life of God is symbolically poured out.

"Your mother"—the gift of this woman to the disciple whom he most intimately loved, the seamless tunic, the vinegar, the yielding of Jesus' "spirit," and the words of Jesus, "It is finished," *all speak of the same thing*. This is the *one thing* which John knows and wishes to communicate (see 1 Jn 1:1-4; 2:20-25). This inclusive gift, which Jesus explicated at length at the supper, will be further developed in the symbolism of the sixth and seventh days. The blood and water which are to flow from the pierced side of Jesus (19:34) will express the sacramental dimension of this gift and its origination from his crucified and pierced body.

Here at the cross the one gift of Jesus is expressed in a Genesis context, a symbolic representation of the garden where man and woman were together at the tree. Golgotha, the hill of the skull, recalls both that garden and the burial place of Adam.[27] In this somber climate, however, there is no direct indication, hardly a glimmer of light to suggest the new creation which is born at this moment.

"It is finished." "Then he bowed his head and gave up his spirit" (19:30). The final "preparation" (see 19:31.42) of the new temple has been completed, in chiastic symmetry with the temple cleansing which began this fifth day. Jesus had prophesied that the temple of his body would be destroyed and then raised up again. On the seventh day he will breathe the Holy Spirit into the disciples who will constitute this new temple, his enduring body on earth; on the sixth day we shall learn more about the indwelling Spirit which will be the life of this temple.

The Piercing, the Blood and Water

The soldiers break the legs of the men crucified at Jesus' left and right side (19:32). Then they come to Jesus, and pierce his side. A grisly and distorted shadow of the mandala is glimpsed. From the center of this figure there come out not just blood, but blood and water.

Can this which the disciple has seen—Jesus stretched upon the tree of the cross, the piercing of his side with a spear and the outflow of blood and water—have remained the *final and definitive sign* (see 19:34-35), which he has written into the very bones of his gospel, in the mandalic structure?

The whole of 19:31-37 is without counterpart or parallel in the synoptics. John's emphasis on the blood and water (19:34; cf. 1 Jn 5:6-8) suggests that these are symbols containing a profound theological meaning. The variety of interpretations which have been proposed for the flow of blood and water testify that this meaning is not obvious.

Blood, in the Old Testament,[28] represents the *life* of an animal, and is consequently sacred. It is not to be eaten, and is given central importance in sacrificial ritual. According to the prescriptions for Jewish sacrifice, the blood of a sacrificial victim should not be allowed to congeal, but should *flow forth* at the moment of death so that it can be sprinkled.[29] In the letter to the Hebrews, it is the blood of Jesus which gives entrance to the interior sanctuary. In John's vision, this final place of arrival—promised land and garden—is the *place* of divine immanence.

A further Mosaic–exodus resonance of our Johannine passage is the water which flowed from the *rock* which was struck by Moses, to give drink to the Israelites in the wilderness (Num 20:11). This event may also be alluded to in the "living water" references in chapters 4 and 7 of John.[30] Related to this water from the rock is the flow of water from the *temple*, in the prophecy of Ezekiel (Ez 47:1), which is certainly reflected in this Johannine crucifixion text, chiastically related to Jesus' declaration that his body was to become the new temple (2:19-21).

In the second creation account (Gen 2:21-22), Eve was taken from the side of the sleeping Adam. Correspondingly the fathers were inclined to see, in the flow of blood and water, the birth of the church from the side of Jesus, dead upon the cross. This interpretation implies a sudden strange congestion of feminine imagery: from the body of Jesus, become "mother," a woman is born.[31] We have already seen, at the supper, Jesus moving by word and gesture into a more "feminine" mode of expression. We may also recall the coming forth of *Sophia*, the feminine Wisdom, from God before the creation (Prov 8:22-27; Wis 7:25; Sir 24:3).

This *birth* interpretation of the blood and water—both of which flow in the process of natural birth—relates well to the thematic of our fifth day. If John encapsulates the new creation of *living* beings in the birth of this woman, this nicely parallels the Genesis narrative.

The man named his wife Eve [a name related to the Hebrew word for *living*] because she was the mother of all living (Gen 3:20).

The wisdom of God, newly immanent in the world, plays a parallel role in the new creation. This "woman," then, flowing forth from within the body of Jesus, is another expression of the one gift. She will be the life-giving continuation of his own presence.

Another persuasive interpretation, adopted by Brown,[32] and based on 1 John 5:6-8, sees the *water* as representing the *baptism of John*, which did not yet confer the Holy Spirit (see 1:31). Only when Jesus had shed his *blood* could the Spirit be given, and in the flow of blood and water John signifies that this Spirit can now be poured out. Through the death of Jesus, this principle of life that comes from above, the "living water," is given, as a source of life for all who believe in him. One of the sayings of the desert fathers extends this interpretation into the life of the disciple: "Give blood and receive Spirit."[33]

Another sacramental interpretation,[34] perhaps the most plausible and profound of all, sees the water as signifying Christian *baptism*, and the blood as denoting the *eucharist*. These two sacraments are deeply woven into the symbolism of John's gospel, as we shall see. A second century author refers to "the twofold cleansing of water and blood, *word and spirit*."[35] Other, similar, overtones of this symbolic pair are light and life, faith and love, birth and death. These various parallels are further expressions of that one *progression* which is the inner movement of John's gospel. The first letter expresses the same progression in terms of light and love.

The Sword and the Cup

When Jesus was about to be arrested in the garden, Peter attempted to defend him: he struck out with his sword and cut off the ear of one of the high priest's servants. Then Jesus turned to Peter and said, "Put your sword back into its sheath; am I not to drink the cup that the Father has given me?" (18:11).

Goettmann[36] sees a pivotal symbolic contrast in these words:

The weapon of the Savior is *the cup*, the cup of the New Covenant, cup of sorrows and of joys, that of the wine of friendship and that of the blood given.... The contrast between the masculine symbol of the sword, sign of separation, and the feminine symbol of the cup, sign of communion, underlies this passage of John's Gospel. It is already present in the Song of Songs and in the visions of the Apocalypse.

We have observed Jesus' symbolic passage from masculine to feminine when, repeating Mary's gesture, he washed the feet of his disciples (a service which *Peter* refused!) and moved into the language of love and of indwelling which filled his supper discourse. His words to Peter in 18:11 express this same transition symbolically, with a brilliant clarity.

Peter and the beloved disciple are continually presented in a comparative way. Peter, the rough-hewn "masculine" figure, is consistently more distant from Jesus than is the disciple, who rests upon Jesus' bosom and communicates intimately with him. Peter, ultimately, will be told to *follow* his Master, while the disciple is to *remain* (21:19-22). The disciple has already, with Jesus, made the passage from a "masculine" dualism or separation-consciousness, which Peter must still make by following Jesus to his death. This comparison between Peter and the disciple, in terms of a masculine-feminine polarity,[37] is evident here in the passion episode. Peter remains outside the high priest's court, until the disciple brings him in by speaking to the *girl* at the door. Peter denies his Lord at the question of a *woman*, a serving maid (18:17). While the disciple remains at the cross with the women, Peter has apparently fled with the other disciples. Finally, to the disciple will be given the *mother* of Jesus. To Peter will later (21:15-17) be entrusted the sheep. The consistent intimacy between the disciple and Jesus, as it is contrasted with the tormented variability of Peter's relationship with his Lord, parallels the positive instances of the disciple's relations with women which John has given us.

Jesus' exterior garments are divided among the *four soldiers*; these men represent the outside world which does not receive the light. The women (three or four in number) may represent, in contrast, the interior world, the disciples who are gifted with the interior sight of faith, the feminine heart of humanity which does receive the light. As we shall see on the sixth day, these women are related to the four rivers which flowed from paradise in Genesis (Gen 2:10-14), and to the four women who mark the four poles of the mandalic figure. More immediately, these sorrowing women reflect the interior process that is taking place in Jesus himself. He is about to give birth from his side, as Adam gave birth to Eve. The sorrowing women are participating in this painful labor with Jesus: they have been able to remain and go through the whole process with him. Woman *"remains"* in John's gospel: it is Magdalene who perseveres at the empty tomb until Jesus appears. The men, meanwhile, go and come, flee and return—even die and come back to life.

The Disciple Whom Jesus Loved

The disciple is the first to experience the divine birth, to awaken as a "child of God" (1:12). He is presented as the realized child of the new creation in whom masculine and feminine, human and divine, have been reconciled. Thus he dwells already at the center, the heart of the mandala. Peter continues to walk behind his Master along the surface, the periphery of the figure, history's way of the cross. The disciple has merely to *remain* at this point where the birth has taken place: it is, as it were, the bosom of the incarnate Word, of Jesus (see 1:38; 20:8;

1:51). It can be said that the essential message of John's gospel and the secret of the Johannine mandala is the knowledge of *this place* which is the center.[38]

The event—and experience—of being *"begotten of God"* is central to John's vision (see Jn 1:12.18; 1 Jn 2:29; 3:9; 4:7; 5:1.4.18). The disciple rests "in the bosom" of Jesus as the Son reposes in the bosom of the Father (Jn 13:23; 1:18). The disciple, therefore, represents those persons who are born anew through faith in Jesus—born precisely *in* Jesus. To this corresponds the significance of the "beginning" for John. The disciple knows the place of birth and the moment before time when it occurs. He knows the beginning and the Word that is in the beginning. The wisdom, the *knowledge* of John, which he communicates in his gospel, would then be simply the consciousness or knowledge emanating from this reality, this fact, of the birth in God, which corresponds to Christian *baptism*.

E. The Burial: 19:31–42

Jesus is buried in a *garden* with a huge quantity of *spices*. Both the garden and the spices suggest the burial of a *king*.[39] John's account of the passion has accentuated the kingly identity of Jesus, and throughout the narrative of his trial, his mockery by the soldiers and his crucifixion, this royalty has been garbed in the darkest irony. As the burial account which concludes this tragic narrative returns us, in chiastic fashion, to a *garden*, recalling the garden where Jesus was arrested, we are given subtle suggestions awakening the fragrance of another, quite different, world which is about to appear.

John has been careful to tell us (18:1) that Jesus crossed the *Kidron* with his disciples to enter the garden where he would be arrested. This brook, which runs between the old city of Jerusalem and the Mount of Olives, mentioned nowhere else in the New Testament, was crossed by the aged King *David* in flight from the forces of Absalom (2 Sam 15).

> The whole country wept aloud as all the people passed by; the king crossed the Wadi Kidron.... But David went up the ascent of the Mount of Olives, weeping as he went, with his head covered; and all the people who were with him covered their heads and went up, weeping as they went. David was told that Ahithophel was among the conspirators with Absalom (2 Sam 15:23.30-31).

This strange procession prefigures, in a quasi-ritual manner, the prelude to Jesus' passion. Ahithophel will play exactly the role of Judas, in betraying David, and then will hang himself. Absalom will be killed in the battle which follows. David will actually, at the end of his life, choose *Solomon*, Bathsheba's child, to succeed him on the throne.

Solomon—his name means *peace* (see Jn 14:27; 16:33; 20:19.21.26) —the much-married son of David, is the proverbial *wise man* of the Old Testament. John subtly uses Solomon to bring the passion and death of Jesus into the *sapiential* context which is proper to his gospel. We are to think of Jesus as David, the departing king of Israel, who is to be succeeded by this "wise man" for whom the great nuptial Song of the Bible is named.

A garden locked is my sister, my bride,
A garden locked, a fountain sealed.
Your shoots are an orchard of pomegranates
With all choicest fruits...
With all trees of frankincense, *myrrh and aloes*,
With all chief spices—
A garden fountain, a well of living water,
And flowing streams from Lebanon (Song of Solomon 4:12-15).

The great quantity of *myrrh and aloes* with which, John tells us, Jesus has been buried, recalling the Song of Solomon, is another hint of the *bride* whom we shall encounter on the sixth day, and of the nuptial climate which will surround the Johannine expression of Jesus' resurrection. The garden of the Song, with its graces, reflects the garden of the new creation to which we shall soon be introduced.

Solomon built the *temple* of the Lord at Jerusalem. This king was the lover of divine wisdom who prayed,

O God of my ancestors and Lord of mercy, who have made all things by your word, and by your wisdom have formed humankind to have dominion over the creatures you have made, and rule the world in holiness and righteousness, and pronounce judgment in uprightness of soul, give me the *wisdom* that sits by your throne... (Wis 9:1-4a).

In Solomon, the kingly vocation of Adam in the world is symbolically fulfilled. The wedding of masculine and feminine, and of a human person with the divine glory, already manifest in King

David, is symbolically brought to fullness. Solomon, the man of peace, represents the complete king, in whom power is wedded to wisdom. The work of Jesus, the new Solomon, has been to build the temple in which this feminine wisdom of God is to dwell. Closing the chiastic ring of the fifth day, we recall the words of Jesus in the temple, "Destroy this temple, and in three days I will raise it up." The new temple will be a *living body*, the body of Jesus himself. The Word, become flesh to dwell among humans, will now be present also as the gentle lady wisdom, the bride, the glory, the Spirit, the life which dwells within the human temple which is the center of the new creation.

$$\oplus$$

We have observed *two great movements* in John's passion account. In conformity with the mandalic pattern of the gospel as a whole, they can be described geometrically. The *vertical* axis consists of the ironic ascent of Jesus into glory through humiliation, mocking, his death and burial in the earth. Jesus rises into his place—the final unitive condition of divine humanity—through his descent as seed into the ground. This paradoxical movement is expressed in the doubly ironic "lifting up" in John's account.

The *horizontal* axis represents the movement of Word and Spirit outward from Jerusalem, from Judaism, from Israel, to the whole world. Jesus, finally rejected as "King of the Jews," is manifested as creative Word and Lord of the universe (see 6:15 and 6:20). The irony persists through this transition, which takes place in the darkness of treachery and humiliation. Jesus is again betrayed by his own, as he is handed over to the Gentiles. These will in turn mock and crucify him; the non-Jewish peoples are not to be drawn to him until the seed has fallen into the ground (see 12:20-24; 12:32). From this seed will spring forth the tree of life which is the continuing presence of Jesus in the world: reaching from earth to heaven and outward to the ends of the earth.

The two traditionally masculine roles of king and of priest have both returned to their universality in the figure of the new Adam, in whom they are united also with the "woman": divine Wisdom. Jesus has become identified with King David, and then with Solomon, the bridegroom of Wisdom. As high Priest, Jesus has identified himself with the lamb of sacrifice and finally with the temple, the habitation of God with humanity. The feminine Wisdom whom

Solomon fervently seeks as his bride is also the divine presence which will dwell in the new temple of the body of Jesus, when he has come into his glory. It is this divine Feminine, bringing humanity to its fullness by dwelling within it, which will generate the sixth day of the new creation.

THE FIFTH DAY: SYNTHETIC REVIEW

Our fifth day of the new creation is the day of *life*, but this life has been consistently manifested under the cloak of irony, and in conflict with a principle of *death*. The ambiguous relation between religion and life has polarized into the struggle between a religion of power—become a religion of death—and the power of life which has appeared in Jesus. The forms of animal life, conceived as created on the fifth day, have been developed by John into a symbolic complex which serves as language for this dramatic struggle between the forces of life and of death. Sheepfold and temple, shepherd, king and priest, are drawn into this development and become polarized across the boundary of this conflict.

In the four great episodes of the fifth day there emerges another microcosm of the mandalic figure of the entire fourth gospel (see Figure 2.2). They constitute a cruciform figure based in the Jerusalem temple with its animal sacrifices, and with its apex in the new temple, the body of Jesus lifted up on the tree. The right arm is constituted by the reversal of the exodus plague upon the Gentiles, with the bringing to life of the royal firstborn. The left arm is the reversal of the plague of legalistic perversion and homicidal infidelity which has weighed upon the Jewish people in the person of their priesthood and custodians of the law, with the bringing to life of the "son of Aaron."

The journey of the fifth day, on which we accompany Jesus up this symbolic tree, is a passage from the juridical and mediated religion of the temple, the religion of the first exodus and the Mosaic *Torah*, to the immediate union of humanity with God in the risen body of Jesus. Fruit of the process of divine incarnation, this deification of humanity constitutes the new creation. Contained within this greater movement is the lesser movement along the horizontal axis—now from left to right—in which this new and immediate union which is in Jesus breaks through the confines of Jewish religion and reaches out to all the nations, and even to the limits of the material cosmos.

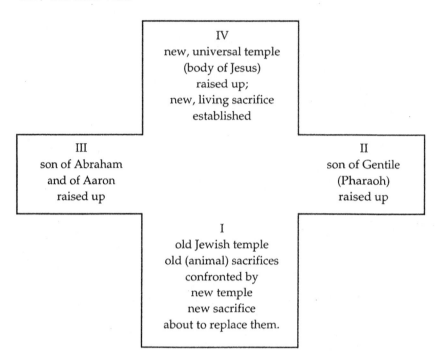

FIGURE 2.2 CHIASTIC STRUCTURE OF THE FIFTH DAY

This movement of the fifth day is embodied in a complex play and interplay of symbolism, as we have seen. The *animal* theme of Genesis becomes the shepherd, sheep and sheepfold theme of John 10, and *shepherd* becomes differentiated into *priest* and *king*, in the Jewish and Gentile worlds which confront one another across the horizontal axis of our figure. As the true realization of each of these two roles begins to emerge in Jesus, the corresponding negative distortion comes clearly into the light—embodied in the Jewish chief priests and in Pilate, the soldiers, and the Roman power which they represent.

Repeatedly, in the course of the fifth day, the reality of *human power*, human authority, emerges in contrast and opposition to the theme of *life*: whether in the Jerusalem temple and its officials and guards, in the royal official who cannot give life to his son, in the Jewish officials who plan to kill both Jesus and Lazarus, or in the high priestly clan and the Roman procurator who do finally crucify Jesus. In contrast to this world of human power stands the Lamb, who does not defend himself because his kingdom is not of this world—and because he must die so that it may be born within this world.

The relation between the passion account and the gospel as a whole is quite different in the synoptic gospels, on the one hand, and in the fourth gospel, on the other. Through its mandalic inner structure and its language of symbolic correspondences, John's gospel *centers itself*[40] in the death and resurrection of Jesus, and in the figure of Jesus upon the cross. Events which, on the narrative level, *precede* Jesus' passion (e.g. the signs of Cana and of Lazarus) reappear on the mandalic-symbolic level as *fruits* of this passion. While John's narrative ends, much like the synoptics, with a series of fugitive appearances of the risen Jesus, the fourth gospel comes to a much fuller resolution upon the mandalic level through the symbolism of the sixth and seventh days of the new creation. Jesus' departure in death will quickly be succeeded by a new fullness of interior presence, expressed both in the centered geometry and in the biblical symbolism of this gospel.

Jesus has now accomplished his *"exodus* at Jerusalem" (Lk 9:31). This new exodus, of the fifth day, from the religous world which had been circumscribed by the first exodus and the Mosaic code, is simultaneously a new creation. It is, paradoxically, a going out into oneness, an exodus not of separation but of immediate union. Jesus' new exodus of union contrasts with the first exodus, therefore, just as Jesus' new unitive creation contrasts with the first creation which took place through a series of separations.[41]

The *body of Jesus*, which concentrates within itself the new creation, becomes the great symbol[42] into which flow a series of biblical images, now that his hour has arrived. At the central place of the tree, all the words and images once again rejoin the original Word and become one reality. Identified with the tree to which it is joined, the body of Jesus is burning bush and tree of life. It becomes the ark of Noah which carries all life within itself through the waters of death. It is temple and house, blood-sprinkled Passover door and door of the sheepfold and itself the sheepfold and living temple. The unitive reality of the Word—one with this body—gathers both the symbols, and then the human and cosmic realities which they represent, into the same body.

Like the ritual observances of the first Covenant, John's symbols "...are only a shadow of what is to come, but the substance belongs to Christ" (Col 2:17). "For in him the whole fullness of deity dwells bodily, and you have come to fullness in him..." (Col 2:9-10). At the end of the fifth day we stand at the opened doorway of this immanent plenitude. As the sixth and seventh days proceed, John will continue to weave his symbolic language, like a living vestment, around the same invisible fullness.

"*Your son lives!*" These words of Jesus to the *basilikos*, echoing Elijah's words to the widow of Zareptha, return to gather up the events of the fifth day. They are spoken to King David as well as to Pharaoh, to the Gentiles as well as the Jews. They are spoken to the mother of Jesus from the cross: "Woman, behold your son." And so they are spoken to the first man and woman, to Adam and to Eve, who transmitted to all their children a life tainted by death. The Son of Man lives, for he is Son of God, for he *is*. When Jesus brings back the *basilikos'* child from the door of death, *at a distance*, he is King David who departs to return in his own son and successor, Solomon. He is also Adam, the father of humanity, who dies to rise again in the Son of Man, now filled with the glory which is his bride. Adam will wake from his sleep to receive his "helper," like to him, the woman who is the Wisdom of God. It is she who will now be his life. In this way John will bring the biblical symbolism together in a final marriage feast—a banquet of wisdom—expressing the fullness of human life.

Chapter Six

The Sixth Day:
In the Image of God He Created Them

So God created humankind in his image,
in the image of God he created them;
male and female he created them.

God blessed them, and God said to them, "Be fruitful and multiply, and fill the earth and subdue it..." (Gen 1:27-28).

The man gave names to all cattle, and to the birds of the air, and to every animal of the field; but for the man there was not found a helper as his partner. So the Lord God caused a deep sleep to fall upon the man, and he slept; then he took one of his ribs and closed up its place with flesh. And the rib that the Lord God had taken from the man he made into a woman and brought her to the man. Then the man said,

"This at last is bone of my bones
and flesh of my flesh;
this one shall be called Woman,
for out of Man this one was taken."

Therefore a man leaves his father and his mother and clings to his wife, and they become one flesh (Gen 2:20-24).

...grace and truth came through Jesus Christ (Jn 1:17b).

The sixth day brings a plenitude. In the account of Genesis 1, God completed his work of creation on this day by making man and woman in his own likeness. John transforms this imagery of man and woman and their union into an expression of the fullness of humanity which blossoms from the death and resurrection of Jesus. The mandalic form of the gospel also comes into its fullness here on the sixth day.

⊕

The *transition* from the fifth to the sixth day moves through an extreme contrast—from the crucifixion and burial of Jesus to the wedding feast of Cana, and from Judea to Galilee. From the sacrificial death of the paschal Lamb we pass immediately to a symbolic representation of the Lamb's wedding feast (see Rev 19:6-9).

SECTION 16: 2:1-12
THE WEDDING AT CANA

I

On the third day there was a wedding at Cana of Galilee, and the mother of Jesus was there... (2:1).

This is the most extreme change of scene that we have experienced. From the horror of the crucifixion and the sorrow of the burial of Jesus, we find ourselves suddenly transported to a village wedding, a scene of celebration. In the narrative order of John's gospel this Cana wedding feast is the "sabbath" which concludes the first week of the new creation.[1] In our mandalic scheme it follows immediately upon the final dramatic crisis of the passion. In either case, it is the *symbolic* meaning of Cana that will be decisive. The time indication which begins the narrative is our first key to this symbolism: the *third day* after Jesus' death is the day of *resurrection*.[2] Jesus' resurrection is first represented by a *wedding*, and this sets the tone for the whole of the sixth day. Each of the four episodes of this day is to be interpreted in a nuptial sense.

The Cana story does not occur in Matthew, Mark or Luke. Its flavor and its meaning are peculiarly Johannine. Cana, the first sign of Jesus, like the prologue and the baptism of Jesus, offers a key of interpretation to the whole of the fourth gospel. The mother of Jesus is mentioned first and singularly among the guests; she is the *woman* who presides at the entrance of the sixth day. This shall be the day of woman, of the revelation of the inner meaning of the feminine.

"When the wine gave out..." These words bear a weight of feeling. One imagines the pain attending such an embarrassment at the great event in the lives of these two poor people. The words resonate on other levels, too. They express something of the profound and manifold sorrow of the human condition. The wine is always giving out. And as the day wears on, we are more and more aware that we cannot replenish it from our own resources. The narrative does not linger with this situation, however, but moves quickly on to the interaction between the woman and the man. There is no mention at this point of the actual bride and groom, but only of Jesus and his mother.

"...the mother of Jesus said to him, 'They have no wine.'" Mary's words are touching both in the compassion they express and in their simplicity. "Woman, what concern is that to you and to me? My hour has not yet come." The various translations from the Greek all express a certain coldness on the part of Jesus. Commentators have written much about this apparent distancing of Jesus both from his mother and from the predicament of their hosts, and also about the possible symbolic meanings of his words. The "distancing"—at this moment— indicates that the fulfillment which is to be symbolized here at the Cana wedding is yet to come. When Jesus' *hour* has come—and in the mandalic order it has now arrived—the eschatological union—both wedding and wine—which is the ultimate *concern* both of Jesus and of this woman (2:4) will be consummated and poured out.

"Do whatever he tells you." Mary plays a double mediating role here, with her words first to Jesus and then to the servants. And yet she adds nothing, brings nothing new—only the inclination of union, which is herself. These simple words to the servants reach, once again, far beyond the concrete situation.

"Now standing there were six stone water jars for the Jewish rites of purification..." We have arrived at the sixth day, and the stone vessels of Israel are full of water. The painful history, the exodus journey through the purifying desert, has been completed and it is time to enter the promised land of Canaan, to bring the ark to ground upon the fertile earth, to drink the fruit of the vine (see Gen 9:20).

The number six signifies the human measure in its natural fullness; that is, the day of man created in the image of God, created king of the universe. It is the number of the first Gen-

esis that the Lord takes up in order to transform it into the
new Genesis under the sign of the seventh day.[3]

These six stone jars, standing there "for the Jewish rites of purification," are multiple in meaning.[4] Their number would ordinarily, in
the biblical usage, signify incompletion upon the threshold of the perfect seven. The seventh, however, this sabbath which is about to be
born in the water, is transcendent, and does not add another vessel.
The sabbath is already here, anticipated on the sixth day, when Jesus
appears at the wedding. Now past are the six days of the week upon
which labor must be done: days of purification, days of penance, ages
of history preceding its consummation, and days of Jesus' labor of
new creation which have led through the cross.

"Now draw some out, and take it to the chief steward." And
when the servants did what Jesus had told them, the water had
become wine. Though we have moved quickly to symbolic meanings,
one can dwell at length within this scene itself, feeding upon its inner
fullness.

"The steward called the bridegroom and said to him, 'Everyone
serves the good wine first... but you have kept the good wine until
now.'" This inversion of order parallels the relation between the
Moses and Jesus, the revelation and religion of the Jews and Jesus, the
Baptist and Jesus. The Son of Man comes late in the day, arrives late
at the wedding, bearing hidden within himself the fullness, the creative fire, of the true beginning. In this fire each thing ripens to its
own fullness.

"Jesus did this, the first of his signs, at Cana of Galilee, and revealed his glory..." This first sign of Jesus, like most of the signs
which are to follow, is at once the filling of a human need and a manifestation of divine glory. Here the joy of a bride and bridegroom, of
two poor families and their friends, is saved and saved grandly with
this abundance of "the good wine." The upwelling of celebration, the
gratuitous gladness of this *first* sign, is expressive of Jesus' final and
definitive sign: the resurrection. Cana expresses the resurrection of
Jesus as *participated* in by men and women.

In this first sign the *need itself* which is met is the need for *glory*,
for the joy which is the crown of love, of the union of man and
woman, the inner chamber and tender secret of human life which is a
direct participation and expression of divine Spirit, divine glory. "So
God created humankind in his own image, in the image of God he
created them; male and female he created them" (Gen 1:27). Here we
are close to that tree which stood in the middle of the garden (Gen

3:3). In the place where glory disappeared into shame, and man and woman covered their bodies and hid themselves from the light, the glory breaks forth once again.

The thing not strictly necessary, the gratuitous thing, the excess which is grace itself, is the essential thing for a life which is truly human. As the stone which the careful builders rejected becomes the cornerstone, so also the beauty, the enchantment of *eros*, the grace of the garden which seems a final crowning touch, the glory of God which is reserved for the final feast, is the indispensable seed without which there is no life. Here on the sixth day we encounter the intimate and mysterious interrelation of spirituality and sexuality.

"Jesus did this, the first of his signs... and revealed his glory; and his disciples believed in him." The wine itself expresses this *glory* which Jesus begins to manifest here. "And the Word became flesh and lived among us, and we have seen his glory, the glory as of the Father's only Son, full of grace and truth." The final verses (1:14-18) of John's prologue open up the symbolic depths of the Cana sign. Here, against the background of Mosaic religion and John's baptism of water, is the pouring forth of the glory of the Son, in which is communicated the wedding of grace and truth.

The Cana sign, like the prologue, is a full recapitulation of John's gospel. The whole coming and dwelling and pouring out of the unitive Word in the world is embodied in this narrative. The fusion of symbols which we experienced in the crucifixion scene is continued here as woman, wine and wedding merge to express the same reality, the one gift.

II

Fyodor Dostoyevsky has understood deeply the meaning of the wedding of Cana and its relationship to resurrection. In his novel *The Brothers Karamazov*, the brief chapter, "Cana of Galilee," and the whole account of Father Zossima, carry with them the taste of the new wine, a tender and ecstatic love which is the fruit and experience of the resurrection of Jesus. This wisdom belongs to the tradition of eastern Christianity.

In the novel, the gospel of Cana marks a point of death and new birth. It is read over the dead body of Father Zossima, the elder monk who was the spiritual father of Alyosha, the youngest Karamazov brother around whom this narrative revolves. During the reading of this gospel Alyosha falls into a reverie in which he finds himself present at the wedding feast and meets Father Zossima there, his eyes shining, rejoicing with the guests. Alyosha awakens, walks out into the night and, in a sudden ecstasy, experiences the unity of heaven and earth, of matter and the Spirit. In what seems to be an initiation into the fullness of the Holy Spirit by the old monk, Alyosha comes suddenly into his manhood, filled with conviction and strength. "He had fallen on the earth a weak boy, but he rose up a resolute champion...."[5]

The author has seen the Cana wedding and its sign as the bridge between one life and another. In this fullness of the Holy Spirit Alyosha tastes the wine of Cana. The spiritual father is, as it were, alive once again in his disciple. The disciple, however, is free in his new strength, and leaves the monastery for the world as his teacher had foretold. Alyosha seems a reincarnation of the beloved disciple, who himself incarnates anew the Word which has come in his Teacher.

When, in our mandalic interpretation of John, we find the Cana wedding and its sign immediately after the passion account, we are firmly directed toward a *sapiential* and *nuptial* interpretation of Jesus' resurrection—through a symbolic of wedding, of woman, of wine. The wedding feast of Cana is, symbolically, the obverse of the death upon the cross which Jesus had spoken of as inseparable from his glory. The wine which Jesus brings forth at Cana flows directly from the piercing of his side upon the cross, and the issue of blood and water. In that hour of his final suffering, Jesus was finally united with the "woman," and there was generated the son who *lives* (see Jn 4:50) anew in the beloved disciple.

Portentous enunciation, syllable
To blessed syllable affined, and sound
Bubbling felicity in cantilene,
Prolific and tormenting tenderness
Of music, as it comes to unison....[6]

⊕

The symbolic harmonics of the changing of the water to wine are numerous: from law to gospel, prophecies to fulfillment, law to wisdom; from exterior truth to an interior and experiential truth. Paul speaks of the passage from law to grace, to freedom, to faith, to Spirit, from letter to Spirit, from dead works to living faith, from exterior to interior, from shadow to substance. From religion on a predominantly ritual and institutional level, we pass to the grace of Christ; from a dualistic and mediated relationship with God to the immediate union of God and the human person; from revelation to incarnation. John's thought leads us continually from the first creation to a new creation which is *unitive*. The wine is this incarnation, this new creation, communicated to humanity—poured out and participated in by human persons.

Melchizedek, that mysterious priest-king who made an offering of bread and wine to God on behalf of Abraham (Gen 14:18), was seen by Philo of Alexandria as the *"priest-logos."* C.H. Dodd interprets the Johannine wine of Cana according to Philo's view of the wine-offering of Melchizedek.

> Thus the *wine* which the Priest-logos brings forth ... stands for God's gifts of grace, joy, virtue, wisdom, and the like; in fact for all those things which for Philo characterize the higher or spiritual life. We may therefore recognize in it an apt symbol for all that the Fourth Evangelist conceives Christ to have brought into the world—without for the present defining it further....
>
> ...What then is the *water* which is replaced by this wine of God? The evangelist has given us a hint when he says that the waterpots were there (for the purifications of the Jews). They stand for the entire system of Jewish ceremonial observance—and by implication for religion on that level, wherever it is found, as distinguished from religion upon the level of *aletheia* (truth) (see 4:23-24). Thus the first of signs already symbolizes the doctrine that (the law was given through Moses, but grace and truth have come about through Jesus Christ) (1:17).[7]

The wine is the very marriage itself, the transformative union,[8] rendered communicable, poured out for people to drink. It is the wine of final union. While this has a *eucharistic* ring, it also corresponds symbolically to the action of Jesus which will soon follow on the seventh day: his *baptism* of his disciples in the Holy Spirit: the solemn conferral of this new divine immanence.

⊕

She is the sunrise in the blood,
Sweet inner resurrection.

The *woman*, who had been taken from Adam's side as he slept, was then brought to Adam to be received as his partner or helper (Gen 2:18), and to receive her name. Jesus has risen from the sleep of death, and at Cana we are given a glimpse of the *glory* which he now receives (see 2:11)—both in the *woman* with whom he is symbolically united now that his hour has come, and in the *wine* which he pours out for the guests. The woman will receive her name, *Mary*, in the matching episode concluding this sixth day. Cana is the ritual celebration of this union, and the symbolic sharing of it with those who believe in him.

If the Cana episode symbolically represents the resurrection, and therefore recapitulates the whole movement and the final fullness of John's gospel, we must give special attention to the *woman*, the "mother of Jesus," whom we encountered at the threshold of this narrative, and who initiated Jesus' action. The fullness which is present in the mother of Jesus is very subtly rendered in John. The fullness which arrived, in and through a woman, in the birth of Jesus, was the anticipated presence of the fullness which has now come through his second birth in the hour of his resurrection: a birth which is to be experienced by those who receive him (see 1:12).

Jesus and his mother are the man and the woman who stand in the place of bridegroom and bride at this wedding. The Baptist had spoken of Jesus as the *bridegroom* (3:29). It is less clear who, ultimately, is this *bride*. Since *Israel*, the people of God, is frequently figured as "bride" of the Lord in the Hebrew scriptures (see Is 50:1; Hos 2:4-9), Christian interpreters have naturally seen the *church*, the "new Israel," in this bride. Spiritual writers have seen the bride also as the individual *person*, and conceived the spiritual life in terms of a nuptial relationship between the Word of God and the "soul." The bride of the Word may also be seen as *humanity* as a whole, or even, in some sense, the *cosmos* itself.

⊕

Another possible interpretation, though radically different, is not incompatible with these traditional ones. It opens up a perspective which is of urgent importance for our own time. Originating in the wisdom literature of the Bible, and developed by Jewish interpreters,[9] it is hardly to be found in the orthodox Christian tradition. Beyond that bride which is the church and the person—and dwelling within both of them—the ultimate bride of the Word is *Sophia, the wisdom of God*, the divine Feminine. For John, this immanent divine wisdom is practically equivalent to the *glory* of Jesus (see also Paul in 1 Cor 2).

The bride of God and of the Word is this eternal Feminine which is the divine *Spirit*. Jesus comes into the world to "baptize with the Holy Spirit" (1:33)—as a man, to win and to impart this "woman" who, in the language of the fathers,[10] completes the "image" of God which is humanity. Again, the true bride and the wine are one. Mary, the mother of Jesus, is the creature, the woman, in whom the wine of *Sophia* becomes incarnate, becomes flesh and blood, then to remain in the world as church, body of Christ. This sophianic wine, the divine–human Feminine, is the inner music of John, a golden thread which has remained almost entirely concealed throughout the subsequent history of Christianity—shining out for a moment from time to time from within the more sapiential currents of our tradition.[11]

⊕

Hagia Sophia in all things is the Divine Life reflected in them, considered as a spontaneous participation, as their invitation to the Wedding Feast.

Sophia is God's sharing of Himself with creatures. His out-pouring, and the Love by which He is given, and known, held and loved.

She is in all things like the air receiving the sunlight. In her they prosper. In her they glorify God. In her they rejoice to reflect Him. In her they are united with Him. She is the union between them. She is the Love that unites them. She is life as communion, life as thanksgiving, life as festival, life as glory.

Because she receives perfectly there is in her no stain. She is love without blemish, and gratitude without self-complacency. All things praise her by being themselves and sharing in the Wedding Feast. She is the Bride and the Feast and the Wedding.[12]

The beauty of this story of the wedding at Cana is not only literary. The little narrative corresponds perfectly with the truth, the inner reality, which it represents, like a wineskin which is one life with its contents. Transition from emptiness to fullness, from flatness to exuberance, from servitude to freedom, from image to reality—the symbolic overtones of this sign are as endless as the variations on a primary musical theme. Though John says nothing of music at this wedding, it was surely there. John's Cana narrative is itself music. This overture to the sixth day, on which God perfects his work of new creation, rises like a Mozart theme, soaring, tender and full. As the water became wine, simple human words break into a fullness which is feast and music as well. The union and the dance of grace and truth are embodied here in the marriage of image and meaning which itself expresses the new creation.

⊕

After the weight, the constriction of heart, the excess of darkness through which the passion narrative led us, the sixth day is experienced as a liberation, an emergence into the freshness of a new land. We have come from Judea into *Galilee* once again—a Galilee which now represents the garden of the new creation. The change is much more radical than we may think: there is a hint of this in the symbolism with which the transition is expressed. There is a dionysian wildness, an "excess" implicit both in wine and in *eros*, in human sexuality, which intimates something of the world which we are entering. The "linearity" of our journey up to this point—even through the planetary days of creation on the mandalic figure—gives way to a different movement, a blossoming upon the completed stem. John's poetry, as he further unfolds the mystery of Cana in the successive episodes of the sixth day, will express this new movement of life.

SECTION 17: 4:4-42
THE WOMAN AT THE WELL

Jesus passes through Samaria. Immediately following the Cana narrative, this is another abrupt change of scene—from Jesus' home locale to a strange land, from the mother of Jesus and the local wedding celebration, with its suggestion of innocence, to this lone woman, a stranger, who has had a wide-ranging past.

The account of Jesus' meeting with the Samaritan woman at the well (ch. 4) brings us quickly in touch with outer *limits*. We have come into the locality of a religious tradition hostile to Judaism, and this woman's apparent sexual promiscuity corresponds to the religious deviation of the Samaritans.[13] When Jesus asks this woman for a drink, the young rabbi himself steps outside the bounds of conventional religion; what John is suggesting, however, goes further than this.

"Jacob's well was there." This *well* will remain, as dominant image, in the background of the dialogue which follows. The well, and the meeting of man and woman at the well, are archetypal motifs. They also have a biblical background which is one key to the understanding of our story. There are several meetings at wells in the Old Testament which are related to espousals and marriages: the servant of Abraham finds a bride for Abraham's son Isaac at a spring (Gen 24:42-67); at the well Jacob encounters Rachel, who becomes his wife (Gen 29:9-30); and it is at a well that Moses meets Zipporah, the daughter of the priest of Midian, whom he soon marries (Ex 2:15-21).

The scene of Jesus' meeting with the Samaritan woman is, then, implicitly a *nuptial* one, despite her past marital adventures and present illicit union. This is *Jacob's* well, and it is probably to the story of Jacob and Rachel that we are referred here. The story follows immediately upon Jacob's dream at Bethel.

Then Jacob went on his journey, and came to the land of the people of the east. As he looked, he saw a well in the field and three flocks of sheep lying there beside it; for out of that well the flocks were watered. The stone on the well's mouth was large, and when all the flocks were gathered there, the shepherds would roll the stone from the mouth of the well, and water the sheep...

The shepherds tell Jacob that they are from Haran, and they point out to him the daughter of his kinsman, Laban, coming toward the well:

"...and here is his [Laban's] daughter Rachel, coming with the sheep." He said, "Look, it is still broad daylight; it is not time for the animals to be gathered together. Water the sheep, and go, pasture them." But they said, "We cannot until all the flocks are gathered together, and the stone is rolled from the mouth of the well; then we water the sheep."

When Rachel came with her father's sheep,

Jacob went up and rolled the stone from the well's mouth, and watered the flock of his mother's brother Laban. Then Jacob kissed Rachel, and wept aloud. And Jacob told Rachel that he was her father's kinsman, and that he was Rebekah's son; and she ran and told her father (Gen 29:1-12).

Jacob and Rachel meet at the well at midday, before the gathering of the flocks. He removes the stone, waters her flocks, and kisses her, and they will become man and wife. When Jesus rises from the tomb, the sun ascends to its zenith in the heavens. The stone is rolled from the well and the living water pours forth to give drink to his flocks; not only to his own disciples but to the "other sheep" (10:16) that will come, who are represented by the Samaritans. The other episodes of the sixth day will also reflect this old story.

Jacob's well was there, and Jesus, tired out by his journey, was sitting by the well.

The mention of Jesus' own physical *need*, here and in his request for a drink, is unusual in John. These statements are not simply indications that Jesus shares the human condition; they have a symbolic weight. It is about the sixth hour: noon, time to break the journey and have something to eat. And so the disciples go off to buy food. Jesus has arrived, symbolically, at the midpoint of his journey, its apogee;

soon he will be traveling again toward Jerusalem and the journey's end.

"A Samaritan woman came to draw water..." Commentators note that noon was not the time when women would likely come to the well to draw water, nor would they come alone, but in a group. The woman who comes alone to the well at noon might well be one who is excluded from the society of the local women—perhaps because of her implied promiscuity.

Jesus said to her, "Give me a drink." Jesus will soon refuse food, but of this *woman* he immediately asks a drink. He speaks of his thirst one other time, from the cross. In his discourse on the bread of life in chapter 6, Jesus will identify himself with food. But for a drink he asks, and he asks a woman. At Cana Jesus seemed at first to repulse "the woman"; here he approaches her, asking for a drink. As the sun begins its decline toward the earth, the return to the feminine begins as well.[14] The strange poignancy of this dialogue arises from the climate of *intimacy* which John has subtly created. The intimacy which we sensed between Jesus and his disciples at the supper emerges here in the very different context of this encounter with the woman at the well.

"Jesus answered her, 'If you knew the gift of God, and who it is...'" A *twofold revelation* begins with these words. To this woman Jesus reveals *himself*, with a surprising candor and fullness. And he speaks, further, of a *living water* which he will give. This water is symbolically reflected not only in her waterpot and in the well of her ancestors, but in the woman herself. Jesus will speak, correspondingly, of a worship both in spirit and in truth.

We sense once again, as at Cana, an extremely close relationship —a fine interweaving—of *word and imagery*. This is an expression of the marriage of the Word with the creation which is the inner matter of the sixth day.

"Sir, you have no bucket, and the well is deep.... Are you greater than our ancestor Jacob?" The woman's words to Jesus recall Jacob's rolling the stone from the well's mouth and watering Rachel's flock. The woman is clinging to the literal level of Jesus' words, but this is about to break beneath her feet. Jesus speaks more clearly of the water that he is to give, and she finally asks him, "Sir, give me this water, so that I may never be thirsty or have to keep coming here to draw water."

This second episode of the sixth day focuses upon a further development of the interface of sexuality and spirituality. The water, that *feminine* unitive that lives within every human person, is stirred at the approach of the Messiah. It is he who is anointed with the unitive divine Spirit, and who promises to impart that same Spirit, the living water. The water of human life reddens at the approach of its destiny as wine.

"Jesus said to her, 'Everyone who drinks of this water will be thirsty again, but those who drink of the water that I will give them will never be thirsty.'" We have heard similar words from him about food: "Your ancestors ate the manna in the wilderness, and they died. This is the bread that comes down from heaven that one may eat of it and not die" (6:49-50). Living bread and living water: Jesus himself and that which he will give. There are resonances of the biblical wisdom literature[15] here, reminding us once again that Jesus is himself the wisdom of God. In the course of this sixth day, John is developing the immanent, "feminine" mode in which this divine wisdom will be present when Jesus has been glorified.

The water that Jesus is to give will root itself in those who believe in him, and "become in them a spring of water gushing up to eternal life." This powerful image develops further Jesus' words in the temple on the third day (7:37), and recalls also the flow of blood and water from his pierced side upon the cross, at the end of the fifth day. The spring flows both from within Jesus and from within the disciple; in this flow the two are one.

In the Cana narrative we found an interweaving of two related symbolic lines: the symbolism of the *marriage* and that of the *wine*. Here in Samaria, similarly, the encounter between man and woman and the image of the living water are present together, and mysteriously related.

"Sir, give me this water, so that I may never be thirsty or have to keep coming here to draw water." What can she be thinking at this point? Her words cannot be taken in their literal sense, and yet do not arrive at the spiritual meaning of Jesus' words.

"Go, call your husband, and come back." Must both man and woman be present together if Jesus is to give this living water? Is it to be received only in unity?

"You are right in saying, 'I have no husband.'" The revelation takes a painfully personal turn. Such are the prophets. "... you have had five husbands, and the one you have now is not your husband.'"[16] The five husbands may represent the five books of the Mosaic *Torah*, which were the only scriptures which the sect of the Samaritans accepted.[17] They did not accept the prophetical books, and this may underlie the woman's acknowledgement of Jesus as a prophet in the next moment.

In a contrasting sense, the five husbands may symbolize the gods of the five pagan nations which had been transplanted into Samaria by the Babylonians,[18] and thus correspond to the "spiritual adultery" of which the Samaritans would be accused by orthodox Jews.

"Sir, I see that you are a prophet. Our ancestors worshiped on this mountain, but you say that the place where people must worship is in Jerusalem." She moves swiftly to redirect the conversation into a less uncomfortable path: here is a theological subject that should interest this too-perceptive young rabbi. Mount Gerizim and Jerusalem were the rival cultic centers of the Samaritans and orthodox Jews.

"Woman, believe me, the hour is coming when you will worship the Father neither on this mountain nor in Jerusalem"—neither on the Mount Gerizim of the sectarians nor on the Mount Zion of the orthodox. This is a shocking statement indeed, and develops further the radical transformation which is emerging on this sixth day. Quite suddenly, to this "half-Gentile" woman who represents the extreme of Jesus' reach beyond the Jews, he discloses his revolutionary program.

In silent contrast to the two rival *mountains* we recall the *well* at the center of this scene, where the two have met at midday. The young Jewish rabbi speaks to this foreign woman of a new worship, "neither on this mountain nor in Jerusalem . . . in spirit and in truth." Neither the religion of the Jews nor that of the Samaritans, neither the old orthodoxy nor the old heterodoxy, neither one patriarchal tradition nor the other, but a worship *springing up from the well at the center of the person*, from the heart, in spirit and in truth. This new, *spiritual* life revealed at the midday of history is "feminine," interior, sapiential, a unitive worship which is one with the human person. The living water which he promises is one with the wine of Cana. The revolution of the sixth day is a gentle explosion, outward and inward at once, transcending dimensionality in presence—from the jealous mountains of collective, tribal worship, to the well which opens within each human person (see 4:14).

As the sun blazes down from its noonday zenith, it is answered by a gleam from the depths of the well, from where the living water will soon fill the earth. As the circle of the light of the Word reaches its maximum amplitude, its limit during Jesus' life, and once again contracts, we are made aware of that other presence of the light and the fire, which will soon be released within. The solar *Logos* will become a well of living water.

⊕

...for wisdom, the fashioner of all things, taught me. There is in her a spirit that is intelligent, holy, unique, manifold, subtle...all powerful, overseeing all, and penetrating through all spirits that are intelligent, pure, and altogether subtle.

For Wisdom is more mobile than any motion; because of her pureness she pervades and penetrates all things. For she is a breath of the power of God, and a pure emanation of the glory of the Almighty; therefore nothing defiled gains entrance into her. For she is a reflection of eternal light, a spotless mirror of the working of God, and an image of his goodness. Although she is but one, she can do all things, and while remaining in herself, she renews all things; in every generation she passes into holy souls and makes them friends of God, and prophets; for God loves nothing so much as the person who lives with wisdom....

She reaches mightily from one end of the earth to the other, and she orders all things well (Wis 7:22–8:1).

"You worship what you *do not know*; we worship what we *know*, for salvation is from the Jews." Here is one side of this twofold revelation, in spirit and truth, Word and Spirit. The tradition of the knowledge of God through his *Word*, entrusted to the Jews, comes to its end in this Jew who speaks to her. And it is through his death at the hands of his own people that this revelation of the Word opens out into the fullness of its dimensions: spirit and truth, interiority and freedom, universality and the concreteness of incarnation. Through him pours the sacred river of wisdom, widening into a sea which is to fill the earth (Sir 24:25-31; see Is 11:9).

"But the hour is coming, and is now here..." As at Cana, the narrative has anticipated this paschal *hour* which now, on the sixth day, has arrived.

"...in spirit and truth..." The prologue had spoken of an outpouring of *grace and truth*[19] through the Word incarnate, which would supersede the law of Moses. Again, Jesus brings a double revelation: the truth which he *is*, and the living water which he will *give*—the divine Spirit. These are the two mediations of God, now known as Father, which are to replace the religious structures symbolized by those two ancient mountains, Zion and Gerizim. These new mediations, however, *are one with God* (see 1:1), within God, and will be one with the person who receives them.

Throughout the nuptial country of the sixth day, and more obviously here at the well in Samaria, there is celebrated the wedding of spirit and truth, of fidelity and freedom, which Jesus brings.

⊕

Her eyes seek his, we imagine, and then turn quickly away, as she speaks once again from the security of her ancestral tradition: "I know that Messiah is coming (who is called Christ); when he comes, he will proclaim all things to us." The Samaritans cherished the expectation of such a Messiah.

"*I Am*, who is speaking to you." These words echo the revelation to Moses from the fiery bush on Sinai; the mountain also recalls Sinai and hence the exodus. It was then that Israel was separated from the nations and given its law. But here we have not fire, and a separation, but water, and a new universal revelation and worship, a new cosmic union. We recall also the "*I Am*" of Jesus as he appeared upon the waters of the sea. Here in Samaria also, we are brought back to the unitive source, the waters of creation which are enkindled by the Spirit. It is the light of the first day of creation, the light of the Word, which flashes at the bottom of the well, where the living water is to spring forth.

⊕

The Sun burns in the sky like the Face of God, but we do not know his countenance as terrible. His light is diffused in the air and the light of God is diffused by Hagia Sophia.

We do not see the Blinding One in black emptiness. He speaks to us gently in ten thousand things, in which His light is one fulness and one Wisdom.

Thus He shines not on them but from within them. Such is the loving-kindness of Wisdom.

All the perfections of created things are also in God; and therefore He is at once Father and Mother. As Father He stands in solitary might surrounded by darkness. As Mother His shining is diffused, embracing all His creatures with merciful tenderness and light. The Diffuse Shining of God is Hagia Sophia. We call her His "glory." In Sophia His power is experienced only as mercy and as love.[20]

⊕

"Just then his disciples came..." The spell of intimacy is broken: as the disciples return, the woman leaves her water jar behind at the well and hurries into town to tell her neighbors of what she has seen and heard. "Come and see a man who told me everything I have ever done! He cannot be the Messiah, can he?"

We recall Eve, and "everything that she did," according to the Genesis history, by accepting and passing on to the man the fruit of the tree which promised knowledge. Now this man comes and discloses within himself a knowledge which embraces the history of woman, of "Eve," and the whole of her being. Here the powerful sexual sense of "knowledge" in the biblical tradition is not excluded but transformed. We are still in the nuptial context of the sixth day. But now it is the fruit of the tree of life which presents itself to the woman in Jesus.

The Samaritan woman has represented both *Eve* as woman in her unredeemed condition, and perhaps primordial *religion* as well. She is woman, primal and eternal, ever coming to this well to find herself, and now she finds one who knows her through and through: "Come, see (cf. Jn 1:39.46) a man who told me *everything I have ever done!*" Having illumined the history of Eve since the beginning, the light now offers to deliver her, with living water, from her curse: from her own thirst and her demonic charism of leading men away from their own life. In this betrothal to the new Adam, and the gift of this water, she is to discover once again the truth of her own inner being.

On the cross, Jesus had cried, "I am thirsty," and been given sour wine by the soldiers. He surprises this woman by asking her, "*Give me a drink.*" Within the obvious meaning of his words may lie more than one layer of symbolic meaning. On one level, he is saying, I thirst for you, for your faith, for your soul[21]—just as the *food* of Jesus in this same narrative (see 4:31-34) is related to the "harvest" of those who are to believe.

Following further in this line, we find in this scene a mutuality, *the meeting of two thirsts*: Jesus' thirst and that of the woman. At the theological core of this meeting at the well, as at Cana, we find both the human feminine, human psyche or interiority, and the divine

Feminine, the fullness, the wine of union. Here, in the middle of Jesus' journey, the sense of plenitude is still more veiled, incipient, as the dialogue takes place over a wider distance.

This woman's insatiable thirst has driven her through one liaison after another; she has come often to the well and is still not satisfied. When Jesus recalled the history of these relationships, he was speaking to her heart, speaking of her own thirst. He had already spoken to her of another water which he himself would give. Jesus thirsts for her faith:[22] that is, for the "water" which is her soul, and which is itself lost, alienated from itself, seeking itself outside itself. This is the human interior feminine, the inner unitive person. It is both psyche, anima, soul, and is "sexuality" in a broad sense. Somewhere beneath and within this human feminine, there move always the living waters of the divine Feminine, the Spirit.

> ...I loved her and sought her from my youth; I desired to take her for my bride, and became enamored of her beauty. She glorifies her noble birth by living with God, and the Lord of all loves her (Wis 8:2-3).

From the fullness of Cana, the final union celebrated in symbol, we have come to this person who is a history of botched unions, aborted union, the personification of unredeemed human desire, "fallen Eve." Jesus comes to her, comes to this well, bearing within himself the secret and the promise of the *fullness of her own being*. The Samaritaness is *woman*, who had offered the fatal nourishment to Adam, and whom Jesus now asks for a drink of water, so that his thirst may find hers and he may restore her to herself, to her destiny as the bearer of divine life.

The Spirit of the Fountain dies not.
It is called the Mysterious Feminine.
The Doorway of the Mysterious Feminine
Is called the Root of Heaven-and-Earth.

Lingering like gossamer, it has only a hint of existence;
And yet when you draw upon it, it is inexhaustible.[23]

⊕

If this story pulls strangely upon the human heart, this is partly owing to the deft and allusive grace with which John has told it, but there is a further reason. Here the deep springs of human longing, human desire, are evoked and brought very subtly into an encounter with the depths of God. The inner spaces of human longing resonate with a music that comes from beyond themselves; against the walls of the dark cave of the human heart leaps the flame of the divine fullness, "*I Am*" (see 4:26).

⊕

"Rabbi, eat something." "I have food to eat that you do not know about" (4:31-32). We have heard of the weariness of Jesus, and then, in connection with the woman, his thirst. Jesus' hunger and his food have to do with the work of *men's* world—with these disciples and with the field of Samaritans ripe for the harvest. "My food is to do the will of him who sent me and to complete his work." The work of God is itself the divine food, and Jesus as Word is somehow one with this work and food; we recall his words at Capernaum by the sea, after he had fed the crowd with bread. We do not hear him complain of hunger.

"I sent you to reap that for which you did not labor; others have labored, and you have entered into their labor." Who are these other laborers who have brought the field to ripeness? Moses and the teachers of Israel, the shepherds and mediators? No doubt. But ultimately Jesus is speaking of the busy arms of God, the Word and the Spirit, which have been at work within all humanity. Soon he will send his disciples to gather in the harvest. Like the Samaritan woman, however, they will not quickly awaken to the presence of the one who works with them, and who runs ahead to carry the word of the new creation.

> ...then I was beside him, like a master workman;
> and I was daily his delight,
> rejoicing before him always,
> rejoicing in his inhabited world
> and delighting in the human race (Prov 8:30-31).

⊕

"It is no longer because of what you said that we believe, for we have heard for ourselves, and we know that this is truly the Savior of the world." This progression of the Samaritan villagers from a mediated to an immediate, interiorized belief corresponds to Jesus' new sophianic revelation. This revelation is symbolized by the woman who runs from the well to tell her neighbors, and at the same time—springing up within their own hearts—it transcends her ministry.

"...we know that this is truly the *Savior of the world.*" With this title, found only here, the Samaritans express the second, outward, dimension of the new revelation. It corresponds to the noonday amplitude of this midpoint of his journey, and expresses the universal and cosmic scope of Jesus' revolution, announced to this woman on the sixth day.

SECTION 18: 12:1-11
THE ANOINTING AT BETHANY

"Six days before the Passover." This episode follows immediately upon the raising of Lazarus, and the mention of the Passover reminds us that it will be followed soon (in the narrative order) by the death of Jesus.

The Cana wedding, at which the mother of Jesus was present, marked the beginning of the public life of Jesus in John's gospel, while the meeting with the Samaritan woman at the sixth hour symbolically represented its midpoint. Now Jesus approaches his sunset, and a woman will anoint his body for burial.

The setting, in the midst of a family who are intimate friends of Jesus, is unusual in the gospel. The supper and its atmosphere remind us both of the Cana wedding and of Jesus' last supper with his disciples. This story, while found only in John, is obviously based on the same event as the story of the anointing with nard in the house of Simon, which is found in all three synoptics. John's version is closer to that of Mark and Matthew than to that of Luke.

> While he was at Bethany in the house of Simon the leper, as he sat at the table, a woman came with an alabaster jar of very costly ointment of nard, and she broke open the jar and poured the ointment on his head. But some were there who said to one another in anger, "Why was the ointment wasted in this way? For this ointment could have been sold for more than three hundred denarii, and the money given to the poor." And they scolded her. But Jesus said, "Let her alone;

why do you trouble her? She has performed a good service for me. For you always have the poor with you, you can show kindness to them whenever you wish; but you will not always have me. She has done what she could; she has anointed my body beforehand for its burial. Truly, I tell you, wherever the gospel is proclaimed in the whole world, what she has done will be told in remembrance of her" (Mk 14:3-9).

The *differences* which appear in John's story are worth examining; often these details shed light on John's theological purpose. John introduces Lazarus, eliminates Simon from the common story and instead introduces Martha, Mary and Lazarus as the hosts. The respective roles of Martha and Mary are consistent with their responses in John 11, and also recall another familiar story in Luke's gospel (Lk 10:38-42). While in Matthew and Mark the woman anoints Jesus' head, in Luke and in John the woman's attentions are exclusively to his feet.

In Matthew and Mark, *Judas* appears only afterward, and immediately goes to the chief priests to betray Jesus; in John it is Judas who reproves Mary for her extravagance. John takes the opportunity to mention that Judas kept the money box and was a thief, and also that he is the one who was to betray Jesus.

Only in John are we told that "the house was filled with the fragrance of the perfume." This may be John's symbolic equivalent to the promise of Jesus in Matthew 26:13 and Mark 14:9 that her act would be remembered wherever in the world the gospel would be preached.

Thus in John's story we have a tighter dramatic economy. The action is limited to a few significant characters: Jesus, Lazarus, Martha, Mary, Judas. This is typical of John. We may wonder if there is another kind of concentration going on here as well—if John is compressing several episodes from the common tradition into one narrative. The *unitive* theology of John may be reflected in an inclination to draw together and integrate various elements from the common tradition, resulting in a kind of unitive synthesis of the other gospels.

Together with the central action—Jesus anointed before his death—John has wound these other threads: the death and raising of Lazarus, the contrasting personalities of Martha and Mary. The anointing itself takes on an entirely new meaning from its association with Jesus' raising of Lazarus. When Mary pours the fragrant oil upon Jesus' feet, she expresses the relationship between these two events: the raising of Lazarus and the imminent death of Jesus.

The perfume filling the house with its fragrance recalls the tomb of Lazarus, which was assumed to be filled with stench, and also the tomb of Jesus, into which, along with his body, a hundred pounds of myrrh and aloes would be put. The pouring and flow of the perfume suggests the gift of new life which passes from one to the other: from Jesus to Lazarus. Again, here on the sixth day, we are beyond the laws of "before and after," of temporal causality, just as we are beyond the counsels of economic prudence. The gift of new *life* which this perfume signifies, however, is not the same mortal life; the quality of this substance speaks of something further: the *eternal* life which is the life of God and of the new creation. Like the wine of Cana, the flowing of this perfume speaks also of a quality of friendship, of communion, in which those who remain with Jesus participate. Martha serves the food which is shared by the guests; Mary's fragrance evokes a more delicate and intimate quality of the same communion. Martha and Mary are juxtaposed like Peter and the beloved disciple, like bread and wine.

The relationships and interactions of these characters are compact, dialectical. Martha and Mary play their familiar parts of service and adoration. The magnanimity of Mary is contrasted with the response which it provokes in Judas. Together at table are Lazarus and Jesus: one has just returned from the tomb and the other will soon be placed in his tomb.

As Jesus speaks to Judas here, we are reminded of the moment at the other supper when Jesus sent Judas forth into the dark on his errand. As Judas went out to betray Jesus soon after Jesus had stripped and bent to wash the feet of his disciples, so Judas responds with an avaricious obtuseness to Mary's parallel gesture of anointing the feet of Jesus at this supper. The parallel expresses the continuity in the inner drama which flows through the two scenes.

⊕

While the king was on his couch, my nard gave forth its fragrance (Song 1:12).[24]

This perfume which fills the house (12:3) recalls the many sweet scents of the Song of Solomon, that nuptial poem which seasons, like an incense, the whole of the sixth day. In the context created by the Song, Mary's anointing of Jesus' feet carries a connotation of sexual union:[25] a symbolic resonance which parallels the gesture's implication of a complete gift of self, an unconditioned devotion. From the tentative and implicit response of the Samaritan woman we have progressed to a gesture of total self-donation. The oil itself has a more sensual and corporeal connotation than the water of that village well.

The sweet odor that fills the house suggests the feminine aura of the Word which is the divine glory. It is the fragrance of a proximate spring, a victory of life, as well as of realized union. The scent, redolent of that mythical garden both of the Song and of Genesis, is music of the earth, nuptial song of the body. Woman, who herself correlates symbolically with garden and earth,[26] expresses in the mute plenitude of her action some obscure knowledge of paradise.

⊕

The audacity of sexual metaphor is permissible here because the sexual symbolism is balanced by the reality of death (see 2:4) and the solemnity of this moment: the sexual metaphor is transposed to another level. Lazarus has just returned from that dark place, and Jesus is about to go there. Human love is here grounded in death, and, in the fullness of this gesture, sings beyond itself.

> Set me as a seal upon your heart,
> as a seal upon your arm;
> for love is strong as death,
> passion fierce as the grave.
> Its flashes are flashes of fire,
> a raging flame.
> Many waters cannot quench love,
> neither can floods drown it.
> If one offered for love
> all the wealth of his house,
> it would be utterly scorned (Song 8:6-7).

This is the language of Mary's gesture, nonsense to Judas. It is the language of John's gospel—where the words and gestures of human love intimate the presence of a *new* love, unbounded and divine.

⊕

The Samaritaness was led toward recognizing in Jesus the Messiah, the Christ. This recognition may also be signified in Mary's anointing.[27] While the Anointed One manifested himself to the Samaritaness in his plenitude of *knowledge* ("Come and see a man who told me

everything that I have ever done! He cannot be the Messiah, can he?"),
at Bethany he identifies himself by a totality of *power*: a power of life
which is stronger than death.

Judas and the chief priests respond in parallel fashion to the
"signs" of Jesus and of Mary of Bethany. It is Judas, in John's account,
who disapproves of the wastefulness of Mary's anointing of Jesus'
feet, and apparently it is at about this point that he decides to betray
Jesus. It is, similarly, the popular acclaim of Jesus after he has brought
Lazarus to life which brings about the decision of the chief priests to
put to death both Jesus and Lazarus (12:10). Soon afterward Judas
and the chief priests will join together to accomplish Jesus' death.

⊕

Between the scene in Samaria and this one in Bethany there is a progression from conversation to physical contact; the sexual symbolism
is intensified, the bodiliness of the encounter is accented. The symbolic nuptial relationship advances to a new stage of intimacy. While at
the well of Samaria we witnessed the meeting of *two thirsts*, here at
Bethany we find the meeting of *two outpourings*, in a context of death
—death overcome in Lazarus and death imminent for Jesus. Now that
his hour has arrived, symbolism verges upon actuality.

In contrast to the scene at the well, the woman here is mute: she
comes to meet the Word in Jesus with that language of immanent
divine wisdom which is the grace of feminine gesture. The symbolic
union is complete, as Mary's ritual action expresses perfectly what
Jesus is about to do in giving himself. This Mary acts with the sophianic sense of Jesus' mother at Cana, a knowledge of fullness which
finds its own language of fullness—approaching the concrete language of Jesus himself at the wedding and on the cross. Her action is
the anticipated feminine reflection of the pouring out of Jesus' own
spirit, his life (see 19:30) and the subsequent pouring out of the Spirit
of grace from his risen body (Jn 20:22). Here death and resurrection
and the sending of the Spirit are not distinguished: they are all
expressed in the one gesture of Mary, reflecting the hidden inner
movement of divine life itself.

⊕

There is in all visible things an invisible fecundity, a dimmed
light, a meek namelessness, a hidden wholeness. This mysterious Unity and Integrity is Wisdom, the Mother of all, *Natura*

naturans. There is in all things an inexhaustible sweetness and purity, a silence that is a fount of action and joy. It rises up in wordless gentleness and flows out to me from the unseen roots of all created being, welcoming me tenderly, saluting me with indescribable humility. This is at once my own being, my own nature, and the Gift of my Creator's Thought and Art within me, speaking as Hagia Sophia, speaking as my sister, Wisdom.[28]

SECTION 19: 20:1-18
IN THE GARDEN

Sec. 19A: 20:1-10
The Disciples at the Tomb

From the interior of the house at Bethany, filled with the fragrance with which the woman had anointed Jesus for the day of his burial, we have arrived at the tomb of Jesus, which now lies open. Here another woman, similarly named Mary, comes seeking the body of Jesus, and finds the tomb empty. John's careful time-indications are significant. Mary arrives at the tomb early on the *first day* of the week, while it is still dark. We recall the first day of creation, and the dark sea-crossing, and the creation of light: that symbolic beginning is evoked here at the tomb, as we await the reappearance of day.

The implications of this scene begin to emerge with John's words, "...the stone had been removed from the tomb," which recall to us the well in Samaria, and the story of Jacob. After *awakening from his sleep* at Bethel, Jacob anointed the stone upon which his head had rested, and continued his journey. When he had come to the land of "the people of the east," he saw a *well* in the middle of a field. Rachel, the daughter of his kinsman, came along, and Jacob *rolled the stone from the mouth of the well* so that she could water her flocks. This woman became Jacob's wife.

The earlier narratives of the sixth day have developed a background for the symbolic development of this hole in the rock which is the tomb of Jesus. The new Jacob has awakened from his sleep in the stone, and removed the stone from the spring. The meeting between Magdalene and Jesus here will be implicitly a nuptial meeting, and the tomb in the rock is to become a spring.

⊕

Mary, in her perplexity and concern for the body of her Teacher, runs to the two disciples. In the first scenes of John's narrative, which will soon introduce us to the seventh day, John the Baptist had pointed out Jesus to two of his disciples, who followed the young rabbi to learn where he was "staying." One of those two disciples was the brother of Peter; the other was unnamed. Now it is "the other disciple, the one whom Jesus loved," who runs with Peter to the tomb. This other disciple arrives first at the tomb, but does not enter it. Peter arrives and goes into the tomb, and the other disciple follows him. John tells us carefully what they see: the linen cloths in which the body had been wrapped and, rolled up in a separate place, the "soudarion," or facecloth, which had been on Jesus' head. We are told that the other disciple "went in, and he saw and *believed.*" Then the two disciples returned to their homes.

What is signified by this complex, formal ritual of the three disciples at the opened tomb? Each of the three is shown elsewhere to be related to Jesus by a particular bond of love, and each will be characterized by a particular role in the communication of that which Jesus has brought. The role of Magdalene here is reminiscent of that of the *Samaritan woman,* who ran from the well to tell her neighbors about the man whom she had seen there. But she also recalls *Rahab* the harlot—a favorite of those fathers[29] who took pleasure in the wilder insinuations of scripture—who offered a hiding place to the two Israelite spies who had been sent to scout the promised land ahead of the others (Jos 2). Peter and the disciple are brought by Magdalene into this feminine enclave of the sixth day, anticipating the seventh day, the sabbath when their fellow disciples too will taste the fruits of the promised land, the resurrection. John's gospel—particularly at this point—is rich in these obscure hints. The veil which covers the "other disciple" throughout this gospel folds to double thickness over the moment of this disciple's descent into the empty tomb.

Taken literally, this narrative of the two disciples at the tomb is as puzzling, inconclusive, and disappointingly poor of significance as are the synoptic stories of the open tomb. Only as we reflect upon it in the light of biblical tradition do its depths of symbolic meaning begin to open to us. We should not be surprised to discover a superabundance of symbolic overtones in this scene of apparent vacancy, if we recall that this hole in the rock is *the place of Jesus' resurrection.* This place, we shall see, has a central symbolic importance for John, as for the beloved disciple of his gospel. Once again—here at Jesus' *hour*—we are at the hub of the wheel, where all the spokes of symbolism converge. This is one of the points in John's narrative at which the central illumination of the first day (section 1) becomes present with particular vigor, so that this *place* of the tomb becomes to some degree interchangeable with the place of the gospel's mandalic center—the dark waters of the sea-crossing.

⊕

While in the synoptic gospels *Peter* stands out alone against the background of the other apostles, John continually presents him in contrast with the *"other disciple"* to whom we attribute the fourth gospel itself. The disciple habitually *sees* and hence *"arrives"* first, because of his close relationship with the Lord—he has a unique gift of knowledge. Peter, however, must *enter* first: this is his prerogative as Rock, as external head. His entering may be merely formal, since we are not told that he then believes. Apparently it is the disciple who believes, as well as knows, before Peter. While Peter is first among the disciples, leader and spokesman for all, it is the disciple who precedes him both in his *intimacy* with Jesus—as we have seen—and in his *vision*.

Peter, however, personifies the movement—and particularly the confession—of *faith*, even in John's gospel. It is he who responds in the moment of general doubt in Jesus, "You have the words of eternal life" (6:68). More generally in the New Testament, Peter represents the cornerstone which is faith in the messianic identity, divinity and resurrection of Jesus. He is also the type of the leader in the church, and of the man of action, that action which is motivated by love for Jesus.

The *disciple*, on the other hand, is distinguished by John as the one who is *loved by Jesus*. The basis of his response is, then, this grace rather than his own love for the Lord. He is characterized not as active but as *receptive* (parallel to Mary of Bethany as contrasted with her sister Martha), as enjoying a particular closeness to Jesus from which derives his peculiar depth and sureness of understanding. He is the disciple who best knows the heart of the Lord.

The *deference* of the disciple to Peter at the tomb recalls that of Jesus to the Baptist in chapter 1, when Jesus came to be baptized by him. The Baptist and Peter compare to Jesus and the disciple somewhat as exterior ritual and symbolic ministry—and perhaps the exterior signification of faith—compare to interior realization and unitive fullness (see Part III, Chapter 7 below). Peter moves still on a level of dualism, and his own primacy is a symbolic, figurative and "institutional" primacy (nonetheless real and necessary for that), while the superiority of the disciple is presented as interior, experiential, sapiential and mystical. This ambivalence of the fourth gospel toward the figure of exterior ecclesial authority is parallel to a similar attitude with regard to the exterior forms of baptism and the eucharist (see below, Part III, Chapters 6 and 7). The external ecclesial realities are not rejected, but John consistently passes over them silently while he proceeds to treat at length the corresponding interior and sapiential realities, which appear much less clearly and amply in the other gospels.

⊕

The rock, the hole in the rock: wide echoes from the Old Testament are evoked here, and we shall see John playing upon them freely, bringing a fullness of meaning out of this strange emptiness. We have already seen reflected here the stone which Jacob rolled from the well for Rachel. In the book of Daniel we hear of a wonderful rock:

> As you looked on, a stone was cut out, not by human hands, and it struck the statue on its feet of iron and clay and broke them in pieces...the stone that struck the statue became a great mountain and filled the whole earth (Dan 2:34-35).

The rock shatters the colossal statue of *idolatry*, of the tyranny of visible figure and image, and becomes the whole earth. In the Christian tradition, the rock of Daniel has been identified with Christ himself.

The first letter of Peter uses the symbol of the *"living stone"* both for Christ and for those who believe in him and are thus built upon him, the cornerstone (1 Pet 2:4-7). This stone which is Christ is also, implicitly, the Word of God, which has been contrasted (quoting Is 40:6-9) with the flesh which is like grass.

As this image of the living stone develops, there is a merging of the images of stone, of seed and of childbirth. Born anew of the imperishable seed which is the Word of God, that stone which abides forever, Christians are newborn babes and at the same time living stones built upon that living stone of Christ, to form a house, a temple, a nation, a priesthood, the whole of which lives with one life. Peter, we should remember, has himself received from Jesus the name of *Rock* (1:42). His vocation and his vision are inseparable from this image of the living stone and the house which grows from it.

Peter himself has a double symbolic role. By his faith in Christ, his love for Christ, he represents the foundation and the core of the Christian life. By his identification with the house, the structure which grows from this rock of faith, confession and kerygma, he is Jacob's memorial stone, the enduring point of orientation for Christian worship. "This is none other than the house of God, and this is the gate of heaven" (Gen 28:17; see 28:18-22).

⊕

The beloved disciple steps into the hole in the rock, steps into the rock, and sees and *believes*. While Peter, in the New Testament writings, seems to *become* the rock itself, planted in this place of the resurrection and growing from it as a living house, this disciple draws our attention to something that happens invisibly *within* the rock. The experience of the beloved disciple—"*he saw and believed*"—has an importance in the fourth gospel far beyond what would be inferred from these few words. Perhaps the disciple himself does not realize, at this point, the meaning of what he has seen and believed. The implication of these words, however, is that *he is the first of the disciples to experience the resurrection of Jesus*: he is the *firstborn*, as Thomas will be the last.

Moses and *Elijah*, who had been seen, according to the synoptic accounts, with Jesus at the transfiguration on the mountain, had both been closely associated with the mountain and the rock. From the rock in the desert, Moses had brought forth water for the people to drink; according to Paul, "the rock was Christ."[30]

Elijah had fled from the wrath of Jezebel into the desert, where he slept by a broom tree. He awoke, was refreshed, and ran to the "mountain of God," where, after a violent wind, an earthquake, and a great fire, the Lord came to him in a small, whispering sound and then spoke to him (1 Kgs 19). Elijah's encounter with God seems to foreshadow a passage from the mediation of external signs and wonders to the intimacy and interiority of the disciple's initiation within the rock tomb.

The empty tomb is further illuminated by *Moses'* encounter with God at Sinai. When Moses asks the Lord, "Show me your *glory*, I pray," the Lord responds,

I will make all my goodness pass before you, and will proclaim before you the name, "The Lord" (Yahweh); and I will be gracious to whom I will be gracious, and will show mercy on whom I will show mercy. But...you cannot see my face, for no one shall see me and live.... See, there is a place by me where you shall stand on the rock, and while my glory passes by I will put you *in a cleft of the rock*, and I will cover you with my hand until I have passed by; then I will take away my hand, and you shall see my back; but my face shall not be seen (Ex 33:18-23).

Moses ascends Mount Sinai once again, stands in a cleft in the rock, and the Lord manifests his *name* to him. Then the Lord makes a covenant with the people through Moses and gives him command-ments, among which is that of keeping the sabbath rest (34:21) on the seventh day. When Moses comes down from the mountain, his face is shining from the encounter with God, and the people are afraid to approach him (34:30). He puts a *veil* on his face so that the people may not be terrified, and removes it when he goes into the tent once again to speak with the Lord.

The experience of the disciple in the tomb, that cleft in the rock, directly reflects this intimate revelation of the Lord to Moses: the rev-elation of his glory, of his name, and the vision of his "back." To the *veil* which Moses put over his face to hide its glory from the people are related the abandoned *burial garments* which the two disciples see in the tomb, and particularly the *headcloth* which lies apart. John's intention in describing these cloths so carefully becomes clearer when we read Paul writing to the Corinthians about the veil of Moses and its symbolic meaning.[31]

The discarded grave clothes lying in the tomb recall the *figures and images* in which the Mystery had been clothed until this moment. The deposed *face cloth* represents that which had concealed the head or face of Christ and has now been laid aside. Now for Paul this *veil*, whatever it is, renders the letter of the *Torah* opaque to the Jews.

But their minds were hardened. Indeed, to this very day, when they hear the reading of the old covenant, that same veil is still there, since only in Christ is it set aside. Indeed, to this very day whenever Moses is read, a veil lies over their minds; but when one turns to the Lord, the veil is removed. Now the Lord is the Spirit, and where the Spirit of the Lord is, there is freedom. And all of us, with unveiled faces, seeing the glory of the Lord as though reflected in a mirror, are being transformed into the same image... (2 Cor 3:14-18; see 1 Jn 3:1-2).

Paul does not tell us precisely what this veil is. In John it is apparently *the figures, images and external symbols themselves* (cf. Jn 16:25: "I have said these things to you in figures of speech. The hour is coming when I will no longer speak to you in figures, but will tell you plainly of the Father"). John is saying, then, through his mention of the head cloth, that the time of *figures* is over now: the reality of Jesus—and therefore of the Father (see 14:9: "Whoever has seen me has seen the Father")—is now revealed openly to those who "see": that is, who believe. The time of figures corresponds to the old covenant, to the religion of Israel, the law.[32]

That which is manifested now that the figures have been superseded is, according to Paul, "the glory of God in the face of Jesus Christ."

For it is the God who said, "Let light shine out of darkness,"
who has shone in our hearts to give the light of the knowledge
of the glory of God in the face of Jesus Christ (2 Cor 4:6).

If the account of the disciple in the tomb is intended to signify that which Paul is expressing more directly in this passage, we have indeed arrived at a *decisive moment* in the fourth gospel. The disciple is presented as the first of Jesus' followers to experience Jesus' resurrection *within himself*. This is the basic and constitutive Christian experience which would soon be associated with baptism and the reception of the Holy Spirit. We shall proceed upon this premise.

The burial clothes which have been laid aside recall also the *garments of skin* which had been supplied to Adam and Eve when they were ejected from the garden of paradise (Gen 3:21). Before they had sinned, man and woman were naked but unashamed. When they had eaten of the fruit of the tree of knowledge, their eyes were opened: they saw that they were naked, and hid themselves from the Lord. They made garments for themselves of fig leaves to cover their nakedness (Gen 3:7).

Here in the tomb, the clothes which have been laid aside signify that this curse has been rescinded. The garden is once more opened to humanity, and the eyes which were once opened ironically, to the shame of human "*nakedness*," are now opened in truth to the *glory* with which man and woman are clothed in the resurrection. Seeing but this empty cave with his eyes, the disciple *sees*—but within himself and filling himself this time—the glory of the Son of Man which the disciples had seen first at Cana (2:11). And he *believes* (see 2:12) but with a new kind of faith.

The Greek word used for this head cloth or face cloth (20:7) is *soudarion*. This word is derived from the Greek term for sweat, and can denote the cloth which a laborer would use for wiping sweat from his face. From this detail there opens a significant further breakthrough to the Genesis or creation level of allusion here. After the sin of the first parents, God said to Adam:

By the *sweat of your face* you shall eat bread until you return to the ground, for out of it you were taken; you are dust, and to dust you shall return (Gen 3:19).

Adam's sentence of hard, sweaty labor for his bread is in continuity with his sentence of death and return to the earth. In his death and burial, Jesus has terminated this sentence and moved beyond it. The *soudarion* laid aside in the tomb is the sign of this. The "sweat-cloth," which had wiped the face of man in his labor and covered it in his death, is no longer needed. The *six days* of labor are now finished, and the sabbath has dawned in the resurrection of Jesus. The breadth and depth of this symbol of the sabbath rest is beautifully exposed by the letter to the Hebrews (ch. 3–4). There God's rest is the entrance into the promised land, equivalent to the "kingdom of God" of the gospels. This is the entering into the heavenly sanctuary, the holy place (Heb 9:2), where Jesus has gone before to open the way. It is, more simply, an entrance into the immediacy of divine union. In our interpretation of John's gospel, it could be called a rebirth in the new divine immanence. That which the first paradise had symbolized is at last open to *Adam*, to humanity, in Jesus.

Here once again, John has moved through the literal history to a level of exodus symbolism (Moses, his theophany and his veil) and then beyond that to a *creation* level: a new creation in which we are reborn in that "beginning" which is the creative Word.

The word *soudarion* is found in one other place in John's gospel—at the raising of Lazarus (11:44). "The dead man came out, his hands and feet bound with strips of cloth, and his *face wrapped in a cloth* (*soudarion*). Jesus said to them, 'Unbind him, and let him go.'" Here used as a face cloth, the cloth corresponds well to the veil of Moses. This use of the word *soudarion* here, combined with its use in 20:7, strengthens the identification of Lazarus with Adam, and invites us to look further into the similarity and contrast between the resurrection of Lazarus and that of Jesus.

> For this reason the Father loves me, because I lay down my life in order to take it again. No one takes it from me, but I lay it down of my own accord. I have power to lay it down and I have power to take it up again (10:17-18).

Jesus' grave clothes lie where he laid them aside; Lazarus must be called forth, and then unbound.

The "removal of the veil," in this context of Genesis 3, at the terminus of our journey back through sacred history, suggests also the removal of the veil of *history* itself, and the veil of the *scriptures* themselves (see 2 Cor 3:12-18). As the veil which renders *symbolic* expression obscure and uncertain gives way to an immediate vision, so also man and woman, the "image of God," will be brought to a new level of relationship with God in which the *sacramental* mediation of marriage will be transformed. The exclusivity, the circumscription and the bondage of sexuality and family relationships are to give way to a full transparency, an unbounded communion. Humanity, the image, will at last become translucent to the divine glory.

The disciple's experience takes place still *within the sixth day* of creation, the day of the full flowering of symbolism, in the nuptial reunion of the image of God. It is, however, an anticipated participation in the sabbath, the "rest of God" which belongs to the *seventh* day and will be shared by the other disciples on the seventh day.

⊕

Now the Wisdom of God, Sophia, comes forth, reaching from "end to end mightily." She wills to be also the unseen pivot of all nature, the center and significance of all the light that is *in* all and *for* all. That which is poorest and humblest, that which is most hidden in all things is nevertheless most obvious in them, and quite manifest, for it is their own self that stands before us, naked and without care.

Sophia, the feminine child, is playing in the world, obvious and unseen, playing at all times before the Creator. Her delights are to be with the children of men. She is their sister. The core of life that exists in all things is tenderness, mercy,

virginity, the Light, the Life considered as passive, as received, as given, as taken, as inexhaustibly renewed by the
Gift of God. Sophia is Gift, is Spirit, *Donum Dei*. She is God-
given and God Himself as Gift. God as all, and God reduced
to Nothing: *exinanivit semetipsum*. Humility as the source of
unfailing light.[33]

⊕

The rock of *Daniel*, "cut out of the mountain without hands," corresponds to our *movement into the Unitive, beyond figures*. That stone
breaks the *figure*, the statue of the king (which can be seen as representing every form of idolatry) into pieces, and then "fills the whole
earth," becomes the whole earth. The age of figures is over—as with
the *soudarion* and the disciple's enlightenment. The seeing of the disciple within the rock is the *unitive* vision in which, one with the Word,
one experiences or realizes God within oneself. This is not any longer
the seeing of a distinct object by a conscious subject, not a dualistic
knowing but an experience of the non-dual light which is the *Logos*
within one.[34] This light itself is the *unitive* reality and understanding
to which we have often referred.

For John the *veil*, or head cloth, represents the *figures*, images,
external symbols and words, through which the Father has heretofore
been revealed, even by Jesus himself. In the rock tomb the disciple
now hears the *plain speech* concerning the Father (16:25) that corresponds to the new *birth* (16:21). It is the light of the Word (1:5.9.14)
that he now sees, and which enlightens the whole of his witness, his
gospel.

⊕

Entering the door in the rock, the disciple sees, believes, and is born.
He is baptized in the earth, as Jesus was baptized first in water and
then in the earth.

> Do you not know that all of us who have been baptized into
> Christ Jesus were baptized into his death? Therefore we have
> been buried with him by baptism into death, so that, just as
> Christ was raised from the dead by the glory of the Father, so
> we too might walk in newness of life. For if we have been
> united with him in a death like his, we will certainly be unit-
> ed with him in a resurrection like his (Rom 6:3-5).

⊕

The disciple is the child of this rock, this earth, this *adamah*, and so himself becomes the Son of Man and beloved in the bosom of the Father (1:18).[35] Now the bosom of Adam, earth, creation, has become also the bosom of the Father, where rests the beloved, the Son, the *Son of Man*, the unitive Child. This has taken place within the feminine enclosure of the sixth day; here the rock has become permeable to the creative power, transparent to the ultimate reality which it symbolizes: Father, Mother, God.

Between the first creation and this new, immanent creation, the body of Jesus was pierced, and so was opened the new passageway into the sanctuary celebrated in the letter to the Hebrews (ch. 9–10). This same body of Jesus, pierced upon the tree, will be soon manifested to Magdalene and then to the disciples in the closed house.

⊕

Paul, in expressing his initiatory experience of Christ, had identified it with the *first day* of creation. "It is the God who said, 'Let light shine out of darkness,' who has shone in our hearts..." (2 Cor 4:6). A little further on in the same letter he will write, "So if anyone is in Christ, there is a *new creation*: everything old has passed away; see, everything has become *new*" (2 Cor 5:17).

While the first creation is a beginning of *material existence*, the new creation is a beginning *"in Christ"*: spiritual, immanent, unitive, and inseparable from faith and love. While the first creation begins with the birth of *light*, the new creation begins with *an inner illumination with the glory of God which is in Christ*. In the tomb episode of John 20, the first day of creation may be implicit in the "seeing" of the disciple: the light has shone out of darkness in his heart, and he believes. This light of the "glory of God" is the light of the creative *Logos*.

Our interpretation of the disciple's "seeing" in the tomb according to 2 Corinthians 3–4 corresponds to a definitive move at this crucial point in the gospel *from exodus to unitive creation* and *from Moses to Christ*. "No one has ever seen God. It is God the only Son, who is in the Father's bosom, who has made him known" (1:18). God is known with the knowledge that is this Son, through birth in this same Son who is ever born in God.

Section 19B: 20:11-18
Jesus and Mary Magdalene

I

Mary Magdalene remains, weeping, at the tomb, after Peter and the other disciple have gone home. When she first looked, she had seen only that the stone had been rolled away and the tomb was empty. Now it has become lighter, and as she looks into the tomb once again, she sees two angels, seated where the head and the feet of Jesus had rested.

Only John mentions the *tears* of Magdalene and the angels' question, "Woman, why are you weeping?"A likely theological motive for this will emerge. Magdalene's blind and distracted seeking for the body of Jesus comes near to comedy as she ignores the angels—who, if not of interest just now, might be expected to be of some help with her problem—and fails to recognize Jesus himself. The power of life emanating from Jesus' resurrection manifests itself as a tide of enormous good humor, releasing disciples from jail while playfully leaving the system in perfect order: gates locked and guards in place (Acts 4:17-26; 12:4-11; 16:24-34). Jesus' body has become the principle of life; seeking it among the dead, Magdalene resembles a blindfolded child about to be surprised.

Magdalene sees Jesus before she hears his voice, but does not recognize him. She recognizes him only when he calls her by her name. Jesus asks her the same question the angels had asked, and she answers him as she had answered the angels. This childlike, obsessive concern with the *body* of Jesus (the Samaritan woman and Mary of Bethany also minister to Jesus' *body*) is characteristic of the *woman* and it is respected by Jesus, who appears to Magdalene first of all the disciples. This attention to Jesus' body reflects the theological centrality of the body in Christianity.[36]

Here we begin once again to be aware of strong echoes of the Song of Solomon.

> Upon my bed at night
> I sought him whom my soul loves;
> I sought him, but found him not....
> "I will rise now, and go about the city,
>   in the streets and in the squares;
> I will seek him whom my soul loves."
> I sought him, but found him not.

The sentinels found me,
>   as they went about in the city.
"Have you seen him whom my soul loves?"
Scarcely had I passed them,
>   when I found him whom my soul loves.
I held him... (Song 3:1-4).

Mary Magdalene is the distraught beloved, the two angels are "the sentinels," and Jesus is "him whom her soul loves." The nuptial meaning of the Johannine scene is established.

Mary first supposes that Jesus is the *gardener*, and in the present context this directs us to Genesis once again. We are once again in the original garden, where Adam was to be the gardener: "The Lord God took the man and put him in the garden of Eden, to till it and keep it" (Gen 2:15).

⊕

"Mary"—When, in the gospel of John, Jesus addresses individuals by their proper names, the naming may communicate more than we would expect: "Lazarus, come out!" At Cana he addressed his mother as *"woman,"* and again at the cross. Only here, when Jesus is risen and once again in the garden of the first creation, does he use this name *"Mary."*

Then the man said, "This at last is bone of my bones and flesh of my flesh; this one shall be called Woman, for out of Man this one was taken" (Gen 2:23).

This naming of Mary is a climactic moment in the gospel, reflecting Jesus' words to his mother at Cana: "Woman, what concern is that to you and to me? My hour has not yet come" (2:4). Jesus' hour has now arrived, and *woman* has become *Mary*. John has not told us of the history of Mary Magdalene, but Mark recounts this same appearance with these words:

Now after he rose early on the first day of the week, he appeared first to Mary Magdalene, *from whom he had cast out seven demons* (16:9).

When Jesus called *Lazarus* by name, he came out of the tomb as Adam restored to the living. When Jesus calls *Mary* by this name, we can understand a parallel symbolic significance. Through the death and resurrection of Jesus, woman—Eve—has been liberated from the power of evil which had inhabited her, as Lazarus had been freed from death. Both actions are to be interpreted as symbolic of the new creation, in its two complementary aspects represented by the man and the woman.

The relation of this encounter in the garden with its twin, the Cana wedding, develops further as we recall the *six vessels filled with water*. Magdalene is the full vessel of the sixth day, purified throughout by her tears: the sorrow of mortality itself, of the first five days (here she is one with Mary of Bethany mourning for her brother Lazarus). Now she is ready to be filled with the new wine which Jesus brings, and this filling is one with the nuptial union represented by the Cana wedding.

In Genesis 3 *man* was sentenced to work the earth until he returned to it in death, while *woman* was sentenced to give birth in suffering: "...in pain you shall bring forth children..." (Gen 3:16). Both Lazarus and Jesus live out this sentence of Adam, while Mary of Bethany and Magdalene live out that of Eve. Here at the tomb there are the pains of labor (see 16:21-22) and then the joy of a birth.

In Genesis, God took woman from the body of Adam while he slept and then brought her to him to be named (Gen 2:21-23). Here on the sixth day of the new creation, God brings to Jesus, the new man, his helper and spouse in the person of Mary. Like Eve in Genesis 2, she appears at this point as the crowning work of the new creation. She recapitulates and embraces within herself everything that has come before her.[37]

Magdalene, in addressing Jesus with the term *"Rabbouni,"* or Teacher, confirms her role as *disciple*. But she also represents the *beloved*, the bride. We have found the same combination of roles in the expression, the *"disciple* whom Jesus *loved."*

> Jesus said to her, "Do not hold on to me, because I have not yet ascended to the Father. But go to my brothers and say to them, 'I am ascending to my Father and your Father, to my God and your God'" (20:17).

In the Song of Solomon, when the woman found her beloved,

> ...I held him, and would not let him go
> until I brought him into my mother's house,
> and into the chamber of her that conceived me (3:4).

The "mother's house," the chamber, is the feminine vessel in which the wisdom of God will dwell, but this can take place only when Jesus has ascended to his Father. The contrast between Father and mother implicit here is meaningful: from the Father is to come the glory which will fill the chamber of the mother. Here it is not a question of the historical moment of the ascension of Jesus but of a symbolic ascent: the glorification of Jesus by which he is empowered to impart the Holy Spirit to those who believe in him. Thus the new relation of the disciples to God the Father follows upon his ascent to the Father (20:17).

Jesus must ascend to the Father, he must be glorified and at the same time physically withdraw from the disciples (see 16:7), *so that the new interiority, the indwelling, may begin*. The initiation of this new indwelling is represented in the next episode when Jesus breathes the Holy Spirit into the disciples.

II

In this second part of the narrative at the tomb, our attention moves from the two disciples to Magdalene. And so we rejoin the explicit *nuptial* symbolic of the sixth day. A number of chiastic symmetries, some exact and some more general, appear between the narratives of the tomb and *Part I* of John's gospel (see Fig. 1.5). The *garden* in which the encounter between Magdalene and Jesus takes place recalls and contrasts with the *wilderness* of the Baptist, where John's narrative began. This journey of the gospel from desert to garden recalls the *new creation* prophesied by Isaiah (see Is 41:18-20; 65:17-18; 66:22).

We have already observed an approximate chiastic relation between, on the one hand, John the Baptist and the two disciples of chapter 1, and on the other hand Mary Magdalene with the two disciples at the tomb in John 20. It is *the Baptist* who points out Jesus to the first two disciples—one of whom is unnamed, and the other is Andrew, Peter's brother. *Magdalene* introduces the two disciples (beloved disciple and Peter) to the mystery of the empty tomb. The "seeking" of Magdalene and the two disciples in John 20 also recalls the seeking of the disciples in John 1, and there are echoes of the Song of Songs in the running of Mary and the disciples, in the actions and words of this episode.[38]

It is early on the first day of the week, and still dark. This is definitely a *beginning*: we are brought back to the prologue and to our mandalic center, the first day, the creation of light. Light is to be born anew from the womb of darkness here in the garden. In Magdalene's encounter with the risen Jesus in the garden there is both a *completion* and a return to the *beginning*. For John, the *end* is a beginning, the initiation of a new creation.

There is still a *further step* to be made: Jesus is to ascend to the Father and then "return" to breathe the Spirit into the disciples and bring them to life, bring about the birth. The *completion* is signified both in the nuptial encounter of man and woman, and in the "naming" of Mary. The fulfillment itself, however, is nothing but *beginning*, birth-giving. Here (as implicitly at the cross, p. 178 above), there is the closing of a ring with Cana, the wedding banquet, the mother of Jesus and the fullness of woman's destiny and being: the glory.

Woman is once again *"mother* of all living" (Gen 3:20), but now immaculate and God-conferring. But as woman gave birth to the single child Jesus, now woman must be a spring of living water, wine, imparting life to the world, "bringing in" the Spirit, the Life, to the center of the person, the heart (see once again the "womb of creation" at the center of the mandalic figure, the scene upon the waters in section 1).

The tears of this woman, who is full of sorrow, are the water which is symbolically transformed into wine. This wine is what we shall see being *poured into the disciples* in the next scene in John 20: their baptism with the Holy Spirit, the in-breathing by which they become the body of Christ, the new Adam, through his sophianic presence within them.

Sophia is the mercy of God in us. She is the tenderness with which the infinitely mysterious power of pardon turns the darkness of our sins into the light of grace. She is the inexhaustible fountain of kindness, and would almost seem to be, in herself, all mercy. So she does in us a greater work than that of Creation: the work of new being in grace, the work of pardon, the work of transformation from brightness to brightness *tamquam a Domini Spiritu*. She is in us the yielding and tender counterpart of the power, justice and creative dynamism of the Father.[39]

The encounter of the risen Jesus with Mary Magdalene has much in common with his three *earlier encounters* with women on the sixth day.

The *tomb* of John 20 is bridal chamber, womb and wellspring: the tomb in the rock is woman. In the three earlier episodes, the wine, the water, the ointment were *external* to the woman who was associated with them. Here the water is *within* Mary; symbolically the water is *identical* with her. The woman has become once again pure water in passing through death with Jesus; and now this water is to be transformed into wine by the interior fire of the risen Jesus. A unitive progression is suggested in the passage from Cana through Samaria and Bethany to the garden. Having passed through these three geographical places, we stand now with man and woman in the one, original place.

Another overtone of the chiastic movement from Cana to the garden, from "woman" to "Mary," is the progression from first to second creation. Woman was the name of Eve, "mother of all the living." The feminine being signified by this name Mary is mother of all those who are born into the new and unitive life, the divine life. The new man is born and lives from this interior fullness which is the eternal bride, eternal woman, divine Feminine, *Sophia*. This is, too, the wine of the union.

The mysterious childbirth foretold by Jesus (Jn 16:20-22) is symbolically accomplished in the four scenes of John 20. In these first two scenes, belonging to the sixth day, the unitive child has been born, in the person of the disciple, and the woman's sorrow has been turned into joy as she encounters the new man who has been brought into the world. On this sixth day, however, boundaries are freely crossed. The woman about to give birth is at once the disciples and these four women and this one woman, and the child will be one disciple and all the disciples, Jesus himself and even the women who have brought him to this birth which is new creation.

$$\oplus$$

At five-thirty in the morning I am dreaming in a very quiet room when a soft voice awakens me from my dream. I am like all mankind awakening from all the dreams that ever were dreamed in all the nights of the world. It is like the One Christ awakening in all the separate selves that ever were separate and isolated and alone in all the lands of the earth. It is like all minds coming back together into awareness from all distractions, cross-purposes and confusions, into unity of love. It is like the first morning of the world (when Adam, at the sweet voice of Wisdom, awoke from nonentity and knew her), and like the Last Morning of the world when all the fragments of Adam will return from death at the voice of Hagia Sophia, and will know where they stand.

It is like being awakened by Eve. It is like being awakened by the Blessed Virgin. It is like coming forth from primordial nothingness and standing in clarity, in Paradise.[40]

⊕

The attentions of Mary of Bethany and Magdalene to the *body* of Jesus, before and after his crucifixion, correspond to the focus of the entire gospel narrative—at this point of his death and resurrection—upon this body from which life is to come into the world. This is both a transition to "feminine language" and a movement of incarnation. Death, sexuality and birth mark this supreme point of density of the corporeal. It is through the *body*, as it is through *woman*, that the new life comes, that it is given and received.

The woman is *mother*: Magdalene's motherhood is suggested here also by the parallel positions of Magdalene and the mother of Jesus in the chiastically related scenes of the garden and the Cana wedding. The new Mary is associated with the open tomb—womb of the earth —at which she lingers. Here at the tomb, the woman is present to represent the *mother of the disciple, of the new man begotten of God*. She is the one who runs to carry to the disciples, "my brothers," the word of Jesus' resurrection and his words about this new brotherhood of theirs, this new unitive relationship by which each of them and all of them are the one Son of God in the bosom of the Father. "I am ascending to my Father and your Father, to my God and your God."

The *open tomb*, hole in the surface of the earth, is symbolically open to the *center*, like the well in Samaria. It reaches into the creative waters of our mandalic center. A passage from the Pauline letter to the Ephesians suggests the cosmic and personal depths of what is happening here: "...what does it mean but that he had also descended into the lower parts of the earth? He who descended is the same one who ascended far above the heavens, so that he might *fill all things*" (Eph 4:9-10). This is "a new tomb where no one had ever been laid" (19:41). It is a virgin tomb, virgin rock, virgin earth, into which Jesus' body is placed. Woman here in John 20 is symbolically parallel to "earth," cosmos, as in the Genesis story (compare Gen 3:16 with 3:17-18). Both earth and Mary Magdalene are "mother."

The seventh day will continue to develop this new birth, in the symbolic language derived from the first chapters of Genesis.

THE SIXTH DAY: SYNTHETIC REVIEW

On the sixth day of creation, our gospel opens out into a fullness, a more perfect symmetry, a four-petalled blossoming of the sapiential-symbolic language of John. These four episodes are more intimately related, and more nearly approach a single image, than do the episodes of any of the other days. It is as if the gospel had suddenly come into focus and its overall symmetrical structure had become apparent all at once.

The four Jesus-woman narratives may be seen as the four *poles* of the mandalic figure, so that the women represent the height and depth, the length and breadth, so to speak, of the Christ-event. We shall see more precisely how both the *intensive* or unitive dimension, and the *extensive* or anthropological-social dimension, are represented by these four women. The four women whom Jesus encounters, then, encompass the whole of humanity with all its possibilities. They are, together, the one bride of the Word. The essentially nuptial character of John's vision is apparent in the simplicity of this convergence.

This nuptial flowering follows immediately upon the death and burial of Jesus, and it represents the obverse of his passion: on the sixth day is symbolized the *glorification* of Jesus. This is to be found not on the literal but on the *symbolic* level, and John has provided plenty of clues pointing in this direction—particularly in the symbolism of the early chapters of Genesis.

$$\oplus$$

Behind the narratives of the sixth day we become aware again and again of the presence of *Adam and Eve*. Out of this Genesis background centered in the first man and woman, John develops his vision of a unitive new creation. After the complex drama and dialectic of the earlier days, the sixth day returns to an elemental simplicity in these scenes of Jesus interacting with woman.

Exodus symbolism remains throughout the whole of the sixth day, however, and will continue until the end of the gospel. Jesus, as long as he is visible in this world, is still an exodus-figure. The chiastic resonances between Jesus and John the Baptist will underline this even on the seventh day. The persistent reminder of Jesus' *hour*, or its equivalent, the sense of anticipation of a union still to be consummated even after Jesus is risen, the "do not hold on to me, because I have not yet ascended..." to the woman, all insist that exodus is still a reality, that, even at the end of the sixth day, a further step remains to be taken. The fullness of union which is indicated by the nuptial imagery of the sixth day must be interiorized and opened to all the other disciples, and this will happen on the seventh day. Meanwhile, in each of these scenes in which Jesus has interacted with woman—as if woman would *prematurely* restore the garden of creation with its sufficiency, its abounding and flowering presence—we found a reminder of the exodus, the journey yet to be completed.

The movement of the fourth gospel proceeds both from *exodus* to new creation and from *first creation* to new creation. One principal function of the abundant exodus symbolism in John is to represent a *mediated* religion: one which depends essentially upon human representatives and religious ritual. The new exodus is a liberation from confinement within the mediating forms of the Mosaic religion which were instituted at the time of the first exodus. Where the first exodus was a *going out* from the "natural worship" or cosmic religion of paganism, the new exodus is the movement into a new interiority: an *entering in*. Where the first exodus was immediately followed by the institution of a legal enclosure around the people of Israel, the new exodus is a going out from this imprisonment within the law (4:21-24; see also Gal 5:1-6). While the first exodus constitutes a *dualistic* worship, the new exodus is a liberating movement into the *unitive*. This is precisely the new and immanent creation. New exodus and new creation are two sides of the same reality.[41]

$$\oplus$$

While there is a progression from one episode to the next during the sixth day, we shall find it more necessary here to *combine* the scenes, to view them synthetically. The Cana narrative, unequaled as a symbol of fulfillment, begins rather than concludes the sixth day. This alerts us to expect, between these "feminine" stories, rather a circular and unitive relationship than a linear one.

A nuptial symbolism, more or less explicit, runs consistently through the four narratives. The principal symbols are, first, *woman*, and, second, some *liquid* of human importance with which woman is associated: whether drinking water or wine or a precious ointment or the tears of mourning. Convergent in meaning, and ultimately *one*, are woman, the life-giving liquid which she ministers, the Spirit which Jesus is to pour out, the glory of God which Jesus is to receive and impart, and the mode of his future presence in his disciples. The central dynamic of John's gospel is expressed, on this sixth day, in a symbolism which is predominantly *sexual*.

Among the evangelists, John, identified with "the disciple whom Jesus loved," is the scholar of love. In his own intimacy with Jesus, sexuality is, symbolically, both expressed and transcended;[42] it is in his dwelling place "in the bosom of Jesus" that the deep tides of *eros* which move through our being open to reveal their source, that love which is divine life. In the experience of this disciple in the tomb, we have found the further movement beyond sexuality and beyond imagery to the ultimate terminus of the *unitive child*. This movement will be further developed on the seventh day.

We have seen that the sexual metaphor in the New Testament has traditionally been interpreted in terms of the union of the Word, as Bridegroom, with that bride who is at once the church, the mother of Jesus and the soul of each believer. This is in continuity with the image of Israel as the bride of God in the Hebrew scriptures. The later biblical tradition which sees the divine wisdom, represented by a feminine figure, as both the companion of God and the companion of man,[43] has had few followers in Christian tradition.[44] When both the Word and wisdom of God were presented by the New Testament authors as conclusively present in the man Jesus, both Word and wisdom took on an apparently definitive masculine identity. Our study of John's gospel suggests that this has been a one-sided development. The symbolic depths of human sexuality exist in God before the creation; both masculine and feminine are present archetypally in the divinity—*God is a wedding*.

Further, John's development of the man-woman relationship, culminating on the sixth day, opens to our exploration the *other side*, the alternative interpretation, of the sexual metaphor in terms of the union of divine and human. He brings forward the biblical revelation of *Sophia* to the point at which the "divine Feminine" expresses the new mode of divine immanence[45] which we have called new creation. The corona of women which blossoms on the sixth day represents this new filling of humanity—and therefore virtually of the cosmos—with the *Shekinah*,[46] the divine *Sophia*, the glory which is God's presence in the creation.

⊕

We can trace a certain consistent *progression* through the four "feminine" episodes of the sixth day. At Cana, several indications mark the narrative as a *beginning*. The presence of Jesus' mother recalls his birth. This, "the *first* of his signs," occurs at the start of Jesus' public life. The meeting with the Samaritaness at midday signifies the "*middle*" of Jesus' life, the point of widest geographical expansion from which it will then contract toward his death. The anointing by Mary at Bethany, "for my burial," marks this third point, the *death* of Jesus. The final tomb episode, with its two parts—the first centered upon the disciple whom Jesus loved and the second upon Magdalene—symbolizes the ultimate point of arrival of the gospel, which is the dawn of the new life, the divine *birth*. This is expressed both in the "child" who is the disciple and in the "mother" who is at once Mary and the divine Spirit, divine wisdom, new wine. Here we must recall Jesus' words to his mother and to the disciple, from the cross (19:26-27).

⊕

This structure seems clear and solid. Is the progression expressed also in a consistent symbolic development of *Adam and Eve*, man and woman, since we have found such frequent reference in John to the narratives of the first chapters of Genesis?

As we study this biblical theology we must keep continually in mind that woman, the feminine, Eve, and man, Adam, are *symbolic* expressions of realities which lie fully within *both* woman and man. At the same time, this "symbolic" duality is written indelibly in the bodies of men and women, and continues to play an undiminished role in human existence and history. The relationship between gender and the fullness of potential of the human person—this precious truth which emerges in our time—is still far from clear.

When, in the Genesis story, God has created Adam and placed him in the garden,

> Then the Lord God said, "It is not good that the man should be alone; I will make him a helper as his partner" (Gen 2:18).

Then God creates the various living creatures, as if they were sketches for such a helper, but "for the man there was not found a helper as his partner." Finally God puts Adam to sleep, and *from within him* takes a rib and fashions from it a woman, whom he brings to the man to be named.

John completes the diptych with a corresponding scene: the encounter of Magdalene and Jesus in the garden, against the background of the earlier episodes of the sixth day. As, in the Genesis story,[47] woman was created so that man might not be "*alone*"—taken from within him and then presented to him as companion—here on the sixth day woman is transformed, created anew, and presented to man (Jesus) to receive her name. Symbolically, woman is about to be *restored to her original interior place.* Now, however, the "interior feminine" is not only part of man's created nature—with her enters *the divine Feminine, Sophia.*

Woman, in Christ, becomes the bearer no longer of the deadly fruit but of the living water, the oil of immortality, the wine of union which corresponds to her own nature, her very femininity. And thus it is once again "through woman" that Christ comes into the world this second time, at his resurrection. It is through the interior femininity of the human person, that *unitive interiority* of the person, that the divine Unitive (i.e. divine Feminine, or Holy Spirit) enters into humanity and creates it anew. It is through the fourfold river of the interior feminine that the new life flows out into all the world. This is the meaning of Cana and of each of the "woman" episodes of the sixth day.

"It is not good that the man should be alone." The *"aloneness"* of humanity is potentially overcome in this gift of the divine Feminine— for this gift is itself relationality, the unitive. As a shattered and alienated humanity becomes the dwelling of this sophianic presence, it is both joined with God and reintegrated within itself.

These four episodes may be seen also, then, as *stages* in the unfolding of the destiny of the feminine: symbolically, of *"woman."* At *Cana* there is present the natural mother of Jesus, of man, Eve who is "mother of all living." In *Samaria* we see Eve, woman, strayed far from her vocation into promiscuity and ignorance, and, at the apogee of this orbit, recalled to her inner meaning by the young prophet at the well. Blazing into her soul like the noonday sun, he tells her "all she ever did" and offers her the mercy of living water from the inner well which is her own core. He gives her the truth of her own living self.

At *Bethany,* we recall that this woman is double. Martha has responded (still on the fifth day) to the death of man on the practical level, going out to meet Jesus with a Petrine confession of faith, while Mary mourned within the house, as if already suffering the pangs of a yet unrecognized birth. Remaining with her sorrow she resembled the disciple whom Jesus loved, and through Magdalene she will become associated with the birth of this disciple in the same tomb where Jesus himself will have been buried. Meanwhile she anoints Jesus for his burial—for this tomb—with a gesture in which wedding celebration and sexual union and death and the pouring out of the divine Feminine, the Spirit, are all expressed. The betrothal made at the well in Samaria is here symbolically consummated, in a perfect feminine ritualization of the paschal transformation and outpouring of the Word. Here sexuality itself descends into the darkness of death to undergo its sea-change, its rebirth into spirituality.

The encounter of Magdalene with Jesus in the *garden* is the icon of this new birth of woman and of sexuality, in which the multiform water which is the feminine, or the human unitive, becomes the wine of divine wisdom, the "embodiment," or materiality, of Spirit, now to be poured out for all the guests.

$$\oplus$$

The movement from Word to Spirit, from a largely dualistic "masculine" revelation of God to the interior "feminine" and unitive revelation (or self-communication) of God, is expressed with incomparable power and subtlety in John's gospel. This dramatic transition can be seen as the *hinge*, the pivotal center, of the entire *biblical history*.[48]

We can also view the development of the world's great *religions* in this perspective, if we postulate a simultaneous "double revelation," corresponding approximately to east and to west (see below, p. 404). In the east, the quest for union with the Divine has for millennia been largely by way of various paths of non-dual interiority,[49] based explicitly or implicitly upon the *immanence* of divinity in the world. In the west, on the other hand, revelation through the *Word* of God has been primary. Only in our own time has the dialectic between these two great revelations articulated itself with clarity. In our time we can see both the urgent necessity and the possibility to develop once again, and with a new comprehensiveness, a *unitive vision within Christianity*. John's gospel offers itself as the primary biblical source for such a development.[50] It is in this culmination of the New Testament revelation that the unitive fullness within the divine Word itself is revealed, and the common root of both eastern and western spiritual traditions is glimpsed.

Taking a further step, we can see the *inner history of humankind* as centered in the pivotal event of the incarnation of the Word, and this event as the entry of God into a new immanence within humanity and thus within the creation. It is not only in John's gospel that this revolution is manifested through a new realization of the *feminine*: it is also in our own contemporary experience, both individual and collective.

⊕

The feminine principle in the world is the inexhaustible source of creative realizations of the Father's glory. She is His manifestation in radiant splendor! But she remains unseen, glimpsed only by a few. Sometimes there are none who know her at all.[51]

Chapter Seven

The Seventh Day:
Into the Place of His Rest

Thus the heavens and the earth were finished, and all their multitude. And on the seventh day God finished the work that he had done, and he rested on the seventh day from all the work that he had done. So God blessed the seventh day and hallowed it, because on it God rested from all the work that he had done in creation (Gen 2:1-3).

... then the Lord God formed man from the dust of the ground, and breathed into his nostrils the breath of life; and the man became a living being. And the Lord God planted a garden in Eden, in the east; and there he put the man whom he had formed. Out of the ground the Lord God made to grow every tree that is pleasant to the sight and good for food, the tree of life also in the midst of the garden, and the tree of the knowledge of good and evil. A river flows out of Eden to water the garden, and from there it divides and becomes four branches (Gen 2:7-10).

Then the Lord God said, "See, the man has become like one of us, knowing good and evil; and now, he might reach out his hand and take also from the tree of life, and eat, and live forever"—therefore the Lord God sent him forth from the garden of Eden, to till the ground from which he was taken. He drove out the man; and at the east of the garden of Eden he placed the cherubim, and a sword flaming and turning to guard the way to the tree of life (Gen 3:22-24).

⊕

For we who have believed enter that rest, just as God has said,

"As in my anger I swore,
'They shall not enter my rest'" (Ps 95:11),

though his works were finished at the foundation of the world. For in one place it speaks about the seventh day as follows, "And God rested on the seventh day from all his works." And again in this place it says, "They shall not enter my rest." Since therefore it remains open for some to enter it, and those who formerly received the good news failed to enter because of disobedience, again he sets a certain day— "today"—saying through David much later, in the words already quoted,

"Today, if you hear his voice,
do not harden your hearts" (Ps 95:7-8).

For if Joshua had given them rest, God would not speak later about another day. So then, a sabbath rest still remains for the people of God; for those who enter God's rest also cease from their labors as God did from his. Let us therefore make every effort to enter that rest... (Heb 4:3-11a).

⊕

No one has ever seen God.
It is God the only Son,
who is in the Father's bosom,
who has made him known (Jn 1:18).

From Mary *Magdalene* with Jesus at the tomb, we return to the *Baptist* by the Jordan River, at the beginning of John's narrative: an abrupt change of scene from the garden to the wilderness of Judea. Garden and desert are mysteriously related, however, and we become aware of a peculiar insistence on *place* as Jesus appears and begins to attract disciples. We soon find ourselves in an atmosphere which is strangely like that of that mythical garden of the sixth day. The fragrance of that garden—of the first garden of Genesis and the meeting of man and woman—is sensed in the delicacy of this first meeting of Jesus with his disciples. Their seeking is reminiscent of Magdalene, seeking the body of Jesus, as well as of the two disciples who ran to the tomb at her word. The union which has flowered so splendidly in the nuptial symbolism of the sixth day will now disappear once again into the everyday of faith to dwell *within* the disciples, on this enduring *today* of Jesus' sabbath, the seventh day of the new creation.

SECTION 20: 1:19-51
THE BAPTIST AND THE FIRST DISCIPLES

The sabbath of the new creation begins in the quiet of the Judean desert, where John is baptizing. From the weeping woman at the empty tomb in the garden, we come to this man by the river in the wilderness. This place does not suggest the fullness we might expect here. John's narrative begins as priests and levites from Jerusalem come to question the Baptist about his mission. For a reply he takes up the words of the prophet Isaiah,

A voice cries out:
"In the wilderness prepare the way of the Lord,
make straight in the desert a highway for our God" (Is 40:3).

In the text of Isaiah, this passage immediately follows the grand opening of the book of consolation:

Comfort, oh comfort my people, says your God.
Speak tenderly to Jerusalem, and cry to her
that she has served her term, that her penalty is paid,
that she has received from the Lord's hand
double for all her sins (Is 40:1-2).

Like Moses, the Baptist leads the people out into the "sabbath" of the desert. Like Moses again, he will not himself lead them into the promised land of consolation, the sabbath of fullness.

John the Baptist appears immediately after the solemn music of the prologue, and it is the same John who initiates the public ministry of Jesus in the other gospels. In the fourth gospel, John is immediately placed within a structure of *contrasts*. The first contrast is suggested by the questioning of the *priests and levites* sent to him from Jerusalem by the Jews. This "man sent from God," preaching repentance in the wilderness with a voice very different from that of official Judaism of the time, constitutes an implicit prophetic indictment of the Jewish religious establishment. Jesus will carry this prophetic confrontation much farther than John, and the mounting conflict between Jesus and the religious authorities will finally lead to his death.

The second contrast is implicit in John's *responses* to the questions of these officials, and is seen more clearly in the Greek. John replies with a series of three negatives to the three questions about his identity: "*I am not the Messiah*"; "*I am not*"; "*No.*" It is in Second Isaiah, to which the Baptist refers, that we find the great affirmations of Yahweh which his own negations reflect.

I, the Lord, am first, and will be (Gr. *egō eimi*) with the last (Is 41:4).

I, I am he (Gr. *egō eimi, egō eimi*) who blots out your transgressions for my own sake, and I will not remember your sins (Is 43:25).

John's negative self-designations place him in precise contrast with the Creator-God of Deutero-Isaiah. Jesus, on the other hand, employs the divine "*I Am*" in identifying himself.[1] It is he, rather than Moses or the Baptist, who opens the way of the final exodus in his own death.

This background of exodus and of the divine "*I Am*" points to the transcendence of symbol and image that is now to prevail, as we enter the sabbath of the Word. A certain parallel is evident between the prohibition of images in the worship of Israel and the quiet, the "apophatic" character of that sabbath day which stood at the center of the covenant worship.[2] As we cross the threshold of the seventh day, the sabbath of the new creation, we shall find the symbolic representations leading beyond themselves into an interior unity.

The focus on the *identity* of the Baptist at the beginning of this episode matches the intense concentration of attention on the identity of Jesus toward its end. John functions as the plain or vacant background, the foil, to that which appears in Jesus. The Baptist is he who is *not*, the voice rather than the Word, the friend of the bridegroom rather than the bridegroom, the lamp rather than the light, and the one who baptizes with water in contrast with the one who will baptize with the Holy Spirit.

⊕

The movement into the seventh day, then, recapitulates the chiastic two-stage history of the exodus time. First there takes place the *exodus* from the old Jerusalem, represented by the Baptist at the Jordan. Then there will be the *entry* into the promised land, or paradise, the garden of the beginning. John the Baptist leads the people out of the old order of an institutional religion which has grown corrupt, into the wilderness of repentance, a personal encounter with the Lord, signified by his baptism with water. In this he resembles *Moses*, leading the Israelites out of Egypt. It is left for Jesus, the new *Joshua*, to lead the people *into* the promised land which is a new and immediate relationship with God.

But if the Baptist, this man in the desert, recalls Moses and the exodus, he also recalls *Adam* and the Genesis story of the creation and the fall. His wilderness contrasts with the *garden* from which the first man and woman were expelled after their sin. Adam, the first man, fallen from his high estate and bereft of the glory of God (see Rom 3:23), sojourns in the wilderness. The Baptist husbands a river of compunction which recalls only faintly the glory, the bride (see Is 43:19-21).

John identifies Jesus as the *Lamb of God* who takes away the sin of the world. This title reflects both the *Passover lamb* of exodus times and the *servant of Yahweh* who appears in Deutero-Isaiah. It contrasts with popular expectations of the messiah, as does the wild Baptist himself.

While John does not recount the *baptism of Jesus* by John in his narrative, he alludes to it very clearly (1:33-34; see Mk 1:9-11). This event, with its theophany, will persist as a dominant image behind both episodes of the seventh day. The dove descending upon Jesus, representing the Holy Spirit, recalls the dove which departed from Noah's ark at the end of the flood and remained on the newly emergent earth. The return of the dove and its remaining upon Jesus indicate that the passage through the waters has been completed and that Jesus is himself the promised land of the new creation. The dove, as Kermode points out, is a figure of "that *pneuma* that brooded over the formless waste of waters in the beginning, at the great threshold between darkness and light"[3]—that is, at the first creation. The seventh day returns us not only to the beginning of John's gospel, but to the first day of creation.

The Spirit descends and *remains* upon Jesus: the word used here (Gr. *menein*) is the same which has been used frequently in John to indicate the way in which the disciples are to relate to Jesus and his word. It will be used again here in a moment. Remain, *dwell*: this corresponds to the sabbath, the seventh day.

There is a particular poignancy and magic in the first dialogue of Jesus with his disciples-to-be (1:37-39). It is at this point that the reader, like the two disciples, may first experience the power which emanates from the person of Jesus. These two disciples seem to "fall in love" with Jesus;[4] his words to them reflect the invitation of divine wisdom. In the order of the narrative this courtship of the first disciples will conclude at the end of the "first week of creation" with the Cana wedding and the pouring out of the good wine. The movement from water to wine corresponds to the progression from the Baptist to Jesus.

"What are you looking for?" These words, in the Johannine context, resound with a metaphysical depth. There are echoes here not only of the Wisdom literature (see Prov 8:34-36; Sir 24:19-21; Wis 6:12-14) but of the concluding chapter of Deutero-Isaiah: "Seek the Lord while he may be found…" (Is 55:6).

Jesus will bring the exodus journey, upon which these disciples of the Baptist have embarked, to its destination. They sense this, and respond with a further pregnant question, "Rabbi, where are you *staying (meneis)*?" The Greek verb *menein*, from the beginning of John's narrative, had borne that connotation of depth which reached its fullest expression at the supper, in Jesus' words about the indwelling, the new immanence which the disciples would experience when he had departed from them.

The *"come and see"* of Jesus echoes Isaiah once again, as well as the woman of the Wisdom books.

> So, everyone who thirsts, come to the waters;
> and you that have no money, come, buy and eat!
> Come, buy wine and milk without money and without
> price… (Is 55:1).

"Come and see." The words are heavy with meaning,[5] recalling the two healings on the fourth day and the experience of the disciple in the tomb. Now these two disciples of the Baptist respond to his invitation—they follow him, they come where he is, they *see*, and very

soon they are apostles of Jesus, summoning others to come and see what they have seen. One by one the others respond to the witness of this power; they come to him, they see and they are his.

"What are you looking for?"—whom do you seek? This question is asked by Jesus in two other places: in the garden of his arrest to those who come to apprehend him, and in the garden of his tomb to Magdalene who seeks his body.

The "*other disciple*," strangely unidentified inasmuch as Andrew is named, is not further mentioned as Jesus gathers Peter, Philip, and Nathanael to himself.

⊕

The meaning of *Nathanael's* exchange with Jesus emerges against the background of a story in the book of Genesis (ch. 28). Jacob, on a journey, stops to rest for the night at Haran.

And he dreamed that there was a ladder set up on the earth, the top of it reaching to heaven; and the angels of God were ascending and descending on it (Gen 28:12).

...Then Jacob woke from his sleep, and said, "Surely the Lord is in this place—and I did not know it!" And he was afraid, and said, "How awesome is this place! This is none other than the house of God, and this is the gate of heaven"(Gen 28:16-17).

Nathanael's exclamation of astonishment at Jesus' knowledge echoes this cry of Jacob. Jesus' final words to Nathanael indicate that it is the *Son of Man* who will be the "house of God and gate of heaven"; where he is, the heavens shall be opened and a new intercourse with God come to be.

Nathanael beneath his tree, Nathanael speaking with contempt of Nazareth: these recurrent allusions to *place* bring us finally to the symbolic *garden and its tree* at the end of this episode. From the garden near Jerusalem with its tomb, at the end of the sixth day, we have made an exodus into the desert of the Baptist, and then come with Jesus into Galilee and to the garden of the beginning, with its tree reaching from earth into heaven.

The outspoken Nathanael, true Israelite *without guile*, is seen by Jesus under the *fig tree*. Adam and Eve, when they had eaten from the tree and saw themselves to be naked, "sewed fig leaves together and made themselves aprons," and then they *"hid* themselves from the presence of the Lord among the trees of the garden" (Gen 3:8).

The connections are not accidental. Nathanael is not only a Jacob/Israel, he is also an *Adam*. This Adam is no longer afraid, no longer hides himself among the trees of the garden. Jesus, when he *sees* him underneath the fig tree, recalls the Creator who walked in the garden in the cool of the day and called to the man, "Where are you?" He promises that Nathanael shall *see* greater things.

At the conclusion of this first chapter of John, we are left with Jesus in the place of the ladder stretched from earth to heaven, and the disciples have seen where he *dwells*, where he is rooted. The fig tree under which he saw Nathanael is also the "cosmic tree" which unites the created world with God.[6]

> You will see greater things than these...you will see heaven opened and the angels of God ascending and descending upon the Son of man (1:51).

Since we do not see this promise of Jesus literally fulfilled anywhere in John's gospel, these very explicit words of Jesus present a difficult problem of interpretation. C.H. Dodd[7] interprets the vision of the angels as a metaphorical expression for the revelation of Jesus' glory through the whole series of his signs and finally his death and resurrection. These words will receive further light from the encounter of Thomas with the risen Jesus in our next episode. There we shall ponder the meaning of this most suggestive title, which Jesus uses for himself, *"the Son of Man."*[8]

These final words of Jesus to Nathanael resonate strangely with the synoptic account of Jesus' baptism.

> In those days Jesus came from Nazareth of Galilee and was baptized by John in the Jordan. And just as he was coming up out of the water, he saw the heavens torn apart and the Spirit descending like a dove on him. And a voice came from heaven, "You are my beloved Son; with you I am well pleased" (Mk 1:9-11).

It is at Jesus' baptism, then, that the *heavens are opened*, and the Spirit *descends* as Jesus *ascends* from the water. The heavenly voice affirms Jesus to be the Son of God, while in John 1:51 he speaks of himself as Son of Man. This final verse of John's first episode is evidently related to that same event to which the Baptist had referred earlier: Jesus' baptism in the Jordan. There is a strong tradition in early Christianity which sees Christian baptism as a participation in the messianic anointing which Jesus received symbolically at the moment of his own baptism.[9]

Since baptism, in the early church, was often seen also as the re-entry into paradise,[10] it is not unreasonable to see a connection between the "heaven opened" here in John 1:51 and the entrance to the promised land which is also the sabbath[11] of the new creation.

John's narrative brings the epiphany at Jesus' baptism in the wilderness together with Jacob's vision of the ladder between heaven and earth—and implicitly with the garden of paradise opened and the tree of life extending from earth to heaven. All of this points forward to that which is to take place when Jesus has died and risen once again. The Son of Man, here declared Son of God, will open a living way between heaven and earth as he ascends to bestow the Spirit upon his disciples,[12] in whom he is present on earth. The "angels of God ascending and descending," which Jacob had seen, give way before this constitutive new "way of the Lord" which is Jesus himself, the tree of life.

SECTION 21: 20:19-31
JESUS APPEARS TO THE GATHERED DISCIPLES

I

They came together that evening in the usual place, and shut the doors securely against the terror that moved like a dark sea in their own hearts. Two claimed that they had seen him, but many other strange things were being said as well. And suddenly he was there in the room. They knew it was he by the sudden change within themselves; there was no need for further evidence. Within the room now a subtle light opened door after door within them. The night upon the sea, when he came to them and said to them, "Do not fear, *I Am*." The supper in the upstairs room. Their minds moved through the corridors of scripture, through door after opened door: huddled darkness of the Passover night, the ark with its living cargo tossing upon the mountainous sea—and the first night, when the Spirit played over the waters like a great bird.

"Peace be with you," he said, and the *I Am* was a bush aflame in their hearts. He showed them the red marks in his wrists and in his side. He moved from one to another, as on the evening when he had washed their feet, but this time he breathed upon each face. He was gone, and when they looked once again at one another, each face was shining from within. Afterward, all they could say was, "We have seen the Lord."

⊕

The meaning of Jesus' appearances to the disciples in the closed house emerges only gradually as we reflect on each of the details of John's narrative, in relationship with all that has gone before.

"On that day, the first day of the week": this expression, as it is used for the day of Jesus' resurrection, opens to a fullness which transcends time itself. This first day, *dies solis*,[13] day of the sun, will become the *one day*, the day of the Lord, the *"today"* of the letter to the Hebrews (4:3-10) and of the liturgy. Jesus himself, risen, is the one day of the new creation. In the synoptic parallels, the disciples are at table, and there is a meal, suggesting the influence—or the origin—of the Christian eucharistic tradition.

⊕

Deutero-Isaiah speaks of the eschatological day of the Lord in words which recall to us the Johannine first day of creation.

> Therefore my people shall know my name; therefore in that day they shall know that it is I (Gr. *egō eimi*) who speak; here am I (Is 52:6).

⊕

The seventh day of creation is the day of *God's rest*, when he has finished his works. The letter to the Hebrews presents the life of God's people as a journey toward that rest, and therefore presents the rest itself, the sabbath, as a *place*.

> ...for if Joshua had given them rest, God would not speak later of another day. So then, a sabbath rest still remains for the people of God... (Heb 4:8-9).

John also imagines the sabbath of creation as a place. It is both promised land and heaven and paradise. It is the image of garden, of paradise, which is most generative here, in keeping with John's basic theme of creation. On the seventh day, the new creation is initiated as God and humanity are united in the place which is the *body* of the Son of Man. This body is presented, in John 20, both as the pierced body of *Jesus*, risen from the dead, and as the body of the *disciples*, into whom Jesus breathes the Holy Spirit.

This image of the *desired place*, place of peace and union, is able to gather into itself much of the imagery of the Hebrew scriptures: the progression through the desert to the promised land in Exodus, as well as the garden of Genesis. The image of the house of God, the tabernacle and temple, is gathered in as well. A further important reference for John here is the place where Jacob encountered God, and to which he gave the name Bethel, house of God. The Johannine sabbath, therefore, is both time and place[14] and at the same time *beyond* time and place. It is here on the seventh day that the dimensions of the first creation and the symbols that germinate from it are *transcended* in the unitive interiority which is the terminus of the gospel journey.

⊕

The place where the disciples are gathered, "... the doors of the house ... locked for fear of the Jews," may have a multiple symbolic value for John. Here, near the end of his gospel, it suggests a drama not yet completed. The closed place recalls the houses where the Israelites sheltered themselves behind closed doors on the Passover night (Ex 12:22-27) as well as the ark of Noah, sealed as it rolled upon the waters of the flood (Gen 7:11–8:19). It recalls the tomb of Jesus and suggests also a child in the womb, just before the moment of birth (see 16:20-22).

"Fear of the Jews" here may be taken in an extended sense: the disciples have not yet been liberated from the weight of the old order, symbolized in John by "the Jews," and particularly the Jewish leaders.[15] The closed house may therefore signify the synagogue, the Jewish religion, Israel, the *temple*—house of God closed to the Gentiles —and the law which, according to Paul as well, governed a religious world characterized by fear rather than by grace or love (see Rom 8:15; 2 Cor 3:6-9; 1 Jn 4:17-18). There is even a contrast with the *body of Jesus* here, which is manifested precisely as *opened*. We recall also the promise of the "heaven opened" which had concluded the matching episode, and the related theophanies of Jacob, of Nathanael and of Thomas: "This is the gate of heaven..."

The closed space suggests also, however, the *interior* of the *person*. Jesus appears in the middle of this closed room as he manifests his presence within the soul, still shut within its fears. Here is an archetypal experience which has been often discussed by spiritual writers.[16]

"Jesus came and stood among them..."(Gr. *eis to meson*, literally, *in the midst*) (20:19). The same expression will be used for the second appearance (20:26), and it recalls the words of John the Baptist in 1:26. The appearance of Jesus *in the midst* of his disciples here has a depth resonance, for it is here that the final interiorization of his presence will take place. John's words, *"eis to meson,"* together with the closed place in these two appearances, suggest more strongly still an *interior* manifestation to the disciples. All of the revelation of *interiority* of John 14 then pours into these scenes. Thomas, the twin, still ignorant of the unitive experience, demands an exterior or "dualistic" manifestation of Jesus. This is granted to him, but along with a much more powerful experience within himself. And so his double cry.

$$\oplus$$

Jesus' greeting to the gathered disciples, "Peace to you" (NRSV: Peace be with you), which will be repeated twice (20:19.21.26), is not a mere wish;[17] it signifies the gift which he is conferring upon them. This word (*shalom* in Hebrew, *eirēnē* in John's Greek), in the light of what has gone before in John's gospel, expresses quite exactly the meaning of the seventh day.

The primary meaning of the Greek word is a state of *rest*,[18] and this corresponds to "God's rest," the *sabbath* which is the seventh day, as well as to the "resting" or dwelling of God in the new temple, inaugurated with the gift of the Holy Spirit. The Hebrew *shalom*, however, has a meaning—basically religious—which reaches much further. *Shalom* is, first of all, a state of well-being which embraces body and soul. In the course of its development in the Old Testament it gradually comes to signify the totality of the blessings which will accompany the coming of the *Messiah*, and thus becomes a global expression of the hope of Israel (Is 9:6-7; see 11:1-9; 57:19; 60:17; 66:12).

In the New Testament, "peace" usually indicates this messianic peace as experienced through Jesus Christ: the eschatological salvation of the whole person.

> May the God of peace himself sanctify you entirely; and may
> your spirit and soul and body be kept sound (or complete)

and blameless at the coming of Our Lord Jesus Christ (1 Thess 5:23).

When Jesus promised his peace to the disciples in the context of their last supper before his death (14:27;16:33), the immediate sense of this word seemed to be an interior tranquillity and strength in the face of a hostile world. As Jesus, now risen from the dead, appears to the disciples, his peace takes on the fuller biblical meaning: it is a communication of his own fullness of life. Solomon, the king of peace, has returned to share the fruits of his victory with those who have followed him. Jesus had concluded his words to them at the supper with: "I have said this to you, so that in me you may have peace. In the world you face persecution. But take courage, I have conquered the world" (16:33). This gift of peace, as he breathes the divine Spirit into them now, is the beginning of a *new* world.

⊕

That Jesus, after his resurrection, showed his *wounds* to the disciples is attested also by Luke, according to whom "...he showed them his hands and his feet" (24:40). John's special attention to the wound in Jesus' *side* may be related to the gift of the Spirit here in the same episode (19:34). This showing of Jesus' wounds verifies his identity: this one who stands before you is the crucified one. The wounds, persisting in his risen body, suggest that his passion and death are somehow woven into the fabric of his risen life, as well as into the life of his followers (see Rom 6:3-8; Gal 2:19-20; 6:14; Col 3:3). By these wounds, Jesus' body has been *opened*; this will be of symbolic importance especially in the Thomas narrative.

⊕

"As the Father has sent me, so I send you." The new relationship of "identity" with Jesus, into which he now brings them (see 20:17), will be expressed immediately in terms of *ministry*. Jesus has used this word "send" both for himself as sent by the Father and for the Spirit which will be sent by the Father (14:26) and by Jesus himself (15:26; 16:7).

When Jesus breathes on the disciples, conferring upon them the Holy Spirit, he brings the dramatic movement of John's gospel symbolically to its *conclusion*: the divine life has finally been given to humanity, and the Spirit of God dwells within the human body as its temple. Jesus' action clearly alludes to the decisive moment of the *creation of Adam/humanity*, in the second Genesis account.

> ...then the Lord God formed man from the dust of the ground, and breathed into his nostrils the breath of life; and the man became a living being (Gen 2:7).

The same gesture recalls the bringing *back* to life of "the whole house of Israel" in one of the visions of Ezekiel:

> "Son of man (NRSV: 'Mortal'), can these bones live?" ... Thus says the Lord God to these bones: "I will cause breath to enter you, and you shall live... and you shall know that I am (*egō eimi*) the Lord" (Ez 37:3-6).

The Son of Man, himself just returned from death, now breathes the divine breath into his demoralized followers, bringing them to new life and to knowledge.

His words "Receive the Holy Spirit. If you forgive the sins of any, they are forgiven..." recall the conferring of the power of the keys in the synoptics (e.g. Mt 16:19). In John, this juridical-sounding power of forgiveness is balanced and deepened by its relation with the new and constitutive interior presence of the Holy Spirit. The recalling of the story of the creation of man in Genesis indicates that this conferral of the power of forgiveness of sins signifies something even *more* than the reconciliation of human persons with their Maker. This gift of the Holy Spirit and the power to communicate the Spirit to others initiates a *new creation*.

And the mission entrusted to the disciples with the giving of the Spirit does not belong only to those who will be called to a specifically "apostolic" ministry, any more than does the gift of the Spirit itself. It is *all* of the disciples, "baptized with the Holy Spirit" (see 1:33), who are to communicate the life of God, and therefore a new existence, to the world.

II

"A week later..." (Greek: "after eight days"). Suggested in this recurrence is a regular gathering on the first day of the week, as in the later eucharistic tradition of the church. The words of the other disciples to

Thomas, "We have seen the Lord," recall Magdalene's "I have seen the Lord" (20:18): this is the original and essential Christian witness, "*Christ is risen!*"

⊕

Thomas' reply, "Unless *I* see...and put *my* finger...and [put] *my* hand, *I* will not believe," suggests that his absence from the community has been more than a physical separation. Such is the deep personal root of his relation to Jesus that he cannot accept the witness of the others, however unanimous and emphatic. He must, like Nathanael, have the confirmation of personal experience. Jesus' appearance to him, like Jesus' words to Nathanael, more than fulfill the demand. Thomas' cry of faith is as intensely personal as his doubt had been: "*My* Lord and *my* God!" (20:28).

Thomas represents all of those who have not been present to see the risen Jesus: "Blessed are those who have not seen..." (20:29). At the same time, Thomas, the twin, upon whom the shadow of death and the cross weighed heavily ("Let us also go, that we may die with him"—11:16), is another *Adam* figure. He is one—bitten by the fruit of the tree of the knowledge of good and evil—whose faith is constricted by the taste of death. Only in seeing the *crucified* Jesus *alive* is he freed from his ambivalence, from this doubleness, and enabled to leap with both feet onto the ground of faith: "My Lord and my God!" His cry echoes that of Nathanael, his counterpart, the Adam-figure who concluded the first half of the seventh day.

The story of *Jacob* at Bethel becomes relevant to our present scene when we remember his cry, "This is none other than the house of God, and this is the gate of heaven" (Gen 28:17). The exclamation of Nathanael echoed Jacob's cry, and now Thomas' exclamation of faith in Jesus echoes it once again. In John 1, it was Jesus himself who was the "place" of Nathanael's epiphany. Here, finally, Thomas sees in the opened body of Jesus both the house of God and the gate of heaven. On this seventh day, the sabbath of God's *rest*, this risen *body* of Jesus is recognized as the final dwelling place, the new temple, of the divine presence on earth.

These two narratives, in chapter 20, of the appearances of the risen Jesus to the disciples and to Thomas are *complementary*, when we regard them together in the light of the transition into the new age of the Spirit. Both stories are situated at the threshold between the direct physical and sensory experience of Jesus, by his contemporaries and his immediate disciples, and the situation of all of those

who would follow, and would have to believe in him on the testimony of others. This is the transition from the time of direct discipleship
to that of "mediated"[19] discipleship, from seeing and believing to
believing without seeing.

Thus Thomas' role as *the absent disciple*, and Jesus' blessing of
those who would believe without seeing him, correspond to the *gift of
the Holy Spirit* at his earlier appearance, which would communicate
the experience of Christ to all of those who would follow and believe
in him without the experience of his physical presence.

⊕

Thomas' insistence on touching the wounds of Jesus resonates strangely with his designation as *the twin*. Given the double or twin structures
which we have discovered frequently in John's gospel, we can expect
that this epithet of twin will carry more than its obvious meaning.
Jesus appears *twice*—in "twin" manifestations to the disciples and to
Thomas here. The entire episode has its *chiastic* twin in the first
episode of the seventh day, John 1:19-51.

Thus Thomas is the chiastic twin of *Nathanael*, who was the "holdout" among the disciples in John 1, and the last to be won over by
Jesus in that narrative. The correspondences between these two narratives are so multiple and strong that we shall have to give them further attention.

Thomas, here at the end, parallels *Mary Magdalene*, first of the disciples to see the risen Jesus, who was similarly preoccupied with the
physical body of the crucified. While Jesus told Magdalene not to
hold him, he invites Thomas to touch his wounds. More significantly,
Thomas appears as twin of the *"disciple whom Jesus loved."* As the disciple who had lain close to Jesus became the first-born when he
believed in the risen Jesus within the tomb, so Thomas, absent here at
Jesus' first appearance, is the last-born, yet born, like the others, upon
this one day of the resurrection. They remain twins in the one birth
from the tomb.

In representing all of those who are *absent*, that is, who are to
come afterward, Thomas symbolizes the whole "other hemisphere"
or *twin era* of the Holy Spirit which is to follow this brief time of the
Word incarnate, during which Jesus has been present in the flesh with
his own and poured out the fullness of his revelation. This will be the
era of the *other Paraclete* (14:16), the "twin" of Jesus, who is to make
Jesus present interiorly to those who believe in him.

We may see the two episodes of the seventh day as centered in the *two baptisms* or births: the new birth of Jesus in the Spirit at his baptism by John, and the new birth of the *disciples* when they are baptized with the Spirit by the risen Jesus. These are two "twin" bodies of Jesus being baptized, "born." And these two baptisms, two births, or two creations enclose the mandalic gospel of John: they are its beginning and its conclusion.

As we shall see, Thomas is the twin of *Jesus himself*, and, like Jacob and Nathanael, struggles with him in the womb and in the night. He is the "outside brother," the Ishmael or Esau, who must labor and wrestle in time's shadows before coming into the light and freedom of full birth. Still further, Thomas is every human person, separated from the one light and life of God.

⊕

Jesus' invitation to Thomas, "Reach out your hand and put it in my side..." (20:27), recalls God's words after the sin of Adam and Eve:

Then the Lord God said, "See, the man has become like one of us, knowing good and evil; and now, *he might reach out his hand and take also from the tree of life, and eat, and live forever"—*therefore the Lord God sent him forth from the garden of Eden, to till the ground from which he was taken. He drove out the man; and at the east of the garden of Eden he placed the cherubim, and a sword flaming and turning to guard the way to the tree of life (Gen 3:22-24).

As we arrive at the conclusion of the fourth gospel's chiastic narrative,[20] its great ring of symmetry closes in the convergence of the twin narratives of Nathanael and of Thomas. The two stories meet, finally, in the *garden* of Genesis. Thomas, as well as Nathanael, stands beneath the ladder which is a tree, in the garden which has, finally, been opened to humanity once again. Indeed heaven itself has been opened (1:51) symbolically through the piercing of Jesus' body upon the cross (see Heb 9:11-12; 10:19). In words which echo the divine decree of banishment, Thomas is invited to stretch forth his hand to the opened body of Jesus and there to take the fruit of the tree of life.

"But these [signs of Jesus] are written that you may come to believe that Jesus is the Messiah, the Son of God, *and that through believing you may have life* in his name." This closing verse is an invitation to the hearer or the reader: one is called to reach out one's hand to the *tree of life*, as Thomas has finally done.

The exclamation of Thomas, this double cry of faith which brings Nathanael's confession to its fulfillment, "My Lord and *my God*," is unique in John's gospel—but for the "It is *God* the only Son" of the prologue (1:18), which is its exact structural parallel (see below, p. 319)—and stands here at the end as its climactic expression of faith. What Thomas has seen in the risen Jesus, he has experienced *within himself*; from somewhere beyond the conflict of his own doubleness, his own stubborn mind and its understanding, springs this cry of total assent.

This narrative of the meeting between Thomas and the risen Jesus, placed at the end of the Johannine chiastic structure, brings together in a conclusive way several texts which we have encountered earlier in the gospel. There is a further resonance with the final prologue verse cited above—specifically with the words which have been translated, *"he has opened the way"* (1:18). An earlier exchange between Jesus and *Thomas*, at the supper, makes this convergence still more powerful.

> "In my Father's house there are many dwelling places. If it were not so, would I have told you that I go to prepare a place for you? And if I go to prepare a place for you, I will come again and will take you to myself, so that where I am, there you may be also. And you know the way to the place where I am going." Thomas said to him, "Lord, we do not know where you are going. *How can we know the way?*" Jesus said to him, "I am the way and the truth and the life. No one comes to the Father except through me..." (14:2-6).

When Jesus shows his opened breast to Thomas, it is the *way that he has opened by his death* (see Heb 11:19-20; 9:11-12), "through himself," that is disclosed to Thomas. The *place* which is prepared and opened now, signified by Jesus' opened body, is both "in the bosom of Jesus" and "in the bosom of the Father," where Jesus himself dwells.

⊕

This cry of faith of Thomas the twin, at the conclusion of John's chiastic narrative, closes not only the chiasm of the fourth gospel but the great chiasm of biblical history. Thomas is *Adam*, humanity bitten by the sword of separation from the divine life, excluded from tree and garden. When Jesus was about to return to Judea to waken his friend Lazarus (who is also Adam, humanity!), Thomas had said with bleak resignation, "Let us go also, that we may die with him" (11:16). These words are prophetic of what is actually happening here, as Jesus takes upon himself the one death of humanity (see Rom 5:15–6:11). There has been a deliberate "twinning" of the Lazarus story and the events of the *hour* of Jesus. The episodes of the death and resuscitation of Lazarus and the supper in Bethany are followed almost immediately by Jesus' last supper and his own death and resurrection. It is the *one human person, Adam, whom Jesus will join to himself in death and then in the new life.* With his exclamation, Thomas emerges from this narrow gate.

The story of Elisha's raising of the Shunammite's child (see pp. 156-157 above) closes the gap between these two sequences.

> When Elisha came into the house, he saw the child lying dead on his bed. So he went in and closed the door on the two of them, and prayed to the Lord. Then he got up on the bed and lay upon the child, putting his mouth upon his mouth, his eyes upon his eyes, and his hands upon his hands; and while he lay bent over him, the child became warm ... the child sneezed seven times, and the child opened his eyes ... (2 Kgs 4:32-35).

As all of the women with whom Jesus interacts in John's gospel are one woman, simply "Woman," or Eve, all of the men (and the boy) whom he heals or raises from the dead are *one man*, simply "Man," or Adam. And this Adam contains within himself, symbolically, all of humanity, as does Jesus, the second Adam.

> When you make the two one, and when you make the inner as the outer and the outer as the inner and the above as the below, and when you make the male and female into a single one ... then shall you enter the Kingdom. [21]

These words of Jesus from the Gospel of Thomas (see below, p. 368) express quite well what we are to understand in this Johannine episode, as the twin sees the opened body of Jesus, returned from the dead, and experiences within himself the divine Unitive, the tree of life. At this moment Thomas enters the garden, the place of the One.

Adam is received into the indivisible life of God, born anew in the one birth of the Word.

⊕

The two appearances of Jesus to the disciples in the place with its doors "locked...for fear of the Jews" recall another night when he had come to them.[22]

> ...they saw Jesus walking on the sea and coming near the boat, and they were terrified. But he said to them, "*I am*; do not be afraid" (6:19-20).

The seventh day recapitulates the *first day* of creation, when the uncreated light had dawned upon the waters. Now they have passed through the sea with him, shared his baptism, and the unitive light (*I Am*) is *within them*. Within them too is the creating Spirit. They are ready now for the sun to rise upon their long day of labor.

The Seventh Day: Synthetic Review

On the seventh day of the new creation, the risen Jesus imparts his *glory* to his disciples. This is the culmination of a series of stages. On the *third* day this glory of Jesus emerged against the background of John the Baptist and the tradition of Israel. On the *fourth* day, at the supper, he explicated the meaning which this glory would have for his disciples, and prayed to the Father for it. On the *fifth* day Jesus emptied himself completely, and the glory was manifested in the irony of total eclipse: in the mockery by the soldiers and then upon the cross. On the *sixth* day Jesus, now victorious, symbolically received the glory as bride. Now on the *seventh* day this glory is distributed to his disciples as he breathes the Holy Spirit upon them.

⊕

These *two episodes* (sections 20 and 21) enclose between them the whole of John's mandalic narrative. As we would expect, their *relationship* to one another is profound and multiple in its aspects. There is symmetry, complementarity, continuity and progression, culminating in the powerful symbolic convergence which we have already observed in the narrative of Jesus' two appearances to his disciples in the closed house. The final symbolic unity is that of Eden—with the creation of humanity through the communication of divine breath, the garden with its tree and rivers of life. All of these symbols finally locate themselves in the crucified and risen *body* of Jesus, which is to be understood as symbolically identical both with the center of the mandala and with the whole figure. This body is opened through Jesus' death so that those who come to him through faith and baptism may enter into the new and unitive creation, the life of divine immanence.

Two great thematic complexes join the two narratives. The *first* parallels John the Baptist, his baptism and his words in chapter 1, with Jesus and his in-breathing of the Spirit in chapter 20. John the Baptist's prediction, in 1:33, of a baptism with the Holy Spirit is fulfilled by Jesus in 20:22. John's designation of Jesus as the "Lamb of God who *takes away the sin* of the world" is similarly verified in 20:23, when the disciples are commissioned and sent to *forgive sins.*

The *second* complex relates the encounter between Jesus and Nathanael to that between Jesus and Thomas, against the symbolic background of the vision of Jacob at Haran and, ultimately, the garden of Eden and the tree of life in its midst.

There is a strong structural and thematic *symmetry* between the two episodes, with their rhythm of successive waves of discovery and acceptance—among virtually the same group of disciples—first of the young Teacher pointed out by John against the background of Jesus' baptism, and then of the risen Jesus. The acclamation of Nathanael (1:49) is echoed by the final acclamation of Thomas (20:28), and the responses of Jesus are also parallel (1:50; 20:29). The gentle suggestion of a quest of *paradise* which we have sensed in the first chapter comes to a sudden focus when Jesus recalls Nathanael's presence beneath the fig tree (1:48.50). We realize that Thomas stands also beneath a tree—the tree of the cross and of life—as Jesus shows him the wounds of his crucifixion. Both episodes are related, by Jesus' words in 1:51, to Jacob's vision at Bethel (Gen 28) of the heavens opened and a ladder extending from heaven to earth. Thomas sees in the body of Jesus, opened and living before him, the ladder and the tree, the "gate of heaven and the house of God" (Gen 28:17), the temple (or paradise) opened to him.

The *week* which concludes at Cana in chapters 1–2 is reflected by the week which elapses between the Easter day appearances and the final appearance to Thomas in chapter 20. Here in John, the week recalls the original seven days of the creation and the planetary progression of the whole gospel.

There is both balance and progression between the two scenes in the closed house (20:19-29). Thomas' presence in the second scene signifies a movement forward and outward from the immediate circle of Jesus' disciples to the larger circle of *all of those who are not present* and will believe through the word of these disciples (17:20). In these two matching scenes are represented the *two faces* of the one comprehensive new situation of these many later disciples, "who have not seen and yet (will) believe." It is the interior gift of the *Spirit* (scene I) which will enable them to *believe, without seeing* the risen Jesus with their eyes (scene II: 20:29).

⊕

Within the white light of the seventh day's sabbath are gathered all the colors of the *six preceding days*. In the two scenes in which Jesus appears to the disciples in the closed house, there will be found some symbolic allusion to each of the earlier stages of the new creation. The in-breathing of the Holy Spirit recalls the Spirit hovering over the waters at the first moment of creation, and the manifestation of the light of the Word is reproduced within each of the disciples in this baptism with the Spirit. The eucharistic bread of life is recalled by the gathering of the disciples on the first day of the week, and by Thomas' "reaching out his hand" to the tree of life which is Jesus, while the new communion which is the inner reality of this sacrament is born in the midst of these disciples. The entering of the glory into its dwelling in the new temple and the opening of the interior river of living water take place here in the house.

It is here also that Jesus' own "grace" or fullness enters into his disciples, and they receive their mission toward the world. These human beings are born, at this moment, into the new life which flows from Jesus' cross. The union of truth and grace, of Word and Spirit, and the new immanence of the divine wisdom occur for the gathered disciples at this moment.

⊕

The seven *signs* of Jesus are also recapitulated in these two scenes. Tracing the paths of biblical symbolism which relate them to the resurrection appearances is an instructive exercise, and confirms the unity of the structure, as well as the symbolic system, of John's gospel. Only a few indications will be given here.

The first sign (in the mandalic order of the gospel)—Jesus' appearance walking upon the water and of the instantaneous arrival at the farther shore—is realized as Jesus *appears* to them once again. Having completed his Passover and his exodus journey, he brings his disciples with him into the promised land. The bread of life—sapiential and eucharistic—has been broken in Jesus' death and now is eaten in this new land by the disciples as he returns to them on the Lord's day and his fullness enters into them. He is the tree of life in their midst, the one bread.

The second Cana sign is verified as the King's first-born Son comes back to life, now in his inclusive person. The paralytic rises and enters the temple, as Jesus "heals a man's whole body" (7:23—see Gen 2:7) on this sabbath. On this Johannine sabbath each disciple, like the man born blind, has the veil of earth, which had both revealed and hidden the reality of Jesus, removed from his eyes as he is washed in the Holy Spirit and *sees* within himself. Lazarus—Adam—returns from the tomb in this Jesus who appears to the disciples.

The sign of Cana is fulfilled as Jesus pours out for his guests the wine of divine union, breathing the Holy Spirit upon these disciples. This first sign at the wedding feast, in which Jesus "revealed his glory," has become, in the order of the seven days, the final sign preparatory to that ultimate "sign"—which communicates reality itself—Jesus' own resurrection and the gift of his Spirit.

When Jesus gives the glory to his disciples by breathing upon them, reproducing the action of God in creating Adam, the first human (Gen 2:7), the work of new creation is essentially completed, as John has presented it. What remains to be achieved is the extension of this new creation to the whole world. *This creation of a new humanity is the central meaning of the seventh day.*

In the first creation account of Genesis 1, man and woman are said to be fashioned in the *image of God*. Abraham Heschel has related this doctrine to the prohibition of images in the worship of Israel[23] (see Deut 27:15; Ex 20:4; Deut 4:9-28). The ultimate reason for this exclusion of representations of other living creatures from temple and worship, he proposes, was that *the human person is the only valid image of God* (see Gen 1:26-27).

The prohibition of images is analogous to our *sabbath* (see p. 244 above), on which we have passed beyond images and figures of speech to the "plain speech of the Father" which Jesus had promised (16:25). *The symbols and images have disappeared into the mystery of the one image of God which is the human person*, this human person finally created on the seventh day.

Unitive Experience and Baptismal Experience

In moving from the dramatic action and variety of the sixth day to the confinement of these two scenes of the seventh day—which one quite naturally expects to be conclusive—the reader may easily experience, at first, an *anticlimax*. The setting of these scenes, within the closed house, does not seem to offer scope for an adequate dramatic climax for John's narrative. The Thomas episode, despite the triumphant cry of faith which is its climax, remains puzzling and insufficiently conclusive in itself, until we penetrate beneath the narrative's surface.

The absence of a dramatically satisfying final event, however, corresponds to the movement from figure, metaphor, symbol, to the *unitive*. On the seventh day in Genesis 2, God rested. This *rest of God* here in John, however, is precisely the unitive immanence of God in humanity which constitutes the new creation. The dramatic *anticlimax*, therefore, is the unitive *climax*, and the consummation of the work of creation. It is this, realized within the human person, which Thomas expresses in his final cry of faith," *My* Lord and *my* God!" The symbolic opulence itself of the sixth day has disappeared into this new immanence.

We have already spoken of the passage beyond images in the experience of the disciple within the open tomb (p. 225), still on the sixth day. We have related this to the *apophatic*[24] tradition which is common to both non-Christian and Christian traditions. God, and the ultimate knowledge of God, are beyond visible representations. The experience of the disciple in the tomb, however—as we have imagined it—remained "incomplete" insofar as it stopped short of this actual *new creation of the human person* in the gift of the Holy Spirit. This further step takes place in the assembled disciples.

The central Christian doctrine of *resurrection* is unique in this embrace of the human person, in its totality of body and spirit, by the creative movement of the Holy Spirit, raising it to a new level of divine-human life. This transformation and divine-human life is what eastern Christian tradition refers to as *"theosis,"* divinization.[25] It is a cornerstone of New Testament faith,[26] a doctrine of extreme importance which has been too much forgotten in the west—in both the

Protestant and the Catholic traditions. When it is forgotten, the theological sky, opened through Jesus' death and resurrection (see Jn 1:51; Heb 9–10), closes once again, and Christianity easily becomes the prisoner of its own structures. With the sealing of this unitive theological eye, faith becomes easy prey to the grim procession of "isms": paternalism, institutionalism, moralism, legalism, provincialism.

The liberating heart of the Christianity of Paul and of John is this faith in a transformative new creation. *Salvation*,[27] the redemptive act of God in Jesus Christ, is ultimately nothing less than a transformation of the cosmos—of the whole of nature—centered in the transformation of the human person and human community through the divine reality which lives and acts within it.[28]

"Receive the Holy Spirit. If you forgive the sins of any, they are forgiven them; if you retain the sins of any, they are retained." This expression seems so limited as to annul the concept of new creation. The baptism of John had been administered "for the forgiveness of sins" (see Mk 1:4); does Jesus' baptism with the Holy Spirit accomplish no more than this?[29]

This conundrum is one with the mystery of baptism and the baptismal experience. *What is added* to the person in the basic Christian experience of baptism? What accrues to the body of the neophyte emerging from the waters? *Nothing* is added except the Holy Spirit, and this Spirit is experienced as light, freedom, new life. The person is liberated from darkness, liberated into a foretaste of *the fullness of its own being*. Baptism is not an addendum to the person, or even an augmentation of the person, but the *birth* of the person.

This new creation is a liberation of the person into the simplicity of its own being in the Word, free of the long shadow of sin, guilt and death (see Heb 12:14-15). At the same time, the newly indwelling Spirit, which is the very "freedom of God," liberates the person into a freedom which is *beyond its own limitations, its own creaturehood* as we know it. The person is liberated into God by the indwelling love of God.

This freedom of the person is most fully expressed in *love*, and love is the characteristic manifestation of the immanent Spirit in the individual and in the community. This primacy of love becomes the distinguishing mark of Christianity;[30] Paul and John are its theologians.

The apophatic itself, as a particular *way*, disappears into the ordinariness of human life. Christian apophatism is not, essentially, a special and segregated tradition, but the life of faith itself. Such is the perfect fit of the grace of divinization with the human person that it proceeds with the quietness of a natural process. Once it flows smoothly in its course, there is no essential experiential remainder, "nothing special." The breath of Jesus which is the Spirit disappears into the bodies of his disciples as his blood had soaked into the earth.

Here there is a parallel with the apophatic as conceived in some traditions of Buddhism: in the zen tradition as expressed, for example, in the well-known "oxherding pictures."[31]

⊕

"Peace be with you." We have already (above, pp. 252) studied the meaning of this word *eirēnē*, or *shalom*. At this point, it is the global meaning of *shalom*, the "well-being of the whole person," which is appropriate to our interpretation. Here, at the inauguration of the creation of the new humanity, Jesus' "Peace be with you" expresses the *totality* which he confers in the gift of the divine Spirit. The peace is a reconciliation, a "union" in the double and cruciform sense of Ephesians.

> For he is our peace; in his flesh he has made both groups (i.e. Jews and Gentiles) into one, and has broken down the dividing wall between us. He has abolished the law with its commandments and ordinances, that he might create in himself one new humanity (lit. one new man, *anthrōpos*) in place of the two, thus making peace, and might reconcile both groups to God in one body through the cross, thus putting to death that hostility through it. So he came and proclaimed peace to you who were far off and peace to those who were near; for through him both of us have access in one Spirit to the Father (Eph 2:14-18).

When Jesus appears to the disciples and shows them his wounds, he places himself before them as *crucified*. The Pauline figure (see p. 24 above) of the crucified Christ—who unites everything in heaven and on earth in himself—is present here in John 20. The figure of the mandalic gospel is present as well, here at the end of the mandalic narrative. The two axes meet in the body of Jesus: the vertical, joining God and humanity, and the horizontal, bringing together Jews and Gentiles—or, more generally, the people of the first revelation and covenant, and the whole of humanity.

"...that he might create in himself *one new humanity* (*anthrōpos*: one new *man*) ..." This is precisely what John indicates by alluding to the creation of Adam (Gen 2:7) when he depicts Jesus breathing the Holy

Spirit into his disciples. Jesus concludes his work of new creation by bringing to life the *"new Adam,"* one with himself, through this gift of the divine Spirit. Jesus' *shalom* denotes the new *fullness of human life in the "divinization" which new creation signifies,* the fullness of life, flowing from the immanent divine Spirit, which constitutes the new humanity.

This new humanity, new Adam, is also the *new temple* which Jesus had promised to build in three days (2:19). The new Solomon ("king of peace") has constructed the house of the Lord, and now the glory, the divine presence for which he prayed (17:1.11.21.24.26), has entered this temple to dwell there.

⊕

"As the Father has sent me, so I send you." The revelation of the *new life* in the Holy Spirit has already been made at the supper. Here Jesus speaks only of *mission,* of the more exterior and "masculine" aspect of the new creation. The unitive transformation is implicit in his words, however. The disciples are sent as Jesus was sent because, in the gift of the Spirit, they *are* Jesus.

One of the servant poems of Deutero-Isaiah, quoted by Jesus to describe his own mission, helps to unfold the sense of this *sending*— first of Jesus and then of the disciples—"for the forgiveness of sins."

> The spirit of the Lord God is upon me,
> because the Lord has anointed me;
> he has *sent me* to bring good news to the oppressed,
> to bind up the brokenhearted,
> to proclaim liberty to the captives,
> and release to the prisoners;
> to proclaim the year of the Lord's favor... (Is 61:1-2a; see Lk 4:18).

⊕

John places Jesus' gift of the Holy Spirit within a context of *"shalom"* and of a *mission* for the forgiveness of sins. The full meaning of this gift, however, only comes forth in the light of the whole of his gospel: everything in John's gospel up to this point has been in preparation for this fullness which is in the gift of the indwelling Spirit. Many of Jesus' words—particularly the words which his listeners have found most difficult, and particularly his words at the supper—have been explication and commentary of the one "Word" which those who believed would receive in this gift of the Spirit. This gift of the Spirit is best understood in the light of the *creation* symbolism which pervades John's gospel.

On the seventh day, a human person breathes the divine Spirit into human persons, re-creating them as the beginning of a new world of divine immanence. "As the Father has sent me, so I send you" (20:21). The disciples are commissioned to *continue this work of new creation;* they are constituted *co-creators* with God and his Christ. The first exercise of this creativity will be the bringing of other persons into the new creation through the communication of this same Spirit, in the forgiveness of their sins. This will occur through the communication of the Word of Christ through the *preaching* of the disciples, and through *baptism*, in which the Spirit itself is to be imparted.

A new spiritual *generativity*—a kind of *reproductive* power—is, then, the primary expression of the divine creativity now imparted to human persons: the power to communicate this same Spirit to others.[32] The gift goes further, however—it includes a new power to participate in the re-creation of humanity and of the world through the various human capacities (see Eph 4:7-13). Central to this work will be the imagination of faith.

⊕

We have already discussed the mysterious final words of Jesus in John's first chapter (see above, p. 248), but this *promise* of Jesus demands further reflection. We have not seen, anywhere in John's gospel, a plausible literal fulfillment of the promise. However there are strong parallels between this text and its chiastic counterpart at the end of Section 21.

Sec. 20   "Rabbi, you are the Son of God! You are the King of Israel!" . . . "Do you believe because I told you that I saw you under the fig tree? You will see greater things than these . . . you will see heaven opened, and the angels of God ascending and descending upon the Son of Man" (1:49-51).

Sec. 21   "My Lord and my God!" . . . "Have you believed because you have seen me? Blessed are those who have not seen and yet have come to believe" (20:27-29).

Because of its final position in John's first episode, Jesus' promise exerts what we may call a strong *chiastic pressure* upon the conclusion of this final episode of the mandalic chiasm (20:29). It may be, in fact, that John has concluded his first episode with the riddle of these words for this reason: to generate a tension corresponding to the transformative leap between the beginning and end of his gospel narrative. If we would find the fulfillment of this promise in Jesus' appearances to the disciples after his resurrection, we are challenged to follow this leap in a symbolic translation which proceeds through *paradox*.

In the light of the strong parallel between the two texts quoted above, is it possible that to "see heaven opened and the angels of God ascending and descending upon the Son of Man" is *equivalent to not seeing and yet believing*? May the promised *seeing* be of such a different kind that it is also a *not-seeing*?

Behind these two passages lies the image of *Jesus' baptism* in the Jordan, to which John has referred only obliquely (1:34).

And just as he was *coming up* (*anabainōn*) out of the water, he saw the heavens torn apart (*schizomenous*, while John has *aneōgota*, "opened") and the Spirit *descending* (*katabainon*) like a dove on him. And a voice came from heaven, "You are my Son, the Beloved; with you I am well pleased" (Mk 1:10-11).

In this Marcan scene, as Jesus, the *Son* of God, *ascends* from the water, he *sees* the *heavens* opened and the Spirit *descending* upon him. In John 20, the "Son of Man" may be, actually, the *disciple* who is baptized by Jesus in the Holy Spirit (1:33). Jesus, the *Word* incarnate, *ascends* to the Father (20:17), and the Spirit *descends* upon the disciple. Son of Man, angels of God, opened heavens and seeing itself are brought to a *new level* of meaning in this final episode, corresponding to the transformation which is worked by this new baptism in the Holy Spirit.[33]

The Son of Man is *Jesus* at his baptism. It is also the *disciple* who is baptized and introduced into the new "seeing" in the Spirit. The Son of Man is also the *church*, the body of disciples which is related to God the Father through the ascent of the Word and the descent of the Spirit. The opening of heaven admits disciple and community to a new and *interior* relationship with the Father, mediated by the "angels of God" which are Word and Spirit. Word and Spirit ascend and descend upon the Son of Man who is Jesus, become a ladder between God and humanity; they ascend and descend upon the Son of Man which is church, the "house of God and gate of heaven" upon earth.

The *glorification of Jesus* and the *giving, or descent, of the Spirit* are two permanent movements relating the church in this world to God. New creation comes about through the progressive elevation of humanity to God and the progressive entrance of God into humanity.

On another, more exterior plane of interpretation, the "angels of God" are the *disciples themselves*—become, in Jesus and the Spirit, the mediators between God and the church on earth. Mark (1:2) quotes Malachi 3:1, in which John the Baptist is called *"aggelos mou,"* my messenger. John omits this quotation but may be presupposing it here. Then, parallel with the chiastic contrast between the two baptisms—with water and with the Holy Spirit—he would be implying a contrast between the "angel of God" who is the *Baptist* and the *disciples* of Jesus who have become, in this Spirit, angels—that is, messengers, intermediaries—of God. The baptismal vision becomes an image of the church, the new Eve, continually giving birth to the collective or total Son of Man with the assistance of these ministers.

Thomas has insisted upon personal contact and even a kind of physical intimacy—placing his finger and hand into Jesus' wounds. Instead, he is given something different which is *more* personal and more intimate: the interior "touch" which is unitive experience of the Spirit. Blessed are those for whom this spiritual contact suffices; they shall be rich in the fullness of the Lord's interior presence, and in the purity and strength of their faith.

Thomas, the twin, has been the *last* holdout among the disciples against this new presence of their Master which is interior and unitive—and which brings with it an actual transformation into the new Adam—as the disciple was the *first* to surrender to it. Now the twin (see the story of Jacob and Esau in Genesis 25–33) is reconciled with his "brother" (see 20:17), and this reconciliation takes place in the *womb* (see Gen 25:21ff) where the one birth of the "Son of Man" takes place.

The passage from one kind of knowledge to another, from the knowledge of external *sight* to the knowledge of *union*, to which Jesus has led these disciples—and last of all Thomas—corresponds to his promise, "...you will see *heaven opened*..."(1:51). It is this initiation into the final unitive knowledge of God which is implied also in the final verse of John's prologue:

No one (i.e. not even Moses; see 1:17) has ever seen God. It is God the only Son, *who is in the Father's bosom*, who has made him known (1:18).

Or, more graphically, "...*who has opened the way*" (see above, p. 54 with the related note 16). The promised *opening of the heavens* is accomplished in the opening of "the Father's bosom" to those who believe in Jesus. This opening of the interior sabbath of God's rest to humanity is symbolized by the opened bosom of Jesus, as we have seen (above, p. 255). This is the promised "*place*" (14:2-4), promised land and paradise. These convergent spatial images, however, all refer to a relationship which is non-spatial, non-dual and beyond all images: the simple divine union.

Two disciples, "twins," are particularly associated with this *place* in John's narrative: Thomas and the *disciple whom Jesus loved*. It is the disciple who rested on Jesus' bosom at the supper (13:23.25), who saw and witnessed to the opening of Jesus' side upon the cross (19:34-35), who is to "remain here until I come" (21:21.23) and who "is testifying to these things and has written them, and we know that his testimony is true" (21:24).

This great crystallizing of implications in the final Thomas narrative contains an important *baptismal* reference. The promise of the "heavens opened" of 1:51 alluded to the baptism of Jesus and probably also, therefore, to the baptismal experience of those who would believe in him. We have just witnessed, here in John 20, after all, the "baptism with the Holy Spirit" of the gathered disciples, and it is through a new birth in water and the Holy Spirit that one must enter this place (see 3:5). The whole of John's gospel has prepared the way toward this *entering*; we shall examine further its relation to the baptismal event (see below, pp. 327, 357).

⊕

In the context of John's mandalic-chiastic structure, then, *Thomas'* exclamation signifies that he, too, at this point in his journey, has found the *center*. The *twin*, in this twinned Johannine narrative which is both linear journey and circular orbit around the *Logos*-center, has now experienced the convergence of these two movements, these two dimensions of life. He upon whom the gravitation of death weighed so heavily has now experienced the final gravitation of the center, of "My God," in the opened body of Jesus.

It is in Thomas, the twin, then, that John brings together, at the end of his narrative, the *two levels of his gospel*: the linear or chronological (the historical journey along with Jesus), and the metaphysical or centric (the relation to the transcendent *Logos* which is in Jesus). The

Johannine figures of Peter and the beloved disciple also correspond to these two movements (see below, p. 386). Through his death and resurrection and the gift of the Spirit, Jesus has achieved this marriage; John expresses it in Thomas' enlightenment and in his conclusive word of faith (20:28).

Thus the Son of Man is *born* in this unitive baptism which closes the chiastic ring of the gospel. The scene of Jesus' appearance to Thomas closes this ring with a representation of the *unitive experience* —and the way—which is *open toward the reader*: *"Blessed are those who have not seen and yet believe"* (20:29). The following two verses, in fact, conclude the narrative by addressing the reader directly in this sense. Beginning and ending in a baptismal context and centered in an epiphany which is symbolically baptismal, the gospel presents itself to the Christian, the new disciple, as an explication of his or her experience. The whole of John's gospel, then, is a mystagogy of the basic Christian, or baptismal experience (see below, Part III, ch. 4).

$$\oplus$$

At the end of John's first episode (1:51), Jesus speaks of the *Son of Man* in words which echo his response to the high priest's formal question at the climactic moment of his trial in Matthew's gospel:

> From now on *you will see the Son of Man* seated at the right hand of Power and coming on the clouds of *heaven* (Mt 26:64).

This is the statement of Jesus which precipitates his condemnation by the assembly. John has placed a similar promise of Jesus in his first episode so that it returns with conclusive force at the end of the entire chiastic gospel narrative. We have seen (above, p. 271) how John relates this prediction to the baptismal experience.

At the end of chapter 20, the promise of 1:51 has the further effect of positioning the "*Son of Man*," together with "My Lord and my God" and "the Messiah, the Son of God" (20:31), as one of the final titles or images of Jesus in the chiastic gospel. *Son of Man* has a special claim to attention here both because of its eschatological connotation (see Dan 7:13-14) and because it has been preferentially used by Jesus himself—but also because it is particularly appropriate to this Johannine *conclusion*.

Irenaeus brings out the "chiastic" biblical-historical relationship between *Adam* and the Son of Man:

That is why the Lord proclaims himself the *Son of Man*, the one who renews in himself *that first man* from whom the race born of woman was formed; as by a man's defeat our race fell into the bondage of death, so by a man's victory we were to rise to life again.[34]

Both Son of God and Son of Adam, he is also, like Jacob/Israel, both an *individual* and a *nation*. While "Son of Man" is a Christological title which refuses to be confined within a single image, it nevertheless manifests a certain structure. This image-beyond-images expands along two coordinates. Along the axis of time it embraces the biblical history from first to second Adam. Along the line of "space" it expands from the individual person Jesus to the whole of humanity. In this way the image develops through the mandalic chiasm's four dimensions, to express the fullness of the whole. From the center which is the crucified Christ, the Son of Man expands into the fullness of history and cosmos—gathering into himself the entirety of that which was created through the Word. For God has planned, in the fullness of time, "to gather up all things in him, things in heaven and things on earth" (Eph 1:10).

The *final sign* with which John leaves us here is Jesus of Nazareth (1:45-51; 20:26-29) risen from the dead, and still manifesting in his wounds the figure of the tree (see Is 55:10-13; Sir 24:8-22). The real terminus of John's gospel, however, is in the unimaginable fullness which is identified with this Son of Man, and participated by those who believe in him.

⊕

The cryptic kernel which is John's *prologue* expresses in a few words of infinite profundity the chiastic progression of the seventh day, from first creation to new creation. The second half of the prologue, including verses 12-18, may be read as a theological explication of that which happens within those disciples gathered in the closed room of John 20.

It is at this moment that the Word becomes flesh in the disciples, making his dwelling in them as in the new temple. Here is experienced the glory of the Father's only Son by the disciples who are born as children of God in him. The fullness which they have seen in Jesus is now experienced as present within themselves; the God who cannot be seen is now known with a new and interior knowledge. The grace which was anticipated in Moses and present in Jesus is now poured into the disciples. Through the Son who is in the bosom of the Father and who is himself the opened way into the Father, these disciples experience themselves in this same ultimate place. The two witnesses, Baptist and disciple, testify to the one who *was* before them. We seem to hear in the Baptist's words also the voice of the first Adam, who is himself recapitulated in the Son of Man. The prologue's concluding verse is taken up in Thomas' exclamation, as he experiences within himself the fullness which is in God.

Chapter Eight

The Continuing Day

A river flows out of Eden to water the garden, and from there it divides and becomes four branches (Gen 2:10).

⊕

The first man did not know wisdom fully, nor will the last one fathom her. For her thoughts are more abundant than the sea, and her counsel deeper than the great abyss. As for me, I was like a canal from a river, like a water channel into a garden. I said, "I will water my garden and drench my flower-beds." And lo, my canal became a river, and my river a sea. I will again make instruction shine forth like the dawn, and I will make it clear from far away. I will again pour out teaching like prophecy, and leave it to all future generations. Observe that I have not labored for myself alone, but for all who seek wisdom (Sir 24:28-34).

⊕

...water was flowing from below the threshold of the temple toward the east.... He said to me, "This water flows toward the eastern region and goes down into the Arabah; and when it enters the sea, the sea of stagnant waters, the water will become fresh. Wherever the river goes, every living creature that swarms will live, and there will be very many fish, once these waters reach there. It will become fresh; and everything will live where the river goes. People will stand fishing beside the sea from En-gedi to En-eglaim; it will be a place for the spreading of nets; its fish will be of a great many kinds, like the fish of the Great Sea" (Ez 47:1.8-10).

SECTION 22: CHAPTER 21
ON THE SEASHORE

The Problem of John 21

This final chapter of the fourth gospel has long presented a problem to exegetes,[1] and it is problematic for our mandalic interpretation as well. Most scholars do not believe that it was part of the original plan of the gospel, although John's gospel appears never to have circulated without it. The final verses of chapter 20 (20:30-31) seem clearly intended as a conclusion, and one would not expect a further narrative—and particularly another of Jesus' *signs*—to follow them.

In the final narrative of John 20, we have seen the creation imagery of the whole gospel drawn together, and we have returned to the beginning in splendidly Johannine fashion—with a strong chiastic symmetry between the final and the first episodes. Addition of a further narrative within the overall chiastic structure tends to obscure these symbolic and structural felicities, diffusing the conclusive force of this chiastic closure. The Galilee narrative of chapter 21 departs from the symbolic language of the early chapters of Genesis, which had become so concentrated in chapter 20. We seem at first to return from a deep immersion in the mystery of Jesus' death and resurrection to a more contingent world of human activity and human biography.

Does, then, chapter 21 belong to the chiastic structure[2] of John's gospel, or has it been appended to the rest of the gospel narrative as an extra-chiastic element like the prologue? Is chapter 21 intended to form part of the symbolic complex of the seven days of creation—either as a component of the seventh day or as a distinct eighth day? These questions will remain present in the background while we study John's final chapter, and we shall finally return to them.

Division of Chapter 21

The narrative may be easily divided into two great sections:

I. 21:1-14.   After Peter and the disciples have fished all night without result, Jesus appears and directs them to a great catch of fish. He invites them to breakfast with him on the shore.

II. 21:15-25.   Jesus questions Peter, foretells his destiny, and tells Peter to follow him. The disciple whom Jesus loved, however, is to remain until his return.

I

With Peter and his companions after a fruitless night of fishing on the Sea of Galilee, we seem once more to be at the beginning of the gospel story.

> When he had finished speaking, he said to Simon, "Put out into the deep water and let down your nets for a catch." Simon answered, "Master, we have worked all night long but have caught nothing. Yet if you say so, I will let down the nets." When they had done this, they caught so many fish that their nets were beginning to break. So they signaled their partners in the other boat to come and help them. And they came and filled both boats, so that they began to sink. But when Simon Peter saw it, he fell down at Jesus' knees, saying, "Go away from me, Lord, for I am a sinful man!" For he and all who were with him were amazed at the catch of fish they had taken; and so also were James and John, sons of Zebedee, who were partners with Simon. Then Jesus said to Simon, "Do not be afraid; from now on you will be catching people." When they had brought their boats to shore, they left everything and followed him (Lk 5:4-11).

All three synoptic gospels recount the call of the first disciples at the Sea of Galilee, and in all three Jesus tells the disciples that they will be "fishers of people" (lit. "men," *anthrōpon*). Only Luke includes the story of the miraculous catch of fish. By returning to the moment when Jesus had called the disciples to their apostolic ministry, John symbolically begins this *new day* of labor. In the fourth gospel the role of Jesus' expression "fishers of people" has been transferred to the narrative itself, so that the catch of fish becomes symbolic of the missionary work of the church throughout the ages to come. It is as if John, with his greater subtlety, has suppressed Jesus' explicit, if figurative, expression—as it is found in the synoptics—and *embodied* it in the "sign" itself of the great catch of fish.

Nor do we find here a solemn pronouncement of the apostolic mission such as that of Matthew: "Go therefore and make disciples of all nations, baptizing them..." (Mt 28:19). Presupposing these clear enunciations conserved by the tradition, John is able to incarnate them in his language of symbolism and inference.

"*Just as day was breaking.*" More than one beginning is recaptured in this final episode of John's gospel. This moment of dawn recalls Magdalene's visit to the tomb, and therefore Jesus' resurrection. Jesus' appearance alongside the sea recalls his earlier appearance walking upon the same waters, while the disciples toiled at the oars (16:16-21). The day of work which is dawning here, now that the seven days of Jesus' work of creation have been completed, evokes the first day and therefore that uncreated light which is the eternal dawn (see 1:1-9). It is through these fishermen that the light will move out into the world, and it is this light which will draw humanity to them (see 12:32).

The gospel *narrative*, on the other hand, began at the Jordan *River*, with John the Baptist and then Jesus and the first two disciples. At the center-point of the chiastic figure of the gospel, we found the disciples struggling in their boat upon the *sea*; here they come to *shore* in the boat, and the narrative concludes with Jesus and two disciples. Through the whole of the gospel, the disciples are in the course of a *sea-journey*, and finally they disembark upon the farther shore. There Jesus awaits them and feeds them, as Yahweh had fed the Israelites in the desert after Moses had led them out of Egypt and through the Red Sea. The sea journey, as we have seen on Day 1, has profound mythic and psychological resonances. In John 21, the journey brings the disciples into the "*whole world*" and into the fullness of their mission. This shore on which Jesus awaits them also suggests the "farther shore" of the kingdom, the final new creation.

⊕

Peter's plunge into the water (21:7), which is only found in John, expresses the urgency of his love for Jesus and probably the fervor of Peter's repentance after denying his Master. It has symbolic resonances as well, however. It was Peter who had repulsed Jesus' gesture of washing his feet, and then cried, "Lord, not my feet only, but also my hands and my head!" (13:6-9). This plunge into the sea may represent a further symbolic washing after his denial of Jesus, a new "baptism." The charcoal fire which Jesus has prepared on the shore, where he will question Peter about his love for him, recalls the similar fire in the high priest's courtyard where Peter was warming himself when he denied Jesus.

⊕

When the risen Jesus appears to his disciples, it is often while they are gathered for a *meal* (Mk 16:14; Lk 24:30; 24:42-43). Only here in John does Jesus himself *provide* the meal; this parallels the feeding of the multitude with bread and fish beside the same Sea of Tiberias in chapter 6 (where even the words used by John are very similar: compare 6:11 and 21:13). A *eucharistic*[3] implication is probable in both places. Together with the baptismal resonance evoked here by the echo of the first day's sea-crossing, therefore, we find a reflection of the second day's eucharist in this meal by the sea. The basic sacramental sense of the first two days of the week of creation is recapitulated here at the end of the gospel. Augustine finds symbolic meaning not only in the bread, but in the *fish* upon the fire.

> The cooked fish is Christ who has suffered, and he is the bread who has come down from heaven.[4]

> The meal on the shore suggests also the eschatological meal[5] which was foretold by Isaiah and other prophets.

⊕

The Greek verb used for Peter's hauling the fish ashore (21:11) is *helkyein*, the same word used in 12:32: "And I, when I am lifted up from the earth, will *draw* all people to myself."[6] John would remind us that it is the power of Jesus, crucified and in glory, which draws people into the company of his disciples—just as it is the presence of Jesus which has filled the nets of Simon and his companions. This subtlety is not unusual for John.

The *hundred and fifty three fish* have exercised not only Peter and his companions, but the commentators. There are many explanations[7] —including some ingenious mathematical ones—for this particular number. A simple and plausible proposal is that this number of fish represents all of the races and nations of the world. According to St. Jerome, Greek zoologists recognized the total number of species of fish as 153.[8]

⊕

This great catch of fish at the end of John's gospel recalls Ezekiel's eschatological vision, in which the water originating from the temple becomes a river of life, flowing into the stagnant sea[9] and producing a multitude of fish (see above pp. 275-276).

The living water flowing from the new temple—the opened body of Jesus—pours into the stagnant waters of the Sea of Tiberias, the world of the Gentiles. This water of the Spirit freshens the sea so that it becomes a *new creation*. Here the narrative of John 21 connects firmly with the creation symbolism of the body of the gospel, and particularly of John 20. This *river*, flowing from the new garden of paradise into the sea, bridges the discontinuity between John's final two chapters. Distilled into this river of living water is the fullness of the creation symbolism, the comprehensive image of the new creation, which now flows out into the immensity of this open world. Our exodus from the tomb and from the interior of the house, "locked for the fear of the Jews," has brought us out also from the enclosed primal garden of John's Genesis symbolism, to the open and active, pragmatic world of Peter. It is the river of living water flowing from that interior Johannine country, however—the Spirit received through baptism—that brings about the great catch of fish. This living river brings to life the living dead and communicates the new creation to the great human world which is Peter's fishing-ground.

II

"Simon, son of John, do you love me more than these?" (21:15). Interpretations of these words have proceeded along three different lines.

- Do you love me more than all these *things*: that is, all that is represented by the boats, nets, the fish, the life to which

you have been accustomed? "And when they had brought
their boats to land, they *left everything* and followed him"
(Lk 5:11; see Mt 4:20-22; Mk 4:18-20).

- Do you love me more than *you love these other disciples?*

- Do you love me more than *these others love me?*

It is the *third* of these interpretations which seems most likely in the
present context, especially when Simon has just left the other disciples
behind to leap into the sea and swim toward his Master. This is not
out of character for Simon Peter, who had said at the last supper,
according to Matthew, "Though all become deserters because of you,
I will never desert you" (26:33). Earlier in Matthew's narrative, when
Jesus appeared to the disciples walking upon the sea, Peter had left
the others behind in the boat while he set out to walk to Jesus over the
water (Mt 14:28-29).

Jesus' words (21:15ff) to Simon Peter, then, may mean, in the language of Matthew: If you wish to be first, then serve the others, as the
Son of Man has come not to lord it over others but to serve them and
give his life for them (see Mt 20:27-28; Jn 13:12-17).

What is the meaning of this strange and abrupt transition from
fisherman to shepherd? Perhaps John is going beyond the synoptic
metaphor of "fishers of people" in emphasizing that the responsibility
of Peter and the other disciples will be a truly *pastoral* care which goes
far beyond merely hauling in the new converts. Typical of John is an
emphasis which goes beyond the more exterior—and therefore quantitative—aspects of life and ministry. When Jesus has fed the disciples
with this bread and fish which he has supplied, he turns to Peter and
repeatedly charges him to feed his lambs, his sheep. This certainly
refers to Peter's ministry of preaching and teaching (we recall that
food, for John, often symbolizes *wisdom*: see Part II, chapter 2 above),
but it also implies something that will approach Jesus' own gift of his
body and blood to his followers. Here John begins to suggest a protracted history—for Peter himself and also for the whole company of
disciples—until finally the Lord returns (see 21:22-23).

Jesus' questioning of Peter's love for him certainly recalls that earlier meal at which Jesus had poured out his teaching on love, and also
had invoked love for himself as the ultimate motive for following his
teaching. "*Those who love me* will keep my word..." (14:23). The awk-
ward grammatical form of Jesus' first question[10] may be due to John's
desire to communicate both senses of the ironical question: Do you

love me more than these do?—and also, Do you love me more than you love these others? Peter must learn to love the others as he loves Jesus—must learn this unitive lesson which is so difficult for him (see above, p. 123). It is in continuing to care for the sheep that he is to follow the Shepherd.

This interaction between Peter and Jesus is clarified by the presence of the silent third person about whom Peter will ask in a moment, the "disciple whom Jesus loved." A curious circularity in the dialogue leads us in this direction. Jesus repeatedly asks Peter about his love for him, and Peter responds, each time: *You know* that I love you. Contrasted with the disciple whom Jesus loved is this disciple who had been so rashly sure that *he loved Jesus*. Peter, the man of initiative and action—"I am going fishing"—the leader, had been confident in his own strength, and in that confidence had abysmally denied his Lord. The other disciple seems to do nothing, but he *knows* Jesus and knows *the love which Jesus has for him*. This little drama is consistent with the earlier one at the supper in accenting this contrast between the two disciples.

Again we encounter that *inversion*, that reversal of order, which we had seen between the Baptist and Jesus, between exodus and creation, and, at the tomb, between Peter who entered first and the disciple who then entered the tomb and saw and *believed*. A later theology would speak of the relationship between nature and grace, human activity and the primal action of God. "Man" acts first, and falls. Then comes the action of that grace which "was in the beginning" (see 1:17). The great catch of fish itself, after the disciples' night of fruitless work, follows this pattern.

> The true light, which enlightens everyone, was coming into
> the world. He was in the world, and the world came into
> being through him; yet the world did not know him (1:9-10).

In Matthew's gospel, Jesus had said to Peter who tried to dissuade him from his dedication to the way of the cross disposed by the Father, "*Get behind me*, Satan...for you are setting your mind not on divine things but on human things (lit. the things of *men—ta tōn anthrōpon*)" (Mt 16:23). You continually forget the source of the light in which you pride yourself, and now you would even instruct me. "*Follow* me" (21:19.22)—don't presume to lead me; you have not yet understood what I am teaching you.

If the disciple is not told by Jesus to follow him, as Peter is, this is because he already understands this lesson—and, too, because his own word is not "follow," but *"remain."* He has already been brought into a place which Peter does not yet know, and what he must do is remain rooted in that place. It is the place of the *beginning.* Simon Peter, on the other hand, identifies the beginning with his own impulse, his own initiative.

The focus, here in John 21, upon the *disciples*—and Peter in particular—rather than upon Jesus himself is a departure from the whole of the fourth gospel up to this point. And yet this narrative is never far from the Johannine Christocentric axis, to which it returns in Jesus' final words to Peter: "Follow *me*" *"... that he remain until I come...."*

John has depicted in the figure of Peter, subtly but powerfully, the perennial shadow of institutional power, of official mediation. Religious authority is ever accompanied by the temptation to mistake one's own will for God's, one's own ideas and agenda for the divine plan. Peter's response to Jesus, "Lord, you know everything; *you know* that I love you," shows that he has learned that he must reach yet deeper in his faith, place his confidence in something beyond itself, beyond himself. This primacy of grace, of the divine initiative that is in Jesus, is not a lesson, however, that is learned once and for all.

This narrative had begun with Peter's initiative, "I am going fishing," and much of the story's meaning is in the transformation which must take place within this man, who is endowed both with an evident personal authority and with Jesus' mandate as chief shepherd. Jesus indicates this transformation in his parabolic words about Peter when *young* and when *old* (21:18). While Jesus certainly refers here to Peter's death on the cross (cf. 21:19), these words also summarize the inner development of his life. The force of Peter's destiny will carry him from his willfulness to the point of surrender. If the fisherman is to become truly a shepherd, he must learn to relate to the other disciples in a way which is almost maternal, and which will progressively involve the laying down of his own life. This way of life is in continuity with its end.

> It will not be so among you; but whoever wishes to be great among you must be your servant, and whoever wishes to be first among you must be your slave; just as the Son of Man came not to be served but to serve and to give his life as a ransom for many (Mt 20:26-28; cf. Mk 10:45).

This little narrative centered in Peter recalls another sea story, that of *Jonah.* When God sent Jonah to preach repentance to the Gentile Ninevites, he took a ship to flee from his mission. To calm a great storm, the seamen threw him into the waters; he was swallowed by a great fish and finally cast up on land once again. A little wiser after this detour, Jonah then went to Nineveh and preached as he had been told; the Ninevites promptly repented and were spared from God's wrath. Peter has much in common with this comic figure, Jonah. In the great catch of fish here in John 21, Peter encounters, as in a parable, his apostolic mission to the Gentile world. Then he comes out of the water to receive his Lord's explicit command, "Feed my sheep."

Peter passes, like Jonah, through the *water*—as he has passed through the catastrophe of his Master's crucifixion—and is then examined by Jesus at the *fire*, where he had earlier failed. As the shepherd must be sheep and lamb, so the fisherman must himself, in passing through the transforming waters of death like his Master, become a fish.[11] These waters are baptismal, unitive, like the gate of the sheepfold with which Jesus identified himself (10:7).

The transformation of Peter which is indicated here corresponds to the drama of Peter and Jesus in the synoptic gospels and the Acts of the Apostles. Peter is rebuked by Jesus for attempting to dissuade him from the journey through death, for still preferring merely human concerns (Mt 16:23; Mk 8:33) to the demanding way of God. The same repulsion will lead him to deny his Lord, before he turns to him once again and finally, in the new fire of the Holy Spirit, preaches Jesus Christ boldly before the same Jerusalem Jews who had crucified him (Acts 2:14-36). It is the "fear of the Jews" (20:19), the shadow of the law, which had imprisoned Peter: fear of the Jewish authorities and a related fear of crossing the boundary of the law toward the Gentiles (see Acts 10:14; Gal 2:11-14).

The drama of Peter and his transformation opens to a more general significance. In his story there is an ecclesial meaning—as well as a personal meaning for each of those who will follow. On the *ecclesial* level, the words of Jesus to Peter indicate a continual process of conversion which must take place in the church's life. This process is parallel also to the experience of Israel during her Babylonian exile. The cold light of recent centuries has exposed more and more fully the "shadow" of the church: a perennial, collective and institutional selfseeking which obscures the gospel both for Christians and for those outside. At the same time Christians are recognizing in their own experience a collective, historical *dark night*,[12] a purificatory sea journey or exile. Like Jonah and Peter, Christians learn today in the darkness their never-ending lesson that the church is called to communicate the truth of Christ by *serving* humankind rather than by dominating it or by complacently preaching the Word to it from outside and above.

We have already seen revealed in John (on the fourth and fifth days) the deep conflict between the power of this world and the power of Jesus and of the Spirit. We have met again and again in the course of John's narrative those official mediators of religion who become the arch-enemies of Jesus in the gospel, and whose opposition to him generates the gospel's central drama.

The *individual* or personal meaning of this passage also resonates deeply with contemporary experience. Some of the more profound schools of psychology are in concord with the millennial spiritual traditions in teaching that each of us must undergo an interior journey— from the level of our superficial self toward a center, toward the realization of a self which is characterized by freedom and openness. We must be ripened out of our egocentricity, our superiority complex, the narrow self-love and tendency to self-exaltation which contaminate our relationships and consequently our ministry. We must find some way of descending to the *common*, the ground of human reality, if we would discover the ultimate remedy which is love. There seems, ultimately, to be no other way there than that which goes through the darkness, through the waters. The disciple, too, must have traveled this road to reach the place where he is now to remain.

⊕

Ellis argues that chapter 21 is an integral part of the structure of the gospel because it was necessary to fill critical gaps in the earlier chapters.

> If chapter 21 had not been part of the original Gospel, the author would have grievously failed his readers by capriciously arousing their expectations and anticipations regarding Peter and then failing to fulfill them. The same can be said for the Beloved Disciple, though not to the same degree.... If chapter 21 had not been part of the original Gospel, so much that was said about the Beloved Disciple would have remained unresolved.[13]

This argument has force. The drama of Simon Peter would clearly have been left inconclusive if his last appearance were that at the empty tomb. On the other hand, the "seeing and believing" of the disciple could conceivably, given John's subtlety, have constituted an adequate finale to the story of the disciple. A *larger symmetry*, however, is achieved when the *disciple*, identified with John and with the source of the gospel, is brought forward as witness at the end of the whole narrative to parallel the witness of John the *Baptist* at the beginning of the gospel. Such is the theological, as well as the literary, power of this symmetry of Baptist and disciple that it may be the strongest argument in favor of the presence of chapter 21 in the original gospel text.

The *disciple whom Jesus loved* appears once more (21:20ff), therefore, to bring the narrative to its close. His question to Jesus at the supper, about the betrayer, is recalled. This reminder of the dramatic interaction at the supper between Jesus, Peter, the disciple, and Judas seems strangely out of place here until we recall that here in John 21 we have been concerned with the leadership, and implicitly with the failure, of Peter. Again the author reminds us of the contrast between the infidelity of Peter, which was a yielding to Satan not incomparable with Judas' betrayal, and the fidelity of the disciple who remained close to Jesus until the end.

Peter's question about the disciple, "Lord, what about him?" (21:21), enables John to bring out, in a few words, the contrasting destiny of the disciple, from whom will originate this gospel itself (21:24). Symbolically, Peter and the disciple represent two intrinsic dimensions, and two enduring traditions, within the community of Jesus' disciples.

"...that he remain *until I come.*" Jesus' words here, like those to Nathanael (1:51), are difficult to take literally, for the disciple has died and Jesus has not yet returned. A reference to the "second coming" of Jesus would be exceptional in John, whose vision is consistently of a "realized eschatology."[14] We have seen that the whole of this final chapter, however—and particularly its concern with specific events to take place in time—departs from John's usual perspective.

"If it is my will that he *remain...*" (21:22). The word *menein,* "remain," appears here for the last time, and once again with theological weight. It is the disciple who rested on Jesus' *bosom* (13:23: Gr. *en tō kolpō,* with an overtone, therefore, of *"in"* that bosom) who stood near his *cross,* and "saw and believed" inside his *tomb,* who is to *remain.* Peter, meanwhile, is to *follow* Jesus. His energy and initiative will be needed, but must operate differently now—*following* Jesus' leading, as Peter himself leads others. This paradoxical union of leadership with following parallels Jesus' joining of master and servant in washing the feet of his disciples—an action which Peter had strenuously resisted. This, however, is the essential corrective to the negative potentialities of Peter's office as well as his personality. It is *sheep* who *follow* their shepherd (see 10:3-4). Jesus, the Shepherd, became also the sheep, the lamb, and so must Peter. He will first learn to follow, as the others follow him, and then journey toward a death of the same form as that of the Passover Lamb.

Joined with the gift of the Spirit by the risen Jesus was the mandate to *forgive sins*: to continue the mission of the Lamb of God (20:21-23; see 1:29). This mission of taking away sins, in the footsteps of Jesus himself, similarly implies a sharing in the destiny of the Lamb: like Jesus, being spent for the "sin of the world" (see Is 53:4-7).

⊕

"This is the disciple who is testifying to these things and has written them..." (21:24). This precious verse establishes the relationship of the disciple whom Jesus loved to the entire gospel of John. Chiastic symmetry between the disciple's witness here at the gospel's end, and the witness of John the Baptist at its beginning, makes it still more probable that we are to understand the disciple's name as *John*.

While contemporary scholarship views with extreme skepticism this identification of the disciple, the apostle John and the author of the gospel,[15] the mainstream of Christian tradition has long seen them as one person. For our purposes it is not the actual identity of the three which is important, but their identification *in the intention of the fourth gospel itself*; and this was faithfully preserved by the tradition. Once again in this case, our concern is not with historical *fact* but with literary—and theological—*intent*.

⊕

But there are also many other things that Jesus did; if every one of them were written down, I suppose that the world itself could not contain the books that would be written (21:25).

This final verse, recalling the "many other signs" of the earlier conclusion (20:30), seems to leave us in an unwarranted cloud of improbability (see 1:51). Perhaps a final surge of chiastic fervor has led the author to return here to the perspective of the prologue:

In the beginning was the Word, and the Word was with God, and the Word was God.... All things came into being through him, and without him not one thing came into being (1:1.3).

He, the Word that was before the world, and through whom the world was created, has come in Jesus to re-create the world. Neither he nor his works, ultimately, are "contained" by the world.

Perhaps our perplexity with this clearly hyperbolic expression comes from attempting to understand it in quantitative terms. Those "books that would be written" to contain the work of Jesus must surely be of *another order* than the books of this world—like those books which are opened for judgment in the presence of the Ancient One, before whom the Son of Man appears (Dan 7:10.13; see Rev 20:12), or the great scroll which "no one in heaven or on earth or under the earth was able to open or to look into" (Rev 5:3). This final verse suggests the total disproportion between "books," even this book of the disciple, and the creative *Word* who has come, in Jesus, to dwell and work in the world.

John 21 and the Chiastic Gospel

From the "ultimate realities" of the paradise symbolism of John 20, this Galilean appearance has brought us back *into history*: a salvation history which is woven into the history of world and empire. We are with the disciples no longer in the closed house (20:19-29), but upon the sea. Both the "Sea of *Tiberias*" and the great catch of fish indicate a context of universality.

While this final chapter continues the revelation and self-communication of Jesus which has been the axis of the whole gospel, it does so in this new *universal* key (see 17:20). The horizon now broadens—from the little circle of persons with whom Jesus has come into personal contact, to the whole world. The new perspective is that of the mission of the disciples to all the nations. First the great mission itself is symbolized in the catch of fish, and then the particular missions or "vocations" of the two arch-disciples are revealed and contrasted.

In a first view, John 21 can be considered a *Petrine appendix* to the Johannine gospel, serving a double purpose. First, it *relates* the mandalic vision of John's gospel, and the Johannine tradition itself, to the "*great church*" which is represented by Peter (thereby also indicating two great traditions in the church). Second, it sketches the vocation, the journey and the destiny of *Peter*.

Indeed, John 21 is centered upon Peter. The other disciples do not individualize themselves, except the disciple whom Jesus loved, and even he remains at the margin of the action. This sustained focus upon the disciples, and upon one disciple, rather than upon Jesus

THE CONTINUING DAY / 289

himself, distinguishes John 21 from the rest of the gospel. It is as if the author or redactor, having completed his unitive and unswervingly Christocentric gospel, found himself confronted with problems and perspectives which demanded a response from a different standpoint. This could easily have come about in the course of his successive encounters with other traditions within the church of the first century, and his experience of the tensions and conflicts between them.

Then, we may imagine, he turned to Peter, representative of this larger church within which the Johannine community was but one current, and added to his nearly completed picture a sketch of the role of Peter in the church and of the newborn church in the world. Finally he places the Johannine vision itself in relationship with the universal church—as well as with its counterpole of external structure and authority—through Jesus' words to Peter about the disciple. With this pregnant word "*remain*," he closes the circle once again. The sureness of construction and consistency of expression with which this is done would indicate that either the author or redactor of the gospel, or someone very close to its origin, must have added this final episode.

The numerous chiastic relations between John 1 and John 21,[16] and particularly the appropriateness of the chiastic symmetry between John the Baptist and the other John who is the disciple loved by Jesus, strengthen the impression that this concluding episode belongs to the final chiastic structure of the gospel,[17] even though that structure appeared to arrive at a satisfactory closure with chapter 20. The new episode, to be joined to the already completed chiastic structure ending at 20:31, may have been crafted in chiastic symmetry with the first episode of the gospel. Finally, therefore, the first narrative episode, section 1 (1:19-51), would have *two* distinct chiastic mates: 20:19-31 and 21:1-25.

John 21 may be conceived as an *epilogue*, therefore, lying neither completely within nor completely outside the gospel's great chiasm. In this it somewhat resembles the *prologue* of John, which is related to the narrative which follows it in John's chapter 1 by the two narrative passages concerning the Baptist within the prologue itself (1:6-8; 1:15). Possibly John's gospel has been deliberately bound with a final—and paradoxical—loop of chiastic symmetry by the relationship between that quintessentially Johannine prologue and this Petrine epilogue.

$$\oplus$$

The way of Peter is to "*follow* me," while that of the beloved disciple is to "*remain* until I come." The first is a journey in history, the second a dwelling at a central place. Here we seem to find recapitulated west and east, chronology and symmetry, linear sequence and mandala, masculine and feminine, dualistic and unitive, active and contemplative, exterior and interior, temporal and transtemporal, center and periphery, walking and dwelling, journey and life, movement and light, gradual progression and original fullness. Explicitly juxtaposed are the witness of martyrdom and the witness of "remaining," of a rooted fidelity. The gospel of John corresponds to the latter series—unitive, interior, contemplative, transtemporal, eastern, symmetrical, feminine, centric, pleromic—and its mandalic inner structure expresses these qualities in a coherent and powerful way.

Our final episode, then, projects several theological structures which are to characterize the life of the church throughout this protracted workday which begins with the breakfast on the shore. The ambiguity of the chiastic relation of chapter 21 to the rest of the gospel, the sharp change in perspective in this chapter, and particularly the abrupt movement from the "rest" of the seventh day to the scene of fishing and the theme of work and mission, permit us to find in this final narrative the sketch of an *eighth day* to be constituted by the active life of the church in history. John's final scene at the sea's edge represents the dawn of this arduous day.

III

GOSPEL, COMMUNITY AND WORLD

Chapter One

Prologue and Gospel Narrative

By way of introduction to the structure and symbolism of John, we briefly considered the prologue before setting out on our journey through the seven days of creation. Now the prologue will provide us with a synthetic perspective from which to look back over the entire gospel narrative.

A. The Center

Prologue: 1:12 (Parallel in narrative—Section 1 [=Part III]: 6:16-21)

> But to all who received him,
> who believed in his name,
> he gave power to become children of God....

The *structural* centers of the chiastic figures of both prologue and gospel narrative are also the *theological* centers of these texts. The prologue center relates well to the narrative's central sea-crossing narrative on its symbolic level. This sea-crossing, we recall, represents both the sea-crossing of the exodus event, and the first day of creation. There the uncreated light of the Word, present in the man Jesus, shone over the waters where the Spirit had hovered in the beginning.

The central verse of the prologue is, "To all who received him, who believed in his name, he gave power to become children of God" (1:12). Verse 13, which is joined with 1:12 to form the central "first day," will be discussed below (pp. 297-303). This *power* is a participation in the being of the one Son of God who is Jesus.

"To all...who believed in his *name*..." (1:12b). Here we must recall the "*I Am*" which Jesus spoke upon the waters, reflecting the name of Yahweh, the *I Am* of Exodus 3 and of Second and Third Isaiah. This *I Am* signifies the infinite well of "identity" into which the children of God are born when they receive Jesus, believing in his name. This *I Am* has in itself a *creative radiance*. It is in Deutero-Isaiah, as the coming salvation of Israel is being proclaimed as a new creation, that the divine *I Am* repeatedly sounds. At the center of the gospel, where the *I Am* appears, we have located the first day of creation: this first day is constituted not by a distinct creative action on Jesus' part, separate from his being itself, but simply by the manifestation of that being and its "reception" by the believing disciples, by the *revelation* (and recognition) of the *I Am* in Jesus.[1]

The prologue center further develops this same event of manifestation and acceptance, revealing it as the event in which the one who believes is reborn as a child of God. This quantum leap of identity is a participation in the divine *I Am* through Jesus' unique participation in the divine identity.

In contrast to the first creation, the new creation which begins with this birth takes place through humanity, through the faith of human persons. The new creation is constituted by a new *immanence*. God dwells in the human person and the human person dwells in God. From the externality of the first creation a person's being is drawn inward, into God's *generation* of the Son. The centrality of this central verse to the mandala figure as a whole, whether of prologue or of gospel, is an expression of this new interiority or immanence.

Both in the center of the gospel and in that of the prologue, it is when Jesus is "received" that the event of transformation, of new creation, takes place. It is belief in Jesus' "name"—receiving him in faith —which brings about the new birth that is a fuller receiving of Jesus. This new birth of the believer is itself precisely a receiving of the being of the Son of God into himself or herself (see 17:26). In the sea-crossing passage, the receiving is indicated by the words, "Then they wanted to take him into the boat" (lit. to *receive* him, *labein*), "and immediately the boat reached the land toward which they were going" (6:21). This arrival is another expression of the transformation which is being signified here: the land to which they are suddenly brought is that of the new creation.

Since the new birth is related both to baptism—recall Jesus' words to Nicodemus, "...no one can enter the kingdom of God with-

out being born of water and the Spirit" (3:5)—and to the consummation of the new creation, it relates closely to the *seventh* day: that is, to
the beginning and the end of the gospel narrative. The words "he
gave them power to become children of God" at the center of the prologue also relate strongly to the seventh day, when Jesus breathed the
Spirit upon his disciples. In the center of the prologue, the new creation which proceeds by stages through the gospel narrative *has
already reached its unitive conclusion.* In the gospel this comes about
only on the final days of the week of creation.

These two centers support the hypothesis that *baptism* is central to
John's gospel, because they both relate to baptism in a most particular
and powerful way. In fact *baptism joins the two centers* anew by associ-
ating the descent into water, the *passage through water,* with the *new
birth as children of God.* It is in baptism, here at the center, that prologue and gospel narrative coincide most clearly and strongly.

B. Quaternity

1. Prologue and Gospel: The Parallel Figures

Let us look first at some of the more general relationships between
the two mandalic figures of prologue and gospel narrative. The parallel which relates the two axes—or four arms—of the prologue mandala to those of the gospel mandala (see Figures 1.5, 1.6, 1.7) is not a
simple one, but requires a step of interpretation. Movement up the
vertical axis of the gospel figure is from the first creation, represented
by the people of Israel, their life and religion, and particularly by John
the Baptist, to the new and unitive creation, represented by the disciples of Jesus and particularly by the disciple. The progression along
the horizontal axis of the gospel from right to left is from the people
who dwell at the margins of Israel to those who preside at its heart,
the religious leaders of the Jews. In the course of this movement a discrimination and polarization takes place between those who believe—
and so become the new Israel—and those who disbelieve, among
whom stand out the leaders of the old Israel.

We have already referred to the prologue a number of times in
our study of the successive episodes of John's gospel in Part II. Seen
through the perspective of the prologue, the gospel narrative is *rein-
terpreted* in terms of the creative Word and of the final unitive fullness
of the new creation. The beginning itself of the prologue relates to

that of the gospel narrative not by simple parallelism, but through an ironic contrast, as we shall see (p. 318 below).

The prologue figure may be read in terms of a succession of *dwelling places of the Word*. In Part I the Word is with God (not yet termed "Father"); in Part II it is in the world; in Part IV it is "among us" in the flesh; in Part V it is the Son (perhaps now to be taken with an implicit inclusivity—see 1:12) in the bosom of the Father. Part III expresses by its geometrical position of *interiority*, as center, the relationship of the creative Word to God, to humanity and to the cosmos. The Word is always *center*, and it is the *unitive* center of humanity and of the world.

The prologue invites us to trace in the gospel narrative the movement of the fundamental Isaian text: 55:8-11. The Word which was with God comes into the world, bears fruit (those who believe in him: the "we" of 1:14) from the ground and brings it back to God (into the bosom of God: into a new intimacy with the Father). In the course of this journey of the Word, God has "opened," so that humans can participate the grace and truth of his interior life: Spirit and Word. The divine fullness has been poured out into human persons, and humanity has been brought into God in the only Son.

The word *plērōma*, or fullness (1:16; see 1:14c), emerges along the upper arm of the prologue mandala, while the symbols of this fullness accumulate in the corresponding part of the gospel.

Parallel to the progression—from a revelation which occurs still within the *first* creation, to the fullness of the *new* creation—which we find in John's prologue and narrative, is the movement within the brief prologue of John's *first letter* (1 Jn 1:1-5). The progression from revelation to communion in the letter prologue corresponds to that from light to *plērōma*, or unitive fullness, in the prologue to the gospel. The creation itself, which begins the gospel prologue, is only suggested very briefly by the first words of the letter: "We declare to you *what was from the beginning...*" (1:1; see Gen 1:1). That which is expressed with such compactness and clarity in the 1 John prologue is woven throughout the whole gospel, with its complex structure of symbolism and narrative. This basic progression in the gospel—from signification to union (or revelation to immanence, Word to Spirit)—is most apparent between its beginning in Part I and its conclusion in Part V, and appears strongly also in the movement through the seven days of creation.

2. The Four Dimensions in John 1:13

...who were born, not of blood
or of the will of the flesh
or of the will of man,
but of God (1:13).

Here at the center of the quaternary figure of the prologue, this verse, with its fourfold development, has a structural function. Following immediately the prologue's theological centerpoint (v. 12, the new birth), v. 13 resumes this center ("who were born...") and then proceeds to indicate the *four dimensions* along which the cruciform figure will extend outward from this center. The lower arm corresponds to "blood," or natural generation; the right arm to "the will of the flesh," or the way of the world (see 1 Jn 2:16); the left arm to "the will of man," which relates antithetically to the revelation of the glory of the Son along this same axis. Finally, "born of God" relates to the upper arm, where to those who believe, God is made known *unitively* by the only Son who is in God. We have already briefly indicated (pp. 48-51 above) the correspondences between these four dimensions of the prologue and the corresponding parts of the mandalic gospel narrative.

The four dimensions of 1:13 and the prologue are disposed in *three tiers*. The lowest is "blood," or the merely natural and involuntary level of existence. The highest is "God." Intermediate between these two is the level of human consciousness and freedom, psyche and mind. This ranges between the two contrasting poles of "will of the flesh" and "will of man."

Behind this quaternary pattern lies, once again, the ultimate quaternity of God, Word, Spirit and cosmos. The human mind and psyche, on the intermediate level, participate in this Word and Spirit—but also oppose themselves to Word and Spirit, thus generating the drama of the prologue. The intermediate—properly human— level, then, is a theater of division, of contrast and drama, of differentiation and irony and judgment.

We find only a vague consistency between the four phrases of 1:13 and the four limbs of the prologue. The four dimensions have only an attenuated life in the prologue itself. They take on their full significance when embodied concretely in the gospel's dramatic narrative, as we shall see.

While the prologue itself proceeds to its conclusion with a calm power which is hardly challenged, rather than with the gospel's crescendo of dramatic conflict, 1:13 contains within it the seeds of the gospel's drama. Contrasted with the birth from *God* here are *blood*, *flesh* and *man*, and in the gospel these three will become three forces opposing the new creation. From this tension emerges the dramatic conflict of the gospel.

The prologue mandala marks a further development beyond the Pauline figures (see Fig. 1.7). Israel ("the Jews") has become the *new* Israel ("we"), and the Gentiles have become the "world" (*kosmos*). The earth has become the totality of the first creation, contrasted with the new creation which is in the place of "God" at the upper pole of the figure. In prologue as well as gospel, the center itself remains the paschal mystery of Jesus crucified (in the gospel narrative, Jesus' death and resurrection are symbolically identical with the central passover sea-crossing of 6:16-21), but seen explicitly as the event of new *creation*.

John's prologue has developed the symbolic geometry of the Pauline mandala,[2] with its predominantly objective vision, in the direction of the *experience* of Jesus' disciples (1:14.16). From the cosmic or creation thematic of the earlier mandala John has introduced a progression to *new creation*, in his own theological sense of unitive immanence. Central to this process is the Johannine new *birth*. The prologue mandala expresses not simply the four dimensions of the one great Christ-event, but its progressive development. The event, in the prologue, has become a *history*.

3. The Four Dimensions in Prologue and Gospel

Now we shall survey the four dimensions or arms of the gospel figure (Parts I, II, IV and V—see Figure 1.5 above) in the light of the corresponding members of verse 13, to see whether this prologue verse offers a synthetic view of the gospel as a whole.

(1) *"not of blood."* Part I: 1:19–4:3. That is, not of human generation. This is a recurrent theme along the lower arm of the gospel mandala which extends from 1:19 to 4:3. The narrative begins with a questioning of the identity or "origin" of the Baptist and his teaching—not his human origin, which is well known, but his divine mandate. Behind this narrative lie vv. 1-2 of the prologue, which affirm the divine origin of Jesus. The question of Jesus' identity and origin soon arises. "Among you stands one whom you do not know" (1:26). "And I myself have seen and have testified that this is the Son of God" (1:34). "We have found the Messiah" (1:41). "We have found

him...Jesus son of Joseph of Nazareth" (1:45). "Can anything good come out of Nazareth?" (1:46). "Rabbi, you are the Son of God!" (1:49). Behind this first episode also is the memory of Jesus' baptism by John; according to the synoptic accounts, the voice of the Father was heard at that time, saying, "You are my beloved Son; with you I am well pleased" (Mk 1:11).

As the story of the Cana wedding opens, we are told immediately that "the *mother* of Jesus was there." The significance of Jesus' first sign makes of this *wedding* itself a sign of another union which is fertile but "not of blood." Jesus' relationship to his human mother is, at the same time, symbolically raised to another level.

When Jesus replies to the Jews, after he has cleansed the temple, "Destroy this temple, and in three days I will raise it up" (2:19), his words imply that the revelation and the worship will no longer be limited by "blood," that is, confined to the nation of Israel whose religious center and symbol was the temple of Jerusalem.

Jesus' dialogue with Nicodemus is, from its first words, intensely concerned with the question of personal origin, descent. "Rabbi, we know that you are a teacher who has come from God..." "...I tell you, no one can see the kingdom of God without being born from above." "...can one enter a second time into the mother's womb and be born?" (3:2.3.4).

The words of Jesus which conclude the final episode of this Part return emphatically to the question of the divine origin and mission of the Son (3:31-36).

⊕

(2) "or of the will of the flesh." Part II: 4:4–6:15. The Samaritaness, with her history of promiscuity, initiates this Part. Jesus would move religion from the level of the flesh to that of spirit and truth (4:23-24). Jesus heals the son of the *basilikos* without the contact of flesh, at a distance. The paralytic is one who is weighed down by the flesh: perhaps even his "mat" has this significance. He never rises to the level of the spirit, and his healing remains on that of the flesh. In the next episode of this Part (5:30-47), Jesus strives in vain to raise the level of understanding of the Jews—who are listening to him from the level of the flesh—to that of the spirit, which is the plane of the Father. Finally, when he has fed the crowd with bread and fishes on the other side of the sea, they interpret his sign on the level of the flesh (see 6:26-27) and try to make him their king. He flees into the solitude of the mountain.

⊕

(3) "or of the will of man." Part IV: 6:22–12:11. The left arm of the gospel mandala, including 6:22–12:11, is indicated in 1:13 by "the will of man." What we find along this arm of the gospel mandala (passing over Part III, the central episode which we have discussed above) is a crescendo of conflict between Jesus and the Jewish leaders. These scribes and Pharisees and chief priests represent this *will of man* opposing the new birth which Jesus has come to bring. In the course of this section the will of Jesus to do the Father's will—by healing, by giving life, ultimately by bringing new life to humanity—is contrasted diametrically with the opposing will of the leaders. We are told again and again that they want to put Jesus to death.

This dramatic conflict is continual and progressive. We shall quote from this section more extensively, for it is here that the contrast sketched by John in 1:13, and with it the drama of the gospel, approaches its decisive climax.

> ...for I have come down from heaven, not to do my own will, but the will of him who sent me. And this is the will of him who sent me, that I should lose nothing at all that he has given me, but raise it up on the last day. This is indeed the will of my Father, that all who see the Son and believe in him may have eternal life... (6:38.39.40).

> He did not wish to go about in Judea because the Jews were looking for an opportunity to kill him (7:1).

> The world cannot hate you but it hates me because I testify against it that its works are evil (7:7).

> Anyone who resolves to do the will of God will know whether the teaching is from God or whether I am speaking on my own. Those who speak on their own seek their own glory; but the one who seeks the glory of him who sent him is true... (7:17-18).

> Why are you looking for an opportunity to kill me?... Who is trying to kill you? (7:19-20).

> Is not this the man they are trying to kill? (7:25).

The dispute about *freedom and slavery*, which Jesus initiates in 8:31, is about the will of man and its liberation by obedience to the word of God. The focus upon the bad will of Jesus' opponents is continual.

...you look for an opportunity to kill me, because there is no place in you for my word (8:37).

You are from your father the devil, and you choose to do your father's desires. He was a murderer from the beginning... (8:44).

If you were blind, you would not have sin. But now that you say, "We see," your sin remains (9:41).

In the story of the blind man, it becomes apparent that the *will of man*—in this sense of a perverse or evil will—*turns light into darkness*.

The basic contrast of this Part IV is expressed clearly in Jesus' discourse on the shepherd and sheep:

The thief comes only to steal and kill and destroy. I came that they may have life and have it abundantly (10:10).

The generosity of Mary's gesture in anointing Jesus (12:3) is contrasted with the "will of man," exemplified by Judas (12:4-6).

So the chief priests planned to put Lazarus to death as well, since it was on account of him that many of the Jews were deserting and were believing in Jesus (12:10-11).

These verses *conclude this Part IV* of the gospel, and the horizontal axis. They are a conclusive expression of this "will of man" which has more and more thoroughly expressed itself as evil in these successive episodes of Part IV. Not only do these men will to put out the light— hating the light which shows "that their deeds are evil" (3:20)—but *this will of man wills to kill man* as well. Lazarus, like Jesus, is not just an individual here: he represents Adam, humanity, everyone.

While the correlation between v. 13 of the prologue and the gospel narrative is *very good* here in Part IV, there is a strong *contrast* between Part IV of the prologue itself and Part IV of the gospel. The prologue here rises to the disciples' vision of the glory of Jesus, while the gospel descends to record these men's *blindness* to this glory and even to the common light of reason—to the extent finally of conspiring to put out the light itself. The differing viewpoints or levels of reflection of prologue and gospel are most apparent here.

In Part II we saw that the *flesh*—corresponding to the "world" and represented by some characters relating only marginally to the Jewish religion—was characterized by *weakness*; the will of *man*, however, here expressed in the *leaders of the Jews*, is characterized by a *force* of malice which is, finally, murderously effective.

⊕

(4) "but of God." Part V: 12:12–20:31. The *hour* of Jesus which occupies this final section of the gospel is to bring about the new birth of the children of God. In this *hour* are embraced both Jesus' *death* and the new *birth* of his resurrection: both to be shared by those who shall believe in him.

The new birth is expressed in the image of the grain of wheat which must die in order to bring forth new life (12:24-26); the death of Jesus, as well as his life, is to be shared by those who follow him.[3] When Jesus speaks of his being lifted up (12:32) and drawing all people to himself, it is the life of the *risen* Christ in which they are to participate. "Children of the light" (12:36): this is more than metaphor; those who believe in the light of God in Jesus will be reborn of it.

Jesus' supper discourse is almost entirely devoted to the *new life* which his disciples are to experience. While the theme of new *birth* becomes explicit only as he concludes his words to them (16:20-27), this final image of childbirth signifies the beginning itself of the new life which he has described at such length, and which he will illuminate further in his prayer to the Father (ch. 17).

The *disciple* whom Jesus loved stands for all of those who shall believe in him, and therefore his words from the cross refer to a birth and new life which all shall experience: "Woman, here is your son"; "Here is your mother" (19:26-27).

The intrusive prominence of *John the Baptist* in the prologue is less surprising if we understand here a structural parallel between two "Johns," who sum up in themselves the whole of Part I and Part V of the gospel, respectively. This symmetry between the two witnesses, Baptist and disciple, may parallel the opposition of the two expressions, "born not of blood" and "born of God." In the gospel of Matthew Jesus says,

Truly I tell you, among those *born of women* no one has arisen greater than John the Baptist; yet *the least in the kingdom of heaven is greater than he* (Mt 11:11).

In the fourth gospel it is the *disciple* who is the prime example of one who has been born into the kingdom of heaven; that is, *born of God*. John the Baptist is presiding witness at the beginning, or "foot" (Part I) of the gospel. "...the one who is of the earth belongs to the earth and speaks about earthly things" (3:31). The disciple, correspondingly, serves as presiding witness upon the upper limb (Part V).

When Jesus says to his disciples, "I am ascending to my Father and your Father, to my God and your God" (20:17), he is telling them that they are, from now on, begotten by his own Father, who is God. Their birth takes place symbolically when he breathes the Holy Spirit upon them in the next scene. This final gesture expresses the "birth from God" perfectly and conclusively. "Adam," humanity, is born anew, but this time by receiving *the very life of God*, rather than the "breath of life" (Gen 2:7).

C. Seven Days of Creation

In Table 3.1, and the accompanying Figure 3.1, the Johannine prologue has been correlated with the seven days of Genesis 1–2 and with the seven days of John's gospel. Assignment of the verses and their divisions to particular days involves uncertainty; some verses could have been located on another day with equal justification. While there are some striking correspondences between pairs of prologue verses, in general the relationships between the different prologue verses assigned to each day of creation are not, by themselves, striking. Nor is the correlation between these seven composite prologue units and the respective verses of Genesis 1–2 convincing by itself. Parallels between the respective prologue verses and the corresponding days of creation—and individual sections—in the *gospel narrative* are numerous and significant, however, as we shall see.

It might be hoped that the prologue verses, in their comparative brevity, would *define* the Johannine days of creation more clearly and concisely than the gospel narrative texts. Consistency of the prologue verses assigned to each day is not good enough to support this with any solidity. The following designations for the seven days, therefore, have been derived by selecting some of the prologue verses for each day (while excluding others) and interpreting them rather freely in the light of the gospel narrative. They are presented only as a preliminary and synthetic sketch of the general prologue–narrative correspondences over the seven days, as we prepare to compare the two Johannine texts in more detail.

DAY I: Beginning of the new creation in the illumination and new birth of the children of God, corresponding to baptism.

DAY II: Divine Wisdom, become a human person, is rejected by his own people, but remains among his new people as eucharistic bread of life.

DAY III: Appearing as light in the world, he dwells among his people as the divine glory, and is proclaimed by his witness.

DAY IV: The divine light, rejected by the darkness of the world, communicates himself fully to his new people, so that they may remain as lights in the world.

DAY V: The divine light, in contrast to the Mosaic law, is the life of all people, as they are born into the Father's only Son.

DAY VI: The creative light, through whom all things were made, comes into the world as grace and truth, so that everyone may come into the fullness of the image of God, becoming one with the creator. In this union in Word and Spirit, the creation itself comes to its fullness.

DAY VII: In the light who is unitive Word and Son, humanity knows God not by exterior sight but by union.

D. The Twenty-One Narrative Sections

Our main objective here is a synthetic view of the gospel narrative through the prologue. We shall not compare the two texts exhaustively, but summarize briefly the chief parallels and correspondences. The reader who would prefer a more rigorous correlation can, starting from Table 3.1, explore the further possible relationships between prologue and individual narrative sections.

TABLE 3.1

SEVEN DAYS OF CREATION IN GENESIS, GOSPEL NARRATIVE, PROLOGUE

GENESIS 1-2 DAY		NARRATIVE SECTION		PROLOGUE VERSE	
I	1	SEA-CROSSING	12		But to all who received him, who believed in his name, he gave power to become children of God,
LIGHT			13		who were born, not of blood or of the will of the flesh or of the will of man, but of God.
II	2	BREAD SIGN	11b		and his own people did not accept him
HEAVENS	3	DISCOURSE	14a		and the Word became flesh
III	4	BAPTIST TO JESUS	6-8		There was a man sent from God, whose name was John. He came as a witness to testify to the light so that all might believe through him. He himself was not the light, but he came to testify to the light.
	5	WITNESSES	11a		He came to what was his own,
EARTH	6	BOOTHS, TEMPLE	14b		and lived among us
	7	JESUS TO JERUSALEM, TO WORLD	15		John testified to him and cried out, "This was he of whom I said, 'He who comes after me ranks ahead of me, for he was before me.'"

Table continued on next page

	8	NICODEMUS	5	The light shines in the darkness, and the darkness did not overcome it.
IV				
	9	PARALYTIC	10bc	and the world came into being through him; yet the world did not know him.
LUMINARIES				
	10	BLIND MAN	14c	and we have seen his glory
	11	SUPPER, DISCOURSE	16	from his fullness we have all received, grace upon grace.

	12	TEMPLE	3c,4	what has come into being in him was life, and the life was the light of all people.
V				
	13	BASILIKOS	10a	He was in the world
LIFE				
	14	LAZARUS	14d	the glory of a father's only son,
	15	TRIAL, DEATH	17a	the law indeed was given through Moses;

	16	CANA WINE	3	All things came into being through him, and without him not one thing came into being.
VI				
	17	SAMARIA	9	the true light, which enlightens everyone, was coming into the world.
HUMANITY				
	18	BETHANY	14e	full of grace and truth
	19	GARDEN	17b	grace and truth came through Jesus Christ.

	20	BAPTIST, FIRST DISCIPLES	1-2	In the beginning was the Word, and the Word was with God, and the Word was God. He was in the beginning with God.
VII				
GOD'S REST				
	21	JESUS APPEARS TO GATHERED DISCIPLES	18	No one has ever seen God. It is God the only Son, who is in the Father's bosom, who has made him known \ opened the way.

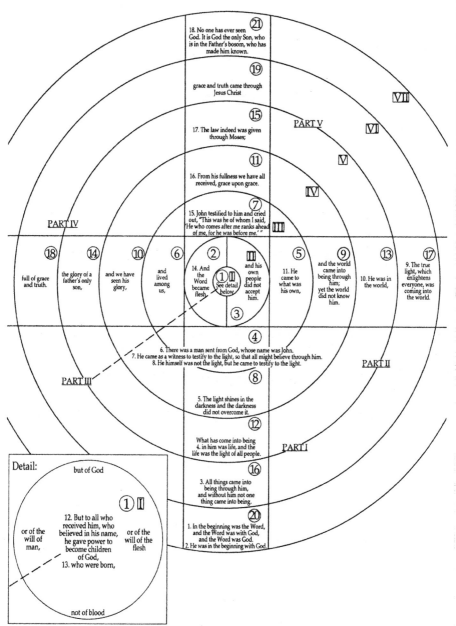

FIGURE 3.1

MANDALA OF JOHN'S PROLOGUE: THE SEVEN DAYS OF CREATION

Day I

SECTION 1   Prologue: 1:12-13   Narrative: 6:16-21

These correspondences have already been discussed (see above, pp. 293-295).

Day II

SECTION 2   Prologue: 1:11b   Narrative: 6:1-15

and his own people did not accept him

It would seem that the Galileans have "accepted" Jesus when, after he has multiplied the bread and fish, they hail him as "the prophet" and are ready to make him their king. Yet Jesus flees from them. This acceptance is *ironic*: they want to take him by force to make of him a king according to their own desires, to achieve their ends by force, by a kind of power which is opposed to the power which is truly his. This irony will become evident during Jesus' discourse on the bread of life after he has crossed the sea. The Galileans have radically misinterpreted the meaning of Jesus' power and the role which God has given him. They have not received his word nor truly accepted his person. They have not, therefore, really eaten the bread of life, the divine Wisdom which is embodied in Jesus. They were content with being "filled with the loaves" (6:26). Jesus' disciples, on the other hand, "wanted to take him into the boat" (6:21), which evidently signifies their genuine desire to "receive" him. The other Galileans remained behind, in the will of the flesh.

SECTION 3   Prologue: 1:14a   Narrative: 6:22-71

and the Word became flesh

The Word became *flesh*; this is what Jesus means by saying "I am the bread of life": he, in the flesh, is this Word which is the food, the life of humanity. If the order of these two verselets is reversed, they read, "and the Word became flesh and his own people did not accept him."

This is precisely what has happened as the people to whom God had revealed his Word in the *Torah*—the "people of the Word," therefore — reject the Word *incarnate* who has come among them. Their resistance to Jesus' words during his discourse on the living bread (6:22-71) is related to his identifying himself with the bread from heaven, and particularly to his insistence that they must eat his flesh (see 6:41.52.60). We must take sections 2 and 3 together if we make this inversion.

This prologue verse may also be reflected in the progression from word to *sacrament* which we have observed in the course of Jesus' discourse on the bread of life (p. 83 above). With 6:51, "...and the bread that I will give for the life of the world is my *flesh*..." the eucharistic sense appears and it is confirmed in the words which follow. When Jesus says, "Those who eat my flesh and drink my blood abide in me, and I in them" (6:56), this eucharistic meaning of "flesh" is related to a new *indwelling*, resonating with 1:14a. The will of man resists this intimacy, this transcending of personal boundaries.

The other side (see "will of flesh") is expressed in 6:63: the flesh is useless. This is the exact balance, counterweight, to 14a. The very concrete language which Jesus has been using makes this clarification necessary. While he insists with great firmness that his words must be understood *of* the flesh in which he stands among them, yet these words can only be understood not *in* the flesh but in the Spirit.

Day III

SECTION 4   Prologue: 1:6-8   Narrative: 3:22–4:3

There was a man sent from God,
whose name was John.
He came as a witness to testify to the light,
so that all might believe through him.
He himself was not the light,
but he came to testify to the light.

Corresponding to this first "John" passage in the prologue, we find in the gospel a return to the subject of John the Baptist: 3:23-30. John speaks of himself as *sent* (3:28; cf. 1:6), and here once again he *witnesses* (28-30) to Jesus. His witness itself here, as he contrasts himself with the bridegroom, reflects v. 8 of the prologue.

SECTION 5   Prologue: 1:11a   Narrative: 5:31-47

He came to what was his own,

Jesus speaks to the Jews, the people of the Word, and refers to the witness of John the Baptist, to whom they had sent to inquire about Jesus. These are "his own" who search the scriptures and put their trust in the *Torah* of Moses, and they do not accept Jesus despite the multiple witness to him.

SECTION 6   Prologue: 1:14b   Narrative: 7:1–8:59

and lived among us

In this section we find a very strong and repeated insistence on *place*: both on the temple, which is the setting of the action, and on the place of origin of Jesus (7:27.28.41.42.52). Jesus himself will speak of the place to which he is going: 7:33-36. The question of Jesus' place comes up again in chapter 8 (vv. 21-23). Later on in the same chapter, the Jews claim to be free persons because they are the descendants of Abraham. Jesus' response involves a subtle play upon the notions of home and *hospitality*: 8:35.40-41.

"About the middle of the feast Jesus went up into the temple and taught" (7:14). These words indicate Jesus' coming into his own place to take up residence and exercise his proper authority. But they are ironic in their reference to the temple of Jerusalem, which will not receive him. The Greek verb which John has used for "lived among us," *eskēnosen*, is related to the Greek name of this feast of Booths, *Skēnopēgia*. As we have moved to the left arm of the mandala—both in the gospel and in the prologue—we have entered a context in which the *dwelling of the Word, or of Jesus, in Israel* is thematically central (see above, p. 296).

SECTION 7   Prologue: 1:15   Narrative: 12:12-50

John testified to him and cried out,
"This was he of whom I said, 'He who
comes after me ranks ahead of me,
for he was before me.'"

The correspondence between prologue and narrative texts here is not immediately obvious, but emerges clearly against the background of *Psalm 118*, source of the acclamation with which the crowd greets Jesus: "Hosanna! Blessed is he who comes in the name of the Lord!" (Ps 118:25-26; cf. Jn 12:13). Earlier in the course of this long *processional* song we find strong resonances both with the gospel narrative of Jesus' entry into Jerusalem and with our prologue verse (1:15):

> Open to me the gates of righteousness, that I may enter through them.... This is the gate of the Lord; the righteous shall enter through it.... The stone that the builders rejected has become the chief cornerstone. This is the Lord's doing; it is marvelous in our eyes (Ps 118:19-20.22-23).

Jesus' entry into Jerusalem is the solemnization of his *coming*. The final disbelief of "his own," represented by the leaders of the Jews, contrasts with his royal reception by the people as well as the words of the Baptist. As Jesus arrives at Jerusalem to begin his *hour*, we have here a dialectic of foundations or *centers*. He who *was and is*, the eternal center, the Word, the one and only *"cornerstone,"* comes to the historical religious center which is the holy city. When he has been rejected and put to death there by the Jerusalem leaders, the "builders," he will replace the city itself just as he is to rebuild its center, the temple (2:19-21). Contrasting with this brittle resistance of the holy city—or, rather, of its religious leaders—is the *Baptist's* faith and openness: his graceful yielding of place to the one who comes after him.

DAY IV

SECTION 8   Prologue: 1:5   Narrative: 3:1-21

> The light shines in the darkness,
> and the darkness did not overcome it.

Nicodemus comes to Jesus out of the *darkness* (3:2), and his dialogue with Jesus orbits around the question of understanding, of seeing the kingdom of God, of learning and teaching in Israel. Jesus says to him, "...no one can *see* the kingdom of God without being *born* from above (anew)" (3:3). There is an absolute separation, incommunicability, between darkness and light. The darkness can neither overcome nor comprehend the light: it must be reborn in the light itself, and this comes only from above, from God. At the end of this Nicodemus discourse, Jesus returns emphatically to the metaphor of *light*, and now it is a question of a light which shines in the darkness (3:19-21) and of people who prefer the darkness to the light. "... the light has come into the world..." (3:19) is almost identical verbally with v. 9, and its sense is very close to that of vv. 9-11 of the prologue.

SECTION 9   Prologue: 1:10bc   Narrative: 5:1-30

> ...and the world came into being through him;
> yet the world did not know him.

This prologue verse is especially applicable to the *paralytic*, who does not know Jesus after he has been healed by him (5:13), and then still does not really know him for who he is (5:15). The scene at the pool of Bethzatha, where the paralytic waited for the water to be stirred, was strangely reminiscent of the first day of creation in Genesis 1. In Jesus the creative Word comes and restores this man to his natural movement.

SECTION 10   Prologue: 1:14c   Narrative: 9:1-41

> ...and we have seen his glory...

The blind man who receives his sight from Jesus also knows something of Jesus' glory, for he believes in him. And for this he is himself cast out of the synagogue by the blind men who are the authorities. This man stands in contrast to his opposite number, the paralytic, who does not awaken to the identity of the man who has healed him. The man born blind believes in Jesus (9:38) and so joins the "we" of the disciples.

SECTION 11   Prologue: 1:16   Narrative: ch. 13–17

> ...from his fullness we have all received,
> grace upon grace.

The *we* of 1:14 returns here (see 1 Jn 1:1-5). Indeed, *we* are *constituted by this fullness*. This is the *plērōma* which contains and integrates within itself also a plenitude of meanings, of dimensions. Here we have arrived at the conclusion of prologue and gospel, just as the *hour* of Jesus is a fullness and a conclusion in the gospel narrative.

This fullness is symbolized by the *supper* itself, with its biblical overtones of messianic banquet, banquet of Wisdom, eschatological banquet. The particular aspects under which John considers this fullness are *union* and *interiority, indwelling* and, finally, the *love* which is *agape*.

At the beginning of the supper discourse, Jesus had said, "Now the Son of Man has been glorified, and God has been glorified in him. If God has been glorified in him, God will also glorify him in himself and will glorify him at once" (13:31-32). The fullness of 1:16 is this fullness of *glory*, and in the prayer which concludes the supper narrative Jesus will pray that this glory (for the biblical writers a golden word comprehending within itself all the riches of God), which is uniquely his, may be given to the disciples; he himself confers it upon them: "The glory that you have given me, I have given them..." (17:22; see 17:22-26). This is the primary meaning of the "grace upon grace" of 1:16: it is the disciples' participation in the fullness which is in the risen Jesus. The expression may also, as John frequently does, contrast the grace of Jesus with that of Moses and the exodus covenant.

DAY V

SECTION 12   Prologue: 1:3c-4   Narrative: 2:13-25

What has come into being in him was life,
and the life was the light of all people.

The new creation will be "life in him," and the new temple will be not a slaughterhouse, a temple of death, but the temple of life which is "in him" by being his own body. Whatever enters this temple enters life. Both the temple and the Jewish law are sometimes presented by John as institutions of death. The new temple of life will be not just for one nation but for *all people*.

SECTION 13   Prologue: 1:10a   Narrative: 4:43-54

He was in the world...

The *basilikos*, like the centurion of the synoptics to whom he is related, represents by his office the "world." Jesus is "in the world," and has royal power over everything in the world, and therefore is able to heal the son of the helpless royal official even at a distance, by a word.

SECTION 14   Prologue: 1:14d   Narrative: ch. 10–11

...the glory of a father's only son...

It is in the culminating sign of the raising of Lazarus that the *glory* of Jesus is particularly to be revealed:

This illness does not lead to death; rather it is for God's glory, so that the Son of God may be glorified through it (11:4).

Did I not tell you that if you believed, you would see the glory of God? (11:40).

The connections between prologue and gospel narrative here are verbal, literal. Perhaps the author has put in the exact verbal correspondences (11:4) as deliberate *clues* to help the reader find the proper parallels, relationships and structure. Lazarus is *Adam*, humanity, to be brought back by Jesus from the corruption of sin and death to the glory of the only Son—in himself.

SECTION 15   Prologue: 1:17a   Narrative: ch. 18–19

The law indeed was given through Moses...

These prologue verses interlock like the links of a chain: Moses was implied in v. 16 and emerges explicitly here in v. 17. The *Mosaic law*, surprisingly, is reflected in the passion narrative of John 18–19. The bulk of the Johannine passion narrative, in fact, is occupied with the *legal proceedings*—first before the high priests and then before the Roman procurator—which led to Jesus' death. But it is the Mosaic *Torah* to which 1:17 specifically refers. The high priests and scribes "sit upon the chair of Moses" and govern the people according to his law. And it is in this capacity that they condemn Jesus to death. "We have a law, and according to that law he ought to die because he has claimed to be the Son of God" (19:7) (see Lev 24:16). Pilate had responded to them, when they hauled Jesus before him in the early morning, "Take him yourselves and judge him according to your law" (18:31).

The Jews, scrupulously observant of the *law*, refrain from entering the court of the Gentile Pilate so that they may not incur a ritual defilement which would prevent them from eating the Passover.

It is dramatically highlighted, in the account of these legal proceedings, that the law which was given through Moses has become, in the hands of these officials, anything but an instrument of grace and truth—and a medium of death rather than life. But even in its purity, the Mosaic law was not "grace and truth" in the Johannine sense, which we shall study further in a moment.

A further connection between passion account and law is the presence here of high priests, of Pilate, and the persistent dispute over the title of "king of the Jews" which Pilate attributes to Jesus. These are legal titles; the formal context is a juridical one. Another significant connection with the "law" of 1:17a is in John's careful attention to the *fulfillment of the scriptural prophecies* in the narrative of Jesus' crucifixion and death: 19:24.28.36.37.

The abundant correspondences to this single prologue verse in the gospel's passion narrative may be intended to accent the dramatic opposition which has emerged between these two great orders: the order of the *law*, or Word of God administered imperfectly through human intermediaries, and the order of the living and immediate, plenary *Word*, which is instituted by Jesus.

DAY VI

SECTION 16   Prologue: 1:3   Narrative: 2:1-12

All things came into being through him,
and without him not one thing came into being.

It is in this verse 3 that the *creation* theme is most explicit in the prologue. In his first sign at Cana, Jesus *"made (epoiēsen) the water wine"* (4:46). This is a strong "creation" gesture, and admirably expresses the relation of the *new* creation to the first creation, appropriately symbolized by water (see Gen 1:2; Jn 6:16-21).

As, in the first creation, "all things came into being through him," now, in the second creation, "*one thing*" comes into being through him: and this is symbolized by the Cana wedding and by its wine. All things become one thing again in the unitive new creation in the Word become flesh. "...and they become *one flesh*" (Gen 2:24).

SECTION 17   Prologue: 1:9   Narrative: 4:4-42

...the true light, which enlightens everyone,
was coming into the world.

The meeting with the Samaritan woman represents Jesus' furthest expedition into the "world" in John's gospel. Jesus tells the woman "all she has ever done," and she begins to perceive him as possibly the Messiah because of the *light* which is in him (see 4:25-26.29.39). Finally the townspeople confess, "...we know for ourselves that this is truly the Savior of the *world*" (4:42). It is high noon, the sixth hour, and the light of Jesus symbolically expands to its full width, over the world. The disciples are surprised that Jesus is talking with this woman, but the light which is in him has come to enlighten *everyone*.

SECTION 18   Prologue: 1:14e   Narrative: 12:1-11

...full of grace and truth.

In the encounter between Jesus and Mary of Bethany, there is a symbolic meeting of truth and grace, Word and outpoured fullness of Spirit. When Mary anoints his feet with a prodigious quantity of precious perfume and the house is *filled* with its fragrance, the glory of the Father's only Son is signified. The fragrance which fills the house reflects also the glory which filled the temple of Solomon, and which is to fill the new temple of Jesus' body when he is risen from the dead.

"You always have the poor with you, but you do not always have me with you" (12:8). The relationship of Jesus' messianic anointing and the *grace* which he brings to the poor and the afflicted (Bethany may signify "house of the afflicted"), to Mary's anointing of Jesus, is illuminated by a passage of Isaiah:

The spirit of the Lord is upon me, because the Lord has anointed me; he has sent me to bring good news to the oppressed, to bind up the brokenhearted, to proclaim liberty to the captives, and release to the prisoners; to proclaim the year of the Lord's favor, and the day of vengeance of our God; to comfort all who mourn; to provide for those who mourn in Zion—to give them a garland instead of ashes, the oil of gladness instead of mourning, the mantle of praise instead of a faint spirit. They will be called oaks of righteousness, the planting of the Lord to display his glory (Is 61:1-3).

Jesus is this anointed one that Mary honors with her own gesture, and he has given liberty to the captive of death ("unbind him and let him go"—11:44—Jesus' last words here), and abundantly consoled those who mourned. Mary's anointing corresponds to this anointing of the true King, and to the grace which he brings.

The "grace and truth" which Mary recognizes in Jesus and symbolizes with her gesture contrast with the *"will of man"* (see p. 301 above) which is manifest in 12:4-6 (in the calculating greed and the deviousness of Judas) and 12:10 (in the malice of the chief priests).

SECTION 19   Prologue: 1:17b   Narrative: 20:1-18

... grace and truth came through Jesus Christ.

The *grace and truth* of 1:17 are the immediate participations in divine life which are experienced through faith in Jesus. These two words, while they reflect the love and fidelity, *hesed* and *emeth* attributed to God in the Old Testament,[4] *go much further* at this point of the critical breakthrough of Jesus' resurrection and the pouring out of his fullness. Grace and truth are divine Spirit and Word (see the "spirit and truth" of 4:23), which now dwell within the human person and inform human life.

In this encounter of Jesus and Magdalene in the garden, *Adam and Eve* are symbolically re-created together. This reference to the first man and woman here is a recalling of the *true or symbolic being of man and of woman*. The true being of woman, or of the feminine, may be expressed as "grace"; the true being of man, or the masculine, as "truth."[5]

When Jesus addresses Magdalene as "Mary," it is as if he gives her the symbolic or "true" name of woman. The one *woman*, who is found with Jesus in the four episodes of the sixth day, is finally restored to her own truth in this encounter with the risen Jesus in the garden narrative.

DAY VII

SECTION 20   Prologue: 1:1-2   Narrative: 1:19-51

In the beginning was the Word,
and the Word was with God,
and the Word was God.
He was in the beginning with God.

At first the divergence between prologue and gospel seems widest here at the beginning of the narrative. The gospel narrative begins in the desert waste with the Baptist and the prologue begins in heaven with God! The two texts are related by this contrast itself, however.

The negative and self-deprecating responses of the Baptist to the questions of the Jerusalem priests and Levites beautifully reflect the great positive and ontological assertion of the identity of the Word—and therefore of Jesus—in the prologue's first verse.

"I am not the Messiah." (*Egō ouk eimi* ho kristos.)
"I am not." (*Ouk eimi.*)
"No." (*Ou.*)

John's replies should be heard against the background of Jesus' repeated words of self-identification, "*I Am*," *egō eimi.* The first two verses of the prologue affirm this same divine identity of the Word which becomes present in Jesus. The repeated "*was*" of 1:1-2 is to be interpreted with this ontological force.[6] This contrast is perfectly consistent with the Baptist's other declarations of his relationship to the "one who comes after me" (e.g. 1:15.30).

A further strong prologue connection is created by the Baptist's reference, still in regard to his own identity, to the first chapter of the Isaian book of consolation (Is 40; see Jn 1:23).

A voice says, "Cry out !"
And I said, "What shall I cry?"

All people are grass,
their constancy is like the flower of the field.
The grass withers, the flower fades,
when the breath of the Lord blows upon it;
surely the people are grass.
The grass withers, the flower fades;
but the *Word of our God* will stand forever! (Is 40:6-8).

John is the *voice*, and he speaks so that this *Word* (1:1-2) may be recognized. "I came baptizing with water that he might be revealed to Israel" (1:31).

"This is he of whom I said, 'After me comes a man who ranks ahead of me because he *was before* me'" (1:30). Jesus, of whom he speaks, is the *Word* who *was* in the *beginning*. The correspondence between the prologue's beginning and the beginning of John's narrative is exact. There is a resonance also between the "In the beginning" of 1:1 and the *baptism of Jesus* which is recalled in this first episode (1:31-33). As we have noted, the baptism of Jesus is sometimes presented in the New Testament as the beginning of the story of Jesus' life.

When, later in the first chapter, the disciples ask Jesus, "Rabbi, where are you staying?" and Jesus replies, "Come and see," there is another strong connection with 1:1 and with 1:2. These words, so charged with mystery, point ultimately to the place where Jesus dwells *with* God (1:1) and *in the Father's bosom* (1:18—chiastic mate of 1:1 within the prologue). The word *menein*, used here for *stay*, is the same word which Jesus will employ at the very end of the narrative when he says of the disciple, "If he is to *remain . . .*"

The prologue, then, is, from the start of the gospel narrative, *interpreting the narrative* on the *level of ultimate, unitive meaning*. The prologue is the *unitive key* to the gospel narrative. These first verses of the prologue gently illumine the first episode of John's narrative—in terms, first, of the *identity of Jesus*, and, second, of the *dwelling place of Jesus*.

SECTION 21   Prologue: 1:18   Narrative: 20:19-31

No one has ever seen God . . .
It is God the only Son,
who is in the Father's bosom,
who has made him known (or *opened the way[7]*).

This final prologue verse expresses the "sabbath" of the new creation in terms of a *place*—the place within the Father's bosom which belongs to the only Son. The final *rest*, the "rest of God," into which those who believe in Jesus are introduced, is beyond images (see above, p. 264), and therefore beyond "seeing."

While Thomas is not satisfied when the other disciples tell him, "We have seen the Lord" (20:25), he finally does experience something which convinces him completely (20:28). He has *seen* (20:29) Jesus—yes, but what his confession expresses is something deeper than what we usually mean by "seeing." Thomas experiences this *place* of the divine sabbath, and so he joins the disciple who had rested on the bosom of Jesus, seen Jesus' breast pierced upon the cross, and finally "seen and believed" in the tomb.

Thomas' experience corresponds also to that which was conferred by Jesus when he breathed the Holy Spirit upon the disciples. This is the *new and reciprocal immanence or indwelling* which Jesus had promised at the supper (see 14:20). It corresponds also to the primal Christian experience which is the new birth of *baptism*.

The prologue intervenes with decisive force here, to interpret the enigmatic scenes in the closed house in terms of the unitive experience of the Son who dwells within the Father. The "grace and truth" which are the patrimony of the Son (1:14)—and which have now come into being in the world of the new creation (1:18)—express this same experience, this same reality.

The recreation of Adam (humanity), which occurs on the conclusive seventh day of the gospel narrative, is the reconstitution of the human person—image of God, male and female—in the grace and truth of the only Son who dwells within the Father. It is the re-creation of humanity *within God*, and filled with the fullness of God which is expressed by this grace and truth.

In the gospel narrative of John 20, it may be that the vision of the risen Jesus, and the disciples' reborn *faith*, correspond to the "truth" of the prologue, and the gift of the Spirit which brings them to life corresponds to the "grace."

This final correspondence, between the two appearances of Jesus to the gathered disciples in ch. 20 and the final verse of the prologue, has conclusive force. If the strongest contributions of the prologue to the reading of the gospel seem to be concentrated at the beginning and the (chiastic) middle and the end of both texts, this may be, in part, because the prologue is concerned with *ultimates*, and in part also because John's geometrical way of thinking tends to place the greatest theological weight at these points.

Chapter Two

Prologue and Baptism

The inner continuum of John's prologue is the divine Unitive which is first expressed as the *Word* and then as the light, as the "he" which denotes Jesus revealing himself in the world and making those who believe in him children of God in himself; then as the fullness of grace and truth, and finally as the Son in the Father's bosom. The prologue is centered in the *event* by which those who believe become children of God and receive this unitive fullness in themselves. This event, as we have seen, *corresponds to the baptismal event.*

The entire prologue surrounds this baptismal event, first building up to it by recounting the *external* revelation of the light of the Word, and then explicating its effect by recalling the *interior* experience of the baptized. Here, particularly, the cautious and conditional discourse of a merely scientific exegesis is alien to the fullness which is implicit in the text.

We shall attempt to suggest something of this fullness of the prologue's baptismal reference through a simulated patristic text. The following is an imaginary instruction for the rite of baptism in a "Johannine community," based upon a reading of the actual prologue text to the persons being baptized.

The baptismal instruction is given in five parts, corresponding to the five divisions of the mandalic prologue. The time of the instruction is during the vigil of Easter, and the baptism itself is presumed to be administered close to the time of sunrise. The place of instruction is the baptistery: a square building surrounding the circular pool where the immersion takes place. The catechumens will face successively in the four directions of the compass, from which points the four sections of the prologue of John: I, II, IV and V, will be read. The actual rite of baptism will take place during the reading of Part III, between v. 12 and v. 13.

I

In the beginning was the Word,
and the Word was with God,
and the Word was God.
He was in the beginning with God.

You have turned from your old life, the road that leads to death, and come to the place of the beginning, so that you may enter into the beginning and be born into a life which does not die. Before the beginning of the world, the Word was in the beginning with God. The Word was born eternally in God, and in this generation of the Word is the beginning of all things. This is the Word of life which has been preached to you, and in whom you believe.

All things came into being through him,
and without him not one thing came into being.

Through him, the Word who is Jesus Christ, all things were created. There is nothing that exists which did not begin in him, and all that exists is one in him. You are to be born anew in this oneness which is the Word, and you shall experience it within your own being. All that exists must once again come together in him, for in him alone is being and life.

What has come into being
in him was life,
and the life was the light of all people.

As you descend into the waters you will enter into his death, and as you ascend from the waters you will rise in his resurrection. You will be life as he is life; from now on you will know your true life as inseparable from your very self. When you come from the waters you will be illumined more fully from within; you will know in its fullness the light of humanity, which illumines all people even when they do not receive it: the light which is their only life and in which they must learn to walk if they are to live. Though not a child of

Abraham by blood, by faith you are a child of God. This light, unlike circumcision and the law, is for all humankind. The inner secret which is hidden within the heart of every man and woman is about to blossom within you.

The light shines in the darkness,
and the darkness did not overcome it.

Through the grace of God in Jesus Christ, you are coming from the darkness into light. You have already seen this light and come forth into it. Now the God who said, "*Let there be light,*" is about to speak his Word in its fullness within your heart, and drive the darkness from it. Now the light of his glory will dawn there, so that you may be wholly light in Christ. From the beginning the light has shone in the darkness; the light has come to you now and will dwell in you so that you too may shine as light in the darkness of this world. The darkness will resist you and fight against you as it fought against him, but it will not prevail, for the light which will be within you is risen, never to be overcome.

There was a man sent from God, whose name was John.
He came as a witness to testify to the light,
so that all might believe through him.
He himself was not the light,
but he came to testify to the light.

It is a man named John[1] who has witnessed to you what he has seen and heard and touched with his hands: Jesus, the Word of life. And you have believed and are about to enter into the fellowship which we have in him, Jesus Christ. The first witness, John the Baptist, immersed Jesus in the water of the Jordan River and the Spirit descended upon him in the form of a dove. You are to be baptized by John, the second witness, in the water which is Spirit, in his name.

John the Baptist was a lamp to the Jewish people, and John who witnessed to you has been a lamp to your steps. But Jesus is the light who will come to you in the water and will dwell within your heart so that you too may be a lamp for others.

You are to be baptized into the only-begotten Son of God, and become the child of God, one with him, one in him. When you come up out of the waters you shall put your foot upon a new earth, the promised land flowing with milk and honey, paradise of the new creation.

It is Jesus who will baptize you with the Holy Spirit, so that you will be born in him. This baptism is an entering into the depths of God, a pouring and entering of God himself into you as his vessel and body and temple, to dwell in you and fill you. It is for this reason that Jesus has chosen to come to you through *waters*.

II

The true light, which enlightens everyone,
was coming into the world.

Although he was already the light enlightening every person within the inner darkness of their heart, he has come anew as one person visible within the world, come among us in the one man Jesus Christ. Coming, he was baptized into the world, baptized into our flesh and blood. Now he comes to dwell within you in his fullness and to illumine you from within.

He was in the world,
and the world came into being through him;
yet the world did not know him.

Although this light which enlightens everyone was already in the world, already in everyone, it was not recognized, not released and shining, until Jesus appeared among us to offer himself to us. The world did not know the one from whom it came; the child did not know the one who gave it birth in his image.

Born of man and woman, you did not know your true source, nor did the creation itself know him. To be re-created you must accept him in faith and enter into the waters of rebirth, which recall the waters of the first day of creation. Created without knowledge, you must be created anew through the knowledge which is in Jesus Christ, through the light of faith and the sunburst of baptism.

He came to what was his own,
and his own people did not accept him.

It was to his own people that the Word of God had been given. They did not accept the Word of God when he came among them as a man, as one like them. You, who came not from among these people but from the darkness outside, have believed in him, and are to be born into him. As you become truly his own, remember those who

were his own and yet did not accept him when he came to them.
Remain faithful.

You are about to step out of the darkness of the world and into
the light of Christ.

III

[Those who are to be baptized turn to the east]

But to all who received him,
who believed in his name,
he gave power to become children of God,

[Here each catechumen descends into the baptismal font at its western end and is baptized in the name of the Father and of the Son and
of the Holy Spirit. The newly baptized ascends from the font toward
the east.]

You have passed through the sea, as the Israelites behind Moses.
You have seen the light which shone new on the first day of creation.
But this light which is within you now, and in which you are a new
creation, is Jesus Christ himself in his glory. You have heard within
the waters his word, "*I Am*," and now, in the beginning which is God,
you have come to be.

who were born, not of blood
or of the will of the flesh
or of the will of man, but of God.

Born out of the world and its concupiscences, you have received
upon your forehead his sign (the cross); you have been sealed with
the oil of his Spirit. Put on his robe of light and keep it unspotted by
walking in the way of his cross, as you have been taught.

IV

And the Word became flesh and lived among us,

You are now the temple and dwelling of God, the body of Christ. As
the Word became flesh when Jesus was born of Mary, so now the
Word becomes flesh in you. You have become one of us, and soon

you will join your brothers and sisters at the table of the flesh and blood of the Lord. The meaning of this food and drink has been explained to you, and you will be further instructed in this as you hear the words of the beloved disciple during the coming weeks.

> and we have seen his glory,
> the glory as of a father's only son,
> full of grace and truth.

The glory of the only Son of God was revealed first at Jesus' baptism, and then in all the signs which he performed. This glory is now revealed in you. Open your eyes to the dear light which dawns within you at this moment. Beloved of the Father, you are robed in his light, and radiant with his beauty. Shortly you will be brought to his table to feast upon the food and drink he has prepared for you. He has given you everything that is his: his Son in whom you live, and the glory of this only Son. The bride is yours, shining at your side.

You have come to the wedding banquet, and grace and truth are wed within you; now you are filled with the wine, and your face shines with its gladness. Heaven and earth, Word and Spirit are wed in you; the light and the joy of God are now yours. May the joy and the light of this moment remain in your heart forever, guiding you in his way every day of your life.

V

> John testified to him and cried out,
> "This was he of whom I said,
> 'He who comes after me ranks ahead of me
> because he was before me.'"

We, who have been witness of Jesus to you, and teacher of his way to you until now, and we by whom you have been baptized, are John.[2] You have descended into the Jordan with Jesus and ascended in him. Now you have received the anointing from him and from now on it abides in you and is your teacher. He, the Word who *was* with God in the beginning, teaches you from within you, he who has come to you in the water and in the oil. We witness to him whom you have received, that he is the true light, Jesus Christ the Son of God. We shall diminish and recede as you learn to know him, and the light grows brighter and brighter within you.

From his fullness we have all received, grace upon grace.

We have instructed you at length about the fullness that is in him. As you have been baptized with him and in him you have received this fullness, now it dwells in you, grace for grace. The true light has dawned, the old is passing away. Behold all things are new. As you become one with us in this fellowship, sharing this fullness, we too come to fulfillment, our joy becomes full.

The law indeed was given through Moses;
grace and truth came through Jesus Christ.

In your weeks of instruction you have heard at length of the Passover, the *Torah*, the circumcision given to the people of God through Moses in former times. These things have now come to an end. When you were baptized into Jesus Christ, every wall was broken down, every mediation was annulled, every law disappeared into the light of the Word which is in you. Your truth and your law are the Son of God, whose bride is the Spirit of grace. The grace which you have received is unbounded; you are freed. The truth now within you is immediate and unshadowed, your very self. When you pierced the waters by descending into them, the heavens were opened and you entered into God. As the heart of Jesus was pierced on the cross so that the divine life might flow forth to us, your heart has now been pierced that the life of God might enter into you. From this moment your law is the law of grace. Your life must be love.

No one has ever seen God.
It is God the only Son,
who is (in the Father's bosom),
who has made him known / *who has opened the way*.[3]

When you entered with faith into the waters, you entered into the bosom of the Son and so into the bosom of God, your Father. You have had no need to see God with your eyes; you have seen him in his Son. And now you see him not before you but within you, not face to face but by dwelling in him as he dwells in you. He is your light, and your light is your very vision, the source of your true world. He is that by which you see whatever you may see, and he is that which, ultimately, you inwardly see.

Born anew in the womb of God, you realize within yourself the meaning of the words which he spoke to you at the supper, "The

hour is coming when I will no longer speak to you in words, but will
tell you plainly of the Father."

Now come, friend, and join us at the table of the Lord. Yours are
his bread and wine, his flesh and blood, yours are the fullness of the
Word and the Spirit. Everything that is in your Father's house is yours.

⊕

The prologue, like the gospel narrative, is constructed in cross-form
around its center, which represents the baptismal new birth. This
reflects the sign of the cross with which the baptized were anointed
when they had ascended from the waters of the font. In early Christianity baptism and the cross of Jesus are often found together.[4]

⊕

The center of the prologue mandala is a *crossing,* a boundary of transition or transformation which corresponds to the baptismal event
itself. Moving along the horizontal axis, the believer becomes separated from the *"world"* and its darkness through baptism, and joins the
company of disciples—the *"we"* who have seen the Lord's glory and
among whom he dwells. Along the vertical axis, the baptismal transition through the center is from the first creation to the new, immanent
creation which is expressed in the language of fullness, grace and
truth, and to the immanent knowledge of the Father.

⊕

"The true light, which *enlightens* everyone, was coming into the
world" (1:9). John uses here the verb *phōtizein.* This word, and other
derivatives of *phōs* (light), will, in the fathers of the second century,
become technical terms for baptism.[5]

⊕

Here in the prologue John creates a powerful alignment of centers,
parallel to that which we have seen in our interpretation of the central
sea-crossing. The prologue as a whole is not only structurally parallel
to the gospel narrative, but—totally related to the baptismal event—
corresponds to the center of the narrative mandalic figure: the sea-crossing

and Jesus' appearance upon the waters as light in the midst of the darkness.

Along the axis of the central movement of the Prologue are aligned these pivotal moments:

I.   The birth of the Word from God (implicit): 1:1-2.

II. The creation of all things: 1:3.

III. The incarnation of the Word both in Jesus and in the disciples: 1:14.

IV. The baptism of Jesus: 1:6-9.14.

V.   The baptismal birth and illumination of the disciple: 1:12-13.14.

Along this same continuum are also indicated:

- The indwelling of the Word/light in the created world from the time of creation: 1:4-5.

- The coming of the Word into the world in Jesus: 1:9-11.

- The experience of the *plērōma* dwelling in the disciples through baptism: 1:16.

- The reciprocal indwelling: the disciples admitted into the bosom of the Father, knowing him in Jesus through unitive knowledge rather than sight: 1:18.

The prologue's overall chiastic structure expresses with elegance this great theological progression: that which is revealed and witnessed to *in Jesus* in the prologue's first half is witnessed to *in the disciples* in the second half. The pivot around which this movement turns is the baptismal new birth of 1:12.

Chapter Three

Gospel, Baptism and Easter Liturgy

The relation between John's gospel and Christian initiation is not, as we have seen, limited to the prologue. In the next chapter we shall bring together the many connections between baptism and the Johannine *narrative*. We have already discovered a number of these baptismal allusions on our journey through the Johannine seven days.

At this point it is necessary to broaden our inquiry to include the *other gospels* as well. We shall focus upon *Mark*, since it is Mark's gospel in which the most extensive affinities to Christian initiation have been found.

Most scholars believe that John is independent of the synoptic gospels, and therefore that relationships between the Johannine text and the texts of Matthew, Mark and Luke are not of great significance for the interpretation of the fourth gospel. One notable exception is C.K. Barrett, who finds strong parallels between the gospel of Mark and that of John.[1] An example (Barrett, pp. 43; 271; 279) is the narrative of Jesus' feeding of the multitude (Mk 6:34-44; Jn 6:1-13) and walking upon the lake (Mk 6:47-52; Jn 6:16-21)—a sequence important for its central position in John as well as for our present sacramental inquiry. The order of events is the same in the narratives of Mark and of John, and a number of the Johannine features are of theological significance.

Parallel Chiastic Structures in Mark and in John

Beyond the parallels between particular episodes and sequences of episodes in the two gospels, there are larger structural parallels. The overall structure of Mark, as well as that of John, has been found to be *chiastic*. A number of authors now agree that Mark's chiastic structure —like the overall Johannine structure discovered by Gerhard and Ellis—consists of *five parts*.[2]

According to Van Iersel,[3] the five sections of the Marcan chiasm (joined by short "hinge" passages) are related to distinct *locations* in Mark's narrative.

A1   In the desert (1:2-13)

B1   In Galilee (1:16–8:21)

C   On the way (8:27–10:45)

B2   In Jerusalem (11:1–15:39)

A2   At the tomb (15:42–16:8)

Some parallels are evident between this topographical scheme and the series of locales or territories which are either specified or connoted in the five parts of John's chiasm. We have found the two "wings," or horizontal arms, of the Johannine figure to be characterized respectively as *Gentile* and *Judean* contexts. These correspond to the Galilee–Jerusalem pair which occupy similar positions in the Marcan chiasm.

John's narrative begins, as does Mark's, in the wilderness with the Baptist, and it soon recalls the *baptism* of Jesus (1:26.32-34; cf. Mk 1:9-11). It concludes, however, not with the women at the tomb, but (setting aside, as usual, John's chapter 21 as extra-chiastic) in the closed house with the disciples. It is here that John's *symbolic* chiasm is closed, as the disciples are *baptized* "with the Holy Spirit" as John the Baptist had foretold (Jn 1:33). Their "baptism" recalls the creation of Adam (Gen 2:7). Thomas, then, sees the garden of paradise opened once again. John's chiastic journey from the desert is not finally to the tomb but to the closed houses of the Israelites on the night of the *Passover* supper, and thence to the *garden* of new creation. As we have seen, this very same two-stage symbolic progression, continually employed by John, is the theological key which discloses the meaning of the central sea-crossing scene.

According to Standaert, the core of Mark's concentric structure is the section 8:27–9:13. This section, in turn, is constructed as a five-part chiasm, centered in Jesus' solemn announcement, to whoever would follow him, of the way of the cross:

> And he called to him the multitude with his disciples, and said to them, "If any man would come after me, let him deny himself and take up his cross and follow me. For whoever would save his life will lose it; and whoever loses his life for my sake and the gospel's will save it. For what does it profit a man, to gain the whole world and forfeit his life? For what can a man give in return for his life? For whoever is ashamed of me and of my words in this adulterous and sinful generation, of him will the Son of Man also be ashamed, when he comes in the glory of his Father with the holy angels." And he said to them, "Truly, I say to you, there are some standing here who will not taste death before they see the kingdom of God come with power" (Mk 8:34–9:1. *RSV*).

These central words of Jesus are preceded by his questioning of his disciples, "Who do you say that I am?" and Peter's confession, "You are the Messiah," and then by Jesus' prediction of his passion and death, and his reproof of Peter (8:27-33). The central speech is followed immediately by the divine confirmation of Jesus' identity in his transfiguration, and a further prediction of his passion. The whole text begins (8:27-28) and ends (9:11-13) with the mention of Elijah and John the Baptist.

Jesus' exposition of the way of the *cross*, here at the center of the entire gospel of Mark, corresponds to the *sea-crossing* narrative at the center of John's narrative. The paschal sea-crossing, we should recall, corresponds to Jesus' death and resurrection. John has centered his cruciform figure of the whole gospel in the sea-crossing.

Another author,[4] similarly finding in Mark a chiastic structure consisting of a prologue, three parts and an epilogue, determines the exact center of this structure to be the words heard from the cloud, "This is my beloved Son; listen to him." For Standaert, the center is not at this moment of glory but in the text on the Way, which is a kind of pivot point between cross and glory (compare Mk 8:34 with 9:1).

Gospel and Baptism

Standaert, besides proposing a thorough five-part chiastic structure in Mark, also argued that Mark's gospel was written specifically *in relation with Christian initiation*.[5] He finds in Mark strong and recurrent *baptismal* resonances, and also echoes of the Christian eucharist.

Mark is an *initiation* book—written to initiate those soon to be baptized into the followership of Jesus. Prologue and epilogue frame the central portion which contains the main teaching of the book, which has to do with following Jesus on the Way of the Cross.[6]

Mark's prologue and epilogue[7] particularly favor the baptismal hypothesis. The prologue (1:1-13) begins with John the Baptist in the wilderness, continues with his baptism of Jesus and concludes with Jesus' temptation by Satan in the wilderness, which probably reflects the baptismal renunciation of Satan.[8] In the epilogue (16:1-8), the women went to the tomb at dawn, and found within the opened tomb, where Jesus' body was expected to be, "a young man ...dressed in a white robe" (16:5). When Jesus was arrested, a "young man" who was following him, and clad only in a linen robe, fled naked, leaving behind the linen robe (14:52). The early rite of baptism by immersion involved disrobing and then, after emerging from the font, putting on a white garment. These two passages, heard before and after the account of Jesus' death, symbolically recall baptism, understood as a dying and rising with Jesus.[9]

Do you not know that all of who have been baptized into Christ Jesus were baptized into his death? Therefore we have been buried with him by baptism into death, so that, just as Christ was raised from the dead by the glory of the Father, so we too might walk in newness of life... (Rom 6:3-4).

Near the beginning of Mark's gospel, we heard the Baptist's words, "...he will baptize you with the Holy Spirit" (1:8; these words are not fulfilled within Mark's narrative). The scene at the tomb, then, stands as a parallel baptismal reminder at the gospel's end, which may have been soon followed by the actual rite of initiation. At Jesus' transfiguration, the words from the cloud, "This is my Son, the Beloved; listen to him!" (9:7), recall with striking exactitude the words from heaven at Jesus' *baptism*: "You are my Son, the Beloved; with you I am well pleased" (1:11). As Jesus was approaching Jerusalem for the last time, he confided to his disciples that he was to be put to death. Shortly after, we hear him saying to the sons of Zebedee, "The cup that I drink you will drink; and with the baptism with which I am baptized, you will be baptized..." (10:39).

While the baptismal allusions in Mark's gospel are numerous, then, we find them particularly concentrated at the beginning and the end of the narrative. With Standaert, we may interpret the chiastically central passage on the way of the cross (8:34–9:1; see above) as a baptismal instruction. A strong parallel is evident with John's narrative, in which we have found strong baptismal indications at the same three points: beginning, chiastic center and end.

It is striking that the central (and sacramentally dense) sixth chapter of John is so closely related to Mark's account of the feeding of the multitude and the crossing of the sea,[10] although this section is not central in Mark. Standaert points out this linking of symbolic allusions to baptism and eucharist, the sacraments of initiation, as a recurrent motif in Mark.[11] As we shall see (below, ch. 6), the same sequence of sacramental allusions recurs frequently in John.

It seems possible that John, in composing his own *gospel* (a form which may itself have been originated by Mark), has taken from Mark not only his basic chiastic structure, with its geographical associations, but also its systematic reference to Christian initiation. John would have further developed both the chiastic structure and the symbolic implications of the narrative episodes (e.g. Jesus' sign of the bread and the sea-crossing), integrating them into an expression of his unitive vision.

Gospel and Paschal Vigil

David Daube proposed in 1958[12] that the earliest forms of Christian gospel derive from the *Jewish Passover Haggadah*: that is, the recitations at the Passover meal which recalled the history of Israel and particularly the exodus events. A few years later John Bowman based upon this same supposition his commentary on Mark's gospel: *The Gospel of Mark: The New Christian Jewish Passover Haggadah.*[13]

It was Benedict Standaert who brought together this Passover context for Mark's gospel with the two other elements we have already considered in this chapter: an overall chiastic structure and an orientation toward Christian initiation. According to Standaert and those who have adopted his view, Mark is a *Christian Passover Haggadah,*[14] composed to be read through during the Easter vigil, and followed by the baptism of the neophytes at sunrise. The Christian community, with those to be baptized in its midst, would have spent the night before the feast of the resurrection in vigil and prayer. The narrative of Mark, which was evidently composed to be read through continuously at one time,[15] would have been read to them as a recitation of the history of Jesus' life—which at the same time gathered together the threads of the biblical history of Israel. The narrative would thus have oriented the community and its catechumens toward the celebration of the sacraments of initiation which, as day broke forth, actualized anew the resurrection of Jesus.

This is a revolutionary interpretation of Mark's gospel, and of great significance for the interpretation of the other gospels as well. It is based upon extensive earlier research upon the early Christian liturgy and the Jewish Passover celebration.[16] We cannot present here much of the evidence and reasoning which underlie this conclusion of Standaert's study,[17] but will discuss one striking expression of this Jewish liturgical tradition which offers to shed light upon the origins of John's gospel as well.

It was on the Passover night that the messianic expectation of the Jewish people burned most brightly as they reviewed their ancestral history.

> The intervention of God at the end of time was imagined as a *New Exodus*, under a new Moses: "The final liberator will be like the first"; or, further, as a restoration of the *life of Paradise*, with the coming of a new *Adam*, who would be without sin and would overcome the powers of evil and of death.[18]

We have encountered something strikingly parallel in our study of John, and particularly of the central sea-crossing episode of John. The symbolic movement is double: first the reference to Moses and the exodus, and then to Adam and the creation narratives of Genesis 1–2.

Exodus 12:42 recalled the first Passover night at the time of exodus, and prescribed that the night be observed for all time:

> That was for the Lord a night of vigil, to bring them out of the land of Egypt. That same night is a vigil to be kept for the Lord by all the Israelites throughout their generations.

In a targum (Aramaic translation and commentary) on this verse there is found a poem which expresses with singular density and beauty the spirit of the Jewish Passover liturgy, with its mixture of historical memory and eschatological expectation. This is the "Hymn of the Four Nights" which has been studied extensively by Roger Le Déaut.[19]

The first night was that upon which Yahweh revealed himself over the world to create it. The earth was waste and empty, and darkness was spread over the face of the abyss. And the Word (*Memra*) of the Lord was the light and it shone. He called it the First Night.

The second night was when Yahweh appeared to Abraham, a hundred years old, and to Sarah his wife, who was ninety years old, to fulfill that which the Scripture says: Will Abraham, at the age of a hundred, beget, and Sarah, at the age of ninety, give birth? Isaac was thirty-seven years old when he was offered upon the altar. The heavens came down and abased themselves; Isaac saw their perfections and his eyes were darkened because of their perfections. He called it the Second Night.

The third night was when Yahweh appeared to the Egyptians in the middle of the night: his hand slew the firstborn of the Egyptians and his right arm protected the firstborn of Israel, so that there might be fulfilled what the Scripture says: My firstborn son is Israel. He called it the Third Night.

The fourth night will be when the world will fulfill its purpose and be dissolved (or be delivered). The iron yokes will be broken, the perverse generations will be destroyed; Moses will come up from the midst of the desert and the Messiah-King will come from above. One of them will walk at the head of the flock (or on the summit of the cloud) and the other will walk at the head of the flock (or on the summit of the cloud). His Word will walk between the two, and they will go forward together. This is the night of the Passover for the name of the Eternal, the night reserved and fixed for the redemption of all the generations of Israel.[20]

Standaert comments on this Passover *haggadah*:

This passage unites in one single "remembrance" the night of the exodus, the first night of the creation, the night of the covenant with Abraham (associated with that of the sacrifice of Isaac), and the night of the messianic coming at the end of time. As we have already shown above, it is characteristic of the liturgical feast to bring together in one great present the time of origins, the time of history, and the time of the end. This system of time constitutes ... one of the most striking points of convergence between the Gospel of Mark and the *Poem*.[21]

Is John's Gospel a Christian Passover *Haggadah*?

This poem has become the centerpiece of Standaert's argument that the gospel of Mark was written as a Christian *haggadah*—a meditative homily on the events of salvation history—for a Passover liturgy which had now become the Easter vigil. He finds strong affinities between the poem and Mark's narrative—and particularly between the fourth night of the poem and the transfiguration narrative which is near the center of Mark's chiastic gospel.[22] While it would be a mistake to place too much weight on this one Jewish text—given, especially, the difficulty in fixing the date and context of its origin[23]—we can confidently take it as an expression of the kind of *haggadic* interpretation of the Passover commemoration which was current in the first or second century. Understood in this way, the poem brings confirmation and a further deepening to our interpretation of John's gospel, and particularly of the central sea-crossing narrative.

If the parallels between the Hymn of the Four Nights and Mark's gospel—especially the transfiguration narrative—are impressive, its parallels with John's gospel—and particularly with the sea-crossing scene which is its center—are even more striking! First of all, the Hymn presents itself at once as a quaternity and as a unity. The four nights are commemorated in the one night of the Passover celebration. We perceive a parallel to the quaternary geometry of the Johannine mandala, as well as to the extreme theological concentration, the centering dynamic, of John.

The sea-crossing of John 6:16-21 takes place *near the Passover* (6:4) and *at night*! We have already seen, in that brief narrative, the symbolic resonances both of the *exodus* crossing of the Red Sea and of the beginning of the first *creation* account in Genesis 1, the creation of light.[24] What we have supposed within the appearance of Jesus upon the dark waters, the Hymn makes explicit: *"And the Word of the Lord was the light and it shone. He called it the First Night."* In John, this is the "first day" of the new creation. The baptismal *illumination* finds in Genesis 1:3 its first biblical anticipation.[25] But this light is the *immanent* light of the Word, received in the waters of baptism (see 2 Cor 3:16-18; 4:6).

The Hymn's *Second Night* advances the notion of *creation* to that of *birth*: the birth of Abraham's son Isaac. It is apparently the impossibility attendant upon the great *age* of Abraham and Sarah which constitutes the night from which the child is to be born. But within this same second night is included also the *sacrifice of Isaac*, with its own wall of hopelessness, of darkness. Since we have not yet pursued in our study of John's gospel the Isaac symbolism which was so central for the rabbinic tradition,[26] we shall need to spend some time with this "second night."

The "binding," or sacrifice, of Isaac was related, in this tradition, directly to the Passover celebration: Passover became a celebration of the deliverance of Isaac from death as well as of the liberation of Israel from captivity in Egypt. The virtual sacrifice of Isaac was even seen as the source of the expiatory value of the death of the Passover lamb.[27] "When I see the blood of the Paschal lamb, I see the blood of *Aqeda* (the sacrifice, or "binding," of Isaac) also."[28]

It is likely that the great tissue of midrashic interpretation which surrounded the Isaac stories was present in the tradition out of which John's gospel grew. The reflections in John's gospel of the Isaac narratives of Genesis are subtle and scattered, but taken together they suggest that, for John, Isaac is an important type of Jesus. To be persuaded of the likelihood of this, it is sufficient to reflect on the centrality of the relationship between *Father and Son* in John's gospel. It is the *Johannine* Jesus who is continually referring to his Father and to his relationship with the Father. The archetypal father-son relationship in the Hebrew scriptures is that between *Abraham and Isaac*!

When the Baptist points out Jesus as the *Lamb of God* who takes away the sin of the world (1:29), the reference is not only to the servant of Yahweh of Isaiah 53, and to the Passover lamb, but to *Isaac*.[29] When John carefully informs us that Jesus went to Golgotha "carrying the cross by himself" (19:17), this recalls Isaac carrying the wood for the burnt offering to the place of sacrifice (Gen 22:6).

When God commands Abraham to take his son Isaac to a remote mountain and immolate him there, his words convey a particular tenderness: "Take your son, your only son Isaac, whom you love (or 'the *beloved*')..." (22:2). In the Septuagint Greek translation, the words "*beloved son*" are identical with the words of the voice which is heard at Jesus' baptism in the synoptic gospels: "You are my beloved Son" (Mk 1:11)! This connection of the sacrifice of Isaac with the baptism of Jesus is further strengthened by a passage in the *Testaments of the Twelve Patriarchs*, a Jewish apocryphal writing which probably originated shortly before the time of Christ. The prophecy, concerning the future of the levitical priesthood, is attributed to the patriarch Levi, and speaks of a priest-Messiah to come.

And then the Lord will raise up a new priest
to whom all the words of the Lord will be revealed....

The heavens will be opened,
and from the temple of glory sanctification will come upon him,
with a fatherly voice, as from Abraham to Isaac.
And the glory of the Most High shall burst forth upon him.
And the spirit of understanding and sanctification
shall rest upon him [in the water].[30]

And in his priesthood the nations shall be multiplied in
    knowledge on the earth,
and they shall be illumined by the grace of the Lord....

And he shall open the gates of paradise;
he shall remove the sword that has threatened since Adam,
and he will grant to the saints to eat of the tree of life.
The spirit of holiness shall be upon them.[31]

The New Testament passages in which one would immediately recognize an affinity to this text are the synoptic accounts of *Jesus' baptism*, to which the *Testaments* bring as background this history of Abraham and Isaac. The synoptic tradition of Jesus' baptism seems to be presupposed in John 1, and the baptism is reflected in John 1 by the "Lamb of God" designation for Jesus (see Gen 22:7-8).

It is more surprising to find, in the final verses quoted above, an anticipation of our interpretation of Jesus' two appearances of the disciples in the house, in John 20. The gift of the Holy Spirit has been recounted by John in his narrative of the first appearance of the risen Jesus to his gathered disciples in 20:19-23. We have seen in the second appearance (20:24-29) precisely the removal of the sword, the opening of the gates of paradise, and the offering of the tree of life to Thomas. The two chiastic *baptismal* passages, then—in John 1 and John 20—appear to be related to this extra-biblical Jewish text. In the first of them, Jesus would be identified with Isaac, the "beloved son."

Other texts in the fourth gospel appear to identify Jesus with Isaac in the context of his paschal death (see also 19:17 in relation to Gen 22:6).

For God so loved the world that he gave his only Son...
(3:16).

For this reason the Father loves me, because I lay down my life in order to take it up again (10:17; cf. Gen 22:16-18).

Not only Jesus but *Lazarus* appears to be identified with Isaac in John's gospel. Jesus' final words in the episode of his raising of Lazarus are too strongly reminiscent of the story of Isaac's near-sacrifice to be accidental: *"Unbind him,* and let him go." Lazarus, then, is not only *Adam,* but *Isaac*—rescued from the mouth of death when God provides another "lamb" for the sacrifice (see Gen 22:13).

It is in the eighth chapter of John, apparently still at the feast of Booths, that Jesus' self-identification with Isaac is most fully developed. Here he continually speaks of himself *in relation to the Father.* He speaks of the freedom of the children of Abraham, in contrast to slavery, much as Paul when speaking of Isaac (Gal 4:21–5:1). Several times Jesus uses the *I am* expression.

Finally, at the end of this long dispute with the Jews, Jesus identifies himself with Isaac and nearly in the same breath speaks from the timeless place of the Word:

> Your ancestor Abraham rejoiced that he would see my day;
> he saw it, and was glad . . . before Abraham was, *I am* (8:56.58).

This luminous word is Jesus' self-identification upon the waters in the central night of the sea-crossing.

It is worthwhile to notice the parallel between the symbolic fusion of the promised *birth* of Isaac with his sacrificial *death* in the Hymn, and the fusion of the death and resurrection of Jesus with the new birth of baptism in John (see for example 3:5 together with 16:20-25). The birth and death of the *Son* are drawn together by the gravitational force of the Passover night, and then by that of the Easter vigil. It is in the baptismal moment at the heart of the Christian paschal liturgy that this new birth of the Son is participated by those who have believed in him.

While no direct correspondences have emerged between the Second Night of the Jewish paschal Hymn and the Johannine paschal sea-crossing, there is a general congruence, centering around the figure of *Isaac.* Isaac is the beloved son who becomes the sacrificial lamb of God, undergoing a kind of ritual baptism upon the altar. In his baptism and in the sacrifice of the cross, Jesus, the Son, is most evidently Isaac. The Johannine sea-crossing is the central text of the gospel in which both the death and resurrection of Jesus (his *Passover* or paschal journey) and Christian baptism are signified. In the *birth* of the newly baptized, the one *beloved child* who has been offered in sacrifice—Isaac and Jesus—returns to live anew in this world. ". . . to all who received him, who believed in his name, he gave power to become children of God" (1:12). Lazarus, returned from the dead, also reflects this "return of Isaac" through Jesus' death (see p. 159 above).

On the Hymn's *Third Night*, the same *Passover-exodus* event which is reflected in the Johannine sea-crossing is recalled—not directly in terms of the crossing of the Red Sea, but rather in terms of the *firstborn son*. The crossing of the sea has been absorbed into this symbolic complex of the son. The firstborn of Pharaoh was slain, the firstborn of Israel were spared, and finally Israel is designated the firstborn son of God. The consistency with the creation-birth axis of the first two nights continues, as the *birth of Israel* in the exodus is recalled. This insistence on *birth*, the birth of an only son or firstborn son, continues the focus of the second night (on Isaac), but now the one firstborn has become a people. In the Johannine paschal sea-crossing—a passage through the waters of baptism—the new Israel is born (see once again 1:12).

The *Fourth Night* of the Hymn makes present on the Passover night the "end of the world," with the eschatological coming of the Messianic King. The ascent of Moses and the descent of the Anointed remind us of the two narratives of the Johannine seventh day, which stand at the base and at the summit of the mandala's vertical axis. Corresponding to the Baptist at the bottom is Jesus anointing his disciples with the Spirit at the top. Standaert[32] points out that the *transfiguration* of Jesus, close to the center of Mark's gospel, responds to this expectation of the "fourth night" of the Jewish paschal vigil, with its scene of the three figures upon the cloud. It is the conclusion of this part, reflecting the appearance of the Word on the first night, which brings us back to the center of *John's* gospel.

> His Word will walk between the two, and they will go forward together. This is the night of the Passover for the name of the Eternal, the night kept and fixed for the redemption of all the generations of Israel. ("Hymn of the Four Nights"; conclusion of the Fourth Night)

We seem to see once again here the night-procession of Israel through the Red Sea at the time of exodus, but now led by the *Word* of God (present again here at the *end* as it was in the *beginning* of the First Night). The "name of the Eternal," in the light of the prologue and John's use of the divine *I Am* and of the divine *"name"* (see above, p. 66), recalls once again the *I Am* of John 6:20.

This timeless *I Am* powerfully expresses the *realized eschatology* of the fourth gospel.[33] John is concerned with *what is to come* only as the manifestation of that which already *is*. During the earthly life of Jesus, it is in his person, coming and going among his disciples, that this present eschatology is concentrated. After his resurrection and departure, this reality is present in a new way: within the disciple and within the community of disciples. The symbolic expressions of this new presence are *baptism and eucharist*. The *I Am* is present, as at the beginning, upon the *waters*.

The "baptismal eschatology" is, as we have seen, a *new creation*.[34] That which was at the beginning returns at the end, but in this new state of divine immanence which has come in the water of baptism. The four phases of the Hymn find a certain parallel in John. Beginning with the first night of *creation*, the Hymn continues through two intermediate *historical* stages of the passage of Isaac and that of the people of Israel, and concludes with the *end* of history. In John's vision, the movement is from first creation (through the Word) to new creation (*in* the Word), through two intermediate historical stages: the first is either Jesus himself or Israel, the second is either the new Israel (the church) or all humankind, "the world." A parallel with the Pauline mandalic scheme—with its horizontal axis running from Israel to the Gentiles—is also apparent.

Beyond the specific parallels between the paschal Hymn and John's paschal sea-crossing narrative, there is a more general correspondence in the axis of *liturgical time* that runs through both texts, bringing together in one moment historical events which—whether in symbolic myth or in reality—are widely separated in time.[35]

Whatever be the historical problems surrounding these targumic texts, the inherent conservatism of Jewish liturgical tradition makes it possible to affirm the existence of this kind of ritual and literary reflection on the Passover night at the time of the writing of John's gospel. It seems very likely, then, that the center of John's chiastic composition, with its paschal and baptismal symbolism, grew out of this *haggadic* tradition.

This tradition, expressed in the Hymn of the Four Nights, brings into direct contact with John's gospel—and precisely at its central point, the sea-crossing narrative—the *center of Jewish liturgical life*, the *Passover* commemoration, which in turn relates the Johannine text to the *Christian Easter vigil* and its baptismal climax. The parallels and more general correspondences between the two texts strongly suggest, as for Mark, that this was the original context of John's gospel.

Our inquiry leaves us with the image of a Night which is one and yet many, historical and beyond time; singular and perennially recurrent: which is the source, matrix, "mother" of all that is, font both of creation and new creation. "In the beginning was the Word..." It is this Night from which light is born, this emptiness from which the fullness comes forth, which John has placed at the center of his gospel.

There is a further piece of evidence suggesting that John's gospel itself may have been composed as a Christian Passover haggadah, a symbolic narrative to be read during the Easter vigil, in preparation for Christian initiation. In some Christian communities of Egypt, the four gospels were read completely during the nocturnal services of Holy Week, with the *gospel of John being read in its entirety during the Easter Vigil*.[36] John's pervasive symbolic allusions to baptism, then, may have originally served a function similar to that of the baptismal allusions of the Marcan narrative: to link the gospel's presentation of the way of the disciple to the sacramental event in which the catechumens would come to new birth as the sun rose on Easter morning.

$$\oplus$$

This proposal for the original matrix and function of John's gospel cannot, obviously, claim to be scientifically rigorous. The relationships which have come to light between John's gospel, Christian baptism, and the paschal vigil liturgy, however, are certainly significant enough to be studied more thoroughly. The *baptismal background* of this gospel, in any event, emerges ever more powerfully.

Our brief survey suggests that the baptismal and paschal elements in John's gospel are *more fully developed than those in Mark*. This seems to be true particularly of the chiastic *center* of the fourth gospel, corresponding to the first day of the new creation. John appears to have transformed his historical material more completely, in the light of Christian baptism and the solemn Night, than has Mark.

John's placing the gift of the Holy Spirit by Jesus to his disciples on the *seventh day* suggests a further interesting possibility. Whether or not John's gospel was written as a paschal *haggadah*, could it have been structured as the basis of a sacramental catechesis which could occupy the seven weeks between the two great feasts of the Christian Passover and of Pentecost? While this can claim to be no more than a conjecture, it will provide us with a framework for a final review of the Johannine narrative from the perspective of Christian initiation, in the next chapter.

As the unitive meaning of John became more and more visible through the gospel's symbolic tapestry in the course of our long journey through the seven days of the new creation, the Unitive nevertheless remained disembodied—an interior spiritual reality still detached from the fabric of ordinary life in the world of space, time and bodily existence. It is the *sacramental* elements in John's gospel—particularly baptism, and implicitly the paschal liturgy—which have closed this gap and brought John's central meaning back into flesh-and-blood human existence, when Jesus is no longer visible among his disciples. The great river of unitive light and life which gathers from all the episodes of John's gospel and flows through the final moments of Jesus' *hour*—supper, passion and resurrection appearances—*pours through the gate of baptism* into world and time.

Chapter Four

John's Narrative as Baptismal Catechesis

As we have read John's prologue anew from the perspective of Christian baptism (in Part III, chapter 2, above), now we shall reread the Johannine narrative in the same way. This time also we shall proceed by means of a literary fiction—in the form of a "patristic" instruction on Christian initiation, intended for the newly baptized. The instruction will be divided into seven parts, corresponding to the seven weeks between Easter and Pentecost. It is assumed that in the course of each of these weeks there are read the sections of the fourth gospel which we have related to the corresponding *day of creation*. The instruction will comment on the narrative sections in the order in which they have been read—therefore in the same order in which we studied them in Part II. The instruction of the first week of Easter, for example, will be based upon the reading of Section 1—the sea-crossing episode of John 6:16-21, which corresponds to the paschal baptismal event itself.

The neophytes have already heard John's gospel, which was read through to them in its narrative order and commented for them during the instruction of the weeks preceding their baptism. The narrative was read through to them once again during the vigil service just preceding their initiation.

Now that the candidates have been baptized, they are conducted through the fourth gospel once again—but in the new, "concentric" order. Their baptismal experience, as will be explained in the instruction, has brought about within them the new divine indwelling and the illumination by which they are enabled now to follow the gospel along the path of its inner meaning. The new creation has been initiated in them through their baptism, and the mandalic structure, centered in the Word, reflects for them both their own person and the entire cosmos, within which this new creation is proceeding. John's gospel now comes into its proper context as the *mystagogy*[1] of the Johannine community, an instruction which leads the newly baptized toward an understanding of the new interior reality which they have received.

Since the neophytes have already been instructed in the Old Testament background of the fourth gospel, with its types and parallels, these relationships will be recalled here only when they illuminate the *correspondence between gospel narrative and baptism* which is the focus of this instruction.

The word *baptism* will not be repeated continually. Wherever the catechist is explaining to the neophytes *their new condition*, and wherever he uses expressions like "you have been..." it can be assumed that he is speaking of their baptism and the new condition consequent upon it.

Since the following is a condensation of the catechesis which would occupy seven weeks, and since it moves continually between the gospel narrative and the sacraments of initiation, the reader will have to bear with a congestion of symbolic interpretations and a certain repetitiveness.

The Paschal Instruction

Now that you have passed through the water and been anointed, and eaten the body and blood of the Lord, you have become one with the gospel. That which Jesus did and suffered has entered into you and is now within you. Within you is that which Jesus was and is. In the light which is now within you, you shall find that the gospel and your life interpret one another. You are anointed and, essentially, no longer need a teacher; the anointing that is within you teaches you everything. The purpose of our words is merely to bring this anointing to consciousness within you, to awaken your heart to the voice of the only Teacher, who is within.

I. First Week: Day I. Reading: Section 1.

Out of the Dark Waters, Light Has Risen Within You

1. When you descended into the waters, you left Egypt behind you and followed the new Moses in his own journey through death to life. Descending into those waters you entered into the night in which the world was created, the darkness of the beginning. The light which filled you is the light of the divine Word himself. For the God who said, "Let light shine out of darkness," has shone in your heart, and you have seen that the light is good. Receiving him within you, you have been filled with gladness. You have heard him pronounce his name within the depths of your being, *I Am*. In that name you have come to be. Now you have come to the land to which your whole journey leads, the new land, the promised land. As you rose from those waters over which the Spirit hovered, the Spirit settled upon you to remain, and you were born a new creature, child of God. You have heard within your heart the Father's voice, saying to you, "You are my beloved child; in you I am well pleased."

From that morning, when the sun of the *Logos* rose within you, the words of the apostolic witness are opened to you. Now you hear the story of the life of Jesus in a new way, because the light that was in him is in you, within your heart. In that light you hear and read his words and his deeds from within. The moment of your baptism in the waters, and the light that filled you then, remain within you as the center of your understanding and of your life. We shall return to this center continually, as we proceed through this week of the new creation. The life of Jesus and his disciples is opened to you, made transparent to you. And your life must become transparent to that same light which is given to you and dwells within your heart. From this light which is within you, the creation of the world begins again.

II. Second Week: Day II. Readings: Sections 2,3.

You Have Eaten the Bread from Heaven

2. Now that you have passed through the sea into light and freedom, you are to be nourished with new food. It is a food which you must learn to eat, the mysterious bread of this new land across the waters.

You shall learn to eat it in the light which awakened within your heart at baptism. Already you have experienced the fullness which belongs to this bread. Wherever there is an urgency for light, for food, the bread swells and multiplies until it fills the space of need. You have known this sufficiency, and you will never hunger again. You yourself will be able to break the bread of Christ's Word to fill the hunger of others.

The boy who has brought the five loaves and two fishes is the Son of Man. His teaching is the new *Torah*—the five loaves—and the two fishes are the mysteries of baptism and eucharist. The Jesus whose life and teachings have been communicated to you in the gospels is these five loaves, and the invisible Word and Spirit are the two fishes.

From this single child who is Isaac—the immolated Lamb, the Son, the only one—has come the bread to feed the whole world, all the people of God. The flowing water of baptism and the broken bread of the eucharist carry the light and life that is in him to the ends of time and the ends of the earth. Now that you have believed and been reborn in him, you know his light and life within you.

He took the bread in his hands as the Creator had taken the earth in his hands in the beginning, to raise one humanity up in Adam with the fire of his breath. Now he has taken in his hands the bread which is himself, to break it for the countless multitude, the whole twelve tribes of humankind. As they eat the bread and fish which are himself, they become again one humanity, one Adam. It is your new birth in the waters which makes this truth live in your hearts and minds. You have been given more than you yourself could eat; you must gather up the fragments and save them, for they belong to all the tribes of Israel, all the nations and races of humankind who are to come.

3. As you have crossed the dark waters with him, you have come to understanding; the mystery of the bread has opened within you. Unlike those who disbelieve, or follow him only for the fulfillment of their earthly needs—who understand his words according to the flesh and not the Spirit—you have seen in Jesus himself the bread of life which has come down from heaven into this world. Jesus is the Wisdom of God come among us in flesh and blood, and this same mystery has entered into you and dwells within you.

He is the *one bread*, the Word of God, the one tree of life. No longer are your eyes veiled when you read the scriptures; now you perceive within them the Christ who has come as light into your own heart. You have been washed and brought inside, brought within the garden of the beginning, where the one tree offers its fruit and where the river of living water flows freely.

You have eaten of the bread of life which is his word, which is himself. As you remained with him and watched him and listened to him, you were nourished, filled. And you knew that he was the Holy One of God, and that there was no one else in heaven or earth to whom you could go. You have renounced Satan and all his empty allurements, and you have joined yourself by vow to the Son of God. You have crossed the waters and come into the garden. Now you have eaten of his flesh and drunk his blood, and been carried far beyond your own light, your own understanding. Understanding not, yet knowing, you remain with him; for in him and in his words is eternal life. You must be faithful to what you have received, faithful to what you have become and are.

III. Third Week: Day III. Readings: Sections 4,5,6,7.

You Have Become the Temple of His Glory

4. John came baptizing with water to prepare the way for that which you have received. He prepared the waters for Jesus to descend into them and place his light and his life in them. The Bridegroom came and entered into the bridal chamber of the waters, and you too have entered there and been joined with him. The Word came into the waters and brought with him the heavenly Bride, the Spirit *Sophia*, the *Shekinah* of the divine glory who dwelt in the holy place. You have received her[2] within you and now she dwells there so that you are the temple of God. Beyond the fulfillment of human marriage, the event of baptism has become the permanent condition of your life.

You have heard the voice of the one who comes from above, the voice of the Bridegroom, and welcomed him into your house. Now he must increase, while you must decrease. You have received the Spirit within you; his testimony speaks in your heart. Eternal life is yours. Let nothing turn your faith and your love from that which you have received.

5. Through the testimony of the beloved disciple John, which has come to you through the church, you have come to him. You rejoiced in the burning and shining lamp that has illuminated you in the one

who has instructed you, in the words of John, in the witness of his gospel. But now that you have come to him and passed through the waters in which his Spirit moves, you have experienced his works— the works of his Father—*within* you. The Father of Jesus Christ, in his one great work, has raised you up in his Son. Now you have not only his Word but his Spirit dwelling within you and testifying to him. The glory of God dwells within you, witnessing to the Son of God. There is no greater witness than this. You have become the lamp of God in the world, and must never allow your light to be dimmed or quenched.

6. The leafy tents of the Jews in the desert, and the annual feast of Booths in Jerusalem, were symbols of that which has taken place in you; crowned with his grace, you begin to flourish in him. Your body has become the dwelling of the Most High, and the body of Jesus is your glorious dwelling. He has come up not visibly but as in secret, has taken up his place within you, and there he teaches. On the sabbath he has made your whole body well, consecrating it to its destined holy function as place of worship, temple of God. The glory which is his dwells there now.

In your thirst you came to him, and now you have drunk of the living water which flows from him. Now that he dwells in you, the rivers of living water flow from within your own heart.

You have continued until now in his Word, and received the Holy Spirit in the waters, and now you are free with the very freedom of the Son of God. The glory which you have received is not that of the sons of Abraham, but of the only Son of God, who dwells hidden within you. Let nothing take this freedom, this glory, from you.

7. As the crowd welcomed Jesus into the holy city with palms in their hands, your soul flourished, a green paradise, when he came into it to make it his dwelling. There at your center he has been lifted up as the noonday sun in the midst of the heavens, the light of the world. There he reigns, drawing all things to himself. Like the prophet in the temple, you have seen his glory—but in the temple of your own body. He has crowned you with his own beauty, and as you grow toward him as a green tree toward the sun, he is living and growing within you.

You have been reborn in him, a child of the light, and must walk in the light as he walked. Like the Lord Jesus, you are that grain of wheat which must fall into the ground, that it may bring forth much fruit. You have become his servant, and now must follow him in the same way of the cross. As you leave behind your life in this world, you step upon the soil of paradise. As you follow him in darkness as in light, his glory, which has blazed within you, will gradually come to fill your whole body and the whole earth.

IV. Fourth Week: Day IV. Readings: Sections 8,9,10,11.

You Are Lights in the World Through Baptism

8. You have put aside the meager light of your own knowledge and recognized the darkness in which you actually walked. Out of that darkness you have come to him, have come into the light. Professing your belief in the name of the only Son of God, you have been born into him—reborn from above, born of water and the Holy Spirit. And so you have entered the kingdom of God, and have seen its glory. Only now can you awaken others and help to bring them into this light, help them to be born anew. Remember that your light and your life itself come from above, not from this earth. You have renounced the wisdom of the serpent who crawls upon this earth, who had deceived your parents at the tree, and have joined yourself solemnly to the wisdom from above, the Son of Man who has been lifted up on the tree before you.

9. The Word of God has come down into the waters and stirred them with the Spirit of life, and you have descended into those waters and come up from them again. Now you have been raised up, and you are able to walk in the way of the Lord. "Stand up, take up your mat and walk," he said to you, and at his words the waters of life flowed once again within you. The energy of God's Spirit has come into your body and your limbs, has come into your spirit and soul, so that now you can rise, take up your life with its burdens, and enter the temple, the kingdom of God. You can walk freely there as a child of God. You have passed from death to life. Your new freedom is a witness to the divine power that is in him. You must never fall back under the power of sin, lest this divine power leave you and death grasp you once again, perhaps forever.

10. You had been blind from your birth and a beggar, when the One who made you walked by and saw you. As he had molded you of earth in the beginning and given you life through his breath, he per-

formed this act of creation once again, making mud of earth and his spittle and placing it upon your eyes. He sent you to wash in the pool of Siloam, the waters sent from God. You went, and you washed, and you saw. When you returned, those who had known you before questioned your healing and your sight, and all you could answer was, "I was blind and now I see." And within you, as for the first time, you knew, "I Am." You have been created anew in the Son of Man. You have believed and been baptized in his name; he is the light in which you see, the life in which you rejoice. Do not be surprised if you are driven from their assembly by those leaders of the people who are blind and yet think that they see. They are envious of the self-revealing light that is within you, and which witnesses to itself so powerfully that they cannot refute it. You, born blind, have become a teacher through simply witnessing to him who is within you. You must never forget that once you were blind and now you see.

11. He bent low to wash your feet. He bathed you in the waters that flow from himself, washed you in his own Spirit, and now you are clean. And he gave you a new commandment to live as he lived, loving one another. He died that he might prepare a place for you in his Father's house, which is his own risen body, and now through the water he has brought you into that place, so that you may dwell there. You do not see him, but you have a better gift: experiencing him and his Father within you, yourself within him and his Father. You do not understand this, but you have a better gift: the union which surpasses understanding as light surpasses the things that you see.

Through his blood and the water of your baptism, you have been grafted into the holy vine. There you must remain, by remaining in love, the love which flows through all the branches. Through sorrow you have come to joy, as you were born in him, and now you remain there in him.

He prayed that you might be consecrated in him, the Word, and then he poured out the waters of consecration from his side to wash you and bring you to birth in him. Now you have received his glory within you, and he is glorified in you. Through your rebirth in the waters you are *one* as he and his Father are one. This is the glory which is given you.

Now you must remain in his truth, in him, in whom you have been sanctified. You do not belong to the world, but he has washed you in the Spirit and sent you into the world. You must keep yourselves from evil, by remaining in him. He has brought you into the place where he dwells, to see his glory. Through his prayer and your new birth, the fullness of God's love is within you and he is within you.

He has seated you beside him at his table and has shared with you his own cup: the wine of divine Wisdom which has raised you out of your senses, out of your old sanity, and opened your mind and heart to the secret of the One. Now everything that he has is yours; all that was in him is within you. You are to be his lights in the darkness of this world, so that the world may believe.

V. Fifth Week: Day V. Readings: Sections 12,13,14,15.

Through Baptism You Died with Him and Live in Him

12. By his death you have been cleansed—not only purified but transformed. You have been destroyed and rebuilt in the waters, and you are now the temple of the Lord, the body of Christ. The Holy Spirit springs up in the middle of this temple as a fountain of living water. The glory of God which dwelt in the temple of Jerusalem dwells in you, but more fully, more intimately, as your very life. Your bodily life itself, from now on, will be the worship of God, your spiritual sacrifice. Washed and brought into the temple of his body, you may now eat of the one sacrifice, the flesh of the Lamb, and drink his blood, and live forever.

13. The royal child, who was at the point of death, has been brought back to life. You have been raised up by the Word of the Master, spoken two thousand years ago in another country. It is through the waters of baptism that the Word and Spirit have traveled through time and distance to bring you back to life. You, child, have died and been brought back to life in the Child, the Son of God. It is the wine of that royal wedding, symbolized at Cana, which now lives within you, and you can no more die. Your royal destiny is fulfilled through the Lord, the Son of God.

14. The Shepherd came to find you, his straying sheep, and followed you even into the grave. He was baptized into death with you so that you might be baptized into life in him. He called you by name, and brought you out of darkness into the freedom of day. Now that you have passed through the living gate that is in the waters, you find

pasture in him. Through baptism you, to whom the word of God had been addressed, have become children of God and "gods" (10:34-35) in the very Word of God who has come to you.

He was bound and led to death for you, so that you might be unbound and set free. It is in the darkness of the waters that you were joined with him, the true Isaac and Lamb of God, so that the life of God might be in you.

It is for the sake of God's glory that you have been brought to life, for the Son of God is glorified in you. This one man has died so that through his death all the people of God, baptized in his name, may live in him.

15. He died, shedding his blood upon a tree, and was buried in a garden, so that through the living waters of baptism you might be created anew in him, the Tree of life. From the tree he gave to you, the disciple whom he loved, his mother: the Wisdom of God. She is mother of all the living, and in taking her to yourself you will find life. She will dwell as a spring of life within your house.

Sealed with the sign of his cross at baptism, you have died with him and risen again with him. The water and blood that flowed from his opened body have given you life in his body. He, the Word of God, became a human person and was baptized into the earth through death, so that you, Adam–earth, might be baptized in the living waters of his Spirit.

VI. Sixth Week (near Ascension): Day VI.
Readings: Sections 16,17,18,19.

Through Baptism the Divine Marriage Feast Is Within You

16. As you were washed externally with the baptismal waters, the wine of the royal wedding sprang forth within you. The good wine, the unitive divine Wisdom, now dwells within you. The marriage is poured out within you and there it copiously flows. The Woman, the Bride, is yours,[3] there within your house, through your immersion in the waters. In her you have a light that never sets and a life that will never be quenched. The light which shone upon you from above and without, the *Logos*-Sun, is now within your very body as fire and wine.

17. Estranged in a far country, with sweat and shame you drew water under the noonday sun, and yet your thirst was never satisfied. Then he came, and you believed and entered the waters in his name. Now you have drunk of his living water, and it has become a spring within you, gushing up to eternal life.

He to whom you were joined was not your husband, but you have renounced him and engaged yourself to the Son of God. Since you descended into the water, and knew within yourself the opening of that deep well, God's gift of grace to you no longer depends magically upon this or that place of worship, this or that ritual or formula of words. Now through Jesus Christ you know the Father, and worship him in spirit and in truth—with the freedom and confidence of his children. The secret of your own being has been revealed and released within you by the one who dwells there. The festive meal which you share is already the fullness, the eucharistic harvest of the time of the Messiah.

18. When he had brought you back from the darkness of death, he placed you beside him at the banquet. Joined with him in death through the dark waters of your baptism, you were now joined with him in life at the wedding banquet. The fragrance of the woman filled the house: baptized into him, you entered into the house of Mary, the place of unitive life. And it was as at the beginning, where the two breathed together the one fragrance of the garden.

Washed in his waters, now you have felt within your own body the sweetness of his anointing, the fragrant oil of his messianic glory and of eternal life. In this Spirit you walk in the world as one newly born from the bondage of darkness into joy and freedom.

19. As the beloved disciple descended into the earth, saw and believed, you descended into the waters and were buried there with the Master. In the waters the light sprang forth: you saw within yourself and fully believed.

⊕

It is as if the waters were also within you, filling you. Now the long time of your grieving is over, and the child has been born. He came to you now not in the familiar way, but as a stranger—as everyone. You are to see him coming to you in everyone you meet. And yet he spoke your name, and you knew him and were born once again. This gardener, the first Man, is ever the stranger, and yet ever whispers to you the most intimate word, the name which is known to nobody else.

You have feasted upon him as upon the tree of life. And yet you may not cling to this delight of his presence, for you are not only in the garden but still in the desert as well, and he is the manna that you must seek each day, your daily bread. You have no need to cling to this experience. Rather, you must find him where he dwells in his brothers and sisters. Go and tell the others the good news: through the waters they are reborn into this garden of the beginning, where his Father is their Father, and they are his brother and sister and mother. Let them look deeply enough into the waters of their grief and they will experience this for themselves: they will find the garden there and he, risen, in its midst.

VII. Seventh Week (near Pentecost): Day VII.
Readings: Sections 20,21.

You Have Entered into God's Rest; You Are His New Creation

20. You have been baptized in the baptism of Jesus in the Jordan, and heard the Father's voice speaking to you: "You are my only-begotten, my beloved child; in you I am well pleased." You have been born of the Father in the waters, received the Holy Spirit, and this voice greets you as you ascend from the waters. As your body was washed in the waters which bathed the body of Jesus, you were physically reborn in him. Your new life in him is a bodily life, and it is to be maintained by eating the fruit of the tree of life which is his word and his eucharistic body. Your bodily birth in him and the nourishment of your continual life in him are inseparable. And so you live by eating the flesh of the paschal Lamb.

You have come and entered the waters, and there you have seen the place where he dwells. Now you are to remain with him there. Under the fig tree you have put off the garments of shame and you have put on Jesus Christ and are robed in his glory. You have come into the light and been baptized into the light; having put on the light, you no longer have any fear. Walk ever in the light, that the power of darkness may never shadow you again.

As you ascended from the waters, born anew in the Son of Man, you have seen the heavens opened and known within yourself the angels of God—Word and Spirit—ascending and descending upon you.

21. You had been baptized into fear and darkness, like the people of Israel closed into their houses on the night of death, the first Passover night. You had been shut in "for the fear of the Jews" when he came and stood in your midst and gave you his peace. He brought you out of the dark house of bondage and fear, out from the shadowy walls of the law, into a place of spaciousness and light. Though you did not see him with your eyes, you believed. Then he breathed the Holy Spirit upon you and you were created anew, and your eyes were opened. It was as if you came from the waters of birth once again, in the simplicity of a newborn child yet in the wisdom and strength of maturity. You feasted upon his presence and his words. With the breath of his Spirit that he breathed into you he gave you the power to forgive sins, and sent you in this Spirit and power to continue his re-creation of the world. This Spirit of God *is* the forgiveness of sins and more: it is the very life of God, in which the world is reborn as one. From the closed house of your fear, you have been sent to carry this new life out into the world. From the paradise of his opened body flow the rivers of life which carry his new creation to the ends of the earth.

With the apostles you have not only been sent out, but *brought in*, as you were baptized into him. Through his opened side, you who were far off and outside have been brought in; through the water and the blood his life is yours. You have entered the garden and he has invited you to stretch forth your hand and eat from the tree of life, take of his body and blood. Eternal life is yours.

Now that his Spirit dwells within you through baptism and you are the temple of God, the sabbath of God surrounds you like a garment throughout the week, wherever you walk in your new freedom. Your going and coming, your eating and drinking must be in him, so that the whole of your life may be worship. For you have been made a new humanity in the Son of God.

VIII. Eighth Week (First Week of the Year)
Reading: Section 22 (chapter 21)

As the waters of new life disappeared into your depths, your life became once again, apparently, an ordinary life. In your own place you had worked all through the night without result when a lone figure called out to you from the distance. You cast as he suggested, and suddenly the nets were filled with fish. It was he! It was like the first time, at the wedding, when he made wine. It was like the time when he broke the bread beside the sea and fed the five thousand. It was like the morning on which you were baptized, and the sun rose within you. Now you must put away the things of childhood, leave behind your own petty concerns—for your Father knows what you need—and labor in his service, for the salvation of humankind. Again and again you will pass through these waters and meet him upon the shore. Again and again you will experience the dawn of his coming and be filled with his bread and fishes. And it will always be as that first time.

The sun has risen once again; the fire burns within your hearts as you walk together along the road, thinking ever of him and all the things he said and did. In the fire and light of that Easter night—his fire and light that are within you through your baptism—all of the scriptures lie open to you now.

As you follow him, yet you remain ever here: here by the water and the fire, the bread and the fish, as the sun rises upon the shore.

Chapter Five

Baptism and the One:
John and Syrian Christianity

There is one current in early Christianity which resonates so deeply with the unitive vision of John's gospel that it seems the continuation and further evolution of that vision. That is the *Syrian* Christianity which has found expression in the Odes of Solomon, and in the writings of Aphrahat, Ephrem and others.[1]

The Odes, together with a few other texts which seem to be nearly contemporary with John's gospel itself, represent the primitive phase of this Syriac Christian tradition, while its fullest development appears in the writings of Ephrem in the fourth century.

To this *semitic* Christianity, the symbolic language of the Bible and of Jesus is still native. The teaching, even as late as Aphrahat and Ephrem, remains unconstrained by the Greek philosophical structures which, with few exceptions, soon came to characterize the theology of both Greek and Latin fathers. These Syrian theologians are free, therefore, to follow the living rhythm of the biblical thought itself. Much of this sapiential writing is in *poetic* form: often in the form of hymns for liturgical use. The doctrine of these writers, still full of the energy and movement of their experience of the Christ-event, expresses itself naturally in musical forms and resists settling into theoretical structures or even into the sobriety of prose discourse. This is theology flowing forth still molten, and its life is often expressed in a shower of sparks: symbolic intuitions glowing with the experience from which they come.

At once startling and alluring is the *unitive* experience which spontaneously found expression in these early Syrian writers. Their favorite symbolic language was that of the paradise story of Genesis: the garden, the tree, the river of life. Adam was seen as the *one* man who contains in himself all of humanity, and Jesus was seen as the person who embodies the very oneness of God, and comes to restore the oneness of humanity and of the universe, as the second Adam.

It is in *baptism* that the believer is plunged into this One, and himself or herself becomes one. So powerful was this sense of *oneness* that, for some communities, baptism implied a commitment to a life of celibacy (see below, p. 369).

These Syriac writings give us a glimpse of a Christian life which is still illumined by the unitive light of the *Logos* and the Spirit. At the same time they offer powerful further witness—and sometimes very explicit witness—to the origin of this unitive Christian vision in the experience of *baptism*. These texts, unlike the canonical gospels focused upon the life of Jesus, are often direct expressions of a personal experience: the new life of the baptized.

⊕

The Odes of Solomon[2] are a series of poems which were apparently written at about the same time as the fourth gospel.[3] Except for fragments previously known, they came to light only at the beginning of the twentieth century, in a Syriac manuscript. It is not certain whether they were originally written in Syriac, however, or in Greek. Their theological vision, in any case, places them in the Syrian tradition.

The Odes are closely related to John's gospel in theological language, symbolism and thought.[4] A large number of parallels between the two texts are evident, even though the difference in languages (the Odes exist primarily in Syriac, while John's gospel is in Greek) tends to suppress the similarities. Such are the affinities between John and the Odes that a leading specialist in these rediscovered poems concludes, "Both reflect the same milieu, probably somewhere in Western Syria, and both were probably composed in the same community."[5]

When scholars discovered the Odes at the beginning of this century, it was as if they had stumbled into the green world of Eden. The poetic exuberance, the profusion of symbolic foliage, of this early Syriac literature witnesses to the invisible *source* which bathes its roots. This is the same spring from which the Gospel of John arose.

> Fill for yourselves water from the living spring of the Lord,
> because it has been opened for you.

And come all you thirsty and take a drink,
and rest beside the spring of the Lord.

Because it is pleasing and sparkling,
and perpetually pleases the soul.

For more refreshing is its water than honey,
and the honeycomb of bees is not to be compared with it;

Because it flowed from the lips of the Lord,
and it (came) from the heart of the Lord.

And it came boundless and invisible,
and until it was set in the middle they knew it not.

Blessed are they who have drunk from it,
and have rested by it (30:1-7).

The scholarly world as a whole has been slow to recognize that the key to the imagery of the Odes is the *baptismal* event.[6] It was J.H. Bernard, one of the first modern commentators on the Odes, who proposed baptism as their origin and central reference. Bernard brought forth a great web of patristic evidence to support his thesis that "They are baptismal hymns intended for use in public worship, either for catechumens or for those who have been recently baptized."[7] While his view had been long dismissed as exaggerated,[8] most scholars now concede that the Odes contain a large number of baptismal references.[9] No comparable key has been found, in the intervening eighty years, to unlock the symbolic language of these poems. The Odes express the inner experience of the person baptized, with a wealth of imagery deriving primarily from the initiation ritual itself.

The language and imagery of the Odes is closely related to that of John's gospel. Two of the most striking common expressions are the *living water* (see Ode 30:1-7 above) and the *Word*.

... The Son of the Most High appeared
in the perfection of his Father.

And light dawned from the Word
that was before time in him (Ode 41:13-14).

...For the subtlety of the Word is inexpressible,
and like his expression so also is his swiftness and acuteness,
for limitless is his path....

...And they were stimulated by the Word,
and knew him who made them,
because they were in harmony.

For the mouth of the Most High spoke to them,
and his exposition was swift through him.

For the dwelling place of the Word is man,
and his truth is love.

Blessed are they who by means of him have recognized
    everything,
and have known the Lord in his truth (Ode 12:5.10-13).

The most luxuriant growth of baptismal imagery is to be found in the eleventh Ode. Much of this symbolism only becomes intelligible when interpreted in the light of other documents—particularly the baptismal rites—from this same early Jewish Christian milieu. Christian baptism was understood as the circumcision of the heart. The mystery of the transformation of sexuality in the Spirit, which we found beneath the symbolism of the fourth gospel, is central to this baptismal poetry.

My heart was pruned and its flower appeared,
then grace sprang up in it,
and it produced fruits for the Lord.

For the Most High circumcised me by his Holy Spirit,
then he uncovered my inward being toward him,
and filled me with his love.

And his circumcising became my salvation,
and I ran in the Way in his peace,
in the Way of truth....

...And speaking waters touched my lips
from the spring of the Lord generously.

And so I drank and became intoxicated,
from the living water that does not die....

...And the Lord renewed me with his garment,
and possessed me by his light....

And from above he gave me immortal rest;
And I became like the land which blossoms and rejoices in its
    fruits.

And the Lord (is) like the sun
upon the face of the land.

My eyes were enlightened,
and my face received the dew;

And my breath was refreshed
by the pleasant fragrance of the Lord.

Through baptism the singer is brought into the garden of the new
creation, which lives and flourishes from these waters.

And he took me to his Paradise,
wherein is the wealth of the Lord's pleasure.

(I contemplated blooming and fruit-bearing trees,
and self-grown was their crown.
Their branches were flourishing
and their fruits were shining (or *laughing*);
their roots (were) from an immortal land.

And a river of gladness was irrigating them,
and the region round about them in the land of eternal life)

...And I said, blessed, O Lord, are they
who are planted in your land,
and who have a place in your Paradise;

And who grow in the growth of your trees,
and have passed from darkness into light....

... Indeed, there is much room in your Paradise.
And there is nothing in it which is barren,
but everything is filled with fruit... (Ode 11:1-3.6-7.11-16.18-
    19.23).

The profusion of baptismal imagery and references in this Ode
includes, besides circumcision itself, the passage from darkness to
light, personal illumination, putting off the old garments and putting
on the garment of Christ, setting out upon the Way, entering the
Lord's rest, receiving the crown, the dew, living water, the garden of
paradise with its river, its trees and their fruit, and the bearing of fruit
by the faithful disciple.[10]
Embracing this lush Genesis imagery—waters, garden, trees—
and invisibly dwelling at its center, is that *unitive reality* which we
have found permeating John's gospel.

And there is nothing outside of the Lord,
because he was before anything came to be (16:18).

Sometimes it is the *Word* which is identified with this unitive reality, sometimes *Christ*.

The Messiah in truth is one.
And he was known before the foundations of the world,
that he might give life to persons forever by the truth of his
    name (41:15).

Sometimes it is the union of the baptized with Christ that is expressed, in the Pauline image of body and head:

His members are with him... (see also Ode 17:16).

In the same poem—as in Paul—the identification with Christ
moves beyond the confines of this image:

... I love the Beloved and I myself love him,
and where his rest is, there also am I....

... I have been united (to him), because the lover has found
    the Beloved,
because I love him that is the Son, I shall become a son.

BAPTISM AND THE ONE / 365

Indeed he who is joined to him who is immortal,
truly will be immortal.

And he who delights in the life
will become living... (Ode 3:2.5.7-9).

In a number of these poems the unitive reality flowing from baptism is reflected in subtle shifts between the voice of the Odist and the
voice of Christ (see Odes 8,15,17,28,36,41,42). The Odist will proclaim
that he "puts on" his Lord (Ode 7:4), and takes on the attributes and
powers of Christ. Often it is not clear when it is the Odist and when it
is Christ who is speaking. The unitive implications of these passages
would often be more evident in the simplicity of the Syriac than in the
English translations.[11] This ambiguity, implying identification of the
speaker with Christ, is sometimes associated with a *new or different
birth*.

I received the face and form of a new person (Ode 17:4).

...I was not their brother, nor was my birth like theirs (Ode
28:17).

All those will be astonished that see me, for of another race
am I (Ode 41:8).

The baptized are often spoken of as *babes*, and the creator Spirit is
a mother[12] who contains them, embraces them, fills them.

As the wings of doves over their nestlings,
and the mouths of their nestlings toward their mouths,
so also are the wings of the Spirit over my heart.

My heart continually refreshes itself and leaps for joy,
like the babe who leaps for joy in his mother's womb....

...And immortal life embraced me,
and kissed me.

And from that (life) is the Spirit which is within me.
And it cannot die because it is life (28:1-2.7-8).

This *feminine* characterization of the stream of unitive life which moves invisibly beneath the Odes' symbolic foliage is reminiscent of John's gospel.

The Odist sings of "raging rivers" that destroy those who despise the Lord, and then he turns to those who walk in faith.

> ...But those who cross them in faith
> shall not be disturbed.

> And those who walk on them faultlessly
> shall not be shaken.

As he continues, speaking of the baptized, his words recall first the ritual of baptism, then the cross of Jesus, and finally the baptismal sea-crossing which is the center of John's mandalic gospel and the Way which is consequent upon that crossing.

> Because the sign on them is the Lord,
> and the sign is the Way for those who cross in the name of the
>   Lord.

> Therefore, put on the name of the Most High and know him,
> and you shall cross without danger;
> because the rivers shall be obedient to you.

> The Lord has bridged them by his word,
> and he walked and crossed them on foot.

> And his footsteps were standing firm upon the waters, and
>   were not destroyed;
> but they are like a beam (or cross) (of wood) that is construct-
>   ed (or firmly fixed) on truth.

> On this side and on that the waves were lifted up, but the
>   footsteps of our Lord Messiah were standing firm.

> And they are neither blotted out,
> nor destroyed.

> And the Way has been appointed for those who cross over
>   after him,
> and for those who adhere to the path of his faith;
> and who adore his name (39:5-13).

⊕

The Gospel of Thomas is another very early text which has been recently rediscovered.[13] While the text unearthed at Nag Hammadi in 1945 is in Coptic, the original language may have been Greek or—very possibly—Syriac. Like the Odes, this collection of sayings of Jesus probably originated in a baptismal context.[14] Here the *unitive* vision which is born from the baptismal experience begins to create its own language.

Jesus said, "The man old in days will not hesitate to ask a little child of seven days about the place of Life, and he will live. For many who are first shall become last and they shall become *a single one*" (logion 4).[15]

Unity (variously translated into English as singleness or solitariness, etc.) is an expression, insistently repeated in Thomas, for the condition toward which Jesus' disciples are to strive. It is apparently a unity *in* Jesus, the Son of Man.

Jesus said, "I shall choose you, one out of a thousand, and two out of ten thousand, and they shall stand as *a single one*" (logion 23).

Jesus said, "Blessed are the *solitary* and elect, for you shall find the Kingdom; because you come from it, and you shall go there again" (logion 49).

Jesus said, "Many are standing at the door, but the *solitary* are the ones who will enter the bridal chamber" (logion 75).

Jesus said, "When you make the two *one*, you shall become sons of Man, and when you say, 'Mountain, be moved,' it will be moved" (logion 106).

Children, or babies, recur often in the Gospel of Thomas. As in the Odes, they are doubtless the newly baptized.

Jesus saw children who were being suckled. He said to his disciples, "These children who are being suckled are like those who enter the Kingdom." They said to him, "Shall we then, being children, enter the Kingdom?" Jesus said to them, "When you make the two *one*, and when you make the inner as the outer and the outer as the inner and the above as the below, and when you make the male and the female into *a single one*, so that the male will not be male and the female not be female... then shall you enter the Kingdom" (logion 22).

This logion 22, which we have quoted only in part, is particularly complex. And yet its movement is precisely a unification. Jesus is presented here as teaching a return of the baptized person to a primordial condition of undividedness preceding the first sin and the "fall" of humankind. This is imagined as a *return to the unity in which Adam was created*, prior even to the division of the sexes.

Stevan Davies[16] finds reflected here the *"baptismal reunification formula"* which had been identified in several Pauline texts (Gal 3:28; 1 Cor 12:13; Col 3:10f) earlier by Wayne Meeks.[17] This formula, proclaiming the annulling of the sexual division of humanity, would have been originally a part of the rite of Christian baptism.[18]

...Galatians 3,28 contains a reference to the "male and female" of Genesis 1,27 and suggests that somehow the act of Christian initiation reverses the fateful division of Genesis 2,21-22. Where the image of God is restored, there, it seems, man is no longer divided—not even by the most fundamental division of all, male and female.[19]

This recurrent motif, in Paul's letters, of the unification of opposites in Christ finds expression in the recurring image of reunification which we have called the *Pauline mandala* (above, pp. 22ff). The intrinsic relation of this "formula" to *baptism* suggests that the mandalic reunification figure is also directly related to the baptismal event. Since our mandalic scheme of John's gospel parallels the Pauline mandala, the likelihood of an essential relationship between John's gospel and baptism is further strengthened.

The association of this reunification (logia 22, 106) with Thomas is strangely reminiscent of our interpretation of the encounter of "the Twin" with Jesus in the final episode of John's chiastic gospel (Jn 20:26-29, pp. 259-260, 270-272 above). It was, symbolically, in the figure of Thomas, we proposed, that finally *the two were made one*.

⊕

The unitive language of these texts, and the unitive baptismal theology itself, is encapsulated in a Syriac word which comes to bear a unique fullness of meaning: *iḥidaya*.

Particularly interesting is the word *iḥidaya*, the Syriac equivalent for both *monogenēs* (only-begotten) and *monachos*,[20] which latter occurs several times, as also the Coptic equivalent, in the *Gospel of Thomas*. As various recent studies have brought out with varying emphasis, there are three elements in the meaning and doctrine of *iḥidayuta*: (1) singleness by leaving family and not marrying; (2) single-mindedness (stressed already by Paul and James!) and (3) a special relationship to the *Iḥidaya*, Christ the Only-begotten Son, whom the consecrated ascetics "put on" in a special way. Those who adopt this way of life form a kind of "church within the Church" called the *Q yama*.[21]

Given the motive power of the unitive reality which this word embodied, it is possible to understand how the apparent linkage between baptismal union with Christ and the two other forms of "singleness" may have led some Syrian Christian communities to require a commitment to celibacy or marital abstinence as a condition for baptism.[22]

On the basis of broad evidence in the early Syriac literature, Robert Murray proposes "a very early Judaeo-Christian *baptismal exhortation* of fairly fixed content" which explained for the neophytes these three meanings of *iḥidayuta*:

(1) becoming "single" by accepting Christ's call to leave dear ones,

(2) becoming single-minded, by accepting "circumcision of heart," and

(3) "putting on" the *Iḥidaya*, Christ, and thus "standing up" for him as a sort of representative, and thereby joining the *Q yama*, the "heart" of the church.[23]

Murray illustrates this hypothesis with one hymnic text which develops with particular clarity these implications of the unitive event of baptism:

See, Our Lord's sword is in the waters,
which divides sons and fathers;
for it is a living sword, which (see!)
makes division of the living among the dead.

See! [people] being baptized and becoming
virgins and consecrated ones [*qaddise*],
for they have gone down, been baptized and have put on
that single Only One [*l-haw ḥad Iḥidaya*].
See, the many rush at him
[with] kinsmen, offspring and riches.
For whoever is baptized and puts on
the Only One, the Lord of the many,
occupies the place of the many,
for Christ becomes his great Treasure.[24]

Baptism is at once a separation and a union for the believer. It is
both *sword* of division—from those who remain in unbelief as well as
from the multiplicity which is the "world"—and *garment* of the unitive life which is Christ.

Gabriele Winkler[25] has studied the meaning of *iḥidaya* in the Syriac writers as it relates to one of the earliest Christian ascetical traditions. She also finds the word frequently linked with the baptismal
unification expressed by Paul in Galatians 3:27-28:

As many of you as were baptized into Christ have clothed
yourselves with Christ. There is no longer Jew or Greek, there
is no longer slave or free; there is no longer male or female;
for all of you are one in Christ Jesus (see above, p. 368).

Quoting logion 17 of the Gospel of Thomas, in which Jesus
promises, "I will give you... what has not arisen in the heart of man,"
she continues:

Aphrahat also alludes to that reality when he says: "Jesus, the
'Only One' (*iḥidaya*), who is from the bosom of the Father,
shall cause 'those who are one' (*iḥidaye*) to rejoice." "What has
not arisen in the heart of man" is nothing less than the reality
of becoming transformed into God's own glory. In Syria this
transformation often is described in biblical language; to be
robed in glory[26] is to put on Christ, for as Paul said... (she
then quotes Galatians 3:27-28, above). This New Testament
theme of "oneness," of becoming one by putting on the
"One," very likely also lies behind the Syrian idea of Christ
being the *Iḥidaya*, the "Only One," whom the *iḥidaye*, "those
who are one," put on at baptism.... [27]

The celibate ascetical life was understood as a direct expression of this putting on the *One* which is the Christ of Galatians 3:27. Aphrahat writes:

> Those that preserve chastity
> are resting in the sanctuary of the Most High.
> The *Iḥidaya* (the "Only One"), who is from the bosom
> of the Father,
> shall cause the *iḥidaye* ("those who are one") to rejoice.
> There is no such thing as male and female.... [28]

These texts—the Letter to the Galatians (3:28), the Gospel of Thomas, the Syrian hymns on Epiphany and Aphrahat's *Demonstrations*—disclose one common theme, *the reintegration and unification of the parts*, of dispersion as such, *into the original totality*.[29]

Thus the *original unity of man* forms the leitmotif of Syria's early reflection on the ascetical life, which, we should not forget, is embedded in their understanding of what the rites of initiation are all about. This unity does not mean a quantitative sum of male and female, but a qualitative transfiguration of male and female into the *One* who is Christ.[30]

In this Syrian vision, baptism is an insertion into *the baptism of Jesus himself*, which in turn reflects the first *creation* when the Holy Spirit hovered over the waters. Jesus, as in Paul's vision (see Rom 5:12-21), is the *new Adam*, and it is in his baptism that the paradise of the new creation is opened. Those who are baptized in Jesus' name are created anew in him, and enter this garden.[31]

We have found a very similar convergence of baptism with the Genesis symbolism in the final chiastic closure of the first and last sections of John's gospel. When the risen Jesus presents his opened body to Thomas the twin, and Thomas believes, he re-enters the *unitive being* of the new Adam, which was first manifest at the baptism of Jesus in the Jordan. The other disciples, gathered in the closed house on the evening of the first Easter, a week earlier, had been baptized—and so born—into this new Adam when Jesus breathed upon them, saying, "Receive the Holy Spirit."

The unitive baptismal theology which is so forcefully expressed by Paul in his letter to the Galatians becomes the center of a literature which has very strong resonances also with John's gospel. The Christian unitive vision of Paul, of the Syrian poet-theologians—*and of John*—is essentially related to *baptism*.

The experience of the baptized (or *"illuminated"*[32]) sometimes brought about a flowering of poetic intuition, naturally expressing itself in verse and song. Gradually these shining waters have once again become visible to us through the teeming green forms of this first garden of the new creation. The same stream of inner experience which has given life to the symbolic narrative of John's gospel has produced this body of poetry in the Syriac tradition. Like that gospel, these odes and hymns draw spontaneously from the deepest veins of biblical symbolism. Never again in Christian history shall we find the unitive center of the Christian experience—which Paul had proclaimed in his letters and John had artfully embodied in his narrative of the life of Jesus—expressed with such fullness and power as in the literature of these early Judeo-Christian communities.

⊕

At the same time when this unitive sacramental theology of the "first church" (a Christianity still enclosed within the limits of *Judaic*, or semitic culture) is being rediscovered, we are observing the decline of the "second church" (that Christianity, dominant since the fourth century, which remains theologically confined within the *Greek and Latin* cultures). And the "third church," or *world* church, a Christianity truly inculturated—and therefore incarnated—in a plurality of cultures, is being born.[33]

We can see before us the moment when, having passed—during these past five centuries—through the crucible of critical discrimination, and having struggled free of the exclusive claims of its European cultural expressions, the Christianity of the west will become conscious once again of the simplicity and power at its core. Then, once again, the living gospel will find itself face to face with the challenge of the original Pentecost day: the cultural plurality of all humankind. It is the unitive reality at the heart of the Pauline and Johannine writings—which from the beginning has been inseparable from *baptism*—that must be consciously realized in the new context so that the long-awaited multiform birth may then take place.

Chapter Six

Sacraments and Interiority

It has sometimes been asserted that the sacraments are deliberately suppressed in the fourth gospel.[1] Such a claim can be made with some plausibility because of the omission in John's narrative of the baptism of Jesus and the institution of the eucharist. The truth, however, is probably exactly the opposite: it is John which, among the four gospels, has been most thoroughly composed in view of these two sacraments of initiation.

The language of John's sacramental theology is *symbolic* and allusive, rather than direct and explicit. This symbolic language, however, together with the concentric mandalic structure, is able to bind the entire Johannine narrative together into a single whole which is centered both in the interior unitive gift of Jesus, and at the same time in the sacramental events of baptism and eucharist. As Jesus was the visible manifestation or "sacrament" of the hidden God, so baptism and eucharist, the unitive sacraments of initiation, are the visible and ritual counterparts to the interior mystery of life in the Word. The characteristic Johannine *literary transformation* which has generated the structural and symbolic intricacies which we have already found everywhere in this gospel also explains the subtle and pervasive sacramental reference.

John has consistently avoided explicit mention of the external rituals—which he could presuppose as well known to the community—probably better to convey, through symbolic implication, the unitive fullness of the spiritual reality to which these rites correspond. We have found in the Odes of Solomon the same paradox: inspired by the experience of Christian initiation and largely woven of poetic allusions to baptism, the Odes do not use the word *baptism* once! Suppression of the literal in favor of oblique and symbolic reference is natural to poetic expression, however—as much of our twentieth century poetry testifies. We might expect this style to be favored particularly in treating the *mysteries*.[2] It is in this literary country that the symbolic and the reductionist-empirical interpretations clash most magnificently.

We have given much attention to the likely baptismal references in the fourth gospel. Does John speak of the *eucharistic* reality with equal fullness and subtlety? Here John's *silence* is even more conspicuous than in the case of baptism, so as to favor—at least by modern readers—that interpretation of "antisacramentalism" which is the exact contrary of the gospel's actual intent. While, from the viewpoint of the community of disciples, Jesus' institution of the eucharist is of primary importance, John has omitted this event—the core of the synoptic supper narratives—completely. Yet he has left us a supper narrative which is enormously longer than that of the synoptics. This Johannine supper narrative consists of a long discourse of Jesus *on precisely the life of interior union which corresponds to the eucharist*. The Johannine silence, given the existence of the synoptic accounts, generates a tension toward deeper understanding, leading the hearer of the gospel from the obvious and literal toward the depths of the mystery.

It has been observed that Mark's gospel contains a number of instances of the *pairing* of a baptismal allusion with a eucharistic allusion.[3] An example, already mentioned, is the sequence of Jesus' feeding of the multitude and his walking on the water (Mk 6:34-44 and 45-52), which occurs also in John (6:1-13 and 16-21). Another is Jesus' raising the daughter of Jairus to life (a miracle understood in a *baptismal* sense in early tradition) followed by his command that she be given something to eat (Mk 5:41-43).[4]

In John we also find a number of these baptismal-eucharistic pairings; in fact they are so numerous as to constitute a basic motif of the narrative. The baptismal references of the beginning, the (chiastic) middle and the end of John's gospel are followed by eucharistic allusions. The Baptist's recollection of Jesus' baptism in John 1 is followed shortly by an allusion to the tree of life in the garden (through Nathanael-Jacob beneath his fig tree), and then by the wedding banquet of Cana. We have just noted the sequence of feeding and sea-crossing in the central sixth chapter. When Jesus appears, in chapter 20, to the disciples gathered in the closed house, the scene itself suggests the regular eucharistic celebration of the early Christian communities on the first day of the week. Jesus' baptism of his disciples with the Holy Spirit is followed, once again, by an allusion to the tree of life and the garden, as Jesus invites Thomas to reach out his hand and put it in his side (see above, p. 257). Jesus' showing of his pierced side to the disciples also recalls baptism and eucharist, in the light of 19:34.

Finally, in chapter 21, we find the disciples upon the *sea* (as in the central sea-crossing). Peter plunges into the water; then there is the *meal* on the shore with its eucharistic connotation. We are reminded at this point that Jesus has chosen for his first disciples these *fishermen*: men who bring forth food from the waters. At this final meal, as at the other meal by the sea (6:1-13), both bread and *fish* are eaten: it seems that no meal in John can be without a reminder of the *water*, of the new creation which is baptism.

The water and the blood which flowed from Jesus' side upon the cross recall baptism and the eucharist. This is another cardinal moment in the gospel narrative, and the disciple witnesses to the double effusion with a solemn declaration (19:34-35). Eating and drinking is implied in several other Johannine scenes, besides those which have been mentioned. At the wedding feast of Cana, the water which becomes wine may signify baptism and eucharist together. There is a progression from the baptism of Jesus, implied in the first scene, to this *banquet* (suggesting eucharist) at which the new wine is poured out for the *guests*. Here we seem to move from the baptism of John to Jesus' baptism, and at the same time from baptism to eucharist. The two sacraments of initiation appear inseparably united at this wedding which expresses the eternal union of Word and Spirit. We must not forget that, in the mandalic sequence, Cana follows immediately the death of Jesus, and expresses his resurrection, poured out for his followers.

The narrative of Jesus' encounter with the Samaritan woman at the well, with his promise of living water, is framed by conversation about *food* (4:8.31-34). Jesus' promise of living water here in chapter 4 is paralleled by his self-identification as the living *bread* in the discourse at Capernaum. The Samaria episode, in the mandalic scheme, is chiastically paralleled by the *supper* at Bethany. The Johannine narrative of Jesus' last supper with his disciples begins with his gesture of *washing their feet*, with its baptismal overtones.

Baptism and eucharist, the water and the bread (or wine, or blood), comprise still another Johannine dyad, or *pair*. We have become used to this double language, which is most obvious in the related pairs of *characters*: Baptist and Jesus, Baptist and beloved disciple, Peter and the disciple, Peter and Judas, paralytic and blind man, *basilikos'* son and Lazarus, Magdalene and the mother of Jesus, Samaritaness and Mary of Bethany, Mary and Martha. But there are also Galilee and Judea, wilderness and garden, Israel and the world. Thomas, the twin, has brought some dramatic resolution to this doubleness in his final confession of faith (20:28), and Peter and the disciple have represented its projection into the subsequent history of the church (21:19-22). The device of chiastic structure has enabled John to weave this pattern through the entire fabric of his gospel.

The mystery of these two which are one—baptism and eucharist—can no more be resolved than can the mystery of Word and Spirit. We are recurrently confronted in John's gospel with pairs of terms which are at once contrasting and immanent in one another—as man and woman. It may be that here we reach the vanishing point of intelligibility—in this world—where expression and signification disappear into the unitive light of the Word itself. Entrance into these mysteries of the two-in-one is ultimately through the receptiveness of a life of faith and love rather than through rational penetration.

Baptism and eucharist are sacramental expressions of the beginning and the end of human life. Jesus' life begins, in our Johannine narrative (as in that of Mark), with his baptism in the Jordan by John. His life ends in his *hour*, the meaning of which is most fully developed in the course of John's supper narrative. Here it is the other John, the disciple whom Jesus loved, who is himself initiated, as he rests "in the bosom" of Jesus. The parallel of Baptist and disciple seems, from this perspective, the relation also of baptism and eucharist, of the water and the wine. It is the disciple who has come and seen where the Master "is staying" (1:38-39), and it is this "place" of which his long supper narrative speaks in its circular, spell-binding chant.

Baptism is the gift as received, the Spirit as come within the believer and dwelling within him or her. Eucharist is the gift become incarnate in the disciple—in the flesh and blood of this person, who becomes himself or herself incarnate gift. We seem to see this at the supper in Bethany, as Mary pours the perfume, thick and precious, upon Jesus' feet. Baptism is the beginning, the birth from the unitive waters; eucharist is the ending, the death into the unitive cup.

Baptism is Spirit, Mother, and eucharist is Word, Christ. And yet baptism is union with Jesus and eucharist is the offering of self in the flame of the Spirit. Baptism is wedding—or betrothal—and eucharist is wedding. Baptism is death as well as birth; eucharist is an awakening in the life of the body as well as a death of self.

This is the one who came by water and blood, Jesus Christ,
not with the water only but with the water and the blood.

And the Spirit is the one that testifies, for the Spirit is the truth. There are three that testify: the Spirit and the water and the blood, and these three agree (1 Jn 5:6-8).

Jesus did not come to confer the divine unitive life merely by speech, by symbol, by contact, or even, in sovereign creative power, by simply embodying this life in a material medium. Rather, "through water and through *blood*"—that is, *a unitive self-communication through suffering and death*, through the human labor pains which are the seal of true union in the language of flesh and blood. By pouring out his blood into the earth, by dying into the soil of humanity, he has filled humanity with the divine Spirit. He has left two ritual and material representations of this salvific death, baptism and the eucharist: the water and the blood. These are the two visible "witnesses"[5] which remain in the church, like the record of Baptist and disciple. These two witnesses are two communal and visible events and also two personal and interior events (experiences) in Christian life. There is, in Johannine language (1 Jn 5:6-8), also a third witness, the Holy Spirit, which is behind these two and within these two. The Spirit, however, *continually indwells* the one who believes in Jesus and has been baptized: "Those who believe in the Son of God have the testimony in their hearts" (1 Jn 5:10). This interior testimony is the ongoing experience of the divine life itself within the human person. A fourth witness is the scriptural word itself, in which the testimony of the disciple is communicated (Jn 21:24).

The two came forth from the opened breast of the One, to become the Alpha and Omega of human life, the river and the tree of life in the interior garden of the new creation.

Then the angel showed me the river of the water of life, bright as crystal, flowing from the throne of God and of the Lamb through the middle of the street of the city. On either side of the river is the tree of life, with its twelve kinds of fruit, producing its fruit each month, and the leaves of the tree are for the healing of the nations (Rev 22:1-2).

Chapter Seven

Two Centers:
Peter and the Beloved Disciple

Several times in the course of John's narrative, Peter and the beloved disciple have been presented together: at the supper, going to the tomb of Jesus, and finally on the shore of the sea in chapter 21. Each time John presents the two figures in deliberate *contrast*. Because of the crucial roles of Peter and the disciple—as chief shepherd and as the witness from whom the fourth gospel is said to originate (21:24)—we can expect this comparison and contrast between them to be of importance for the interpretation of John's gospel. More so, since the contrast's final appearance is at the very conclusion of the narrative.

In the doctrinal polemics that have rationalized the division of western Christianity since the time of the reformation, Peter and the sacraments of the church have played analogous roles. Both Peter and the sacramental system have been identified with the *institutional* side of Christianity, and with Roman Catholicism. Protestant interpreters have often seen in John's gospel both a subordination of baptism and eucharist to some more individualistic or spiritual element, and a subordination of Peter to the beloved disciple. As the controversy continues,[1] the roles of the two disciples as they are presented by John emerge into sharper clarity.

We have already observed the relationship between the two disciples at three points in the narrative. Now let us look at the Johannine presentation of the two in a more synthetic way, and make a final attempt at extracting the meaning which their relationship is meant to convey.

As the interpretive debate has disclosed, the relationship between Peter and the disciple is somewhat parallel to the relationship between the sacramental rites of baptism and eucharist on one hand, and John's gospel on the other. John appears to move away from the view of Peter in the synoptic gospels—where he stands out much less ambiguously as the leader among Jesus' disciples—in the same direction in which he moves away from the external rites of the two sacraments. Peter, in his office of chief shepherd, belongs to the external church as do the two sacramental rites.

We have interpreted John's gospel in terms of the divine *Unitive* coming into the world in Jesus. From this viewpoint, Simon Peter, the *Rock*, represents the continuing *external principle of unity* of the disciples of Jesus in the world: that is, of the new humanity, the body of Christ (see Jn 15). The beloved disciple, in contrast, can be seen from this same viewpoint as representing the *interior principle of unity* of the new humanity, understood either as the unitive knowledge or the *koinōnia*, the communion of the disciples (see 1 Jn 1:1-3). The relationship of these two principles can be visualized quite well through the geological terms *epicenter*[2] and *center*.

Peter, this representative of the external principle of unity, the "Petrine principle," is certainly presented in a *critical* light by the author of the fourth gospel, as he narrates the story of Peter in his following of Jesus. We hear very little of Peter—merely his naming and his confession of faith—until Jesus' *hour*, and then Peter's lack of understanding and his denial of Jesus are presented with bold emphasis. Meanwhile the beloved disciple is continually present with implicit or explicit contrast.

It is hard to avoid the conclusion that this presence of the disciple, who manifests a deeper understanding and a more stable love for Jesus, underlines again and again Peter's shallowness and instability. The disciple, on the other hand, is presented as the one who is gifted with quickness of insight, with depth of understanding, and with fidelity to his Master. We do not see him failing to understand or failing to stand firm in his witness. Were it not for the recognition of grace in the appellation itself—"the disciple *whom Jesus loved*"—we could hardly help but hear in the voice of "John" an echo of Luke's Pharisee (Lk 18:11) comparing himself favorably with the publican. It may be, however, that we are to understand these two figures principally in their *symbolic* sense, as representing enduring realities in the community of disciples and within each disciple. It is interesting that *Paul*, too, presents himself favorably in contrast to Peter (Gal 2:11-14), in his vindication of Christian freedom against the dietary restrictions of the Jewish law.

With Beatrice Bruteau, we have interpreted Peter's refusal to allow Jesus to wash his feet (13:6-8; see above, p. 123) as a resistance to Jesus' "Holy Thursday revolution": that radical shift from the old order of domination and subjection, to the new order of communion. Peter's recalcitrance stems from his *attachment to the old, the merely human order*—as is clear from Jesus' rebuke in the synoptics: "...you are setting your mind not on divine things but on human things" (Mk 8:33). This old order is the order of "this world"—a world ruled by *external* structures and forces. It is Peter whose *inner* vision has not been awakened, despite the deep faith in Jesus and love for Jesus with which he has been gifted.

And so Peter, who is to occupy Jesus' place as chief shepherd, becomes, in the Johannine narrative, also symbolic of the *old, external and unmoving order*. In this he is contrasted with the beloved disciple, who has been awakened and come to birth in the new and transformative order which evolves from within.

This stubborn adherence of Peter to the old order of *"this world"* has emerged very clearly—but with John's characteristic subtlety— from two passages in the account of Jesus' arrest and trial. It is *Peter* who draws his sword in the garden and cuts off the ear of the high priest's servant (18:10). A little later, when Jesus stands before Pilate, he responds to the procurator:

My kingdom is not from this world. *If my kingdom were from this world, my followers would be fighting to keep me from being handed over to the Jews...* (18:36).[3]

Peter is designated by Jesus as rock and *shepherd*—he is to be the leader, while the disciple remains only a witness. Yet Peter must learn from the disciple, who is closer to Jesus and knows Jesus more deeply (13:23-25; 21:7). Peter is the one who professes *his love* for Jesus, while the disciple is identified as the one *loved by* Jesus. The disciple, who *receives* knowledge (though he also witnesses)—is also the one who *receives* love. He contrasts with Peter who is to *act* as shepherd (leader, teacher, pastor) and who *"loves"* Jesus. Peter and the disciple are distinguished by their active and receptive roles.

Peter is to *follow* Jesus, while the disciple is to *remain* (21:19-22). We are told that here Jesus speaks of the death which Peter is to die. Peter will be crucified, as was Jesus. There may be something else here also. As Jesus was handed over by the Jews to the Gentile Romans to be killed, so Peter will go to *Rome*, where he will die. Perhaps this is where this Galilean fisherman would rather not go, but he must be the highly visible, symbolic epicenter not just for Jewish Christians but for the Gentiles as well.

Jesus' command to Peter, *"Follow me,"* may also relate to the attachment of Peter to "this world" which we have recently discussed. As the chief shepherd Peter will have to occupy—and defend —a particular *place in this world*. A tension, painful and perennial, will develop between this worldly position of Peter and the transformative dynamism of the gospel. The universality of Peter's mission, and the revolutionary nature of the gospel which he must preach, will call upon him to follow Jesus like an exile and pilgrim. His inclination, on the contrary, will be to materialize and particularize his mandate so that it becomes transformed in the likeness of an earthly kingdom or empire.

The Johannine music is contrapuntal, dialectic: very often we ourselves must supply, from our knowledge of the biblical tradition, the harmonic background of a particular narrative. To what extent does John expect us to listen to his narrative against the background of an existing gospel tradition? This question arises again in connection with a complex of relationships between two passages in John's and Matthew's narratives of Peter and Jesus at Caesarea Philippi.

In the much-discussed text of Matthew 16:16-19, it is Simon Peter who responds to Jesus' question by confessing, "You are the Messiah, the Son of the living God."

And Jesus answered him, "Blessed are you, Simon son of Jonah! For flesh and blood has not revealed this to you, but my Father in heaven. And I tell you, you are Peter, and on this rock I shall build my church, and the gates of Hades will not prevail against it. I will give you the keys of the kingdom of heaven, and whatever you bind on earth will be bound in heaven, and whatever you loose on earth will be loosed in heaven" (Mt 16:17-19). (See also Mt 18:18, where the power of binding and loosing is given not only to Peter but to the other disciples as well.)

Here we have elements of *two chiastic Johannine passages*: first, Jesus' naming of Peter—"You are Simon, son of John...you are to be called Cephas (which is translated Peter, that is Rock)" (1:42)—and, second, Jesus' conferring upon the gathered disciples both the Holy Spirit and the power of forgiving sins (20:21-23). Matthew has put together the naming of Peter, "Rock," and the promise of the "power of the keys"—the authority to bind and to loose on earth and in heaven—while John has placed the two events in a chiastic relationship at opposite ends of his narrative.

In contrast to Matthew's account, John does not speak of the *keys*. Instead, John presents Jesus conferring the power of the *forgiveness of sins*, which has a less juridical ring and is open to an interpretation in terms of Genesis symbolism: forgiveness of sins as reversing the effects of the original fault and pointing to a new creation through the immanence of the divine Spirit in humanity. In Matthew the power is given to Peter alone; in John, the corresponding power is given to the gathered disciples, who apparently include the twelve less Thomas.

In John, then, the *power* is different in these ways: it is one with the interior gift of the Holy Spirit, and therefore with the basic baptismal gift of new life in Christ; it is a power specifically for the forgiveness and retaining of sins; it is given not to one, Peter, but to the gathered "college" of disciples.

In addition to these explicit differences there are the Johannine symbolic resonances. Chief among these is the definite allusion to Genesis 2:7: God's creation of Adam by breathing the spirit of life into a bit of earth. Both Johannine passages probably also reflect another story from Genesis, which we have mentioned earlier (above, p. 247)—Jacob, on his way to Paddam-aram to find a wife (Gen 28), stops and sleeps with his head upon "one of the stones of the place." After dreaming of the ladder reaching to heaven, with the angels upon it, and the Lord's promise of the land, he awakens and sets the stone up for a pillar, anointing it with oil. Finally, he vows, "...and this stone, which I have set up for a pillar, shall be God's house..." (Gen 28:10-22).

It is in John 1:42 that Simon is called, by Jesus, the *rock*. The words which immediately follow this naming in Matthew, "...and on this rock I shall build my church..." (Mt 16:18), directly correspond to the words of Jacob as he anoints the stone as *"God's house"* (Gen 28:22), and correspond, in John, to Jesus' "anointing" of the disciples with the Holy Spirit, after he has awakened from the sleep of death. The gift, however, is given not only to Peter but to the other disciples as well. (The mention of the "twelve" in John 20:24 recalls the twelve sons of Jacob, eponymic patriarchs of the twelve tribes.) And the power of binding and loosing—of forgiving and holding sins—is conferred upon all of these disciples also. We should remember that this takes place within the house where the doors were still "locked for fear of the Jews," recalling the Passover night in Egypt.

It would seem likely that the power of forgiving or retaining sins (which in Matthew was the power of opening or closing the kingdom of heaven) is the power of admitting into this new *house of God* or excluding from it. Admittance into this house of God and gate of heaven (Gen 28:17), however, is related by John to the liberation of the Jews from the constriction of Egyptian slavery—now realized in the liberation of Jesus' disciples from the "fear of the Jews" and the Jewish law. It is related also to the reopening of the garden of paradise and admittance to the tree of life. When Jesus shows his wounds—shows his *opened body*—to the disciples gathered in the *closed house*, there is implied a *double opening*. The house of slavery is opened for their exodus, and the house of God, or paradise, is opened for their entry.

Matthew's narrative conveys the image of an institutional church which has replaced the institution of the religion of Israel, and which now, in its place, represents the kingdom of heaven and determines who will enter that kingdom. This authoritative church is presided over by Peter the Rock, who by the gift of his faith and the Lord's designation has become joined to it both as foundation stone and authoritative head.

From John's gospel we receive a different image. As Jesus anoints the stone of this place (recalling also the "dust of the ground" of Gen 2:7) with the oil of the Holy Spirit, it becomes the house of God. This stone, however, is not Peter only, but all the gathered disciples, signifying all the twelve tribes and ultimately all the nations of humanity. Like the earth which came alive when the breath of God entered it to become Adam, the first human, this earth or stone which is Peter and the other disciples comes alive through the Holy Spirit to become the new body of Jesus (the new temple of 2:21). This body of Jesus is the *new creation*, and this new birth in the Spirit corresponds to baptism. The body's members abide in it and grow as they partake of the eucharistic tree of life which is the Word become flesh—here signified in the bodily presence of Jesus among the disciples, and especially this bodily presence offered to Thomas.

Matthew's text depicts an ecclesial body which is solid as stone and clearly defined as a walled fortress, standing fast in this world—against its demonic counterpart—through the divine power which dwells in it. The Johannine passages project an image which is less distinct but at once more intimate, more vital and more inclusive. The power of the Spirit which is infused into these men from the risen body of Jesus begins a re-creation of the cosmos to be propagated through the "forgiveness of sins." Once again, John refuses to leave before us an image of the community of Jesus' followers which is not open and in movement toward this *cosmic* re-creation.

In contrast with the figure of Peter, representing "external church"—as an external and institutional center of unity—John has presented his great complex of images representing the interior reality of communion and new birth or new creation, and this interior world is correlated with the beloved disciple. We might imagine the community of Jesus' disciples, then, in the form of an *ellipse*, with its *two centers* or foci. In our earlier and more differentiated image, this community has both a visible center, or epicenter, and an invisible center. The symbolic *epicenter* is Peter, as chief shepherd in Jesus' place, head of the visible community. The deep or *invisible center* is the symbolic John, the beloved disciple. This disciple who rested "in the bosom" of Jesus represents the interior reality of this same community: the unitive light and the communion which are the gift and presence of Christ. These two disciples represent the complementary exoteric and esoteric aspects of the one Christ-mystery. *Both* Peter and the disciple are essential to the sacramental church of Christ—as body and spirit are both essential to the human person.

A further comparison is offered by the two texts which we have excluded from our mandalic presentation of the fourth gospel: the *prologue* and the final chapter which we have called the *epilogue*. The relationship between these two very different texts parallels the relationship which we have just discussed between the disciple and Peter. The prologue, centered in the Word and entirely permeated with unitive reflection, approaches concrete narrative only in the verses concerning the Baptist. This seems a quintessentially *Johannine* text. The epilogue, on the other hand, seemed to us from the start less "Johannine" than the rest of the gospel narrative. It begins with Peter's "I am going fishing," and revolves continually around Peter—more than around Jesus, upon whom the rest of John's narrative is so emphatically centered. We are here in a *Petrine* world, and we hear of Peter's vocation, his ministry, his personal relationship with Jesus, his destiny. In contrast to the sublime world of the prologue, we are here immersed in the structures of history, the history of a "Petrine church."

In the prologue we began on a plane of high abstraction, with an eagle's eye view of the Christ-event. In the epilogue we find ourselves returning to the world—at first, as if Peter and the others had never met their Teacher! We found the prologue to be probably a *baptismal* text. The epilogue, on the other hand, seems to speak symbolically both of baptism and of *eucharist*: even a kind of eschatological eucharist when the nations have finally been gathered together. Jesus' words to Peter about *feeding* his sheep reinforce the eucharistic sense while they relate it both to Peter's ministry and to his death.

Epilogue and prologue, therefore, project an historical church and an interior and spiritual community, respectively—parallel to what we have inferred from the figures of Peter and the beloved disciple. While both texts have implicit sacramental reference, the epilogue presents baptism and eucharist in a symbolic and dramatic language which reflects the more exterior church and its history, while the prologue's music sounds from the interior experience of the same unitive mystery.

Stepping outside John's gospel itself, one can quickly confirm this impression of the contrast between a Petrine and a Johannine vision of Christ-event and Christian community by comparing the first letter of Peter with the first letter of John.[4] 1 John is written in a language which seems saturated with the unitive experience of knowledge and communion, while 1 Peter speaks of the same Christ-event in a language largely woven from Old Testament symbols and prophecies, and with a more specific and practical attention to the problems and trials of the journey. In 1 Peter we hear the voice of the tested shepherd, the rock; in 1 John we are listening to a voice directly expressive of that more interior center of unity: "the anointing which you have received."

⊕

The visible church and its sacraments both carry through the coming of the unitive divine reality into the world, by incarnating and perpetuating the presence of this unitive reality in the world. John creates a unique equilibrium in his gospel. On the one hand he places everywhere in it unobtrusive sacramental allusions, and several times he centers attention upon the figure of Peter. On the other hand he carefully avoids explicit sacramental statements of the kind that we find in the synoptics and in Paul, and he presents the beloved disciple continually in juxtaposition with Peter.

As we have seen, the allusions to baptism and to eucharist are both numerous and oblique. The allusions are oblique because they are symbolic, and their multiplicity is expressive of the fullness within the gospel's *unitive core*, of which these two sacraments are representations. We have found the "meaning of John's gospel" concentrated in a river of unitive divinity which flows through the gospel's center to pour from the opened body of Jesus and then to be breathed into his disciples on the seventh day. Baptism and eucharist represent the material embodiment of this unitive reality, and therefore they are the physical medium of the new creation of the cosmos. If the re-creation of the universe begins in the eucharistic presence and is itself a eucharistic transformation, we need not be surprised to find a multiplicity of eucharistic references in John. The same may be said of baptism.

This Johannine sacramental vision, while it seems inconceivable to many western scholars, both Catholic and Protestant, has long been quite at home in the tradition of eastern Christianity. The ecclesial vision of the early fathers—continuing still today in the eastern church—is of a church which, essentially, is *wisdom* and is *communion*. These are the twin expressions of that divine Unitive which is revealed in the Johannine writings.[5]

Peter and the beloved disciple will be two *different witnesses* to the same Jesus; they will communicate two varying but complementary visions of the same reality. At the same time, they themselves will be *complementary images of Jesus and of discipleship*. Peter is the disciple who follows his Lord with faith and love, yet in darkness and not without falling. Both shepherd and sheep, he presents the image of the normal and outward life of a disciple walking in the footsteps of Jesus.

The beloved disciple, on the other hand, represents the person who lives *within* each disciple. This is the *new* person, reborn in Jesus and remaining in him. This is the *child*, beloved son, who has received everything and has but to remain at the center, in the heart of Christ. This is the person who is not so much walking and growing as continually being born. His vocation is identical with the divine presence in which he remains.

Chapter Eight

The Sevenfold Day:
One Hundred and Fifty–Three Fish

The gospel which unfolded from the one night of baptismal illumination, at the center of our figure, is finally gathered into the unitive light of the one day of the resurrection, the enduring sabbath of new creation.

The comprehensiveness and power of the single dramatic movement of John's gospel is seen when we regard successively each of the seven days of the new creation from a dynamic perspective, as a *revolution* or transformation.

I. In Jesus the unitive *beginning* has come into the world; we are born into that beginning and remain there, so that the unitive beginning is taking place in us everywhere and at every moment.

II. Against the background of the various partial forms of human knowledge, Jesus appears in the world as the plenary divine *Wisdom*, communicating himself in the darkness of faith as a knowledge which is living, personal and unitive. Within the world there becomes present a new point of orientation which is the Wisdom from which the world originated, a new center which draws the world together in itself. The wise become blind and the blind see.

III. In the human person of Jesus the inalienable *glory* of God is present and is communicated to the totality of those who believe—to humanity and to the human person, body, soul and spirit. This glory is communicated not from outside and above

387

but from within and below. The unimaginable and completely ungraspable is possessed in the darkness of faith and interiority.

IV.   All traditions of the teaching and *transmission* of religious realities are transcended and relativized—even inverted—in Jesus' unitive gift of himself. Mediation has been taken up within the immediacy and totality of this new relationship between humanity and God.

V.   Jesus revolutionizes human *life* and relationships as, through his death, he pours the unitive and eternal divine life into those who believe in him. Now that which is below feeds upon that which is above, rather than, as always before, the greater feeding upon the lesser. The law of death which had dominated human life is overcome by the law of an indestructible divine life. Gradually human life is transformed by this seed of divine life within it.

VI.   Through the communication of the divine unitive *Feminine* (the Holy Spirit), Jesus liberates and transforms the interior unitive human feminine, so that the movement toward realization of this unitive feminine then becomes one with the inner spring of history itself—of the development of human society and the human psyche.

VII.   In the unitive simplicity of his own person, the one *man* Jesus brings together God and humanity, so that all people become the one dwelling place of God which is his human body, and so that human life itself is able to become worship.

⊕

These seven "revolutions" or dramatic transformations are complementary aspects of the *one* event initiated by Jesus and progressively accomplished in Jesus, which is the movement from the first creation to a new *unitive* creation.

ONE HUNDRED AND FIFTY–THREE FISH[1]

1. The movement is beyond dualism to the unitive center. The term *revolution*, while useful for expressing the dynamic quality of this Event, fails to convey its essential *unitive* quality.

2. To this one movement correspond the various *inversions* which are conspicuous in John's gospel. To it also corresponds the progression from linear to mandalic movement, from surface to center or to a centered geometry.

3. *"The Unitive"*[2] is a *partial* expression for God. Incomplete as it is, the "name" of God which is the One, or the Unitive, expresses something of primary importance to the human person and to the human community. In the New Testament this same reality, divine and human, is expressed in terms such as love (*agape*), communion (*koinōnia*), *one* (Jn 17).

4. Corresponding to this unitive revolution, in the life of human persons and of society, is the movement from selfishness, egocentricity, to love.

5. The unitive revolution is basically *baptismal*, communicated and experienced in the *new birth in the one beginning* which is baptism. It also corresponds to the *eucharist*, however, as a *partaking of the end*, the glorified and communal body of Christ.

6. Thus the *sabbath* enters into the week, permeating each of the days of ordinary life. The chord of light is completed as the prismatic colors of the successive days disappear into the clear and invisible light of this sabbath.

7. While Peter follows the Master on the way of the shepherd, the disciple remains by the water and the fire. In the water and the fire is the life.

⊕

8. The Johannine community is constituted by a communion of faith and of love. "Church," *ekklēsia*, is not a Johannine category: the word does not appear in the fourth gospel (although it is found in Revelation and in the third letter of John). The reality which corre-

sponds to this word, however, is central to John's gospel.[3] Here, as with baptism and eucharist, we find the *implicit* and symbolic language of John to be primary. And his interest appears to be not in order nor structure but in the actual fabric of human relationship which constitutes the community.

9. Deeper still, the community is constituted by a communion of grace. This is the grace which flows from Jesus and is expressed symbolically—in the very corporeal language of water and blood.

10. The Johannine church or community is the continuing presence of the *unitive divine Word* in the world, incarnate in the disciples of Jesus. The community consists of those who believe in Jesus and then abide in him through faith and love. It is the being *in Jesus* which is primary and constitutive.

11. The relationship of the community with Jesus is expressed in terms of faith and love, and in terms of sacramental union through baptism and eucharist.

12. This community, or *koinōnia* (1 Jn 1:3), is a unitive and creative ferment in the world, first fruits and leaven of the new creation.

13. The community lives in a perpetual tension between the creative and regressive forces within it. The Holy Spirit dwelling in its midst tends to draw the world to a new birth, transforming it into the community (into *koinōnia*), while at the same time the world tends to convert the community of believers back into itself, into the fallen and unredeemed first creation. This struggle has been foreshadowed in the history of Israel. The exterior forms and structures and offices of the community are particularly susceptible to this subversion by which they harden into the structures of power and domination of the old world. This regression is favored often by the challenges—and especially the opposition—which the community encounters in the world.

14. The church is the presence of the divine Wisdom in the world, incarnating itself in the communion of human persons. Two conceptions of the church are of primary importance, therefore: church as *wisdom* and church as *communion*.

15. It is not possible to return to the fullness and vigor of the beginning through separation, but only through union. As the church has evolved further and further from its origins, there have been repeated attempts to return to what was conceived as the purity, simplicity and authenticity of its origins. The attempt to achieve this return by focusing on one element, or one complex of elements, conceived as the essence of Christianity, however, has often resulted in further division.[4]

16. While the conception of the church as *communion* has remained primary in the Christian east, it was eclipsed by an institutional model[5] in the medieval west. The decentralizing Protestant communities were born in a reaction against this exteriorizing and hardening of ecclesial union. The re-emergence of the communion vision of the church in our time is expressed in Roman Catholicism by the Constitution on the Church of the Second Vatican Council. Here the Johannine *Unitive* is glimpsed once again as the church is defined as the sacrament of the union of humanity with God and of the union of human persons with one another.[6]

17. As the divine Word becomes communion on earth (see 1 Jn 1:1-3), the divine presence, the temple, becomes the embodied human person. A new community is planted in the world to represent and embody this new reality of *communion, koinōnia*, the divine Unitive, in the world. The central sacramental realization of this communion is the supper of the Lord, the eucharist.

18. This church, like Jesus, is *mediator of the immediate*, bringing together God and humanity not only through itself but *in* itself. In this role the church is feminine, *woman*, Eve, "mother of all living." Yet, while the mediation is essentially unitive, immanent, "feminine," it must be visibly represented—and its institutional representations are largely borrowed from the surrounding cultures; the church takes on their forms. Thus, at one or another time in history it comes to be forgotten that the church is the people of God. At some times the institutional church has taken from secular institutions not only the external forms but the corresponding attitudes, so that its officials could begin to think, and govern, and express themselves in the language of emperor and imperial court.

19. The true divinization of humanity is suppressed as the church reinterprets itself in terms of the structures and ornament of secular power. These external forms are very enduring, since they wear upon themselves the glow of the Christ-anointing, and consequently the

authority of God and his Christ. But to the extent that the church understands itself and governs itself in terms of these forms, structures and categories, there is a suppression of the divine glory within the heart of the common persons to whom the communion belongs. Only exceptionally, then, does the human person become aware of his or her freedom, and of the divine anointing which he or she has received.

20. Neither the unitive side nor the creative side of this gift of divinization is realized in the shadow of such borrowed power and magnificence. The "feminine," more interior side of the gift of Christ, which is inner Unitive, or communion, is blocked by the opaque mediation. Nor does there exist within the church a space in which may be realized the "masculine," more active and exterior side of the gift—which is the creative energy and light to transform the world. Both the unitive and creative sides of the Christian charism are too threatening to a predominantly institutional religion.

21. The re-creation of the world in the divine Unitive proceeds simultaneously upon personal, communal and cosmic levels. These may be envisioned as concentric circles. The innermost circle would represent the individual person; next would come the successive human communities, and finally, as the outermost circles, all living creatures and the material creation or cosmos itself. The personal and individual realization of this Unitive may be called the *baptismal* level. We have seen this everywhere—though most often implicitly—in John's gospel, and have found it most clearly expressed in the early *Syrian* tradition. The communal experience of the Unitive, the *koinōnia* of the first letter of John, may be called a *eucharistic* realization—as may also the experience or intuition of *cosmic* unity.

22. The great spiritual traditions, both of east and of west, are concerned with achieving the *unity of the person*. This is true whether the particular way is explicitly conceived in this language of personal unity or not.[7] This unitive core of the person, referred to conveniently as the *center*,[8] is the particular focus of the *monastic* traditions.

23. Monasticism is a way of life which, through "blessed simplicity,"[9] promotes the realization of this unitive human center. This is implied by the word itself, derived from *"monos,"* *one.* Such practices as celibacy, solitude, poverty, silence and meditation function as means toward a progressive *interiorization*, and hence toward realization of the unitive center.

24. Contemplation, "enlightenment," or unitive experience,[10] is the realization of the unity of the person, and the activation of this center. The revolution in consciousness which thus occurs is a participation in the one unitive revolution.

25. Contemplation, then, is an experience of the ground of consciousness itself, the invisible basis of all awareness, reflection and thought.[11] Paradoxically, this unitive experience is usually regarded as a rare and isolated mystical experience.

26. Realization of this unity of the person is accompanied by the progressive quieting or integration of the "passions," or disordered emotions,[12] and so is manifested in a deep peace or *hēsychia*.[13]

27. The more profound schools of contemporary western psychology[14] have penetrated through the surface of human experience to discover once again the unitary *Self*. At this point they rejoin the ancient religious traditions of Asia.

28. In the true maturing of the person, the seat of consciousness progresses from the surface toward the center, so that all of life is informed by the unitive light which resides there. The progression from the literal level of the scriptural narrative to the unitive center is analogous to this movement from the surface to the center of the person.

29. The vocation of the human person in the world, rooted in this unitive center, can be conceived as a reintegration of the divided world within one's own person. With the coming of the unitive Word into the world in a human person (Jesus), and then progressively in other persons, this vocation of "microcosm and mediator"[15] takes on a new fullness.

⊕

30. The coming of the unitive Word into the world, and the gift of the divine Spirit, introduce a new order of *freedom* into humanity. Freedom, so valued in the modern west, is a complex reality. There is external freedom—political, economic; there is a psychological free-

dom—from complexes, compulsions, obsessions, dependencies; and there is a spiritual freedom. The freedom brought by Christ operates on all of these levels, but on each at a different pace. The spiritual freedom conferred by the Holy Spirit was experienced immediately by early Christians, and brought with it a psychological freedom. The ideal of political, economic and cultural freedom for all has only become a goal of practical action much later.

31. The concept itself of freedom has become very ambiguous in modern individualistic, or atomized, societies.[16] Here, beneath an appearance of complete personal (political and economic) freedom, walls of isolation and the bonds of addiction and unconscious dependencies paralyze the hearts and minds of great numbers of persons to the extent that they often behave as anonymous masses.

32. Human freedom will only be complete on the other side of death, when the body itself is transformed in the Spirit (Rom 8:21). Meanwhile it is the *spiritual* freedom, immediate fruit of this indwelling Spirit which is the concern of the New Testament and of John. The roots of this freedom are that Spirit which is the very freedom of God, and the unitive Word in which the person is radically re-created. The "freedom of the glory of the children of God" (Rom 8:21) is the royal freedom of the Son of God, shared by those who are baptized into him.

33. Interior *freedom* is equivalent to the *unity* of the person: these are two faces of the same reality. This unity does not begin within the person but is, at its root, the divine unity itself; and here is rooted not only the person but all of creation. The children of God are radically freed into the kingdom of their Father—made free, at the core of their being, in all that which belongs to the Creator.

⊕

34. *Glory*, in the New Testament revelation, becomes the inner life of the human heart.[17] Glory is the obverse—the secret name—of faith and hope, and the precise ironical sum of our state of eclipse. Glory is not a word to which we can immediately respond in a time of disillusion, of grim realisms, of human emptiness.

35. *Scientism*[18] has imposed upon many people in our time a "single vision"[19] which has banished both beauty and spiritual presence

from the world. Under this shadow *glory* can easily seem but the tarnished gold of past ages of privilege. Or it is seen as the product of a pathology—comic and familiar—the projection of a starved soul which has somehow been frustrated in the fulfillment of its needs. If we are loyal pupils of our culture, we are likely to believe that it is only the *needs*—the palpable, down-to-earth needs—that are real.

36. We live today at the apogee of glory. At the full length of the sun's arm, in a time of deconstruction and disillusion, of "hermeneutic suspicion," all the old glory is drowned in disgrace and disgust. For it has not, finally, lifted up the human heart. The glory of past great ones, of the towering nobles, of the elite, which oppressed the common truth for so long, has been discarded.

37. It has proved very difficult to conceive of the glory of *God* freed from the weight of human inflation, self-serving and complacency, and still more difficult to allow *human* glory to exist, to be imagined, in the light of faith. The regal glory which the fathers saw in the Son of Man was inflated into caricature in the interests of self-serving institutional religion, the institutional ego. The glory of Adam was forgotten, as the beginning too was swallowed by the dark theological cloud of traditional guilt. We have frequently made the glory of God and the true glory of the human person incompatible, mutually contradictory, in our meanness of imagination. But in proportion as glory is excluded from the Christian vision, the heart of Christianity is suffocated.

38. Christian religion has often appeared the enemy of glory, as its ministers preached with too little enlightenment a gospel of renunciation and human subjection. A grim and legalistic religion has often been a stranger to the heart and served to turn the modern world away from the light of the Word within its own heart, turning the wine into water once again. But glory is the *raison d'être* of Christianity, the beginning and end of sacred history, the inner spark of faith.

39. For glory dwells within the *Word*. It is the recognition of the divine glory in the human person Jesus that is the new birth of faith. And it is the Word, become man in Jesus, who baptizes with the veritable glory. He is the new Adam who has risen from the waters of death and put on once again the wedding garment, and poured out his new wine for the guests. He is David, whose anointing rises up within his followers, and lights them secretly from within. He brings a *revolution* of glory, which no longer comes from above, but *rises up from within* earth and body, common as water and free as the air.

40. Glory is the secret thread of all our hope. It is the hope too great to hope, the thrilling hidden string of every dramatic triumph which reflects "that which God has prepared..." (1 Cor 2:7-10). Glory is the music of resurrection in the human heart, that which we desire with every conscious breath.

41. Glory is essentially related to the *feminine*—and at the same time it is the crown of the masculine. It is the sun's glint on the edge of courage, of enterprise, of exploit—and the interior spring of love. There is a marriage here, and its wine.

42. Within language there is a knowledge of glory. This knowledge tends toward the realization of glory as the stem tends toward the rose blossom. The words of the poet aspire to glory as grass rising through the earth toward the sun. Whenever poetry finds its voice once again, what is heard is glory or its echo. Poetry brings to theology its sense of glory—something urgently needed in our time.

43. In the darkness of our time, when our hunger and thirst for glory is nearly forgotten, our secret inner knowledge of the glory comes to a crystalline clarity and sureness once again. We often seem to live in an exile, a dark night, of glory, when our splendid temple with its remembered gold is but a mockery, and human fires glow only briefly until they die. These things must diminish so that the true glory may appear in its truth.

44. Glory is precisely the unseen face of faith, the hidden focus of our vital movement, the golden denouement of the drama of dramas which is ordinary life. In the wise roots of our faith a sureness gathers. Glory and justice are hiddenly one; humanity and the invisible glory are co-extensive: Glory and human life are related with the logic, the organic inevitability of flower and stem. Glory is the beginning and the end of our day of life. Words, like pebbles turning in the hem of the moving sea, glimmer for a moment and are still. And then we hear only the cries of children and of birds, as the sun descends to meet that gleaming sea. Day whispers to day the huge and unspeakable birth toward which we move.

⊕

45. *Love* **and the unitive are two names, or two sides, of the same reality.** Inconceivable as it would be to interpret John's gospel without mentioning *love*, we have given little attention to this central Johannine term. Instead, we have spoken continually of the *unitive*. The divine Unitive is the beginning and end, the basis and the goal of love. Divine love would seem to be the divine Unitive in its active expression: the Unitive *asserted* or considered dynamically.

46. The new *commandment* **of love is inseparable from the** *gift* **of love.** In John's gospel, Jesus' explicit teaching on love is heard only at the end of his life, during the *supper*. It is at this time that the divine Unitive is about to be poured into the world—as the *new reality* in the world which will make this *new commandment* possible. We can be enjoined to love one another in truth only when this love can move within a pre-existing unity, can be the actualization of that which is already latent, invisibly present.

47. Jesus, the new Adam, gathers humanity into himself; his commandment of love is a corollary of this action of the unitive Word. "Abide in me as I abide in you. . . . I am the vine, you are the branches. Those who abide in me and I in them bear much fruit..." (15:4-5). Here, in the metaphor of the vine, we see once again how the sacramentality of John is not primarily a matter of distinct references to baptism and eucharist, here and there in the gospel. The eucharistic reality permeates this whole discourse on love and communion, on indwelling and on this inherence in the body of Jesus.

⊕

48. In Jesus Christ the creative Word of God has come into the world. If we have often forgotten that Jesus is the *Logos*, the Word, we have systematically forgotten that Jesus is the *creative* Word. It is in the modern west, where the unitive *Logos* seems to have gone into total eclipse, that we have witnessed an unprecedented flourishing of *human* creativity, as if this eclipse of the unitive center were the necessary condition for the liberation of the creative potential of humanity into its outward expression.

49. After this historic blossoming of human creativity it is not possible for us to return to the constrictions of an earlier age of supposedly "unitive" culture. Rather we must rediscover, within our own creativity, the creative light and energy of God.

50. Two contrasting forces operate in history: counter to the gravitational force pulling back toward the unitive source and center is the outward, centrifugal force of creativity. It is in the modern west that this conflict has become most evident and that the creative force has achieved an unprecedented dominance. It has been particularly difficult for the great religious institutions of Christianity to recognize and affirm this creative movement working within human history. Institutional voices and conservative currents both in the Orthodox churches and the Roman Catholic Church have resisted the creative movement as anti-religious and contrary to the spirit of faith. Only very recently[20] has the Catholic Church been able to turn about and express itself as favoring the creative activities of humanity—particularly in science and technology.

51. The incarnation of the *Logos* is the pivot around which turns the history of the world. In the vision of Owen Barfield, this history is understood in terms of human *creativity*. Before the incarnation of the Word in Jesus Christ, humanity was the pupil of the cosmos—taking into itself that which the visible world had to teach it. When Jesus appeared, this dynamic was *reversed*. Jesus brought into the world the creative light and energy of the divine Word, and injected this like yeast into the dough of humanity. From that time forward, *the human person is creator* in the world, and the divine creative light and energy flow out from him into the rest of creation.[21] The *beginning* comes also into *my* mind and hands—so that I myself may become a creator, and participate in the new creation of the world.

52. The revolution in human life which consists in the discovery of a creative power within the person now expresses itself not only in scientific achievements or in the products of the poetic imagination, but in broad, highly conscious movements toward the actual *transformation of society and culture*. This is a key turning point in history and in the development of human consciousness, opening the way to a true anticipation of the "new creation" in this world.

53. To the extent that such a new birth is to take place through human efforts, it will demand the activation not only of this cre-

ative power but of the two companion gifts as well: the primary sense of communion and prophetic critical insight.

54. Poetry witnesses to—and sometimes enacts—the beginning, the new creation that is within the human breast and that must ignite the world around with its flame. While poetry seems—today, particularly—the weakest of things, it paradoxically expresses something essential to a life which is truly human. We would die in the weight of oldness without the breeze and glimmer of the "thoughts of the heart," without some reminder of that which is born freshly within us at each moment. *Imagination*, then, becomes the garden at whose center the tree greens and blossoms anew. And its green fire kindles the world at its core. In the creative act, everything is drawn together for a moment into the unitive energy of this center.

55. A meaningful *history* of Christianity could be written in terms of *the Unitive* and its vicissitudes throughout the centuries. As we look at a few of the critical crystallizations and junctures in this history, our starting place is with the unitive vision of John and the early Syriac tradition, which we have just examined. Here we find a consciousness and a vision of life still centered and illumined by this new unitive reality which has come into the world in Jesus and been received by the individual and the community through faith and baptism.

56. A second moment or face of this history is in the patristic theology centered in the Word of God, the *Logos* incarnate in Jesus Christ. This tradition is directly and obviously *Johannine*, and it is taught already by the church fathers of the second century. Greatest among these is Irenaeus of Lyons, who has been called the father of Christian theology. Irenaeus' vision is of a breadth and vigor comparable only to that of John himself; being, like that of the early Syrians, almost entirely free from intrusive philosophical structures, his thought moves with the Word itself.

57. The *recapitulation*[22] of all things in the incarnate Word—that central concept of Irenaeus' theology—corresponds to the gathering into the Word of everything which was created through the Word. Thus, as we have seen in our study of John, the first creation—divided and scattered—is drawn together into a *unitive* new creation. The power and comprehensive simplicity of Irenaeus' *recapitulation* are often lost

when it is analyzed into a series of concepts as if it were a system, a conceptual structure, rather than a synthetic insight corresponding to the scope and movement of the *Logos* itself.

58. Cosmos and history intersect in the unitive *Logos*. This Word of God, from which the cosmos has sprung and which is still present within it, enters the world anew in the inspired utterances of certain persons, and finally in the form of one specific human person (see Heb 1:1-3). The humans who populate this world determine their own destinies by their response to this Word: whether the immanent Word or the Word as revealed in the biblical Word and finally in Jesus. And out of this encounter of cosmos and historical Word, a new cosmos begins to be born. This new creation in the unitive Word is the movement of John's gospel—and gives birth to a new vision of *history*.

59. Human history itself moves between these two worlds of first creation and new creation, and the principal tensions and conflicts of history are expressions of the basic tension between these two worlds. The new world which is coming into being in the awareness and acceptance of the Word is ever opposed by a world which refuses this transformation and remains centered in itself and, therefore, ultimately in nothingness. In the New Testament this great drama is enacted in a plurality of symbolic forms—but principally in the struggle between the new Israel and the old Israel.

60. An *apophatic*[23] theology, or theology of unknowing, is the essential counterbalance to a *Logos* theology. Without the corrective of this divine darkness, even the unitive revelation is easily appropriated by the collective ego and transformed into human power.
In the Christian tradition Pseudo-Dionysius[24] is the pioneer explorer of this uncharted wilderness. Here union takes place beyond knowing. The apophatic current has deep roots in the religious tradition of Israel. Both the prohibition of images in the worship of Israel, and the development of the sabbath, reflect the awareness that God is *beyond* every representation, every mediation, every image and symbol and even every form of worship, every official mediation. This transcendence is implicit in the monotheism itself of Israel.[25]

61. In the religious traditions of Asia, an awareness that the Absolute is beyond every representation has been present from very early times. It is particularly important in *Buddhism*, which might be called the apophatic religion. Awareness of the immateriality and utter transcendence of ultimate reality is close to constituting the heart itself of Buddhism. It accounts for the silence which permeates Buddhist language, the indirectness and reticence with which Buddhism speaks of the final reality.

62. The apophatic dimension of Christian spirituality corresponds to the *Father*—that is, to the invisible *God*. Word and Spirit also, however, transcend all of their particular manifestations and expressions, and hence remain "unknown" even as they are known. This unknowing is, finally, *inherent in our knowledge of God*, whether as Father, Word or Spirit. This is obviously true in the life of faith; some of the fathers insist[26] that it will continue in the next life.

63. It is in the *Christian east* that the theology of unknowing has been most carefully preserved, and it is central to this tradition as it is central to monasticism. Vladimir Lossky speaks of "that apophatism which constitutes the fundamental characteristic of the whole theological tradition of the Eastern Church."[27]

64. *John the Baptist* is the archetypal figure of the apophatic in Christian tradition. He is the man of the wilderness who replies, "*I am not*," and who must decrease so that the Christ may increase. *Monasticism*, Christian or non-Christian, finds its basic orientation in the apophatic. It is the "apophatic life."

65. The apophatic and the unitive are two aspects of the same reality. It is only that One which is beyond every particularity who can contain all particularities. Philosophically this has been expressed in terms of the relationship of Being to beings, or of *esse*, or existence, to particular essence or quality. A corollary in the spiritual life is the inseparability of holiness or freedom or love from *detachment*.

66. Meister Eckhart[28] is the prime exponent of a unitive mysticism in western Christian tradition. His theology of principial, or unitive, consciousness is rooted in the Johannine doctrine of the Word that is eternally born of the Father. The Word, or Son, is born of a human mother in this world, and it is *in him* that we are born in God and God is born in us.

67. The eclipse of unitive vision in the modern world has been directly related to the movement *from wisdom to science* which has

transformed western theology since the thirteenth century.[29] While the ancient religious traditions, which have suddenly become present to us today, remain largely *wisdom* traditions (this is especially true, and most obvious, of the Asian traditions: Hinduism and Buddhism), Christianity (the larger historic churches, at least, and particularly Roman Catholicism) has appeared to the world in recent centuries largely as religious *institution*. The thought and preaching of Christianity in modern times have often either transmitted the doctrine of an authoritative institution in the terms of a theology claiming to be a science (i.e. scholasticism), or employed the concepts and theology of newer sciences to deconstruct this orthodox doctrine and to propose alternative visions.

68. With the division of eastern and western Christianity, the unitive Center of *Logos-Koinōnia* became quickly inconceivable to western theology. As the ever-delicate equilibrium between Johannine principle and Petrine principle was destroyed, ecclesiastical *authority* became more and more the sole point of orientation for the church.

69. The growth of this radical imbalance between the interior and exterior principles of unity constituted a decisive shift in the center of gravity of the western church, as represented by Roman Catholicism. The ontological primacy of the interior presence of a superior order of reality, the *koinōnia* of *Logos* and Spirit, was largely replaced by an institutional primacy: the absolute authority of official dogma and of hierarchy and its magisterium.[30] With increasing centralization of the church, this became more and more the magisterium and the authority of Rome.

70. The center, or principle of orientation, within Christianity has disappeared for a majority of the people of the west in *two stages*: first, the replacement of *Logos* and *koinōnia* by the vertical institutional principle, and, second, the discrediting of this vertical principle. In our own time, the credibility of the Roman principle of orientation has been challenged and diminished even for many within the Catholic Church.[31] This had already happened in the sixteenth century for those who joined the Protestant reform.

71. We live today in a situation of polarization consequent upon this loss of center, and in need of a new vision, a Christian unitive wisdom capable of bringing meaning to the creative movement of the world's historical development. Western Christianity tends to be torn between two opposing forces and two hostile camps. One extreme party immobilizes itself in one or another form of fundamentalism—biblical or institutional—and rejects all but superficial questioning. At the other extreme are those who have definitively rejected both the institutional center and the authority of scripture.

⊕

72. A theological vision which is—at least relatively—*unitive* is natural to eastern Christianity. Eastern Christianity may be called Johannine, in contrast to a Petrine Roman Catholic Christianity, though such simplifications must be used with caution.

73. The theology of eastern Christianity, while less conditioned by institutional elements than the western vision, is constricted by its own cultural boundaries. The Greek theological tradition, for example, is conditioned by the intellectualism, the dualism and patriarchal or masculine bias of the Greek philosophers. Much eastern thought has been colored both by Platonism and by Neoplatonism. If *institution* has been the primary constricting factor in the Roman Catholic Church, it is *tradition* which has played the same conservative role in the east.[32]

74. Eastern Christianity offers a unified theological vision which faithfully reflects the Johannine teaching—also in its *unitive* depth and its cosmic scope. At the same time, the *historical and developmental* dimension which is implicit in John as well as in Paul usually finds too little place in eastern thought. It is as if the holy *koinōnia* of the church, once established by Jesus, were to *remain*, unchanged (see Jn 21:22), until his return.

75. It is in the *Russian* east that the *historical* drama of Christianity does find expression.[33] At the same time there is a much fuller realization of the *sophianic feminine* than could ever find expression in the Byzantine tradition.[34]

76. Russian writers also complete the Greek patristic tradition—with its platonic intellectualism and monastic angelism—by restoring an incarnational balance. The Russians translate a Byzantine anthropology centered in the spiritual intellect or *nous* into a vision of the human person which is centered in the *heart*—as the biblical tradition had maintained.

77. Russia has, in this way, played a mediatory role between east and west—bringing together the crystalline theological nucleus of Byzantine theology and the sense of historical progression and destiny which lives in the western soul. Russian writers have, in several ways then, brought the Johannine tradition of eastern Christianity back into the context of the fullness and the materiality of human life. There is great potential for the west in this spiritual and theological tradition which is once again a practical and *experiential* Christianity, and which relates to the feminine, the heart, the body and the earth.[35]

78. Among the world's great religious traditions we may distinguish (1) the religions of the *Word*—Judaism, Christianity, Islam— which are based upon a divine revelation through the Word; and (2) the religions of *immanence*: that is of a cosmic or immanent or interior and non-dual manifestation[36] of God or of ultimate reality (see above, p. 239). Hinduism and Buddhism would belong to this second group.[37] The religions of immanence are, for us, the religions of the *east*, while it is chiefly in the *west* that the religions of the Word have spread. Consequently *east*, for Christians and Jews, easily connotes *divine immanence*, whether this is explicit, as in Hinduism, or only expressed through paradox, as in Buddhism.

79. Among the western religions themselves—and within each of them—there is discernible a further spectrum: between a faith which bases itself upon a hard and literal interpretation of the biblical Word, and therefore may be called *fundamentalistic*, and a faith which develops through symbolic and unitive senses of the Word, and is therefore *sapiential*. The sapiential tradition represents an integration of Word and immanence. It is *John* which is the gospel of this sapiential tradition—and of the marriage of Word and immanence—in Christianity. This integrative potency of John's gospel (with which should be joined the first letter) remains, in the twentieth century, what it was in the second century.

80. Today it is largely through contact with the non-Christian religious traditions of the east that the western world becomes once again aware of unitive mystical experience and unitive vision. It is from the east that we hear the ancient language of the uncarved block, the beginning, the unitive source.

81. If a new Christian theological wisdom is to be born from this encounter of west and east, it is likely that the pivotal center of this

new development will be, once again, the unitive and immanent *Word* of John's gospel.[38] It is obvious that John's vision has never been fully assimilated in Christian tradition. This Johannine "hermeneutic problem," if we may call it that, has reached an unprecedented acuteness in the rationalist-empiricist culture of our own century. As, through contact with the east, however, we become once more aware of the unitive reality, the possibility emerges that the Johannine unitive Word may be glimpsed in the west in something more like its full dimensions. It is a west not of the fourth century or the twelfth century, however, but of the twentieth century, that encounters this unitive Word now. It is a differentiated—and often a fragmented—consciousness and person who awakens to this Word.

⊕

82. **Human sexuality occupies a central place in the dynamic of new creation in Christ.** In Christianity, therefore, should emerge the first fruits of a new human sexuality, in which the glory of God begins to appear. And yet this theological truth has never yet been confronted broadly and openly by the church, and this potential has rarely been realized. An understanding of this eschatological destiny of sexuality has been developed primarily in terms of a life of virginity or celibacy. The positive and creative potential of relationship between man and woman has, until now, remained unexplored by theology and—without a context of understanding and support—too seldom realized among Christians.

Here the paradox and tension of *incarnation* are most acute. The war between "flesh" and spirit is most continually and intimately experienced in the sphere of sexuality (see Rom 7:14–8:13; Gal 5:16-26).

Nowhere does Christianity find its encounter with the modern world more difficult than in the two—intimately related—areas of sexuality and of authority. The confrontation and controversy around sexual issues exists *within* the church also, becoming one of the chief causes of division and disaffection. While the inability to realize the creative potential of human sexuality is not peculiar to Christianity, our reading of John's gospel has suggested that it is in the mystery of Christ that the key to this realization is offered to us.

83. **The gospel's realization in the world depends upon a transformation of the relationship between man and woman.** "There is no longer Jew or Greek, there is no longer slave or free, there is no longer male or female; for all of you are one in Christ Jesus" (Gal 3:28). Of

the three lines of unitive revolution projected in these words of Paul, the transcending of the *gender* distinction is probably the deepest and most difficult and slowest of accomplishment. Sexuality is written more deeply and indelibly into the embodied being of humanity than race or social class.

84. The church, founded upon this gospel of the primacy of communion, finds its deepest identity to be "feminine." The external forms and the organizational structures of the Christian churches are cast in predominantly patriarchal forms. This is particularly apparent in Orthodoxy and Catholicism, where all the institutional power is vested ultimately in a male celibate hierarchy. It is difficult for the transforming presence of communion, which is the heart of the church, to realize itself with any fullness and freedom through these frameworks.

85. It is the thoroughly masculine, patriarchal tradition of the biblical revelation and the culture of Israel which is the background for the appearance of Jesus and his revelation. The biblical literature itself is thoroughly pervaded by the patriarchal spirit of the culture in which it was written, and its image of God is emphatically masculine. Aside from a few scattered expressions, it is only in the *Sophia* of the late wisdom tradition (and parallel images such as the *Shekinah*) that the feminine aspect of God emerges.

86. At the turning point of history, in the unitive revolution of Jesus, the gift of the unitive divine Feminine liberates the human unitive feminine into its destined place. Human sexuality is thus radically renewed, and released to rise to its creative function. At the same time sexuality is interiorized; through the symbol the unitive reality is manifested and freed.

87. The revelation of the divine unitive Feminine, of the new *Sophia*, is expressed only in an implicit and cryptic form in the New Testament. This is true even in the gospel of John, where its expression is fullest. Despite the consistent masculine code of expression of the Hebrew and Christian scriptures, an identification of the Holy Spirit with the immanent divine Wisdom, and consequently with the divine Feminine, can be inferred.

Among the New Testament writings, only John's gospel reveals the sexual-spiritual revolution which Jesus has set afoot, and this usually in an implicit manner. This revelation is of extreme and direct importance to our situation and our problems at the end of this second millennium.

88. In the Christian east, and with less continuity in the west,[39] **a sophianic theology gradually evolves.** A pivotal—though little recognized—western development of this New Testament revelation appears in the poetry of Dante Alighieri. The feminine mediation of divinity, the sacramentality and spiritual vocation of woman, the divine Feminine which lies behind these expressions, emerge to the light in Dante's vision of Beatrice and the poetry which it generates.[40]

89. Feminine consciousness and feminine psyche are characterized by their *unitive* and *interior* modalities[41]**—as well as by the life-favoring qualities which have long been attributed to the feminine.** The new science of psychology which was born at the threshold of the twentieth century, out of the desperate situation of repression and oblivion in which the psyche had been placed in the west, has inaugurated a new discovery of the psyche itself and with it a gradually developing new knowledge of the feminine.

90. Among the major cultural changes happening today around the world, the emergence of woman and of the feminine may be the most broadly and deeply significant. It urges us to take a new look into the depths of the New Testament revelation, the work of Jesus—and particularly into John's gospel. The fullness of humanity is to be realized in the marriage of masculine and feminine, as an epiphany of the eternal marriage of *Logos* and *Sophia*, and as an expression of the wedding of the creation with its God. The emergence and liberation of the feminine is, from our viewpoint, the historical axis of this development, and arrives at a quantum threshold in our time. And so a fresh face of Christianity—and of Christ—begins to appear today.

91. Today it is largely through the voice of *Sophia*, the immanent feminine divine Wisdom, that God speaks to us. The modality of divine revelation is not totally fixed, but is varied in the course of history. In the nearly two millennia since the writing of John's gospel, the Sun of the *Logos* which rose in the east has crossed the sky and disappeared once again into the earth. Now the revelation comes to us largely *from below and from within.* And yet it has *ever* been this divine Wisdom which has made present the Unitive within the world.

At a time when half of the western world has been thoroughly immunized to the *word*, preached from outside, this voice is heard from *within*. This is the revelation that is happening all the time, coming up through the ground like water, or like the shoots of new life reaching into the sunlight. This revelation is to be discovered *within* ourselves and within one another,[42] and *through* ourselves and one another.

92. This immanent revelation is at once unitive and creative, feminine and masculine. The creative imagination and audacious energy (the divine creativity now immanent in human persons) by which the world is gradually transformed into a home for humanity and for all the living creatures is the active partner. Within this innovative intelligence dwells its guide and animatrix, the immanent feminine which is the unitive faculty of human personality, and within which, in turn, dwells the unitive divine Feminine, *Sophia*.

93. Corresponding to the emergent feminine, we find in John's gospel indications of a new realization of the *masculine*—this too with particular relevance to the problems of today.
We have presented the drama of John's gospel largely in terms of the emergence of a unitive *feminine* principle. In the context of our own patriarchal civilization and its history, this accent on liberation and integration of the long-obscured feminine has been natural at the present moment. It would also have been possible, however, to consider the same theological drama in terms of a newly emergent *masculine*. The Johannine figures of John the Baptist and Jesus contain the elements of a vision of the masculine side of human character which is as significant for our time (marked by a "crisis of masculinity") as is the image of the feminine which we have found in John.
We can distinguish three aspects or dimensions in "the masculine" as manifested by the Johannine Jesus. The first two are also evident in John the Baptist, as he is presented in the fourth gospel.

a. taking a stand against the "world";

b. a transparency of self; a transparent identity;

c. an immanent creative relation to the world (cosmos, creation), expressed in a transformative power which operates within other persons and, more broadly, within the creation itself.

As, early in the synoptic gospels, we see John the Baptist preaching repentance in the wilderness to those who come out to him from the "world," he is an unsurpassed example of the first characteristic (a). In the spirit of the prophets, he accuses the world and its rulers of their sins, and this costs him his life. John typifies the masculine "voice in the wilderness" or "light in the darkness": witnessing to the truth, without support, in an indifferent or hostile world. In Jesus we see the same prophetic witness and confrontation continued to its logical climax upon the cross. It is a *masculine* vocation, this heroic dualism—this standing for one world within another world which is opposed to it.

This requires a transparency of soul (b), for its truth is possible only for the man who seeks not his own glory but the glory of the One who sent him. This transparency is expressed in the Baptist's negative responses to those who ask about him and his mandate (1:19-23), and in his giving way before the one who comes after him. John administers the symbol of a similar transparency in baptizing with water those who come to him confessing their sins. When Jesus receives this baptism, the scene is illumined by the manifestation of his identity as beloved Son (synoptics). In John's gospel this divine identity is expressed at every turn. Jesus' transparency goes further than this, however, for he incessantly speaks of the Father and attributes everything he has and does to the Father. The transparency is the obverse of the light of knowledge: the Baptist and Jesus, in very different degrees, know the One who has sent them.

The *signs* of Jesus (the Baptist "did no signs") point to something beyond these two characteristics. John was the friend of the Bridegroom; Jesus is the Bridegroom himself. That is, he has the Bride—that is, the Spirit. And therefore he has the Bride that is the church, that is humanity, that is the cosmos itself. Jesus' signs are the indications that the time has come for the transformation of the world to begin. This is the third aspect (c) of the dualistic vocation of man (which, in each case—and most perfectly in Jesus—is in the service of the *Unitive*), this mediation between two worlds which is the tree-like masculine life. From within the old world, Jesus brings the new world into being. In the midst of darkness, he stands as light and creates the light.[43]

The new masculine which is fully evident in the *risen* Jesus is the *non-dual*, or "wedded" masculine, whose tidal grasp is *within* all beings—particularly the human beings who have received his Spirit. This is the final "dramatic hero" whose appearance itself stirs all things *from within*, whose power is the immanent unitive.

It is *this* "*masculine*" which belongs to those who believe in Christ —and yet which is so tragically lacking today in the church and in the western world itself. Christianity, if it would flourish once again, must come to know itself, distinguish itself from the "world" around it by its knowledge of that which is within it. And then it must make present in the world this Christ whose creative power operates not from above and outside humanity but from deep within—beyond every negation, in the unitive core of the human person.

⊕

94. The human person is a knowledge-creature, a truth-being, and lives always within the paradox of a knowing ignorance and an ignorant knowledge. Human life moves upon this line of consciousness, of the assimilation of the *light* as food, as growth, becoming, birth, as self. We are beings of light, though we come knowing not whence we come. Our end, or good, or salvation, our hope or our life, comes to us as light, as illumination. And so theology speaks of *revelation*, and our deeper life is a life of *faith* which begins with a *Word* of God.

95. Jesus comes as *personal unitive Word*: the Word in which God becomes one with the person who receives it. And this is a totally *new* event in the world, even though it culminates a history of lesser self-communications of God through his Word, in the history of Israel.

96. Today, in the west, the tension and the irony of knowledge and ignorance has reached a climactic intensity. We have wrested from nature a knowledge which empowers us to transform—and virtually to destroy—the world, and yet we have become progressively more estranged from the knowledge which relates most deeply and personally to ourselves, to the center of our being—the knowledge which is life and fullness. The western polarization between *science* and *wisdom* has come to full maturity.

97. Meanwhile the west, in the light of the immanent Word, has developed for humanity indispensable tools: a sharp critical reason, a ruthless grasp of factual and empirical truth; and in the west there begins to emerge a broad human self-possession as *creator*. Another gain, paradoxically, is an experiential awareness of the value of the human person and the richness and profundity of individual experience.

98. The old, unworldly wisdoms were often pre-critical and unconcerned with distinguishing symbol or myth from existential reality.

A purely symbolic biblical interpretation easily accommodates itself to the old structures and dynamics of power and exploitation, leaving undisturbed the incumbency of the strong and the wealthy. When the gospel word is heard at once with simplicity and with the *critical realism* which has developed in the west, it becomes again a sword cutting straight through to the heart and threatening the roots of social injustice. The way to the transformation of human society begins to be cleared.

99. As the Word joins itself, in Jesus, to the human person and to the cosmos itself, the *entire spectrum* of knowledge becomes illumined and oriented. Unitive knowledge, symbolic knowledge, rational knowledge and sense knowledge shine with a new intensity in the presence of the unitive light of the immanent Word.

100. In the incarnation of the Word there is initiated a *marriage* of reason, rationality, the bright masculine daylight knowledge, with the dark immanent feminine, concrete knowledge which is most familiar in symbolic art, in poetic literature. Today there emerges once again the aspiration toward such an integration of science with imagination, vision with music, and knowledge with the heart. It is both from the side of our poets and from that of our scientists that movements toward such a reunion appear.

101. Not only reason or mind, but *psyche* is eye and ear, organ of knowledge. In our modern western world, however, psyche has been isolated—ignored, suppressed, so that its gentle inner voice could not be heard, and consequently *"man's"* knowledge has become shallow, metallic, opaque and brittle.

102. Heartless *power*—disguised with varying degrees of subtlety and success—still rules the world, and knowledge is its priest and sorcerer. There is an analytical knowledge which is perfectly indifferent to genuine human values, and so is able to adapt itself perfectly to the ends of ruthless self-interest. Characteristic of this ironic knowledge is its *divisiveness*. This is the knowledge which becomes ever sharper, and ever more blind. The known is gradually disintegrated into a pyramid of sand, ultimately meaningless. Humanity itself, in the course of the same process, becomes divided into living atoms; these in turn become mindlessly aggregated into progressively more ominous political monsters. Meanwhile the fabric of human communication becomes dampened until the spark of truth can no longer start a fire. The orchestrators of darkness are smooth, appealing, bulging with high purpose.

103. The knowledge which has come into the world in Jesus is a knowledge which ripens into *communion.* This is its distinctive fruit and work. This knowledge is continually dying into that knowledge which surpasses it, which is love. This is the *power* which stands in perennial contrast and confrontation with the power of the world. Jesus brings at once the sword of critical, prophetic insight and the cup of communion.

104. The west knows a history of social and political revolutions in which, at some level, there has worked the ferment of this knowledge of communion which came in Jesus. This *incarnate unitive knowledge* embodied—still inarticulate—in the people, in the poor, more widely finds a voice today. Networks of communication and common concern come into being. Courageous voices speak this truth of fire again and again, giving hope that the new creation of humanity is afoot on a larger scale than ever before.

105. In contrast to a western rationalistic knowledge which has become separated from life, the wisdom traditions propose that *knowledge is life.* For Christianity, *faith* is that knowledge which is life; but Christians of earlier centuries knew also an experiential *gnōsis* which accompanies growth in the life of faith.

106. Besides the unitive wisdom of the Spirit and the dualistic knowledge of science, there is also a knowledge or consciousness, born in the shadow of the fatal tree and therefore in the shadow of death, which is essentially egocentric and paranoid. Human life is fundamentally altered by the fact of death, the concrete and inescapable sign of our "fallen state," which ever exerts upon the human heart its forces of fear and anxiety, of selfish concern and greed, generating hostility and division (see the "works of the flesh" in Gal 5:19-21; Heb 2:14-15; Jas 3:14-15). This mentality is basically invasive and exploitative, seeking advantage and concentrating wealth and power. Standing in contrast to this is that knowledge—or wisdom—of the fundamental gratuitousness of being, and the basic unity of all being and life, which expresses itself in favoring life, giving life.

107. When, as in our modern west, human rationality becomes completely removed from the context of wisdom, it becomes easily enlist-

ed in the service of power and privilege: of self-seeking interests which are the perennial enemies of life, communion and human development. Thus the gift of *human creativity* becomes itself turned against that movement of new creation in the world which is animated by the Holy Spirit. This has been very evident in our time as science and technology have become largely appropriated to the service of the great military-industrial-political establishments which are inherently indifferent—and therefore in effect hostile—to the values of human life.

⊕

108. The gospel of John becomes a key to the reading of the whole corpus of the Bible. This role is analogous to that of the prologue with respect to the gospel narrative.

109. It is the Johannine revelation of the *unitive Word* of God, incarnate in the world in Jesus Christ, and identified with the fullness of the revelation and self-communication of God, which opens the scriptures to their inner meaning. When Jesus is conceived as embodying the divine Unitive, revealing it and communicating it to humanity, many of the difficulties of Jesus' words as recorded in the gospels can be resolved.[44]

110. The *interior unitive divine Feminine*—identified with the unitive Word and hidden within it—is a second interpretive key. This is the inner reality of the Word and of God, which remains concealed in the Bible until inferred through sympathetic intuition, implication and symbolic inference. A sense of this principle makes possible the opening up of the thoroughly "patriarchal" exterior shell of the biblical word to its essentially communicative and unitive core: the sophianic wine.

111. The New Testament is *ironic*, and this in a subtle and pervasive way—this is ultimately not a stylistic but a theological quality. The words of Jesus which seem so hard—conveying to our naive imaginations the image of a harsh and merciless God (see especially Jesus' parables in the synoptic gospels)—are tuned to our own deep paranoia. To pierce to their interior meaning is to experience a liberating revolution, a penetration into the loving innocence deep in our own hearts (see n. 109 above and the corresponding note 44). This irony of the words of Jesus is analogous to the paradox of the zen Buddhist *koan*, or the paradoxes of other wisdom traditions. The humor and

sapiential salt which we often find in the literature of these traditions appears to be missing in the gospels—until we grasp this principle of Jesus' irony. The humor of the gospels is deep and mixed with sorrow and tragedy: it rests upon the basic paradox of the light shining, unseen, in a darkness which believes itself to be light.

The seeds of this irony are present in the very core of the New Testament—consider Philippians 2:6-11, the Pauline text so central to the liturgy of Holy Week, or the Johannine words, of equal theological importance, "*The Word became flesh.*" The "word of the cross" is *essentially* an ironic word, as Paul's own words make very clear (1 Cor 1:18–2:8).

The *Johannine* irony is pervasive, deriving from the fullness of unitive light and life which is present in Jesus and flashes out at each confrontation with the puniness and the malice of human minds and hearts. The "realized eschatology" of John demands an ironic language.

112. In John's gospel, the *symbolic* language of the Bible is brought back to its source in the Word. The centrality and finality of the Genesis symbolism in John—the images of garden, river and tree, of man and woman in the glory of innocence—express this new closeness of creation and Creator, the intimacy which lies within the creation vision and which, in Jesus, becomes union. And so John becomes also a key to the *symbolism* of the scriptures.

113. Two parallel expressions of the *materialization* of the biblical word in modern times are an over-analytical scientistic method and the fundamentalism which is a reaction to this critical method. A primary attention to the unity of the Word and to its symbolic language is needed to confront both these forms of literalism.

114. A contemporary *sapiential* method of interpretation would allow the scientific-critical method to play its proper role—and would employ its results—while integrating these results in a perspective of *theological imagination* which corresponds to the nature of the biblical literature itself.

115. John's gospel distinguishes itself from the other three gospels by its radical *Christocentricity.* The Johannine Jesus teaches nothing which is not himself—what should he communicate but the Word? His only moral teachings are faith and love, which are modes of union with his own being, modes of living in the unitive Word. This absolute or unitive Christology becomes a knife which cuts through many complexities elsewhere in the New Testament: Jesus himself is the light to which all questions must be brought for their resolution.

116. **Related to this maximal Christology is the more general** *maximalism* **of John.** If our interpretation of the fourth gospel has continually seemed to skirt the border of excess, this appearance of exaggeration reflects the absolute quality of the Christ-event in the Johannine vision itself. We have attempted to express this in terms of a new creation and of the one unitive revolution. The words of Jesus in Revelation, "See, I am making all things *new*" (Rev 21:5), would not be inappropriate to the Jesus of the fourth gospel. The power and glory contained in the "news" that John is communicating are smothered much more successfully by a disintegrative analysis than by hermeneutic "optimism" or poetic lyricism.

117. **The Pauline and Johannine expressions of the one Christ-mystery are complementary and dialectical, and their relationship may be conceived in terms of the** *masculine* **and** *feminine* **poles of consciousness.** Both Paul and John return again and again both to the *center* and to the *whole* of this Christ-mystery or Christ-event. Paul, however, tends to focus upon one or another expression of the center, while John tends to bring out the presence of the whole at each point in his text. Both for Paul and for John it is Jesus Christ who is center, and who also embraces the whole within himself. Paul, however, tends to see the center itself more distinctly, standing out from the whole. While from his objective or cosmic perspective this center will most likely be presented as Jesus Christ on the cross, Paul will sometimes write on a more subjective and personal level, and then the center may be the decisive moment of faith and illumination. For John, this center—the Word, the *I Am* which is incarnate in Jesus, the paschal crossing of his death and resurrection, the personal experience of faith and baptism—is continually seen as *identical* with the whole, drawing the whole into itself. John's vision remains more consistently a *unitive* vision than does that of Paul. While Paul returns from time to time to a consideration of linear history in the light of its dramatic break in Christ, in John we seem to hear rather of the final emergence of that which has been latent—and obscurely known—from the beginning. The communal perspective in John remains more simple and undifferentiated than in Paul—who is, after all, often providing specific moral instruction for his communities. John's discourse itself seems to be permeated with a unitive light which would quite naturally express itself in *koinōnia*. Differences are largely soft-

ened if not dissolved in the unbounded light of the *Logos* which bathes his entire field of vision. It is natural that *Protestantism*, with its masculine selective focus and dualism, its emphasis on individual faith, should have originated in connection with the doctrine of Paul, while *Orthodoxy*, with its primal unitive perspective and "feminine" disregard for focus and for univocal structures, should remain ever the Johannine church.

118. It is love for the scriptures, and engagement with the word of God, which invokes the light of interpretation. An enthusiasm for the word, which is, at the same time, an open passion for the truth, is the subjective "principle of interpretation" which gathers in the harvest.

⊕

119. The rediscovery of the unitive sense of John's gospel invites Christians to rediscover, in turn, *the baptismal reality*. Within each baptized person there dwells a new *beginning* which is to be drawn from again and again throughout life.

120. Discovery of the fullness of *eucharist* today would appear to be a still more difficult challenge: humanity is called to open itself to a unity which embraces all the peoples of the earth.[45] On the other hand, the essential human eucharistic acts—thanksgiving, self-offering and love—are what they were at the beginning, as revealed to us in the New Testament writings.

121. John's centric gospel is an initiation into this new sacramental life, which consists of finding the water and the fire once again at every point in the narrative of our life and of the history of our own time.

122. Practices of meditation originating in the Asian traditions have reintroduced the Unitive as an actuality for many westerners. Silent meditation is a way of descending to the level of unitive consciousness, so that one may live from this center. It does not supplant the Word, however. The two are complementary.

123. The Charismatic or Pentecostal movement has begun to rediscover the experiential reality of baptism, in its "baptism in the Holy Spirit." The movement is attended by dangers of a narrow conservatism and a fundamentalist interpretation of scripture, however, and is in need of the complement of a symbolic and sapiential theology. The unitive experience of the Spirit demands the full unitive scope of the Word and a psychological wisdom if it is to bring forth a genuine growth rather than surrendering its own inner law of freedom to an ironic confirmation of static cultural and psychological attitudes.

124. A Johannine spirituality would be a Christianity lived in the depth of unitive vision—lived from the unitive center which is the Word.

125. Basic to this way would be the regular *reading of scripture*— **and particularly the New Testament writings—with full attention to symbolism and unitive meaning.** To enter into the Word in depth may not be possible without some form of unitive meditation or prayer: a descent into the silent depths of the heart.

126. The Johannine Word is the *creative* **Word, and a Johannine spirituality will not be a system but a creative response to life and history from the unitive center.**

127. Along this way one *follows* **Jesus with Peter and, with the beloved disciple,** *remains* **at the place of the center: the fire and the meal by the sea.**

128. And one moves back and forth between the two poles of baptism and the eucharist. The movement alternates between the renewal of repentance and interiority which is its beginning, and the life of self-forgetful service and love which is its end.

$$\oplus$$

129. Along with the widespread rejection of institutional religious authority today, there is a widespread sense of the solidarity of all humanity, a sense of *communitas*[46] **or of communion.** Consciousness of the issues of social justice, and the concern for world peace, have grown so that for the first time a true popular *revolution*, on a broad basis, begins to be conceivable in our civilization.

130. There is a growing sense, in our time, of the sanctity of life and of the solidarity of all life. Sometimes this amounts to a worship of life. At the same time our civilization has attained a very considerable ability both to preserve and favor biological life—and to destroy it.

The rediscovery of our communion of life with the other creatures has secrets to reveal to us. In the light of the Word, we find here a glimpse into the Adamic vocation, the role of humanity in the world.

131. **A very significant expression of this new and unitive consciousness which is dawning at present was the Second Vatican Council as, in beginning to transcend a monolithic institutional vision of the church, it began to embrace the diversity of humanity. A truly *"world church"*[47] begins to be conceivable in Christianity.** This would be a church which truly incarnates itself in all the diversity of human cultures, rather than attempting to impose upon all peoples a single religious culture. In Vatican II the Catholic Church begins also to recognize the solidarity of all humankind, the positive value of all religious traditions and of all constructive human efforts.

132. **At the end of the second millennium the rediscovery of the *interior* unitive reality is accompanied by a new realization of the unity of human life on *planet earth*.** Technological achievements, while they have magnified the violence of human conflicts, have drawn the world together and made possible the beginning of a shared consciousness and vision.

133. **From different sides the unitive vision advances, extends its influence.** The energy of growing consciousness begins to glow along a broad horizon. In the midst of massive disillusionment, and despite failure after failure, new shoots of courage and imagination arise; across the ruined walls from face to face there begins to be communicated a new hope. Humanity begins to awaken, to become conscious of itself.

134. **To the poets of our time belongs the pregnant night.** But poetry must now rise from out of the earth: "no ideas but in things."[48] No spirit but that which breathes in the clay, patient, anonymous. Here in this dark, this soil, is our eucharist, roots feeding deep together. Blind process is our certainty, when one cannot yet speak of birth.

⊕

135. **The unitive Event is constitutive of a new creation. This is the basis of a radical *sacramentalism*.**

136. **Baptism and eucharist, in this view, represent the continuing *incarnation* of the Word and the equivalent process for the Spirit.**

Baptism and eucharist become the symbols and ecclesial media of this new creation which is an *immanent* creation.

137. The expression "Christian *initiation*" illuminates these two sacraments in expressing the *totality* which is involved in both of them. But the expression may be misleading insofar as it seems to limit the action of the two sacraments—or baptism, at least—to the *beginning* of Christian life. Both baptism and eucharist become the *continuing* source of new life or new creation, in the individual person, in the community and in the world.

138. Perhaps the eucharist represents the continuing incarnation of the Word in the new creation, and baptism represents the continuing indwelling and action of the Spirit in the new creation. The two sacraments relate as body and soul, matter and energy, but inseparably. Each of the two is continually discovered in the other. Baptism would correspond to the *feminine* dimension of God (*Sophia*) and of humanity and creation. The Spirit, entering within the person, brings the person to birth as mother, illumines the person as glory, and transforms the person as interior fire. The Spirit works invisibly, from the interior darkness. Eucharist would correspond to the *masculine* dimension of God (*Logos*) and of humanity and creation. The Word becomes one with the person as light, idea, image and food, working from the level of mystery but continually becoming visible or intelligible, and through this visibility and intelligibility nourishing the person and transforming the person into itself. The *sacramental* view, then, converges with the *sophianic* vision.

139. The characteristic *double language* of John's gospel is rooted in this dual emanation of Word and Spirit from the invisible Father or Godhead. These two are manifested in multiple and interchanging forms, and finally in the symbolic language of Genesis: man and woman, tree of life and river of living water (see Rev 21–22 and Jn 20).

140. This sacramental view stands in radical confrontation to the *scientism* and *literalism* of our modern west.[49] To find a sacramental realism which is adequate to the Johannine vision, one must return to the eastern Christian, and finally to the Syriac, tradition. Today this radical sacramentalism finds an ally, in its opposition to literalist scientism, in the *new paradigm* thought,[50] which opposes itself to a Cartesian-Newtonian reductionist worldview.

141. Radical sacramentalism and contemplative *poetry* are related as two aspects of the same reality.[51] They are two different expressions of the same union between God and creation—which we have expressed elsewhere in terms of immanent *Sophia*.

The classical Greek patristic expression of this meeting was the "natural contemplation," or *theōria physikē*, of Evagrius, Maximus Confessor and others.[52] This concept has been revived in our time by Thomas Merton under the name of *active contemplation*.[53]

142. John's prologue is, in a sense, the gospel, or good news, of the poet. From the creative Word come both the cosmos, the material creation itself, with all its variety and beauty, and also the unitive light which dwells within the human heart. These begin together in the Word and in the creative act of the Word; they come together again within the poet and the act of unitive imagination, like an echo of the creation itself happening within the human person, human language, the human world.

143. Now we can distinguish four *liberating perspectives* which are implicit in John's gospel:

a. the *apophatic principle*: God is beyond image, concept, word, and therefore beyond any institutional mediation.

b. the *creative Logos*, the Word: there is a knowledge accessible to the human person which is unitive, pleromic, divine—and the source both of creation and of creativity.

c. *immanent Sophia*: corresponding to the divine *Logos* is an *immanent* feminine principle through which we discover this same fullness *within* us and within all creation. In this immanent principle, the divine becomes one with our own being.

d. *sacramental new creation*: rooted in baptism and eucharist, this divine action continues the incarnation of the Word in us and in the cosmos.

144. The Second Vatican Council took a step in the direction of a new and radical contemporary sacramentalism when it described the church as the sacrament of communion with God and of human unity.[54] These conceptions have not, however, given rise to a radical sacramental *realism* approaching that of the early eastern traditions.

145. There appears to be an inverse relationship between the depth and fullness of sacramental vision and the consolidation of institutional control. This may be either the political control of empire or the domination of the institutional elements within the church.

146. The sacramental sense is eclipsed by the unintegrated growth of human *power*. This may be the power of kingdom or empire, which solidifies more and more with the growth of civilization, or the power of science and technology. The centralization and consolidation of human power—also in the church—renders the earth, the cosmos, the body, creation, *opaque*. Human consciousness loses its responsiveness to environment as well as to the interior voice as it surrenders to the dominant culture, the official story, the single authoritative voice.

147. Christians today find themselves between *two sacramental visions*. According to an *ecclesial* sacramental theology, the divine life of communion flows into humanity through the two sacraments of baptism and eucharist. From the perspective of a *cosmic* sacramentalism, on the other hand, the whole created world is a medium of divine revelation, union and life.

While the two are not mutually contradictory, they are not easily reconciled conceptually. One way of thinking one's way out of the dilemma is suggested by Karl Rahner's conception of the *church as sacrament of God in the world*[55]—and therefore radiating the revelation of God and the grace of salvation also to those outside, who do not have the benefit of the ecclesial sacraments of baptism and eucharist. We may not, however, limit this effect to those who *consciously experience* this presence of the church.

148. The sacraments were, for early Christians, the *mysteries*, the *arcana*, the secret inner sanctuary of their new life.[56] One evidence that these were not merely literary expressions is the well-known fact that the unbaptized were dismissed from the assembly when the eucharistic liturgy itself was about to begin. Probably the sacraments are *implicit* in John partly for this reason: that they are the *mystēria*. Whether or not John is concerned about *concealing* them from outsiders, he carefully positions them beneath the surface of his narrative. He passes over the obvious *external* features of baptism and eucharist in order to open entrances to the interior mysteries themselves.

Baptism and eucharist relate to *us* from the same hidden place. We become accustomed to them as standard rituals, and we easily come to assume that the church presents them to us as something which is thoroughly understood. The reality is the opposite: they represent the dark core of unitive mystery within the church's life, beneath the level of word and concept. The sacramental mysteries, from this invisible center beneath the visible rituals, illuminate all the words; in them dwell the light and the fire of the Word itself.

149. These two sacraments, then, lead us back to the *boundary of mystery*, of *the Mystery*, at which we began in our consideration of the Johannine first day of creation, and of baptism. Here we encounter once again the *child*, and the invisible Christ-mystery, the continuing incarnation, the eternal birth which is taking place within and among us, which is being undergone by the universe itself (see Rom 8:19-23).

$$\oplus$$

150. It is in John's gospel that Jesus' imperative to turn and become a *child* is carried to its ultimate point: the *"beginner's mind"*[57] which we are to acquire consists of a continual birth in the Word, the Son of God.

151. It is particularly in the beginnings of life that psychology joins Christian theology—and, in a particular way, the Johannine vision. Contemporary psychology has, from its beginning, focused upon the experience of the *child* as the key both to the illnesses and to the healing of the psyche. Gradually it has recognized the permanent presence of the "child" within the human person: the child with its infinite potential for new beginnings, for growth and for creativity. The salvation that is revealed in John's gospel is a new birth of the person in God which is at the same time a birth of God within the human person.

152. The unitive revelation invites us to a new *simplicity*, in the midst of our complex contemporary world and its demands. This would be discouraging, were it demanded and not also *given* to us.

153. At the end of the road is a purified hope. An expectation broad and patient as the earth itself grows warm as the time of birth approaches. Now that all hopes and plans, all schemes and projects, have returned to dust, and the world has grown old without understanding and without changing, it is time to begin. Christ burns within to be born.

Epilogue

In the course of this long journey we have spent much of our time off the familiar road of John's narrative, cutting paths across country and through dense woods. Now it is time to consider how this work may serve us as we continue with the gospel of John.

The mandalic scheme, first of all, raises a question. Am I to read John according to this complex geometrical reconstruction, rather than in the order of the narrative itself? When it comes, as it must, to simply reading the gospel, is the mandalic scheme not an obstacle rather than an aid? Are we forced to make a choice between story and geometry, continuity and symmetry?

We must return, as always, to the beginning. The *narrative* itself is our text, and it is the narrative order which remains primary. The chiastic and mandalic structures and the patterns of symbolic resonance mediate for us between the multiplex concrete detail of the narrative and the unitary mystery of the Word which is beneath and within it. Again and again, we must return to the narrative detail, and recommence from there our journey toward the center.

We do not very often sit down and read through the whole gospel, however, nor even through a series of successive episodes. One scene or discourse, one dramatic encounter, is usually a more fruitful subject of reflection than a series of them, and this is the form in which the scriptures are presented to us also in the liturgy.

The general outline of the mandalic scheme can be memorized without very much effort—and perhaps this is why it is there. Then, as its various internal resonances are consciously realized, one by one, the structure is personally interiorized on a deeper level. This is a delightful continuing experience of discovery. After a while, as we read one particular episode of the gospel, the whole gospel with its internal structure will be at hand, condensed in this simple geometrical framework. The network of relationships which surrounds each text will be accessible to us, brought into relief by the alignments and symmetries of the figure.

As we travel through John the mandalic arrangement serves first, then, as a map or compass. A map supplies us with a bird's eye view of the whole country, and quickly shows us how to travel from where we are to each of the other places. A compass magically orients us in relationship to the form of the whole earth, as we inch along over the particularities of its surface. Reading along with the mandalic figure at hand, one may remain in touch, at each point, both with the center and with the overall structure of the Johannine vision.

For it seems to have been in the plan of its author that our reading of the fourth gospel should be a *double* reading—consistent with the structure of human, and Christian, existence itself. As we read and live the historical narrative—of the gospel text or of our personal life—we are aware continually of another level of reality and presence beneath that surface, within that history. We are continually in relation *both* with the varied surface of life and with the light which dwells at its center.

The teaching of John, reduced to its simplest expression, is the disclosure of the identity of this central light which is the Word. The unitive light of this Word unlocks both gospel and life to their essential form and meaning. As we, like Peter, gradually awaken to follow Jesus through the journey of his life, we are at the same time, like the disciple, to remain here at the center where he dwells.

The presence of this Word beneath the moving surface of John's gospel provides the continual opportunity for a *unitive reading*, which will challenge our mind's boundaries with its profundity and simplicity at once. Inseparable from this unitive sense of the text is the *personal encounter* with the Word which is both beginning and end of our reading. "Remain here until I come."

The great "*method*" is to immerse oneself in the text—to read it with a conviction of the fullness that is in it. One may explore it like a new country, set loose one's imagination to prospect everywhere around it, dwell in it, invest one's time and attention in it, return to it anew with new questions, trusting that sooner or later it will open abundantly. The journey we have embarked upon is also a lifetime *relationship*: this word is to be taken quite literally.

⊕

The commentaries can be of great help in getting the facts straight, in familiarizing oneself with the text and its context. They also help to train us in the distinctions and comparisons and the multitude of reasonings by which we may acquire a grasp of the text. The careful and learned commentaries of Brown, of Barrett,[1] of Schnackenburg, can guide us into a realistic and responsible relation to the text itself, as we prepare to enter more deeply into the Word. We must not expect from the commentators more than they have set out to do, however. The leading commentators of today usually limit themselves to an exegesis which will distinguish the authentic literal sense of the text. This is already a very great service! They tend to be very cautious, however, in precisely those resonant sectors of the literary keyboard where the depth and fullness of John's music are produced. It remains for the biblical literary criticism now being developed,[2] together with a symbolic and contemplative biblical theology, to pursue these further paths of structural and symbolic relationship.

Works of biblical theology[3] bring us a step beyond the scientific commentaries. Here we will find immediate help in expanding the symbolic range of the things, events and people of the Bible. Here the poetic overtones and the fuller inner meaning of the text begin to appear, as well as the theological structure of the Mystery itself.

A comparative reading of the synoptic gospels and of Paul, as we have seen, brings much light to our reading of John. It is not difficult, with a synopsis, to become aware of the particular Johannine features of a text. This often casts a light on the intent—and theological slant—of the author, as well as on his compositional artistry. It is also necessary to read the other gospels in order to balance one's vision of the Christian mystery. The existence of four gospels rather than only one —Johannine—gospel is not just another example of biblical untidiness. As a glance at the sermon on the mount in Matthew (Mt 5:1–7:29) will show, there are many vital elements of Jesus' teaching that John, counting on the wider gospel tradition, has not communicated to us in his own work.

It is not surprising that a large number of more meditative or contemplative works have been written, in the course of the centuries, on John's gospel. Some of the Christian authors with deepest insight into the Johannine vision have been those of the east. Not only the Syrian but the Greek fathers, as well as Russian writers of recent centuries, are very often closer to John's unitive and sapiential vision of the Christian mystery than are comparable western authors, whether Catholic or Protestant. The theology of eastern Christianity has ever been more Johannine than that of the west.[4]

Among the recent western writers, of a more meditative than scientific bent, who have seen deeply into John, several heirs of a classical Catholic tradition of symbolic exegesis[5] should be mentioned. Other writers, standing outside both Catholic and Protestant traditions and often influenced by the Asian religions, have written with insight of the fourth gospel.[6]

⊕

We shall find surprising resonances between John—especially the prologue of John—and some of the writings of the Asian sapiential traditions: the *Upanishads*, the *Bhagavad Gita*, the *Tao Te Ching*, with their unitive and contemplative wisdom. Christians may find that they can make these texts their own by approaching them through the door of John's gospel and the unitive *Logos*.

⊕

One need not be too "serious" with this gospel—serious in the wrong way. It is better if the mind learns to play, to move with the music of the text. For this it requires space and freedom. An obsessive concern with the limits of orthodoxy, or an over-eagerness to extract a clear meaning from the text, can block this sapiential play of mind and feeling, which is both an abundant spring of understanding, and enables us to fall in love with the gospel, to be gripped and held in its movement.

Related to this space of play is the space of silence, of simple listening. It is here that the Word is continually reborn, in ever fresh expressions, ever new lights. It is here that we are able to hear the Word not as text but as a word spoken—the speaking of a creative Word in which all is suddenly new once again. Silent meditation, a resting in the quiet of interiority, is the best and most enduring companion for the reading of John.

⊕

If we have not spoken of a *Johannine spirituality*, this corresponds to our *unitive* interpretation of John. Christian spirituality is at once more unitary and more diverse than such a title would suggest. So personal is the relationship with God—the spiritual journey—that its features are unique for each individual, and the maps and ladders of former times no longer carry conviction for us. On the other hand, the unitive Word is the principle not only of understanding but of life and action. For John, as for Paul,[7] it is the *vision* which is primary, and the disciple's response is determined by this vision rather than constituting a distinct program.

In the Christian wisdom tradition which derives primarily from John, theology and spiritual life and ordinary life are not separable. It is the Word which informs life, and one's personal life is to become more and more filled with the Word. Such is the fullness and power of the Word which John has seen and heard and absorbed, that both vision and response are awakened *together* by its transforming influence, like the two disciples in his gospel.

⊕

This book obviously represents an unfinished journey, a work-in-progress. Some of its major proposals will, I trust, be vindicated by time. Others will be corrected, and some will surely fall by the wayside. The option for interpretive power rather than relative certainty has been deliberate—a principle of method which I believe is necessary if we are to hear the Johannine music once again. It is a new and plenary way of knowing that John would reveal to us in this Word of life.

Geometrical methods of reflection, such as that used here, are irresistibly attractive to some persons[8] and seem to interest others little if at all. The mandalic affliction is, for some of us, progressive and irreversible. It can become quite impossible, after a time, to climb out of this geometrical perspective and regard its results with anything like the critical detachment which others will so readily bring to the matter.

It is evident that the mandalic interpretation of John, together with the symbolic-unitive approach, finds a nearly unparalleled wealth of *meaning* in the fourth gospel. It is for each reader to verify by personal experience the correspondence of this meaning with the *truth* which the Johannine Word awakens in his or her heart. Truth, however, is at once more simple, more varied and imaginative—and more brilliantly *alive*—than we have supposed.

Endnotes

INTRODUCTION

1. This current usage of the expression *paradigm* derives from the work of Thomas S. Kuhn, *The Structure of Scientific Revolutions*. Discussions of the *new paradigm* will be found in: Marilyn Ferguson, *The Aquarian Conspiracy*; Fritjof Capra, *The Turning Point*; Ken Wilber, *Eye to Eye*; Stanislav Grof, *Beyond the Brain*, ch. 1, "The Nature of Reality: Dawning of a New Paradigm," pp. 1-91.

2. *The other disciple:* see Jn 20:2.3.4.8. Throughout the book we shall treat as synonymous the expressions *John, the other disciple,* and *the disciple whom Jesus loved* (or *the beloved disciple*). We do not assume that these persons were historically identical, but that it is the intention of the author of the fourth gospel that they be *understood* as one and the same person. Sometimes we shall refer to this person simply as *the disciple*. This person is also understood to be, if not the final author or redactor, at least the original source of John's gospel.

John is an *other gospel* not in the sense in which Paul condemns a radically erroneous teaching which vitiates the Christian mystery (Gal 1:6-9), but in the sense of a more profoundly realized view of the same Christ-mystery, the same essential reality and event.

3. *Christ-Mystery:* this global term (see Eph 3:4.9) is intended to signify the totality of the person, the work and the "event" of Jesus Christ, with all of its ecclesial and cosmic scope. See Eph 2–3, Col 1, etc. Discussions of the term *mystery* will be found in B. Rigaux and P. Grelot, *DBT*, 374-377; Vagaggini, *Theological Dimensions*, pp. 598-611, 969-972.

4. In reading the gospel (i.e., John's gospel), one is drawn into a literary world created by the author from materials drawn from life and history as well as imagination and reflection. Culpepper, *Anatomy of the Fourth Gospel*, p. 231.

...the Fourth Gospel as a whole is a "fantastic" book, deliberately full of mysteries and more provocative contradictions than are found in other works of earliest Christian literature. Hengel, *Johannine Question*, p. 130.

5. First among the critical works to which I am indebted is Raymond E. Brown's *The Gospel According to John*. This excellent example of historical-critical Johannine scholarship integrates much of the best of earlier work. A compact and inexpensive distillation of Brown's Johannine interpretation is the more recent *The Gospel and Epistles of John: A Concise Commentary*.

6. *Sapiential exegesis:* This is the symbolic interpretation of scripture according to its "spiritual sense" which was dominant in both east and west until the thirteenth century. See Leclerq, *The Love of Learning and the Desire for God*, ch. 9, "Monastic Theology," pp. 233-286; Daniélou, *From Shadows to Reality*; de Lubac, *The Sources of Revelation*.

7. There are a number of verse-by-verse commentaries available, ranging from a popular level to the exhaustive scholarly works of Brown and Schnackenburg. See note 1 to Epilogue. Sloyan's *What Are They Saying About John?* (1991) is a useful guide to the principal contemporary commentaries as well as, more generally, to the Johannine scholarship between 1970 and 1990.

8. *Lectio divina*, "holy reading," is the meditative practice of biblical reading, central to the Christian monastic tradition. It is oriented toward a contemplative penetration of the scriptures. See Leclerq, *The Love of Learning*, especially ch. 5, "Sacred Learning," pp. 87-110; Tunink, *Vision of Peace*, ch. 24, pp. 265-274; Peifer, *Monastic Spirituality*, pp. 392-405; Cummings, *Monastic Practices*, pp. 7-23; Louf, *The Cistercian Way*, pp. 74-79; Panimolle, *Like the Deer That Yearns*.

9. *The Holy Bible, New Revised Standard Version*: see Bibliography.

Part I

Chapter 1

1. See Thomas Merton's Introduction to his *Gandhi on Non-Violence*, New York, New Directions, 1965: "Gandhi and the One-Eyed Giant," pp. 1-20.

2. *Sapiential* derives from the Latin *sapientia*, meaning wisdom. It

is roughly equivalent to the Greek *sophia*. See note 6 to Introduction, above.

3. Brown I, Introduction, D. Wisdom Motifs, p. CXXXII.

4. Brown I, Appendix II, "The 'Word,'" p. 524.

5. Frank Kermode, "John," in *The Literary Guide to the Bible*, p. 441.

6. Epistemology—i.e. the basic question of the *ways in which we can know*—is a primary, though usually unmentioned, point of division in Johannine interpretation. Contemporary interpreters most often do not cross the threshold which leads into the sapiential thought of John's gospel because they are committed—perhaps unconsciously—to certain limiting presuppositions about knowledge and consequently about communication. John can *only* mean *this*, because *only this* (often something crisply conceptual, and therefore anachronistic) *can* be thought and said. Akin to this is the tendency to apply an inappropriate *either-or* mentality to a Johannine statement: because he says A, he cannot also be saying B. But John can be—and frequently is—saying A+B+C+ . . .

John's gospel presents us from the beginning with a Jesus who is the living and divine *Word* of God, containing within itself the power which created the universe and which is now creating it anew. When we read the gospel, this transformative power of the Word is effective immediately in our minds, opening them to *a new way of knowing*. It must be insisted again and again that only through a transformation of our way of thinking—a change which is itself beyond our understanding—will we enter deeply into John's meaning.

7. William Blake: ". . . may God us keep / From single vision and Newton's Sleep." See note below to Part III, ch. 8.

8. There are few studies of the theme of *oneness* in John's gospel. The *TDNT* article *eis* by E. Stauffer, while useful in its discussion of the oneness theme in the Pauline letters, touches on the Johannine writings only in passing. The one substantial work that I have found on this theme in John is Mark Appold's *The Oneness Motif in the Fourth Gospel* (1976). Appold's focus is upon the *explicit* oneness motif: that is, on expressions using some form of the Greek word *eis* (one). His attention is given principally to five passages in which forms of *eis* are used with distinctly theological implications. These are Jn 10:16; 10:30; 11:52; 17:11; 17:21-23. In his review (pp. 13-17) of previous studies relating in various ways to his theme of oneness in John, the author dismisses those inquiries which interpret the theme in a mystical or metaphysical sense. Correspondingly, his own study avoids these aspects as well as ignoring expressions of the theme in the symbolism and literary structure of John's gospel.

Appold clearly recognizes the centrality of this theme in John:

In constantly varying approaches and modulations, the motif of oneness emerges as the most prominent and pervasive qualifying characteristic of the Fourth Gospel's theological concerns (p. 280).

And, speaking of the five explicit texts he has chosen to study,

Here the oneness motif appears as a theological abbreviation for the evangelist's deepest concerns (p. 262).

The basic form of this oneness is *Christological*: the oneness of Jesus with his Father (10:30). From this derive the soteriological and ecclesiological expressions of oneness.

The resulting oneness relation with the Revealer is not just a spiritual or an internal relation invisible to others around. It has instead concrete, perceivable manifestations, central among which is the corresponding oneness among the believers. The picture here is not so much that of a vertical-horizontal dimension (the author is here rejecting R. Brown's presentation of the oneness theme in Jn. 17: see Brown II, p. 776), but rather that of an emanative sequence or a chain of action whereby oneness describes, as point of origin, the relational/revelational correspondence of Father and Son, and then successively but interconnectedly the relation of Revealer and believer, and also believer and believer. Thus the line leads from christology to soteriology to ecclesiology, and oneness serves as the theological abbreviation for the constitutive aspects of all three (p. 285).

The author's insistence on seeing the oneness only as *relational* in a rather linear sense (first in 10:30 and then consistently elsewhere) rather than intensive, metaphysical and participative (as we see it especially in the prologue: e.g. in the *Logos* of 1:1-4), confines his treatment to a relatively external level of John's thought. The study is clear and is convincing in its positive assertions about the oneness theme. It suffers throughout from its excessively dualistic (*either-or*) approach, systematically excluding the less easily conceptualized (e.g. the cosmic) dimensions of the Johannine unitive.

Thus, typical of the majority of contemporary biblical studies, the book remains within the limits of a narrow implicit epistemology which systematically excludes the breadth and depth of a sapiential interpretation. This is especially evident—and unfortunate—in dealing with the Johannine *oneness* (or Unitive), which is itself the key to a sapiential epistemology and which, in one or another of its implicit and symbolic expressions, pervades every part of John's gospel. Nevertheless, Appold has drawn attention to the centrality of the Johannine unitive theme and has demonstrated the structure of relationships between its clearest, most explicit affirmations.

9. See Kelley, *Meister Eckhart on Divine Knowledge*.

10. On this sapiential unitive knowledge see Nasr, *Knowledge and the Sacred*, pp. 1ff, 130ff, 148ff.

11. We shall frequently use the word *unitive*: unitive experience or knowledge, the Johannine Unitive, etc. *Unitive* is intended here in a metaphysical sense which, like the terms "being," or "God," goes beyond the limits of precise conceptual definition. The Unitive is a fullness—sometimes experienced as such—and yet, with a paradoxical logic, is known "apophatically," in an unknowing. The meaning of the term is maximally inclusive: the Divinity conceived as the unity of all being. This central meaning is then modulated and specified by the other words used: e.g. "knowledge" or "event."

The "Johannine Unitive" is the *Word* of the prologue, and it is also the indwelling *Spirit* (14:17), the *koinōnia* (1 Jn 1:3) and the *anointing* (1 Jn 2:27). It is the one divine Gift which is the central revelation of the fourth gospel. One may best become initiated into the meaning of this unitive language by meditation on some biblical texts: Wis 7:21–8:1; Jn 1:1-4.14.16-18; Jn 17:20-23, and the various *I Am* texts of John's gospel, e.g. 8:12 (9:5); 6:35 (6:51); 14:6; 6:20. The language of John's first letter (like that of the gospel's prologue) is frequently saturated with the sense of this unitive reality: see 1 Jn 1:1-3; 3:1-3; 4:16b-17.

The eternal One, source of the universe, becomes newly present and manifest within the world in Jesus, gathering the world into itself through faith in him. Those who believe in him and realize this unity through love are gathered into him, and through him into the One. The fullness of the One, in turn, becomes present in them, participated as light and as communion. Thus the One is further manifested in the world.

The "Johannine Unitive" is God conceived as this One, and manifest alternately (or simultaneously) as Father, Word or Son, and Holy Spirit: Source, manifestation, and immanent fullness. The One is

434 / THE GOOD WINE

thus manifested, participated, and gathers the creation into itself in a new and reciprocal immanence.

12. Aquinas, *Summa Theologica*, Pt. I, Q. 1, A. 10. New York, Benziger, 1946, vol. I, p. 7.

13. See Berdyaev, *The Meaning of the Creative Act.*

14. The Johannine symbolism is itself *centripetal*, as we shall see. An event in John's narrative will often reflect an event on the level of *Torah*—the exodus history—which is embedded deeply in the structure of the biblical word. Then the same Johannine story will open to disclose a still deeper symbolic implication on the level of the *creation* narratives of the first chapters of Genesis. Entering, finally, this inner symbolic garden, we find the Genesis symbolism flooded with the unitive light of the center, the creative *Word*.

15. This convergent dynamism in John's gospel is an intensified instance of the *centripetal* movement which Northrop Frye finds to be primary in all literature, and particularly in the Bible. He contrasts this with the *centrifugal* aspect—the external reference—of a written work.

> The principle involved here applies to all books but applies with considerable force to the Bible because the Bible is so deeply rooted in the characteristics of words and of language. The centripetal aspect of a verbal structure is its primary aspect, because the only thing that words can do with any real precision or accuracy is hang together....
>
> ... The events the Bible describes are what some scholars call "language events," brought to us only through words; and it is the words themselves that have the authority, not the event they describe....
>
> ... All verbal structures have a centripetal and a centrifugal aspect, and we can call the centripetal aspect the literary aspect.... The primary and literal meaning of the Bible, then, is its centripetal or poetic meaning. It is only when we are reading as we do when we read poetry that we can take the word "literal" seriously, accepting every word given us without question. This primary meaning, which arises simply from the interconnection of the words, is the metaphorical meaning. There are various secondary meanings, derived from its centrifugal perspective, that may take the form of concepts, predications, propositions, or a sequence of historical or

biographical events, that are always subordinate to the metaphorical meaning... (*The Great Code*, pp. 60-61).

16. While this approach is certainly open to the perils of excess subjectivity, the purely "objective" methods, when applied to John, leave us with a feeling that we have not yet encountered the text on its own level. On this hermeneutic problem both Northrop Frye and Frank Kermode have written with penetration. See Frye, *The Great Code*, xvii and elsewhere; Kermode, "John" in *The Literary Guide*, pp. 440-444, and Nasr, *Knowledge and the Sacred*, p. 149.

17. See note 8 to Introduction, above.

Chapter 2

1. See Robert Lawlor, *Sacred Geometry*.

2. The Latin cross is contrasted here with the Greek or equilateral cross. See Cahill, "Johannine Logos as Center," p. 62.

3. The phrase *lumen orientale* is attributed to William of St. Thierry: "As the brethren of Mont-Dieu (i.e. Carthusian monks) introduce to our Western darkness and French cold the *light of the East...*" *The Golden Epistle*, Book 1, Introduction, p. 9.

4. See Pseudo-Chrysostom, "Sermon VI for Holy Week," quoted in de Lubac, *Catholicism*, pp. 282-283. See also Hayes, *The Hidden Center*, pp. 200-202.

5. The classic western treatment of an Asian mandala tradition is Tucci's *Theory and Practice of the Mandala*.

6. See *Collected Works of C.G. Jung*, General Index (vol. 20), s.v. *mandala*; particularly, "Concerning Mandala Symbolism," vol. 9/1, pp. 355-384; Appendix "Mandalas," vol. 9/1, pp. 387-390; "Commentary on *The Secret of the Golden Flower*," vol. 13, pp. 1-56 (+ plates). See also Marie Louise von Franz, *C.G. Jung: His Myth in Our Time*, Ch VII, "The Mandala," pp. 139-157; Jolande Jacobi, *The Psychology of C.G. Jung*, pp. 136-141.

7. Jung, CW 9/1, p. 387.

8. Jacobi, *The Psychology of Jung*, pp. 138f.

9. Jung, CW 9/1, p. 388.

10. Jung, CW 9/1, p. 357.

11. Jung, quoted in von Franz, *Jung: His Myth*, p. 140.

12. Here the form of the cross is implicitly present, despite the difficulty of imagining the four dimensions spatially as they are rendered

in the text itself. The fathers would have no difficulty perceiving the image of the cross in these words.

13. The mandalic figure can also be found in other Pauline texts; for example, Phil 2:6-11 (here the horizontal is found compressed in vv. 10-11); Col 2:12-14 (Paul himself here represents the Jews, and the Colossians represent the Gentiles; in the joining of these two groups, once again, the fullness is signified). The figure is probably present also, though it does not settle into a single fixed form, in Paul's proclamation of the *word of the cross*, in 1 Corinthians 1:17-25.

14. Parallel, though not identical, to the two terms *ontological* and *historical* here are *synchronic* and *diachronic*.

15. As Jesus tells the Samaritan woman in 4:22, "... salvation is *from the Jews...*"

16. The word *fullness*, as we use it here, is equivalent to the Greek *plēroma* (see Jn 1:16), and signifies the fullness *of God*. See Col 2:9 (quoted below). When, elsewhere, we use the word *fullness* in another sense, this should be evident from the context.

17. Jung repeatedly cites the figure—frequent in Christian art—of Christ surrounded by the four evangelists, as an example of mandala in a western tradition.

18. Irenaeus, *Against Heresies* III, 8, p. 429.

19. Irenaeus, *Against Heresies* V, 3, pp. 545f.

20. Irenaeus, *Proof*, ch. 34, pp. 69-70. See also notes 168 through 173, pp. 171-173 of the same volume.

21. Irenaeus, *Against Heresies*, IV, 20, n. 1-4, pp. 487-488. Here the *center* of the Pauline vision is eclipsed, as Irenaeus expresses the whole mystery in terms of the figure's four *poles*.

22. Northrop Frye, *T.S. Eliot*, p. 77. Aside from its inner presence in Eliot's *Four Quartets*, the figure of the mandala appears again and again in Frye's writings, as if a motif woven into the texture of his thought. Frye uses it to illustrate the inner dimensions both of the Bible and of secular literature. Most often Frye envisions its center at the intersection of time (or history or narrative order) and the *axis mundi*. It appears that myth and metaphor—the two great literary modes which generate Frye's literary cosmos, develop perpendicularly from the same central point. See his *Anatomy of Criticism*, p. 162; *Words With Power*, pp. 47, 83, 95, 139, 151-153, 175-176.

23. The relationship between this recurrent Christian mandalic figure and the mandalas of the other religious traditions, noted earlier, is clarified by the work of *Jung* and his followers. As with Northrop Frye (himself indebted to Jung), Jung's thought often suggests a man-

dalic figure even when this is not made explicit. For example, the Jungian quartet of faculties of the personality—intuition, feeling, thinking and sensing—may be represented graphically in the form of a mandala, which then becomes an image of the fullness of the human psyche or Self. It is essentially this Self which, for Jung, is represented by the mandalas of dream, art, myth and religious meditation.

24. Ellis (p. 17) speaks of the "spiral" movement of John's thought and relates it to the gospel's chiastic structure. This spiral movement, in the light of the "sacred geometry" of ancient religious traditions, is suggestive. A spiral path, for example, was common to the structural design of many temples in the ancient Near East. See Frye, *Words With Power*, p. 153.

Chapter 3

1. Boismard, *St. John's Prologue*; Culpepper, *The Pivot of John's Prologue*.

2. Ellis, *The Genius of John*.

3. For the use of chiasm in general, see Stock, "Chiastic Awareness and Education in Antiquity," *BTB 14* (1984), pp. 23-27. For OT and NT chiastic structures, see references in Ellis, *The Genius of John*, note 27 to Introduction, p. 314. Specific studies of NT chiasm include Lund, *Chiasmus in the New Testament*; Ellis, *Matthew: His Mind and Message*; Scott, *Chiastic Structure* (chiasm in Mark's gospel; see also Part III, ch. 3 below); Talbert, *Literary Patterns, Theological Themes and the Genre of Luke-Acts*; Fiorenza, *Composition and Structure of the Revelation of John*; Ellis, *Seven Pauline Letters*; Bligh, *Galatians*; Vanhoye, *La structure litteraire de l'Epitre aux Hebreux*; for a brief review, in English, of Vanhoye's structural proposals for Hebrews, see Attridge, *Hebrews*, pp. 15-16 (note 128).

4. Ellis, *The Genius of John*, pp. 12-14.

5. Ellis, p. 13.

6. Ellis, pp. 16-17. This method's fruitfulness is then verified throughout the commentary on John which follows.

7. Ellis, p. 111.

8. The importance of this principle of a *center* will gradually emerge during our study of the fourth gospel. We have already glimpsed the power of the center in the prologue: the further dimensions which open from this archetype of center in John's prologue are powerfully brought out by Cahill, in "The Johannine Logos as Center."

Chapter 4

1. Ellis, p. 10.

2. Chapter 21 was excluded from the chiastic scheme because the symbolic system of the gospel narrative seemed to arrive at a conclusive closure in chapter 20, and chapter 21 introduced a new perspective and new subject matter (the life of Peter and of the "other disciple"). This question will be discussed more fully in Part II, ch. 8 below.

3. Ellis develops *four levels* of chiastic relationship in John's gospel:

> 1) Part to part within the whole gospel: e.g. between Part I and Part V.
> 2) Sequence to sequence within the whole gospel: e.g. between seq. 1 and seq. 21.
> 3) Sequence to sequence within each part: e.g. between seq. 1 and seq. 5.
> 4) Section to section within each sequence: e.g. between sec. a and sec. a' of seq. 1 (Ellis, p. 30).

In this book we shall develop the chiastic relationships between parts and between sequences (called *sections* in the present book) within the context of the whole gospel, and ordinarily disregard the third and fourth levels of parallelism. The purpose of our divergence from Ellis' rigorous procedure is to secure a sufficient space of freedom in our interpretation to explore the other literary relationships in the gospel, particularly the *symbolic* resonances. The chiastic structures, less dominant in the present work, will be found to serve as a framework for the major symbolic elements in John's design. It is the theological significance of these elements, and of the relationships between them, which will be our principal concern.

4. See chapter 2, above. The *geometrical* parallel which we have pointed out between the mandalic structures in some of the Pauline letters (e.g. Eph 2:6.13-22; Eph 3:17-19; Eph 4:10-14; Col 1:15-22) and the structure here proposed for John's gospel expresses a common inner *theological* structure in these New Testament writings.

5. Scholars continue to differ on the precise meaning-in-context of the Hebrew words with which God identifies himself to Moses in Exodus 3:14. In Deutero-Isaiah and in later Judaism, however, there is no doubt that the expression *I Am* (Septuagint Greek *egō eimi*) is used as a *name of God*. When Jesus uses the expression *I Am*, without predicate, in John's gospel, therefore, it is intended to join him with the

divine name, and hence with the Divinity itself. This is sometimes confirmed by the reaction of his listeners, as in 8:58 and 18:15. See Brown I, p. 537.

6. The development from linear narrative order to mandalic order may be seen as taking place in three successive steps.

1) chiastic *symmetry* determines the form of the gospel (Gerhard-Ellis);

2) the *center* is accented: relating to the other elements, and to the gospel as a whole, as a center of *meaning*;

3) *quaternity* emerges, producing a *mandalic* figure.

At each of these successive stages in development of its *form*, the gospel acquires a greater depth and intensity of *meaning*. Among two-dimensional geometrical figures, the mandala is unique in its archetypal fullness of meaning (see ch. 2 above).

7. The two events of creation and of the exodus are not often related explicitly to one another by the Old Testament writers, even though they represent, in the biblical history, two great *beginnings*: the beginning of the world itself and the beginning of Israel as the people of God's covenant. The two moments are brought together in Deutero-Isaiah. See Stuhlmueller, *Creative Redemption*.

8. George Mlakuzhyil, in *The Christocentric Literary Structure of the Fourth Gospel*, made a detailed survey of the structural proposals for John's gospel, up to the time of his writing. He was able to distinguish twenty-four *species* of structural hypothesis!

Chapter 5

1. Brown I, pp. 20-21.

2. Sanders (in *NT Christological Hymns*) finds evidence of pre-existing Christological hymns in the following NT passages: Phil 2:6-11; Col 1:15-20; Eph 2:14-16; 1 Tim 3:16; 1 Pet 3:18-22; Heb 1:3 and Jn 1:1-5 + 1:9-11. See also Brown I, pp. 20-21.

3. See chapter 1 above, p. 10. Kermode, *The Literary Guide*, pp. 443f.

4. The history of chiastic studies of the prologue is summarized by Culpepper in "The Pivot," pp. 2-6.

5. Ellis, p. 20.

6. Ellis, p. 21.

7. In Part III, chapter 1, we shall correlate the prologue verses with corresponding sections of the gospel narrative and explore the relation of the prologue to the scheme of the seven days of creation.

8. See Rahner, "Theology of the Symbol," pp. 221-252, and Wong, *Logos-Symbol*.

9. See note 11 to Chapter 1 above.

10. This unitive pre-knowledge may be regarded either from a philosophical viewpoint (e.g. as the knowledge of absolute being which is intrinsic to human knowing—see Rahner, *Spirit in the World*, pp. 406-408) or from a theological perspective, such as the presence of the Holy Spirit—and therefore of the unitive fullness itself—in the individual hearer or reader of the scriptures. See Breck, *Power of the Word*, pp. 43-47.

11. This Hellenistic tradition includes threads of both Platonic and Stoic thought, against the dark background of Heraclitus' *Logos*-doctrine.

12. See Dodd, *Interpretation*, pp. 73, 133; Brown I, pp. lviif.

13. Brown I, p. 524. For a more ample development of the meaning of the Johannine *Logos*, see Brown I, Appendix II, "The 'Word,'" pp. 519-524; Dodd, *Interpretation*, pp. 263-288 (with special attention to Philo); Boismard, *Prologue*, passim; A. Feuillet and P. Grelot, *DBT*, pp. 666-670; G. Kittel and Kleinknecht in *TDNT*, vol. 4, pp. 77-136.

14. See Brown I, pp. cxxii-cxxv, 25, 29, 30, 33; Dodd, *Interpretation*, pp. 274-275; Boismard, *Prologue*, pp. 74-76.

15. See, for example, Keating et al., *Finding Grace at the Center*; Pennington, *Centering Prayer*; Panikkar, *Blessed Simplicity*.

> One instance of a symbolism omnipresent in man's religious history is the symbolism of the center, the locus which "is pre-eminently the zone of the sacred, the zone of absolute reality" (Cahill, "Johannine Logos as Center," p. 54, with quotation from M. Eliade, *Cosmos and History*, p. 17).

> ... our theme is *the center*, that is, the place of meeting of the human spirit and the divine Spirit, and, in that meeting, the place where the Christian at prayer meets the whole of reality, divine and human, persons and things, time and space, nature and history, evil and good (Thomas E. Clarke, in Keating et al., *Finding Grace at the Center*, p. 50).

16. The reading of the final words of the prologue (1:18) as *he has opened the way* is proposed by Ignace de la Potterie (1988). René Robert (1987) had suggested that the Greek verb form *exēgēsato* which

concludes 1:18 and the prologue contains *two meanings*, rather than one. In addition to the usual translation, "he has explicated," the word would convey also the sense "he has guided." See also Robert, 1989, 1990.

De la Potterie, in the light of the preceding verselet of 1:18 ("It is God the only Son, who is in the bosom of the Father"), as well as in the context of John's gospel as a whole, has offered the reading which we have adopted: *he has opened the way*. We shall return to these very important concluding words of the prologue more than once.

17. The expression *children of God* may today evoke echoes of paternalism, authoritarianism, suppression of the development of the individual person. In John, however, the context of this expression again and again makes it evident that it is related not to authority and subjection but to a divine *generation*: the influx of a new and unbounded life. In contrast to Hebrews 12:4-11, for example, the Johannine sense of *children of God* connotes less a movement of obedient submission than one of personal emergence and liberation in the discovery of a gift of life.

18. Among later Christian writers, it is probably Meister Eckhart who has most cogently set forth the Christian's participation in the generation of the Son by the Father. See Kelley, *Divine Knowledge*, pp. 129-130.

Chapter 6

1. Jesus' baptism by John is recounted by all three synoptics: Mt 3:13-17; Mk 1:9-11; Lk 3:21-22. In each of these three gospels, the baptism represents the solemn initiation of Jesus' public life and ministry. After the baptism he immediately retires into the wilderness to be tempted by Satan, and then returns to begin his life of teaching and healing. The baptism is presented as an initiation by the Holy Spirit, formally inaugurating the journey of Jesus and the drama of his life.

2. The symbolism of baptism and particularly of the baptism of Jesus has been most fully explored and poetically developed by the theologian-poets of the *Syriac* tradition: from the Odes of Solomon to Aphrahat and Ephrem. See Duncan, *Baptism*; Brock, *Syrian Orthodox Baptismal Liturgy*; Brock, *The Holy Spirit in the Syrian Baptismal Tradition*.

PART II

Chapter 1

1. Ellis, pp. 110-111.

2. For the Christian liturgical tradition and for the fathers, this sea-crossing is perhaps the most important of all the OT prefigurations of Jesus' work of salvation. See Daniélou, *From Shadows to Reality*, pp. 153-226.

3. Carroll Stuhlmueller has investigated the joining of exodus and creation in Second Isaiah's vision of the future redemption of Israel from exile, in his study *Creative Redemption in Deutero-Isaiah*.

4. In 6:21 it is not clear whether the disciples *receive* Jesus into the boat or not before it comes to land; there is good reason for believing that he did not get into the boat. John makes it clear, however, that they *"wanted to take him into* the boat," which suffices for the correspondence with 1:12.

5. *"Uncreated light"* is an expression used often in eastern Christian tradition for the divine self-communication. See Lossky, *Mystical Theology*, ch. 4, pp. 67-90.

6. See Part III, chapter 1 below for a fuller development of the relationship between prologue and gospel narrative.

7. See Brown I, Appendix IV, pp. 533-538. John's mention of the *name* of Jesus at the center of his prologue, 1:12, correlates with the *I Am* spoken by Jesus at the chiastic center of the gospel, in 6:20.

8. See the Jung essay in note 9 below, and McGann, *The Journeying Self*. The basic study of the *night sea journey* is Leo Frobenius, *Das Zeitalter des Sonnengottes*, Berlin, 1904.

9. Jung, "The Psychology of the Unconscious," in *CW* 7, *The Archetypes of the Collective Unconscious*, p. 99.

10. John does not mention the *sign of Jonah*, of which Jesus speaks in the synoptic gospels (Mt 12:39-41; 16:4; Lk 11:29-32). Jesus' paschal journey through death follows this path, however, and we shall hear in John 21 that "Simon, son of Jonah" must travel it behind his master. See also John 12:20-26, Jesus' teaching on the occasion of the coming of the Gentiles ("Greeks") to him.

11. Some of Jung's writings on the mandala are quoted above (Part I, ch. 2) and references to them are indicated in the notes to that chapter.

12. See Vandana's *Waters of Fire*. This book is entirely devoted to the study of the symbolism of *water* in John's gospel, from the perspective of the Indian religious tradition.

13. *Apophatic* or *negative* theology is that which speaks of the Absolute, of the ultimate reality, not directly and through positive symbols and concepts, but through negative statement ("God is not this...") and paradox. See below, Part II, ch. 7 and Part III, ch. 8.
14. Sahi, *A Comparison between the Johannine Structure of Image Sign and the Buddhist-Hindu Mandala.*
15. Sahi, p. 90.
16. Sahi, p. 88.

Chapter 2

1. Alternative translations of this word: *firmament* (KJV, RSV), *vault* (JB, NJB, NEB). "God inserts an immense concave plate in the midst of the all-encompassing waters, creating a vast hollow between the upper and the lower waters" (R.J. Clifford in *NJBC*, p. 11).
2. Alternative translation of this word: *heaven* (KJV, RSV, NEB, JB, NJB).
3. This recalls Sahi's vision of a unitive new creation by Jesus which brings together that which had been separated in the first creation. See ch. 1 above.
4. See Feuillet, *Johannine Studies*, pp. 78-80.
5. Among the OT texts of a sapiential character which are strongly reflected in John 6 are the following: Sir 24:21; Prov 9:5; Sir 15:3; Is 54:13; Is 55. See Brown I, pp. 273-274; Feuillet, *Johannine Studies*, pp. 81-83.
6. See below, p. 297.
7. We shall often use the verb *participate* transitively, and without the preposition *in*: e.g. "the human person *participates* divine wisdom." The verb is used without the preposition where a more *intensive* sense is desired— e.g. in connection with the divine Unitive.
8. Traherne, *Centuries*, Cent. I, nos. 44, 45, p. 21.

Chapter 3

1. While Jesus seems to originate from Nazareth of Galilee (1:46), according to the synoptics he was actually born in Bethlehem (Mt 2:1; see Jn 7:42). It is on the *symbolic* level that Jerusalem is his own city: he is the Messiah, the "Son of David."
2. See J.C. Rylaarsdam, *IDB* vol. 1, pp. 455-458.

3. The narrative of Jesus and the woman caught in adultery, Jn 8:1-11, is not found in the earliest manuscripts of John's gospel and is therefore considered a later addition to John. Accordingly we have not included it in our mandalic scheme and will not comment upon it.

4. See D. Mollat, *DBT*, pp. 202-205.

5. D. Mollat, *DBT*, p. 203.

6. See Terrien, *The Elusive Presence*.

7. The *land of unlikeness, regio dissimilitudinis*, is a patristic-medieval metaphor for the "fallen condition" of humanity. See Gilson, *Mystical Theology*, pp. 115-117 and note 43, p. 224. The expression is found in the *Confessions* of St. Augustine, Bk. VII, ch. 10, and later in St. Bernard's *Sermo 42 De Diversis*, nn. 2-3.

8. See Pss 2:2 and 45:8.

9. See John Bradshaw's popular treatment of "toxic shame" in *Healing the Shame That Binds You*, and *Homecoming: Reclaiming and Championing Your Inner Child*.

10. It is Vladimir Soloviev who has probably come closest to creating a Christian theology of love and beauty. See his *The Meaning of Love*, and "Beauty, Sexuality and Love," and Hans Urs von Balthasar, "Soloviev," in *The Glory of the Lord*, vol. 3, pp. 279-352.

11. See Rosemary Haughton, *The Passionate God*, and Charles Williams, *The Figure of Beatrice: A Study of Dante*.

Chapter 4

1. Origen, "Homily 1 on Genesis," trans. Ronald E. Heine, *FOC*, vol. 71 (1981), pp. 54-55. This typical patristic interpretation of the fourth day of Genesis 1 is in the same line as John's development of the fourth day.

2. *Archōn*: the word is very suggestive because of its etymological relation to *archē*: "In the beginning (*archē*) was the Word..." This elder or "first one," "teacher in Israel," must learn from the Son of Man who is ever the Word "in the beginning" to become a beginner once again, to be born anew. See G. Delling, *TDNT*, vol. 1, pp. 478-484, 488-489.

3. See Barfield, *Rediscovery of Meaning*, pp. 233-235; *Saving the Appearances*, pp. 131-132, 145-147, 169-172, 181; *Romanticism*, pp. 102-103, 231.

4. See M-F. Lacan, *DBT*, pp. 88-90; H. Schlier, *TDNT* (s.v. *parrēsia*), vol. 5, pp. 871-886.

5. This expression, *the disciple*, will be used for the anonymous "disciple whom Jesus loved" (21:20-24), to whom the fourth gospel is attributed (21:24).

6. Bruteau, "The Holy Thursday Revolution" (1978); "Neo-feminism as Communion Consciousness" (1978). Both articles are reprinted in *Neo-Feminism and Communion Consciousness*.

7. See Bruteau, "Neo-feminism as Communion Consciousness."

8. See Brown II, pp. 598-601; Ellis, pp. 209-210.

9. The five-part chiastic structure of the supper narrative is outlined by Ellis on pp. 210-211. We have adopted the same division.

10. See Bauckham, *The Parable of the Vine*.

11. In dreams, the archetypal *child* is often a symbol of integration, wholeness, the unity of the Self. See Jung, *Psychology of the Child Archetype*.

12. *Begotten of God*: this expression occurs in the center of the prologue and often in 1 John. Whenever Jesus has spoken, at the supper, of the new relationship which the disciples are to have with the Father, of their dwelling in the Father or in the Father's house, or of Jesus' or the Father's dwelling in them, this divine generation is implied.

13. This movement beyond images will be discussed in ch. 6 and ch. 7 of Part II.

14. See the parallel accounts of Solomon's prayer of consecration for the Jerusalem *temple* in 1 Kgs 8:12-61 and 2 Chr 6:14-42. The temple is repeatedly called the house, or place, for God's *name*: e.g. 1 Kgs 8:16.17.18.19.20.29; 2 Chr 6:20.24.26.32.33.34.38. Cf. Jn 17:6.11.12.26, where Jesus, in his prayer, repeatedly associates the *disciples* with God's name.

15. Wis 9:1-18.

16. See note 9 above.

Chapter 5

1. "The Temple worship was essentially the offering of animal sacrifices" (Sandmel, *Judaism and Christian Beginnings*, p. 132).

2. See, for example, 1 Kgs 8:62-64.

3. See the synoptic texts on avarice and wealth: Mt 6:24; 13:22; 19:21f; Lk 6:24; 12:15-21; also E. Beaucamp and J. Guillet, *DBT*, p. 650.

4. The words of Jesus, "Destroy this temple" (2:29), however, probably refer *both* to the temple of Jerusalem—which the Jewish offi-

cials are bringing to destruction by their infidelity—and to Jesus' own body.

5. We propose the following chiastic division of these two chapters (some possible thematic symmetries are indicated):

A. 10:1-21:   discourse on shepherd and sheep; the *gate*.
B. 10:22-42: feast of reconsecration of temple; attempt on Jesus' life.
C. 11:1-44:   raising of Lazarus (human body raised as new temple).
D. 11:45-53: decision to put Jesus to death to save "holy place."
E. 11:54-57: Jesus secluded with disciples; Passover (the redemptive exodus, or *going out* is at hand).

6. The Greek term *hagiazein*—to sanctify or consecrate—is used both in 10:36 and in 17:17.19.

7. Goettmann (*Saint Jean*, pp. 156-157), following Bruckberger, revives the identification of Mary of Bethany both with Mary Magdalene (see Lk 8:1-3; 23:55; 24:10; Mk 15:40.47; 16:1-10; Jn 19:25; 20:1-18) and with the "sinful woman" who anointed Jesus with perfume in Luke's gospel (Lk 7:55–8:2; cf. Jn 11:2).

8. Compare the internal and external "labor" to which, as a result of the first sin, woman and man are bound in Gen 3:16-19.

9. Ellis, p. 247.

10. Fulgentius of Ruspe, Epist. 14, nn. 36-37, *CCL 91*, pp. 429-431, in *Liturgy of the Hours*, vol. III, p. 97.

11. "*Spirit in the World*" is the title of Karl Rahner's foundational study of the epistemology of St. Thomas Aquinas. The anthropological principle condensed in this title, and the anthropology sketched in this book, become the basis of Rahner's later theological work.

12. This seven-part chiastic structure, which according to Ellis (p. 260) occurs nowhere else in John's gospel, may allude to Rome, with its seven hills.

13. Goettmann, pp. 235ff.

14. Goettmann, p. 236.

15. Goettmann, p. 236.

16. Ellis, p. 258.

17. Ellis, pp. 253, 259-260.

18. See P. Grelot, *DBT*, pp. 288-290 (*king*); A. George, *DBT*, pp. 459-462 (*priesthood*).

19. Meeks, *The Prophet-King*.

20. "The house of Annas is notorious in rabbinic literature for its corruption" (Brown [1988], p. 88).

21. Vann, *The Eagle's Word*, Introduction, p. 107.

22. According to Philo of Alexandria, the Israelite priest does not rend his garments because these garments reflect the clothing that the *logos* makes for itself from the universe; *De fuga* XX, nn. 110-112, cited in Brown II, p. 921. St. Cyprian of Carthage sees in the garments of Jesus, divided into four parts, "a symbol of the four corners of the earth, while the seamless tunic represents the undivided Church" (Brown II, p. 921). Brown (ibid.) recalls also the rabbinic idea that God gave both to Adam and to Moses a seamless tunic.

23. At least from the time of the division of eastern and western Christianity in the sixteenth century, Catholic *eucharistic* spirituality underwent a similar one-sided development: accenting the sacrifice of Jesus and the union of the individual believer with the divine Victim, while allowing the fullness of the eucharistic *koinōnia* (communion) to fall into eclipse.

24. "Up to Carolingian times, the equilateral or Greek cross was the usual form, and therefore the mandala was indirectly implied. But in the course of time the center moved upward until the cross took on the Latin form, with the stake and crossbeam, that is customary today. The development is important because it corresponds to the inward development of Christianity up to the high middle ages. In simple terms, it symbolized the tendency to remove the center of man and his faith from the earth and to 'elevate' it into the spiritual sphere"—Jaffe, "Symbolism in the Visual Arts," in Jung et al., *Man and His Symbols*, p. 273 (cited in Cahill, "Logos as Center," p. 62).

25. See Brown I, pp. 99f, 108-109; II, pp. 924-927; Barrett, *Gospel*, p. 191.

26. See D. Mollat, *DBT*, p. 203.

27. See Brown II, pp. 899-900.

28. See C. Spicq and P. Grelot, *DBT*, p. 52.

29. Brown II, p. 951.

30. See Brown II, pp. 949-950.

31. See Nancy K. Hill, "The Savior as Woman": "My thesis is simple: Jesus Christ died in childbirth" (p. 1).

32. Brown II, pp. 950-951.

33. See Ward, *The Desert Christian*, Longinus n. 5, p. 123.

34. Brown II, pp. 951-952; Cullmann, *Early Christian Worship*, pp. 114-116.

35. Brown II, p. 952.

36. Goettmann, pp. 233-234.

37. It would be a crude oversimplification to infer a *superiority* of feminine over masculine in John's vision. The contrast between Peter

and the disciple might better be considered—to borrow a modern terminology—in terms of a masculine which is either alienated from or integrated with the interior feminine.

38. See Cahill, "Logos as Center," passim.

39. See Brown II, p. 960.

40. We conceive these events at the *three Passovers* of Jesus' public life to be related in such a way that not only the sea-crossing but also the two others may be sometimes conceived as the center of the mandalic figure:

1) section 1 (6:16-21):   the central sea-crossing.
2) section 12 (2:13-25):   Jesus cleanses the temple.
3) section 15 (ch. 18–19): Jesus' passion and death.

Both the *figure* itself of the cross and the theological significance of Jesus' death (in which it is parallel to the exodus sea-crossing), added to that death's proximity to the Passover celebration itself, strongly urge that Jesus' death on the cross be imagined in the center of the mandala. There is a very strong theological convergence upon the *cross* as *center* (see the Pauline mandalas in Part I, ch. 2).

The appropriateness of the temple-cleansing episode (2:19-21) as center is not so immediately obvious. The strongest motive for seeing the temple, or divine dwelling, as central to the mandala is the recurrent Johannine allusion to a central or interior *place*, together with the fact that the new creation is characterized by a new divine *immanence* in the human person. John also deliberately relates the temple cleansing to the paschal journey of Jesus: his death and resurrection (2:19.21).

41. See R.J. Clifford in *NJBC*, ch. 2, pp. 10-11; Boadt, *Reading the Old Testament*, p. 114.

42. See Rahner, "The Theology of the Symbol," pp. 245ff.

Chapter 6

1. Brown (1988), pp. 28-29.

2. See Goettmann, p. 63.

3. Goettmann, p. 64.

4. St. Augustine sees in these six vessels of water the six ages of history which extend from the first Adam to the second Adam who is Christ. The great figures of these six ages foreshadow Christ, and "In order that the water become wine, it is necessary only that Christ be recognized in all of this prophecy" (Augustine, Homily on John 9:6, *NPNF* I Series, vol. 7, p. 65, quoted in Goettmann, p. 64). Bernard of Clairvaux, on the other hand, interprets the six vessels of water "for

the purification of the Jews" in terms of a series of ascetical practices of the monks to whom he is speaking ("Sermon I for the First Sunday after the Octave of the Epiphany"; see also Sermon 55, *De Diversis*, "les six jarres de purification," in *Saint Bernard, Sermons divers*, vol. 2, pp. 46-50).

5. Dostoyevsky, *The Brothers Karamazov*, pp. 380-381.

6. Wallace Stevens, "The Comedian as the Letter C," Part VI, *Collected Poems*, New York, Knopf, 1982, p. 43.

7. Dodd, *Interpretation*, p. 299. The passages quoted in parentheses appear in *Greek* in Dodd's text.

8. The expression *transforming union* is used in the Carmelite spiritual tradition to signify divine union and transformation in the individual soul.

9. In the Jewish Kabbalah, the *Shekinah* replaces the *Sophia* of the OT and Gnosticism as the feminine element in God, daughter and bride of God in the world. See Scholem, *Major Trends in Jewish Mysticism*, pp. 229-233, and Patai, *The Hebrew Goddess*, passim, especially pp. 96-111, 135-160.

10. While *image* and *likeness* are synonyms in the narrative of Genesis 1, the fathers often distinguished the two. They would see the image as persisting in fallen humanity while the likeness was lost through sin and regained only through grace and a life of virtuous effort. In Wisdom 7:26, *Wisdom* is called the *likeness of God*. This text is applied to Jesus in the NT: Heb 1:3; Col 1:15.

11. The unitive *rest* of the seventh day goes beyond the *symbolism* —e.g. the sexual or nuptial symbolism—but not beyond the *reality* (the fullness and union) represented by the Cana narrative.

12. Merton, "Hagia Sophia," pp. 368-369.

13. Sexual promiscuity is often used by the prophets as a metaphor for spiritual infidelity and contamination, and particularly for idolatry. See Brown I, p. 171 and M.-F. Lacan, *DBT*, pp. 9-10.

14. See Tarnas, *The Passion of the Western Mind*, where the history of western thought is recapitulated as the parabolic trajectory of the solar masculine mind—ascending through an unprecedented development to an isolated clarity and brilliance in our time, then inevitably to descend (see Tarnas' Epilogue, pp. 441-445) toward the common "ground" in its reunion with the feminine.

15. See Brown I, pp. 178-179.

16. Brown (I, p. 171) points out that *three* marriages were the maximum number allowed by the Jewish law. Whatever be the tradition of the Samaritans, this woman is well outside the bounds of orthodox morality.

17. Brown I, p. 171; B.J. Roberts, *IDB*, vol. 4, p. 190; T.H. Gaster, *IDB*, vol. 4, pp. 193-194. See also John Macdonald, *The Theology of the Samaritans*, London, SCM Press, 1964.

18. Brown I, p. 171.

19. While the pairing of these two words, *grace and truth*, reflects the OT dyad of *hesed* and *'emet* (i.e. covenant love and fidelity—Brown I, p. 14), John probably intends a further echo here—of *Word* and *Spirit*. The prologue's movement parallels the progression of the gospel narrative to the final pouring out of the "fullness" which takes place in Jesus' giving of the Holy Spirit.

20. Merton, *Hagia Sophia*, pp. 366-367.

21. A further possible connotation of Jesus' *thirst* here and in his words upon the cross: thirst for that *glory* which he had before the world was made—which is associated with the eternal *Sophia* and which he is to pour out within those who believe in him.

22. "But the one who was asking for a drink of water was thirsting for her faith," and "the gift of God is the Holy Spirit"—St. Augustine, *Homilies on the Gospel of John*, Tractate 15, nn. 11-12, *NPNF* Ser. I, vol. 7, p. 102 (quoted in *Liturgy of the Hours*, vol. 2, p. 13).

The same affirmation—that the thirst of Jesus is for the Samaritan woman's faith—is found in the Preface for the Third Sunday of Lent in the *Sacramentary* of the Roman Catholic rite.

23. Lao Tzu, *Tao Teh Ching*, ch. 6, p. 13.

24. Note that Mary anoints Jesus' feet with *nard*. See also Song 5:5; 8:6-7; 4:9-15.

25. Possible sexual connotations of the anointing of Jesus' feet are suggested by the associations both of the *feet* and of an anointing with *nard* in the cultural milieu of the ancient Near East. See Pope, *Song of Songs*, pp. 38, 110, 349.

26. See Frye, *Words with Power*, pp. 195-196.

27. See Pss 45:8; 2:7; see P.-E. Bonnard and P. Grelot in *DBT*, p. 355.

28. Merton, *Hagia Sophia*, p. 363.

29. See Daniélou, *From Shadows to Reality*, pp. 244-260.

30. See M. Prat, *DBT*, pp. 509-510.

31. For the interpretation of the head cloth of John 20:7 which follows, I am indebted to Robert, "Du suaire de Lazare à celui de Jesus," *RThom. 88* (1988), pp. 410-420.

32. This conception of the transition from Old to New Testament as a passage *from figures to reality* is a basic principle of patristic exegesis. See Daniélou, *From Shadows to Reality*, passim; de Lubac, *The Sources of Revelation*, passim.

33. Merton, *Hagia Sophia*, pp. 367-368.

34. Non-dual knowledge is central to the more mystical developments of the spiritual traditions of Hinduism and Buddhism. See Loy,
Nonduality. It is probably most powerfully expressed in the Christian
tradition by Meister Eckhart.

35. Beyond the ordinary meaning of "close to the Father's heart"
(NRSV) or "at the Father's side" (NAB 1986), John's Greek expression
eis ton kolpon signifies the *interiority* of the Son in the Father, into
which Jesus introduces his disciples—and, first among them, the
beloved disciple.

36. This central place of the human body in Christianity (see Vagaggini, *The Flesh*) has, through the centuries, largely been eclipsed.
This is especially evident in the western church during the past few
hundred years.

37. This image of woman corresponds to a vision of the *church*
which was frequent in the fathers. Vladimir Soloviev interprets
human sexual love, and the vocation of woman, in a similar way. See
his "Beauty, Sexuality and Love," pp. 124-128.

38. See Ellis, pp. 288-289.

39. Merton, *Hagia Sophia*, p. 369.

40. Merton, *Hagia Sophia*, pp. 363-364.

41. See Stuhlmueller, *Creative Redemption*.

42. There is here probably an implicit reference to the friendship of
Jonathan and David: see 1 Sam 18–20.

43. See Prov 8:27-31; Wis 7–9; Swidler, *Biblical Affirmations of
Woman*, pp. 35-49, especially 47-48.

44. For the biblical tradition of *Sophia*, see Swidler, ibid. A general
overview of the Christian sophianic tradition—including the Russian
sophiologists—is provided by Tavard, *Woman in Christian Tradition*,
pp. 159-167, 194. A good example of modern Russian sophiology
available in English translation is Bulgakov's *The Wisdom of God*.

During recent years the feminist movement has brought about
a revival of interest in *Sophia* and a fresh examination of the sophianic
traditions. See, with bibliographies, Engelsman, *The Feminine Dimension of the Divine*; Virginia R. Mollenkott, *The Divine Feminine: The Biblical Imagery of God as Female*; Cady, Ronan and Taussig, *Sophia: The
Future of Feminist Spirituality*.

A very extensive attempt to bring together the various strands
of the *Sophia* tradition is Schipflinger's *Sophia-Maria*. Schipflinger also
describes analogous developments in Hinduism, Buddhism and Taoism. A passionate assimilation of the *Sophia* traditions to contemporary cult of "The Goddess" is Matthews' *Sophia, Goddess of Wisdom*.

The Divine Feminine from Black Goddess to World-Soul. The author brings together a wealth of material relevant to *Sophia* which is often passed over in the more orthodox works.

The present chapter has been punctuated by passages from Thomas Merton's prose poem *Hagia Sophia*, expressing a new understanding of the feminine which was emerging into Merton's consciousness during the later years of his life. Some of the personal experiences which entered into the genesis of *Hagia Sophia* are related by Merton's biographer, Michael Mott, in *The Seven Mountains of Thomas Merton*, pp. 307-308, 312-313, 326-327, 361-364.

45. The relationship of the feminine with human *interiority* is confirmed by contemporary Jungian psychology. Comparative studies of the consciousness of man and woman also characterize the feminine consciousness as being more *unitive* than analytic or objective (in the dualistic sense of perceiving an object as completely distinct from the subject). See Ulanov, *The Feminine in Jungian Psychology and in Christian Theology* (e.g. p. 334), and *Receiving Woman* (e.g. pp. 76-80).

46. For the later Kabbalistic doctrine of the *Shekinah*, see references above to Scholem (especially pp. 227-335) and Patai. See also Terrien, *The Elusive Presence*, pp. 404, 409 (note 63), 420, 442-443 (note 22).

47. Before the division of the sexes, Adam is apparently seen here in Genesis as containing in "himself" the fullness of humanity.

48. It is Paul who presents this dramatic and abrupt *transition* with greatest clarity and power. He expresses it as a movement from law to grace, slavery to freedom, letter to Spirit, old to new creation, etc. See Rom 5:1-21; 6:1-11; 8:1-23; 2 Cor 3:7-18; 4:6; Gal 2:19-21; 3:23-28; 4:1-9; Phil 3:7-11.

49. See D. Loy, *Nonduality*.

50. Some studies of John in relation to the Asian traditions will be listed below: see Part III, ch. 8, note 38, p. 469 below.

51. Merton, *Hagia Sophia*, p. 369.

Chapter 7

1. See Brown I, pp. 533-538.
2. See Heschel, *The Sabbath*, passim.
3. Kermode, *The Literary Guide*, p. 448.
4. See Sebastian Moore, *The Fire and the Rose Are One.*
5. Recall Jesus' words to Nicodemus: you cannot *enter*, cannot *see* the kingdom unless . . . ; and the two complementary healings: the paralytic enabled to walk and enter the temple, the blind man given his

sight. There may be a certain parallel also with Peter, always ready to move, and the beloved disciple, who sees.

6. See Frye, *Words with Power*, pp. 154-155; Jung, "The Philosophical Tree"; Cook, *The Tree of Life*; de Lubac, *Aspects of Buddhism*, ch. 2: Two Cosmic Trees, pp. 53-85.

7. Dodd, *Interpretation*, p. 294.

8. *Son of Man* is a title for Jesus which appears seventy times in the NT, and twelve times in John's gospel—the last of which is 13:31: "Now the Son of Man has been glorified, and God has been glorified in him." In John, this title is used only by Jesus of himself. The major OT occurrence of the title is in Daniel 7, where it denotes the mysterious figure who appears before the Ancient One to receive power and glory.

> To him was given dominion and glory and kingship, that all peoples, nations and languages should serve him. His dominion is an everlasting dominion that shall not pass away, and his kingship is one that shall never be destroyed (Dan 7:14).

The "one like a son of man" appears to be a *collective* figure as well, merging with the "people of the Most High" who share his dominion.

> The kingship and dominion and the greatness of the kingdoms under the whole heaven shall be given to the people of the holy ones of the Most High; their kingdom shall be an everlasting kingdom, and all dominions shall serve and obey them (Dan 7:27).

See also Lindars, *Jesus Son of Man*.

9. See Beggiani, *Early Syriac Theology*, pp. 113-115. The words *Messiah* and *Christ* mean, literally, *the Anointed One*. This anointing consists, essentially, in the gift of the divine Spirit itself.

10. Daniélou, *From Shadows to Reality*, ch. 2, pp. 11-65. And see below, Part III, ch. 5.

11. See Heb 3:7–4:11.

12. Here the title *Son of Man* may refer not only to Jesus himself, but also to those who believe in him and who, now one with him, will remain on earth when he has returned to the Father.

13. *Dies solis—sun day*: see Regan, "The Day of the Sun," and Bacchiocchi, *From Sabbath to Sunday*.

14. Heschel, *The Sabbath*, pp. 13-24.

454 / THE GOOD WINE

15. See Rom 8:1-17; Gal 3:21–4:11.

16. See the "visits of the Word" spoken of by Bernard of Clairvaux: Sermon 32 on the Song of Songs, n. 2, *Works*, vol. 3, p. 135; Gilson, *Mystical Theology*, p. 241.

17. "...many translators have 'Peace *be* to (or with) you,' a rendering implying the wish that peace be restored or granted. In this eschatological moment, however, Jesus' words are not a wish but a statement of fact" (Brown II, p. 1021).

18. Foerster, *TDNT*, vol. 2, pp. 401, 406.

19. Paradoxically, through Jesus' resurrection—as we have seen—the nature of Christian discipleship is also transformed by a radical interiorization, in the new *immediacy* of the Spirit.

20. It is possible, however, that chapter 21 also belongs to this chiastic structure, as Ellis affirms (p. 292). We shall consider this question further when we study John 21 in the next chapter.

21. Logion 22, Guillaumont et al., *Gospel of Thomas*, pp. 17-18.

22. Brown (II, p. 1021) mentions that some translations (Vulgate and Peshitta) of Luke's gospel add to Jesus' repeated greeting of "Peace be with you" in Lk 24:36, the words "It is I (*egō eimi*, *I am*); do not be afraid." These are the same words Jesus spoke to his disciples when he appeared to them walking upon the waters of the lake: Jn 6:20; Mk 6:50; Mt 14:27. Luke tends to associate, therefore, the appearance of the risen Jesus to the gathered disciples with his earlier appearance upon the lake, as recorded in the other gospels. From the perspective of the Johannine *seven days of creation*, this is suggestive: the seventh day becomes associated or identified with the first day.

23. Heschel, *Quest for God*, pp. 119-127.

24. *Apophatic* theology proceeds not by affirmations about God but by *negations*, insisting that the divine Reality *transcends* all concepts, images and finite beings. See Lossky, *The Vision of God*; Lossky, *Mystical Theology*, ch. 2, "The Divine Darkness," pp. 23-43, and also pp. 238-247; Louth, *Origins of the Christian Mystical Tradition*, ch. 8 and 9, pp. 159-190, 197.

25. See Lossky, *Mystical Theology*, pp. 154f, 196-216, 238; Louth, *Origins*, pp. 73, 78, 124, 170, 197; Lossky, *Image and Likeness*, ch. 5, "Redemption and Deification," pp. 97-110; Meyendorff, *Palamas*, pp. 40-47; Mantzaridis, *Deification of Man*.

26. See Jn 17:20-23; 20:17; 2 Cor 3:18; 2 Pet 1:4; 1 Jn 3:1-2.

27. *Salvation*—see C. Lesquivit and P. Grelot, *DBT*, pp. 518-522. The Hebrew terms for "salvation" used in the OT already communicate the sense of a *totality* of human good: see *DBT*, p. 519. The unitive

fullness of the *sōtēria*, *salus*, salvation brought by Christ is expressed in the eastern Christian tradition: e.g. Lossky, *Mystical Theology*, pp. 135ff. See the references on *deification* in note 25 above.

28. See Rom 8:19-23 and Irenaeus:

> ...it was for this end that the Word of God was made man and He who was the Son of God became the Son of man, that man, having been taken into the Word, and receiving the adoption, might become the son of God ("Against Heresies," III, 19, 1, *ANF*, vol. 1, p. 448).

Vladimir Lossky writes:

> Man was created last, according to the Greek Fathers, in order that he might be introduced into the universe like a king into his palace (*Mystical Theology*, p. 111).

> In the parousia, and the eschatological fulfilment of history, the whole created universe will enter into perfect union with God (*Mystical Theology*, p. 235).

29. See Lampe, *Seal of the Spirit*, pp. 33, 46.

30. See 1 Cor 13; 1 Jn 2:9-11; 3:10-24; 4:7-21. "Agape constitutes the being and the life of the Christian.... This, then, is the heart of Christianity and the spring of Christian morality: 'to be in charity' (Eph 1:4)" (Spicq, *Charity and Liberty*, p. 8).

"Johannine thought takes all metaphors and symbols of salvation and unifies them in Jesus. He is the one about whom all symbols speak.... Similarly, the teaching of Jesus is unified in the single commandment of love" (Pheme Perkins, *Love Commands*, p. 105).

31. The ten ox-herding pictures will be found, with brief commentaries in prose and verse, in Kapleau, *Three Pillars of Zen*, pp. 301-313.

32. This spiritual generativity (see 1 Cor 4:14-15) bears a certain analogy to human fatherhood in that it initiates a life which is not further dependent upon it—paradoxically communicating a new relationship with God which is *immediate*: essentially free of the need for any human mediation.

33. See Part III, ch. 2 and ch. 4 for similar transpositions of meaning related to baptism.

34. Irenaeus of Lyons, *Against Heresies* V, 21, 1: *ANF*, vol. 1, p. 549.

Chapter 8

1. Brown II, pp. 1077-1082.
2. Ellis (pp. 290, 292, 310-312) sees chapter 21 as an integral part of the chiasm of the gospel as a whole. He finds both an internal chiasm within each of the two sections of ch. 21, and a chiastic symmetry between these two sections and two sections of John 20—20:24-29 and 20:19-23, respectively. Ellis sees the final five-part chiastic unit of the gospel as extending from 20:19 to 21:25, with its central section in 20:30-31.

A more recent marshaling of evidence for the presence of chapter 21 in the original design of the fourth gospel will be found in *St. Vladimir's Theological Quarterly*, vol. 36 (1992), pp. 3-49: (1) A review of the question (Editorial, otherwise untitled) by John Breck, pp. 3-5; (2) M. Franzmann and M. Klinger, "The Call Stories of John 1 and John 21," pp. 7-15; (3) P.F. Ellis, "The Authenticity of John 21," pp. 17-25; (4) J. Breck, "John 21: Appendix, Epilogue or Conclusion?" pp. 27-49.

3. Brown II, pp. 1099f.
4. St. Augustine, *Homilies on the Gospel of John*, CXXIII, NPNF Series I, vol. 7, n. 2, p. 444; quoted in Brown II, p. 1099.
5. See Is 25:6; 49:9-10; 55:1-2; 65:13; Feuillet, *Johannine Studies*, pp. 70-72, and P.-M. Galopin in *DBT*, p. 344.
6. See Ellis, p. 301.
7. See Brown II, pp. 1074-1076.
8. St. Jerome, "Commentary on Ezechiel," XLVII, 6-13; *PL* 25:1474C, Brown II, p. 1074.
9. In Ezekiel 47:8, the water from the temple flows first into the *arabah* and then into the Dead Sea. The *arabah* is a great depression in the earth which extends south from the Sea of Galilee through the Dead Sea to the Gulf of Aqabah. See S. Cohen in *IDB*, vol. 1, pp. 177-179.
10. Brown II, pp. 1102-1104.
11. See Jung, "AION: The Fish in Alchemy," especially pp. 127, 149-152; Leach, "Fishing for Men."
12. See E. Leclerc, *The People of God in the Night*.
13. Ellis, p. 303.
14. *Realized eschatology*: a conception of the "last things" as already present. For John, the fullness of the new creation is present in Jesus and—through Jesus—in the believer. See Brown I, Introduction, pp. cxvi-cxxi. For a review of more recent study, see Carroll, "Present and Future in Fourth Gospel Eschatology."

15. See Brown I, Introduction, pp. lxxxvii-cii; Brown (1988), pp. 9-12; Ellis, pp. 2-3; Hengel, *Johannine Question*, passim.
16. Ellis, pp. 310-312.
17. It is to be remembered that Ellis places chapter 21 firmly in the *original* chiastic structure of the gospel: see Ellis (1984), p.292 and (1992), pp. 17-25.

PART III

Chapter 1

1. We are not suggesting that the disciples reflected upon the theological implications of Jesus' words, *I Am*, but that the presence of the One to whom this expression traditionally belonged impressed itself upon their minds and hearts when Jesus appeared to them upon the waters. Of first importance to us, however, is not what the disciples experienced or thought at that moment, but what John intends to evoke in his reader at this point in his gospel.
2. It is possible, of course, that the Johannine mandala has developed independently of the Pauline figure.
3. "Whoever serves me must *follow me*, and where I am, there will my servant be also" (12:26). The words "follow me" here refer to *any* disciple, while in 21:19.22 the same words are addressed only to *Peter*, and with some particular implications (see 21:18-19).
4. See note above on Part II, ch. 6, and Brown I, p. 14.
5. Here once again we must be careful to avoid confusing two distinct levels of sexual reference: the *symbolic* masculine–feminine polarity and the fact of gender in the individual person.
6. Kermode in *Literary Guide*, pp. 445-446, 452-453.
7. See note 16 to Pt. I, ch. 5, on pp. 440f above.

Chapter 2

1. In this supposed "Johannine community" the central evangelical instruction has been given through *John's* gospel. Extending this continuity still further, we suppose that the representative of the community who administers the baptism itself is here called *John*.
2. See note 1 above.

3. See note 16 to Pt. I, ch. 5, on pp. 440f, and pp. 258, 319.

4. Mt 28:19; Rom 6:3-8. See Lampe, *The Seal of the Spirit*, ch. 13, pp. 261-283; Hamman, *Baptism*, e.g. p. 10.

5. *phōtizein* is found in Heb 6:4 and 10:32:

> "... the reference being to the beginning of Christian life.... Baptism is in view." "The technical use of *phōtismos* for baptism, which does not occur in the NT, is developed by Justin: Apol. 61,12; cf 65,1; Dial. 122,5. Another explanation is offered by Clement of Alexandria: Paed. I, 6,26,2, where baptism is *phōtisma*." H.G. Conzelmann, *TDNT* vol. 9, pp. 355, 357-358. See also Hamman, *Baptism*, pp. 18-19.

Chapter 3

1. Barrett, "John and the Synoptic Gospels"; Barrett, *Gospel*, pp. 15-18, 42-54.

2. Standaert, *Marc: composition et genre litteraire* (1978), and *Marc: Commentaire* (1983); Scott, "Chiastic Structure: A Key to the Interpretation of Mark's Gospel" (1985); van Iersel, *Reading Mark* (1988); Stock, *Method and Message of Mark* (1989). Standaert, van Iersel and Stock propose virtually the same five-part chiastic structure for Mark, while Scott proposes a five-part chiasm divided according to a different principle.

3. van Iersel, *Reading Mark*, pp. 20-26.

4. Scott, "Chiastic Structure"; see note 2 above.

5. Standaert (1978), Part III, pp. 496-540.

6. Stock, *Method and Message*, Introduction, p. 16.

7. These authors differ slightly in their division of the gospel's chiastic sections. Here, following Standaert (1978 and 1983), we shall take the *prologue* as including Mk 1:1-13 and the *epilogue* as including Mk 16:1-8.

8. Stock, *Method and Message*, p. 17.

9. Stock, ibid., pp. 18-19. See also Scroggs and Groff, "Baptism in Mark," p. 540.

10. See Barrett, *Gospel*, pp. 43, 271, 279.

11. McVann, "Baptism, Miracles and Boundary-Jumping in Mark," p. 155.

12. Daube, "The Earliest Structure of the Gospels," and *The New Testament and Rabbinic Judaism.*

13. Leiden, E.J. Brill, 1965.

14. Stock, *Method and Message*, pp. 12-19.

15. Stock, ibid., p. 16.

16. See references in Standaert (1978), p. 542. Of first importance was Le Déaut, *La nuit pascale: Essai sur la signification de la Pâque juive à partir du Targum d'Exode XII 42* (1963). Also available is a shorter account by the same author, "Pâque juive et Nouveau Testament" (1969).

17. See Standaert (1978), pp. 496-626, summarized in English by Stock, in *Method and Message*, Introduction, pp. 12-35.

18. Standaert (1978), p. 570.

19. See the two works by Le Déaut listed in note 16 above.

20. From Targum on Exodus XII,42: original text in Diez Macho, *Neofiti I.* French translation in Standaert (1978), pp. 545-546.

21. Standaert (1978), pp. 546-547.

22. Standaert (1978), pp. 574-579; Standaert (1983), p. 74.

23. On the complex problem of *dating* the Targums, and particularly *Codex Neofiti I*, which contains the "Poem of the Four Nights," see Le Déaut, "The Current State of Targumic Studies," *BTB* 4 (1974), pp. 5, 22-24. "It seems, however, that the bulk of it (*Codex Neofiti I*) comes from the I/II Cent. A.D." (p. 5).

Le Déaut brings together a number of parallels which have been discovered between the targumic literature and John's gospel in "Targumic Literature and NT Interpretation" (1974). On Targums and John's gospel see also McNamara, *Palestinian Judaism and the New Testament*, pp. 234-241.

24. As Le Déaut (1969, p. 28) points out, there is reason to believe that the three-year cycle of readings in the Palestinian synagogues for Passover time included *Genesis 1* in the first year, and *Exodus 12* in the second year. At present, the first creation account and the narrative of the Passover night, from these same two chapters, are read each year in the Roman Catholic Easter vigil liturgy.

25. See Le Déaut (1969), p. 29.

26. See Le Déaut (1969), pp. 38-40 and Le Déaut, *nuit pascale*, chs. 2 and 3.

27. See J.E. Wood, "Isaac Typology in the New Testament," p. 587.

28. *Mechilta ad Exodus*, VIII, quoted in J. Daniélou, *From Shadows to Reality*, p. 119.

29. Wood, "Isaac Typology," pp. 586-587.

30. The words in brackets are probably a Christian addition to the text.

31. "Testament of the Twelve Patriarchs," Levi 18, in Charlesworth, *Pseudepigrapha*, vol. 1, pp. 794-795.

32. Standaert (1978), pp. 573-579; Standaert (1983), p. 74.

33. *Realized eschatology:* see note 14 to Pt. II, ch. 8.

34. See Le Déaut (1969), p. 32, and chapter 5 below.

35. See the passage quoted above from Standaert, on the conflation of different historical moments in the *Poem* and in Mark.

36. Standaert (1978), p. 607, citing both Burmester, "Le lectionnaire de la semaine sainte," p. 433, and Baumstark, *Nocturna laus*, p. 43.

Chapter 4

1. *Mystagogy:* guidance into the mysteries. This term was sometimes used in the patristic age for the instructions on the Christian sacramental mysteries preached to catechumens or the newly baptized (e.g. the "Mystical Catecheses," or post-baptismal instructions, of St. Cyril of Jerusalem). See E. Mazza, *Mystagogy*. The term has been used in a more general, non-sacramental sense by James J. Bacik, in *Apologetics and the Eclipse of Mystery: Mystagogy according to Karl Rahner*.

2. This language expresses the mystery of baptism from a *male* viewpoint. The "sacred marriage" realized or inaugurated in baptism, from the viewpoint of a *woman*, could be conceived rather in terms of a union with the Word-Bridegroom. From either perspective, through a new indwelling of the Spirit in the baptized person, the conjunction of Word and Spirit is newly realized in this person.

3. See note 2 above. Here again the perspective is a masculine one. A woman might conceive of the indwelling Bride (the Spirit) as now *one* with her own being, so that she herself can relate as bride to the *Logos*-Bridegroom. Of course the *Logos* too, from either viewpoint, is interior as well as exterior. In referring to the episodes of the Samaritan woman at the well and of Magdalene in the garden, we shall now move to the feminine perspective.

Chapter 5

1. "The Odes of Solomon," ed. Charlesworth, 1978 and 1985.

A brief introduction to the Syrian spiritual tradition, with bibliography, will be found in Jones, Wainwright and Yarnold, *The Study of Spirituality*, pp. 199-215. A fuller introduction to the Syrian tradition is provided in Brock's *The Syriac Fathers on Prayer and the Spiritual Life*. A copious treatment of the tradition, centered around the book's ecclesial focus, is Murray's *Symbols of Church and Kingdom: A Study in Early Syriac Tradition*. Also useful is the brief study of Beggiani, *Early Syriac Theology, with Special Reference to the Maronite Tradition*.

The works of Aphrahat and Ephrem, the two principal early Syrian writers, will be found—though in an antiquated translation—in *NPNF* Series II, vol. 2. A number of valuable translations and studies of the Syriac writings by Sebastian Brock and Robert Murray have appeared, over the years, in *Eastern Churches Review* and *Sobornost*, and then in *Sobornost/ECR* (see Bibliography). See also Sebastian Brock's translation of twelve poems of St. Ephrem, *The Harp of the Spirit*, and his *The Luminous Eye. The Spiritual World Vision of St. Ephrem the Syrian*.

2. See note 1 above.

3. "...the Odes were probably composed sometime around 100 A.D." (Charlesworth, *Pseudepigrapha*, vol. 2, Introduction to the Odes, p. 727).

4. See Charlesworth and Culpepper, "The Odes of Solomon and the Gospel of John."

5. Ibid., p. 320.

6. The controversy about baptismal references in the Odes is recounted by Robert C. Stroud in *The Odes of Solomon: Sacramental Prophetism in the Church's First Hymnal*, pp. 45-53.

7. Bernard, *The Odes of Solomon* (1912), p. 42.

8. The controversy between those who find an abundance of baptismal allusions in the Odes and those who minimize the baptismal reference offers an interesting parallel to the dispute about the sacramental references in John's gospel. In both cases, it is the very *abundance* and the symbolic *depth* of these baptismal connections (both contributing to their implausibility for the skeptic) which point to an actual *totality* of baptismal reference. This theology of incarnation and of cosmic new creation is essentially and integrally sacramental!

9. "...the Odes are a window through which we can occasionally glimpse the earliest Christians at worship; especially their apparent stress on baptism...." "Bernard recognized, but exaggerated, the importance of baptism in the Odes...." Charlesworth, in his introduction to the Odes in *Pseudepigrapha*, vol. 2 (1985), p. 728.

"...many of them (the Odes) are generally agreed to be baptismal in character." Brock, *Holy Spirit in Syrian Baptismal Tradition* (1979), p. 27.

462 / The Good Wine

"Scholarly interpretation has gradually returned to a baptismal interpretation of much of the imagery, as proposed by J.H. Bernard before the more sceptical commentary of Rendel Harris and Mingana." Murray, *Symbols* (1975), p. 25.

10. See Bernard, "The Odes of Solomon" (1910), pp. 4-14.

11. Ode 36:3, for example, appears in Charlesworth's translation as

(The Spirit) brought me forth before the Lord's face,
and because I was the Son of Man,
I was named the Light, the Son of God.

Bernard, "The Odes of Solomon" (1921), p. 90, translated the same verse in this way:

She (sc. the Holy Spirit) brought me forth before the face
of the Lord; and although a son of man, I have been
named a luminary, a son of God.

12. The Holy Spirit is characterized as *feminine* particularly in Odes 19, 28 and 36. See Murray, *Symbols*, pp. 142-150.

13. See Guillaumont, *Gospel According to Thomas*. Another English translation of *Thomas*, by David R. Cartlidge, is supplied in Davies' *Thomas and Christian Wisdom*, pp. 158-171.

14. "The sayings in the Gospel of Thomas had a function in early Christian communities connected with the rite of baptism. Thomas is neither a baptismal text itself, nor does it contain very many obviously liturgical passages; only (Logion) 22 and the ritualized questions and responses of (Logion) 50 probably played a part in actual baptismal rites....

... Thomas is probably part of the post-baptismal instruction of new Christians and was probably read aloud to such persons, with explanations and interpretations added orally for at least the more difficult sayings. Thomas is not, therefore, a purely intellectual document; it is based on a rite, an event, a ritual transformation. To discover the meaning of the sayings, as advocated in Logion 1, is to discover the meaning of the rite" (Davies, *Thomas*, p. 136).

These last affirmations of Davies about the Gospel of Thomas may be also applicable in large part to the gospel of John.

15. Guillaumont, *Thomas*, p. 3 (the italics are ours). The further passages of the Gospel of Thomas in the present chapter will also be quoted from the English translation of Guillaumont et al. in the same volume.

16. Davies, *Thomas*, p. 127.

17. Meeks, "The Image of the Androgyne," pp. 180-181.

18. Meeks, ibid., p. 182.

19. Meeks, ibid., p. 185; quoted by Davies, *Thomas*, p. 128.

20. Both the Syriac *iḥidaya* and the Greek *monachos*, which may derive from it, came to be used as technical terms for ascetics or monks.

21. Murray, *Symbols*, p. 13. See also Murray, "Exhortation."

22. Murray, *Symbols*, p. 15; "Exhortation," pp. 59, 79-80.

23. Murray, *Symbols*, p. 16.

24. *Hymns on the Epiphany*, No. 8, quoted in Murray, *Symbols*, p. 16.

25. Winkler, "The Origins and Idiosyncrasies of the Earliest Form of Asceticism."

26. This image of the baptismal robe of glory, very common in the Syriac literature, is discussed by Duncan, *Baptism in the Demonstrations of Aphraates*, pp. 43-49, Brock, *Holy Spirit*, pp. 48-52, and Beggiani, *Early Syriac Theology*, pp. 108-110.

27. Winkler, "Origins," p. 33.

28. Aphrahat, *Demonstrations*, as quoted in Winkler, p. 35.

29. Winkler, p. 35.

30. Winkler, p. 35.

31. See Winkler, pp. 35-37.

32. See Conzelmann, *TDNT*, vol. 9, pp. 357-358; Hamman, *Baptism*, pp. 18-19.

33. This three-phase history of the church is proposed in Rahner's essay, "Basic Theological Interpretation of the Second Vatican Council."

Chapter 6

1. At one end of the spectrum of opinion concerning John's relationship to baptism and the eucharist stands Bultmann (*Gospel of John*, p. 472), who posits an anti-sacramental bias in the evangelist. The opposite pole is represented by Cullmann (*Early Christian Worship*, p. 116), for whom reference to worship (i.e. the two sacraments) appears in "an astonishingly large number of passages which are given a *decisive* place in the structure of the whole Gospel."

See also the discussion in Barrett, *Gospel*, pp. 82-85, and especially the evaluation of evidence for the various positions in Brown I, pp. cxi-cxiv.

2. For *the mysteries*, see Vagaggini, *Theological Dimensions*, pp. 598-611. The *disciplina arcana*, or code of secrecy, was the practice of reserving full instruction in, or exposure to, the church's sacramental

mysteries to the baptized. This practice, however, did not yet exist during the first two centuries of the church. See Jungmann, *Early Liturgy*, p. 159.

3. McVann, p. 155. McVann here quotes Quentin Quesnell, *The Mind of Mark: Interpretation and Method in the Exegesis of Mark 6:52*, Analecta Biblica 38, Rome, Biblical Institute Press, 1969, p. 202.

4. McVann, ibid.

5. According to the Jewish law, the testimony of two witnesses was required and sufficient to establish a truth. See M. Prat and P. Grelot, *DBT*, p. 661.

Chapter 7

1. See Brown II, pp. 1006-1007; Maynard, "The Role of Peter in the Fourth Gospel"; Droge, "The Status of Peter in the Fourth Gospel." Further bibliography will be found in these two articles.

2. The *epicenter* is the *visible* point on the surface of the earth directly above the actual (underground) *center*: e.g. of an earthquake.

3. See Droge, pp. 309-310.

4. Regardless of the precise authorship of these two letters, they very likely express the visions of Petrine and Johannine traditions at a point close to their respective origins.

5. Eastern Christianity has continued to understand the church primarily as communion rather than institution. See, for example, Staniloae, *Theology and the Church*. Contemporary western writers who do exemplify a vision of cosmic sacramentality include A.M. Allchin (e.g. *The World Is a Wedding*) and Rosemary Haughton (e.g. *The Passionate God*).

Chapter 8

1. Evagrius Ponticus (345-399) was apparently the first to adopt John's one hundred and fifty-three fish as a literary form, in his 153 *Chapters on Prayer* (see *Evagrius Ponticus: The Praktikos and Chapters on Prayer*). Since the 153 large fish of John 21 apparently refer to the fullness of humanity—the totality of the nations—to be harvested by the disciples of Jesus throughout history, they may serve also to denote a series of theological reflections on history in the light of the Johannine Unitive.

2. At the beginning of our study, we explored the term *Unitive* in the light of a series of scriptural texts (see note 11 to Part I, ch. 1). Now, at the end, it may be useful to suggest a few unitive conceptions from outside the biblical world which reflect one or another feature of the Johannine Unitive.

We observe in the contemporary western world a broad encounter with a variety of Asian spiritual traditions. At the heart of several of the more influential of these eastern traditions (Hindu Vedanta and Advaitan philosophy, Taoism, Buddhism) there lies an experience and a consciousness of *non-duality* which is deeply resonant with the Johannine Unitive, especially along the lines of baptismal experience and contemplative experience. See D. Loy, *Nonduality*; K. Wilber, *Spectrum of Consciousness.*

This eastern unitive experience has been brought into relationship with western psychology and spirituality (G. May, *Will and Spirit*; T. Merton, "Inner Experience"). Related to eastern integrative conceptions of the human person (*Atman*) are unitive contemporary western conceptions of the person such as the Jungian *Self*.

Among not only poets but scientists as well, a need is felt to overcome the acute *subject-object* duality of the modern west—especially in the sense of our contemporary alienation from nature. See R. Bly, *News from the Universe*; Mary C. Richards, *Centering*, R. Sheldrake, *The Rebirth of Nature*. New Paradigm thinkers insist on a *holistic* perspective: the unity and interconnectedness of all beings. See F. Capra, *Turning Point*; K. Wilber, *Eye to Eye*.

A few western writers—including Teilhard de Chardin and Owen Barfield—have brought human history and the evolution of life into the light of the Unitive. Much of Teilhard's speculative writing is permeated by his passion for unitive vision, and he sees all human efforts—and human history itself—as moving toward a final unity. The unitive perspective is evident in some of the principal Teilhardian concepts: the *Omega*, the *Centric*, the *Divine Milieu*. His quest for a unitive spirituality may be seen particularly in *The Divine Milieu* and in Ursula King's *Towards a New Mysticism*.

Christ is the unitive center of the evolutionary visions of both Teilhard de Chardin and Owen Barfield. Barfield sees human history as a long and gradual movement from a passive *original participation* in the divine unity to a conscious and creative *final participation* of human persons in the same divine unity. This is analogous to the progression which Teilhard proposes from the *Road of the East* (a return to an undifferentiated original unity through withdrawal from the world and its multiplicity) to the *Road of the West* (a forward movement into final unity through further personal differentiation, through love, and through interaction with the material universe itself). See U. King, *Towards a New Mysticism*, ch. 6, pp. 123-143.

Attempts to reconcile or integrate the Christian (e.g. Johannine) unitive vision with other unitive perspectives must face the peculiar union of *inclusiveness* and *particularity* which is at the core of Christianity. This has many expressions. The future of the world pivots about the particular human person who is Jesus Christ, and about the concrete bit of history which is his life, death and resurrection. The destiny of an individual person may pivot around that person's response of faith to a particular divine revelation and invitation. This paradoxical fusion of totality and particularity which we find in the NT is most evident in the Pauline and Johannine writings, where the unitive cosmic scope of the Christ-mystery becomes most explicit. The paradox is condensed in the prologue's affirmation, *"The Word became flesh"*—the divine Source of the universe came into this world newly and uniquely in the one very concrete and specific human person who is Jesus of Nazareth.

Through this man's death and resurrection, the unitive Divinity is newly opened to human participation: through experience and knowledge, through love and ultimately through an ontological union in which the human person is opened to its divine destiny. This unitive divinity, dwelling at the heart of cosmos and of history, becomes the force which carries the world toward its transformation and fulfillment.

While the inclusive or cosmic or unitive aspect of this mystery has a wide appeal, the obverse side of the mystery—the "scandal of particularity"—is the great obstacle to belief both for Christians and non-Christians. The obstacle may be encountered in the form of the historical Jesus, of an actual church community or church institution, in the materiality of the sacraments, or in the apparent hopelessness of one's own existence. An understanding of the Johannine Unitive which did not confront this concrete incarnational challenge would be partial and delusive.

3. "There is scarcely another book in the NT where the presence and role of the church is so strongly exerted and felt as in the Fourth Gospel. And yet traditional church terminology is absent. Just as the salvation-history perspective is missing...so also any reference to structured order, ranks, and offices within the church." M. Appold, *The Oneness Motif*, p. 264.

4. The apparent simplicity of the reformation's *sola gratia, sola fide, sola scriptura* masks an actual dichotomizing of the Christ-mystery and consequently of the Unity. See Lortz, "Reformation," in *Sacramentum Mundi*, vol. 5, pp. 215-233; Rahner, *Foundations of Christian Faith*, pp. 359-366.

5. This language of *institution* and of *communion* models of the church is that of Avery Dulles, in his *Models of the Church*. In this well-known book Dulles proposes three other models as well: church as *sacrament*, as *herald* and as *servant*. In his sequel, *A Church To Believe In*, he finds most adequate and inclusive a further model: the *community of disciples*. This latter, developed in a *sapiential* direction, would relate well (as does the *communion* model) to our interpretation of John's gospel.

6. "Dogmatic Constitution on the Church," in Flannery, p. 350.

7. Among modern spiritual writers who use the explicit language of personal unity are Underhill (*Mysticism*, ch. X, "The Unitive Life," pp. 413-443, and Merton, "The Inner Experience (I)," *CS 18* (1983), pp. 3-15.

8. See Panikkar, *Blessed Simplicity*, pp. 15-18.

9. Panikkar, ibid., pp. 29-35.

10. See Merton, "Inner Experience (I)," cited above, and further installments of the same work in successive issues of *Cistercian Studies* during 1983 and 1984; Gerald May, *Will and Spirit*, ch. 3, "Unitive Experience: A Paradigm for Contemplative Spirituality," pp. 52-68; Underhill, *Mysticism*, pp. 329ff.

11. See Rahner, *Foundations*, pp. 14-23; Ken Wilber, *Spectrum of Consciousness*, pp. 106ff; May, *Will and Spirit*, ch. 3, pp. 52-68.

12. See Bamberger, Introduction to *Evagrius Ponticus*, pp. lxxxii-lxxxvii.

13. See Bamberger, ibid, pp. xii-xiii; Irenee Hausherr, S.J., "L'hesychasme"; George Maloney, *Russian Hesychasm*; Louis Bouyer, *Spirituality of NT and Fathers*, pp. 378, 505.

14. See the various contributions in Moustakas, *The Self*; see Jung, *Aion*.

15. *Microcosm and Mediator* is the title of an important study of Maximus Confessor by Lars Thunberg. Thunberg has more recently published, also in English, a shorter overview of Maximus' theology, *Man and the Cosmos*.

Maximus (ca. 580-662), one of the most powerful synthetic thinkers of the Christian east, sees the human person at the center of the process of re-establishing the unity of the entire creation in Christ.

Thomas Merton, in our time, envisions a similar unitive role for the individual person.

If I can unite *in myself* the thought and devotion of Eastern and Western Christendom, the Greek and the Latin
Fathers, the Russians with the Spanish mystics, I can
prepare in myself the reunion of divided Christians.
From that secret and unspoken unity in myself can
eventually come a visible and manifest unity of all
Christians.... We must contain all divided worlds in
ourselves and transcend them in Christ (T. Merton, *Conjectures*, p. 12).

Merton's conception of this inner work of unification was not,
it is evident, limited to the world of Christianity.

16. See Bellah, *Habits of the Heart*, a study of American individualism and its fruits.

17. See Jn 17:22-23; 1 Cor 2:7; 2 Cor 4:6.

18. *Scientism:* the unreflective and uncritical mentality—a caricature
of true scientific intelligence—which presupposes that the empirical and
rational knowledge of science is the supreme and comprehensive—the
only ultimately valid—human knowledge.

19. 'Tis fourfold in my supreme delight
And threefold in soft Beulah's night
And twofold always. May God us keep
From single vision and Newton's sleep.

These verses were included by William Blake in a letter to Thomas
Butts of November 22, 1802. See *Blake: Complete Writings*, p. 818.

The "single vision" of modern scientific rationalism is studied
by Barfield (*Saving the Appearances*, passim), by Roszak (*Where the
Wasteland Ends*, Part 2, "Single Vision and Newton's Sleep," pp. 99ff),
and by Frye (*Double Vision*).

20. The document signaling this official change in attitude is
Gaudium et Spes, "The Pastoral Constitution on the Church in the
Modern World," Flannery, pp. 903-1001.

21. See Barfield, *Rediscovery of Meaning*, pp. 233-235, and further
Barfield references above in note 3 to Part II, ch. 4.

22. The term *recapitulation* (Gr. *anakephalaiōsis*) derives from the
Pauline writings (Eph 1:10), but Irenaeus' use of it in conjunction with
the *Word* is closer to Johannine thought.

23. *Apophatic* theology: see note 24 to Part II, ch. 7 above.

24. See *Pseudo-Dionysius. The Complete Works*, with its introductory
essays.

25. See Deut 27:15; Ex 20:1-4; Deut 4:9-28. See also P.Lamarche, *DBT*, p. 252 and Abraham Heschel, *Quest for God*, ch. 5. "Symbolism," pp. 115-144.

26. See Gregory of Nyssa, *Life of Moses* (1978), nn. 162-164 (pp. 94-95); nn. 219-239 (pp. 111-116); Daniélou, *From Glory to Glory*, Introduction, pp. 23-32; text, pp. 118, 142-148. See also the text from Gregory's "On the Song of Songs" quoted by Lossky, *Mystical Theology*, p. 35, and the passage from Gregory Palamas, *Theophanes*, quoted by Lossky in the same book, p. 37.

27. Lossky, *Mystical Theology*, p. 26. Consistent with this affirmation, Lossky devotes the first chapter of this synthesis of eastern theology to "the divine *darkness.*"

28. *Meister Eckhart: Sermons and Treatises*, ed. Walshe. Generous selections from Eckhart have also been recently published in two volumes of the Paulist Western Spirituality series, *Meister Eckhart: The Essential Sermons, Commentaries, Treatises and Defense* (1981) and *Meister Eckhart: Teacher and Preacher* (1986).

29. See Rahner, *Sacramentum Mundi*, vol. 6, p. 243 (Aquinas), pp. 234-238; Vagaggini, *Theological Dimensions*, pp. 626-628.

30. The *magisterium* in Roman Catholic usage is the official and authoritative teaching function of the church. See Rahner, *Sacramentum Mundi*, vol. 3, pp. 351-358.

31. See Gilkey, *Catholicism Confronts Modernity.*

32. One expression of such a materializing and absolutizing of "tradition" is the principle, widely held in Orthodoxy, that the development of church doctrine ended with the last of the great ecumenical councils. The result of such a view is an effort to immobilize the life of the church in one particular historical age.

33. This historical sense of Russian thinkers is exemplified by the writings of V. Soloviev and N. Berdyaev.

34. See Tavard, *Woman in Christian Tradition*, pp. 155-170.

35. See Fedotov, *A Treasury of Russian Spirituality*, and Schmemann, *Ultimate Questions.*

36. We have not used the word *revelation* here because this concept is characteristic of the traditions of the *Word.*

37. It is possible to categorize the Hindu and Buddhist traditions in this general way, despite the great variety of paths that are gathered under the name Hinduism, and the resistance to verbal expression—the apophatism—of Buddhism.

38. Affinities between the Johannine writings and the Asian traditions have been explored by a number of writers in recent decades. A

few examples will be cited here without evaluation: Bruns, *The Art and Thought of John* (1969); Bruns, *The Christian Buddhism of St. John* (1971); Duraisingh and Hargreaves, *India's Search for Reality and the Relevance of the Gospel of John* (1975); Abhishikhtananda, *Saccidananda. A Christian Approach to Advaitic Experience* (1974) (the book as a whole, however, is not focused upon John); Abhishikhtananda, *Hindu-Christian Meeting Point* (1976), ch. 6 , "The Johannine Upanishads," pp. 77-93; Viereck, *The Lotus and the Word: Key Parallels in the Saddharma Pundarika Sutra and the Gospel According to John* (1973); Malatesta, *Interiority and Covenant* (1978), Appendix: "Indwelling in the Bhagavad Gita," pp. 325-331, with a bibliography of earlier writings on John and the east; Vandana, *Waters of Fire* (1988); Ravindra, *The Yoga of the Christ in the Gospel According to St. John* (1990).

39. The western contributions are treated most amply by Schipflinger, *Sophia-Maria*. Several presentations of Jacob Boehme are now available in English.

40. See Williams, *The Figure of Beatrice*, and Haughton, *The Passionate God*.

41. See Ulanov, *The Feminine* and *Receiving Woman*.

42. See Rahner, "Experience of God Today"; "Experience of Self and Experience of God."

43. This power of Jesus is strongly reflected in our central episode of the *sea-crossing*. The emergent masculine is this Jesus who stands upon the waters (in the synoptic versions) at the center of the universe and says *I Am*; says *Be still*, and the surging chaos quiets at the sound of his voice. He is the creative Word whose appearance itself is authority; who is the *ground*, so that whoever reaches out to receive him is already touching the farther shore, the new earth. First he is merely this light in the darkness of the night sea: the witness, *I Am*. Then he is the author of the *new creation* which begins in those who "received him, who believed in his name," and which consists in the imparting of his own unitive being so that the kingdom is born within those who believe.

This Jesus of the *beginning* is the same Jesus who appears to his disciples in the house after his resurrection and breathes the Spirit into them.

44. The interpretive power of this unitive principle can be demonstrated by reading a number of the synoptic parables from the unitive perspective. This often brings about an inversion through which the harsh and sometimes absurd imagery of the story opens to reveal another expression of the one revelation of the divine love in Jesus.

Consider in this light, for example, the Matthean parable of the two servants (Mt 18:23-35), and that of the vineyard workers (Mt 20:1-15).

45. Ironically, eucharistic celebration in the churches, because of its—only partly inevitable—exclusiveness, witnesses not only to the separation of Christians from other people but to the divisions among Christians themselves.

46. The Latin word *communitas* was appropriated by Victor Turner to express the extraordinary sense of communion or solidarity and of freedom from separative social structures which is experienced in certain situations of marginalization, of transition and anonymity which he calls *liminal* situations. See Turner, *The Ritual Process*, p. 96.

47. See Rahner, "Basic Theological Interpretation."

48. This well-known literary slogan was originated by William Carlos Williams, the twentieth century American poet.

49. See Barfield, *Saving the Appearances*, cited above. This book is largely devoted to a criticism of the rigid literalism of much contemporary thought, dominated by scientism. He calls this literalism *idolatry*.

50. See note 1 to Introduction, above.

51. See Allchin, *The World Is a Wedding*; Brock, "Poet as Theologian."

52. See Bamberger, Introduction to *Evagrius Ponticus*, pp. lxxxviii-lxxxix; *Praktikos* n. 1 and 2, pp. 15-16.

53. Merton, "The Inner Experience" (IV), *CS 18* (1983), pp. 289-298.

54. Vatican II *Constitution on the Church*, n. 1, Flannery, p. 350.

55. See Rahner, "The New Image of the Church," especially pp. 12-24 on church as *sacrament*.

56. See De Waal, "Towards a Renewed Sacramental Theology," p. 705.

57. *Zen Mind, Beginner's Mind* is the work of Shunryu Suzuki Roshi, a contemporary Soto Zen teacher.

Epilogue

1. See Bibliography: Barrett, Brown, Ellis, Haenchen, Perkins, Schnackenburg.

2. See Bibliography: Culpepper, Frye, Kermode. Particularly useful is the *Literary Guide to the Bible* edited by Alter and Kermode. A concise classification and review of particular methods of literary criticism in use during recent decades is provided by Schneiders, "Literary Criticism."

3. An excellent example is the *Dictionary of Biblical Theology* (*DBT*) edited by Léon-Dufour, to which we have often referred. For readers with some Greek, the *Theological Dictionary of the New Testament* (*TDNT*), edited by Kittel and Friedrich in nine volumes, offers abundant background information.

More specific in focus are Terrien's *The Elusive Presence* (useful for background and context of the Johannine writings) and the various thematic articles collected in *A Companion to John: Readings in Johannine Theology*, edited by Taylor.

4. See Lossky, Meyendorff, Mantzaridis, Schmemann, Staniloae. Periodicals featuring eastern Christian theology include *Sobornost/ ECR* and *St. Vladimir's Theological Quarterly*; in French, *Contacts. Revue Orthodoxe de Theologie et de Spiritualité*, Paris.

5. This tradition is especially rich in the French language, with scholars such as Henri De Lubac, Jean Daniélou, Louis Bouyer, M.-E. Boismard, André Feuillet, René Robert, Ignace de la Potterie, and Jacques Goettmann.

6. See Kühlewind, *Becoming Aware of the Logos*, Ravindra, *The Yoga of Christ*, and Christopher Bamford's reflections appended to John Scotus Eriugena, *The Voice of the Eagle*.

7. In most of the Pauline letters we find a consistent two-part structure. First there is a doctrinal section, an exposition of the Christ-Mystery and the grace which has come from it to these believers, and then an exhortation in which the ethical imperatives deriving from this grace are spelled out.

8. Howard Gardner (*Artful Scribbles*, p. 47) discovered that young children, in their preference for particular ways of playing, sorted themselves into two groups, *dramatists* and *patterners*. Unlike their more outward-going fellows of the first group, the patterners occupy themselves with "the configurations they can discern, the patterns and regularities they encounter..." (quoted by Anthony Storr, *Solitude*, p. 90).

Bibliography

I. Biblical

The Holy Bible, Containing the Old and New Testaments with the Apocryphal/Deuterocanonical Books, New Revised Standard Version, New York, Collins, 1989.

Alter and Kermode, *The Literary Guide to the Bible*, Cambridge, Harvard University Press, 1987.

Appold, *The Oneness Motif in the Fourth Gospel. Motif Analysis and Exegetical Probe into the Theology of John*, Tübingen, J.C.B. Mohr (Paul Siebeck), 1976.

Attridge, Harold W., *The Epistle to the Hebrews*, Philadelphia, Fortress (Hermeneia series), 1989.

Barrett, Charles Kingsley, "John and the Synoptic Gospels," *The Expository Times*, 85 (1974), 228-233.

Barrett, C.K., *The Gospel According to St. John*, 2nd rev. ed., Philadelphia, Westminster, 1978.

Bauckham, Richard, "The Parable of the Vine: Rediscovering a Lost Parable of Jesus," *NTS* 33 (1987), 84-101.

Bligh, John, *Galatians: A Discussion of St. Paul's Epistle*, London, St. Paul Publications, 1970.

Boadt, Lawrence, *Reading the Old Testament: An Introduction*, New York, Paulist, 1984.

Boismard, M.-E., *St. John's Prologue*, Westminster, Newman Press, 1957.

Bowman, John, *The Gospel of Mark: The New Christian Jewish Passover Haggadah*, Leiden, E.J. Brill, 1965.

Braun, F.-M., OP, *Jean le théologien et son Evangile dans l'Eglise ancienne*, coll. Études Bibliques, Paris, Gabalda, 1959.

Breck, John, *The Power of the Word in the Worshiping Church*, Crestwood, St. Vladimir's Press, 1986.

Breck, John, "John 21: Appendix, Epilogue or Conclusion?" *St. Vladimir's Theological Quarterly*, 36 (1992), 27-49.

Breck, John, editorial (untitled), *St. Vladimir's Theological Quarterly*, vol. 36 (1992), 3-5.

Brown, Raymond Edward, *The Gospel According to John*, 2 vols, Garden City, Doubleday Anchor Bible 29 and 29A, 1966 and 1970.

Brown, Raymond, *The Gospel and Epistles of John: A Concise Commentary*, Collegeville, Liturgical Press, 1988.

Brown, Raymond E., *The Epistles of John*, Garden City, Doubleday Anchor Bible 30, 1982.

Brown, R.E., J.A. Fitzmyer and R.E. Murphy, eds., *The New Jerome Biblical Commentary*, Englewood Cliffs, Prentice-Hall, 1990.

Bruns, J. Edgar, *The Art and Thought of John*, New York, 1969.

Bruns, J.E., *The Christian Buddhism of St. John: New Insights into the Fourth Gospel*, New York, Paulist Press, 1971.

Bultmann, Rudolf, *The Gospel of John*, Philadelphia, Westminster, 1971.

Cahill, P. Joseph, "The Johannine Logos as Center," *CBQ* 38 (1976), 54-72.

Carroll, John T., "Present and Future in Fourth Gospel Eschatology," *BTB* 19 (1989), 63-69.

Charlesworth, J.H., ed., *The Old Testament Pseudepigrapha*, 2 vols, Garden City, Doubleday, 1983.

Charlesworth, J.H. and R.A. Culpepper, "The Odes of Solomon and the Gospel of John," *CBQ* 35 (1973), 298-322.

Countryman, L. William, *The Mystical Way in the Fourth Gospel. Crossing Over into God*, Philadelphia, Fortress, 1987.

Cullmann, Oscar, *Early Christian Worship*, London, SCM Press, 1963.

Culpepper, R. Alan, *Anatomy of the Fourth Gospel. A Study in Literary Design*, Philadelphia, Fortress, 1983.

Culpepper, R. Alan, "The Pivot of John's Prologue," *NTS* 27 (1980), 1-31.

Daniélou, Jean, *From Shadows to Reality*, London, Burns & Oates, 1960.

Daube, David, *The New Testament and Rabbinic Judaism*, London, Athlone Press, 1956.

Daube, David, "The Earliest Structure of the Gospels," *NTS* 5 (1958), 174-187.

Diez Macho, A., *Neofiti I. Targum palestinense, Ms do la Biblioteca Vaticana*, 6 vols., Barcelona/Madrid, 1968-1979.

Dodd, Charles H., *The Interpretation of the Fourth Gospel*, Cambridge, University Press, 1953.

Droge, Arthur J., "The Status of Peter in the Fourth Gospel: A Note on John 18:1-11," *JBL* 109/2 (1990), 307-311.

Duraisingh, C. and C. Hargreaves, *India's Search for Reality and the Relevance of the Gospel of John*, Papers from a Conference held in Pune in February 1974, edited by Christopher Duraisingh and Cecil Hargreaves, Delhi, ISPCK, 1975.

Ellis, Peter F., "The Authenticity of John 21," *St. Vladimir's Theological Quarterly*, 36 (1992), 17-25.

Ellis, Peter F., *Matthew: His Mind and His Message*, Collegeville, Liturgical Press, 1974.

Ellis, Peter F., *The Genius of John, A Composition-Critical Commentary on the Fourth Gospel*, Collegeville, Liturgical Press, 1984.

Ellis, Peter F., *Seven Pauline Letters*, Collegeville, Liturgical Press, 1982.

Eriugena, John Scotus, *The Voice of the Eagle: Homily on the Prologue to the Gospel of John*, ed. and with reflections by Christopher Bamford, Hudson, Lindisfarne Press, 1990.

Feuillet, André, *Johannine Studies*, Staten Island, Alba House (St. Paul Publications), 1964.

Fiorenza, Elizabeth S., "Composition and Structure of the Revelation of John," *CBQ* 39 (1977), 344-366.

Franzmann, M. and M. Klinger, "The Call Stories of John 1 and John 21," *St. Vladimir's Theological Quarterly*, 36 (1992) 7-15.

Frye, Northrop, *The Great Code: The Bible and Literature*, New York, Harcourt Brace Jovanovich, 1982.

Frye, Northrop, *Words with Power: Being a Second Study of the Bible and Literature*, New York, Harcourt Brace Jovanovich, 1990.

Gerhard, J., *The Literary Unity and the Compositional Methods of the Gospel of John*, unpublished dissertation. Washington, Catholic University of America, 1975.

Glasson, T. Francis, *Moses in the Fourth Gospel*, London, SCM Press, 1963.

Goettmann, Jacques, *Saint Jean. Évangile de la Nouvelle Genese*, Cerf-Pneumatheque, 1982.

Gregory of Nyssa, *The Life of Moses*, trans., intro. and notes by Abraham J. Malherbe and Everett Ferguson, New York, Paulist, 1978.

Guilding, Aileen, *The Fourth Gospel and Jewish Worship*, Oxford, Clarendon, 1960.

Haenchen, Ernst, *John 1* and *John 2*, Hermeneia series, Philadelphia, Fortress, 1984.

Hengel, Martin, *The Johannine Question*, London, SCM Press, 1989.

Hill, Nancy Klenk, "The Savior as Woman," *Cross Currents* 39 (1989), 1-9.

Iersel, Bas van, *Reading Mark*, Collegeville, Liturgical Press, 1988.

Interpreter's Dictionary of the Bible (cited as *IDB*), ed. G.A. Buttrick et al., 4 vols., New York, Abingdon Press, 1962; Supplementary Volume 1976.

Kermode, Frank, *The Genesis of Secrecy. On the Interpretation of Narrative*, Cambridge, Harvard University Press, 1979.

Kermode, Frank, "John," in Alter and Kermode, *The Literary Guide*, 440-466.

Kittel, Gerhard, and Gerhard Friedrich, eds., *Theological Dictionary of the New Testament* (cited as *TDNT*), 10 vols, Grand Rapids, Eerdmans, 1964–.

Kühlewind, Georg, *Becoming Aware of the Logos: The Way of St. John the Evangelist*, trans. by Friedemann and Schwarzkopf, ed. by Christopher Bamford, Hudson, Lindisfarne Press, 1985.

Lampe, G.W.H., *The Seal of the Spirit. A Study in the Doctrine of Baptism and Confirmation in the New Testament and the Fathers*, 2nd ed., London, SPCK, 1967.

Leach, Edmund, "Fishing for Men on the Edge of the Wilderness," in Alter and Kermode, *Literary Guide*, 579-597.

Leclerc, Eloi, *The People of God in the Night*, Chicago, Franciscan Publications, 1979.

Le Déaut, Roger, "The Current State of Targumic Studies," *BTB* 4 (1974), 3-32.

Le Déaut, Roger, "Targumic Literature and NT Interpretation," *BTB* 4 (1974), 243-289.

Le Déaut, Roger, "Pâque juive et Nouveau Testament," in *Studies on the Jewish Background of the New Testament*, Assen, 1969, 22-43.

Le Déaut, Roger, *La nuit pascale: Essai sur la signification de la Pâque juive à partir du Targum d'Exode XII 42*, Rome, 1963.

Léon-Dufour, Xavier, SJ, ed., *Dictionary of Biblical Theology*, 2nd ed., New York, Seabury, 1973.

Lindars, Barnabas, SSF, *Jesus Son of Man. A Fresh Examination of the Son of Man Sayings in the Gospels in the Light of Recent Research*, Grand Rapids, Eerdmans, 1984.

Lubac, Henri de, *The Sources of Revelation*, New York, Herder & Herder, 1968.

Lund, Nils W., *Chiasmus in the New Testament*, Chapel Hill, University of North Carolina Press, 1942.

McGann, Diarmuid, *The Journeying Self: The Gospel of Mark Through a Jungian Perspective*, New York, Paulist, 1985.

McNamara, Martin, *Palestinian Judaism and the New Testament*, Wilmington, Michael Glazier, 1983.

McVann, Mark, "Baptism, Miracles and Boundary-Jumping in Mark," *BTB* 21 (1991), 151-157.

Malatesta, Edward, SJ, *Interiority and Covenant: a study of einai en and menein en in the first letter of St. John*, Rome, Biblical Institute Press, 1978.

Maynard, Arthur H., "The Role of Peter in the Fourth Gospel," *NTS* 30 (1984), 531-548.

Meeks, Wayne, "The Image of the Androgyne: Some Uses of a Symbol in Earliest Christianity," *History of Religions*, 13 (1974), 165-208.

Meeks, Wayne, *The Prophet-King: Moses Traditions and the Johannine Christology*, Leiden, E.J. Brill, 1967.

Mlakuzhyil, George, SJ, *The Christocentric Literary Structure of the Fourth Gospel*, Rome, Editrice Pontificio Istituto Biblico, 1987.

Mollenkott, Virginia R., *The Divine Feminine: The Biblical Imagery of God as Female*, New York, Crossroad, 1983.

Panimolle, Salvatore, ed., *Like the Deer That Yearns: Listening to the Word and Prayer*, Middlegreen, England, St. Paul Publ., 1990.

Perkins, Pheme, *The Gospel According to St. John. A Theological Commentary*, Chicago, Franciscan Herald, 1978.

Perkins, Pheme, *Love Commands in the New Testament*, New York, Paulist, 1982.

Pope, Marvin, *Song of Songs. A New Translation with Introduction and Commentary by Marvin H. Pope*, Garden City, Doubleday, 1977.

Potterie, Ignace de la, "'C'est lui qui a ouvert la voie'. La finale du prologue johannique," *Bib* 69 (1988), 340-370.

Ravindra, Ravi, *The Yoga of the Christ in the Gospel According to St. John*, Longmead, Shaftesbury, Dorset, Element Books, 1990.

Robert, René, "La double intention du mot final du prologue johannique," *RThom* 87 (1987), 435-451.

Robert, René, "Le mot finale du prologue johannique. À propos d'un article récent," *RThom* 89 (1989), 279-288.

Robert, René, "Un précédent platonicien à l'équivoque de Jean 1,18," *RThom* 90 (1990), 634-639.

Sahi, Jyoti, "A Comparison between the Johannine Structure of Image Sign and the Buddhist-Hindu Mandala," in Duraisingh and Hargreaves, *India's Search for Reality*, 84-92.

Sanders, Jack T., *The New Testament Christological Hymns: Their Historical Religious Background*, Cambridge, University Press, 1971.

Sandmel, Samuel, *Judaism and Christian Beginnings*, New York, Oxford University Press, 1978.

Schnackenburg, Rudolf, *The Gospel According to John*, 3 vols., New York, Crossroad, 1968-82.

Schneiders, Sandra, "Literary Criticism," in *NJBC*, ch. 71, 1158-1160.

Scott, M. Philip, OCSO, "Chiastic Structure: A Key to the Interpretation of Mark's Gospel," *BTB* 15 (1985) 17-26.

Scroggs, R. and K.I. Groff, "Baptism in Mark: Dying and Rising with Christ," *JBL* 92 (1973) 531-548.

Sloyan, Gerard S., *What Are They Saying About John?* New York, Paulist, 1991.

Spicq, Ceslaus, OP, *Charity and Liberty in the New Testament*, New York, Alba, 1965.

Standaert, Benoît, OSB, *L'Évangile Selon Marc: composition et genre litteraire*, Brugge, Zevenkerken, 1978.

Standaert, Benoît, *L'Évangile Selon Marc: Commentaire*, Paris, Cerf, 1983.

Stauffer, E., *"eis," TDNT*, vol. 2, 434-442.

Stock, Augustine, "Chiastic Awareness and Education in Antiquity," *BTB* 14 (1984) 23-27.

Stock, A., *The Method and Message of Mark*, Wilmington, Michael Glazier, 1989.

Stuhlmueller, Carroll, *Creative Redemption in Deutero-Isaiah*, Rome, Biblical Institute Press, 1970.

Swidler, Leonard, *Biblical Affirmations of Woman*, Philadelphia, Westminster, 1979.

Talbert, C.H., *Literary Patterns, Theological Themes and the Genre of Luke-Acts.* Missoula, Scholar's Press, 1974.

Taylor, Michael J., ed., *A Companion to John: Readings in Johannine Theology*, New York, Alba House, 1977.

Terrien, Samuel, *The Elusive Presence. The Heart of Biblical Theology*, New York, Harper & Row, 1978.

Vandana, Sister, *Waters of Fire*, Warwick, Amity House, 1988.

Vanhoye, Albert, SJ, *La structure litteraire de l'Épitre aux Hebreux* (Stud. Neot. 1), Paris, Desclée de Brouwer, 1963.

Vann, Gerald, *The Eagle's Word. A Presentation of the Gospel According to St. John with an Introductory Essay by Gerald Vann, O.P.*, New York, Harcourt, Brace & World, 1961.

Viereck, V., *The Lotus and the Word: Key Parallels in the Saddharma Pundarika Sutra and the Gospel According to John*, rev. ed., Cambridge, Cambridge Buddhist Association, 1973.

Welch, John W., *Chiasmus in Antiquity. Structures, Analysis, Exegesis*, Hildesheim, Gerstenberg Verlag, 1981.

Wood, J.E., "Isaac Typology in the New Testament," *NTS* 14 (1967-1968), 583-589.

II. General

Abhishikhtananda (Henri Le Saux), *Saccidananda. A Christian Approach to Advaitic Experience*, Delhi, ISPCK, 1974.

Abhishikhtananda, *Hindu-Christian Meeting Point. Within the Cave of the Heart*, Delhi, ISPCK, 1976.

Abrams, Jeremiah, *Reclaiming the Inner Child*, Los Angeles, Tarcher, 1990.

Allchin, A.M., *The World Is a Wedding: Explorations in Christian Spirituality*, New York, Oxford, 1978.

Aphrahat, selected *Demonstrations: NPNF*, Ser. II, vol. 2, 345-412.

Bacchiocchi, Samuele, *From Sabbath to Sunday: A Historical Investigation of the Rise of Sunday Observance in Early Christianity*, Rome, Pontifical Gregorian University Press, 1977.

Bacik, James J., *Apologetics and the Eclipse of Mystery: Mystagogy according to Karl Rahner*, Notre Dame, University of Notre Dame Press, 1980.

Balthasar, Hans urs von, *The Glory of the Lord*, San Francisco, Ignatius Press, 4 vols., 1983-1989.

Balthasar, Hans urs von, "Soloviev," in *The Glory of the Lord*, vol 3, "Studies in Theological Style: Lay Styles," San Francisco, Ignatius Press, 1986, 279-352.

Barfield, Owen, *Romanticism Comes of Age*, Middletown, Wesleyan, 1966.

Barfield, Owen, *The Rediscovery of Meaning and Other Essays*, Middletown, Wesleyan, 1977.

Barfield, Owen, *Saving the Appearances. A Study in Idolatry*, New York, Harcourt Brace Jovanovich, 1983.

Baumstark, A., *Nocturna laus: Typen frühchristlicher Vigilienfeier und ihr Fortleben vor allem in Römischen und monastischen Ritus*, Münster Westfalen, Aschendorffsche, 1957.

Beggiani, Seely J., *Early Syriac Theology, with Special Reference to the Maronite Tradition*, New York, University Press of America, 1983.

Bellah, Robert, *Habits of the Heart. Individualism and Commitment in American Life*, Berkeley, University of California Press, 1985.

Berdyaev, Nicholas, *The Meaning of the Creative Act*, New York, Collier, 1962.

Saint Bernard, Sermons divers, intro. and trans. by Pierre-Yves Emery, 2 vols, Paris, Desclée de Brouwer, 1982.

Bernard of Clairvaux, *The Works of Bernard of Clairvaux*, vol. 3, "On the Song of Songs," II, Kalamazoo, Cistercian Publications, 1976.

Bernard, J.H., "The Odes of Solomon," *JTS* (1910), 1-31.

Bernard, J.H., *The Odes of Solomon*, Texts and Studies 8, no. 3, Cambridge, University Press, 1912.

Bernard, J.H., "The Odes of Solomon," in *The Expositor*, 22 (1921), 81-93.

Blake, William, *Blake: Complete Writings*, ed. Goeffrey Keynes, London, Oxford University Press, 1969.

Bly, Robert, *News of the Universe. Poems of Twofold Consciousness*, San Francisco, Sierra Club, 1980.

Bouyer, Louis, *The Spirituality of the New Testament and the Fathers*, New York, Desclée/Burns & Oates, 1963.

Bradshaw, John, *Homecoming: Reclaiming and Championing Your Inner Child*, New York, Bantam, 1990.

Bradshaw, John, *Healing the Shame That Binds You*, Deerfield Beach, Health Communications Inc., 1988.

Brock, Sebastian, "Studies in the Early History of the Syrian Orthodox Baptismal Liturgy," *JTS* 23 (1972), 16-64.

Brock, S., *The Harp of the Spirit: Twelve Poems of Saint Ephrem*, with introduction and translation by Sebastian Brock, Studies Supplementary to Sobornost No. 4, London, Fellowship of St. Alban and St. Sergius, 1975.

Brock, S., *The Luminous Eye. The Spiritual World Vision of St. Ephrem the Syrian* (Cistercian Studies series no. 124), Kalamazoo, Cistercian Publications, 1992.

Brock, S., "The Poet as Theologian," *Sobornost*, 7:4 (1977), 243-250.

Brock, S., *The Holy Spirit in the Syrian Baptismal Tradition*, Poona, The Syrian Churches Series, vol. 9, 1979.

Brock, S., *The Syriac Fathers on Prayer and the Spiritual Life*, intro. and trans. by Sebastian Brock, Kalamazoo, Cistercian Publications, 1987.

Bruteau, Beatrice, "The Holy Thursday Revolution," *Liturgy*, July 1978.

Bruteau, Beatrice, "Neo-feminism as Communion Consciousness," *Anima*, Fall 1978.

Bruteau, Beatrice, *Neo-Feminism and Communion Consciousness; Essays by Beatrice Bruteau* (undated), Anima Publications, 1053 Wilson Ave., Chambersburg PA 17201.

Bulgakov, Serge, *The Wisdom of God*, London, Williams & Norgate, and New York, Paisley Press, 1937.

Burmester, O.H.E., "La lectionnaire de la semaine sainte," *P.O.* XXV, Part 2.

Cady, Susan, Marian Ronan and Hal Taussig, *Sophia: The Future of Feminist Spirituality*, New York, Harper & Row, 1986.

Capra, Fritjof, *The Turning Point: Science, Society and the Rising Culture*, New York, Simon and Schuster, 1982.

Cook, Roger, *The Tree of Life. Image for the Cosmos*, New York, Avon, 1974.

Cummings, Charles, OCSO, *Monastic Practices*, Kalamazoo, Cistercian Publications, 1986.

Cyril of Jerusalem, "Mystical Catecheses," *Works of St. Cyril of Jerusalem*, vol. 2, Catholic University of America Press, 1970, 143-203; SC no. 126, Paris, Cerf, 1966.

Daniélou, J., *From Glory to Glory. Texts from Gregory of Nyssa's Mystical Writings*, selected and with an introduction by Jean Daniélou, SJ, New York, Scribner's, 1961.

Davies, Stevan L., *The Gospel of Thomas and Christian Wisdom*, New York, Seabury, 1983.

Pseudo-Dionysius. The Complete Works, translated by Colm Luibheid and Paul Rorem, introductions by Jaroslav Pelikan, Jean Leclerq and Karlfried Froehlich, New York, Paulist Press, 1987.

Dostoyevsky, Fyodor, *The Brothers Karamazov*, trans. Constance Garnett, New York, The Modern Library, Random House, undated.

Dulles, Avery, *Models of the Church*, Garden City, Doubleday, 1974.

Dulles, Avery, *A Church To Believe In: Imaging the Church for the 1980's—Discipleship and the Dynamics of Freedom*. New York, Crossroad, 1982.

Duncan, Edward J., *Baptism in the Demonstrations of Aphraates the Persian Sage*, Washington, D.C., Catholic University of America Press, 1945.

Eckhart, Meister: *Meister Eckhart: The Essential Sermons, Commentaries, Treatises and Defense*, trans. and intro. by Edmund Colledge and Bernard McGinn, New York, Paulist, 1981.

Eckhart, Meister: *Meister Eckhart: Teacher and Preacher*, edited by Bernard McGinn, Frank Tobin and Elvira Borgstadt, New York, Paulist, 1986.

Eckhart, Meister: *Meister Eckhart: Sermons and Treatises*, translated and edited by M. O'C. Walshe, 3 vols., Longmead, Shaftesbury, Dorset and Rockport, 1987-1991.

Eliade, M., *Cosmos and History*, New York, Harper, 1959.

Engelsman, Joan C., *The Feminine Dimension of the Divine*, Philadelphia, 1979 and Wilmette, Chiron Publ., 1989.

Ephrem, selected works, *NPNF* Ser. II, vol. 2, 167-341.

Evagrius Ponticus, *The Praktikos and Chapters on Prayer*, trans. with introduction and notes by John Eudes Bamberger, OCSO, Spencer, Cistercian Publications, 1970.

Fedotov, G., *A Treasury of Russian Spirituality*, compiled and edited by George Fedotov, Belmont, Nordland, 1975.

Ferguson, Marilyn, *The Aquarian Conspiracy: Personal and Social Transformation in the 1980's*, Los Angeles, Tarcher, 1980.

Franz, Marie Louise von, C.G. *Jung: His Myth in Our Time*, New York, publ. G.P. Putnam's Sons for the C.G. Jung Foundation, 1975.

Frye, Northrop, *The Double Vision: Language and Meaning in Religion*, Toronto, University of Toronto Press, 1991.

Frye, Northrop, *T.S. Eliot: An Introduction*, Chicago, University of Chicago Press, 1981.

Frye, Northrop, *Anatomy of Criticism. Four Essays*, Princeton, Princeton University Press, 1957.

Gardner, Howard, *Artful Scribbles: The Significance of Children's Drawings*, New York, Basic Books, 1980.

Gilkey, Langton, *Catholicism Confronts Modernity*, New York, Seabury, 1975.

Gilson, Etienne, *The Mystical Theology of St. Bernard*, repr. Kalamazoo, Cistercian Publications, 1990.

The Gospel According to Thomas, ed. and trans. by A. Guillaumont et al., New York, Harper & Row, 1959.

Grof, Stanislav, *Beyond the Brain: Birth, Death and Transcendence in Psychotherapy*, Albany, SUNY Press, 1985.

Hamman, André, OFM, *Baptism: Ancient Liturgies and Patristic Texts*, Staten Island, Alba House, 1967.

Haughton, Rosemary, *The Passionate God*, Ramsey, Paulist Press, 1981.

Hausherr, Irenée, SJ, "L'hesychasme, étude de spiritualité," *OCP* 22 (1956), 5-40, 247-285.

Hausherr, Irenée, "Hesychasm, a Study in Eastern Monastic Tradition" (unpublished English translation of "L'hesychasme").

Hayes, Zachary, OFM, *The Hidden Center: Spirituality and Speculative Christology in St. Bonaventure*, New York, Paulist, 1981.

Heschel, Abraham Joshua, *The Sabbath: Its Meaning for Modern Man*, New York, Farrar, Straus and Giroux, 1951.

Heschel, A.J., *Quest for God. Studies in Prayer and Symbolism*, New York, Crossroad, 1982.

Irenaeus of Lyons, *Proof of the Apostolic Preaching*, trans. Joseph P. Smith, *Ancient Christian Writers*, No. 16, New York, Newman (Paulist), 1952.

Irenaeus of Lyons, "Against Heresies," in *The Ante-Nicene Fathers*, repr. Grand Rapids, Eerdmans, 1981, vol. 1.

Jacobi, Jolande, *The Psychology of C.G. Jung*, New Haven, Yale University Press, 8th ed., 1973.

Jones, Cheslyn, Goeffrey Wainwright and Edward Yarnold, *The Study of Spirituality*, New York, Oxford University Press, 1986.

Jung, Carl G., *The Collected Works of C.G. Jung* (cited as *CW*), edited by Sir Herbert Read, Michael Fordham, Gerhard Adler and William McGuire, translated by R.F.C. Hull (except vol. 2). New York/ Princeton (Bollingen Series XX), Princeton University Press, 20 vols., 1953–.

Jung, C.G., "The Psychology of the Child Archetype," *CW* 9/1, 151-181, excerpted in Abrams, *Reclaiming the Inner Child*, 25-30.

Jung, C.G., *Aion. Researches into the Phenomenology of the Self.* 2nd ed., *CW* 9/2, 1968.

Jung, C.G., "AION: The Fish in Alchemy," *CW* 9/2 (1968), 137-145.

Jung, C.G., "The Philosophical Tree," *CW* 13, 251-349.

Jung, C.G. et al., *Man and His Symbols*, ed. J. Freeman, New York, Dell, 1970.

Jungmann, Joseph, *The Early Liturgy to the Time of Gregory the Great*, Notre Dame, University of Notre Dame Press, 1959.

Kapleau, P., *The Three Pillars of Zen*, compiled and edited by Philip Kapleau, Boston, Beacon Press, 1967.

Keating, Thomas, Basil Pennington and Thomas Clark, *Finding Grace at the Center*, Still River, St. Bede Publications, 1978.

Kelley, C.F., *Meister Eckhart on Divine Knowledge*, New Haven, Yale University Press, 1977.

King, Ursula, *Towards a New Mysticism. Teilhard de Chardin & Eastern Religions*, New York, Seabury, 1981.

Kuhn, Thomas S., *The Structure of Scientific Revolutions*, 2nd ed., Chicago, University of Chicago Press, 1970.

Lao Tzu, *Tao Teh Ching*, trans. John C. Wu, Boston, Shambhala, 1989.

Lawlor, Robert, *Sacred Geometry*, London, Thames & Hudson, 1981; New York, Crossroad, 1982.

Leclerq, Jean, OSB, *The Love of Learning and the Desire for God*, New York, Fordham University Press, 1961; rev. ed. 1974.

Liturgy of the Hours according to the Roman Rite, 4 vols., New York, Catholic Book Publishing Co., 1975.

Lossky, Vladimir, *The Vision of God*, London, Faith Press, 1963.

Lossky, V., *In the Image and Likeness of God*, Crestwood, St. Vladimir's Seminary Press, 1974.

Lossky, V., *The Mystical Theology of the Eastern Church*, Crestwood, St. Vladimir's, 1976.

Louf, André, OCSO, *The Cistercian Way*, Kalamazoo, Cistercian Publications, 1989.

Louth, Andrew, *The Origins of the Christian Mystical Tradition from Plato to Denys*, Oxford, Clarendon Press, 1981.

Loy, David, *Nonduality*, New Haven, Yale University Press, 1988.

Lubac, Henri de, *Catholicism*, New York, Longmans Green, 1950.

Lubac, H. de, *Aspects of Buddhism*, New York, Sheed & Ward, 1954.

Maloney, George, *Russian Hesychasm: The Spirituality of Nil Sorskij*, The Hague, Mouton Publ., 1973.

Mantzaridis, Georgios I., *The Deification of Man: St. Gregory Palamas and the Orthodox Tradition*, Crestwood, St. Vladimir's, 1984.

Matthews, Caitlin, *Sophia, Goddess of Wisdom. The Divine Feminine from Black Goddess to World-Soul*, London, Mandala (Harper Collins), 1991.

May, Gerald, *Will and Spirit: A Contemplative Psychology*, San Francisco, Harper Collins, 1982.

Mazza, Enrico, *Mystagogy: A Theology of Liturgy in the Patristic Age*, New York, Pueblo, 1989.

Merton, Thomas, *Conjectures of a Guilty Bystander*, Garden City, Doubleday, 1966.

Merton, T., "Hagia Sophia," in *The Collected Poems of Thomas Merton*, New York, New Directions, 1977, 363-371.

Merton, T., "The Inner Experience: Notes on Contemplation" (Parts I-VIII), *Cistercian Studies* 18-19, 1983-1984.

Meyendorff, John, *St. Gregory Palamas and Orthodox Spirituality*, Crestwood, St. Vladimir's, 1974.

Moore, Sebastian, *The Fire and the Rose Are One*, New York, Seabury, 1980.

Mott, Michael, *The Seven Mountains of Thomas Merton*, Boston, Houghton Mifflin, 1984.

Moustakas, Clark E., ed., *The Self: Explorations in Personal Growth*, New York, Harper, 1956.

Murray, Robert, "Mary, the Second Eve in the Early Syriac Fathers," *ECR* 3-4 (1971), 372-384.

Murray, R., "An Exhortation to Candidates for Ascetical Vows at Baptism in the Ancient Syriac Church," *NTS* 21 (1974), 59-80.

Murray, Robert, *Symbols of Church and Kingdom: A Study in Early Syriac Tradition*, Cambridge, University Press, 2nd ed., 1975.

Nasr, Seyed Hossein, *Knowledge and the Sacred*, New York, Crossroad, 1981.

The Odes of Solomon, trans. and ed. by J.H. Charlesworth, Society of Biblical Literature Texts and Translations 13, Pseudepigrapha Series 7, Missoula, Scholars Press, 1978.

The Odes of Solomon, ed. by J.H. Charlesworth, in *The Old Testament Pseudepigrapha*, vol. II, 1985, 725-771.

Panikkar, Raimundo, *Blessed Simplicity: The Monk as Universal Archetype*, New York, Seabury, 1982.

Patai, Raphael, *The Hebrew Goddess*, 3rd ed. enlarged, Detroit, Wayne University Press, 1990.

Peifer, Claude, OSB, *Monastic Spirituality*, New York, Sheed and Ward, 1966.

Pennington, Basil, *Centering Prayer*, Garden City, Doubleday, 1980.

Rahner, Karl, *Spirit in the World*, New York, Herder & Herder/ Seabury Press, 1968.

Rahner, K., *Sacramentum Mundi: An Encyclopedia of Theology*, 6 vols., ed. by Karl Rahner et al., New York, Seabury Press, 1968-1970.

Rahner, K., *Theological Investigations* (cited as *TI*), vols. 1-20, London, Darton, Longman and Todd, 1961-1981 and New York, Seabury Press/Crossroad, 1974-1981.

Rahner, K., "The Theology of the Symbol," *TI*, vol. 4 (1966), 221-252.

Rahner, K., "The New Image of the Church," *TI*, vol. 10 (1973), 3-29.

Rahner, K., "The Experience of God Today," *TI*, vol. 11 (1974), 149-165.

Rahner, K., "Experience of Self and Experience of God," *TI*, vol. 13 (1975), 122-132.

Rahner, K., *Foundations of Christian Faith. An Introduction to the Idea of Christianity*, New York, Seabury, 1978.

Rahner, K., "Basic Theological Interpretation of the Second Vatican Council," *TI*, vol. 20 (1981), 77-89.

Regan, F.A., "The Day of the Sun," chapter 4 of *Dies Dominica and Dies Solis. The Beginning of the Lord's Day in Christian Antiquity*, a doctoral dissertation at Catholic University of America, Washington D.C., 1961 (only chapter 4 has been published).

Richards, Mary C., *Centering: In Pottery, Poetry, and the Person*, Middletown, Wesleyan University Press, 1962.

Roszak, Theodore, *Where the Wasteland Ends. Politics and Transcendence in Postindustrial Society*, Garden City, Doubleday Anchor, 1973.

Schipflinger, Thomas, *Sophia-Maria. Eine ganzheitliche Vision der Schöpfung*, Munich, Verlag Neue Stadt, 1988.

Schmemann, Alexander, *For the Life of the World: Sacraments and Orthodoxy*, 2nd ed., Crestwood, St. Vladimir's Seminary Press, 1973.

Schmemann, A., *Ultimate Questions: An Anthology of Modern Russian Religious Thought*, edited and with an introduction by Alexander Schmemann, New York, Holt, Rinehart and Winston, 1965.

Scholem, Gershom, *Major Trends in Jewish Mysticism*, New York, Schocken, 1961.

Sheldrake, Rupert, *The Rebirth of Nature. The Greening of Science and God*, New York, Bantam, 1991.

Soloviev, Vladimir, *The Meaning of Love*, West Stockbridge, Lindisfarne Press, 1985.

Soloviev, Vladimir, "Beauty, Sexuality and Love," in Schmemann, *Ultimate Questions*, op. cit.

Staniloae, Dumitru, *Theology and the Church*, trans. Robert Barringer, Crestwood, St. Vladimir's, 1980.

Storr, Anthony, *Solitude: A Return to the Self*, New York, Ballantine, 1988.

Stroud, Robert C., *The Odes of Solomon: Sacramental Prophetism in the Church's First Hymnal*, unpublished master's thesis, Jesuit School of Theology at Berkeley, 1984.

Suzuki, Shunryu, *Zen Mind, Beginner's Mind*, New York, Weatherhill, 1971.

Tarnas, Richard T., *The Passion of the Western Mind. Understanding the Ideas That Have Shaped Our World View*, New York, Crown/Harmony, 1991.

Tavard, George H., *Woman in Christian Tradition*, Notre Dame, University of Notre Dame Press, 1973.

Teilhard de Chardin, Pierre, *The Divine Milieu*, New York, Harper, 1960.

Teilhard de Chardin, P., "Centrology: an essay in a dialectic of union," in *Activation of Energy*, London, Collins, 1970, 97-127.

Thunberg, Lars, *Microcosm and Mediator. The Theological Anthropology of Maximus the Confessor*, Lund, C.W.K. Gleerup, and Copenhagen, Einar Munksgaard, 1965.

Thunberg, Lars, *Man and the Cosmos: The Vision of St. Maximus Confessor*, Crestwood, St. Vladimir's, 1985.

Traherne, Thomas, *Centuries*, Wilton, Morehouse Publ., 1986.

Tucci, Giuseppe, *The Theory and Practice of the Mandala*, New York, Samuel Weiser, 1970.

Tunink, Wilfrid, OSB, *Vision of Peace: A Study of Benedictine Monastic Life*, New York, Farrar, Straus, 1963.

Turner, Victor, *The Ritual Process: Structure and Anti-Structure*, Ithaca, Cornell University Press, 1977.

Ulanov, Ann, *The Feminine in Jungian Psychology and in Christian Theology*, Evanston, Northwestern University, 1971.

Ulanov, Ann, *Receiving Woman: Studies in the Psychology and Theology of the Feminine*, Philadelphia, Westminster, 1981.

Underhill, Evelyn, *Mysticism*, New York, Meridian, 1955.

Vagaggini, Cipriano, OSB, *The Flesh, Instrument of Salvation. A Theology of the Human Body*, New York, Alba House, 1969.

Vagaggini, Cipriano, *Theological Dimensions of the Liturgy*, Collegeville, Liturgical Press, 4th ed., 1976.

Vatican Council II: The Conciliar and Post Conciliar Documents, ed. Austin Flannery O.P., Northport, Costello, 1975.

Waal, Victor De, "Towards a Renewed Sacramental Theology," *Sobornost*, 6:10 (1974), 697-708.

Ward, Benedicta, *The Desert Christian. Sayings of the Desert Fathers. The Alphabetical Collection*, trans. and with a Foreword by Benedicta Ward, SLG, New York, Macmillan, 1980.

Wilber, Ken, *The Spectrum of Consciousness*, Wheaton, Theosophical Publishing House, 1977.

Wilber, Ken, *Eye to Eye: The Quest for the New Paradigm*, Garden City, Doubleday, 1983.

William of St. Thierry, *The Golden Epistle: A Letter to the Brethren at Mont Dieu*, trans. by Theodore Berkeley, OCSO, Spencer, Cistercian Publications, 1971.

Williams, Charles, *The Figure of Beatrice: A Study of Dante*, New York, Noonday Press, 1961; Octagon Books, 1972.

Winkler, Gabriele, "The Origins and Idiosyncrasies of the Earliest Form of Asceticism," in *The Continuing Quest for God: Monastic Spirituality in Tradition and Transition*, William Skudlarek, OSB, ed., Collegeville, 1981, 9-43.

Wong, Joseph H.P., *Logos-Symbol in the Christology of Karl Rahner*, Rome, Libreria Ateneo Salesiano, 1984.

Abbreviations

Old Testament

Gen	Genesis	Eccl	Ecclesiastes
Ex	Exodus	Song	Song of Solomon
Lev	Leviticus	Is	Isaiah
Num	Numbers	Jer	Jeremiah
Deut	Deuteronomy	Lam	Lamentations
Jos	Joshua	Ez	Ezekiel
Jgs	Judges	Dan	Daniel
Ru	Ruth	Hos	Hosea
1 Sam	1 Samuel	Jl	Joel
2 Sam	2 Samuel	Am	Amos
1 Kgs	1 Kings	Ob	Obadiah
2 Kgs	2 Kings	Jon	Jonah
1 Chr	1 Chronicles	Mic	Micah
2 Chr	2 Chronicles	Nah	Nahum
Ezr	Ezra	Hab	Habakkuk
Neh	Nehemiah	Zep	Zephaniah
Est	Esther	Hag	Haggai
Job	Job	Zech	Zechariah
Ps	Psalms	Mal	Malachi
Prov	Proverbs		

Apocryphal/Deuterocanonical Books

Wis	Wisdom
Sir	Sirach (Ecclesiasticus)
Bar	Baruch

New Testament

Mt	Matthew	1 Tim	1 Timothy
Mk	Mark	2 Tim	2 Timothy
Lk	Luke	Tit	Titus
Jn	John	Phlm	Philemon
Acts	Acts of the Apostles	Heb	Hebrews
Rom	Romans	Jas	James
1 Cor	1 Corinthians	1 Pet	1 Peter
2 Cor	2 Corinthians	2 Pet	2 Peter
Gal	Galatians	1 Jn	1 John
Eph	Ephesians	2 Jn	2 John
Phil	Philippians	3 Jn	3 John
Col	Colossians	Jude	Jude
1 Thess	1 Thessalonians	Rev	Revelation
2 Thess	2 Thessalonians		

II. OTHER

ANF	Ante-Nicene Fathers
Bib	Biblica
BTB	Biblical Theology Bulletin
CBQ	Catholic Biblical Quarterly
CCL	Corpus Christianorum, series latina
CS	Cistercian Studies
CSEL	Corpus Scriptorum Ecclesiasticorum Latinorum
CW	Collected Works of C.G. Jung
DBT	Dictionary of Biblical Theology, X. Léon-Dufour ed.
ECR	Eastern Churches Review
ET	Expository Times
FOC	Fathers of the Church Series, Catholic U. of America Press
Gr.	Greek
Heb.	Hebrew
IDB	Interpreter's Dictionary of the Bible
JB	Jerusalem Bible
JBL	Journal of Biblical Literature
JTS	Journal of Theological Studies
KJV	King James Version
LXX	Septuagint Greek Translation of Old Testament
NAB	New American Bible
NEB	New English Bible

NJB	New Jerusalem Bible
NJBC	New Jerome Biblical Commentary
NovT	Novum Testamentum
NPNF	Nicene and Post-Nicene Fathers, Series I and II
NRSV	New Revised Standard Version
NT	New Testament
NTS	New Testament Studies
OCP	Orientalia Christiana Periodica
OT	Old Testament
PG	Patrologia Graeca-Latina (Migne)
PL	Patrologia Latina (Migne)
PO	Patrologia Orientalis
RB	Revue Biblique
RSV	Revised Standard Version
RThom	Revue Thomiste
SC	Sources Chrétiennes
TDNT	Theological Dictionary of the New Testament, Kittel and Gerhard eds.
TI	Theological Investigations of Karl Rahner
TS	Theological Studies

Index of Authors

Abhishikhtananda (H. Le Saux),
470 n.38.
Alighieri, Dante, 407, 470 n.40.
Allchin, A.M., 464 n.5, 471 n.51.
Alter, R., 471 n.2.
Aphrahat (Aphraates), 359, 371,
441 n.2, 461 n.1, 463 n.28.
Appold, M.L., 431(n.8)-433, 466
n.3.
Aquinas, Thomas (St.), 434 n.12,
446 n.11, 469 n.29.
Attridge, H.W., 437 n.3.
Augustine (St.), 279, 444 n.7, 448
n.4, 450 n.22, 456 n.4.

Bacchiocchi, S., 453 n.13.
Bacik, J.J., 460 n.1.
Balthasar, H. Urs von, 444 n.10.
Bamberger, J.-E., 467 nn.12,13, 471
n.52.
Bamford, C., 472 n.6.
Barfield, O., 112, 444 n.3, 465 n.2,
468 n.19, 471 n.49.
Barrett, C.K., 330, 425, 447 n.25, 458
nn.1,10, 463 n.1, 471 n.1.
Bauckham, R., 445 n.10.
Baumstark, A., 460 n.36.
Beaucamp, E., 445 n.3.
Beggiani, S.J., 453 n.9, 461 n.1, 463
n.26.
Bellah, R., 468 n.16.

Berdyaev, N., 434 n.13, 469 n.33.
Bernard (St.), 444 n.7, 448 n.4, 454
n.16.
Bernard, J.H., 361, 461 nn.7,9, 462
nn.9,10,11.
Blake, W., 431 n.7, 468 n.19.
Bligh, J., 437 n.3.
Bly, R., 465 n.2.
Boadt, L., 448 n.41.
Boehme, J., 470 n.39.
Boismard, M.-E., 437 n.1, 440 n.13,
472 n.5.
Bonnard, P.-E., 450 n.27.
Bouyer, L., 467 n.13, 472 n.5.
Bowman, J., 334, 459 n.13.
Bradshaw, J., 444 n.9.
Breck, J., 440 n.10, 456 n.2.
Brock, S., 441 n.2, 461 nn.1,9, 463
n.26, 471 n.51.
Brown, R.E., 9, 82, 425, 430 n.5, 431
nn.3,4, 432 n.8, 439 n.1, 440
n.13, 442 n.7, 443 n.5, 445 n.8,
446 n.20, 447 nn.22,25,27,29,
30,32,34,35, 448 n.39, 449 n.13,
450 nn.17,18, 452 n.1, 454
nn.17,22, 456 n.1, 457 nn.15,4,
463 n.1, 464 n.1, 471 n.1.
Bruckberger, 446 n.7.
Bruns, J.E., 470 n.38.
Bruteau, B., 122, 380, 445 n.6.
Bulgakov, S., 451 n.44.

Malatesta, E., 470 n.38.
Maloney, G., 467 n.13.
Mantzaridis, G.I., 454 n.25, 472 n.4.
Matthews, C., 451 n.44.
Maximus Confessor (St.), 11, 420, 467 n.15.
May, G., 465 n.2, 467 n.10.
Maynard, A.H., 464 n.1.
Mazza, E., 460 n.1.
McGann, D., 442 n.8.
McNamara, M., 459 n.23.
McVann, M., 458 n.11, 464 n.3.
Meeks, W., 368, 446 n.19, 463 nn.17,18,19.
Merton, T., 420, 430 n.1, 449 n.12, 450 nn.20,28, 451 nn.33,39, 40, 452 nn.44,51, 465 n.2, 467 nn. 7,10,15, 468 n.15, 471 n.53.
Meyendorff, J., 454 n.25, 472 n.4.
Mingana, A., 462 n.9.
Mlakuzhyil, G., 439 n.8.
Mollat, D., 444 nn.4,5.
Mollenkott, V.R., 451 n.44.
Moore, S., 452 n.4.
Mott, M., 452 n.44.
Moustakas, C.E., 467 n.14.
Murray, R., 369, 461 n.1, 462 n.12, 463 nn.21,22,23.

Nasr, S.H., 433 n.10, 435 n.16.

Origen, 11, 444 n.1.

Palamas, G. (St.), 469 n.26.
Panikkar, R., 440 n.15, 467 n.8.
Panimolle, S., 430 n.8.
Patai, R., 449 n.9, 452 n.46.
Peifer, C., 430 n.8.
Pennington, B., 440 n.15.
Perkins, P., 455 n.30, 471 n.1.
Philo of Alexandria, 52, 197, 440 n.13, 446 n.22.

Pope, M., 450 n.25.
Potterie, I. de la, 440 n.16, 472 n.5.
Prat, M., 450 n.30, 464 n.5.

Quesnell, Q., 464 n.3.

Rahner, K., 421, 440 nn.8,10, 446 n.11, 448 n.42, 460 n.1, 463 n.33, 467 n.11, 469 n.29, 470 n.42, 471 n.55.
Ravindra, R., 470 n.38, 472 n.6.
Regan, F.A., 453 n.13.
Richards, M.C., 465 n.2.
Rigaux, B., 429 n.3.
Robert, R., 440(n.16)-441, 450 n.31, 472 n.5.
Roberts, B.J., 450 n.17.
Ronan, M., 451 n.44.
Roszak, T., 468 n.19.
Rylaarsdam, J.C., 443 n.2.

Sahi, J., 72, 443 nn.14,15,16.
Sanders, J.T., 439 n.2.
Sandmel, S., 445 n.1.
Schipflinger, T., 451 n.44, 470 n.39.
Schlier, H., 444 n.4.
Schmemann, A., 469 n.35, 472 n.4.
Schnackenburg, R., 425, 430 n.7, 471 n.1.
Schneiders, S., 471 n.2.
Scholem, G., 449 n.9, 452 n.46.
Scott, M.P., 437 n.3, 458 nn.2,4.
Scotus, J. Eriugena, 472 n.6.
Sheldrake, R., 465 n.2.
Sloyan, G.S., 430 n.7.
Soloviev, V., 444 n.10, 451 n.37, 469 n.33.
Spicq, C., 447 n.28, 455 n.30.
Standaert, B., 331-337, 341, 458 nn.2,5,7, 459 nn.16,17,18,20,21, 22, 460 nn.32,35,36.
Staniloae, D., 464 n.5, 472 n.4.

Index of Subjects

Blind man, cf. also Blindness;
as Adam, 116;
entered, 125;
healing of, 41, 113-120, 172, 263,
312, 352;
illumination of, 139;
and Lazarus, 164;
and paralytic, 114, 118, 375;
and Pharisees, 139;
witness of, 130.
Blindness, 108, 113-120;
the common, 117, 351;
and glory of God, 120;
and guilt, 301;
of Judas, 125, 126;
and knowledge, 411;
of the leaders, 352;
physical, 113;
physical and spiritual, 119;
of the dark priesthood, 174;
spiritual, 90, 116-118, 301;
wise become blind, 387.
Blood,
in biblical tradition, 180, 447 n.28;
"born not of blood..." (1:13),
297-299, 302, 305, 325;
"by water and by blood..." (1 Jn
5:6-8), 376-377, 390;
drinking b. of Jesus, 82-84, 140,
309, 349, 353;
flesh and b. (general), 381;
flesh and b. of Jesus, 46, 51, 82,
133, 155, 348, 376;
of Jesus poured out on earth,
130, 266, 377;
of Jesus poured out, salvific
power of, 145, 155, 180,
352, 354;
of Jesus, unification through, 22-
23;
new creation through b. of Jesus,
91, 176;

of passover lamb, 154-155, 189,
338;
of sacrificed animals, 145-146,
173, 180;
ritual participation in body and
b. of Jesus, 135, 281, 326,
328, 346, 349, 353, 357;
of the vine, 136;
and water from Jesus' side, 180-
182, 196, 204, 354, 357, 375;
waters of Nile turned to, 149.
Book of Consolation, 77-78, 243,
318.
Book of glory, 94, 120, 152.
Book of signs, 94, 152.
Booths, Feast of, 90-93, 310, 340,
350.
"Born ... of God" (1:13), 297-298,
302-303.
Bosom (e.g. as dwelling),
of Abraham, 157;
of Adam, 226;
of the Father, 48, 70, 184, 226,
233, 242, 258, 270, 271, 274,
296, 319-321, 327, 329, 370-
371;
of Jesus, 70, 165, 182-184, 236,
258, 271, 286, 320, 327, 376,
384.
Bread,
come down from heaven, 76-77,
80-81, 101, 204, 279, 309,
347;
eucharist as breaking of, 135-136;
and fish (Jn 21), 279, 281, 358,
375;
given by Jesus to Judas, 126;
multiplied by Jesus, 55, 64, 75,
210, 279, 299, 308, 334, 348,
358;
the one, 263, 348;
as symbol, 51, 77-86;

created on third day, 87, 95, 101;
death as return to, 164, 223;
and heaven joined in cross &
mandala, 18, 23-24, 28;
by Jesus, 85, 266;
by Jesus as ladder, as tree, 54,
77-78, 86, 130, 186, 247-
249, 261;
humanity as, 121;
as mother, 233;
new, 101-102, 323;
as Jesus, 95-96;
as body of Jesus, 95, 102;
"the one who is of earth" (3:31),
303;
"the whole earth is full of his
glory" (Is 6:3c), 95.
Eastern Christianity, 195, 386, 401,
403-404, 425, 464 n.5, 469
nn.26,27,33-35, 472 n.4.
Eden, see Paradise.
Egò eimi, see I Am.
Egypt, see Pharaoh, Exodus;
plagues, 149, 152, 154, 187.
Eighth day, 276, 290, 357-358.
Eleazar, see Lazarus, name of.
Elijah, 72, 98, 149, 152, 156, 190,
220, 332.
Elisha, 149, 156, 259.
Emergence,
as movement in John's gospel,
13-14, 33, 56.
Empowerment (on the fourth day),
104, 107, 109-110, 140.
Epilogue (Jn 21), 39, 289, 384-385.
Eschatology, realized, 286, 341-
342, 414, 456 n.14.
Eucharist,
and appearances to gathered disciples (Jn 20), 254, 262;
and baptism, 417-419, 421;
in John, 342, 348, 373-379, 384-
385, 390;

in Mark, 334, 374;
John's silence, 219, 373-374,
378, 385, 390, 397;
from baptism to, in John, 83, 375;
blood (19:34) as, 182;
bread of life (Jn 6) as, 82-83;
and Cana wedding banquet, 198;
and faith, 84;
and footwashing (Jn 13), 135;
institution of, 120-122, 126, 374;
in Jn 20, 254, 262;
in Jn 21, 279;
and meal on the seashore (Jn 21),
279;
and new creation, 419-420;
and prologue, 309;
rediscovery of fullness of, 416;
ritual of, 83, 374, 421;
and supper discourse, 374, 397;
and Unitive, 389, 391-392;
from wisdom to (Jn 6), 83, 139-
140;
of the Word, 120.
Eve, cf. also Adam; 137, 164, 181,
233;
and Adam, 98, 115, 124, 127, 137-
138, 177-178, 183, 190, 198,
209, 222, 229, 234, 237, 247,
257, 317;
born from the side of Adam, 181,
183;
Church as new, 270, 391;
the new, 165;
liberated through Jesus' resurrection, 229;
and Mary of Bethany, 229, 238;
and Mary Magdalene, 229, 238;
and mother of Jesus, 238;
and Samaritan woman, 208-209,
238;
as symbol, 237;
as "Woman," 177, 232, 259.
exēgesato (he has told, he has

232, 236, 238-239, 403, 406,
407, 408;
emergence, liberation, 407-408;
gesture (anointing), ritualization,
215, 239;
as glory, aura of Word, 214, 396;
as grace, 317;
and history, 239;
human unitive, 183, 203, 208,
209, 238-239, 388, 406;
images in John, 131, 181, 182;
immanent, concrete knowledge,
411;
immanent f. principle, 420;
immanent revelation, 407-408;
in *Odes of Solomon*, 366;
integration with masculine, 183,
185, 407;
as interior unitive wisdom, 205;
Jesus' return to, 203;
language of the gospel, 233;
mediation (unitive), 391-392, 407;
mode of Jesus, 121, 181, 182;
mother of those born into new
creation, 232;
as movement, life, 130;
given one name, Mary, 177;
perspective of the gospel, 415;
as principle of biblical interpretation, 413;
revelation of meaning of, 193;
ring of episodes in John's gospel,
35;
as symbol, 237.
Fire,
in Easter vigil liturgy, 71;
in high priest's courtyard (Jn 18),
166, 170, 279;
of the Holy Spirit, 284, 348;
on the shore (Jn 21), 279, 284,
358, 389, 417;
and water, 416.

Fifth day, 143-190, 353-354.
Firmament, see Heaven.
First day, 63-73, 347.
Fish, cf. also Jonah;
multiplication of bread and (in
Jn 6), 42, 64, 72, 75-76, 279,
299, 308, 348, 375;
great catch of, in Jn 21, 277-278,
288, 357;
one hundred fifty-three, 280, 389-
422, 464 n.1;
killed in the Nile, 149;
on the fire (Jn 21), 279;
symbolism of, 348, 456 n.11;
vivified by water of life (Ezek
47), 275-276, 280.
Fishers, fishermen, 70, 165, 375;
from, to fish 284;
of people, 277-278, 281, 284;
Peter, 280, 282-283, 380, 384;
from, to shepherd, 281-283.
Flesh,
and blood, 46, 51, 82-83, 133, 324,
344, 199;
(body) in Christianity, 227, 451
n.36;
of Jesus to be eaten, 82-84, 140,
309, 326, 328, 349, 356, 376;
of Jesus as bread of life, 84, 96;
"they become one flesh" (Gen
2:24), 191, 316;
and the spirit, 348, 405;
the flesh (negative), 108;
works of (Gal 5:19-21), 412;
"the flesh is useless" (6:63), 309;
"will of the flesh" (1:13), 297-299,
302, 308, 325;
"the Word became flesh" (1:14),
28, 46, 47, 74, 82, 121, 186,
195, 273 (in disciples) 296,
308, 325, 414, 466 n.2.
Food, see Bread.

Sixth day, 191-240, 354-356.
Solomon, 117, 134, 144, 178, 185-187, 190;
    king of peace, 253, 267.
Son, cf. also Abraham, Child, Children of God, Isaac;
    beloved, 58, 99, 226, 248, 269, 299, 326, 332-333, 340, 356, 386, 409;
    beloved, Isaac and Jesus, 159, 338-340;
    of David, cf. also Messiah, Solomon; 153, 185;
    of God, 26-27, 56, 58, 93, 106, 116, 120, 153, 160, 190, 233, 248-249, 257, 268-269, 272-273, 293-294, 298-299, 314-315, 323, 326-327, 341, 349-351, 353-355, 357, 377, 394, 422, 455 n.28, 462 n.11;
    of Man, 48, 54, 75, 84-86, 89, 93, 96-98, 101, 102, 106, 110, 111, 112, 115, 120, 123, 124, 127, 134, 159, 170, 190, 194, 226, 233, 247-249, 251, 254, 268-270, 272-274, 281, 283, 288, 313, 332, 348, 351-352, 356, 367, 395, 444 n.2, 453 nn.8,12, 455 n.28, 462 n.11.
Sophia (wisdom), cf. also Feminine, Wisdom; 53, 79, 83, 99, 181, 199, 211, 215, 231-232, 236, 238, 349, 449 nn.9,10, 451 nn.37,43,44, 452 nn. 45,46;
    "Hagia Sophia" (T. Merton poem), 199, 207-208, 216, 224-225, 231, 232-233, 449-452 nn.12,20,28,33,39,40, 44,51;

in Christian tradition, life, 403, 406-408, 413, 419, 420, 470 nn.39,40,41.
Soudarion (facecloth, headcloth - of Jesus, of Lazarus), 223, 225, 450 n.31.
Speech, cf. also Word;
    plain, of Jesus (16:25), 132-133, 222, 225, 264, 328.
Spiral movement in John's gospel, 437 n.24.
Spirit, Holy, Spirit of God, see Holy Spirit.
Sword and cup, 182-183.
Symmetry, see Chiasm, Mandala, Parallellism.
Symbolic, cf. also Interpretation;
    biblical theology, 425;
    convergence in Jn, 175;
    double s. movement in Jn, 80, 331, 335;
    episodes as s. wholes in Jn, 37;
    imagination, 2, 45;
    method, 10, 13, 427, 438 n.3;
    relationships in Jn, 33.
Symbolism,
    baptismal, in Jn, 321-329, 343, 345-358, 373-376, 457 n.1 - 458 n.5, 460 nn.1-3, 463 nn.1,2, 464 nn.3-5;
    baptismal, in Syrians, 360-372, 461 nn.6-9, 462 nn. 14,16, 463 nn.17-32;
    Christian, 18;
    cosmic, in Jn, 72;
    and critical reason, 410;
    Genesis creation s. in Jn, 76, 83-84; in Syrians, 360;
    Johannine, 10, 33, 34, 37 45, 51-52, 54-55, 57, 67, 68, 79, 390;
    unitive, in Jn, cf. also Unitive; 45, 55, 76, 334.

Symbols,
of fullness in Jn, 296, 313;
God beyond, cf. also Apophatic;
400;
and incarnation in Jn, 82;
of Jn centered in Word, 52, 55,
69, 414;
role of, in Jn, 423.
Synagogue, 33, 108, 251;
at Capernaum, 76-77, 82;
expulsion from, 114-115, 131,
312;
readings, 459 n.24.

Tabernacles (tents), Feast of, see
Booths.
Tao, Taoism, 89, 426.
Tao te ching, 209, 426, 450 n.23.
Targum (Aramaic translation of
OT), 335-342, 459 nn.16,19-
23.
Temple, cf. also Place;
animal sacrifices in, 144-146;
animals driven from by Jesus,
150-152;
as center, 96;
cleansed by Jesus, 3-34, 55, 69,
128, 134, 162, 176, 299;
conflict of two, 147;
currency, commerce, cf. also
Money, 147;
dedication of (feast), 144, 153,
160;
destruction of, 146;
dwelling of glory, 98;
exclusion from, 131;
as Father's house, 128;
in mandala, 33-34, 42;
Jesus teaching in, 96, 110, 310;
new temple, 91;
and baptism, 353;
consecration of, 134, 169;

consecratory prayer of (John
17), 144;
as divine life, 145, 313;
and glory, 179, 262, 316, 349;
of human body, humanity, 91,
145-146, 148, 159, 254,
261, 267, 273, 325, 349,
353;
and indwelling, interiority,
129;
of Jesus' body, 55, 91, 96, 112,
145-147, 160, 181, 186-187,
255, 313, 383;
as living t., t. of life, 54, 167,
313;
and Peter, 219, 383;
as the one *place*, 251, 310;
unitive, 115, 146, 155, 160;
water flowing from (Ezek 47),
146, 181, 275, 280;
prayer of Solomon to consecrate,
445 n.14;
prayer of Solomon for wisdom to
build, 135, 178, 185-186,
445 n.15;
replaced, 96;
as symbol, 33, 91, 146;
vision of Isaiah in (Is 6:1-4), 94-
96.
Testimony, see Witness.
Theological,
center of NT and the first day,
37;
centrality of body, 227;
center of prologue, 297;
and structural centers of prologue & gospel, 293;
core of John's gospel, 41;
intent of John, origin of gospel,
287;
mandala in Christian t. tradition,
27.

conflict of Spirit and, 390;
creation of, 67, 70;
fallen, 137, 148;
"God so loved the w." (3:16),
    106, 339;
hatred of, 131, 253, 300;
and history, 156, 400;
humanity expands into fullness
    of, 273;
human person as king and priest
    of, 173;
human person as "spirit in the
    w.," 168, 446 n.11;
"I have conquered the w."
    (16:33), 253;
"I have sent them into the w."
    (17:18), 134, 172;
Jesus' symbolic movement to
    center of w., 170;
Johannine, 2, 16, 45, 51, 76, 99;
joined with Word in Jesus, 411;
"judgment of this w." (12, 31),
    94, 131;
"lamb ... who takes away the sin
    of the w." (1:29), cf. Lamb;
    171, 245, 261, 287, 338;
in mandala, quaternity, 23, 25,
    186, 297;
mission of disciples to, 262, 278,
    280, 288;
new, new creation of, cf. Cre-
    ation; 253, 268, 320, 383,
    385, 390, 392, 400, 420;
new creative role of humanity
    toward, 112, 398, 408;
new relationship of humanity
    with, 111;
newly filled with divine pres-
    ence, 236;
participates in new life, 168;
Peter and, 380-381;

power of, cf. also Power; 285, 411;
in prologue, 47-48, 51, 54-55, 296,
    298, 328-329;
rebirth of, 69;
represented by mandala figure,
    19, 27, 29;
    Johannine mandala, 346;
"ruler of this w." (12:31), cf.
    Satan; 125, 174;
"Savior of the w." (4:42), 211,
    316;
symbolically related to woman,
    233;
transformed, 265;
two worlds, 400, 409;
vocation of human person in,
    173, 393, 418.
Worship, cf. also Sacrifice, Temple;
and commerce, 147;
from dualistic to unitive, 235;
human life, bodily life as, 145,
    148, 350, 353, 357, 388;
images, prohibition in Jewish,
    263, 400, 454 n.23;
natural, 235;
from old to new, 144-148, 176,
    205-207;
Peter & Christian w., 220;
sabbath in Jewish w., 244, 452
    n.2;
in spirit and in truth (4:23), 145,
    147, 152, 173, 203, 355;
spiritual, 145, 173;
universal, 147, 150-151.
Wound in Jesus' side, cf. also
    Blood, Bosom, Place; 146,
    180-181, 183, 196, 198, 204,
    250, 253, 257-259, 261, 270-
    274, 352, 357, 375, 383.

Zion, 205, 206, 317.

Printed in Great Britain
by Amazon